Managing
Intercollegiate
Athletics

Daniel Covell

WESTERN NEW ENGLAND COLLEGE

Carol A. Barr

UNIVERSITY OF MASSACHUSETTS AMHERST

Holcomb Hathaway, Publishers

Scottsdale, Arizona 85250

Library of Congress Cataloging-in-Publication Data

Covell, Daniel.
  Managing intercollegiate athletics / Daniel Covell, Carol A. Barr.
    p. cm.
  ISBN 978-1-934432-02-0
    1. College sports—United States—Management.   2. Sports administration—United States.
  I. Barr, Carol A. II. Title.
  GV351.C68 2010
  796.04'3—dc22

                                                                 2010012978

Throughout this text, the authors were able to use materials from the following publications, with their permission. Where that usage allowed a credit line, such as when accompanying an exhibit, we have done so. For those instances where the material is used in text, as an extract, we include the following credits:

Material used from *The New York Times* (pp. 234, 238, 305, 371): Copyright © 2005, 2006, 2007, 2008, 2009 *The New York Times*. All rights reserved. Used by permission and protected by the Copyright Laws of the United States. The printing, copying, redistribution, or retransmission of the Material without express written permission is prohibited.

Material used from *USA Today* (pp. 49, 167, 189): Copyright © 2003, 2005, 2006 from *USA Today*, a division of Gannett Co., Inc. Reprinted with permission.

Material used from *The Chronicle of Higher Education* (pp. 59, 166): Copyright © 2007, 2008 *The Chronicle of Higher Education*. Reprinted with permission.

Material used from NCAA publications, © NCAA, is reprinted with the generous permission of the NCAA.

Please note: The author and publisher have made every effort to provide current information and website addresses in this book. However, because of the dynamic nature of this book's subject matter, it is inevitable that some of the information, such as affiliations, job titles, and URLs included here will change following publication of this book.

Consulting Editor: Packianathan Chelladurai

Holcomb Hathaway, Publishers, Inc.
6207 North Cattletrack Rd.
Scottsdale, Arizona 85250
480-991-7881
www.hh-pub.com

10 9 8 7 6 5 4 3 2 1

ISBN 978-1-934432-02-0

Brief Contents

Contents

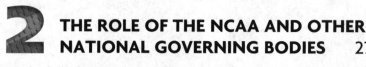

2 THE ROLE OF THE NCAA AND OTHER NATIONAL GOVERNING BODIES   27

3 THE ROLE OF CONFERENCES   71

4 INSTITUTIONAL AND DEPARTMENTAL MISSIONS AND GOALS   97

5 DEPARTMENTAL ORGANIZATIONAL STRUCTURE AND HUMAN RESOURCE MANAGEMENT   125

FINANCES   157

RECRUITING   211

COMPLIANCE AND ENFORCEMENT   249

9 ACADEMIC STANDARDS   271

10 STUDENT-ATHLETE WELL-BEING   301

TITLE IX AND GENDER EQUITY   329

Preface

The topic of managing intercollegiate athletics is a dynamic one, which makes it both interesting and exciting to study and to teach. While many of the underlying management principles and issues remain constant, personnel across collegiate athletic departments and programs must constantly adapt the ways in which they manage these issues to internal and external environmental variations.

When teaching aspects of intercollegiate athletic management, to help convey facets of this dynamic and complex topic to students, you may have brought together a series of articles from various websites, newspapers, journals, research studies, and magazines. And, if you're like the authors of this book, you may have compiled all these sources into a reading packet each semester to be distributed to your students. While this method offers the benefit of current resources, it is time-consuming for the instructor and fails to provide students with a unified and organized approach to the study of intercollegiate athletics. Having taught the subject at both the undergraduate and graduate levels, the authors have experimented not only with the use of reading packets but also with various popular press books on intercollegiate athletics, only to come to the conclusion that a comprehensive textbook on the topic was needed.

This book, *Managing Intercollegiate Athletics,* was created to provide unique, relevant course material to enhance the preparation of future intercollegiate athletic managers. As authors with both academic and practitioner backgrounds, we sought to combine relevant examples with theoretical concepts and important practitioner observations in a unified pedagogical textbook format. We believe the final product has been researched, written, and organized in such a way as to assist you and your students to understand more completely the unique and dynamic factors that shape this significant segment of the American sport industry landscape.

This book will have broad appeal to all sport management programs offering a specific course or portion of a course on college athletics—for example, the book offers relevant information for courses covering topics such as the history of college athletics; organizational structure and governance; the NCAA, member divisions, and conferences; athletic department administration and finances; responsibilities and management of athletic directors and coaches and their staff; and management of student-athletes including recruitment, compliance and enforcement, academic standards, and their well-being.

ORGANIZATION AND FEATURES

In each chapter of this book we seek to understand how the system was created and has evolved, showing how those who work in the industry use the unique qualities of college athletics to impact and influence the management and operation of this sport industry segment. Chapters include the following information:

- Introduction to the topic
- Terminology/definitions
- History (if applicable)
- Factual information (current rules, application, information)
- Examples, models, exhibits
- Case studies
- Practitioner Perspectives
- Questions to consider
- References and resources

Our primary goal for this book was to compile practical, relevant information about intercollegiate athletics, supported by interesting examples of actual challenges in the field. As one reviewer of the manuscript for this book said, "Athletic administration is FAR less about theory, concepts, and scholarship of the administrator and much more about practice, . . . communication, hard work, [and] organization." With that in mind, we include one or more case studies in each chapter to provide an in-depth look inside athletic departments at large and small two- and four-year colleges across the country as they deal with such challenges as the process of changing NCAA divisions, the evolution of Title IX enforcement, the practice of using intercollegiate athletics to boost enrollment, the plight of lower-revenue football programs, international recruiting, the financial landscape, and many more of the environmental changes and challenges and their impact on this industry. Questions follow each case to help readers understand and apply what they've read.

One of this book's important and unique features is "Practitioner Perspectives," for which an athletic administrator was interviewed or contributed a piece focusing on how they encountered and solved a problem—or developed a unique program or creative idea—concerning the chapter content being discussed. This feature provides readers with current and creative problem-solving ideas and information, and exemplifies how chapter material is being applied and handled by an athletic administrator. Interviewees include Myles Brand, former President of the NCAA; E. Gordon Gee, President, The Ohio State University; Stefanie Pemper, head women's basketball coach, United States Naval Academy; four student-athletes on the hockey team of an NCAA Division III school; and many others.

In addition to the case studies and Practitioner Perspectives, each chapter offers a multitude of examples and exhibits to assist readers as they learn and to act as tools and resources for them as they complete course work and move into the field.

This book contains a wealth of information for readers seeking to understand the management of intercollegiate athletics. It will act as a resource for them as they study and work in this important and dynamic field. Due to the nature of this field of study and the level of detail we've provided, it is unavoidable that readers will encounter names, positions, and other such information that has changed since we compiled it. Despite such changes, we believe that the book's purpose and its relevancy for courses in intercollegiate athletics will be apparent.

ACKNOWLEDGMENTS

We would like to thank all those individuals who agreed to be interviewed and provided their personal insight as part of the Practitioner Perspectives portion of this book. They are truly "in the trenches" of intercollegiate athletic management and provided valuable firsthand knowledge and experiences to guide the learning and preparation of the intercollegiate athletic administrators of tomorrow.

We would also like to thank the following reviewers, who offered constructive feedback at various stages as we wrote this book: James Antony, University of Washington; Laura Barnum, University at Buffalo; Josh Berlo, University of Notre Dame; John Clark, Robert Morris University; Richard McNeil, Michigan State University; J. Douglas Toma, University of Georgia; and Roy E. Yarbrough, California University of Pennsylvania. The book is better as a result of their contributions, and we appreciate their help.

About the Authors

Dan Covell is an associate professor of sport management in the School of Business at Western New England College. He earned his B.A. from Bowdoin College in 1986 (where he majored in studio art and lettered in football). After working in secondary education as a coach, teacher, and athletic administrator, Covell earned his Masters in sport management from the University of Massachusetts Amherst in 1995. Covell then earned his Ph.D. in 1999, having served as an administrative intern in the Harvard University athletic department.

His research interests focus mainly on management issues in intercollegiate and secondary school athletics. His recent publications include "Perspectives on image and identity in organizational adaptation: A case study of the New England Small College Athletic Conference," *Applied Research in Coaching and Athletics;* "The Yankee Elimination Project: A case study consideration of linking community relations and sponsorship," *Sport Marketing Quarterly;* "Attachment, allegiance and a convergent application of stakeholder theory: Assessing the impact of winning on athletic donations in the Ivy League," *Sport Marketing Quarterly.*

Carol A. Barr currently serves as associate dean for Undergraduate Programs and Campus Relations in the Isenberg School of Management at the University of Massachusetts Amherst. In this role she serves as the academic dean for all business school students at UMass Amherst and represents the Isenberg School on various committees throughout the university. She holds a B.S. in Athletic Administration from the University of Iowa, and an M.S. and Ph.D. in sport management from the University of Massachusetts Amherst.

Barr holds an associate professor position in the Department of Sport Management. Her research interests lie in the areas of management issues and gender equity within collegiate athletics. She has published articles in the *Journal of Sport Management, Sport Marketing Quarterly, Journal of Higher Education, Journal of Business Ethics, Sex Roles,* and the *International Sports Journal.* Barr has also published more than 40 articles for sport practitioners in publications such as *Athletic Business* and *Street & Smith's SportsBusiness Journal.* She has performed consulting work for the National Collegiate Athletic Association and has been involved in legal research surrounding gender equity, concentrating on its application to the collegiate athletic arena.

Barr has served on the Executive Council of the North American Society for Sport Management, serving as president in 2006–07, and on the editorial board of the *Journal of Sport Management.*

Acronym List

AAHPER	American Association for Health, Physical Education, and Recreation (now AAHPERD American Alliance for Health, Physical Education, Recreation, and Dance)	**DGWS**	Division of Girls' and Women's Sports
		D-I	Division I
		D-II	Division II
		D-III	Division III
AAU	Amateur Athletic Union	**EA**	Electronic Arts
AAWU	Athletic Association of Western Universities	**FAR**	Faculty Athletics Representative
ACC	Atlantic Coast Conference	**FBS**	Football Bowl Subdivision
ACE	American Council on Education	**GA**	Graduate Assistant
AD	Athletic Director	**GIA**	Grant-In-Aid
AIAW	Association for Intercollegiate Athletics for Women	**GNAC**	Great Northwest Athletic Conference *or* Greater Northeast Athletic Conference
AMCC	Allegheny Mountain Collegiate Conference	**GPA**	Grade Point Average
APR	Academic Progress Rate	**GSAC**	Golden State Athletic Conference
BCA	Black Coaches & Administrators	**HBCUs**	Historically Black Colleges and Universities
BCS	Bowl Championship Series	**HEW**	United States Department of Health, Education, and Welfare (now HHS, United States Department of Health and Human Services)
BEOG	Basic Educational Opportunity Grant		
BHAG	Big, Hairy, Audacious Goals		
BS	Bowl Subdivision	**HR**	Human Resources
BTN	Big Ten Network	**IAAUS**	Intercollegiate Athletic Association of the United States
CAA	Colonial Athletic Association		
CBO	Congressional Budget Office	**IFA**	Intercollegiate Football Association
CCHA	Central Collegiate Hockey Association	**ISSG**	Institution Self-Study Guide
CFA	College Football Association	**LSN**	Longhorn Sports Network
CIAW	Commission on Intercollegiate Athletics for Women	**MAAC**	Metro Atlantic Athletic Conference
		MLB	Major League Baseball
CLC	Collegiate Licensing Company	**MOA**	Memorandum of Agreement
COIA	Coalition on Intercollegiate Athletics	**MWC**	Mountain West Conference
CS	Championship Subdivision	**NAAF**	National Amateur Athletic Federation
CSFL	Collegiate Sprint Football League	**NACDA**	National Association of Collegiate Directors of Athletics
CSSG	Conference Self-Study Guide		
C-USA	Conference USA	**NAGWS**	National Association for Girls and Women in Sport

NAIA	National Association of Intercollegiate Athletics	**POPL**	Publication of Proposed Legislation
NBA	National Basketball Association	**SAAC**	Student-Athlete Advisory Committee
NCAA	National Collegiate Athletic Association	**SAOF**	Student-Athlete Opportunity Fund
NESCAC	New England Small College Athletic Conference	**SEC**	Southeastern Conference
		SWA	Senior Woman Administrator
NFL	National Football League	**SWAC**	Southwestern Athletic Conference
NJCAA	National Junior College Athletic Association	**TS**	Traditional Season
NTS	Nontraditional Season	**UAA**	University Athletic Association
OCCAC	Ohio Community College Athletic Conference	**WAC**	Western Athletic Conference
		WCHA	Western Collegiate Hockey Association
OCR	Office for Civil Rights	**WIAC**	Wisconsin Intercollegiate Athletic Conference
PCC	Pacific Coast Conference		

SCHOOLS

Note: This includes the school abbreviations used specifically in this book. Other schools may fall under the same abbreviations but may not be included in this list.

ASU	Appalachian State University	**SMU**	Southern Methodist University
ASU	Arizona State University	**TCU**	Texas Christian University
BC	Boston College	**TTU**	Texas Tech University
BSC	Birmingham-Southern College	**TWC**	Texas Western College (Now UTEP)
BYU	Brigham Young University	**UA**	University of Arizona
CSUC	California State University, Chico	**UCD**	University of California, Davis
CU	University of Colorado	**UCLA**	University of California, Los Angeles
ESU	East Stroudsburg University	**UConn**	University of Connecticut
FGCU	Florida Gulf Coast University	**U of L**	University of Louisville
FIU	Florida International University	**UNCC**	University of North Carolina, Charlotte
GCSU	Georgia College and State University	**UND**	University of North Dakota
ISU	Idaho State University	**UNM**	University of New Mexico
IU	Indiana University	**UNO**	University of Nebraska at Omaha
KU	University of Kansas	**UO**	University of Oregon
KUA	Kimball Union Academy	**USC**	University of Southern California
LSU	Louisiana State University	**USM**	University of Southern Maine
MSU	Michigan State	**USM**	University of Southern Mississippi
MSU	Montana State University	**UT**	University of Tennessee
ND	University of Notre Dame	**UTEP**	University of Texas at El Paso
NYU	New York University	**UVM**	University of Vermont
OSU	The Ohio State University	**W&M**	College of William and Mary
OSU	Oklahoma State University	**WVU**	West Virginia University
SHU	Seaton Hall University		

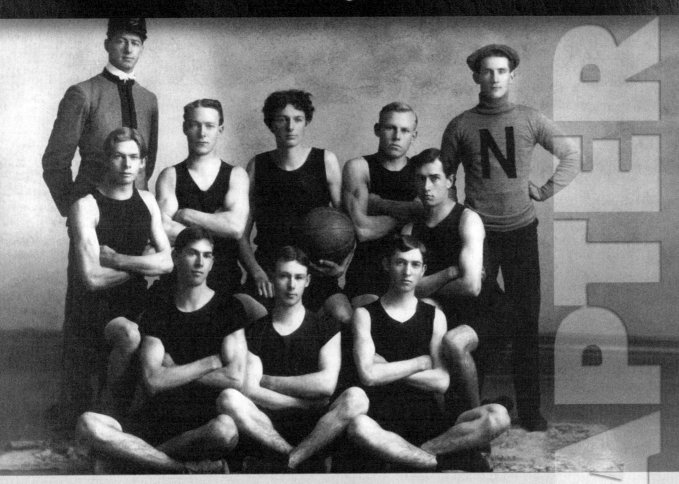

Key concepts to keep in mind while you read the chapter:

- How schools determine the appropriate role of intercollegiate athletics on their campuses.

- The historical elements that influenced the development of intercollegiate athletic management.

- The elements that led to the need to control violence and injuries in football.

- Emergence of the National Collegiate Athletic Association (NCAA) as a rule-making and enforcement body.

- How intercollegiate athletic experiences differed for students based on gender, race, and ethnicity.

Introduction

From before the inception of intercollegiate athletics, and since the very first contest between teams from different schools, the appropriate role of athletics in higher education has been actively debated. Although students first initiated and organized athletic programs for health and fitness reasons, the focus quickly shifted from participation-based programs toward institution-maintained programs that sought to achieve primacy over rival institutions. Proponents of the development of "big-time" athletic programs, as embodied today by those at many National Collegiate Athletic Association's (NCAA) Division I institutions, cite the ability of these programs to create a sense of community among campus constituencies and to promote the institution in general, while critics note that academic integrity is often sacrificed in the pursuit of athletic success, and that institutional resources are misdirected away from academics to support athletics.

Whatever your point of view, intercollegiate athletics in the United States clearly have evolved to mean different things to different stakeholder groups: students, faculty, administrators, coaches, parents, boosters, alumni, and the general public. These diverse collections seek varied outcomes from intercollegiate athletics, including entertainment, as a way to create bonds with the institution, a chance for physical activity, and an opportunity for professional advancement. Some seek the notion of a classic ideal of the student-athlete, one like Bill Bradley, a men's basketball star at Princeton University in New Jersey. Bradley was not only a star player who led his team to the NCAA Final Four but also was a Rhodes Scholar, led the 1964 Olympic gold-medal basketball team, and became an NBA player, a U.S. Senator, and a presidential candidate. The noted writer John McPhee (1978) described Bradley glowingly:

> He is as fluidly graceful as any basketball player I have ever seen . . . a truly complete basketball player. . . . Bradley is easily the most widely admired student on campus and probably the best liked. . . . The most interesting thing about Bill Bradley was not just that he was a great basketball player, but that he succeeded so amply in other things he was doing at the same time, reached a more promising level of attainment, and in the end, put basketball aside because he had something better to do. (pp. 8, 13, 39, 41)

What makes the management of intercollegiate athletics programs so challenging is that, regardless of the size of the school and the number and success level of programs, most institutions expect their athletic programs to meet the expectations of all stakeholders and all anticipated outcomes, some of which are to adhere to a code and a standard that was set by individuals like the seemingly superhuman Bradley. What we will seek to understand in this chapter is how the system was created and evolved in light of these expectations so those who work in the industry can understand how the unique qualities that characterized the formation of the intercollegiate athletics enterprise influence its management and operation.

THE INCEPTION OF UNIVERSITIES

askins (1957) notes that universities were founded by students to fight the threat of high rents and to pressure ineffective professors, as in Bologna, Italy (generally noted as the first such "university" in Europe) in the mid-12th century. The emergence of the university has as much to do with creating financial leverage to be wielded by students as for the furthering of any educational purposes. From its earliest inception at Harvard College (now University), located in Cambridge, Massachusetts, American institutions of higher education have sought to integrate all facets of life into the collegiate experience. Turner (1984) found that Harvard's founders intentionally chose the English collegiate system, where students and masters lived, ate, studied, worshipped, and played together, rather than the European or Scottish model, where students lived and boarded in the community and not on a single unified campus. This choice was based first on academic and religious principles to form a sense of community within the school. In much the same manner, intercollegiate athletics later would be used to build and promote school loyalties. This institutionalizing of non-academic student life would inevitably give rise to the college's involvement in sponsoring, at least by virtue of its responsibility of *in loco parentis*, the extracurriculum, those non-academic activities that were emerging on college campuses.

THE DEVELOPMENT OF INTERCOLLEGIATE ATHLETICS

early a century before the advent of intercollegiate athletics, students formed literary societies and Greek-letter fraternal organizations, and they organized on-campus "intramural" athletics. Faculties, however, usually decried athletics, as evidenced as early as 1787, when Princeton's faculty forbade students to participate in "shinny," a form of hockey, because it was "low and unbecoming gentlemen and scholars" (Rudolph, 1990, p. 151). Nonetheless, an annual junior class versus sophomore class shinny game at Princeton was quite popular, and students there also played "baste ball," an early form of baseball, as early as 1786 (Sheldon, 1969; Seymour, 1989).

But students persisted, for the most part because, as one Amherst (Massachusetts) College student of the day noted, such activities "served to vary the monotony, and relieve the dryness of college duties" (Smith, 1988, p. 15). Students participated in exercise regimens as a precipitate of the gymnasium movement of the 1820s, with colleges opting then to formally incorporate such programs by mid-century. Amherst was the first school to add a Department of Hygiene and Physical Education, in 1860, in hopes of channeling student activity to these areas. Soon, though, students perceived the movement as "so mechanical, so business-like" (Rudolph, 1990, p. 153). Even some presidents criticized the movement, as Paul Chadbourne, president of Massachusetts Agricultural College (now the University of Massachusetts), sniffed: "I would rather a man spend an hour digging out a stump than rolling over in a shed and calling it gymnastics" (Rand, 1933, p. 129).

The first intercollegiate athletic contest

In response to the disinterest in gymnastics but a continued and growing interest in physical activity, students chose instead to compete in sports such as baseball, crew, track, and football. At Yale University in New Haven, Connecticut, under-graduates formed a boat-racing club in 1843. As sports grew on campus, students began to look beyond the campus boundaries for challenges. But before Army–Navy, UCLA–USC, Auburn–Alabama, Ohio State–Michigan, Texas–Texas A&M, DePauw–Wabash, and any of the other hundreds of rivalries that populate the intercollegiate athletic landscape, there was Harvard–Yale. And in what sport was this notion of rivalries born? Not in football, or basketball, or baseball, but in a crew race, and not on the Charles River just a stone's throw from Harvard Yard, or in New Haven's harbor, but at Center Harbor on New Hampshire's Lake Win-nipesaukee in August 1852. Why there? The offer to sponsor the race came from James Elkins, a superintendent for the Boston, Concord, and Montreal Railroad. Elkins and the railroad company believed that spectators keen on watching such a race would secure passage on the train to the site, so they paid for the travel and week's lodging for the two teams, who saw the junket as a "jolly lark" (Smith, 1988, p. 28). The company's speculation proved correct, as about a thousand spec-tators, including future U. S. president Franklin Pierce, watched the Harvard men guide their boat, the *Oneida*, to a win in the morning's 1.5-mile practice race. After a respite of lunch, mineral water, ale, brandy, and cigars, Harvard won the official 2-mile afternoon race as well. For their efforts, the victors took home a handsome pair of black, silver-tipped walnut oars (Smith, 1988).

Other crew regattas would follow, as would expansion into intercollegiate events in other sports as well. By 1870, Sheldon (1969, p. 195) reported that "athletics had won a recognized place in college life," and by 1900, "a greater portion of the public know(s) a college almost exclusively through its athletic records, for three-fourths of the news items concerning student life deal with sport . . . intercollegiate contests play by far the largest part in the daily life and talk (of undergraduates)" (p. 230). Rudolph (1990) aptly summarized:

> For the American college student the gymnasium, the boat club, the baseball team (and before long the track team, the football team, the cricket team) were necessary for the fullest enjoyment of life. They were the institutions in which the student embedded his values, the values of worldly success; institutions in which he clarified the nature of distance that stretched between his view of life and the view that the college purveyed. . . . At last the American college and university had discovered something that all sorts of people cared about passionately. (pp. 154–155)

Early intercollegiate athletic management

Student-run organizations still operated athletic programs well into the early 20th century, paying for programs through dues-assessing athletic associations, fund-raising drives, alumni donations, and gate receipts. The games on the field were run by team captains, increasingly with support and direction from paid or unpaid coaches, and the off-field managerial aspects were run by students. In the 1860s and 1870s, the faculty imposed its will on athletic programs when it perceived that athletic matters were infringing upon students' academic activities.

In 1881, however, Princeton formed the first faculty committee to gain control of college athletics from students (Smith, 1988). One of the reasons was concern over the injuries and deaths in football. Another reason was the potential for publicity and cultivation of off-campus constituencies. Many educators also feared that, as the continent was settled when the century's end drew near, American society would become soft. Sport was promoted by political and religious leaders as part of the "Muscular Christianity" movement in response to American boys, who were perceived to be "an apathetic-brained, a pale pasty-faced, narrow-chested, spindle-shanked, dwarfed race—mere walking manikins to advertise the last cut of the fashionable tailor" (Lewis, 1970, p. 225). To this end, one critic at Harvard complained, "Will a kind fortune ever bring the day when the first scholar of his class can also claim the high honor of being the stoutest oarsman of the College?" (p. 225).

Football in particular became popular on campuses, as "it reinforced elite standards within an educational setting . . . (and) stood as a means of expressing, or even inculcating, the qualities of strength, endurance, and valor deemed highly honorable by generations of cultural commentators" (Miller, 1997, p. 292). At Harvard, without the support and over the objections of President Charles W. Eliot, intercollegiate athletics, specifically football, was engaged as a tool for creating "manly" students. Ira Hollis, professor of engineering and head of Harvard's athletic committee, noted that football "teaches some of the manly virtues admirably, and it exercises a moral restraint upon a large body of youths who might without it drift into all kinds of dissipation" (Townsend, 1996, p. 107). Even though Harvard physical educator Dudley Sargent promoted a comprehensive physical education program as more beneficial for creating his ideal of a Harvard man, "a gentleman who was well balanced and self possessed" (pp. 110–111), this was, as Townsend (1996) notes, not in step with the growing commercialization of intercollegiate athletics. Harvard was spending $112,000 on team sports for 200 athletes, while spending only $12,000 for physical education programs for the entire 2,000-man student body.

The era of student-run teams was coming to an end as well, with Yale's hiring of the first professional coach in 1864. William Wood, a New York City gymnastics and physical education instructor, was brought to New Haven to train the school's crew team. The move to professional coaches helped Yale become the dominant athletic power in many sports well into the 20th century, although Cornell University crew coach Charles Courtney and Harvard football coach Bill Reid were other early notables, some earning more than the highest paid professors at their schools and becoming better known than their school's president (Smith, 1988).

Chu (1989, p. 58) wrote that "American faculty were a major source of opposition to the formal incorporation of athletics into the structure of American higher education," in part due to their influence by the English ideals of amateurism, but Wilson (1994, p. 289) points out that this influence was "muted, however, because the faculty were so weak politically." Barr (1998) wrote that "the formation of faculty athletics committees was a direct result of the vast amount of time faculty found themselves devoting to the discussion of issues regarding intercollegiate athletics" (p. 4). Initial concerns raised included professional coaches and payment of student-athletes. Barr identified the period of formation of the National Collegiate Athletic Association and the founding of faculty-led athletic conferences (1895–1914) as the "high point for faculty control in intercollegiate athletics" (p. 5). The initial conference charter of what today is the Big Ten Conference required

case study 1.A

By the end of the 19th century, football had become the dominant sport on college campuses. For decades, annual contests such as "Bloody Monday" at Harvard were loosely based on soccer but in reality nothing more than an opportunity for hazing freshmen by the beatings of upperclassmen. These "games" evolved into intercollegiate contests, the first of which was joined in 1869 by teams from Princeton and Rutgers University in New Jersey, with Rutgers prevailing, 6–4. A version of the game closer to rugby emerged at Harvard, with rules allowing players to carry the ball rather than just kick or punch it. The Harvard version eventually won converts at Princeton and Yale, and by 1876, the three schools, along with Columbia University (located in New York City), formed the Intercollegiate Football Association (IFA) to adopt standard rules. The IFA's annual Thanksgiving Day championship game became the seminal event toward launching the sport into the nation's consciousness, drawing tens of thousands of fans to the contests held in New York City (Smith, 1988).

Many, including some school presidents, extolled the virtue of athletics, specifically football, in addressing the need to establish the virility of American males, as Williams College president Harry Garfield warned: "Here, as generally in American colleges, there is grave danger of departure from the essential idea of a college as distinguished from an institute of physical culture" (Rudolph, 1990, p. 378). Playing football, said Massachusetts Institute of Technology president Francis A. Walker, demands "courage, coolness, steadiness of nerve, quickness of apprehension, resourcefulness, self-knowledge, self-reliance, . . . [and] something akin to patriotism and public spirit" (Telander, 1989, p. 32). This emphasis was fueled by alumni and students, as University of Michigan president James G. Angell found when he and the Michigan faculty supported rules that would rein in the recruiting tactics by Wolverines football coach Fielding Yost. Heeding the protests of students and alumni, the university's Board of Regents took control of the athletic program away from Angell and the faculty (Sack & Staurowsky, 1998).

To this end, Yale, under the direction of Walter Camp, emerged as the dominant football program of the sport's formative era. Yale squads lost only 14 games in the 34-year span from 1876 to 1909 (including a record of 124–3–3 from 1986 to 1995, with the 1888 team outscoring opponents 698–0). Camp had captained the Yale team as an undergraduate, then stayed aligned with the program as coach and advisor. Camp was also a powerful force on the national scene, lending his influence toward shaping the rules and tactics of the game on the field (Smith, 1988; Gems, 2000).

The resulting developments related to the rise in the popularity of football were identified by Michael Oriard, a historian and former football player at the University of Notre Dame, in his book, *King Football: Sport and Spectacle in the Golden Age of Radio and Newsreels, Movies and Magazines, the Weekly and the Daily Press.* Oriard (2001) concludes that:

> From the initial discovery, in the 1880s and 1890s, that college football games could attract thousands of spectators with no direct connection to the competing universities, football served disparate interests. For many university officials, building a big-time football program meant a Faustian bargain: prestige and growth in return for surrendering control of the sport to the demands of popular entertainment. (p. 67)

One of the elements that proved difficult to control was on-field, in-game violence. At the turn of the 20th century, such violence seriously threatened the existence of college football. Contributing factors were dangerous game tactics, including momentum plays such as the flying wedge and lineman lining up in the backfield, and mass plays in which teammates pushed and pulled a ballcarrier down the field (even picking up and hurling one through the air was legal). Other dangerous tactics included the lack of the forward pass, and rules that called for ballcarriers to verbally call themselves "down," allowing defenders to pile on until the "down" call was made, as well as the inability or unwillingness of the sport's power programs and managers to curb these tactics. As a result, severe injuries were frequent and fatalities common. In 1905, at least three men died and 168 were seriously injured playing college football, although some press reports put the death toll at 25. In October of that year, U. S. president Theodore Roosevelt, a Harvard grad and parent of a son who suffered a broken nose during a frosh game at his alma mater that year, summoned coaches from Harvard,

Princeton, and Yale to the White House to lobby these leading programs to reform the sport.

Notwithstanding Roosevelt's efforts (he ultimately had no power to compel changes in the game), the death of Union College player Harold Moore by cerebral hemorrhage after making a tackle in a November game against New York University (NYU) would prove to be a seminal occurrence (Yaeger, 1991; Gems, 2000; Watterson, 2000). In response to Moore's death, NYU Chancellor Henry McCracken, who had witnessed the incident, sought to convene a meeting of school leaders to discuss reforming the sport. The so-called "McCracken Group" met twice in New York City the next month, with 13 schools represented on the 9th, then with 68 on the 29th.

In a letter to a colleague, Nicholas Butler, president of Columbia, stated that the efforts were "the first step in a general overhauling of the whole athletic situation in American colleges" (Smith, 1988, p. 140). The conference delegates would later name their conclave to reflect these lofty aims: the Inter Collegiate Athletic Association of the United States (ICAAUS). The ICAAUS would be renamed the National Collegiate Athletic As-

sociation (NCAA) in 1910. Eventually, rules changes were instituted, which allowed for the forward pass, a neutral zone at the line of scrimmage with a minimum of seven men required on the line, and elimination of mass (pushing and pulling ballcarries) and momentum (e.g., the flying wedge) plays. These alterations helped to create a more exciting game and to usher in decades of growing popularity for college football (Smith, 1988; Gems, 2000; Watterson, 2000).

questions for you to consider

1. Identify and explain how intercollegiate athletic management at that time complicated efforts to control on-field, in-game violence in college football.

2. Explain and give examples of any factors in the way intercollegiate games are played today that threaten the health and safety of participants.

3. Identify and explain how schools and governing bodies have attempted to address these issues, and whether these efforts have been successful.

that each member school "appoint a committee on college athletics who shall take general supervision of all athletic matters" (Lester, 1995, p. 212). But, as athletic conferences became more powerful and schools began to hire Directors of Physical Education, the precursor to the position of athletic director, athletics "were soon controlled by the powerful coaches and Directors of Physical Education" (Barr, 1998, p. 6). In his study of intercollegiate athletics in the late 1800s at the University of Wisconsin, Smith (1971) noted that

> as intercollegiate athletics assumed a progressively greater importance in student life, faculty members, except in a few isolated instances, remained disinterested. Perhaps they thought athletics unworthy of serious consideration because they were unrelated to academics. . . . Perhaps, also, traces of Puritanism lingered, that any activity which was "fun," must be frivolous. . . . In any case, the professors apparently failed to see the significance and importance of burgeoning student athletics and to perceive that repercussions would be felt in the future. . . . [T]he failure of faculty (to effect later the development of intercollegiate athletics) lay not in any lack of convictions but in the failure to transpose these convictions into concerted actions. (p. 62)

One faculty member at Wisconsin during this period, noted frontier historian Frederick Jackson Turner, took an activist stand on what many faculty members perceived as the excesses of intercollegiate athletics, specifically football. Turner, also a Wisconsin alumnus, worked to rally support in the faculties at other Big Ten schools for the suspension of football. Students on the Wisconsin campus protested to keep the sport and considered burning Turner in effigy, and his proposals were rejected by faculties at other conference schools (Watterson, 2000).

In the early part of the 20th century, some college faculties continued to voice opposition to intercollegiate athletic expansion, but with few results. For example, at the 1918 NCAA Convention, faculty delegates approved of the deemphasis on sports instituted because of World War I manpower and resource shortages and voiced "the unanimous opinion (that) after the war there will be no return to the commercialized systems," including athletically related aid (Sperber, 1993, p. 85). Then, in 1926, the American Association of University Professors published a bulletin condemning football for its hysteria, drinking, betting, overpaid coaches, and professional temptations (Betts, 1974).

THE NCAA'S EVOLUTION INTO A MEANINGFUL GOVERNING BODY

Although schools finally coalesced to deal with the violent and injurious play in football through the rubric of the nascent NCAA, the Association was unable to come to grips fully with the managerial challenges associated with these efforts. Smith (1988) blames this on several factors, the most important being that football's established power brokers didn't want to give up their hegemony over the game (and consequentially potentially weaken their on-field proficiency), along with the recognition that most schools were loath to cede their institutional autonomy in rules making and enforcing.

Since its founding, the NCAA, through its membership, has established thousands upon thousands of rules pertaining to the administration of intercollegiate athletics, most of which focus on setting policy relating to curbing abuses and perceived unfair institutional advantages in recruiting, financial aid, and issues of amateurism. But the idea of the student-athlete—the student who is also an athlete—is the change that is central to the entire intercollegiate athletic enterprise. Much of what the NCAA has done has been an effort to preserve and protect this concept. Stakeholders who support this idea favorably compare the college "game product"—the contests as played by amateur student-athletes—to the professional game product, because to them college athletes play to represent their alma mater with pride, and they play not for money but for the love of the game. However naive these beliefs may seem to many, they do persist, and with great power. Thus, Division I schools, charged with maintaining winning and profitable programs within stated academic boundaries, are also charged with maintaining this ideal notion of the student-athlete, to maintain the popular and commercial appeal of its programs and to satisfy the demand that results from creating sport that is popular entertainment. One critical area of concern for membership in the NCAA has been the struggle to determine the appropriate combination of academic achievement and athletic prowess to be required of Division I student-athletes.

Arbiter for eligibility requirements

The NCAA assumed slowly the role of arbiter for initial eligibility academic requirements, over the reservations of many member institutions. The primary goal of such a system would be to assure that all institutions would use the same minimum academic standards by which to assess prospective student-athletes in determining athletic eligibility, and, in some cases, the appropriate financial aid award. Such an association-wide standard would "level the playing field" for all schools, so a student not admitted or eligible at school A would not later be deemed eligible at school B, and suit up and compete for B against A.

Former Harvard president Derek Bok would refer to the need for broadly applied regulations because "many institutions will find it very hard to maintain reasonable academic standards if their competitors refuse to do likewise" (Bok, 1985, p. 208). No school or president, no matter how willing to tether academics and athletics, would do so alone at the risk of athletic ruin. In addition, such rules ran counter to trends in American higher education, "which is remarkable for its decentralized arrangement characterized by institutional autonomy, voluntary association, and relatively little government regulation" (Thelin, 1996, p. 10), contributing to the overall sense of institutional incongruence and contradiction in the constituency-based system.

At the 1906 NCAA Convention, a policy concerning academic eligibility was adopted, citing that "no student shall represent a college or university in any inter-collegiate game or contest who is not taking a full schedule of work as prescribed in the catalogue of the institution" (Falla, 1981, p. 144). It was left to individual student-athletes to voluntarily report any possible infractions. Smith (1988) points out that the group was formed on "the principle of individual (institutional) au-tonomy," and that "home rule dominated the NCAA for the first half-century of its existence. The individual colleges agreed collectively to act individually" (p. 207). From these modest beginnings, the NCAA eventually would move toward stronger national initial eligibility legislation and enforcement procedures, but the process would take the better part of 50 years.

By the early 1920s, most major conferences deemed freshmen ineligible for varsity-level intercollegiate contests. Many dismantled these frosh restrictions in conjunction with the manpower shortages that accompanied World War II and the Korean War, but some conferences reestablished them soon thereafter. Even though freshmen were ineligible to participate in varsity competition at certain schools, they still were eligible to receive athletically related aid. Not until 1972 did the NCAA finally approve full freshmen eligibility in all sports.

In 1939, the NCAA established initial participant eligibility standards for its national championship competitions. These rules were made more specific in 1946, stating that only those student-athletes admitted to their schools under the same admission standards as all other students would be eligible for NCAA postseason play, and that a participant must be enrolled in a full course of study as defined by his school at the time of competition (Falla, 1981; Mott, 1995; Sack & Staurowsky, 1998). Although these regulations were well intentioned, their impact was questionable, as no enforcement mechanisms yet existed.

The "Sanity Code"

The NCAA's first step in the enforcement process would come later in 1946. At a "conference of conferences" in Chicago attended by faculty members and school presidents, the attendees crafted a set of governing principles to deal with an acceleration of unsavory recruiting practices and athlete subsidies that had followed the conclusion of World War II. These were then sent to the NCAA membership for consideration. These principles came to be known as the "Sanity Code," because of a "prevailing belief that adherence to such principles [was] necessary to restore sanity to the conduct of intercollegiate athletics" (Falla, 1981, pp. 132–133). However, the only penalty the NCAA could impose against schools that failed to comply was expulsion from the association (Fleisher et al., 1992; Helman, 1989). Specifically, the Sanity Code stated that a prospect

- could receive tuition and fees if he showed financial need and met the school's ordinary admission standards, and
- could receive aid regardless of need if he ranked in the upper 25 percent of his high school class or maintained a "B" average in college.

However, many school presidents criticized the Sanity Code because of concerns that the NCAA could enforce the rule only selectively, thereby leaving some schools at a competitive disadvantage compared to others. No president relished the idea of losing a program on his campus, and several school presidents indicated that their school would refuse to comply. Although seven schools (Boston College, the Citadel, the University of Maryland, Villanova University, the University of Virginia, Virginia Military Institute, and Virginia Polytechnic Institute) were cited for violations of the code and recommended for expulsion by the Compliance Committee, they were retained when a vote of the full NCAA membership failed to secure the necessary two-thirds majority.

At the 1951 Convention, large Northern schools and schools from the South lobbied successfully to eviscerate the code. The bulk of other NCAA legislation over the next decade dealt with recruiting and compensation issues, including several proposals to severely restrict the scope of recruiting activities. Increased revenues from its football television contracts gave the Association the resources necessary to establish its enforcement activities, which other accrediting organizations had been threatening to establish in the early 1950s (Lawrence, 1987; Watterson, 2000).

Television contract negotiations

The NCAA began to develop significant powers in 1952, when the Association, under the direction of its first executive director, Walter Byers, negotiated the first college football television contract with NBC for a total rights fee of just over $1 million for 12 games. Thirty years later, the last such contract would net the membership more than $281 million (over $74 million in 1983 alone). Two years before, the University of Notre Dame and the University of Pennsylvania had inked separate TV deals with the ABC and DuMont networks, respectively. The rest of membership, fearful that a supply of free football viewing on television would hurt gate receipts, opted to cede the right to negotiate their own deals and allow Byers and the leadership to craft a national package to sell to the highest bidder. Notre Dame's president, Father Edmund Joyce, ridiculed the plan as socialistic, and Pennsylvania considered challenging the NCAA's authority on this issue. When four schools on their schedules refused to play them if they ignored the NCAA's vote, however, both Pennsylvania and Notre Dame relented (Dunnavant, 2004).

The package restricted the number of times a school could appear on TV in a given time period and distributed funds more or less equally among the members. According to Dunnavant (2004), "the televised game captured the fascination of millions who had been aware of it only through radio or newspapers—or not at all. . . . It was a moment in time where the game became a commodity, elevated by television to a whole new level of popularity" (p. 32). Over time this popularity would continue to grow, aided by the innovative coverage and uses of technological advances such as slow-motion replays. As a result, schools such as the University of Oklahoma and the University of Georgia—those with more prominent programs and legions of rabid fans—believed the NCAA-controlled plan, which limited their exposure, was keeping them from realizing more revenues related to broadcasts.

Sixty-one such schools coalesced in 1976 to form the College Football Association (CFA), whose members would threaten to leave the NCAA entirely over the TV issue but eventually opted to challenge the NCAA in court for the right to sell their own games for broadcast. In 1984, the U.S. Supreme Court found for the CFA on anti-trust grounds, decreeing that the NCAA limited the output of games to raise prices, that the games were the property of the schools, and that the NCAA could not sell them if the schools wanted to do so. The NCAA still owned the rights to its postseason men's Division I basketball tournament, however, and signed a landmark eight-year deal with CBS in 1995, bringing the membership nearly $2 billion (Byers, 1995; Sandomir, 1995; Dunnavant, 2004).

Evolution of academic eligibility rules

Another significant occurrence that impacted the NCAA during the late 20th century was the continuing struggle over academic eligibility legislation. Following the demise of the Sanity Code, the membership passed two similar attempts to govern initial eligibility: the "1.600 Rule" in 1965, and the "2.0 Rule" in 1973. At the 1965 Convention, the membership passed the Association's first-ever minimum academic standards for the awarding of athletically related financial aid. The 1.600 rule required that member institutions could not offer athletically related financial aid to student-athletes who did not have a predicted grade-point average (GPA) of 1.600 (based on a maximum 4.000 scale) in the student-athletes' sixth, seventh, or eighth semester in high school (1964-65 Yearbook, 1965). Standardized test scores on either the SAT or the ACT also were utilized in determining eligibility, which, according to Byers (1995), the longtime Executive Director, "provided an essential national comparative standard" (p. 158).

NCAA president (not the current position that serves as head of the organization) Alan Chapman defended 1.600 as "one of the few pieces of legislation we have on the books that does try to protect the student-athlete from exploitation for athletic purposes" (Proceedings, 1972, p. 167). However, the membership voted to repeal the rule in 1973, opting to replace it with a weaker version, the 2.0 rule. The new rule required that student-athletes who graduated from high school with a 2.0 accumulative sixth, seventh, or eighth semester GPA (based on a maximum 4.0 scale), regardless of course content and test scores, were to be deemed eligible for participation and athletically related aid (A History, 1980).

The relaxing of standards resulting from passage of the 2.0 rule led to shifts in constituent perceptions of intercollegiate athletics. According to Thelin (1996), "by 1978, the national press had once again rediscovered problems with coaching and recruiting excesses. . . . [D]espite the avoidance shown by some faculty senates and university presidents, academics and athletics would be intertwined in institutional and national policy debates" (p. 178).

Concerns regarding athlete exploitation would gradually become a significant issue in the formation of future initial eligibility legislation. The renewal of constituent concern in response to issues such as low graduation rates, star athletes who couldn't read or never attended class, and schools discarding untrained and uneducated athletes as soon as their athletic eligibility expired, would afford interested presidents the opportunity to assume a leadership role in leading the debate and to address these concerns through the NCAA for reestablishing a nationwide initial-eligibility standard. They would be the ones most able to deal with these problems in reestablishing the bonds between athletics and academics that had been loosened over the previous decades. As these bonds were destroyed, the result was damaging to the perception of the ideals notions of the student-athlete and intercollegiate athletics.

In 1982, school presidents took a prominent role in promoting and establishing new, stricter initial eligibility rules. A proposal to confront the issue of initial eligibility requirements came forth from a college presidents' lobbying organization, the American Council on Education's Ad Hoc Committee on the Problems of Major Intercollegiate Athletic Programs, chaired by Harvard president Derek Bok. The committee cited the lack of control by presidents and trustees as one factor in the rise in intercollegiate athletic problems, and called for increases in presidential involvement in athletic matters. The most substantive proposal put forth by the committee dealt with initial eligibility requirements. The proposal retained the concept of the 2.0 GPA Division I eligibility floor but stipulated that the GPA would be computed from coursework "in a core curriculum of at least 11 academic courses including at least three in English, two in mathematics, two in social science and two in natural or physical science (including at least one laboratory class, if offered by the high school) . . . as well as a 700 combined score on the SAT verbal and math sections or a 15 composite on the ACT" (*Proceedings*, 1983, p. A-35).

Academic concerns were legitimate, as the graduation rates for athletes in high-profile sports were indeed poor. An NCAA study conducted from 1975 through 1980 discovered that only 42.9 percent of Division I-A football players graduated. A similar study conducted by the *Sporting News* found that 45 percent earned degrees, including a high of 100 percent in the Ivy League, to a low of 16.7 percent in the now-defunct Southwest Conference (Morris, 1992). At the 1983 Convention, the proposal, known as Proposition 48, was passed in spite of the concerns voiced by many that the standardized test score thresholds would be disproportionately detrimental to minority prospects, who tended to score lower than their white counterparts on such assessment tools. Proposition 48 was amended several times over the next few years, but its basic premise—to establish an Association-wide standard to determine the initial eligibility of prospects and the awarding of athletically related aid—is still intact. More detail on initial and continuing academic eligibility is provided in Chapter 8.

Amateurism rules

Yet another significant occurrence that impacted the NCAA was the battle over maintaining and enforcing the Association's amateurism rules, which came to a head in the 1980s in the case of cash payments to football players at Southern Methodist University (SMU). Over the course of more than a decade beginning in the 1970s, boosters, coaches, and school administrators—including board of trustees head and future Texas governor Bill Clements—conspired to create an intricate system of paying star players. At the time, SMU football was riding high as one of the power teams in the country. Led by future NFL Hall of Fame running back Eric Dickerson, the Mustangs finished second in national polls in 1982. This success was attributable in part to the payments delivered to recruits and players by the Mustang Club boosters. Head coach Ron Meyer, who came to the school in 1976, would meet with high school prospects, "pull out a plump money clip and peel off a hundred-dollar bill. He would get up, walk to a nearby bulletin board, pin up the C-note, and announce: 'Young man, this is my calling card'" (Byers, 1995, p. 19).

In 1985, SMU's program was placed on NCAA probation for the fourth time in 11 years because of cash payments (with monthly disbursements ranging from $85 to $750), gifts, cars, and no-show jobs provided to football players. But the payments continued to the tune of $61,000 over the next 18 months. Mostly because the program had done such a good job in developing the system, those involved could wean neither the boosters nor the players from the payments. In 1987, NCAA investigators, faced with additional reams of damning evidence and institutional intransigence and intractability, leveled what a later SMU football coach called "the atomic bomb" (Layden, 2002) but what is most often referred to as "the death penalty": SMU's football program was shut down for two years, and then allowed to return only with severe restrictions on recruiting and grants-in-aid (Byers, 1995; Layden, 2002).

The case has served as an example of the hammer that an NCAA investigation can wield, as noted by John Lombardi, president of Louisiana's state university system: "The results were so catastrophic that now we'll do anything to avoid dropping another one" (Drape, 2009, p. B11). Several schools have come close to the sentence—most notably a similar case of booster payments to football players at the University of Alabama in 2002. According to Thomas Yeager, then-chair of the NCAA's Infractions Committee (see Chapter 8), the violations at Alabama were "some of the worst, most serious, that have ever occurred" (Drape, 2009, p. B11). Yet the death penalty was not levied. David Berst, former head of the NCAA's enforcement operations (now vice president for Division I), summarized the impact of the SMU case this way: "At the time, there was a culture of cheating in intercollegiate athletics. . . . There was a perception that people needed to cheat to compete" (Drape, 2009, p. B11).

These developments—the institution of rules for initial academic eligibility requirements, recruiting and subsidizing practices and amateurism—combined with the lucrative television deal for the men's Division I basketball tournament, solidified the NCAA's preeminent role in governing American intercollegiate athletics.

THE EXPERIENCES OF WOMEN
IN INTERCOLLEGIATE ATHLETICS

The early decades of intercollegiate athletics were mostly the preserve of the affluent. This is hardly surprising given that well into the 20th century, only 5 percent of American men went to college. By 1920, nearly half of all college students were women, but even though the number of women on campuses was significant, their opportunities to participate in intercollegiate athletics were far fewer and usually quite restricted. Gems (2000) notes that the entrée of women into the previously masculine sphere of physical activity was seen as threatening by many males. Football was considered to be the antidote to an encroaching effeminacy hastened by the lack of physical challenges available in the modern world. This mindset proffered that a woman's role in athletics was to serve as a supporter to brothers, sons, and boyfriends.

The development of women's sports was also hampered by the notion that strenuous physical activity was severely detrimental to the delicate constitutions of women and could cause debilitating injuries, rendering them unable to rear children. Suggs (2005) points out a myth commonly held into the 20th century that "being athletic would cause a woman's uterus to fall out" (p. 20). As a result of these and other concerns, Suggs summarizes that women's programs were kept "low key" because female teacher-coaches "wanted to preserve young women's modesty and accommodate their perceived daintiness," and because of "a general suspicion of competition, particularly as it was being practiced in men's sports" (p. 23).

In spite of these restrictions, many women, like their male counterparts decades before, sought more exciting pursuits, and the sport of basketball became a popular activity for collegiate women, forming what Grundy (2001) deemed to be "a central part of student life at many women's institutions" (p. 41). Initially males saw the sport as less physical, and therefore less threatening to them if women chose to play it. At Smith College in Northampton, Massachusetts, physical educator Senda Berensen devised a version of the game wherein movement was more limited than for men. The floor was divided into three sections and players were not allowed to move into the other two or allowed to dribble more than once.

To many, however, the idea of young women running, jumping, sweating, and yelling in a public forum was highly distasteful and borderline immoral. This was during a time when a woman's sexual reputation was called into question if her skirt failed to touch the ground, so much so that men were barred entry from many of these early contests lest the passions of the moment cause irreparable harm to all parties. Grundy (2001) reports that this notion of propriety was held even more strongly at African-American women's colleges, where women not only had to adhere to roles deemed appropriate for women but also to appear all the more upright to gain approval from the dominant White culture. African-Americans still were seen as "highly sensual and with little control over their impulses" (p. 63) by many Whites of the time, so the idea that the reputation of African-American women would be damaged further by unrestrained sport activities was a concern for their teachers, who sought to help their charges become successfully integrated into White society.

These factors were combined with a mindset of many early female physical educators that the commercial model of men's intercollegiate athletics was inherently corrupt and damaging to its participants, and therefore was a blueprint to be ignored when shaping appropriate programs for women. As a result, in 1924, the Women's Division of the National Amateur Athletic Federation, one of many such organizations composed of educators and coaches at the time, created a series of guidelines for what was deemed to be the proper direction for women's athletic programs. The guidelines called for programs to "stress enjoyment of the sport and the development of sportsmanship, and to minimize the emphasis placed on individual accomplishments and the winning of championships" (Suggs, 2005, p. 25). This mindset would serve to deemphasize the model of intercollegiate competition for men's sports in lieu of the "play day" concept, in which groups of women from various schools would convene at a campus site and create teams composed randomly of women from all in attendance, with the teams then competing in various sports such as field hockey, basketball, and volleyball. The concept valued the social element of sport as much as the competitive element and "play days" became popular in the 1930s and were common well into the 1960s (Suggs, 2005).

Unlike the NCAA, which early in the 20th century established its position as the preeminent governing body for men's intercollegiate athletics and gradually strengthened that position over time, several organizations were involved in fostering the development of women's programs. Much of the debate and focus centered on how best to deal with the prickly issue of postseason championship contests. Suggs (2005) points out that in 1957, several such organizations formed the National Joint Committee on Extramural Sports for College Women to sanction events and championships for varsity-style teams, but this organization proved unwieldy, and in 1965 its functions were ceded to the Division of Girls' and Women's Sports (DGWS) of the American Association for Health, Physical Education, and Recreation (AAHPER), a group that itself had been formed from a merger of the American Physical Education Association's Committee on Women's Athletics and the Women's Division of the NAAF.

In turn, the DWGS created the Commission on Intercollegiate Athletics for Women (CIAW) in 1967 to deal with the issue of national championships for women. In 1972, the CIAW became the Association for Intercollegiate Athletics for Women (AIAW), composed of physical education teachers, to promote better coaching and competition. It became the most prominent governing body and encouraged competition within the bounds of higher education and amateurism. The AIAW's Policy Statement, adopted in 1974, stated that the importance of "the enrichment of the life of the participant is the focus and reason for the existence of any athletic program," and that "separate but comparable teams should be provided for women and men." Suggs (2005) commented that while the AIAW "wanted their fair share of funding, they really wanted to maintain the independence to conduct their own sports programs with their own values" (p. 51).

The growth of women's programs was aided in large part by passage of Title IX of the Education Amendments of 1972, a federal law that sought to increase equity for women in federally funded educational programs (see Chapter 11). This growth, when combined with the AIAW's stated desire for both equity with and separation from men's programs, led to an inevitable conflict with their male counterparts and the NCAA. The AIAW permitted athletic scholarships in 1973 to keep members from moving to the NCAA, but in 1980 the NCAA began to hold championships in women's sports, with the membership voting to expand committees and allocate positions to women. The AIAW sued the NCAA to prevent it from starting championships, asserting that the NCAA was exercising an illegal monopoly over intercollegiate athletics, but the lawsuit failed. Legendary women's basketball coach Pat Summit, who began her career at the University of Tennessee in 1974, had this to say about the two organizations:

> I definitely saw (the AIAW model of governance and recruiting) as restrictive. Players had to come to you. . . . [Recruiting in the NCAA] has really brought about an opportunity for [female] student-athletes to have choices, because they can, regardless of financial background, select colleges of the greatest interest, visit, and have their way paid. It just opened up the door of opportunity. (Suggs, 2005, p. 65)

THE EXPERIENCES OF ETHNIC AND RACIAL MINORITIES IN INTERCOLLEGIATE ATHLETICS

The trials faced by ethnic and racial minority student-athletes, both males and females, in their efforts to participate in intercollegiate athletics were significant as well. Sport involvement, both as participant and as spectator, has always served as a way for recent immigrant groups to integrate into the greater American society. To play American games such as baseball and football meant to be fully a part of the American experience. Intercollegiate athletics were less accessible initially because of the comparatively small number of Americans who had the means to attend schools. Actually, a sense of elitism was actively pursued by the progenitors of early football. Their game was supreme because it was played by amateur gentlemen, and for years college football coaches vehemently denounced the professional version of the game as corrupt, seedy, and loutish (Gems, 2000; Oriard, 1993).

As European ethnic minority groups—Irish, German, Polish, Italian, Czech—slowly gained admittance to higher education institutions, their influence was soon felt in intercollegiate athletics. Perhaps the greatest player in the early era of football was Jim Thorpe, an American Indian Sauk and Fox tribe member from Oklahoma. He played for the Carlisle (Pennsylvania) Indian Industrial School, one of several such institutions nationally founded for the purpose of helping American Indians shed their tribal ways and make the transition into White culture. Carlisle, a boarding school founded in 1879 to teach trades, English language, and other skills to males and females, housed as many as 1,200 students from 76 different tribes. Teams led by Thorpe, Albert Exendine (part Cherokee, part Delaware, also from Oklahoma), Joe Guyon (from the White Earth reservation in Minnesota), and others, under the direction of renowned and innovative head coach Glenn S. "Pop" Warner, became one of the country's strongest programs in the early 20th century. During its peak—1911 through 1913—Carlisle went 38–3 against the era's toughest foes, utilizing the newly legalized forward pass as a key component of its offensive arsenal. Also, the program that would become synonymous with college football success—the University of Notre Dame—achieved its lofty perch in its early decades with a large percentage of players who were of immigrant and Catholic lineage (Gems, 2000; Jenkins, 2007; Oriard, 2001; Sperber, 1993).

For African-Americans, the athletic experiences occurred in separate spheres: at segregated schools and as minorities at mostly White schools. At segregated "historically Black colleges" (HBCs, now HBCUs to include universities), located mostly in the Southeast, laws required that HBCs play only each other, with programs developing at Johnson C. Smith University (Charlotte, North Carolina), Howard University (Washington, DC), Lincoln University (Oxford, Pennsylvania), and Livingstone College (Salisbury, North Carolina). Grundy (2001) notes that "officials at black colleges had looked to sports to build race pride and solidarity . . . at the same time athletic contests gave community cultural endeavors a place within the symbolically potent sphere of educational pursuits" (pp. 179–180). As late as the 1960s, these issues were still powerful for HBCs, as reported by former NBA player and coach Al Attles, a 1960 graduate of North Carolina A&T: "The most important aspect, I feel, was the pride of this small segment of the educational world showing what Black people can do with their own energies and determination" (p. 184).

Significant challenges faced the African-American athletes who played in integrated programs. At predominantly White schools in the North, a few football players gained prominence in the late 19th century, including William Henry Lewis at Amherst (who later became an Assistant U.S. Attorney General). In the early 20th century, others followed, such as Fritz Pollard at Brown University and Paul Robeson at Rutgers, the first African-Americans to be named All-American. But African-American players often were not allowed to suit up against teams from Southern schools, many of which fielded all-White squads into the 1970s. In fact, the 1969 University of Texas squad was the last all-White team to be named national champion in football (Fitzpatrick, 1999).

Many Southern politicians, most notably Alabama governor George Wallace and Mississippi Governor Ross Barnett, saw this issue as a way to make political hay with their state's segregation-minded constituents. Georgia governor Marvin Griffin, however, found himself on the wrong side of public opinion when he sought to bar the Georgia Institute of Technology from playing the University of Pittsburgh and its African-American star Bobby Grier in the 1956 Sugar Bowl. Griffin, who had once said of the integration movement, "We cannot make the slightest concession to the enemy in this dark and lamentable hour of struggle. . . . There is no difference in compromising the integrity of race on the playing field than in doing so in the classroom. . . . One break in the dyke and the relentless sea will rush in and destroy us," pressured Georgia Tech's trustees to keep the team from playing, but thousands of Tech students, relishing the opportunity for national recognition, demonstrated in the streets of downtown Atlanta, many toting "To Hell with Griffin" placards. The school's president allowed the team to go, but the state's legislature still passed a law banning interracial contests within Georgia's borders (Watterson, 2000, pp. 316–317).

In some cases when integrated Northern teams played their all-White Southern rivals, the political battles turned into on-field violence, as experienced in 1951 by Johnny Bright, a running back at Drake University (Des Moines, Iowa). On the first play from scrimmage in a game against Oklahoma A&M (now Oklahoma State University), while standing 5 yards behind his team's ballcarrier, Bright suffered a broken jaw from a violent forearm to the face inflicted by an opponent. At first the A&M coach denied that the play was dirty or racially motivated, but when the game film was made public, the evidence showed otherwise and the coach apologized publicly (Watterson, 2000).

During the 1960s, when civil rights issues began to inch into the nation's consciousness, pioneers such as Wilbur Hackett at the University of Kentucky, Darryl Hill at the University of Maryland, and Jerry LeVias at SMU were among the first African-Americans to integrate Southern football teams. The process was far from easy. These players were shunned by most of their teammates, faced death threats from supposed assassins, and endured racial taunts from opponents and teammates alike (Watterson, 2000; Wolff, 2005).

The experience of an African-American integrating a White program is especially well related by former Auburn (Alabama) University football player Thom Gossom, Jr. Auburn's men's basketball team was integrated by Henry Harris in 1968, and the next year James Owens joined the football team. They were the first African-American players in their sport admitted to a prominent program in the so-called "Deep South" (Alabama, Georgia, Louisiana, Mississippi). At the time Harris was being recruited, the school's president, Dr. Harry Philpott, told the school's board of trustees of his impending matriculation. One trustee responded, "Oh, we can't do that. The state isn't ready for that." When others in the room explained to him that the move was inevitable—especially as Auburn's Southeastern Conference rivals were doing the same, he said, "All right. I won't say anything more. It probably is time." Owens was followed the next year by Gossom, who came to the school as an unrecruited "walk-on," hoping to make the team and earn an athletic grant-in-aid (a.k.a., a scholarship—see Chapter 7). At his first day of practice, Gossom (2008) described what happened: "There was one water break. . . . We were still only a few years removed from legally designated 'white and colored' water fountains. . . . After I drank, two (white) guys behind me decided they weren't thirsty" (p. 44).

Once he made the team, earned a grant-in-aid, and became a starter, Gossom gained the respect of his teammates and coaches but reported that he became close friends with only one Caucasian teammate. Gossom described the team's composition this way: "We had a few hardcore racists. These guys I avoided. At best we were teammates." Gossom explained that most of these "hardcore racist" teammates' prejudices were a result of "ignorance and their sheltered upbringings," and the fact that they had never played with, socialized, or even knew any African-Americans. One such player, whom Gossom described as a country boy who kept to himself and didn't bother anybody, would never sit next to an African-American teammate in the team's dorm dining hall. Gossom attempted to sit next to him once, and the player got up and moved, without a word. Gossom notes that over time the player and he "never became friends, but we became friendly. . . . He had a long journey to travel. He came a long way" (pp. 125–126).

Nonetheless, Gossom still endured more subtle forms of racism. Players would call other African-Americans "niggers" in front of Gossom, apologize, but continue to use the derogatory term. At the end of the third quarter at home games, Gossom (2008) noted:

> [T]he players and fans would stand at attention. The band would play "Dixie" as the Confederate flag flying over the stadium while the U.S. flag was lowered. Most of the fans stood with a hand over their heart. It was a moment right out of the old

South. Once the flag was lowered, the place erupted into cheers. Whenever we got to this moment in the game, I became terribly uncomfortable, if not pissed. . . . I never made a deal out of it to anyone, but I would not, could not honor the tradition. (p. 143)

As a result, Gossom participated in campus protests calling for better treatment for African-Americans on the campus. When asked about his experiences at Auburn, Gossom notes that he was asked many times, "'Well, why didn't you leave?' The simple answer is that we were on a mission. We believed we could make a difference" (p. 71). Gossom reinforced this notion in describing another scene from home football games. He recalls that when the team passed the seating section reserved for the all-African-American members of the school's buildings and grounds staff,

the men's eyes were always riveted on [my roommate] and me. Many of the men reminded me of my dad and the men from my neighborhood. Not only were we getting an opportunity they'd never had, they had to sit and watch us on bleachers that were the equivalent of them sitting on the back of the bus. [My roommate] and I represented their opportunity. Many times I felt I carried the weight of their dreams on my shoulders. (p. 143)

After his Auburn career, Gossom was selected by the New England Patriots in the 14th round of the 1975 NFL draft.

During this time, African-American athletes at some schools outside the South were also feeling the sting of racism, particularly when seeking the right to political expression. One notable case involved 14 African-American football players at the University of Wyoming. The players had asked head coach Lloyd Eaton for permission to wear armbands in their game against Brigham Young University, which is formally aligned with the Church of Jesus Christ of Latter Day Saints (a.k.a., the Mormon Church), to protest the fact that African-Americans were, at the time, banned from joining the Mormon faith. Eaton forbade all his players, regardless of race, from participating in political protests, commenting, "No [Wyoming] football player . . . could be a competent student, an excellent athlete, and still devote himself to such actions as political and social movements." In response to the requests of his African-American players, he not only denied permission, but he kicked the 14 off the team, commenting that if they did not want to play by his rules, they could go on "Negro relief," play for an HBC, or "go back to picking cotton" (Oriard, 2009, p. 105).

The specific experiences of individual African-American student-athletes aside, the event that stands out to many as the seminal moment in the struggle for racial equality in intercollegiate athletics occurred in men's basketball on March 19, 1966, at Cole Field House on the campus of the University of Maryland. It was the final of the 28th NCAA men's basketball championship. Before the opening tip, scheduled for 10 P.M., University of Kentucky coach and future Hall of Famer Adolph Rupp was preparing his Wildcats to take on the decidedly underdog Miners from Texas Western College (now the University of Texas-El Paso), led by head coach Don Haskins. Historian Frank Fitzpatrick (1999) describes the scene moments before the tip:

A confederate flag can be seen amid the tightly packed rows of mostly white shirts. The crowd appears to be entirely white. So are the two officials and all the reporters on press row. After Kentucky's three white coaches wrap up their final instructions, the Wildcat starters, five white players in white uniforms, walk toward midcourt. And then, moving casually toward them with the slow stride of history, come the Texas Western starters. . . . All five of them are black. (p. 24)

Fitzpatrick (1999) notes that NCAA championship teams at that time had started three and even four African-American players, but "no major college team had broken the invisible barrier by starting five" (p. 25). Given that fact, the game took on an added meaning because Texas Western's opponent was mighty Kentucky, which was all White (including future NBA coach Pat Riley), and led by Rupp, whom most considered to be an avowed racist. The Miners, who had five Whites on the 12-man roster, had to take on more than Kentucky that night. The team had to face the stereotypical perceptions that African-Americans, while seen as stronger and more athletic than Whites, couldn't play a team-oriented game, were undisciplined, were ignorant, and would give up if they got behind.

The game stayed close until the 7-minute mark of the second half, when the Miners, who shot well from the foul line, took a 9-point lead, finally winning by a 72–65 score. After the game, TWC guard Bobby Joe Hill's brother Virgil congratulated him, telling him the win was a historic one. "What do you mean?" Bobby Joe asked his brother. "Virgil said, 'It's the first time five blacks had beaten five whites in a game like this.' I hadn't thought about that until then. All I could do was smile and say, 'Wow' . . . [but] everyone got it wrong. That's the thing. The story is messed up. It was Kentucky that was different, not us. We didn't make it white against black" (Fitzpatrick, p. 220). A long-time friend of Rupp put this perspective on the game: "Adolph hated each and every loss in his career. But that one hit him like a ton of bricks. . . . The man was under pressure for not recruiting blacks, he was being criticized for that even at his own school. Then he goes out and loses the NCAA championship to an all-black team. . . . He was repudiated" (pp. 217–218). If the TWC game was powerful enough to impact the infamous Rupp to this extent, it is hardly an exaggeration to call it historic.

The move to integrate schools that had either banned African-Americans from playing or had demonstrated minimal interest in their recruitment *did* impact some schools negatively, specifically the HBCUs. Scholar Michael Oriard (2009) points out that schools such as Florida A&M University, Grambling State University, and Southern University in Louisiana, Morgan State University in Maryland, and Jackson State University in Alabama (which had 11 players drafted by NFL teams in 1968) now were losing their prized recruits to schools such as Alabama and Auburn. Some African-American players also were criticized by their friends and community members for turning their backs on the HBCs, "regarding them as Uncle Toms and wondering why historically black colleges like Grambling, Prairie View, and Florida A&M suddenly weren't good enough" (Wolff, 2005, p. 67).

As a result of the developments outlined above, intercollegiate athletic teams today are far more representative of the demographic make-up of the nation as a whole than those of a century earlier, and far more Americans can access the stated benefits of participation in intercollegiate athletics. Many of these changes were made through great personal sacrifices by those who first sought these enhanced participation opportunities.

THE POPULARITY OF INTERCOLLEGIATE ATHLETICS: AN INSTITUTIONAL PERSPECTIVE

Smith (1971) stated that as student bodies approached heterogeneity, "the sole community of interest began to reside in attendance at sporting events and a few other social pastimes" (p. 65). Handlin and Handlin (1970) noted that "the athletic contest was a great ritual event which drew together students and alumni and, in the zest of the effort to beat the other side, developed a consciousness of their identity" (p. 59). Said Higgs (1995): "The sporting spirit became virtually synonymous with the college spirit, in a mixture of competition, achievement, and leadership" (p. 102). Said Smith (1971): "By the mid 1920s, the foundations of intercollegiate athletics as they exist today has been cemented" (p. 70).

Simon (1971) argues that universities and colleges do not have to host intercollegiate athletic programs, and that "scholarship can proceed quite well without having athletic departments, football weekends, the NCAA basketball tournament, or baseball games with a crosstown rival" (p. 48), and Chu (1989) cites the need for community, student involvement, a cultural interest in clearly defined success, and the desire to perceive the potential for success as the salient redeeming qualities. Former Harvard president Derek Bok (1985) observed this keenly in writing:

> America is different. Its universities are unique in their efforts to please many constituencies—prospective students, donors, legislators, the general public.... The growth of intercollegiate sports aptly illustrates the strengths and weaknesses of a constituency-oriented system of higher education. With enthusiastic support from students, alumni, and even government officials, our colleges have developed athletic programs that have brought great satisfaction to thousands of athletes and millions of spectators. Few aspects of college life have done so much to win the favor of the public, build the loyalties of alumni, and engender lasting memories in the minds of student-athletes. (p. 124)

Novak (1976), concurred, noting that "in varsity sports, universities give the nation the most profound and nourishing popular arts accessible to all our citizens" (p. 284).

These popular arts did not come without costs, though. Sperber (1998) indicated that "toward the end of the nineteenth century, two conflicting trends occurred: colleges and universities began to raise their academic standards, and the proponents of college sports increasingly demanded winning teams, (and) athletes who could perform at the highest possible level and beat their opponents. The search for the scholar athletes began" (p. 11).

The emergence of the land-grant college coincided with the increasing acceptance and proliferation of intercollegiate athletics. Land-grant schools are those founded with public funds as decreed under federal law soon after the Civil War to provide greater access to higher education—initially, mostly in agricultural and technical studies programs. Both land-grant schools and intercollegiate athletics were in a sense manifestations of democratic trends in 19th-century American education, and land-grant schools were "probably the greatest beneficiaries of the sports movement," as they "could compete in these area as equals with the traditional colleges" (Turner, 1984, pp. 158–160). A school need not acquire the strongest faculty or the most pristine and agreeable campus and grounds, or conjure up a litany of athletic successes. A school need only get the chance for its students (not necessarily undergraduates or apt scholars) to knock heads against those from another institution.

The land-grant movement also diminished the air of privilege that had permeated most campuses, which helped change attitudes about athletic excellence and professionalism. Industrial expansion, changing demographics, and expanding cities also created markets and the demand for leisure and entertainment opportunities. Professional and intercollegiate athletics both filled these needs nicely. Many institutions were founded by towns in the Midwest and West in the 19th century to promote emigration and local development. As a result, as noted with the linkage of the land-grant ideal and athletics, in 1924 six of the top nine schools in football attendance were non-Eastern schools (Notre Dame, Michigan, University of California, Berkeley, Ohio State University, University of Chicago, University of Illinois). In that year, 90,000 patrons witnessed the California–Stanford University grid battle, and in 1928 more than 120,000 fans—still the largest college football crowd ever—packed Chicago's Soldier Field for the game between Notre Dame and the University of Southern California. Between 1924 and 1940, four Eastern teams and 37 non-Eastern teams were considered as possible football national champions (Lester, 1995; Sack & Staurowsky, 1998; Sperber, 1993).

Presidents at some of these new powers actively promoted athletics as a vehicle to publicize the institution at large in competing for students and donations among the burgeoning ranks of higher education institutions. Four notable cases are William R. Harper at the University of Chicago (later to be undone under the tenure of Robert M. Hutchins), John A. Hannah at Michigan State University, H.C. "Curly" Byrd at Maryland (who once served as the school's head football coach), and Herman Lee Donovan at Kentucky (Lawson & Ingham, 1980; Shapiro, 1983; Thelin, 1996; Sperber, 1998). A final perspective on the American phenomenon is offered by Sack and Staurowsky (1998), who conclude that athletics was and is "a bridge which could link the high culture of the university with the mass culture of the broader society. . . . Nothing could better attract the attention of mass media, and nothing had a greater appeal to the practical-minded business leaders who provided financial support and who increasingly came to dominate academe's governing boards" (p. 20).

These are the realities that make American intercollegiate athletics what they are. They serve as a framework for the challenges facing intercollegiate athletic managers.

CONCLUSION

Students first initiated and organized athletic programs for health and fitness reasons, but the focus quickly shifted from participation-based programs toward institution-maintained programs that sought to achieve primacy over rival institutions. Intercollegiate athletics since has evolved to mean different things to each stakeholder group: students, faculty, administrators, coaches, parents, boosters, alumni, the general public. These diverse collections seek varied outcomes from intercollegiate athletics, including entertainment, a way to create bonds with the institution, a chance for physical activity, and an opportunity for professional advancement.

Since the establishment of Harvard College in 1636, American institutions of higher education have sought to integrate all facets of life into the collegiate experience. This institutionalizing of non-academic student life inevitably would give rise to the college's involvement in sponsoring intercollegiate athletics, emerging with a crew race between Harvard and Yale in 1852. By 1870, intercollegiate athletics had won a recognized place in college life. Student-run organizations operated athletic programs well into the early 20th century, but the era of solely student-run programs ended in 1864 with Yale's hiring of the first professional coach.

By the end of the 19th century, football had become the dominant sport on college campuses. Many, including some school presidents, extolled the virtue of athletics, specifically football, but on-field violence seriously threatened the existence of the game. Eventually, pushed by the newly founded NCAA, rule changes were instituted, which helped to create a safer, more exciting game and to usher in decades of growing popularity for college football.

The NCAA's membership has since established thousands of rules pertaining to the administration of intercollegiate athletics, most of which focus on setting policy relating to and curbing abuses and perceived unfair institutional advantages in recruiting, financial aid, and issues of amateurism. The NCAA slowly assumed the role of arbiter for initial eligibility academic requirements. In 1952, the NCAA began to develop significant powers, when the association negotiated the first college football television contract with NBC for a total rights fee of just over $1 million for 12 games.

The early decades of intercollegiate athletics were mostly the preserve of affluent White males. By 1920, nearly half of all college students were women, but while the numbers of women on campus were significant, their opportunities to participate in intercollegiate athletics were far fewer and more restrictive. The growth in women's programs was aided in large part to passage of Title IX of the Education Amendments of 1972, a federal law that sought to increase equity for women in federally funded educational programs. As European minority groups slowly gained admittance to higher education institutions, their influence soon was felt in intercollegiate athletics, as was that of American Indians and African Americans.

PRACTITIONER perspective:

STEVE STAPLES, Harvard Assistant Athletic Director for Marketing and Communications

Working in the shadow of history: Athletic sales and marketing at Harvard University

Although the chapter indicated the important role of Harvard University in founding what had become American intercollegiate athletics, the school since has chosen to turn away from the more commercialized aspects of big-time intercollegiate athletics, along with the seven other members of the Ivy League, or more precisely, the Council of Ivy Group Presidents, the league's official title. League membership includes eight renowned and well-established institutions: Brown, Columbia, Cornell, Dartmouth, Harvard, Princeton, Pennsylvania, and Yale. As noted in the chapter, these schools individually and collectively have had a significant impact on the genesis and development of American intercollegiate athletics. But as the development of intercollegiate athletics programs accelerated into entertainment offerings for both on- and off-campus stakeholders in the mid-20th century, the Ivies elected to eschew this course. The Ivies chose instead to focus on fostering intercollegiate athletics on a scale targeted neither toward public entertainment nor inextricably linked with overt commercialism, and according to many, *de facto* professionalism, the contexts that defined the management of other Division I intercollegiate athletic programs. The schools did this by banning athletic scholarships, restricting out-of-season practice, and affirming the observance of common academic standards and eligibility requirements (Timeline, 1999).

However, the Ivies are still members of the NCAA's Division I, and still compete for national titles in many sports, but they do so while trying to maintain a high number of participation opportunities. Today, Harvard maintains varsity intercollegiate athletic programs in 41 sports for 1,500 student-athletes, with annual expenses for these programs exceeding $4 million. Former Harvard athletic director Bill Cleary once referred to the Nike "swoosh," the ubiquitous corporate cipher found on numerous Division I uniforms and coaches' apparel, as a symbolic representation of the phrase, "I own you." Many applaud this stance and view it as "clean" in relation to what is decried as the over-commercialization of Division I athletics, but since even Harvard is not immune to the financial pressures facing contemporary intercollegiate athletic programs, the athletic department must seek to maximize revenues to continue to offer student-athletes a top-notch athletic experience. The balancing of these potentially conflicting tasks fell to Dr. Steve Staples, the assistant athletic director for marketing and communications. Staples, who attended the University of Kentucky as an undergraduate, earned his doctorate from the University of Illinois and worked there and at Utah State University before moving to Harvard. Staples has since moved on to the development office at Princeton. At Harvard, Staples oversaw ticket sales, marketing efforts, and departmental community outreach efforts. Department revenue sources included ticket sales from football, men's and women's basketball, men's and women's ice hockey, and men's lacrosse, concessions sales from these events, merchandise sales, a limited amount of revenues from sales of ads on programs and on schedule cards, and from ads on radio and TV broadcasts.

Staples made it clear to companies looking to affiliate with Harvard athletics that they will never be known as an official sponsor. The distinction had to be made, he says, "because the university has made it very clear that we don't endorse any products." This is because the school and its leadership are uncomfortable with the perception of commercialism tied to athletics. "The provost's office looks at it and says, 'What are the natural products of your department? Tickets? OK, you can sell tickets, and merchandise.' But when you start to have corporate relationships with a bank, or an investment company, they'll ask, 'Why? What's the reason?'" It is a distinction that is made to keep the operation of the athletic department in line with Harvard's educational mission.

Like all American higher education institutions, Harvard courts individual donors for money. When comparing individual donor giving to athletics and corporate involvement, Staples offered that the concern in distancing the department from corporate involvement is to diffuse the perception of corporate control of the department—recalling Bill Cleary's decrying of the "swoosh." Staples said, "I think it gets a little scary. Having worked at a couple of different places, access by corporations is gained. But what access here? Access to better seats? Hey, maybe they deserve better seats, and better parking. But access to decision making? No, and that's the line people worry about here. Are the companies going to have so much power that they're going to want answers, specific results, and decisions based on what's best for Nike rather than what's best for the student-athlete?" Harvard's alumni are very much in support of the department's approach to corporate partnerships. "I've been in plenty of meetings with alums," Staples said, "and they're adamant about Harvard staying the way it is. They don't want us to do the things that other schools are doing. A lot of them don't see that as the right way to do it."

In summarizing the Harvard approach, Staples said, "I don't view corporate sales as marketing, although it may be in terms of exposure, but it's more exposure for corporate entities than it is for the university of the athletic department. Here, I'm in the business of creating new relationships with groups, and exposing to these groups our athletes and our teams to these groups. We focus all our efforts on people that have an affiliation with Harvard—faculty, staff, undergrads, graduate students, alums." The Harvard approach reveals a clear sense of institutional focus, to communicate an image of the university through the workings of its athletic program.

questions TO CONSIDER

1. We learned that early intercollegiate athletic programs were run by students. Can you identify any advantages of having intercollegiate athletic programs run by students rather than professional managers, or is the current model for management far superior?

2. Is the rationale for the value of intercollegiate athletic programs the same today as it was in both the late 19th century and mid-20th century? Why or why not?

3. How are the challenges faced by the NCAA in both the early and middle years of the 20th century different from those faced by the organization and its membership today?

4. Are the contemporary athletic participation opportunities for women and ethnic and racial minorities equal to those of White males? Explain.

5. Can you envision a college or university that would choose not to offer intercollegiate athletic programs? What might be the rationale for such a decision?

references

A History of Academic Legislation. (1980, December 15). *NCAA News*, pp. 2–3.

Barr, C.A. (1998). *The faculty athletics representative: A survey of the membership*. Overland Park, KS: National Collegiate Athletic Association.

Betts, J.R. (1974). *America's sporting heritage: 1850–1950*. Reading, MA: Addison Wesley.

Bok, D. (1985). Intercollegiate athletics. In J.B. Bennett & J.W. Peltason (Eds.), *Contemporary issues in higher education* (pp. 123–146). New York: Macmillan.

Byers, W., with Hammer, C. (1995). *Unsportsmanlike conduct: Exploiting college athletes*. Ann Arbor: University of Michigan Press.

Chu, D. (1989). *The character of American higher education and intercollegiate sport*. Albany: State University of New York Press.

Drape, J. (2009, December 24). New life at S.M.U. with a bowl to play. *New York Times*, p. B11.

Dunnavant, K. (2004). *The fifty-year seduction: How television manipulated college football, from the birth of the modern NCAA to the creation of the BCS*. New York: St. Martin's Press.

Falla, J. (1981). *NCAA: Voice of college sports*. Shawnee Mission, KS: National Collegiate Athletic Association.

Fitzpatrick, F. (1999). *And the walls came tumbling down: Kentucky, Texas Western, and the game that changed American sports*. New York: Simon and Schuster.

Fleisher, A.A., Goff, B.L., and Tollison, R.D. (1992). *The National Collegiate Athletic Association: A study in cartel behavior*. Chicago: The University of Chicago Press.

Gems, G.R. (2000). *For pride, profit, and patriarchy: Football and the incorporation of American cultural values*. Latham, MD: Scarecrow Press.

Gossom, Jr., T. (2008). *Walk-on: My reluctant journey to integration at Auburn University—A memoir*. Ann Arbor, MI: State Street Press.

Grundy, P. (2001). *Learning to win: Sports, education, and social change in twentieth-century North Carolina*. Chapel Hill: University of North Carolina Press.

Handlin, O., & Handlin, M.F. (1970). *The American college and American culture: Socialization as a function of higher education*. New York: McGraw-Hill.

Haskins, C.H. (1957). *The rise of the universities* (Rev. ed.). Ithaca, NY: Cornell University Press.

Helman, J.W. (1989). *A history of American intercollegiate athletic eligibility: Educational compromises to competitive interests*. Unpublished doctoral dissertation. Pennsylvania State University.

Higgs, R.J. (1995). *God in the stadium: Sports and religion in America*. Lexington: University of Kentucky Press.

Jenkins, S. (2007). *The real All-Americans: The team that changed a game, a people, a nation*. New York: Doubleday.

Lawrence, P.L. (1987). *Unsportsmanlike conduct: The National Collegiate Athletic Association and the business of college football*. New York: Praeger.

Lawson, H.A., & Ingham, A.G. (1980, Winter). Conflicting ideologies concerning the Princeton, NJ: Council of Ivy Group Presidents.

Layden, T. (2002, November 18). The loneliest losers. *Sports Illustrated*, pp. 69–71.

Lester, R. (1995). *Stagg's University: The rise, decline, and fall of big-time football at Chicago*. Urbana: University of Illinois Press.

Lewis, G. (1970, Summer). The beginning of organized collegiate sport. *American Quarterly*, 2(1), pp. 220–229.

McPhee, J. (1978). *A sense of where you are*. New York: Farrar, Straus and Giroux.

Miller, P.B. (1997, Fall). The manly, the moral, and the proficient: College sport in the new South. *Journal of Sport History*, 24(3), pp. 285–316.

Morris, W. (1992). *The courting of Marcus Dupree* (Rev. ed.). Jackson: University of Mississippi Press.

Mott, R.D. (1995, January 4). The 100-year debate. *NCAA News supplement: 89th convention issue*, pp. 1, 10, 11.

1964-1965 Yearbook of the National Collegiate Athletic Association. (1965). Kansas City: National Collegiate Athletic Association.

Novak, M. (1976). *The joy of sports*. New York: Basic Books.

Oriard, M. (1993). *Reading football: How the popular press created an American spectacle*. Chapel Hill: University of North Carolina Press.

Oriard, M. (2001). *King football: Sports and spectacle in the golden age of radio and newsreels, movies and magazines, the weekly and the daily press*. Chapel Hill, NC: University of North Carolina Press.

Oriard, M. (2009). *Bowled over: Big-time college football from the sixties to the BCS era*. Chapel Hill, NC: University of North Carolina Press.

Proceedings of the 66th annual convention of the National Collegiate Athletic Association (1972). Mission, KS: National Collegiate Athletic Association.

Proceedings of the 77th annual convention of the National Collegiate Athletic Association (1983). Mission, KS: National Collegiate Athletic Association.

Rand, F. P. (1933). *Yesterdays at Massachusetts State College*. Amherst, MA: Associate Alumni of Massachusetts State College.

Rudolph, F. (1990). *The American college and university: A history* (Rev. ed). Athens: University of Georgia Press.

Sack, A. L., & Staurowsky, E. J. (1998). *College athletes for hire: The evolution and legacy of the NCAA's amateur myth*. Westport, CT: Praeger.

Sandomir, R. (1995, March 17). TV sports: CBS's basketball bet is biggest one of all. *New York Times*. Accessed June 2, 2009, from: http://www.nytimes.com/1995/03/17/sports/tv-sports-cbs-s-basketball-bet-is-the-biggest-one-of-all.html

Seymour, H. (1989). *Baseball: The early years*. New York: Oxford University Press.

Shapiro, B.J. (1983, Winter). John Hannah and the growth of big-time intercollegiate athletics at Michigan State University. *Journal of Sport History*, 10(3), pp. 24–40.

Sheldon, H.D. (1969). *Student life and customs (Rev. ed.)*. New York: Arno Press.

Simon, R.L. (1991). Intercollegiate athletics: Do they belong on campus? In J. Andre & D.N. James (Eds.), *Rethinking college athletics* (pp. 43–68). Philadelphia: Temple University Press.

Smith, M.D. (1971, December). Origins of faculty attitudes toward intercollegiate athletics: The University of Wisconsin. *Canadian Journal of Sport and Physical Education*, 2(2), pp. 61–72.

Smith, R.A. (1988). *Sports and freedom: The rise of big-time college athletics*. New York: Oxford University Press.

Sperber, M. (1993). *Shake down the thunder: The creation of Notre Dame football*. New York: Henry Holt.

Sperber, M. (1998). *Onward to victory: The crises that shaped college sports*. New York: Henry Holt.

Suggs, W. (2005). *A place on the team*. Princeton, NJ: Princeton University Press.

Telander, R. (1989). *The hundred yard lie*. New York: Simon and Schuster

Thelin, J.R. (1996). *Games colleges play: Scandal and reform in intercollegiate athletics*. Baltimore: Johns Hopkins University Press.

Timeline: Council of Ivy Group presidents. (1999). *The Ivy League directory and record book*. University and intercollegiate athletics: Harper and Hutchins at Chicago, 1892–1940. *Journal of Sport History*, 7(3), pp. 37–67.

Townsend, K. (1996). *Manhood at Harvard: William James and others*. Cambridge, MA: Harvard University Press.

Turner, P.V. (1984). *Campus: An American planning tradition*. New York: Architectural History Foundation.

Watterson, J.S. (2000). *College football: History, spectacle, controversy*. Baltimore, MD: Johns Hopkins University Press.

Wilson, J. (1994). *Playing by the rules: Sport, society, and the state*. Detroit: Wayne State University Press.

Wolff, A. (2005, November 7). Ground breakers. *Sports Illustrated*, pp. 58–67.

Yaeger, D. (1991). *Undue process: The NCAA's injustice for all*. Champaign, IL: Sagamore Publishing.

The role of the NCAA and other national governing bodies

2

Key concepts to keep in mind while you read the chapter:

- The structure of and various managerial roles unique to the National Collegiate Athletic Association (NCAA).

- How the NCAA's Principles of Conduct influence how the organization fulfills its purposes and mission.

- The specifics pertaining to the NCAA's rule-making process.

- The nature of each of the NCAA's three divisional classifications.

- How other significant governing bodies— the National Association of Intercollegiate Athletics (NAIA) and the National Junior College Athletic Association (NJCAA)—are structured to serve their specific memberships.

Introduction

The National Collegiate Athletic Association (NCAA) is a critical organization in shaping and controlling this industry segment. The NCAA evolved into a rule-making and governing body initially in response to issues relating to injuries and fatalities in football. The organization then adapted in response to issues pertaining to recruiting, academic standards, and later, the emerging technological and financial impact of television. Where does that leave the organization today? How can we define it so we can understand its role in the management of intercollegiate athletics? A simple definition is that the NCAA is the rule-making body for intercollegiate athletics; however, two other such organizations are also involved in overseeing a segment of intercollegiate athletics: the National Association of Intercollegiate Athletics (NAIA) and the National Junior College Athletic Association (NJCAA). In this chapter we will first look at the purpose and methods of the NCAA, and then examine the other two governing bodies for comparison.

THE ROLE OF THE NCAA

To help you understand the role of the NCAA in intercollegiate athletics, we will discuss the following topics: its mission, purpose, principles of conduct, membership, legislative process, national office, leadership, divisional classifications, and the processes of certification, self-study, and evaluation.

Mission and purpose

The contemporary NCAA has evolved into the most significant intercollegiate athletics governing body in the United States. It is a voluntary association (that is, its members choose to join) consisting of more than 1,000 institutions, conferences, organizations, and individuals. It is organized into three divisional classifications based on the stated philosophical direction of each school's intercollegiate athletic program. Each of its divisionally specific operations manuals first defines its basic purpose as part of its fundamental policy under Article 1 of its Constitution, codified as follows:

> The competitive athletics programs of member institutions are designed to be a vital part of the educational system. A basic purpose of this Association is to maintain intercollegiate athletics as an integral part of the educational program and the athlete as an integral part of the student body and, by so doing, retain a clear line of demarcation between intercollegiate athletics and professional sports. (*2008–09 NCAA Division I Manual*, 2008, p. 1)

In examining this definition, the NCAA sets forth as its goals for the intercollegiate athletic programs it seeks to maintain (*2008–09 NCAA Division I Manual*, 2008, p. 1):

- That athletics are to be maintained as an integral part of the educational program—meaning that the NCAA expects athletic programs to be teaching and learning experiences.

- That the above expectation can be achieved only if athletes are an integral part of the student body.
- That athletes can be part of the student body only if the clear demarcation between intercollegiate and professional athletics is maintained.

Understanding these goals can help to reveal the reasoning behind certain NCAA actions and policies. Sometimes, though, these suggestions are well-meaning and based on well-reasoned rationale but clearly at odds with the essential basic purpose of the Association. The members of the NCAA determine the rules by which they must abide.

So why has the membership, in its wisdom, decreed that the line between intercollegiate and professional athletics be so sharply defined? Critics of the NCAA say that the membership has drawn this line based on some antiquated concept of the purity of amateur sport and the notion that student-athletes play for nothing other than "love of the game." These critics also usually note that if athletic departments don't have to compensate student-athletes, the departments can operate at a lower cost, even as head coaches in many sports receive multi-millions of dollars in salaries, bonuses, and perks. Supporters of the current system argue that the athletes are students first and foremost, the vast majority of whom are part of teams and programs that generate no revenue whatsoever, and that many students at the Division I level receive an opportunity for a free or discounted education based on their participation in athletics—an arrangement that could be worth several hundreds of thousands of dollars, depending on the cost of attendance at a specific institution.

The challenge for us as we consider the unique nature of the NCAA and the task of managing the idiosyncratic world of American intercollegiate athletics is that the current system is at times an imperfect one, meant to govern a membership that has a wide and often disparate range of goals and objectives to be achieved by maintaining their intercollegiate athletic programs (many of which we will consider in Chapter 4). Since the founding of the NCAA, the membership has established thousands upon thousands of rules pertaining to the administration of intercollegiate athletics, most of which focus on setting policies relating to and curbing abuses and perceived unfair institutional advantages in recruiting, financial aid, and issues of amateurism to create the concept of the "level playing field."

Former NCAA executive director Cedric Dempsey understood some of the negative perceptions regarding the NCAA when he commented: "The public has a hard time understanding that all of these rules have been made by the membership. We're only responsible for implementing those rules. . . . Those rules have been made because of mistrust within the membership for each other" (Rushin, 1997, p. 2). In response to all these rules, and the corresponding enforcement of them, Dempsey also opined that for the NCAA to be effective as an organization, "We need to ask 'What is our mission? And what are the minimum standards to meet that mission?'"

As we consider the Association of today, we have to contemplate the managerial implications of these concepts. In an effort to clarify the NCAA's goals and its role in managing intercollegiate athletics, the first pages of its divisional manuals list nine more specific purposes that further illustrate the roles and actions of the Association. These purposes are listed in Exhibit 2.1.

EXHIBIT   2.1   Purposes of the NCAA.

- To initiate, stimulate, and improve intercollegiate athletics programs for student-athletes and to promote and develop educational leadership, physical fitness, athletics excellence and athletics participation as a recreational pursuit.
- To uphold the principle of institutional control of, and responsibility for, all intercollegiate sports in conformity with the constitution and bylaws of the association.
- To encourage its members to adopt eligibility rules that comply with satisfactory standards of scholarship, sportsmanship, and amateurism.
- To formulate, copyright, and publish rules of play governing intercollegiate athletics.
- To preserve intercollegiate athletic records.
- To supervise the conduct of, and establish eligibility rules for, regional and national athletic events under the auspices of the Association.
- To cooperate with other amateur athletics organizations in promoting and conducting national and international athletics events.
- To legislate, through bylaws or by resolutions of a Convention, upon any subject of general concern to the members related to the administration of intercollegiate athletics.
- To study in general all phases of competitive intercollegiate athletics and establish standards whereby the colleges and universities in the United States can maintain their athletics programs at a high level.

Source: 2008–09 NCAA Division I Manual, 2008, p. 1.

At the bottom of page 1 of the divisional manuals, the reader will find Bylaw 1.3.2, the obligations of member institutions, which reads that the Association will pass and apply legislation pertaining to admissions, financial aid, eligibility, and recruiting, and that "member institutions shall be obligated to apply and enforce this legislation, and the enforcement procedures of the Association shall be applied to an institution when it fails to fulfill this obligation" (*2008–09 NCAA Division I Manual,* 2008, p. 1). This bylaw serves as a warning that all intercollegiate athletic teams, conferences, coaches, administrators, student-athletes, and other member stakeholders participating and involved in NCAA-sponsored sports must abide by its rules or face the consequences as meted out through the enforcement process (outlined in detail in Chapter 8).

Principles for conduct of intercollegiate athletics

As outlined above, the purposes stated in Article 1 of the NCAA Constitution relate to general areas of managerial operations. These are codified operationally in 16 principles of conduct in Article 2 of the Constitution. This article attempts to convey the rationale behind all Association legislation, or its rules, so the membership can better understand how to operate its programs in compliance with NCAA guidelines and objectives. The guiding premise that underscores each of the 16 principles is that all legislation enacted by the NCAA be designed to advance one or more of these basic principles. As we examine these principles in the order in which they are presented in each divisional manual, followed by a discussion of how each influences managerial operations, it is helpful to think about the rationale behind the inclusion of each, the issues each is intended to address, how each relates to the others, and which are most critical for consideration by intercollegiate athletic managers.

Principle of institutional control and responsibility

Under this first principle, each member institution is responsible for controlling its intercollegiate athletics program in compliance with the rules and regulations of the Association, with the ultimate responsibility for the conduct and expenditures of the athletic department resting with the school's president. In addition, the institution's responsibility includes overseeing the actions of its own staff members, "and for the actions of any individual or organization involved in the athletic interests of the institution" (*2008–09 NCAA Division I Manual*, 2008, p. 3).

The issue of institutional control is often cited in infractions cases, when rules violations have given a school a competitive or recruiting advantage. Because athletic departments are responsible for the actions of those not employed by the department, this is also often a factor in infractions cases, when the actions of alumni, boosters, or fans run counter to stated NCAA legislation. Later in the manual, under Article 6, the concept of institutional control is further defined and emphasized, with requirements outlined as to the proper conduct of managerial personnel on campus and their responsibilities to ensure that this principle can be upheld.

Principle of student-athlete well-being

As we will learn later, many critics of the intercollegiate athletics enterprise claim that student-athletes are exploited by athletic departments, and that they are used for their athletic abilities with little regard for and attention to their other needs. The principle of student-athlete well-being attempts to address this concern by stating that intercollegiate athletics programs should be conducted in a manner designed "to protect and enhance the physical and educational well-being of student-athletes" (*2008–09 NCAA Division I Manual*, 2008, p. 3). This is to be attained by attention to the specific critical aspects of the student-athlete experience presented in Exhibit 2.2.

Areas to be addressed to ensure student-athlete well-being under Article 2.2 of the NCAA Constitution.	EXHIBIT 2.2

- The overall educational experience, where all activities are conducted as an integral part of educational well-being of the student-athlete
- Maintaining an environment where cultural diversity and gender equity are valued
- Protecting the health and safety of student-athletes
- Maintaining and fostering an environment where the student-athlete/coach relationship is positive
- Assuring fairness, openness, and honesty in the relationship between administrators and student-athletes
- Allowing student-athlete involvement in matters that affect their lives

Source: 2008–09 NCAA Division I Manual, 2008.

Principle of gender equity

In connection with one of the areas noted in Exhibit 2.2, this principle states that each member institution is responsible for complying with federal and state laws regarding gender equity, that the Association should not pass legislation preventing schools from complying with these laws, and that the activities of the Association should be conducted in a manner free of gender bias (*2008–09 NCAA Division I Manual*, 2008). The key federal law in question here is Title IX of the Education Amendments of 1972. The issue of gender equity can be defined loosely as whether team members of one gender would accept treatment and support similar to that received by the other gender, and vice versa. Efforts to achieve gender equity have had a history of contentiousness for athletic managers, so it is not surprising that the membership has sought to formalize statements that show the organization is committed to pursuing equity.

Principle of sportsmanship and ethical conduct

This principle requires that if athletic departments are to promote character development, to enhance the integrity of higher education, and to promote civility in society, everyone associated with athletic departments should adhere to fundamental values such as respect, fairness, civility, honesty, and responsibility. To meet these goals, athletic departments are required to establish policies that are consistent with the educational mission and goals of the institution in which they are housed. It is clear to see how the issues addressed in this principle are applied to on-field and administrative actions, but given the increased concerns regarding student-athlete behavior off the field (as discussed later in the book), this principle may have to be adapted to help address issues in these areas. Current NCAA legislation does not extend to off-field transgressions that do not include performance-enhancing substances and some recreational drugs identified as part of the Association's mandatory drug-testing program.

Principle of sound academic standards

Using language similar to that outlining the basic purpose of the Association in Article 1, this principle specifies that intercollegiate athletics programs be maintained as a vital component of the educational program and that student-athletes be an integral part of the student body. To meet this stated objective, the principle further asserts that the admission, academic standing, and academic progress of student-athletes be the same as the policies and standards adopted by the institution for the general student body (*2008–09 NCAA Division I Manual*, 2008). Much of what the Association and its members identify as the essential characteristic of intercollegiate athletics is that it be a participatory and educatory opportunity for non-professionals housed within institutions of higher education. As such, it is critical that intercollegiate athletes be perceived as and actually be full-time students.

Principle of nondiscrimination

Under this principle, which is related conceptually to the principle of student-athlete well-being and the principle of gender equity, the Association is charged with promoting an atmosphere of respect for and sensitivity to the dignity of every person. The Association will seek to meet this goal by refraining from discrimination with respect to its governance policies, educational programs, activities, and employment policies; and individual athletic departments will assist by creating their own policies and procedures. The categories identified include age, color, disability, gender, national origin, race, religion, creed, and sexual orientation (*2008–09 NCAA Division I Manual*, 2008).

Principle of diversity within governance structures

As another principle that addresses diversity issues, this principle requires that the Association promote ethnic and gender diversity of representation among the membership in the various divisional governance and administrative structures and substructures (*2008–09 NCAA Division I Manual*, 2008). Traditionally underrepresented groups such as women and non-Whites are to be considered closely for leadership positions within the Association.

Principle of rules compliance

Under this principle, related to the principle of institutional control, each member institution pledges to comply with all applicable Association rules and regulations in operating its athletic department. Athletic departments also are responsible for monitoring programs to assure compliance with rules and for reporting instances in which compliance was not achieved. In these cases, schools must cooperate fully with any associated investigation, and take the appropriate corrective actions based on the investigation's findings (*2008–09 NCAA Division I Manual*, 2008, p. 4). The compliance and enforcement function of the Association has evolved into one of its key roles because, if rules are in place, there also must be mechanisms to assure that the rules are followed, and if not, an appropriate system must exist to uncover such actions and to punish those who act in such a fashion. Without such a system, those inclined to operate outside the rules would have little incentive to do otherwise.

Principle of amateurism

Reinforcing another concept outlined in the Association's basic purpose, this principle declares that student-athletes must be amateurs and their participation should be motivated primarily by education and by the physical, mental, and social benefits to be derived. Participation in intercollegiate athletics should be an "avocation." To maintain athletics as an avocation, the Association, member conferences, and athletic departments have to protect student-athletes from exploitation by professional and commercial enterprises. Under the basic purpose, the Association seeks to "retain a clear line of distinction between intercollegiate athletics and professional sports" (*2008–09 NCAA Division I Manual*, 2008, pp. 1, 5). Through the commitment to maintain student-athlete amateurism, this clear line of distinction is demarcated. The staunch commitment to retaining this line, however, exposes the Association and its membership to claims that it is exploiting student-athletes by not allowing them to share in the levels of revenue generated by the intercollegiate athletics enterprise. (These issues are discussed in more detail in Chapters 6 and 10.)

Principle of competitive equity

The concept of the "level playing field" is at the heart of this principle: "The structure and programs of the Association and the activities of its members shall promote opportunity for equity in competition to assure that individual student-athletes and institutions will not be prevented unfairly from achieving the benefits inherent in participation in intercollegiate athletics" (*2008–09 NCAA Division I Manual*, 2008, p. 5).

So how does the legislative process assure that everybody plays under the same rules in important activities such as recruiting, academic eligibility, and financing intercollegiate athletic operations? Also, does the opportunity to win represent the prized benefit that this principle seeks to protect? Or are there other principles beyond winning? Throughout the text we will see examples of how each segment of the intercollegiate athletic enterprise deals with defining and attaining these benefits within the unique framework of institutions of higher learning.

Principle governing recruiting

To speak to some of the competitive equity concepts outlined in the competitive equity principle, the principle governing recruiting states that this process "involves a balancing of the interests of prospective student-athletes, their educational institutions and the Association's member institutions," and that recruiting regulations are in place to promote equity during recruiting and to shield prospects from undue pressures that may interfere with the academic or athletic interests of both the prospect and the institutions (*2008–09 NCAA Division I Manual*, 2008, p. 5). When considering this principle, what kinds of interests are in question, and why do they have to be balanced by NCAA legislation? The acquisition of talented players is the main challenge for intercollegiate athletics coaches and departments (see Chapter 7). As a result, the competition to acquire this important resource is stiff indeed, for the programs that win are often those with the best players. And many coaches know that if they don't win, they will be looking for another job in short order. So when it comes to winning games and job security and the revenue enhancement that accompanies both of these factors, it is not surprising that a myriad of rules have evolved to try to reinforce the primacy of this principle.

Principle governing eligibility

This principle is meant to guide the membership and its legislation to craft eligibility requirements that assure the proper emphasis on educational objectives, promote competitive equity, and prevent exploitation of student-athletes (*2008–09 NCAA Division I Manual*, 2008). Often when the term "exploitation" is used in the context of critiquing the intercollegiate athletic enterprise, it is in conjunction with the belief that student-athletes should be able to share in the revenues that their efforts help to generate. But what about those thousands of student-athletes who either have no real prospects for professional careers or whose programs generate no revenues? How can it be claimed that these individuals are being exploited? The claim can be valid unless eligibility rules are crafted in such a way that student-athletes are capable and are afforded the opportunity of making the most of the educational opportunities that institutions are supposed to be providing, so the student-athletes can complete their education and graduate.

The athletics grant-in-aid, commonly referred to as an "athletic scholarship," is not a payment for athletic services but, rather, a promise that if prospects participate in intercollegiate athletics, they will be allowed to pursue a degree in conjunction with their athletic commitments. Thus, eligibility rules (Chapter 9) are in place so the Association and its members are not allowed to operate under a system of academic exploitation in which student-athletes are neither allowed nor encouraged to pursue academic programs that will lead them to a diploma.

Principle governing financial aid

This principle specifics that student-athletes can receive athletically related financial aid provided that the amount does not exceed the cost of education, and that all sources of financial assistance, "except that received from one upon the student-athlete is naturally or legally dependant," are prohibited (*2008–09 NCAA Division I Manual*, 2008, p. 5). Legislation to limit outside financial inducements from boosters and agents (see Chapters 6, 7, and 10) is based on this principle. Nonetheless, because the principle maintains that aid cannot exceed the actual costs associated with attendance, the Association is prone to receive criticism concerning financial exploitation. (Athletic aid is reviewed in Chapter 6.)

Principle governing playing and practice seasons

In an effort to bring specificity to the wished-for balance in experience that allows student-athletes to pursue their education, this principle declares that the time required to participate in athletic activities shall be regulated so student-athletes have an opportunity to acquire a quality education consistent with that provided to the rest of the student body (*2008–09 NCAA Division I Manual*, 2008).

In support of this principle, Article 17 of the *Division I Manual* (p. 214) outlines specific guidelines for daily and weekly practices and competitive activities, and the length of playing and practice seasons for all NCAA-sanctioned sports. For example, under Bylaw 17.1.6, Time Limits for Athletically Related Activities, all student-athletes are limited to 4 hours a day and 20 hours a week of athletically related activities during their sport's playing season. All student-athletes must have one full day off per week from all such activities (two days a week are required out of season). When out of season during the school year, student-athletes in sports other than football are required to attend only weight training, conditioning, and skills instruction for no more than 8 hours a week. Football student-athletes also are limited to 8 hours a week, of which no more than 2 hours can consist of viewing of film. In sports other than Championship Subdivision football, student-athletes are not allowed to participate in any countable athletic activities out of season during an institutional vacation period and/or during the summer.

Further elements of this bylaw define what qualifies as athletically related activity, and for what amount of time. For example, all competition and any associated athletically related activities on the day of a competition count as 3 hours regardless of the actual duration of these activities. Divisions II and III have no weekly limit on the number of hours of athletically related activities but do have requirements concerning days off per week. Division III student-athletes are not permitted to take part in any athletically related activities while not in season, and Division II student-athletes can participate in conditioning activities, (Chapter 4 provides further identification of divisional classification elements.)

The guidelines that have been crafted to meet the objectives of this principle seem to indicate that participation in intercollegiate athletics is a part-time endeavor, and as such, it should allow student-athletes to balance their time between athletics and academics. The periods over which student-athletes at the Division I level are asked to be in season, however, are expansive and have been growing at the other levels as well. Exhibit 2.3 compares play and practice information for football across Divisions I, II, and III, as an example. Appendices A.1, A.2, and A.3 summarize playing season data for other sports for each division.

What does the play and practice information reveal? Is the playing and practice season for football too long, or is it appropriate? Can student-athletes manage the demands of their athletic and academic schedule? This is a difficult balance, because classroom teachers are expecting that students put a full-time effort into the requirements for their classes, while coaches are expecting the same level of dedication from their players. Often, the student-athlete is caught between these conflicting sets of demands, regardless of the intent of this specific principle.

EXHIBIT 2.3	Contest, playing, and practice season information comparison for football, Divisions I, II, and III.

SPORT	FIRST PRACTICE DATE	FIRST CONTEST DATE	MAXIMUM NUMBER OF CONTESTS/ DATES OF COMPETITION	END OF REGULAR PLAYING SEASON	LENGTH OF PLAYING SEASON
DIVISION I					
Football	Date that permits 40 "practice units" before first scheduled contest	Sept. 3, 2009; Sept. 2, 2010	12 (BS) 11 (CS)	Second Saturday or Sunday in December	
DIVISION II					
Football	Regular season: 21 days prior to first contest Spring: February 15	Regular season: Thursday preceding August 30 Spring: None allowed	11	Regular season: Conclusion of DII Championship; Spring: No later than 7 calendar days prior to date of final exams	
DIVISION III					
Football	Date that permits 25 practice opportunities prior to first inter-collegiate contest	The Friday or Saturday 11 weeks before the first round of the D-III championship or the Thursday prior to Labor Day when the first permissible contest falls on Labor Day weekend	10	Conclusion of D-III Championship	18 weeks between start of preseason and end of regular season

Note: See book Appendices A.1, A.2, and A.3 for related information about other NCAA sports.

Source: 2008–09 NCAA Division I Manual, 2008.

Principle governing postseason competitions and contests sponsored by non-collegiate organizations

This principle, related to the previous principle, states that the NCAA shall control the conditions under which postseason competitions occur to ensure that benefits flow fairly to all participants, to prevent unjust intrusions on student-athletes and their academic endeavors, and "to protect student-athletes from exploitation by professional and commercial enterprises" (*2008–09 NCAA Division I Manual*, 2008, p. 5). Again we see a reference to concerns of student-athlete exploitation, but how do we see this occurring within the context of postseason competitions that are not sponsored by collegiate organizations? To what does this refer? Bowl games come to mind first, but is the involvement of so-called professional and commercial interests in bowl games significantly different from those attached to NCAA-controlled and administered championships? As we will see in Chapter 6, the financial demands of operating intercollegiate athletic events and programs, coupled with the reality that fans have become ardent consumers of products and services associated with intercollegiate athletics, have meant that professional and commercial interests are indeed interested in aligning with intercollegiate athletics to meet the needs and wants of these consumers. The question of exploitation emerges again here because of the revenues associated with these events and the time commitments that these events demand.

Principle governing the economy of athletics program operation

This final principle informs member institutions that intercollegiate athletic programs should be administered "in keeping with prudent management and fiscal practices to assure the financial stability necessary for providing student-athletes with adequate opportunities for athletics competition as an integral part of a quality educational experience" (*2008–09 NCAA Division I Manual*, 2008, p. 5). As we will learn in later chapters, the issue of budgets and finances has emerged as flashpoints of concern for intercollegiate athletics managers and institutional administrators. The question remains that in working to rein in these costs, are managers and administrators preserving the fiscal stability necessary to provide not just adequate opportunities but those at a level of quality within the framework of an educational experience?

Although a level of interpretation may be required to understand fully the issues to which these principles relate, we will raise these issues throughout the text and determine how managers and administrators must consider and address them. In the balance of this chapter we will examine further the specifics relating to how the NCAA and other governing bodies work on a national level to enable member institutions to manage their athletic programs successfully.

NCAA membership

Article 3 of the NCAA Constitution allows for the organization to offer five types of membership, which are defined and explained in Exhibit 2.4, with the corresponding annual dues fee, payable by September 1 of each year.

EXHIBIT	2.4	Types of NCAA memberships.

ACTIVE

- Open to four-year and two-year institutions accredited by the appropriate regional accrediting agency.
- Have the right to compete in NCAA championships, to vote on legislation and other issues.
- Also includes an athletics consortium, which consists of one member institution and neighboring member or non-member institutions. The student-athletes of combined institutions are permitted to compete on NCAA member teams as long as they meet all institutional and NCAA eligibility requirements.
- Annual dues: Division I: $1,800; Division II: $900; Division III: $900.

PROVISIONAL

- Open to four-year and two-year institutions accredited by the appropriate regional accrediting agency seeking active membership.
- Is a prerequisite to active membership and is limited to a seven-year period for Division I schools, a minimum of two years in Division II, and four years for Division III.
- Provisional members receive all publications and mailings received by active members.
- No voting privileges, but can be represented at any Convention.
- Can apply for full membership after an exploratory period and a process by which prospective members must meet specific criteria each year. One requirement is that the school must sponsor at least one sport involving an all-male team or a mixed team of males and females and at least one sport involving a female team in every sport season.
- No dues assessed.

MEMBER CONFERENCES

- Open to intercollegiate athletic conferences.
- Must conduct conference competitions and determine conference champions (through a postseason tournament or round-robin regular-season play) in one or more sports in which NCAA conducts championships.
- Must sponsor competitions in four sports for men, with one in each season, and four sports for women, with one in each season.
- Have all the privileges of active members, but only those conferences that act as a competitive body (conduct competition among members and hold championships) and as a legislative body (develop and maintain rules to govern member athletics programs), have at least six members who can have full voting privileges.
- Annual dues: Division I: $900; Division II: $450; Division III: $450.

AFFILIATED

- Available to a nonprofit group or organization whose function and purpose are directly related to one or more sports in which the NCAA conducts championships or identifies as an emerging sport (e.g., United States Olympic Committee, Women's Basketball Coaches Association).
- Entitled to be represented by one non-voting delegate at any Convention of the Association.
- Annual dues: $225.

CORRESPONDING

- Open to any institution, conference, or nonprofit organization that is not eligible for the previous four memberships but wants to receive the NCAA publications and mailings.
- Annual dues: $225.

Source: 2008–09 NCAA Division I Manual, 2008, pp. 9–16; 2008–09 NCAA Division II Manual, 2008, p. 18; 2008–09 NCAA Division III Manual, 2008, p. 8.

The legislative process

As can be seen throughout a review of the various types of NCAA membership, the key difference among members is the right to vote on all Association legislation. This legislative process reveals that all the rules in each of the divisional manuals are there because the schools and conferences themselves have approved them. Article 5 of the Constitution explains that "all legislation of the Association that governs the conduct of intercollegiate athletics programs of its member institutions shall be adopted by the membership in Convention assembled, or by the presidential administrative groups and the divisional management councils." Issues are voted upon at the Annual Convention, held the second week in January, and at specially convened meetings. The legislative rules specify that each member with voting privileges has only one vote, and the individual selected to cast that vote must be properly certified (*2008–09 NCAA Division I Manual*, 2008, p. 29).

Prior to 1998, all Association legislation was heard and acted upon with a one-member, one-vote policy on all issues regardless of the content of a motion during the Annual Convention. This procedure was changed in 1997, when the legislative and organizational processes were restructured to create a voting system in which members will vote based on how motions impact their specified divisional membership. Under the old format, members could get up and speak on behalf of or against any legislation in a kind of town meeting format. The NCAA itself was coordinated by the following committees, outlined in Exhibit 2.5.

Elements of the NCAA's organizational and legislative structure prior to August 1997.   **EXHIBIT 2.5**

- The NCAA Council, a group of 46 Division I, II, and III members, who were charged with establishing and directing the general policy of the NCAA in the interim between Conventions.
- The Joint Policy Board, which consisted of NCAA personnel, the Executive Director position (now referred to as President), and officers of the Presidents Commission (see below), responsible for review of the Association's budget, the legislative process and convention agenda, and evaluated and supervised the Executive Director.
- The Presidents Commission, composed of 44 institutional presidents or CEOs from all three divisions, was responsible for commissioning studies on intercollegiate athletics, proposed legislation to the Convention, placed any matter of concern on the agenda of any Council or Convention meeting, and reviewed the activity of the NCAA Advisory Board.
- The Executive Committee, 16 members composed of school presidents and chancellors from all divisions including the President and Secretary-Treasurer of the NCAA, responsible for the business affairs of the NCAA, adopting a budget, and employing an executive director.
- The Administrative Committee, composed of the officers and executive director of the NCAA, responsible for necessary items of business in between meetings of the Council and the Executive Committee.
- Other committees for running championships and overseeing specific sports (much as they do under the current structure).

The current organizational and legislative structure

Restructuring of the Association's organization and legislative process was voted upon and approved at the 1996 NCAA Convention and took effect in August 1997. It gave the NCAA more focus on divisional issues controlled by members affiliated with that division. The restructuring eliminated the one-member, one-vote "town meeting" process. In large part this occurred because the Division I schools had long complained that their legislative actions could be counteracted by votes from the Division II and III members, which always have outnumbered those in Division I. Under the current system, legislative and organizational power now rests with the presidential boards and management councils within each division. D-I members were able to get agreement for restructuring by the D-II and D-III members as a result of Bylaw 4.01.2.1. This bylaw guaranteed that these members would continue to receive millions of dollars from the television contracts that the NCAA has through the Association's revenue-sharing program from the general operating revenues that existed as of January 9, 1996. This includes money from the NCAA's lucrative contract for the broadcast rights to the Division I men's basketball championship, but it does not include any money from broadcast rights to bowl games or to any future Division I Bowl Subdivision NCAA-sanctioned playoff, as specified in Bylaw 4.01.2.2.1. The Division I-A (now Bowl Subdivision) schools had threatened that if this proposal was not passed, they would jump ship and leave the NCAA, form their own separate governing body, and take their television money with them.

The resulting governance structure that emerged is outlined in Exhibit 2.6. Under this structure, the Executive Committee has oversight over the presidential boards and management councils for each division. All members are institutional presidents or CEOs, and the four ex-officio/nonvoting members are the president and chairs of all the divisional management councils. The move to this format was made to ensure that each division would operate consistent with the basic purpose, policies, and principles of the NCAA and their specific divisional philosophy statements. The Presidents Commission and the NCAA Council were eliminated and replaced with presidential boards and management councils for each division.

Division I structure. (See Exhibit 2.7.) In Division I, the Board of Directors consists of 18 presidents and CEOs, of which 11 members are representatives of each of the following conferences: Atlantic Coast, Big East, Big Ten, Big 12, Conference USA, Mid-American, Mountain West, Pacific-10, Southeastern, Sun Belt, and Western Athletic. The other seven are from the remaining 20 Division I conferences, and no conference may be represented by more than one member. The board must also have one member who is considered an ethnic minority and one who is female, with a single member not able to meet both minimums. Duties of this board include the responsibility to establish and direct general policy, establish a strategic plan, adopt administrative bylaws and regulations, and delegate to the Management Council responsibilities for matters it deems appropriate. The Management Council consists of 49 athletic directors (ADs), faculty athletic representatives (FARs), and institutional administrators. Bylaw 4.5.1 further specifies that 20 percent of this body must be ethnic minorities, and 35 percent of persons from each gender.

NCAA governance structure.

EXHIBIT 2.6

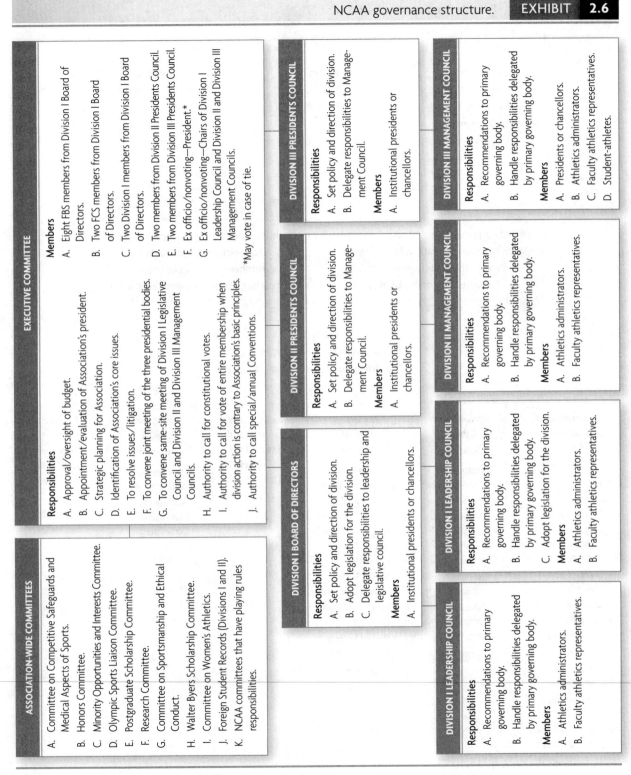

ASSOCIATION-WIDE COMMITTEES

A. Committee on Competitive Safeguards and Medical Aspects of Sports.
B. Honors Committee.
C. Minority Opportunities and Interests Committee.
D. Olympic Sports Liaison Committee.
E. Postgraduate Scholarship Committee.
F. Research Committee.
G. Committee on Sportsmanship and Ethical Conduct.
H. Walter Byers Scholarship Committee.
I. Committee on Women's Athletics.
J. Foreign Student Records (Divisions I and II).
K. NCAA committees that have playing rules responsibilities.

EXECUTIVE COMMITTEE

Responsibilities

A. Approval/oversight of budget.
B. Appointment/evaluation of Association's president.
C. Strategic planning for Association.
D. Identification of Association's core issues.
E. To resolve issues/litigation.
F. To convene joint meeting of the three presidential bodies.
G. To convene same-site meeting of Division I Legislative Council and Division II and Division III Management Councils.
H. Authority to call for constitutional votes.
I. Authority to call for vote of entire membership when division action is contrary to Association's basic principles.
J. Authority to call special/annual Conventions.

Members

A. Eight FBS members from Division I Board of Directors.
B. Two FCS members from Division I Board of Directors.
C. Two Division I members from Division I Board of Directors.
D. Two members from Division II Presidents Council.
E. Two members from Division III Presidents Council.
F. Ex officio/nonvoting—President.*
G. Ex officio/nonvoting—Chairs of Division I Leadership Council and Division II and Division III Management Councils.

*May vote in case of tie.

DIVISION I BOARD OF DIRECTORS

Responsibilities

A. Set policy and direction of division.
B. Adopt legislation for the division.
C. Delegate responsibilities to leadership and legislative council.

Members

A. Institutional presidents or chancellors.

DIVISION I LEADERSHIP COUNCIL

Responsibilities

A. Recommendations to primary governing body.
B. Handle responsibilities delegated by primary governing body.

Members

A. Athletics administrators.
B. Faculty athletics representatives.

DIVISION II PRESIDENTS COUNCIL

Responsibilities

A. Set policy and direction of division.
B. Delegate responsibilities to Management Council.

Members

A. Institutional presidents or chancellors.

DIVISION II MANAGEMENT COUNCIL

Responsibilities

A. Recommendations to primary governing body.
B. Handle responsibilities delegated by primary governing body.

Members

A. Athletics administrators.
B. Faculty athletics representatives.

DIVISION III PRESIDENTS COUNCIL

Responsibilities

A. Set policy and direction of division.
B. Delegate responsibilities to Management Council.

Members

A. Institutional presidents or chancellors.

DIVISION III MANAGEMENT COUNCIL

Responsibilities

A. Recommendations to primary governing body.
B. Handle responsibilities delegated by primary governing body.

Members

A. Presidents or chancellors.
B. Athletics administrators.
C. Faculty athletics representatives.
D. Student-athletes.

Source: 2008–09 NCAA Division I Manual, 2008, p. 27.

EXHIBIT 2.7   Division I governance structure.

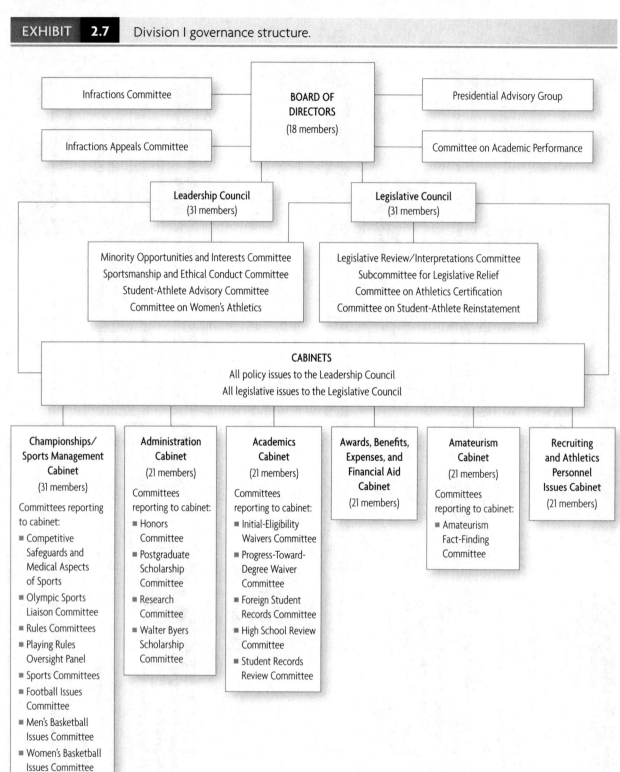

Source: 2008–09 NCAA Division I Manual, 2008, p. 26.

This bylaw also stipulates that three individuals be from the following conferences (Atlantic Coast, Big East, Big Ten, Big 12, Conference USA, Pacific-10, Southeastern), one from each of the Mid-American, Mountain West, Sun Belt, and Western Athletic conferences, and one from each of the remaining 20 conferences. Duties of this group include to adopt operating bylaws and rules as ratified by the Board of Directors, take final action on matters referred to it by the Board of Directors, make interpretations of the bylaws, and develop and administer the annual budget with the approval of the Board of Directors (*2008–09 NCAA Division I Manual*, 2008, pp. 19–20, 22–23).

Division II and III structures. (See Exhibits 2.8 and 2.9.) The primary governance and policy committees in Divisions II and III are the Presidents Councils. In D-II it is composed of one president and chancellor per region for every 22 institutions in that region (Division II is divided into four geographic regions), with an additional two at-large members to represent diversity interests and independent institutions. The D-III Presidents Council is composed of 15 presidents and chancellors, with at least two members from each of the four geographic regions, and seven members serving in an at-large capacity. Also at least two members must represent institutions with full-time undergraduate enrollments of at least 4,000, at least two members must represent institutions with full-time undergraduate enrollments of lower than 2,000, at least two members must represent private institutions, at least two must represent public institutions, at least three members must be women, and at least two must be ethnic minorities. The major responsibilities of the Presidents Councils are much the same as the Division I Board of Directors.

The Division II and III Management Councils serve much the same purposes as the D-I version. The D-II body must consist of one administrator from each of the multi-sport voting conferences, and two at-large members to assure diversity. The Council also must include at least four ADs, four senior women administrators (SWAs, see Chapter 5), at least four faculty athletics representatives, and at least one conference administrator. The D-III Management Council has to include 19 presidents and chancellors, ADs, senior women administrators, conference representatives, and student-athletes. At least nine members of this group must be ADs or SWAs, at least two must be presidents or chancellors, at least two must be FARs, at least three must be ethnic minorities, and it must be staffed by at least eight men and eight women (*2008–09 NCAA Division II Manual*, 2008, pp. 23–25; *2008–09 NCAA Division III Manual*, 2008, pp. 21–23).

Issues with the current structure. The current structure gives more control to each division to govern its own affairs. At the same time it preserves the opportunity for all members to vote on certain types of legislation. This system does have some concerns, however. Specifically, it allows the "rich and powerful" schools to become richer and more powerful by keeping the vast majority of NCAA-derived revenues, and it places more distance between these schools and the remaining members, as opposed to the former "one school, one vote" model.

There is also the issue of access to the governance structure, and the apprehension that by doing away with the one-member, one-vote system, schools not represented on the presidential boards or management councils will not be heard. Student-athletes were assured representation on the Division III Management

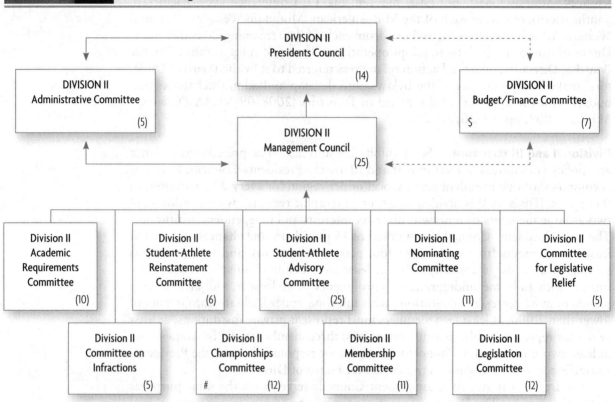

EXHIBIT   2.8   Division II governance structure.

( ) The number in the parenthetical represents the number of individuals serving on this group or committee.

Division II sports committees report and make recommendations directly to the Division II Championships Committee. Such Division II sports committees include the following: Baseball; Men's Basketball; Women's Basketball; Field Hockey; Football; Men's Golf; Women's Golf; Men's Lacrosse; Women's Lacrosse; Women's Rowing; Men's Soccer; Women's Soccer; Women's Softball; Swimming and Diving; Tennis; Track and Field; Women's Volleyball; and Wrestling.

$ The Division II Budget/Finance Committee is a group that advises both the Division II Presidents Council and Management Council regarding the division's financial affairs.

Source: 2008–09 NCAA Division II Manual, 2008, p. 26.

Council but not on the Division I or II versions. In keeping with the principle of diversity within governance structures, positions on the primary governance and policy committees have been reserved for traditionally underrepresented groups.

Passage of legislation

Although the 1997 restructuring did not do away totally with the voting processes at the Annual Convention, the process did allow for members to vote on issues pertaining to their own divisions without the inclusion of other divisional members. Restructuring, however, does allow for bylaws applicable to a division to be adopted or amended at any meeting of the Boards of Directors, Presidents Councils, or Management Councils. The concerns of representation noted above are legitimate,

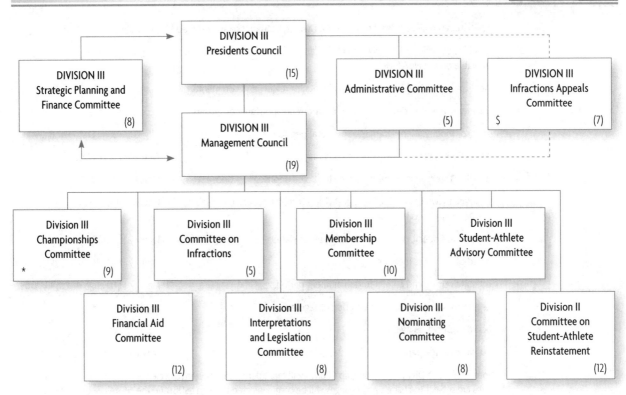

( ) Represents the number of individuals who will serve on this committee.

* All Division III sports committees report up to the Division III Championships Committee.

$ The Division III Infractions Appeals Committee shall hear and act on an institution's appeal of the findings of major violations by the Division III Committee on Infractions. It is composed of two members of the Division III Presidents Council and five members of the Division III Management Council.

Note: The following are common committees with playing rules and championships responsibilities for National Collegiate Championships—Men's Lacrosse, Men's and Women's Rifle, Men's and Women's Skiing, Men's and Women's Swimming and Diving, Men's and Women's Track and Field, Men's Water Polo and Wrestling.

Source: 2008–09 NCAA Division III Manual, 2008, p. 24.

and in addition the NCAA publishes a legislative activity calendar in each divisional manual, outlining the timeframes in which proposed rules and amendments must be submitted to receive review. Exhibit 2.10 shows the 2008–09 calendar for Division I. Tables outlining the legislative process for Divisions II and III are included in Appendices A.4 and A.5.

The NCAA national office

The NCAA's national office is located in Indianapolis, Indiana, having moved from suburban Kansas City, Missouri, to that location in 2000. The NCAA employs a staff of approximately 250, which administers the policies and decisions/legislation approved by the membership, and provides administrative services to all

EXHIBIT	2.10	Division I legislative activity calendar for 2008–09.

Legislation submission deadline for NCAA Division I conference and cabinets.	July 15, 2008
Deadline by which NCAA Division I Publicaton of Proposed Legislation is available on the NCAA website.	Augsut 15, 2008
Applicable proposals forwarded to cabinets for review and comment.	August 15, 2008
Cabinet review and development of positions on applicable proposals.	September 2008
Sponsor modification/alternative proposal period.	July 15 through October 21, 2008
NCAA Division I Legislative Council meeting.	October 20-21, 2008
Board of Directors meeting. Deadline for Board-sponsored proposals.	October 30, 2008
Deadline by which the 2009 NCAA Division I Official Notice is available on the NCAA website.	November 15, 2008
Legislative Council initial consideration of legislation.	January 15, 2009
Board of Directors meeting.	January 17, 2009
60-day override and comment/amendment periods.	January 18 through March 18, 2009
Legislative Council final consideration of legislation.	April 20-21, 2009
Board of Directors meeting.	April 30, 2009
60-day override period.	May 1 through June 29, 2009

Note: The NCAA Division I Leadership Council will meet during the legislative cycle to comment on select proposals. Dates are subject to change. Any changes will be communicated through LSDBi and the NCAA's website at ncaa.org.

Source: 2008–09 NCAA Division I Manual, 2008, p. 42.

NCAA committees. The national office is organized into nine departments: Administration; Business; Championships; Communications; Compliance; Enforcement; Publishing; Legislative Services; Visitors Center/Special Projects.

NCAA leadership

Throughout its history, actions of the NCAA have been shaped by its leadership, specifically by the individuals who have served in the post of executive director (now president). The following section summarizes the actions and influences of these significant individuals.

Walter Byers

From 1951 to 1987, the Association was headed by Walter Byers, who was responsible for much of the growth of the Association through development of television rights fees, first from football and later from the Division I men's basketball tournament. When hired at age 29 after a stint as a journalist, Byers was the NCAA's only employee, its secretary-treasurer, and he worked out of the Big Ten's offices in the LaSalle Hotel in Chicago. When he became NCAA head, he established the

Association's headquarters in Kansas City, his hometown. In subsequent years the offices would move to new facilities in the neighboring towns of Mission and Overland Park (Selcraig, McCallum, & Keteyian, 1986).

Byers was involved early in establishing the Association's enforcement capabilities, as well as negotiating TV rights fees, an area in which Byers excelled. According to Dave Gavitt, a former Division I head basketball coach and first commissioner of the Big East Conference, Byers was not afraid to take a hard line in talks, as was the case in 1981 when executives from NBC were trying to finalize a deal to keep the rights to the Division I men's basketball tournament. Said Gavitt, who was part of the committee reviewing the bids:

> (NBC's negotiators) came in and basically tried to poor-mouth what was going on. They were saying it's hard to sell, hard to clear, blah blah blah. It wasn't where we thought we were. We thought (the tournament) had wings for the future. The meeting was classic Byers. He stood up and closed his notebook, and he said to them, "I want to apologize to my colleagues who I brought in from around the country to listen to that. This meeting is over." (Davis, 2009, p. 244)

Byers' abruptness was not just a negotiating ploy, as it led to opening of the bidding to other networks. CBS was quick to offer $48 million over the next three years (a 60 percent increase over the previous deal with NBC). The next time around, CBS kept NBC out of the bidding entirely by re-upping for another three years for $96 million—double the value of its previous deal (Davis, 2009).

Byers also could be aptly described as a micro-manager, as he crafted organizational policies specifying that each employee had to be at his or her desk by 8:30 A.M. (or risk being marked tardy), and could not leave until 5 P.M., at which time all desks had to be cleared and window drapes drawn. Drinks were not allowed at desks, nor were personal items such as photographs. Former NCAA investigation staff member Curt Hamakawa, now a sport management faculty member at Western New England College in Springfield, Massachusetts, related that if a staffer were to bring in an unauthorized picture or wall decoration, it would disappear overnight, its whereabouts unknown, and no explanation given as to why it was removed.

Byers also was influential in staffing and selecting members of the NCAA Council, the key legislative authority in the Association's former governance structure, so much so that former University of Illinois AD Neale Stoner complained: "The NCAA is a strong central organization that has control over its members. If you think the members put together the legislation, you're crazy" (Rushin, 1997, p. 4). During Byers' time, the Association also was criticized for overzealous enforcement efforts in some cases, most notably a years-long investigation surrounding the men's basketball program at the University of Nevada–Las Vegas and its infamous and successful head coach, Jerry Tarkanian. Of these criticisms, Byers responded in 1986: "We have more investigators than ever before. But you cannot police college athletics properly unless the universities are going to make a solid effort to apply and enforce the rules. That's the only way the system will work, if the [presidents] give hands-on administration" (Selcraig, McCallum, & Keteyian, 1986, p. 12).

As discussed in Selcraig, McCallum, and Keteyian (1986), former Big Ten Commissioner Wayne Duke summarized Byers' influence over the NCAA this way: "The NCAA prospered, in my opinion, because of three factors: Enforcement, football on television and the [Division I men's] basketball tournament. And Walter was the architect of all three" (p. 7). Donna Lopiano, former women's AD at the University of Texas and later head of the Women's Sports Foundation, who opposed Byers while she headed the Association of Intercollegiate Athletics for Women (see Chapter 2), asserted that "the NCAA was nothing until Walter Byers." However, after his retirement, Byers published a book damning much of the NCAA's operational practices. Of the organization he largely created, Byers said, "The NCAA, with its mammoth rule book, controls individual athletes in a manner I think is illegal. It denies athletes the freedom other students have" (Selcraig, McCallum, & Keteyian, 1986, p. 4).

Richard Schultz and Cedric Dempsey

Byers was replaced in 1987 by Richard Schultz, who had been AD at the University of Virginia after stints at Cornell University and the University of Iowa, and had served on several high-level NCAA committees. Schultz was forced to resign in 1993 after it was revealed that NCAA violations pertaining to improper loans made to student-athletes occurred while he was at Virginia, some of which he knew about. Cedric Dempsey, who headed the organization from 1994 to 2002, moved to the NCAA from the AD position at the University of Arizona. Dempsey created a more informal working environment, which included eradicating the Association's dress code (which was outlined in the Association's Office Conduct sections of its 100-page *Office Policies and Procedures* and required that male administrators wear "suits or sport coats and slacks, shirts and ties," and that female administrators and nonadministrative employees "wear dresses, suits, skirts or slacks and blouses," and that all such blouses "cover the waistline and below at all times") (Rushin, 1997, p. 4).

Myles Brand

Dr. Myles Brand served as NCAA President from 2003 until his death from pancreatic cancer in 2009. He was the first former college president to serve as the head of the Association. Brand was president at both the University of Oregon (where he had also served as a philosophy professor and provost) and Indiana University. According to Brand, when he took over as president, many ADs were wary and suspicious of him because of his background (Nethery, 2004). While he was president at Indiana, Brand had fired legendary men's basketball coach Bob Knight in 2000 after Knight committed a series of on- and off-court transgressions.

The president's power and influence. Many view the NCAA as an omnipotent force within intercollegiate athletics and therefore conclude that the one in charge wields all the power. As we learned, however, the president does sit on the Association's Executive Council but has no franchise to vote on the matters before it. Big Ten Conference commissioner James Delany describes the exercising of power in the NCAA this way:

> If you want to limit influence, you divide up the power. There are a lot of checks and balances in the NCAA. . . . when it comes to the actual authority to change policy, or to right a wrong, or to deal with systematic problems, no one really has that authority. . . . [A]t the end of the day, [a president] can't do any more or less than what the schools are willing to do collectively. (Nethery, 2004, p. 28)

When Brand assumed the president's mantle, many familiar with the inter-collegiate athletics enterprise noted that his experiences at Indiana and Oregon would work in his favor within the newly constructed governance and legislative NCAA organization to deal with the following major issues facing the Association (Lapointe, 2003; Wieberg, 2003a):

- continuing to manage Title IX expectations (see Chapter 11)
- the relative absence of African-American football coaches
- control of athletics by school presidents
- the quandary surrounding the Bowl Championship Series in Division I football
- containing the ever-expanding expenses associated with the enterprise

Brand's efforts to control expenses. Brand chose to take on expanding expenses as a key emphasis early in his tenure, which he chose to bolster through the NCAA's periodic collection of financial data coordinated by Daniel Fulks, professor of ac-counting and faculty athletics representative at Transylvania (Kentucky) University. Athletic spending had increased in Division I since 1997, and these increases were leading to a growing gap between the schools already investing heavily in their athletic programs and those who were not, and these increased investments were not yielding high returns. Brand noted that if schools value the experiences that intercollegiate athletics can bring, schools might fund intercollegiate athletics pro-grams like any other institutional department, with the same extent of budgetary oversight, and with less concern for profit. Said Brand:

> We have to bring [intercollegiate athletics] into the university. If you want to bring it into the university, you have to think about it in a different way, and that includes how you budget it. . . . Presidents and others have to examine the rate at which they want to expend their funds for athletics [and] they have to weigh that against the fact that the vast majority of them are going to operate in the red. They can't recapture, even [at Division I schools with Bowl Subdivision football programs], for the most part, the amounts of money they're spending. Those are hard priority deci-sions. (Wieberg, 2003b, p. 11C; 2003c, p. 1C)

Two years after taking office, Brand launched a campaign for fiscal responsibil-ity at the Annual Convention, because, as he observed in a Convention address, the spending spiral had not abated. Brand expressed particular concern with the justifica-tion for athletics facility projects, in which schools were looking to have facilities that would outdo those of pro league franchises. He then qualified his stance, stating:

> I'm not talking about cutbacks. I'm not even talking about staying at the same level. I expect there to be growth in athletic budgets just as there is growth in the rest of the university. What I'm talking about is the rate of growth and whether the rate of growth is justified. The rate of expenditure being higher than the university on aver-age . . . is not a sustainable business plan. (Wieberg, 2005, pp. 1–2)

Nonetheless, many ADs expressed doubt over whether Brand and the NCAA could have an impact on the trend. University of Texas AD DeLoss Dodds said, "The presidents, I guess, could agree in principle that they want to (rein in spending), but in practicality I don't know how it happens" (Wieberg, 2005, p. 2). Brand seems to have looked to his former presidential colleagues to advance his vision for the future of college sports, as evidenced by *The Second-Century Imperatives: Presidential Leadership—Institutional Accountability,* a report released in 2006 by the NCAA's Presidential Task Force on the Future of Division I Athletics (NCAA, 2006).

Jim Isch and Mark Emmert

Former NCAA CFO Jim Isch replaced Brand on an interim basis but was not a candidate to replace him permanently. As to what the next president would be facing upon taking office, Big East Conference commissioner John Marinatto noted that the job had become more attractive to prospective replacements because it had "more teeth," but that it also was more challenging than when Brand took office in 2003 because the financial issues facing the membership were more complex (Smith, 2009, p. 25). When asked by *Street & Smith's SportsBusiness Journal* writer Michael Smith to identify the other pressing issues that the next president would have to take on, NCAA executives, media rights holders, conference commissioners, and ADs listed the following:

- fiscal responsibility,
- the NCAA's next championship media rights negotiations (which was settled in 2010 when the Association reached an agreement with CBS and Turner Broadcasting for a $10.8 billion deal that would run through 2024 [Sandomir & Thamel, 2010]),
- the revenue disparity among Division I schools as a result of Bowl Championship Series affiliation,
- a possible playoff to replace the bowls in the Football Bowl Subdivision (FBS), and
- diversity in hiring head coaches at FBS schools.

In April 2010, the Association named University of Washington President Mark Emmert to the post of President. Emmert, president at Washington since 2004, was previously chancellor at Louisiana State University from 1999–2004. Emmert also was chief operating and academic officer at the University of Connecticut (1995–99), provost and vice president for academic affairs at Montana State University (1992–95), and associate vice chancellor for academic affairs at the University of Colorado (1985–92). He earned his B.A. degree in political science from Washington, and has both a master's and a Ph.D. in public administration from Syracuse University (Mark Emmert Selected, 2001).

NCAA divisional classifications

We have referred to the three divisional classifications that the NCAA uses to categorize member schools. Exhibit 2.11 reviews some of the basic programmatic requirements necessary to fulfill divisional status guidelines, and in the next chapter we will examine more closely the philosophical underpinnings of these separate classifications.

The divisional requirements in general seem to demand that schools make departmental resource commitments to offer certain numbers of teams for both men and women, and in Divisions I and II, that these programs be supported by a minimum level of athletic aid based on the limits specified for each division. Further, Division I schools with Bowl Subdivision football programs are expected to show evidence of public support through a minimum attendance threshold. What are the reasons for these requirements? Why has the membership stipulated that

| General NCAA divisional classification requirements. | **EXHIBIT** | **2.11** |

DIVISION I GENERAL:

- Sponsor seven male or mixed teams of which at least two are team sports, and seven female teams of which at least two are team sports, OR
- Sponsor six male or mixed teams of which at least two are team sports, and eight female teams of which at least two are team sports.
- Must award 50 percent of allowable grants-in-aid for each sport, OR
- Minimum aggregate expenditures of $1,049, 022 with at least $525,511 in women's sports (excluding grants in football and men's and women's basketball)—grant value may not be less than 28 full grants (with 19 for women), OR
- Equivalent of 25 full grants-in-aid in men's sports and 25 full grants-in-aid for women's sports (excluding grants in football and men's and women's basketball).

DIVISION I WITH BOWL SUBDIVISION FOOTBALL:

- 16 total sports: At least six male or mixed teams, including football, of which two are team sports; and at least eight female teams of which at least two are team sports.
- Need to have averaged 15,000 in actual or paid attendance per home football game in a rolling two-year period.
- In addition to Division I aid requirements above, must provide an average of at least 90 percent of permissible maximum number of football grants-in-aid over a rolling two-year period, AND
- Annually offer a minimum of 200 athletic grants-in-aid or spend $4 million on athletic grants-in-aid.

DIVISION I WITH CHAMPIONSHIP SUBDIVISION FOOTBALL:

- Sponsor seven male or mixed teams of which at least two are team sports, and seven female teams of which at least two are team sports, OR
- Sponsor six male or mixed teams of which at least two are team sports, and eight female teams of which at least two are team sports.
- In addition to Division I aid requirements above, must provide an average of at least 90 percent of permissible maximum number of football grants-in-aid over a rolling two-year period, AND
- Annually offer a minimum of 200 athletic grants-in-aid or spend $4 million on athletic grants-in-aid.

DIVISION II:

- Sponsor five male or mixed teams of which at least two are team sports, and five female teams of which at least two are team sports, OR
- Sponsor four male or mixed teams of which at least two are team sports, and six female teams of which at least two are team sports.
- Must sponsor at least one sport, per gender, per season.
- Must award a minimum of 50 percent of the maximum allowable equivalencies in four separate sports, at least two of which must be female women's sports, OR
- A minimum of 20 total full equivalency grants with at least 10 total full equivalency grants in women's sports, OR
- A minimum total expenditure of $250,000 in athletically related financial aid with at least $125,000 in women's sports.

DIVISION III:

- Sponsor five male or mixed teams (increased to six in August 2010), of which at least three are team sports, and five female teams (increased to six in August 2010), of which at least three are team sports.
- Athletically related financial aid is not permitted.

Source: 2008–09 NCAA Division I Manual, 2008, p. 323; *2008–09 NCAA Division II Manual*, 2008, p. 216; *2008–09 NCAA Division III Manual*, 2008, pp. 265, 270.

schools offer programs in a mandatory minimum number of sports based on its classification, as well as the level and dispersal of athletic aid to these sports? On the one hand, if it was not required, schools might concentrate all resources on one or two sports at the highest level possible and not provide the broad-based programs to the greatest number of student-athletes, as outlined in the principles discussed above. On the other hand, it also is reasonable to conclude that schools with existing Division I Bowl Subdivision football programs are seeking to limit the number of competitors in their classification by demanding that would-be competitors not only meet specific standards relative to football attendance and aid requirements but also that these schools spend resources to provide opportunities and athletic aid to other male and female student-athletes. One could conclude that these requirements are benchmarks set to provide the best possible participation experience to student-athletes, but one could also view them as barriers to entry for schools with limited resources that may wish to compete at the highest level in only a limited number of sports.

BIRMINGHAM SOUTHERN COLLEGE AND THE PROCESS FOR CHANGING DIVISIONS

case study 2.A

Each division has stated procedures in its manual, outlining the process of changing divisions. An example is the case of Birmingham Southern College (BSC), a private, liberal arts school with 1,300 students, in Birmingham, Alabama. In 1999, the school left the NAIA for membership in the NCAA's Division I, and then decided to reclassify its programs to Division III status eight years later. According to current BSC president G. David Pollock, who took over in 2004, the move to D-I was made as the school looked to boost its image as a nationally known liberal arts institution and D-I athletics were seen as a complement to those efforts. Pollock also noted that the exceptional stock market returns common at the time made the move seem financially viable. By 2007, however, the school was running an annual deficit of $6 million, of which much was attributed to athletics spending, resulting in downgrading the institution's bond rating to junk bond status. In 2007, the $6.5 million spent on athletics (which included 116 grants-in-aid) represented 15 percent of the school's $42 million operating budget. The financial shortfalls experienced by BSC are common for schools upon moving to D-I status, as NCAA data show that such schools typically run deficits of $3 million a year for the first five years in D-I (June, 2007). As a result of the shortfalls, BSC decided to change its classification from D-I to D-III.

The initial reaction to the move from D-I, approved by the school's board of trustees, was, in Pollock's words, "mean and ugly" (June, 2007, p. A33). Students protested, and coaches and student-athletes complained that they were not consulted. Several coaches quit, 60 student-athletes transferred, and the college's enrollment fell from 1,500 to 1,300. To change classifications from I to III, schools are required to apply for reclassification to the Membership Committee of the NCAA's national office, and are charged a fee of $20,000. No more than four institutions can join or be reclassified in any given year, and they are selected based on whether the geographic area in which the school in question is located either needs or can accept new members, existing or potential membership in an active Division III conference, and the school's broad-based sports sponsorship profile. If elected to reclassify, schools are given "reclassified membership" status, which will last no fewer than four years, during which time the school must meet specific requirements pertaining to Division III rules compliance and termination of athletically related financial aid awards. If all criteria are fulfilled, the school is awarded active membership status (*2008–09 NCAA Division III Manual*, 2008, pp. 209, 211).

In addition, the school's move to D-III and membership in the Southern Collegiate Athletic Conference required additional upfront expenditures, as the school planned to spend $6.5 million on the first phase of a construction program for a facility for several of the school's new programs (football, men's and women's lacrosse, men's and women's track and field). The new programs, says Pollock, would enable the school to provide more participation opportunities and attract more students, helping the school to grow to a desired enrollment of 1,800 by 2014. Once the move to D-III is complete, the school expects to save $1.75 million a year on its athletics expenditures. However, the school expects to pay for the new facility through donations and by drawing on its $125 million endowment, which the school says it will pay back.

Moody's Investors Services, the company that provides bond ratings, is not so sure about the school's approach to alleviate its overall institutional debt of $31.7 million. A Moody's analyst said: "Management has a plan, and it's unproven. But I would view it as a positive that they have a plan. . . . [The reliance on tapping the endowment] continues to be a challenge and a risk." Of this assessment, Pollock responded: "They're looking at us year to year, and the problem didn't occur in one year. I can't do anything about it in a year. But I think they respect everything we're doing" (June, 2007, p. A34).

questions for you to consider

1. Compare the benefits of BSC staying as a member of Division I to the drawbacks of remaining in that classification.
2. Now do the same for the benefits and drawbacks of joining Division III.
3. Based on the factors you identified in the previous questions, explain whether BSC's decision to change classifications is correct.

Certification and self-study and evaluation

Much of what we have learned thus far about the NCAA has focused on the Association's stated operational principles and how these principles are delineated though national legislation and managerial actions from within the NCAA. Member schools must operate according to the NCAA's principles, and the Association provides the means for them to undergo a certification of evaluation process depending on their division, to ensure that they are operating in accordance with the principles.

Division I: Certification

The Association took several measures to enable Division I member schools to review their operations internally to assess whether their programs were operating within the Association's stated principles. This was an effort to help schools avoid running into situations in which the Association's enforcement procedures would have to be called into action. This process, identified as Athletics Certification, took effect in 1994, under an identified general purpose "to validate the fundamental integrity of member institutions' athletics programs through a verified and evaluated institutional self-study." Each Division I member institution must complete an institutional self-study at least once every 10 years, which must be "verified and evaluated through external peer review." Members must submit to the NCAA a status report every five years (*2008–09 NCAA Division I Manual*, 2008, p. 345).

Committee on Athletics Certification. The certification process is overseen by the Committee on Athletics Certification, which is appointed by the Division I Management Council. The committee must have a minimum of 12 members on staff at active Division I members, and must include one president or chancellor, one faculty athletic representative, one AD, one senior woman administrator, and one conference commissioner. The committee is responsible for establishing a pool of peer reviewers, determining the certification review schedule, and modifying and refining standards and procedures for the evaluation visits as necessary.

Peer review process. The review process takes about 18 months, from formation of an internal review committee, collection of information, writing of the report, peer review team visit, and correspondence with NCAA (schools are given 8 to 10 months to complete the report). The external peer review team, composed of two to four members and one NCAA staff member, is responsible for reviewing the institution's self-study report, conducting campus visits, and offering comments to the review team's chair. Peer reviewers are to be from a Division I institution or conference and must have general knowledge of intercollegiate athletics, recognized expertise, skills, or experience in the specific areas addressed in the certification process, and be a school president, faculty athletics representative, AD, or senior female administrator. The peer review team is charged with determining whether the self-study process involved campus-wide participation, and that the self-study report reflects accurately the operations of the school's athletic program and the school's performance in relation to the fundamental operating principles in three basic areas: Governance and commitment to rules compliance; academic integrity; and gender, diversity, and student-athlete well-being (*2007–08 NCAA Division I Manual*, 2007, pp. 345, 411–421).

Governance and commitment to rules compliance. The review determines the extent to which a school demonstrates institutional control by judging whether the institution's governing board provides broad athletic policy oversight in a manner consistent with the overall institution, whether the president is the ultimate authority over operation of the athletic department, and whether the appropriate campus constituencies have an opportunity to provide input into formation of athletic policy. In terms of rules compliance, it must be shown that written policies and procedures assigning specific responsibilities in the area of rule compliance are in place, that these procedures involve input from the appropriate personnel outside the athletic department, and that the rules-compliance program is the subject of evaluation by an authority outside athletics at least once every four years (*2008–09 NCAA Division I Manual*, 2008, pp. 345–346).

Academic integrity. In this area, an institution must show the following (*2008–09 NCAA Division I Manual*, 2008, pp. 347–348):

- It admits only those student-athletes who have reasonable expectations of obtaining academic degrees.
- If the academic performance or retention of student-athletes, as a whole or for any student-athlete subgroup, are lower than the rest of the student body, the disparity must be analyzed and explained by the appropriate institutional authorities.
- Adequate academic support is provided to student-athletes.
- Support services are evaluated at least once every four years by the appropriate institutional authorities.

Gender, diversity, and student-athlete well-being. In this area, institutions must do the following (*2008–09 NCAA Division I Manual*, 2008, pp. 349–350):

- Have a plan in place to conduct and promote its athletic program free from gender bias.

- Demonstrate a commitment to and progress toward the fair treatment of all student-athletes and athletic department personnel with diverse racial, ethnic, and other backgrounds.

- Formally adopt a program that works toward these outcomes.

- Provide evidence that the well-being of student-athletes and the fairness of their treatment is monitored, evaluated, and addressed on a continuing basis.

- Have in place programs that protect the health of and provide a safe and in-clusive environment for each of its student-athletes.

Certification decisions. The Committee on Athletics Certification bases its decision regarding the certification of an institution's athletic program on information contained in the institution's self-study report, the peer-review team's written report, the institution's written response to the review team's report, comments by the review team in relation to the institution's response, evidence presented at hearings or in-person appearances before the Committee. The categories of final certification determination are (*2008–09 NCAA Division I Manual*, 2008, p. 348):

- *Certified* (where an institution has been deemed to have been in substantial conformity with the operating principles under review)

- *Certified with Conditions* (where an institution must fulfill certain corrective actions in a reasonable, specified period of time)

- *Not Certified* (where an institution is deemed not to be in substantial conformity with the review areas given a certain time period to comply)

If a member fails to take corrective action, it may be denied certification, in which case the institution is placed in a restricted-membership category. If, after having an additional time-period deadline placed on the institution, the problems still exist, the institution is placed in a corresponding membership category. As a result, NCAA member schools are asked to refrain from competing against schools that are not certified, with the resulting implications being forfeiture of revenue from games not being played (*2008–09 NCAA Division I Manual*, 2008).

Divisions II and III: Institutional self-study and evaluation

Division II and III institutions are required under Bylaw 6.3 to conduct a self-study and evaluation of their athletic programs at least once every five years, using the Institutional Self-Study Guide (ISSG) composed by the Association. The information gathering for and the composition of the report are to be performed by administrative personnel outside the athletic department. The main areas to be examined under the D-II ISSG are presented in Exhibit 2.12, and the areas for Division III in Exhibit 2.13.

| EXHIBIT | 2.12 | Subject areas to be covered by Division II Institutional Self-Study and Evaluation. |

- Institutional purpose and athletics philosophy
- The authority of the president and institutional oversight of athletics
- Athletic program organization and administration
- Finances
- Personnel
- Sports programs
- Recruiting policies
- Services for student-athletes
- Student-athlete profiles

Source: 2008–09 NCAA Division II Manual, 2008, p. 44.

For example, under the section examining Institutional Purpose and Athletics Philosophy, schools are asked to address questions such as: Is the athletics department's written philosophy statement given wide circulation within the institution and made available to its external constituencies? And does the institution's written statement of athletics program philosophy provide explicit reference to the principles of fair play and amateur athletics competition, as defined by NCAA legislation (*Self-Study Guide,* 2007)?

If, during the self-study, a question area in the ISSG elicits a response indicating an issue that has to be addressed by athletic managers, the ISSG requires an action plan outlining how such issues will be addressed. For example, in 2007, at Western New England College, a Division III member of the Commonwealth Coast Conference with a full-time undergraduate enrollment of 2,500, in Springfield, Massachusetts, a faculty member teaching a class in intercollegiate athletic management coordinated the composition of the report with his students and cam-

| EXHIBIT | 2.13 | Subject areas to be covered by Division III Institutional Self-Study and Evaluation. |

- Institutional purpose and athletics philosophy
- Principles of sportsmanship and ethical conduct
- The authority of the president and institutional oversight of athletics
- Institutional control and accountability of athletics programs
- Athletic program organization and administration
- Employment of athletics department personnel
- Sports programs
- Sports medicine
- Recruiting, admissions, financial aid, and academic eligibility
- Institutional student services
- Student-athlete profiles

Source: 2008–09 NCAA Division III Manual, 2008, p. 42.

| Action plan item from 2007 ISSG report from Western New England College. | **EXHIBIT** | **2.14** |

Issue to be resolved:

Is the athletics department's written philosophy statement given wide circulation within the institution and made available to its external constituencies?

Actions to address specific issues listed above:

If the written statement is distributed and published more widely within the athletic department, both internal and external stakeholders will become conversant and educated about the college's philosophy. It will also allow representatives of the faculty the ability to review changes and new publications of Western New England College's athletic program philosophy, and allow student-athletes to become familiar with the philosophy that they embody on and off the field of play.

Task(s) to be completed:

To address these issues, the easiest and most widespread remedy is to post the written statement within athletic facilities, in game programs, and in team media guides.

Timeline:

By the end of the 2007–08 academic year.

Person(s) responsible:

Athletic department administrative staff.

---

pus administrators. In the process, they discovered that in addressing Question 2 of Section I, the institution's written philosophy statement was not given wide circulation. In addressing the issue, the school's report included the action plan shown in Exhibit 2.14.

The completed report and the supporting documentation are to be made available for examination upon request by an authorized representative of the Association and may be reviewed by the division Membership Committee with a focus on legislative issues and action plans in areas of deficiencies. The final report also must be reviewed and signed off by the school president, chief financial officer, admissions director, athletic director, and other campus administrative personnel. If a Division II school fails to submit the ISSG by the conclusion of the academic year in which the report was due, it will not be eligible to receive Division II Enhancement Fund proceeds and will be placed on probation. If the school fails to complete the report during the probationary period, it will be fined $1,000, placed on restricted membership status, will not be eligible to receive Division II Enhancement Fund proceeds, and will be ineligible for divisional championships in all sports (*2008–09 NCAA Division II Manual*, 2008, pp. 44–45). If a Division III school fails to submit the ISSG by the conclusion of the academic year in which the report was due, it will be ineligible for divisional grant and initiative funding and its entire athletic program will be placed on probation for one year, beginning with the next academic year after the failed submission. A school also may be afforded the probationary period once every 10 years, which begins with the September following the academic year in which the submission failure occurred (*2008–09 NCAA Division III Manual*, 2008, pp. 42–43).

THE ROLE AND FUNCTIONS OF OTHER NATIONAL GOVERNING BODIES

Although much of the content of this chapter is devoted to the role and authority of the NCAA, two similar organizations are charged with national coordination of intercollegiate athletics activities: the National Association of Intercollegiate Athletics (NAIA), and the National Junior College Athletic Association (NJCAA). The NJCAA's mission and constituency would seem to be directed at serving solely two-year institutions. Less clear from its name is where the differences lie between the NAIA and the NCAA. In the remainder of this chapter we will examine these organizations to determine their roles in managing contemporary intercollegiate athletics.

National Association of Intercollegiate Athletics

The roots of the NAIA originate in a 1937 national basketball tournament formed by Dr. James Naismith, inventor of the sport. The NAIA claims nearly 300 member institutions from the United States and Canada. Headquartered in Kansas City, Missouri, its membership is divided into 14 regions, including these schools:

- Azusa Pacific University (California)
- University of British Columbia (Vancouver, British Columbia, Canada)
- Cornerstone University (Grand Rapids, Michigan)
- Dillard University (New Orleans, Louisiana)
- Graceland University (Lamoni, Iowa)
- Haskell Indian Nations University (Lawrence, Kansas)
- Illinois Institute of Technology (Chicago)
- University of Maine at Machias
- Mid-Continent University (Mayfield, Kentucky)
- Oklahoma City University (Oklahoma)
- Savannah College of Art and Design (Georgia)
- South Dakota School of Mines and Technology (Rapid City)
- Tennessee Wesleyan College (Athens)
- Wilberforce University (Ohio)

The NAIA serves 50,000 student-athletes and offers 23 championships in 13 sports (with two divisions each for men's and women's basketball).

Mission and purpose

The organization, which held its first convention in 1940, states that it was the first such governing body to offer membership to historically Black institutions, and to sponsor championships for both men's and women's sports. The organization defines its purpose as "to promote the education and development of students through intercollegiate athletic participation," and its mission as "to advance character-driven intercollegiate athletics." The NAIA also cites "the importance of the individuality of each member institution, (and) the value of the conference and regional structure" (About the NAIA, 2005, p. 1).

In supporting this key component of valuing institutional individuality, NAIA President and CEO Jim Carr described this approach in his State of the Association address at the group's 2008 annual conference in Louisville, Kentucky, as "the NAIA Way . . . how we encourage interaction between student-athletes and coaches, how we give autonomy and flexibility to members, our commitment to character and the straightforward approach to intercollegiate athletics" (Carr, 2008, pp. 1–2).

Leadership

Jim Carr was named to head the organization in 2006, after serving as its general council since 1998. Previously he had worked in athletic fundraising at the University of Nevada–Las Vegas, and was a men's basketball student-athlete at Millsaps College, an NCAA Division III member institution with just over 1,000 undergraduates, located in Jackson, Mississippi.

Organizational strengths and challenges

When Carr took over, many perceived the NAIA to be in trouble, having lost nearly half of its members over the previous 20 years, most of which jumped to the NCAA. When asked why a school president should choose NAIA membership over the NCAA, Carr responded:

> We're like the NCAA, only smaller. . . . NCAA Division II budgets are about twice what NAIA budgets are. The NCAA has certain requirements for scholarships, facilities, and staffing. You can come in here and be competitive against Division II programs, but do it in an economic way and keep college athletics in the proper perspective. (Wolverton, 2007, p. 1)

Richard Artman, president of Viterbo University, an NAIA member school with 2,500 undergraduates located in LaCrosse, Wisconsin, and a member of the Midwest Collegiate Conference, who also has served as the head of the organization's Council of Presidents, agrees with this approach, commenting, "There's no way we can compete with the resources the NCAA has. But [Carr] knows we can be a viable alternative by getting away from the big-money, win-at-all-costs mentality" (Wolverton, 2007, p. 2). The organization, however is still losing members, such as Birmingham Southern College (see Case Study 2.A, p. 52), Newman University, located in Wichita, Kansas, which had been an NAIA member for 30 years but moved to NCAA Division II status in 2006; and Georgia College & State University (GCSU), another longtime member, located in Milledgeville, Georgia. Randy Dunn, GCSU AD, said the school made the move in 2005 after many of the schools in its conference had jumped. The school is now a member of the Peach Belt Conference, an 11-member D-II group with schools in Georgia, North Carolina, and South Carolina. As the NAIA's membership dwindled, Dunn worried about the organization's long-term viability and solvency (the NAIA's entire budget was $4 million, compared to more than $500 million for the NCAA). "I told my president, what happens if the NAIA closes their door? We've made scholarship commitments to kids, we have games to schedule, and we need to think about the future" (Wolverton, 2007, p. 3).

One significant financial challenge facing the organization is that it pays championship expenses only for football and baseball teams, whereas the NCAA pays championship expenses for all its sports. This policy was another factor that pushed GCSU to the NCAA. Dunn stated, "Our budgets are not at the point where we could hold back $60,000 (needed to travel to championships). We need that money to run our programs" (Wolverton, 2007, p. 3). There has also been some degree of competition between the NAIA and the more resourced NCAA. Carr notes that Division II representatives attempted to recruit an entire NAIA conference membership to jump to the NCAA's Division II in 2006, thereby swelling the ranks of the NCAA's smallest divisional classification. NCAA officials deny the effort, claiming that they want the NAIA to survive to serve smaller schools that do not fit their model. Carr disagrees: "It's a little hollow for the NCAA to say they want a strong NAIA if their actions don't show that" (Wolverton, 2007, p. 5).

The smaller NAIA is seen as a benefit to some, as it can respond to questions and challenges quickly. This is verified by Debby DeAngelis, AD at California State University–East Bay, a school of just over 12,000 undergrads, located east of San Francisco in Hayward, California, which has dual membership in the NAIA and NCAA: "The NAIA has capable people who are responsive to the membership. That's part of the reason I see them as viable" (Wolverton, 2007, p. 4). Some ADs also see the NAIA rulebook as far simpler, but others complain that its small size hinders its rules-enforcement program. Just two of the NAIA's two dozen employees work on enforcement issues (compared to an enforcement staff of 24 in the NCAA), and the NAIA's policy that schools must self-report violations doesn't mean that they get reported. Some member schools are looking for the NAIA to ramp up its enforcement approach (after decades of some derisively pronouncing that "NAIA" stood for "National Association of Ineligible Athletes"). Said Jim Redd, AD at William Jewel College, a school with 1,000 undergraduates located in Liberty, Missouri: "When there are allegations, someone other than the institution needs to look into them" (Wolverton, 2007, p. 4).

To increase membership, Carr noted that the organization needed to define itself, stating: "We pride ourselves on institutional autonomy—we don't require schools to sponsor a certain number of sports, for example—and we don't want to change that. But we're basing our organization on character-driven intercollegiate athletics programs, and with that comes a responsibility to govern programs with integrity" (Wolverton, 2006, pp. 1–2).

To meet this goal, Carr helped the organization develop the "Champions of Character" program, designed to teach coaches and student-athletes five core values: respect, responsibility, integrity, servant leadership (defined as "serving the common good"), and sportsmanship. The program calls for member schools to hold character-training seminars for coaches and student-athletes, who then go to local schools and youth sports organizations to teach respecting competitors. Buffalo Funds, a Kansas City–based mutual funds company, provides funding for the efforts. "This program doesn't generate any business for us," says company president John Kornitzer. "We sponsor it because we see an erosion of character in sports, and the NAIA seems to be the only one teaching it" (Wolverton, 2007, p. 3).

In his State of the Association address at the 2008 national conference, Carr outlined other elements geared toward defining the organizing and strengthening its niche, including expanding presidential leadership and strengthening the role of conferences. He also addressed the issue of competition with the NCAA:

> If we wish to predict the future, we must shape it. We must be unafraid to engage in it. As a result, we have worked purposefully and in a sustained way in the last two years to engage the NCAA directly, to state its intentions, its position with regard to the NAIA in intercollegiate athletics . . . in short, to create intentional discussions with the NCAA about the interests and agenda of the NAIA. My final comments on our relationship with the NCAA is that you need to know that representatives of the Council of Presidents have made it clear in every discussion that retaining our identity, keeping the NAIA intact, is a priority. NCAA representatives understand our position and are willing to proceed. (Carr, 2008, pp. 5–7)

The decision of the NCAA to end discussions about the creation of a Division IV could also serve to preserve the NAIA. In response to Carr's comments and the discussions between the two groups, Bernard Franklin, the NCAA's executive vice president for governance and membership (also a former school president), commented: "We are looking for ways to collaborate and have partnerships that better serve student-athletes across the country, irrespective of what association they belong to" (Wolverton, 2008, p. A15).

Whether Carr and his membership will be able to meet the challenges facing the NAIA (in addition to the idea the NCAA may be interested in acquiring it) and to maintain and strengthen its organizational niche will be demonstrated through NAIA actions over the next several years. The Association did add 11 new members in 2007–08, including Cincinnati Christian College, the College of Santa Fe, Talladega (Alabama) College, and the University of Maine–Presque Isle. If this trend continues, the NAIA can survive. However, the NAIA may have to deal with further attrition, as the membership of the Golden State Athletic Conference (GSAC) moved in August 2009 to begin gathering information regarding NCAA Division II membership. The GSAC was established in 1986 by 11 Christian colleges located throughout central and southern California, and member institutions have captured 33 NAIA national championships in the conference's 23-year history. Its current membership includes Azusa Pacific University, Biola University (La Mirada), California Baptist University (Riverside), Concordia University (Irvine), Fresno Pacific University, Hope International University (Fullerton), Master's College (Santa Clarita), Point Loma Nazarene University, San Diego Christian College, Vanguard University (Costa Mesa), and Westmont College (Santa Barbara).

According to the GSAC website, the athletic directors of all 11 member schools were considering the move. As a first step they agreed to initiate fact-gathering processes specific to each campus and to report their findings to their respective presidents. The ADs did not set a specific timeline for the process, and the individual schools and the conference as a whole made no commitment to apply for NCAA membership. GSAC commissioner Dr. Cliff Hamlow said the following about the process: "We are proud members of the NAIA and are grateful for what the association has meant in the development of our conference. We are conducting some homework and charting our future, and nothing more should be construed by our actions. We are unique in our competitiveness and camaraderie, and it is not unusual for us to act together as a conference on a number of activities and decisions" (GSAC Addresses Its Future, 2009, p. 1). The website also commented that GSAC members agreed that current ongoing talks between administrative staffs of the NAIA and NCAA are important and are looking forward to an established direction of those conversations (GSAC Addresses, 2009).

National Junior College Athletic Association

Like the NAIA, the National Junior College Athletic Association (NJCAA) traces its roots back to 1937, when a handful of California-based junior college representatives met to organize an association to promote and supervise nationally intercollegiate athletic activities for two-year schools. The organization was formally approved the next year. In 1949 the Association was reorganized by dividing the nation into 16 regions (which grew to 19 in 1968, to 21 in 1973, and to 24 in 1983), and was organized as a nonprofit corporation. By 1973, the membership had grown to a high of 533. In 1975, the Association began offering championships for women's sports and its women's membership grew to a high of 490 by 1980. School presidents were first named to the Association's Board of Directors in 1987. The Association currently has a membership exceeding 500, divided into 24 geographic regions across the country (except in California, whose two-year schools have formed their own governing body) (About NJCAA—Today, 2009). The membership includes the institutions such as:

- AIB College of Business (Des Moines, Iowa)
- Anne Arundel Community College (Arnold, Maryland)
- Bossier Parish Community College (Bossier City, Louisiana)
- Carl Sandburg College (Galesville, Illinois)
- Coastal Georgia Community College (Brunswick, Georgia)
- The Fashion Institute of Technology (New York)
- Hiawassee College (Madisonville, Tennessee)
- Itasca Community College (Grand Rapids, Minnesota)
- Little Bighorn College (Crow Agency, Montana)
- New Mexico Military Institute (Roswell, New Mexico)
- Snow College (Ephraim, Utah)
- State Fair Community College (Sedalin, Missouri)
- Vincennes University (Vincennes, Indiana)
- The Williamson Free School of Mechanical Trades (Media, Pennsylvania)

The NJCAA sponsors championships in 13 men's sports and 13 women's sports, some of which offer competitions in three separate divisions. The divisions are defined based on the amount of athletically related financial aid that schools can award: Division I schools can provide tuition and room and board; Division II schools can provide tuition only; Division III can award no athletically related aid (About NJCAA—Today, 2009).

Mission and purpose

The NJCAA defines itself as "the governing body of intercollegiate athletics for two-year colleges. As such, its programs are designed to meet the unique needs of a diverse group of student-athletes who come from both traditional and non-traditional backgrounds and whose purpose in selecting a two-year college may be as varied as their experiences before attending college" (About NJCAA—Today, 2009, p. 1). According to its mission statement, the NJCAA exists "to foster a national program of athletic participation in an environment that supports equitable opportunities consistent with the educational objectives of member colleges" (p. 1).

Leadership

The current acting executive director of the NJCAA is Mary Ellen Leicht, who has worked for the association in various capacities since 1989. The president of the Association is Art Becker, former AD at Scottsdale (Arizona) Community College and a former professional basketball player in the now-defunct American Basketball Association (About NJCAA—Today, 2009).

Athletics on individual member campuses

There has been a growth trend in two-year schools offering intercollegiate athletic programs (see Chapter 3) in an effort to boost student matriculation and retention. Many programs at two-year junior colleges (or "jucos," as they are alternatively known), however, serve as feeders for high-profile NCAA programs. Hundreds of Division I and II players in many sports began their collegiate careers at jucos, mostly because they were unable to meet the NCAA's initial eligibility academic standards. Students who meet certain progress requirements at jucos can become eligible to participate at NCAA schools (see Chapter 9). Greg Hinze, AD at Blinn College (Benham, Texas), a school with an enrollment of 14,000 full- and part-time undergraduates, with traditionally strong men's basketball and football programs, described the mission for his programs: "We provide an opportunity to those kids who don't meet NCAA academic requirements, to enable them to continue their athletic careers" (Powell, 2007, p. 27). Established pro stars such as the NBA's Ben Wallace (Cuyahoga Community College, Cleveland), and the NFL's Chad Ochocinco (formerly Johnson) (Santa Monica College, California), are two who utilized the juco system to further their education and their athletic careers. In fact, 32 former juco players, including three from Seminole (Oklahoma) State College—Nick Blackburn (Minnesota Twins), Ryan Franklin (St. Louis Cardinals), and Reggie Willits (Los Angeles Angels of Anaheim)—made the rosters of the eight teams that qualified for MLB's 2009 postseason (Plenty of NJCAA Representation, 2009; Powell, 2007).

Although many juco programs are run on tight budgets, some schools, such as Tyler (Texas) Junior College and Modesto (California) Junior College, provide comprehensive programs that rival many in the NCAA. Tyler boasts a pleasant campus and on-campus housing for 600 students, and, according to Mike Marquis, head coach of the school's men's basketball team, "Kids are coming here over some four year institutions just because it's so nice" (Powell, 2007, p. 27). Modesto fields teams in 21 sports, serving 400 student-athletes from a student population of 18,000. At Broward College in Davie, Florida, the women's tennis team won three national championships over four years and routinely sends players on to Division I programs, even though the team practices on a concrete court in a parking lot. The program looks for talent locally first (which is a harder sell), but reserves two spots (the maximum allowed under NJCAA rules) for international players. The school can pay for tuition ($70 a credit for in-state residents, $242 for out-of-state students) and room and board (with a limited number of student-athletes living in apartments rented by the school). The recruiting message was heard by Alyona Tsutskova, a native of Ukraine and formerly internationally ranked player. She had attended a residential tennis academy in nearby Miami, hoping to turn pro, but then hurt her back. At age 21, she went to Broward to improve her grades—studying business administration after years of focusing solely on her tennis career—so she could get the attention of a Division I coach to earn a grant-in-aid (Powell, 2007).

While schools like Tyler and Modesto often field strong programs such as football, basketball, and baseball (which, in turn, feed prospects to NCAA programs), some programs draw players that are representative of other segments of a school's undergraduate population. At Modesto, AD William Kaiser notes that the women's golf team consists of middle-aged women who are taking a few academic units just so they can play golf. "People say, 'How come our teams are always old women?'" Kaiser says. "I tell them it's because old women are the only ones we can find to play" (Powell, 2007, p. 28).

Unlike the NAIA membership, members of the NJCAA can see a direct benefit in association with the NCAA, as many juco student-athletes are looking to develop their academic and athletic profiles so they can continue these pursuits after completing one or two years at the junior college level. As we will learn in Chapter 9, this path may become more common as the NCAA adjusts its initial eligibility requirements to limit the number of courses that can be taken at private prep schools to qualify for immediate eligibility. Much as the NAIA is seeking to do, the NJCAA has seemed to define more clearly its niche in the intercollegiate athletic landscape. As a result, it seems to be thriving as it serves several specific populations.

CONCLUSION

The NCAA is the national governing body most responsible for shaping and controlling U.S. intercollegiate athletics, even while the NAIA and the NJCAA operate and serve other related constituencies. The NCAA defines its basic purposes as maintaining intercollegiate athletics as an integral part of the educational program and the athlete as an integral part of the student body, and retaining a clear line of distinction between intercollegiate athletics and professional sports. Members of the NCAA determine the rules by which they must abide. The guiding premise that underscores all legislation is that it must be designed to advance one or more of the Association's 16 basic principles.

The organization offers five types of membership, with the key difference among members as the right to vote on all Association legislation. Prior to 1998, all Association legislation was heard and acted upon with a one-member, one-vote policy on all issues regardless of the content of a motion during the Annual Convention. This procedure was changed in 1997, when the legislative and organizational processes were restructured to create a voting system in which members would vote based on how motions would impact their specified divisional membership. Under the current structure, the Executive Committee has oversight over the presidential boards and management councils for each division. All members are institutional presidents or CEOs, and the four ex-officio/non-voting members are the president and the chairs of all the divisional Management Councils.

The NCAA's national office, in Indianapolis, Indiana, currently employs a staff of approximately 250, which administers the policies and decisions/legislation approved by the membership and provides administrative services to all NCAA committees. The NCAA uses three divisional classifications to categorize member schools.

In 1994, the Association began the Athletics Certification process to enable Division I member schools to review their operations internally to assess whether its programs are operating within the Association's stated principles and thereby help schools avoid situations in which the Association's enforcement procedures would have to be called into action. Division II and III schools are required to conduct a self-study and evaluation of their athletic programs at least once every five years, using the Institutional Self-Study Guide compiled by the Association. The information gathering for and the composition of the report is to be performed by administrative personnel outside of the athletic department.

Even though to many individuals, the NCAA is the rule-making body for intercollegiate athletics, two other such organizations are doing much the same thing: the National Association of Intercollegiate Athletics (NAIA) and the National Junior College Athletic Association (NJCAA). The NJCAA has a clearly defined niche in the intercollegiate athletic landscape, while the NAIA seems to be struggling with maintaining and strengthening its niche.

PRACTITIONER perspective:

MYLES BRAND, former NCAA President

Dr. Myles Brand served as NCAA president from 2003 until his death in 2009. Much occurred during his tenure. Greg Shaheen, the NCAA's senior vice-president of basketball and business strategies, eulogized Brand with these words: "Those of us who worked directly with Myles are left with a charge to carry the momentum forward with the same spirit and absolute determination he brought to everything. I am humbled to have experienced his friendship, personally and professionally" (Shaheen, 2009, p. 55).

In the months before his death, Brand agreed to respond to questions for this book to address his perspectives on some of the issues discussed in this and in subsequent chapters, as well as other relevant observations, having served at the acme of intercollegiate athletics management. Our questions and his responses follow.

Q: *We learned in our research that several ADs and conference commissioners agreed with you that the position of president has little direct authority. Do you believe the NCAA would operate more effectively if you had more such authority?*

A: The NCAA has no more "power" than what colleges and universities that belong to the Association cede to it. There are issues—diversity hiring, rate of growth in athletic budgets, academic support development—for which it would be wonderful to have dictatorial authority—but that is not how higher education works, and that is the reason our governance structure is the way it is. The thousand colleges and universities that belong to the NCAA vary in how they meet their common mission to educate, in what resources are available to them, in the relative importance of athletics to the campus, and in a number of other ways. The governance process must listen to all of those voices. Most decisions are the result of reaching a practical consensus.

My role is to offer a leadership approach that at times will encourage new ways of thinking, at times will press for allegiance to founding principles, and at times will negotiate consensus among opposing positions. I have the bully pulpit on a national platform to try to influence decisions, and significant responsibility goes with that opportunity, but higher education is far too diverse to be served by the governance of a single individual.

Later in this book we will look at the issue of academic eligibility and the role played by school presidents to form more strident regulations governing this area. Why have school presidents been more successful in instituting academic legislation than in other legislative areas?

Academic success is so central to institutional mission that there is little room for argument about the worthiness of the effort. We expect student-athletes to meet minimal academic standards to participate in athletics. In common parlance, the need for standards of academic eligibility is a "no brainer." Academic achievement also doesn't compete with other interests that are protected by state and federal law. For example, NCAA legislation that would limit the compensation of athletics personnel would likely be in conflict with anti-trust legislation or laws that would protect against artificial restraints on trade. As a result, presidents haven't had the benefit of NCAA legislation to bolster their own attempts at restraints and often can't overcome local pressure to try to "spend" an institution into competitive equity.

In the absence of a national policy that mandates a certain benchmark for achievement, presidents have difficulty taking unilateral action in correcting athletics ills. And national policy is not possible where it would conflict with state or federal law that protects the rights of individuals or institutions to pursue what, in the end, may be perceived economic benefits.

Speaking of financial issues, which we will look at more closely in Chapter 6. Why is the issue of tax-exempt status so important for the intercollegiate athletics enterprise?

The issue of tax-exempt status is important for intercollegiate athletics for the same reason that it is important to higher education. The U.S. Congress has recognized that there are certain endeavors of such significance to the public good that revenue accruing to those endeavors shouldn't be taxed in the same way that profits for businesses are taxed as long as those revenues are used to further the purpose for which the revenue exists. Education is one of those endeavors, and colleges and universities are exempt from paying taxes on revenues used to advance the mission of higher education.

Intercollegiate athletics has great educational value for students who participate in sports and in the same way as students who participate in the university symphony or on the student newspaper. The fact that some athletics programs, the most competitive in one or two sports, draw lots of fan and media attention, and have been able to generate significant revenue streams as a result, doesn't change the purpose of college sports—providing educational value to students. The revenue—even in terms of millions of dollars—from gate and media receipts for the most popular sports *helps* to offset (but rarely fully covers) the cost of other sports that generate little or no revenue. This cross-subsidization is exactly the way the rest of higher education works. Large lecture sections in English and psychology that generate significant tuition revenue help to offset the cost of providing smaller courses in philosophy or art.

Higher education and intercollegiate athletics have very aggressive revenue-generation initiatives. They want to—and in fact must—develop millions and even billions of dollars to ensure that they meet their educational mission. The philosophical underpinning of tax-exempt status is that those revenues shouldn't be taxed because they don't go to profits for owners or shareholders but, rather, to offset the costs of advancing a purpose that benefits the public good.

In Chapter 3 we will be examining the role of conferences in intercollegiate athletics. You commented in a recent article that conference commissioners do the business of college sports. On what is this comment based, and how does it impact how you perform your duties as president?

For decades, football has been the major source of revenue for most athletic programs, primarily from gate receipts. In the last 20 years, however, the revenues from media and corporate sponsorship relationships in football have grown significantly. When the U.S. Supreme Court found the NCAA football television contract, which managed the appearance of college football teams on telecasts, in violation of anti-trust laws in 1984 (see Chapter 1), conferences and their commissioners were quickly thrust into the role of television negotiation and business development. The opportunity for revenue growth from these sources quickly became the expectation of universities and their presidents who were faced with increased demands for program expansion and declining public support to underwrite the expansion.

All these factors have combined to create a significant change in the role of conference commissioners in the last two decades. Conferences still conduct championships and operate all the traditional league initiatives, but the commissioners also have had to assume the added responsibility of exploiting the business opportunities that intercollegiate athletics present to help their member institutions provide broad sports participation opportunities with as little impact as possible on campus general funds.

The NCAA has a similar responsibility on a national level. The media contracts with CBS and ESPN are vital in terms of the revenue generated to underwrite fully 88 championships in 23 sports and to return dollars to conferences and member institutions for programmatic support and academic enhancement.

Later in the text we will be reviewing the motivation behind the creation of and the subsequent impact of The Second-Century Imperatives: Presidential Leadership— Institutional Accountability, *the 2006 report composed by the NCAA Presidential Task Force on the Future of Division I Athletics. What has been the reaction from intercollegiate athletic administrators to the report and its recommendations?*

One of the reasons for bringing together the task force of presidents who generated the report was that myth-busting research studies on the financial behavior of Division I intercollegiate athletics were being ignored. Peter and Jonathan Orszag had produced an extraordinary study and cost/benefit analysis of spending on athletics in 2003 that, among other findings, showed that increasing spending does not result in increased wins and increased wins do not result in increased revenues. In fact, they found that one dollar of new spending resulted in only one dollar of new revenue. This should have been a wake-up call for institutions that the budget growth of athletics programs that on average were double or triple the growth of the university would not yield commensurate benefits, but it was not.

As the task force finished its year-long review, it became apparent that the rate of growth in athletics, while not likely to ever put the university in a crisis mode,

could neither be justified in terms of increased benefits nor sustained over the long term. *The Second-Century Imperatives* report was designed to reassert both the need to moderate the spending growth of Division I athletics and the authority for presidents to lead this initiative. The report also promised new tools to assist presidents in this effort, specifically the "dashboard indicators" that would for the first time provide comparative data that is transparent in the aggregate so that institutions can see how their spending compares with those of their peers. The indicators were released for the first time in the spring of 2008, and it is still too early to know how effective or useful they will be for presidents.

Frankly, the greatest impediment to broad implementation of a growth moderation approach to athletics budgeting is the lack of a financial crisis. [Note that the interview took place prior to the recession in the late 2000s.] Even though the rate of growth has been as much as four times that of the rest of the university in some cases, the percentage of athletics spending compared to the whole continues to remain under 5 percent and has yet to so dramatically draw from a university's general funds for subsidization of athletics that the academic mission has been threatened. My sense is that most presidents and athletic directors know that the positions outlined in *The Second-Century Imperatives* are accurate, and the need for presidential leadership and institutional accountability is obvious, but unfortunately, a critical mass of institutions has not experienced enough financial pain to change behaviors.

Since you are the first former school president to take over as head of the NCAA, what do you wish you had known or been told before taking over as president that would have helped you operate successfully?

Although I had served in various administrative positions with a number of large state universities and had a good understanding of athletics, I was still surprised at how entrenched some of the "old" thinking was. It became apparent to me early on that athletic programs had to be reintegrated with the academic side of the campus. They were not so much at odds with each other as they were estranged one from the other. The revenue development potential of athletics that had become apparent in the 1990s was welcome relief for many universities struggling to meet growing budgets with declining public support. The trade-off for athletic programs to pay more of their own way through media and sponsorship packages was greater autonomy to explore and to develop new revenue sources, but the effect often was that athletic programs were pushed away from most of the policy development and strategic development for the rest of the campus.

Athletic directors, increasingly under pressure to expand both participation opportunities and the revenue to do so, seldom sat on campus-wide senior staff bodies and occasionally lost touch with the decision-making process for the campus as a whole. The isolation that many, if not most, athletic programs were experiencing created considerable innovation in terms of revenue development, but little progress in terms of keeping pace with new processes for the rest of the campus.

Immediately I began advocating for general integration, urging presidents to include athletic directors on their leadership cabinets, and encouraging athletic directors to seek greater interaction with their peers in the administration of other programs in the university. I had taken both steps as president at Indiana University. Much progress has been made in the last five years, but we are still catching up. Knowing earlier about the drift of athletic programs from the rest of the campus might not have changed how and when the issue could be addressed, but it would have been good to know coming in.

Would you recommend that your successor have experiences as a school president or CEO?

The value of having a former university president serving as CEO of the NCAA is in the deep understanding of the higher educational context that comes with that experience. It was clear to me when I was hired that the NCAA Executive Committee wanted that perspective at the top of the Association. It has helped enormously, I believe, in achieving the full implementation of academic reform, in pressing for the reintegration of intercollegiate athletics with higher education, and in delivering messages to a range of audiences about the educational values of athletics participation.

When the NCAA restructured its governance model in 1997 to put presidents in charge of developing national policy for the conduct of intercollegiate athletics, the role of the national office changed from what was almost exclusively a service role to one in which presidents on the Association's governing boards expected clear, practical leadership. While that shift doesn't exclusively mandate that former university presidents should head the NCAA, it clearly is a benefit in the relationship between the national office and the presidentially composed governance bodies.

questions TO CONSIDER

1. Of the NCAA's 16 Principles of Conduct for Intercollegiate Athletics, which three are most critical to ensuring positive participation experiences for student-athletes?

2. Why have so much effort and detail been expended to maintain the NCAA's organizational structure and legislative process?

3. Given what you now know about the NCAA's divisional classification structure, does your school's current classification allow for your school's athletic programs to meet its goals and objectives, or would a different classification make more sense?

4. If your school decides to reassess its athletic program and must choose between membership in one of the three national governing bodies outlined in the chapter, which of the three do you think would enable the athletic department to best meet its goals and objectives?

5. Identify whom the NCAA membership has chosen to replace Dr. Brand, and outline his or her qualifications. How do they compare with those Brand possessed before taking office, and do you believe the successor has the skills and abilities required to help the Association address its most important challenges?

references

About NJCAA–History. (2008). National Junior College Athletic Association. Accessed February 20, 2008, from: http://www.njcaa.org/history.cfm

About NJCAA—Today. (2009). National Junior College Athletic Association. Accessed June 5, 2009, from: http://njcaa.org/todaysNJCAA.cfm

About the NAIA. (2005). National Association of Intercollegiate Athletics. Accessed July 8, 2008, from: http://naia.cstv.com/member-services/about.htm

Carr, J. (2008, April 13). 2008 NAIA State of the Association address. Accessed July 8, 2008, from: http://naia.cstv.com/member-services/2008NAIAStateoftheAssociation Address.htm

Davis, S. (2009). *When March went mad: The game that transformed basketball.* New York: Henry Holt.

GSAC Addresses Its Future. (2009). Accessed August 24, 2009, from: http://gsacsports.org/wordpress/?p=1817

June, A.W. (2007, May 18). After costly foray into big-time sports, a college returns to its roots. *Chronicle of Higher Education*, pp. A33–34.

Lapointe, J. (2003, February 9). New chief brings college presidential seal to the N.C.A.A. *New York Times*, pp. 8–7.

Mark Emmert Selected as NCAA President. (2010, April 27). *The NCAA News.* Accessed April 28, 2010, from: http://ncaa.org/wps/portal/ncaahome?WCM_GLOBAL_CONTEXT=/ncaa/ncaa/ncaa+news/ncaa+news+online/2010/association.

Member Institutions. (2008). National Association of Intercollegiate Athletics. Accessed July 8, 2008, from: http://naia.cstv.com/member-services/about/members.htm

NAIA History. (2005). National Association of Intercollegiate Athletics. Accessed July 8, 2008, from: http://naia.cstv.com/member-services/about/history.htm

NCAA presidential task force on the future of Division I intercollegiate athletics (2006). *The Second Century imperatives: Presidential leadership—institutional accountability.* Indianapolis, IN: National Collegiate Athletic Association.

Nethery, R. (2004, December 6–12). Cutting a deal in college sports. *Street & Smith's SportsBusiness Journal*, pp. 28–31.

Plenty of NJCAA Representation in 2009 MLB Playoffs. (2009, October 9). National Junior College Athletic Association. Accessed October 13, 2009, from: http://www.njcaa.org/newsArticle.cfm?articleId=9371

Powell, R.A. (2007, April 22). Tennis in a parking lot. *New York Times Education Life*, pp. 26–27.

Rushin, S. (2007, March 3). Inside the moat. *Sports Illustrated.* Accessed August 7, 2008, from: http://find.galegroup.com/itx

Sandomir, R., & Thamel, P. (2010, April 23). 68: Tournament stays at CBS, adding cable and 3 teams. *New York Times*, pp. B9, B12.

Selcraig, B., McCallum, J., & Keteyian, A. (1986, October 6). In the kingdom of the solitary man. *Sports Illustrated.* Accessed August 7, 2008, from: http://find.galegroup.com/itx

Self-Study Guide. (2007). Indianapolis, IN: National Collegiate Athletic Association.

Shaheen, G. (2009, December 7–13). Brand's voice will be missed, but his vision for NCAA endures. *Street & Smith's SportsBusiness Journal*, p. 55.

Smith, M. (2009, December 7–13). 5 issues for the next NCAA president. *Street & Smith's SportsBusiness Journal*, pp. 1, 25–27, 29–30.

2007 Institutional Self-Study Report. (2007). Springfield, MA: Western New England College.

2007–08 NCAA Division I Manual. (2007). Indianapolis, IN: National Collegiate Athletic Association.

2008–09 NCAA Division I Manual. (2008). Indianapolis, IN: National Collegiate Athletic Association.

2008–09 NCAA Division II Manual. (2008). Indianapolis, IN: National Collegiate Athletic Association.

2008–09 NCAA Division IIII Manual. (2008). Indianapolis, IN: National Collegiate Athletic Association.

Wieberg, S. (2003a, January 10). Brand takes control, such as it is, of NCAA. *USA Today*, p. 11C.

Wieberg, S. (2003b, August 5). Brand: Athletics pricey, worthy. *USA Today*, p. 11C.

Wieberg, S. (2003c, August 15). NCAA's Brand: Fiscal fitness up to schools. *USA Today*, p. 1C.

Wieberg, S. (2005, January 8). Brand focused on containing costs in NCAA. *USA Today.* Accessed January 13, 2005 from: http://www.usatoday.com/sports/college/other/2005-01-08-ncaa-convention_x.htm

Wolverton, B. (2006, October 6). New head of governing body for athletics programs lays out his goals. *Chronicle of Higher Education.* Accessed February 19, 2008, from: http://find.galegroup.com/itx/start.do?prodId=AONE

Wolverton, B. (2007, March 23). A small athletics association tries to revamp its image. *Chronicle of Higher Education.* Accessed February 19, 2008, from: http://find.galegroup.com/itx/start.do?prodId=AONE

Wolverton, B. (2008, May 23). 2 athletics associations consider joining forces. *Chronicle of Higher Education*, p. A15.

The role of conferences

3

Key concepts to keep in mind as you read the chapter:

- The organizational, managerial, and operational importance of conferences for intercollegiate athletic managers.

- Historical factors influencing conference formations and affiliations, and how those and other emerging factors impact contemporary affiliations and reconfigurations.

- The key tasks and responsibilities performed by conference personnel, and how these actions support the vision, mission, and goals of its members.

71

Introduction

Intercollegiate athletic conferences, described by Bowen and Levin (2003) as "orbits of competition," were developed primarily for the formulation and enforcement of rules governing student-athlete eligibility, ease and convenience of travel and scheduling, and "lifting some of the political burden away from the individual member institutions" (Quarterman, 1994, p. 129). To support this assertion, Thelin (1996) states:

> The conference is the crucial unit in shaping and regulating intercollegiate athletics because it can have more impact on shaping athletic policies than the NCAA . . . (and) is the locus where a small group of institutions in voluntary association agree to work together, to compete while showing some sign of mutual respect and comparable academic standards. (p. 129)

Kjeldsen (1992) furthers the notion of a sense of a shared organizational identity with members of intercollegiate athletic conferences, noting:

> Structuring alliances with other organizations having like-minded management can reinforce the expectations which are extant in the organization. . . . [S]chools with similar concerns have formed leagues with rules which operationalize their common philosophy and put their athletes and coaches in social circumstances where they will be dealing with people and similar expectations and constraints. (p. 27)

But conferences, these so-called competitive orbits that operate between the like-minded for the betterment of all members, also demonstrate that participating schools must simultaneously cooperate and compete. Member schools come together and cooperate in the ways described above, but they also compete. They compete for wins in games, for media attention, for prospective student-athletes and coaching personnel, and for revenues and resources to run their programs. This competition is what can be a potential source of conflict between schools. Scholar Michael Oriard (2009) notes that schools that seek to institute rules and regulations on their own campuses put themselves at risk because of the "short-term advantage it could give the most direct institutional rivals in recruitment of students," and that any meaningful regulatory effort depends on schools identifying their true competitive "peers," and trusting them to conduct programs in a like manner (p. 277).

Intraconference competition also serves as a measuring stick. When one school in the conference wins, it comes at the expense of another conference member. Steven Lewis, Jr., former president of Carleton College, a private school with 2,000 undergraduates located in Northfield, Minnesota, and a member of the Division III Minnesota Intercollegiate Athletic Conference, expressed this concerning the role of conferences: "In athletics . . . students don't just compete against a standard of excellence as they might in music or theater. They compete against teams from other schools. Therefore . . . we need to act in concert with other colleges whose goals and values are similar" (Lewis, 2001, p. 9).

Lewis's comment expresses the realities of intercollegiate athletic management as schools look to coordinate programs beyond the boundaries of their own teams and departments. The intercollegiate landscape is segmented distinctly by discrete groupings of peer institutions that operate to manage these like-minded spheres of competition. They include organizations such as the Golden State Athletic Conference (GSAC), which restricts its membership to NAIA member schools located in California that are "faith-based colleges and universities of a similar size" (Golden State, 2008, p. 2). Other examples include the Rocky Mountain Athletic Conference (RMAC), a collection of 14 NCAA Division II schools located in Colorado (Adams State College, Colorado Christian University, Colorado School of Mines, Colorado State University–Pueblo, Fort Lewis College, Mesa State College, Metropolitan State College of Denver, Regis University, University of Colorado at Colorado Springs, Western State College), Nebraska (Chadron State College, University of Nebraska–Kearney), and New Mexico (New Mexico Highlands University and Western New Mexico University).

According to its conference code, the RMAC "is organized to maintain a group of collegiate institutions with comparable objectives for the purpose of governing intercollegiate athletic competition and making the athletic program a part of the educational plan," and that "opportunities for athletic participation shall be provided for any student in good academic standing regardless of ethnic group, race, religion, or sex" (2008–09 Rocky Mountain, 2008, p. 1). Another example is the Ohio Community College Athletic Conference (OCCAC), which under its bylaws outlines that the purpose of the organization is "to promote and foster community college intercollegiate athletics for men and women on the [Ohio] state level," and that its members must be "colleges having received state and regional accreditation" that have been approved for membership in the National Junior College Athletic Association (Ohio Community College, 2006, p. 1). Membership of the OCCAC includes Cincinnati State Technical and Community College, Columbus State Community College, Cuyahoga Community College, Edison Community College, Lakeland Community College, Lorain County Community College, Owens Community College, and Sinclair Community College.

In Chapter 2 we explored the role of national governing bodies such as the NCAA and how these organizations impact the management of intercollegiate athletics on a macro level. In this chapter we seek to understand the nature of conference affiliations and how such affiliations have impacted and continue to impact the direction and application of intercollegiate athletic management.

HISTORICAL PERSPECTIVES

As we learned in Chapter 1, intercollegiate athletic competition dates back to 1852, with the landmark rowing competition between Harvard and Yale. During the formative years of the enterprise, students controlled all managerial aspects of intercollegiate athletics, but then faculty and professional coaches absorbed these critical tasks. The rapid rise in popularity of intercollegiate athletics, especially football, with stakeholders groups—students, alumni, the general public—meant increased concern over the wins and losses of individual programs. With the stakes of game outcomes increased, Harvard, Yale, and Princeton, along with Columbia University, formed the Intercollegiate Football Association (IFA) to adopt standard rules.

However, as Rudolph (1990) noted, intercollegiate athletics quickly evolved to a system in which "once the sport had been accepted, the games had to be won"

(p. 381). Supporting Rudolph's realization of the primacy of victory, Smith (1988) underscored the fact that to win those games, "from an early period in American intercollegiate athletic history, there was pressure to bring in athletes with little regard for academic considerations" (p. 175). Early conflicts developed over the participation of first-year, graduate, and non-degree "special" students, student residency requirements, and students transferring solely for athletic purposes. For roughly the first century of intercollegiate athletics, many colleges and universities maintained a separate admissions standard for athletes without abiding by the school's regular admissions policies.

The early roles of conferences

In light of these conflicts and pressures, some schools began to exert greater control over their athletic programs and took actions on their own to deal with academic issues, eventually working together with faculty and managers from other schools to create a more controllable and desired system. The 1895 "Chicago Conference," attended by faculty representatives from the seven schools that later founded what would become the Big Ten Conference (Helman, 1989), was one such successful early effort to control and regulate the eligibility of student-athletes, as was the 1898 "Brown Conference," attended by students, faculty, and alumni from nearly all schools of the present-day Ivy League. The latter conclave in part sought to "'weed out' a 'student who has entered the university for athletic purposes only'" (Smith, 1988, p. 140). For many years thereafter, conference organizations rather than the nascent NCAA would continue to serve as the main arbiter for such academic rules, with varying degrees of effectiveness. We will learn more about such academic rules in Chapter 9.

In the case of punishing member schools for transgressions against specific codes, again, conferences rather than the NCAA remained the main enforcer in such matters. One notable example followed a spate of point-shaving in men's basketball in 1951, which involved players at several schools, including Bradley University, the City College of New York, Long Island University, Manhattan College, the University of Toledo, and the University of Kentucky. It was discovered that Kentucky players and head coach Adolph Rupp had placed bets on games and altered the outcome of games to win these bets when three Kentucky players admitted fixing games in the course of a federal trial. As a result, the Southeastern Conference banned Kentucky from conference play for the 1952–53 season and called for the firing of Rupp, a call that was rejected by the school. Following the imposition of additional NCAA sanctions, Kentucky president Herman Lee Donovan, an enthusiastic supporter of the program, moved to cancel the entire season (Rosen, 1999).

The role of competition in conference formation and management

The stakes and nature of intra-group competition in conference formation and management are observed from the time when the Pacific Coast Conference (PCC), a progenitor of the current Pac-10 Conference, faced an organizational crisis in the 1950s, which challenged the maintenance of its shared orbit of competition. The conference was founded in 1915 by the University of California, Berkeley (Cal), the University of Washington, the University of Oregon, and Oregon State College (now University). In 1917, Washington State College (now University) was accepted into the conference, and Stanford University joined the next year. In 1922, the PCC expanded to eight with the admission of the University of Southern California (USC) and the University of Idaho. The University of Montana joined in 1924, and the conference grew to 10 members in 1928 with the addition of the University of California, Los Angeles (UCLA). In 1950, Montana resigned from the PCC and joined the Mountain States Conference (About Pac-10, 2006).

In the early and mid-1950s, press coverage reported that four member schools (Cal, UCLA, USC, and Washington) maintained slush funds for payments to football players, systems much like that which would occur at Southern Methodist in the 1970s and 1980s, as described in Chapter 1. Oregon also was accused of offering money and clothing to promising recruits. Payments to prospects had been occurring in the PCC since the late 1930s. In 1938, a faculty-hired investigator, Edwin Atherton, took two years (at the cost of $40,000—more than half a million in today's dollars) to reveal problems and create possible solutions. Because of his work, Atherton was hired as the PCC's first commissioner to enforce recently passed recruiting guidelines, which were intended to rein in alumni/booster feting of prospects and to prohibit coaches from contacting prospects off campus. Any violation of these rules would bar the prospect from attending the offending school. "We intend to have the boy select the college, and stop the college selecting the boy," Atherton said (Johnson, 2006, p. 86).

Atherton's hiring did not stop these practices, however. After the announcement and enforcement of the PCC-mandated penalties against UCLA, its chancellor, Raymond Allen, called for the penalties to be reconsidered while claiming to have information of similar wrongdoings at other PCC schools (albeit without proof). Soon thereafter, Edwin Pauley, a member of the University of California's Board of Regents (and the man for whom UCLA's storied basketball venue is named), expressed disdain for the conference's northern membership and suggested that the California schools should leave the PCC to form a "California Conference." Others agreed, citing that the PCC's rules were too restrictive for the California schools looking to play "big football." Local Los Angeles politicians even called for a state investigation of the PCC's moves, claiming that "the northern schools couldn't beat UCLA on the field, 'so they beat them this way'" (Johnson, 2006, p. 86). These comments and actions put additional strain on relations between the California schools and the rest of the PCC membership. Even though the faculty athletic representatives had voted in 1957 to allow aid for needy student-athletes, and scaled back the probation penalties, Cal, UCLA, and USC voted to leave the conference. Washington left the next year, and the five remaining schools opted to dissolve the conference soon thereafter (Thelin, 1996; Watterson, 2000).

Thelin (1996) attributes the fall of the PCC to lack of unified agreement about amateur athletics among stakeholders of the member institutions as many PCC managers sought to "commercialize" their athletic programs. Whether the commercialization of intercollegiate athletics is good or bad is a secondary point in the case of the PCC. The main factor that brought its end was the disagreement over program management among the membership. The reason it regrouped was as basic as the reasons conferences are created in the first place: to maintain and to regulate a manageable orbit of competition among similarly situated institutions. Watterson (2000) notes that the schools (sans Idaho) chose to reconvene because the California state-supported schools couldn't make a go of a three-member conference.

Following dissolution of the PCC, each of these now independent schools chose to maintain their athletic programs, which meant that the need for rules governing student-athlete eligibility, ease and convenience of travel and scheduling, and "lifting some of the political burden away from the individual member institutions" still existed. The resulting question was with whom these schools now would seek to align to create their future orbit of competition. The four penalized schools along with Stanford formed a loose coalition soon after, with the University of Oregon, Oregon State University, and Washington State University rejoining later, establishing what would be known first as the Athletic Association of Western Universities (AAWU), and then as the Pac-8. The University of Arizona and Arizona State University joined in 1978 to round out the current membership, with the resultant renaming of the group to the "Pac-10."

ORGANIZATIONAL STRUCTURE AND GOVERNANCE

As we will see later in the chapter, most conferences are operated with a functional organizational structure; that is, a separate unit or department of specialists is created to perform each function essential for achieving the organization's goals (Covell et al., 2007). We will learn more about the concepts that influence organizational structure in Chapter 5. Most intercollegiate athletic conferences are staffed by a commissioner, and at least one (and in many cases several) associate or assistant commissioners. Operations of the conference are generally divided by specific task areas, with managers within the department having responsibilities for oversight of these areas (as outlined in their position descriptions). While these staffers have the charge of operating the functions of the conference, individual personnel from the member schools, usually ADs and school presidents, have the ultimate power and responsibility to formulate conference vision, mission, and policies.

Contemporary conference formation and structuring

To gain insights into a more contemporary formation and structuring of an intercollegiate athletic conference, let's examine the case of the New England Small College Athletic Conference (NESCAC). The review of NESCAC's organizational evolution provides an intriguing and instructive example of conference formation and the evolution of organizational structure and governance, and the need to develop conference operations based on the changing expectations of member schools.

NESCAC'S FORMATION AND EVOLUTION | **case study** 3.A

The schools that would come to comprise NESCAC's membership were integral in establishing the system of American intercollegiate athletics in the 19th century. In July 1859, Amherst beat Williams, 73–33, in Pittsfield, Massachusetts, in the nation's first intercollegiate baseball game. Students at Bowdoin, Hamilton, Middlebury, and Trinity all formed baseball teams before the Civil War. In 1873, Amherst's Otis Benton finished third out of three in the first intercollegiate track meet, a 2-mile run held in Springfield, Massachusetts. In 1875, Tufts beat Harvard, 1–0, in the first solely American intercollegiate rugby-football contest. In 1883, Trinity and Amherst took part in the first intercollegiate tennis tournament. Amherst, Trinity, and Wesleyan participated in the first intercollegiate gymnastics meet in 1899 (Smith, 1988).

As NESCACs were establishing intercollegiate athletics as a part of American culture, "the proponents of college sports increasingly demanded winning teams, athletes who could perform at the highest possible level and beat their opponents" (Sperber, 1998, p. 11). While many schools heeded these competitive demands, thereby transforming American intercollegiate sport into popular spectacle, the schools that would come to comprise the current NESCAC membership opted eventually to eschew this course and elected rather to focus on fostering intercollegiate athletics on a scale targeted neither toward public entertainment nor linked with overt commercialism and, according to many, virtual professionalism.

As with the Ivies, in the 1940s and 1950s, teams from future NESCACs were no longer national powers. In the 1940s, four future NESCAC members (Amherst, Bowdoin, Williams, and Wesleyan) and future Ivy League member Dartmouth College allied to form the "Pentagonal Agreement" for intercollegiate competition in an attempt to formulate their own orbit. When Dartmouth left to join the formally organized Ivy League, the four remaining schools re-formed their association on a basis similar to that crafted by the Ivies, due in part to the perceived institutional similarities between the four and the Ivy membership.

The NESCACs created similar institutional and collective identities through their formal association around athletic policy. The four remaining "Pentagonals" reaffirmed their athletic association, drafting the Joint Agreement on Athletic Policy in 1955. The agreement adopted many of the aspects cited by the Ivies and specified that athletic scholarships would be prohibited, that members would have full scheduling freedom, and that presidents would be "the definitive regulators of policy" (Velez, 1997, p. 3). The commitment to academics for future NESCACs was a longstanding one, as in 1906 Williams and Wesleyan had agreed to ban frosh from athletic participation if they were deficient in high school Carnegie units. By the late 1960s, other like schools in the region sought to join the remaining Pentagonals because, as cited in a 1967 letter to Bowdoin president James Coles from Trinity president Albert Jacobs, the continued expansion and commercialization of American intercollegiate athletics left Trinity and other like schools at a competitive disadvantage (Velez, 1997).

An official proposal for league expansion was drafted by a committee of athletic directors and presented to school presidents in 1969. The proposal was formally adopted as the conference agreement on March 21, 1971, two years before formal establishment of the Division III classification by the NCAA membership. The agreement formally codified that athletics were to be kept "in harmony" with institutional educational purposes, that student-athletes be representative of their institution's student body, and that presidents would have the ultimate authority over athletics. The original bylaws prohibited conference championships or standings to dissuade overt emphasis on competition (NESCAC Agreement, 1971). The original bylaws also banned athletically related financial aid, strictly limited off-campus recruiting activities, did not require that conference members schedule other conference members, set limits on length of playing seasons and the number of allowable athletic events, and marked that postseason competition was "not to be understood as automatic . . . (it) is exceptional and the decision on whether to participate lies wholly within each individual institution" (NESCAC Agreement, 1971, p. 4).

Institutional autonomy, freedom, and flexibility were also valued, as then-Middlebury AD Richard Coleman noted that NESCAC should be based on "mutual trust and confidence (rather) than a network of tight rules and regulations" (Velez, 1997, p. 7). This approach was valued because presidents were not interested in overseeing the details of conference operation. The NESCAC structure was tested by a dispute in which Union College (Schenectady, NY), a founding member, opted to leave the conference in 1977 rather than abide by conference recruiting and amateurism rules. While Union claimed it left on its own accord, former Wesleyan AD Donald Russell commented, "They were kicked out for cheating at hockey" (Looney, 1994, p. 79). In this case, the conference showed it could regulate itself without an elaborate rules-compliance mechanism (Velez, 1997).

NESCAC has revised its Agreement multiple times since its inception. The basic principles were expanded in 1981, and championships in certain sports were introduced in 1982. Although post-season participation for individual student-athletes had always been allowed under the Agreement, initially NESCAC specifically limited team participation to "regional tournaments . . . played on college campuses which do not lead to further competition or conflict with examination schedules, provided such tournaments do not extend the season more than 7 calendar days beyond the Saturday of the final week of scheduled competition" (NESCAC Agreement, 1975, p. 6).

Although these restrictions did not specifically name NCAA competitions, the limitations made participation in them impossible. However, NCAA's formal establishment of the Division III classification in 1973 created an opportunity for postseason competition against similar schools. Many coaches of NESCAC team sports then began to advocate for the chance to play in NCAA championships, most actively in the late 1980s and early 1990s, citing that such participation would aid recruiting and would enhance "the total athletic/academic experience of the student-athlete and significantly promote NESCAC standards throughout the country" (Velez, 1997, p. 18).

The presidents turned to address the real and perceived inequities of the postseason policy and, in 1993, the Agreement was amended by the Presidents' Executive Committee to permit participation in NCAA postseason championships for a three-year experimental period, beginning in the fall of 1993. The experiment was to be reviewed in 1997, and would be extended only by an affirmative vote of three-quarters of school presidents. Football was to remain banned from any postseason participation.

The decision by the presidents to extend participation was delayed until April 1998. At that meeting the presidents acted on this and other important motions. Regarding NCAA postseason play, the presidents chose to

> . . . evolve into a qualified playing conference . . . (except football) . . . (and to) create appropriate mechanisms to determine a conference champion in all sports where it is practical. . . . We will allow only the conference champion to pursue post-season competition on one venue deemed appropriate - normally NCAA Division III. . . . These changes will lessen conflicts with academic schedules. (NESCAC Presidents, 1998, p. 1)

The presidents had made what many would later identify as a compromise decision. Rather than end postseason participation entirely, or keep full participation, they took the middle ground. After word of this proposed return to the postseason ban leaked out, NESCAC stakeholders voiced considerable concern. Student-athletes in particular were quite vocal in expressing their support for maintaining the opportunity to participate in NCAA championships, using the school newspapers as a forum to voice their concerns. Said Bowdoin student-athlete Ryan Buckley: "By cutting short bids for NCAA play, we are also cutting short certain invaluable lessons that can be taught nowhere else.

After all, do we cut short a student's potential for cum laude? Certainly not" (Orient Forum, 1997, p. 9).

Local members of the mainstream media also questioned the proposed policy change. Mike Szostak of the *Providence (RI) Journal* singled out the school presidents rumored to be in favor of the ban: "Why do the presidents of Amherst, Bates, Bowdoin, Colby, and Connecticut College want to ban New England Small College Athletic Conference teams from NCAA tournaments? . . . Sports are important at these small, elite colleges. Students should be encouraged to go as far as their talents will take them, even if they develop those talents on playing fields in addition to classrooms" (1997, p. 6B). This was a new twist to the issue. NESCAC schools enjoyed success, and the merits were topics of discussion on school campuses and among school alumni. But seldom, if ever, did the mainstream media cover, let alone criticize, the conference and its policies. This would serve only to stoke further opposition from student-athletes, parents, and alumni.

The presidents also were hearing displeasure from their own athletic staffs. Athletic administrators were publicly expressing disfavor with the compromise and its anticipated impact on limiting postseason participation. Payne read the comments of Brian Katten, sports information director at Wesleyan, who commented to interested students in an online chatroom: "I don't think there is an SID among us who does not feel the intended NESCAC restriction on postseason play is a farce" (Katten, 1999, personal comm.). Conference ADs also expressed opposition to the presidents' decision publicly. One AD said: "We were getting five and six teams in the NCAA. Now we're going to get one."

The issues and debate relating to their decision regarding NCAA postseason competition were clearly the single most significant event in influencing the immediate present and future of NESCAC. This process was helping them to assess the direction of future athletic policy more effectively. One president read the situation this way:

> Clearly [the championships issue] was the most important factor that began to force us as presidents [to think about], well, what are we? What does it mean to be in this conference? And how extensive should it be? What's the proper relationship between the presidents and the athletic directors? A lot of things forced us to think about the future and direction of the conference, . . . and then we realized we have to deal with this issue of postseason play, and our relationship to the NCAA, and all that. And I'm optimistic. I think we came through that episode sort of confirming the importance of NESCAC. (Covell, 1999, p. 193)

The presidents believed that the compromise plan was enacted because, due to varying personal and philosophical beliefs held by the group, the conference was in danger of dissolving over this issue. One president described his decision this way: "I've supported these reforms, including the latest ones, because I felt we we're about to split up over this championship issue, and I myself compromised. I'm a purist. I'm a 'no-championship' type in my personal attitude, but I felt the compromise was a sensible one. . . . All the other schools . . . went along compromising, too. So it saved us" (Covell, 1999, p. 193).

Overall, the presidents believed the postseason controversy had reaffirmed the ties and bonds within the conference. Presidents had increased their reliance on each other in sharing information regarding both general institutional and athletic policies. This sharing of information, the presidents hoped, could serve to address questions among presidents about potentially contentious issues within the conference, as well as to prepare the group more fully to deal with external questions and criticisms regarding the intercollegiate athletic policy process and resulting decisions.

The NESCAC model is one of ultimate presidential control over athletic decisions, but as the postseason controversy illustrated, one that also must be responsive ultimately to the input and perspectives of all stakeholder groups. The model of direct presidential control is championed by many as the best way to keep intercollegiate athletics securely centered within the rubric of the mission of higher education, but this method is not without its challenges. A major pitfall to this system is the question of whether school presidents are capable of and/or interested in devoting the time and energy necessary to manage these programs effectively. Even at Division III, these programs garner substantial resources and stakeholder interests, so they cannot be managed with any amount of benign neglect. As the NESCAC postseason issue illustrates, any president who chooses to act in such a way does so at his or her peril.

questions for you to consider

1. Are the factors that led to the formation of NESCAC still impacting intercollegiate athletic departments today?

2. Are the issues that led to the increased formalization of NESCAC applicable to your school's athletic department?

3. What are the benefits and drawbacks of presidential control over intercollegiate athletics?

4. Why did the presidents seek to limit postseason play? What would the result of such a move be on your campus?

Division I conference management models

Now that we have examined the formation and structuring of a conference, let's examine how they are managed by comparing two Division I conference management models.

The Big Ten

Earlier in the chapter we learned that the Big Ten was one of the first formal conferences organized to manage inter-school athletic relationships. After coming together as the Western Conference in 1895, the Office of the Commissioner of Athletics was created in 1922 "to study athletic problems of the various Western Conference universities and assist in enforcing the eligibility rules which govern Big Ten athletics" (Big Ten History, 2006, p. 1). To fill this need, the conference hired Major John Griffith, who served in that position until his death in 1944. Kenneth "Tug" Wilson, former director of athletics at conference member Northwestern University, served from 1944 until he retired in 1961, followed by Bill Reed (1961–1971), and Wayne Duke (1971–1989) (Big Ten History, 2006).

James Delany succeeded Duke after 10 years as Ohio Valley Conference commissioner. Delany's career in intercollegiate athletics management began at the

NCAA, where he was employed as an enforcement representative from 1975 to 1979. After taking the helm of the Big Ten, Delany was described in a 2007 *Business Week* profile as one of the 100 most influential people in sport. He took on "all comers—university presidents, athletic directors, crazed fans, Congress—all, [Delany] says, with the aim of improving college sports" (Big Ten Conference Staff, 2009). Former NCAA president Myles Brand once said that Delany is "part of the Big Ten team. He's going to do everything in his power to make sure his team wins" (Gloeckler, 2007, p. 59). Because of these attributes, a 2008 poll of industry executives rated Delany the fourth-most powerful person in intercollegiate athletics, behind Brand, Duke University men's basketball coach Mike Krzyzewski, and Southeastern Conference commissioner Mike Slive (About Pac-10, 2006; SBJ/SBD, 2008). Delany also has advocated for gender equity efforts and negotiated broadcast deals that have increased the Conference's revenues by nearly $100 million. Lee Corso, former head football coach at Indiana University, and now better known as the mascot head–wearing prognosticator on ESPN's "College Gameday" program, summed up Delany's impact this way: "The Big Ten has become a major corporation, and it's because Jim Delany runs it that way" (Gloeckler, 2007, p. 59).

Exhibit 3.1 lists the managerial positions within the Big Ten office, headquartered in Park Ridge, Illinois, a suburb of Chicago. This office supervises competitions in 25 conference sports.

EXHIBIT 3.1	Big Ten Conference administrative positions.

Deputy Commissioner

Associate Commissioner (4 positions): Officiating Programs, Governance, Television Administration

Assistant Commissioners (5 positions): Branding, Championships, Compliance, Communications, Technology

Controller

Director of Branding

Director Budget and Finance

Associate Director of Communications (2 positions)

Associate Director of Championships (2 positions)

Assistant Director of Compliance

Production Coordinator / Building Administrator

Executive Assistant to the Commissioner

Administrative Assistants (4 positions)

Robert Hammel Communications Intern

C. D. Henry Intern

Web Intern (2 positions)

Governance Intern

Video Coordinator

Coordinator of Officials—Football

Source: Big Ten Conference Staff, 2009.

Colonial Athletic Association

By comparison, Exhibit 3.2 lists the departmental structure and positions of the Colonial Athletic Association (CAA). With offices in Richmond, Virginia, the CAA is a Division I conference (with Championship Subdivision football programs) composed of 12 members dispersed along the East Coast from Boston (North-eastern University) to Atlanta (Georgia State University), and sponsors conference play in 21 sports.

The Big Ten and the CAA both have managers in the functional areas such as finance and marketing, along with specialists in the areas of communications and media relations, postseason conference championships, and conference and NCAA rules compliance (and in the case of the Big Ten, coordination of on-field game officials). The primary difference between these two structures is the greater number of staff members employed by the Big Ten, which can be attributed less to the number of programs overseen than to the amount of public interest generated by the programs at member institutions. This higher interest level means that the conference office has more responsibility in terms of managing relationships with corporate sponsors. For the Big Ten, this includes Cooper Tires, Liberty Mutual Insurance, Ramada hotels, 7-Up, U.S. Bank, Gatorade, Under Armor, and Xbox Live. In addition, both associations have responsibilities and duties connected with national and local media outlets and broadcast partners included in the following discussion.

Colonial Athletic Association staff.   EXHIBIT 3.2

Commissioner
Deputy Commissioner for Basketball
Senior Associate Commissioner – Internal Operations/Senior Women's Administrator
Senior Associate Commissioner – Marketing/Development
Associate Commissioner – Communications
Associate Commissioner – Broadcast Services
Assistant Commissioner – Championships (2 positions)
Director of Basketball Strategies
Director of Communications
Director of Football Communications
Director of Operations
Director of Video Services
Assistant Director of Video Services
Administrative Assistant
Support Services Coordinator
Communications Intern
Compliance and Administrative Intern

Source: Staff Directory, 2009.

KEY ORGANIZATIONAL ACTIVITIES

he Big Ten and the CAA are tasked with compliance with rules and with managing conflict. The following discussion addresses these functions.

Compliance

As we will discuss in Chapter 8, compliance with both NCAA and conference rules is a major component of managing an intercollegiate athletic department. Given the complexity of these duties, conferences have hired compliance personnel and developed mechanisms to aid members in learning and applying these rules to their programs. One such example can be found at the Pac-10's website, www.pac-10.org, under the "Compliance" link. This link directs the user to the site's "Compliance Corner," which is organized to communicate compliance-related information to members in a timely manner. Information is divided based on content such as legislation, deregulation, and emerging issues such as recent NCAA committee decisions. Under "Legislation," the conference posts important information and updates, including NCAA Division I governance agendas and anticipated action items.

Reports are also available via home pages of various governance committees such as the Board of Directors, the Management Council, the Academics/Eligibility/ Compliance Cabinet, and the Championships/Competition Cabinet. And the site contains reports such as that year's Division I Publication of Proposed Legislation. The site, too, provides access to the conference's Legislation Timeline to follow the course of specific pieces of NCAA legislation as far back as 1997, as well as summaries of current legislation. The site offers technical assistance to keep members' *NCAA Manual* current and reminds members of key dates in the compliance and legislative processes, as outlined in Exhibit 3.3.

Broadcast agreements

The landscape for generating revenues related to broadcasting is generally controlled and managed at the conference level. Consider the agreement between the Southeastern Conference (SEC), CBS, and ESPN to broadcast SEC football. Beginning with the 2009 season, the networks agreed to pay conference members $3 billion over 15 years, guaranteeing each of the 12 members nearly $17 million a year (Wolverton, 2009)—well above what many professional league franchises earn in such revenues. According to SEC commissioner Mike Slive, when he approached the networks with a list of demands, both were anxious to keep SEC games, especially because conferences such as the Big Ten and Mountain West have formed their own networks. Slive says the networks gave him everything he wanted: "There's no downside to this deal. . . . What I try to sell to people is that [conference schools] are inexorably tied to one another, and our success helps all of us." SEC will not have to put up start-up costs for its own network or work to sell advertising slots. In addition, in the first week of the 2009 season alone, ESPN broadcast seven games involving SEC teams, giving the league an unprecedented national reach for viewers and prospective recruits (Wolverton, 2009, p. A27).

We have introduced the management structure of the Big Ten Conference and its commissioner, James Delany. One of his key roles is to manage the Big Ten's media contracts, from which the conference and its members garner a significant portion

| | EXHIBIT | 3.3 |
| Pac-10 Conference's instructional timeline for adoption of NCAA legislation. | | |

EVENT	DATE
Conference, cabinet legislation submission deadline	July 15, 2008
Management Council Administrative Committee referral to cabinets; initial web-based publication of legislation	August 15, 2008
Cabinet review	September 2008
Initial amendment period ends	October 27, 2008
Deadline for submission of proposals initiated by Board of Directors	October 26, 2008
Online Publication of Official Notice	November 15, 2008
Legislative Council Meeting at NCAA Convention	January 14–15, 2009
Board of Directors meeting at NCAA Convention	January 17, 2009
60-day comment/amendment period ends	March 18, 2009
Legislative Council meeting for final consideration of legislative proposals	April 20, 2009
Board of Directors meeting for review of Legislative Council proposals	April 30, 2009
60-day override period ends	June 25, 2009

Source: Key Dates, 2009.

of its revenue to pay for its athletic programs. Said Delany, "There's no enthusiasm for funding these programs by the central administrations, so basically we're on our own. . . . I've found it much easier to generate revenue than to cut costs. I'm being honest with you" (Sandomir, 2006, p. 8–8; Thomas, 2009, p. B15). In total the conference distributes nearly $22 million a year back to its members—a twofold increase since Delany took over (Greenstein, 2010).

Delany's pursuit of revenue for the conference has led to his identification as a major impediment to creation of a playoff for the Division I Bowl Subdivision. Delany cites the Big Ten's self-interests as his rationale for defending the current conference-controlled Bowl Championship Series (BCS), which includes the regular season champions from the most powerful conferences (Atlantic Coast Conference [ACC], Big East, Big 10, Big 12, Pac-10, Southeastern). "It's simply to create a theoretical national champion, and allows these conferences to retain the lion's share of the resultant media revenues. We started the BCS to create a healthier bowl environment. We didn't see it as a first step toward a full-fledged NFL-style playoff" (Gloeckler, 2007, p. 60). We will learn more about the structure of bowl games and the importance of associated revenues in Chapter 6.

In addition to preserving the BCS and its concomitant revenues, a task facing Delany was to create contacts and negotiate with potential broadcast partners to generate the additional funds his member schools needed. He has been successful in this role. In June 2006, after moving to secure the rights to four of the five BCS bowl games through 2010 (at a cost of $83 million annually), the Fox cable networks agreed to a partnership with the Big Ten to create the Big Ten Network (BTN), a sports network intended to appeal to fans and alumni, not only in the Midwest but also throughout the country. Fifty-one percent of the channel is owned by the conference, and 49 percent by Fox's parent company, News Corp, with the channel having rights to 35 football games, as well as 105 men's basketball games, live coverage of other conference sports, and other programming such as coaches' shows. This deal came in addition to the broadcast deal the conference renewed with ESPN and ABC for $100 million annually over the next decade, giving the outlets exclusive rights to 41 football games and 59 men's basketball games, as well as rights relating to new media such as cellphones and online broadband coverage. The two deals will guarantee each of the 11 members at least $7.5 million annually. "We have maybe three or four athletic departments in red ink, and this sops it up," said Delany (Sandomir, 2006, p. 8-8). Fox was motivated to partner with the Big Ten in large part because, in the words of Bob Thompson, president of Fox Sports Networks, the organization's collection of regional sports networks, "College football generates a level of passion you don't see in other sports. With its long history of successful schools and teams, and the size and strength of their TV markets, the Big Ten is extremely important" (Gardiner, 2007, p. 10C; Heistand, 2006; Wolverton, 2007).

Why should the Big Ten choose this route rather than taking more in direct rights payments from broadcasters? Delany recalls a meeting several years before with executives from Disney, owners of both ABC and ESPN, when the parties were beginning to negotiate the terms of a new football broadcast deal (the deal at the time paid the Big Ten $1 billion in rights fees): "They told us we were flat. Maybe it was just a negotiating ploy. I don't know. But suffice it to say they weren't very encouraging" (Sandomir, 2006, p. 8-8). This was the catalyst in looking to launch the new venture.

When it was launched in August 2007, the BTN had agreements set with 40 small cable companies and DirecTV's basic satellite package but had not yet inked basic carriage deals with larger cable companies such as Comcast and Time Warner because of disputes over the fees the Big Ten was seeking to charge. Soon thereafter, though, the network switched to Dish Network, which allowed the BTN to reach 28.5 million households nationwide.

Delany has attempted to cajole reluctant cable executives into carrying the BTN as part of basic cable packages, asking for around $1 per subscriber per month. One industry expert says only eight networks get more than 50 cents per subscriber (a typical cable network such as CNN or TBS generally charges 30 cents per subscriber, while ESPN charges 10 times this rate), and didn't believe Delany could get the rate he wanted, especially since the BTN would have mostly "filler content" as ABC and ESPN had rights to the best games already. However, when a 2007 conference matchup between top-ranked Ohio State and No. 21 Wisconsin was available only on BTN, the 60 percent of fans in Ohio and 75 percent of fans in Wisconsin who couldn't watch the game were miffed. Mark Silverman, president of BTN, put the blame on the cable companies for missing the game (Sandomir, 2007). The conference's agreement with ABC/ESPN doesn't allow BTN first choice of games to broadcast but does guarantee at least one conference game per member school.

When asked in October 2008 about the progress of the network in reaching viewers and its future challenges, Delany had this to say: "We need to reestablish that good relationship between the fan bases and the 11 schools, (so) we can build better audiences, get more reliability in audiences, get better ratings" (De Avila, 2008, p. 1).

In the last quarter of 2008, the BTN posted a profit. By early 2010 (after cable companies Time Warner and Comcast picked up the channel) the network was returning $66 million a year to the conference, based on the fact that the BTN was receiving 70 to 80 cents per subscriber from carriers (Jones, 2010). The network has been so successful that it is believed that the conference may expand by as many as five new members to broaden its market and network viewers with the conference's potential new footprint growing from its current contiguous eight-state area to stretch from the Atlantic Ocean to the Rocky Mountains (Jones, 2010). The conference hired a Chicago-based investment firm in 2010 to analyze whether any such expansion would create enough revenue to justify the move (Greenstein, 2010). We will discuss more about Conference expansion and realignment below.

Will this be a trend, with all Division I conferences following the Big Ten's lead and creating their own networks? Fox's Bob Thompson says no, although the Mountain West Conference launched a similar venture in 2006 in conjunction with CSTV and Comcast. "Not all conferences are created equal," said Thompson. "Some are spread over large geographic areas; some may not have enough television households in the territory" (Gardiner, 2007, p. 10C). The fact that broadcast rights for games are controlled by the conference and not by the individual member schools also aided forming the venture. Exhibit 3.4 outlines the broadcast deals for the four other BCS conferences.

Managing conflict

As much as conferences and conference managers try to maintain solid relations with stakeholders and outside organizations, the often-intense nature of on-field competition, combined with the variables that shape and influence the outcomes of these competitions, occasionally force conference managers to address relational breeches. Sometimes these disputes arise based on revenues. Conference and school personnel (including some school presidents) and even politicians have railed against the exclusive conference tie-ins that define the BCS structure and have sought ways to gain access to the millions in revenue available exclusively to the BCS-member schools.

Other disputes are far more specific in terms of impacting department personnel and student-athletes. Consider the case of the 2006 University of Oklahoma–University of Oregon football game, played at Oregon's Autzen Stadium in Eugene. Trailing 33–20 with just over 3 minutes remaining in the game, the Ducks rallied to defeat the Sooners, 34–33, aided in large part by two incorrect decisions made by the officiating and video replay crews (who are assigned by the Pac-10, Oregon's conference, in accordance with written league rules). Video replays clearly showed TV viewers that an

---

Broadcast agreements for BCS conferences.   **EXHIBIT 3.4**

- Atlantic Coast Conference: ABC/ESPN, $258 million (2003/04 through 2010/11); Raycom Sports, $300 million for basketball (2000/01 through 2010/11)
- Big 12 Conference: ABC/ESPN, $480 million (2007/08 through 2015/16); Fox Sports Net, $78 million (2007/08 through 2011/12)
- Big East Conference: ABC/ESPN, $200 million (2007/08 through 2013)
- Pac-10 Conference: ABC/ESPN, $125 million for football (2006/07 through 2011/12); $52.5 million for basketball (2005/06 through 2011/12); Fox Sports Net, $97 million for football (2006/07 through 2011/12).

Source: Major Conferences, 2009.

Oregon player touched an on-side kick before that ball had traveled 10 yards (which Oregon recovered), and that an Oregon pass was deflected at the line of scrimmage, which would have negated a pass interference call against Oklahoma (although the replay official, Gordon Riese, later told reporters that he never saw the most conclusive replay footage, which was confirmed by his supervisor). Soon after the end of the season, Reise, who endured public embarrassment, harassment, and even death threats, was told by his supervisors that he would no longer serve as a replay official (Canzano, 2006; Replay Referee Dismissed, 2007).

In college football, officials are trained and assigned by conferences, which many see as a potential source of dispute. According to former University of Michigan head football coach Lloyd Carr, "I don't think there's any question when you're going on the road . . . you run into some of those issues" pertaining to potential officiating bias (Michaelis, 2006, p. 12C). Pac-10 rules specify that conference officials work all conference member home games. Oklahoma's complaints about the calls after the game were strident, and included a letter from school president David Boren to then-Big 12 commissioner Kevin Weiberg, calling the outcome an "outrageous injustice" and for him to have the game outcome nullified (Weiberg declined, stating, "There is no provision under NCAA or conference rules for a game result to be reversed or changed as a result of officiating errors, nor do I believe there should be. Officiating decisions are part of the game just as decisions of coaches and athletes, and determining what errors should result in overturning results would be chaotic"). Boren's letter requested that Weiberg, in his role as conference representative "vigorously demand that our teams be treated fairly when participating in non-conference games" (Boren, 2006, personal communication).

In response to the subsequent torrent of commentary and criticism, Pac-10 commissioner Tom Hansen issued a statement that read, "Errors clearly were made and not corrected. . . . [I]t is regrettable that the outcome of the contest was affected by the officiating" (O'Toole, 2006, p. 8C). Hansen also announced that the crews would be slapped with a one-week suspension. In response to the actions, Stoops said: "A one-game suspension compared to the way our season now is altered, I don't know if that fits the situation" (Pac-10 Apologizes, 2006, p. D2). Stoops later said that Oklahoma would "reconsider" a trip to Seattle to play the University of Washington in 2008 if the Pac-10's official assignment policy was not changed. Oklahoma kept the game, and won, 55–14, but as of this writing had no Pac-10 opponents scheduled through 2015 (Helsley, 2006).

Both Hansen and Weiberg were forced to address the issue by the gross errors of game officials and the impassioned complaints of the wronged Oklahoma stakeholders. Weiberg could have argued more forcibly that the game's outcome be stricken from the record books. He recognized, however, that incorrect official decisions, even with the best advances of technology available to them, are an unfortunate part of games and can never be eradicated fully. Knowing this (and also knowing that Oklahoma had benefited from a timekeeper's error in a 2003 men's basketball game, which allowed the Sooners additional time at the end of the game to eventually defeat conference opponent Texas Tech), Weiberg sought to maintain amicable relations with a fellow conference's administrators and stakeholders and chose not to bend to the pressure laid on him by his member institution. However, Weiberg did state that he would address the Oklahoma president's complaint with the proper officials (O'Toole, 2006).

Some of the proposed changes to the conference model of official assignments include a model employed in basketball, in which conferences combine and maintain pools of officials who work games for multiple conferences (Sooners See, 2006). According to Barry Mano, president of the National Association of Sports Officials, the notion that any official sways calls in favor of the employing conference is "fiction," but he does agree that such a regional pooling model could address the issue of bias (Michaelis, 2006). In late 2007, the NCAA and 11 of the Division I football conferences announced the formation of a supervising body to improve areas such as the use of replay. The cost is projected to be about $1 million over five years (Wieberg, 2007).

SHIFTS IN CONFERENCE ALIGNMENT

During the last decade or so, Division I conferences have experienced an unprecedented wave of affiliation upheaval. When the dust settled in late 2003, Boston College, Virginia Polytechnic University, and the University of Miami had left the Big East for the Atlantic Coast Conference (ACC). The Big East replaced these defectors with the University of Cincinnati, the University of Louisville, the University of South Florida, DePaul University, and Marquette University, all of which jumped from Conference USA (C-USA). C-USA in turn filled its openings with the University of Central Florida, Marshall University, and the University of Tulsa. Much of the realignment frenzy was attributed to efforts to boost revenues from television broadcast deals that would include conference championship games in football (restricted to conferences with 12 or more members) and new TV markets associated with new members.

**TEXAS CHRISTIAN UNIVERSITY'S
RATIONALE FOR REALIGNMENT**

case study 3.B

One school that serves as an instructive example of the rationale behind the jumbling of conference composition is Texas Christian University (TCU), a private institution of approximately 9,000 undergraduates affiliated with the Christian Church (Disciples of Christ), located in Fort Worth, Texas. TCU was part of the defunct Southwestern Conference (SWC), which disintegrated in 1996 after the University of Arkansas left to join the Southeastern Conference, and recruiting and amateurism scandals plagued the membership, most notably at Southern Methodist University (SMU) (see Chapters 1 and 8). TCU had its own infractions issue relating to booster payments to football players as well, forfeiting 35 grants-in-aid in the late 1980s (Evans, 2006).

When SWC members Baylor, the University of Texas, Texas A&M, and Texas Tech left in 1996 for the newly expanded Big 8 Conference (which then was rechristened "Big 12") TCU along with SMU, the University of Houston, and Rice University were left without a viable conference in which to play. At that point, these four Texas schools opted to join an expanded Western Athletic Conference (WAC), but two years later, eight other schools broke away from that group to create the Mountain West Conference (MWC). TCU then opted to leave the WAC and join Conference USA (C-USA), a collection that at the time included schools such as East Carolina University, Cincinnati, Louisville, and Tulane University. But in 2005, TCU decided to leave C-USA (which had by then also admitted former SWC members Houston, Rice, and SMU) to rejoin the schools that had left the WAC to form the MWC (see Exhibit 3.5).

According to TCU officials, the decision to leave C-USA was based primarily on the ability of Mountain West's football teams to compete for a spot in the Bowl

Championship Series (and to gain access to the substantial revenues associated with such an appearance). MWC member Utah had done so in 2004 and in 2009, becoming the first school from a conference other than the ACC, Big East, Big Ten, Big 12, Pac-10, or SEC to crash the BCS party. TCU AD Danny Morrison stated that the new affiliation "places [TCU] with a conference that has made unbelievable progress in a short period of time. . . . [I]t's well-positioned nationally for a BCS berth" (Harris, 2005, p. 5C). Former TCU AD Eric Hyman, who shepherded the school's shift to the Mountain West before leaving to take the AD post at the University of South Carolina, justified the move this way:

> I'm not trying to be disrespectful to any schools, but nobody had ever heard of some of the [C-USA] schools like East Carolina and South Florida [which has since moved on to the Big East]. But everyone is familiar with Utah, BYU, and Air Force. . . . If you go back to the goals and objectives of what TCU laid out several years ago, they wanted to be a nationally prominent program. What we tried to do was build a road map to try and achieve those objectives. (Harris, 2005, p. 5C)

But a road map, according to critics, is exactly what TCU now needed, as it left behind affiliations with closely proximate state rivals SMU (40 miles away), and Houston and Rice (266 miles away), to travel to conference contests in Utah (Utah and Brigham Young—each more than 1,200 miles away) and California (San Diego State University, 1,321 miles away). Hyman responded that the new conference meant only an additional $200,000 in travel expenses for TCU's 19 intercollegiate programs. MWC commissioner Craig Thompson noted that a boost in revenues would more than make up for this increase, with conference members receiving $2.6 million per school from football allocations in 2004. The MWC hoped that this amount would increase further with the addition of the Dallas/Fort Worth television market to its broadcast partners. But in its last year in C-USA, TCU received $1.7 million in conference revenue and in the 2006–07 year, it got only $138,000 from its new affiliation. By comparison, in the same year the members of C-USA received roughly $2.2 million in comparative payments (Harris, 2005; Major Conferences, 2008).

questions for you to consider

1. Based on the facts in the case, identify the forces that were driving TCU to change conference affiliation in 1996 versus the driving forces it faced in 2005.

2. Identify the forces that were working against a conference change in 2005, and based on your conclusions in these two questions, determine whether the move to the Mountain West Conference made sense for TCU.

EXHIBIT 3.5   Mountain West Conference membership.

Brigham Young University (Provo, Utah)

Colorado State University (Fort Collins, Colorado)

San Diego State University (San Diego, California)

Texas Christian University (Fort Worth, Texas)

United States Air Force Academy (Colorado Springs, Colorado)

University of Nevada–Las Vegas

University of New Mexico (Albuquerque, New Mexico)

University of Utah (Salt Lake City, Utah)

University of Wyoming (Laramie, Wyoming)

Results of realignment

What has been the result of the realignment flurry for others? It depends on the schools and conferences. According to John Swofford, commissioner of the ACC, expansion "has done the job from a revenue standpoint. [It's] about as balanced now as any conference in the country. Our basketball revenue streams are the best in the country. Football is coming up" (Smith, 2008a, p. 27). The data seem to support this claim. In 2003–04 (the last year before expansion) to 2006–07, conference revenues grew 44.5 percent, from $110.6 million to $159.8 million. By comparison, Big Ten revenues grew 42.2 percent, SEC 14.5 percent, and Big 12 8 percent. ACC football revenues then slightly exceeded those from basketball. Expansion allowed the ACC to increase its television revenue 60 percent, to $37 million per season. However, conference payouts to member schools increased by only $1 million annually to $12.2 million, because the money now has to be shared by a dozen schools instead of nine (Smith, 2008a).

As a result, some of the pre-merger members were lukewarm about the expansion. Former Duke University AD Joe Alleva (who then became AD at Louisiana State), put it this way:

> The reason for expansion was football, to improve the league's situation, to expand our footprint and enhance our TV market. From that standpoint, expansion has been very good. You want as many eyeballs watching as you can get . . . (but) from a Duke perspective, it didn't enhance much at all. From a scheduling department, I don't think it was a good thing. We went from playing a rival like North Carolina State twice a year in basketball as part of a round-robin format to playing them once a year for many years because they're in a different division. (Smith, 2008a, pp. 27, 30)

Conversely, athletic department personnel at Virginia Tech were ecstatic about their new alliance. Now they are able to sell out football home games against ACC foes, tickets that were far less desirable for many former Big East opponents. According to Jim Weaver, Virginia Tech's AD, "the ACC is the place our people wanted to be since 1953, when the ACC was formed. . . . [W]e were always a part of the footprint for the league" (Smith, 2008a, p. 33). Proximity to new opponents also has decreased travel costs, another benefit. "We basically went from an airplane league in the Big East to a bus league in the ACC," said Weaver (p. 33).

However, Smith (2008a) points out that measuring the success of conference realignment is not simply assessing changes in television revenue but also looking at less tangible factors such as donations, growing the school's fan base, enhancing its brand, and garnering more interest from potential corporate partners. In this light, Georgia Tech AD Dan Radakovich added this perspective: "While some of the new teams that came in might not have had great basketball histories, they've brought a lot of other things to the table, whether it's in football or other sports. If the tide lifts up even the smallest boat, that's important" (p. 33). But, to most, the ultimate measures remain tied to finances. According to former ABC Sports executive Loren Matthews, "In the end, it's about revenue and a bigger footprint" (p. 33).

Potential future realignments

Are any other conferences still looking to realign? Some speculate that the Pac-10 and Big Ten both might grow to a dozen or more to have a football playoff, with the Pac-10 getting to 12 by adding schools such as current MWC members Utah and Brigham Young. Some suspect that the MWC will seek to get to 12 by scooping up football-strong WAC members Boise State University and Fresno State University, but the interest seems to be minimal.

CONCLUSION

Intercollegiate athletic conferences were developed primarily for the formulation and enforcement of rules governing student-athlete eligibility, ease and convenience of travel and scheduling, and lifting some of the political burden of establishment and enforcement of rules from the individual member institutions.

Early conflicts between schools developed concerning the participation of freshmen, graduate and non-degree "special" students, student residency requirements, and students transferring solely for athletic purposes. To deal with this conflict, some schools began to exhibit greater control over athletics and took actions on their own to deal with academics, eventually working together with faculty and managers from other schools to create a more controllable and desired system. The 1895 "Chicago Conference," attended by faculty representatives from the seven schools that later founded what would become the Big Ten Conference, was one such successful early effort to control and regulate the eligibility of student-athletes. Another was the 1898 "Brown Conference," attended by students, faculty, and alumni from nearly all schools of the present-day Ivy League. In punishing member schools for transgressions against specific codes, the conference rather than the NCAA has been the main enforcer in matters of rules violations.

The New England Small College Athletic Conference, the Big Ten Conference, and the Colonial Athletic Association provide evidence of the variety of issues relating to organizational structure faced by intercollegiate athletic conferences. Issues relating to marketing, compliance, membership realignment, and managing conflict between the Pac-10 and Big 12 conferences give insights into the range and scope of other important conference-level functions.

PRACTITIONER perspective:

JONATHAN LECRONE, Commissioner of the Horizon League

Throughout the chapter we have examined a range of issues pertaining to conference organization and control that intercollegiate athletic managers face at the both the institutional and conference level. Not all issues impact each conference to the same extent, however. Because of stated divisional and philosophical guidelines, personnel associated with NESCAC will not deal with the same types of managerial challenges as do their Division I colleagues. But even within Division I, conferences differ in terms of managerial operations. In this chapter we learned of some of the recent actions of leaders from the Big Ten and Pac-10 in managing financial and operational situations, and how managers at Texas Christian worked to procure the conference affiliation that allows the department to meet its stated objectives. We also learned of the administrative structure of the Colonial Athletic Association, a so-called "mid-major" conference, one that is a collection of Division I institutions but lacks the level of popular support from fans and alumni that garner it the degree of notoriety entertained by the so-called "big-time" conferences like the ACC, the Big East, the Big 12, the Big Ten, the Pac-10, and the SEC.

Because of this "mid-major" status, personnel associated with this group have differing issues and perspectives on intercollegiate athletic management. To learn more about these perspectives, and of other issues of importance to conference commissioners, we sought information and feedback from Horizon League commissioner Jon LeCrone. The Horizon League, founded in 1979 as the Midwestern Collegiate Conference, currently has 10 member schools in Illinois (Loyola University Chicago and the University of Illinois–Chicago), Indiana (Butler University and Valparaiso University), Michigan (University of Detroit Mercy), Ohio (Cleveland State University, Wright State University, and Youngstown University) and Wisconsin (the University of Wisconsin–Green Bay and the University of Wisconsin–Milwaukee). League members are located in five of the top 35 U.S. media markets (Chicago, Cleveland, Detroit, Indianapolis, and Milwaukee). The combined enrollment of the 10 schools is 130,000, with claims of a quarter-million alumni living in the region. The league sponsors competition in 19 sports and receives automatic bids to NCAA championships in baseball, men's and women's basketball, men's golf, men's and women's soccer, softball, men's and women's tennis, and women's volleyball. The league is headquartered in Indianapolis, Indiana, and is governed by a Board of Directors composed of the 10 member schools' chief executive officers (Horizon League, 2008).

LeCrone has been in his current post since 1992, prior to which he spent nine years as assistant commissioner in the Atlantic Coast Conference, where he was responsible for projects relating to television, marketing, revenue generation, and public relations. Prior to his ACC work, LeCrone was Assistant AD at ACC-member Wake Forest University, and was business manager for the Wichita Cubs, the then-AAA minor league affiliate for the Chicago Cubs. In addition to his commissioner's job, LeCrone has served on the NCAA Division I Leadership Council, the NCAA Division I Men's Basketball Committee, and the NCAA Division I Men's Soccer Committee (three years as chair) (Profile, 2008). Here are our questions to LeCrone and his responses:

Q: *In this chapter we outlined many of the job responsibilities of commissioners. From your perspective, what are the key assets, skills, and personality traits of a successful commissioner?*

A: Dealing with volunteer boards, being able to know when to follow, when to lead, when to build consensus, and how to build consensus. One also needs to be able to understand and evaluate threats and opportunities on each campus. Even though institutions might look similar, they are generally quite different, with different sets of political, economic, and leadership challenges. To be able to identity trends and mold those into conference initiatives takes a pretty good amount of skills. For successful commissioners, they probably are able to attract and to hire very effective staff people who take on lots of the operational challenges so the commissioner can focus on strategic initiatives. My position then becomes a strategic planning and forecasting position if I have the ability to hire skilled people who can really help on the operational side and provide all the services that institutions want. As this business continues to change, I think future commissioners have to be focused on customer service. It is a customer service industry. We work at the pleasure of 10 to 16 member schools. Being in touch with those schools about their needs, and then being able to assess the fluidity of those needs and orchestrate a plan to meet those needs takes a staff with multiple kinds of skills.

What is the most important function you perform as commissioner?

To identify threats and opportunities, to understand the regional and national landscapes, what's going on in each and every state, and to understand the nuances of public and private institutions in each state and the stresses and strains they are under. I need to understand how these issues might impact intercollegiate athletics to help school CEOs and athletic directors make the best informed decisions. That's the strategic overview. After gaining that information, I need to identify opportunities and threats for member schools to move forward collectively, and to identify an action plan to help schools respond to those threats in a proactive rather than reactive way. Secondarily, I really need to engage with our member schools on some of their critical hires in a support role rather than an influencing or decision-making capacity to help a president, AD, or search firm make sure they are attracting the right people for the right jobs.

Is there an element of your job over which you'd like to have greater authority, and how would this be of benefit to the conference?

Philosophically, I'm not sure that concentrated power in one area is good for any organization. I like the fact that there are checks and balances in place. I like the fact that conference offices are structured where the commissioner reports to a board of presidents. This works best because there is a level of oversight. Everything that works top-down is not necessarily best for our business, because we are managing groups of schools that are competing with one another. There is natural tension because they are not always pulling in the same direction. What might be good for Kentucky might not be good for Alabama. I think a shared governance structure works best rather than a military structure where what the general says goes.

My practitioner view, after 30 years of experience, is that a shared governance model for what we do seems to work, but we should always look for ways to improve it. When you are in a shared governance structure, especially in this information age in which we work, one of the skill sets that new commissioners will need to have is how to streamline the shared governance structure and keep its advantages in place, and at the same time work through the disadvantage that it is a fairly slow-moving process. One way to do this is by delegating some authority to small subgroups, because absolutely everything we do from this office doesn't have to be signed off on by every single board we have. I think that's a political skill that a Division I commissioner has to learn. But certainly that's going to be different in the ACC, the Horizon, or the Pac-10. Each of those political structures, although essentially the same, has its differences and nuances. The successful commissioner has to figure that out, because there are different times when we have to move a lot more quickly than shared governance might allow.

What has been your biggest challenge as commissioner, and how have you attempted to solve that challenge?

The biggest challenge that all of us have on a daily basis is the management and allocation of resources, which are time, money, and people. All of those ebb and flow, but the skilled commissioner has to understand how to manage financial resources, how to maximize revenues, how to control expenses, and how to understand that something as far away as the price of a barrel of oil can affect your enterprise. It's being a little bit in touch with the big picture, but not being so overwhelmed by the big picture that you're worrying about it. Let me give an example. When the SEC is thinking about an SEC network, or the Big Ten deploys the Big Ten Network, I'm thinking, how are those going to affect everyone else's world? It's being in touch with those things. The people piece is important, too, because I deal with CEOs of major educational institutions. They're going to come and go. They're going to be in and out. The conference board is going to change, athletic directors and coaches are going to change, so I have to understand the fluidity of those positions. I also need to understand the time element of what we work with each day, and how we want staff time to be focused so we can achieve what we want to achieve, because we can't achieve everything. We're limited by time, money, and people. It's not how much we get done; it's what we get done in terms of having connection with the people for whom we work, and understanding the priorities. It's not about working hard but, rather, understanding the differences between inputs and outputs. It's understanding that you're working toward outputs. It's not about the number of hours you work; it's about working on the right things. It comes back to understanding how to manage time, money, and people to meet agreed-upon goals.

In the chapter, we identified conferences like the Horizon League as a "mid-major" conference. Is there a concern about this kind of status, and does this status affect your ability to meet conference goals?

We're limited only by what we think of ourselves. We're not limited by what other people think or say about us. There are lots of days when I'm very proud to be called a "mid-major" conference or a "mid-major" commissioner. For instance, I wouldn't be successful in this job if I try to take the approach for success the ACC has, even though that's the conference I came from. I understand that level and how the ACC operates. If I came here and tried to replicate that approach, I would miss a lot of points. The most basic one I'd miss is that we don't have the same amount of money and number of people, but we do have the same time. The successful commissioner tries to create successful approaches based upon the conference and what those in the conference hold as believable, conceivable, and achievable.

So can the Horizon League have eight teams in the men's basketball tournament and four teams in the Final Four every year? That's probably not believable, conceivable, and achievable. That might be for the SEC. They can think about that and put resources behind that and really get after that. Every conference has status that is self-imposed or imposed by others. The SEC has a reputation; the ACC, the Pac-10, the Atlantic 10 all have reputations. Successful commissioners need to think about their own definition of success and pursue that, rather than have some other group—colleagues, conferences—define success for them. And that's what we've tried to do. The first place we have started is in planning—a skill that all successful commissioners need to develop to work with their conferences. Commissioners need to say to their members, "Listen, I'd like to propose to you my definition of success. But I've gotten a definition of success by talking with you, and thinking about and vetting what I've heard. Do you think that if this is our approach, we could be successful? Could we all agree to this? Is it believable, conceivable, and achievable? And can we pay for it?"

And your approach for success now has benchmarks against which you can measure your progress, so when ESPN commentator Andy Katz says, "The Horizon League didn't even get a team to the Sweet 16 this year. They're not successful," I can counter that by saying, "Hey, Andy, that's not our measure. Here are our measures, and by our measures we were very successful this year. These are the places we did well, these are the places where we've continued to improve, and here's where we're headed."

In this chapter we discussed the realignment spate that occurred in many Division I conferences. What was the intended goal of these actions, and has it been met?

I can give you a practical reason as to why the Horizon League expanded. When the Horizon League added Valparaiso, we did it because we were a nine-team league, and that didn't work very well for us from a scheduling perspective in men's basketball, which is our flagship sport. The move also added another private school and created more balance in our league, as we now have six public and four private schools. There

was a geographic fit in adding Valparaiso, so when we added Valparaiso, it didn't end up costing us more. It actually helped in a lot of ways because it was a convenient travel partner. Valparaiso also had the right mix of sports for our conference, and their athletic budget fit in the context of those at other member schools. So Valparaiso wasn't going to come in and dominate our conference, but at the same time they had enough funding not to be in last place. I was at the ACC when they [first] expanded and added Florida State University. Schools are members of the ACC and SEC because they get a lot of money. And that's why other conferences have added schools, because they add market share and generate income.

If you walk in the door and sit in the chairs of any conference commissioner, and you're not cognizant of membership movement and how to see that as a threat or an opportunity to manage, you're probably not going to be really effective. For us, that means understanding that the Big Ten could expand, and if they start talking about that, then understanding how that might impact us. If a commissioner is not actively engaged in talking about the downside of members leaving your conference and the upside of attracting new members, I don't think you're adding value to your membership.

What career advice would you give to someone who would one day like to become a conference commissioner?

I'm a real believer in a liberal arts background. You have to be able to read, to comprehend, and to understand. You have to be able to communicate effectively, be it speaking or writing. You have to be able to communicate effectively in meetings. Those skill sets can be learned. A graduate degree is absolutely essential. A focused graduate degree in either education or business would be excellent. Any practical experience you can get in coaching is helpful. If you have the ability to get a Ph.D. or a J.D., that can't hurt you. I would recommend that anyone reading this textbook as an undergraduate, if you are going to pursue an advanced degree, pursue it immediately. You have to get practical work experience in any way you can while you're on your college campus. That might mean volunteering and showing up and saying, I'm here, I'd like to work. Whatever type of school in which you are enrolled, there are actual athletic administration activities in which to get involved from a volunteer standpoint.

questions TO CONSIDER

1. Are the issues that led to conference formation in the late 1800s still important for contemporary conference managers? What significant issues have emerged that have supplanted some of these early issues?

2. Check the athletics page on your school's website. What sort of information or links convey information about your school's athletic conference? If there is a link to the conference home page, what sort of goals and objectives are available for review on the conference site? How do these goals and objectives match those of your school's athletic department?

3. Based on what you have read in the chapter, does your school have significant driving forces that push your school toward switching conference affiliation? If so, what are they? If not, what are the forces restraining such a move?

4. Based on the comments of Jon LeCrone and the information related in the chapter, what does the Horizon League have to do to shed its "mid-major" status to be seen as equal to the ACC, Big Ten, and other similar Division I conferences?

5. In your own career planning, would you seek to work at a conference or at an individual school athletic department? What are the factors influencing this decision?

references

About Pac-10. (2006). Pacific 10 Conference. Accessed June 17, 2006, from: http://www.pac-10.org/school-bio/pac10-school-bio.html

Big 12 Conference Commissioner Kevin Weiberg Statement. (2006). Accessed September 18, 2006, from: http:www.cstv.com/printable/schools/big12/sports/m-football/spec-rel/091806aae.html

Big Ten Conference Staff. (2009). Big Ten Conference. Accessed July 29, 2009, from: http://bigten.cstv.com/school-bio/big10-staff.html

Big Ten History. (2006). Big Ten Conference. Accessed June 28, 2006, from: http://bigten.cstv.com/trads/big10-trads.html

Big Ten Network Expands Reach with Addition of Dish Network. (2007, September 6). *Sports Illustrated.* Accessed September 6, 2007, from: http: www.si.com/bigtennetwork/html

Bowen, W.G., & Levin, S.A. (2003). *Reclaiming the game: College sports and educational values.* Princeton, NJ: Princeton University Press.

Canzano, J. (2006, September 19). Football is just a game, until you're on the clock. *Oregonian.* Accessed September 19, 2006, from: http://oregonlive.com/printer/printer.ssf?/base/sports/1158639907304430.xml&coll=7

Carey, J. (2006, September 19). Pac-10 suspends officials, apologizes to Oklahoma. *USA Today,* p. 1C.

Covell, D.D. (1999). *"To keep a proper perspective on the role of athletics": An examination of the perceived role of intercollegiate athletics in the New England Small College Athletic Conference.* Unpublished doctoral dissertation: The University of Massachusetts.

Covell, D., Walker, S., Siciliano, J., and Hess, P. (2007). *Managing sports organizations* (2nd ed.). Burlington, MA: Butterworth-Heinemann.

De Avila, J. (2008, October 1). Long toss: Questions for Jim Delany. *Wall Street Journal.* Accessed December 3, 2008, from: http://0-proquest.umi.com.wildpac.wnec.edu

Delany, James E. (2006). Big Ten Conference. Accessed June 28, 2006, from: http://bigten.cstv.com/school-bio/delany-bio.html#resume

Evans, T. (2006, September 22). That other Texas team craves the spotlight. *New York Times,* p. C14.

Gardiner, A. (2007, August 29). Big Ten extends its brand with new network. *USA Today,* p. 10C.

Gloeckler, G. (2007, October 8). Profiles: Jim Delany. *Business Week,* pp. 59–60.

Golden State Athletic Conference Constitution and Bylaws. (2008, February 15). Accessed August 24, 2009, from: http://groups.apu.edu/gsacsports/GSACpolicies/gsacbylaws.pdf

Greenstein, T. (2010, March 1). Big Ten told it's safe to expand horizons. *Chicago Tribune.* Accessed March 10, 2010, from: http://www.chicagotribune.com/sports/college.

Harris, T. (2005, July 7). There's a method to TCU's madness. *Houston Chronicle,* p. 5C.

Heistand, M. (2006, June 22). Big Ten, News Corp. to create cable channel. *USA Today*, p. 13C.

Helman, J.W. (1989). *A history of American intercollegiate athletic eligibility: Educational compromises to competitive interests*. Unpublished doctoral dissertation, Pennsylvania State University.

Helsley, J. (2006, September 20). Stoops threatens pullout if policy stays. Accessed September 20, 2006, from: http://newsok.com/article/2850278/?print=1

Horizon League: Raise your sights. (2008). Accessed September 23, 2008, from: http://cstv.com/printable/schools/hori/school-bio/hori-about-story.html

Johnson, J.W. (2006). *The wow boys: A coach, a team, and a turning point in college football*. Lincoln: University of Nebraska Press.

Katz, B. (1998). NESCAC schools work hard together to create forum. *Williams Record*. Accessed November 17, 1998, from: http://record.williams.edu/articles/10800.htm

Key Dates: Pac-10 Conference Compliance Corner. (2009). Pacific 10 Conference. Accessed July 29, 2009, from: http://www.pac-10.org/compliance/legis/legis.html#Key%20Dates

Kjeldsen, E. (1992). *The manager's role in the development and maintenance of ethical behavior in sport organizations*. Unpublished manuscript, University of Massachusetts, Amherst.

Jones, D. (2010, March 7). How the Big Ten Network makes expansion more likely this time around. *The Patriot-News*. Accessed March 10, 2010, from: http://pennlive.com/davidjones

Lewis, Jr., S. R. (2001, Spring). The game of life. *Carleton College Voice*, pp. 9, 56.

Looney, D.S. (1994, October 31). Pure and simple. *Sports Illustrated*, pp. 66–80.

Major Conferences Before and After Realignment. (2008, December 8–14). *Street & Smith's SportsBusiness Journal*, p. 28.

Major Conferences' TV Deals. (2009, September 4). *Chronicle of Higher Education*, p. A28.

Michaelis, V. (2006, September 20). Possible bias of officials concerns fans, teams. *USA Today*, p. 12C.

NCAA Forum Follow-up: Statement from Williams College Council. (1998). Accessed November 20, 1998, from: http://record.williams.edu/forum/10800.htm

NESCAC Agreement. (1971). New England Small College Athletic Conference.

NESCAC Agreement (Rev. ed.) (1975). New England Small College Athletic Conference.

NESCAC Presidents Adopt New Mission Statement and Make Decisions Regarding Post-season Competition. (1998, April 23). New England Small College Athletic Conference.

Nocera, J. (2007, October 6). Of tiers, football and dollars. *New York Times*, pp. C1, C6.

Ohio Community College Athletic Conference Constitution. (2006). Accessed August 24, 2009, from: http://www.occac.org/documents.html

Oriard, M. (2009). *Bowled over: Big-time college football from the Sixties to the BCS era*. Chapel Hill: University of North Carolina Press.

Orient Forum: The Future of NESCAC in the NCAA Postseason. (1997, November 7). *Bowdoin Orient*, p. 9.

O'Toole, T. (2006, September 19). Stoops still upset about refs' call in Oregon loss. *USA Today*, p. 8C.

Pac-10 Apologizes, Suspends Officials. (2006, September 19). *Boston Globe*, p. D2.

Profile: Jonathan B. LeCrone. (2008). Accessed September 23, 2008, from: http://cstv.com/printable/schools/hori/genrel/blecrone_jonathan00.html

Quarterman, J. (1994). Managerial role profiles of intercollegiate athletic conference commissioners. *Journal of Sport Management*, 8, pp. 129–139.

Replay Referee Dismissed. (2007, February 7). *New York Times*, p. C20.

Rosen, C. (1999). *Scandals of '51: How the gamblers almost killed college basketball*. New York: Seven Stories Press.

Rudolph, F. (1990). *The American college and university: a history* (Rev. ed). Athens: University of Georgia Press.

Sander, L. (2009, September 4). Big Ten Conference's TV network starts to pay off. *Chronicle of Higher Education*, p. A28.

Sandomir, R. (2006, August 27). Fox is the newest student of the college game. *New York Times*, p. 8–8.

Sandomir, R. (2007, November 2). Channeling the bigger games to the lesser networks. *New York Times*, p. C13.

SBJ/SBD Reader Survey. (2008, November 24–30). *Street & Smith's SportsBusiness Journal*, pp. 20–30.

Schmidt, R. (2007). *Shaping college football: The transformation of an American sport, 1919–1930*. Syracuse, NY: Syracuse University Press.

Smith, M. (2008a, December 8–14). Has realignment worked? *Street & Smith's SportsBusiness Journal*, pp. 1, 27, 30.

Smith, M. (2008b, December 8–14). Who's next for realignment? *Street & Smith's SportsBusiness Journal*, pp. 1, 27, 30.

Smith, R. A. (1988). *Sports and freedom: The rise of big-time college athletics*. New York: Oxford University Press.

Sooners See the Other Side of Replay Controversy. (2006, September 26). *New York Times*, p. C14.

Spanberg, E. (2008, December 8–14). Conference realignments bring cultural shifts. *Street & Smith's SportsBusiness Journal*, p. 31.

Sperber, M. (1998). *Onward to victory: The crises that shaped college sports*. New York: Henry Holt.

Staff Directory. (2009). Colonial Athletic Association. Accessed July 29, 2009, from: http://www.caasports.com/info/staff/

Statement of Presidents of the New England Small College Athletic Conference. (1997). New England Small College Athletic Conference.

Szostak, M. (1997, November 8). College picks. *Providence (RI) Journal*, p. 6B.

Thelin, J.R. (1996). *Games colleges play: Scandal and reform in intercollegiate athletics*. Baltimore: Johns Hopkins University Press.

Thomas, K. (2009, October 30). Call to curb athletic spending strikes some as unrealistic. *New York Times*, p. B15.

2008–09 Rocky Mountain Athletic Conference Code. (2008). Accessed August 24, 2009, from: http://static.psbin.com/9/q/rrbdsu0v2tlj42/0809_rmac_code.pdf

Velez, K. (1997). *The New England Small College Athletic Conference, 1971–1997: A retrospective*. Unpublished manuscript, Williams College.

Watterson, J.S. (2000). *College football: History, spectacle, controversy*. Baltimore: Johns Hopkins University Press.

Wieberg, S. (2007, December 28). NCAA, football powers seek better officiating. *USA Today*. Accessed March 3, 2010, from http://www.usatoday.com/sports/college/football/2007-12-28-football-officiating_N.htm

Wolverton, B. (2007, July 6). Big Ten Network faces tough questions as it nears start date. *Chronicle of Higher Education*, p. A32.

Wolverton, B. (2009, September 4). A powerful league piles up its advantages. *Chronicle of Higher Education*, pp. A1, A26–A28.

Institutional and departmental missions and goals

Key concepts to keep in mind while you read the chapter:

- Key differences in the philosophy statements of the three NCAA divisional classifications.

- The relationship between an athletic department's vision, mission, and goals, and its chosen divisional classification.

- How specific departmental operations are impacted by their vision, mission, and goals.

- How specific environmental factors influence both departmental missions and operations.

Introduction

As discussed in Chapter 1, the appropriate role of athletics in higher education has been a frequent point of debate among stakeholder groups. Recall that back in the mid-1800s, students initiated and organized athletic programs for health and fitness reasons, but that management model and focus quickly shifted to institution-maintained programs that sought to achieve primacy over rival institutions. You also learned that the development of "big-time" athletic programs, as embodied today by those at many NCAA Division I institutions, are credited with creating a sense of community among campus constituencies and promoting the institution in general. The current system is not without its critics, who say that academic integrity is often sacrificed in the pursuit of athletic success, and that institutional resources are misdirected from academics to support athletics.

One example of athletics stakeholder interests and potential conflicts with the academic mission of an institution occurred at the University of Tennessee (UT), a public school with 20,000 undergraduates located in Knoxville, and a member of the Division I Southeastern Conference. Linda Bensel-Meyers, director of the school's writing program, found incidents of plagiarism that had been ignored involving multiple grade changes that had been filed in favor of many of the school's football players. When she tried to address the issue with school administrators, she was ignored. She then turned to an investigative reporter from ESPN to publicize the story, thinking that the revelations would force reform of the issue. However, the post-ESPN-story stakeholder response from Tennessee fans was very much against her, as evidenced by the following e-mails sent to her. Wrote one: "You're forgetting that a lot of people go to UT because of their athletic program and (that their) tuition pays your salary. I would have fired you by now." Wrote another: "Give it a rest! The taxpayers of Tennessee like winning teams. The players pay your salary. Go to Harvard or Yale or some private college and teach if you want a perfect institution" (Dowling, 2007, pp. 114–115). Later, Bensel-Meyers did leave UT for the University of Denver, and became involved with the Drake Group, a reform group consisting of faculty members seeking to address academic integrity issues relating to intercollegiate athletics (Kuharsky, 2003).

Were these comments representative of Tennessee fans in general? Tennessee residents? We know from Chapter 1 that there has always been a tension between producing winning teams and operating programs within the framework of higher education. What we will seek to understand in this chapter is how the wide variations of American higher education institutions use intercollegiate athletics to meet the expectations of all stakeholders, and how the missions and goals of athletic programs must match those of the institution as a whole.

THE NCAA'S DIVISIONAL CLASSIFICATION STRUCTURE AND ITS IMPACT ON INSTITUTIONAL MISSION AND GOALS

n Chapter 2 you were introduced to the NCAA's separate three-tier divisional classification system, which was established in 1973. The formal establishment of separate classifications acknowledged the existing disparity in institutional missions and goals relating to intercollegiate athletics, created an opportunity for regular and postseason competition against similar schools, and established a more stratified approach to awarding athletically related financial assistance.

Many fans and observers can identify the "big-time" intercollegiate programs—the ones that garner the lion's share of public interest, media attention, and TV broadcast time. You may be taking this course at just such an institution, and may take great pride in the successes of your school's teams. But, as we learned in Chapter 2, NCAA Division I membership is only a fraction of the total number of intercollegiate athletic programs. What really distinguishes a Division I institution from a Division II? A II from a III? And a III from a I? It isn't necessarily size, as is often cited as a distinguishing characteristic. Several D-I institutions, such as the College of the Holy Cross in Worcester, Massachusetts, and Lafayette College in Easton, Pennsylvania—both members of the Patriot League—have fewer than 3,000 full-time undergraduate students. In contrast, the majority of the schools in the D-III Wisconsin Intercollegiate Athletic Conference (WIAC)—state-supported institutions such as the University of Wisconsin–Stevens Point (8,750), Wisconsin–Whitewater (10,600), and Wisconsin–Oshkosh (11,000)—have more than three times the number of full-time undergraduates at Holy Cross and Lafayette. Although enrollment does serve to distinguish this Eastern pair from the Wisconsin schools, the factors that are more relevant in determining the direction of and differences in their athletic programs relate to the institutions' choice of NCAA divisional classification. A summary of the key elements of the philosophy statements for each division helps to clarify the specific difference between each divisional classification (see Exhibit 4.1).

Having examined elements from the three distinct statements, take a moment to identify some of the key differences. Consider the following questions: What

Key elements of NCAA divisional philosophy statements.	EXHIBIT 4.1

DIVISION I

- Strives for regional and national prominence
- Serves both the university and the general public
- Sponsors at the highest level possible the spectator-oriented, income-producing sports of football and basketball
- Strives to finance the athletic program through revenues generated

DIVISION II

- Strives for broad participation and competitive excellence, encouraging sportsmanship
- Serves the campus and the general public
- Believes in permitting athletically related aid but on a more modest basis than Division I

DIVISION III

- Encourages participation
- Places special importance on the impact of athletics on the participants rather than the spectators and the entertainment needs of the general public
- Gives primary emphasis to in-season competition
- Awards no athletically related financial aid

makes Division I unique? What about Divisions II and III? Later in the chapter, we will discuss what may have led to a recent discussion within the NCAA about the proposed creation of a fourth divisional classification, which ended when the criteria for this new classification could not be determined.

How are these existing classifications distinct? For starters, it is hoped that certain Division I programs, specifically football and men's basketball, will generate revenues sufficient to fund the operation of the rest of the athletic department offerings, but the other two statements do not mention income and revenues. D-I programs are expected to provide spectator-oriented offerings, while D-III programs are run first and foremost for the benefit of the participants. What does this mean, and where does D-II fit in with this factor?

In recognizing and explaining these similarities and distinctions, we can begin to think about how these factors impact athletic programs on each individual campus and understand how managers on each campus apply these concepts in determining their own specific mission and goals.

INDIVIDUAL DEPARTMENTAL MISSION AND GOALS: AN OVERVIEW

Management expert Peter Drucker has suggested that "it is the first responsibility of the manager . . . to give others vision and the ability to perform" (1973, p. 3). He defined vision as the clear, shared sense of direction that allows organizations to achieve a common purpose. He insisted that vision is the first contribution of management because a shared sense of direction makes possible the cooperation and commitment necessary for organizations to succeed. And only with a common vision can individuals and groups perform with a clear sense of the destination they are working toward and a clear sense of the direction of the organization.

More recently, management thinkers James Collins and Jerry Porras (1998) described a well-conceived vision as having two parts: core ideology and envisioned future. They defined core ideology as the enduring characteristics of an organization, including core values and core purposes. Core values, they proposed, are those values an organization would keep even if it were penalized for retaining them, and core purpose as what defines an organization's reason for being. The envisioned future includes BHAGs, or "big, hairy, audacious goals," bold long-range goals that influence the direction of an organization for 10 to 30 years, and a vivid description of what achieving these BHAGs will mean.

The starting point of the strategic management process is a clear, compelling sense of direction; it is management's responsibility to give the organization this sense of its own enduring purpose (Carlson-Thomas, 1992). The most common way that organizations attempt to communicate this sense of purpose or direction is through a mission statement.

The mission statement

The mission statement is a summary of what an organization does or seeks to do, and often includes a statement of its philosophy and values. The mission statement reveals an organization's long-term vision—what it wants to be and whom it wants to serve. An effective mission statement provides a sense of direction for every individual and group in an organization.

Focus of the business

It may appear strange at first that we think about intercollegiate athletic programs as a "business," but we know from our review of the divisional philosophy statements that Division I programs are managed under the expectations of revenues and income production, and, as we will learn in Chapter 6, financial and budgetary issues are a major concern for intercollegiate athletic managers at all levels. So should mission statements for Division I programs focus only on the need for athletic departments to operate their programs to turn a profit? To answer this question, consider whether such a statement provides direction and/or keeps the program focused on its various stakeholders. Do student-athletes, faculty, or fans care if the department makes money? A departmental mission statement should clearly answer the questions, "What do we do, and why do we exist?" and "What do we hope to do down the road?" What makes this process more complex for intercollegiate athletic managers is that the answers to these questions will vary not only based on the school but also based on the divisional classification the school has chosen.

Philosophy and values

Beyond the operations and programs that an athletic department runs or seeks to run, a mission statement should define the department's philosophy—its basic beliefs, values, and priorities. The mission statement, then, defines for coaches, student-athletes, departmental employees, parents, fans, and all other stakeholders the department's highest and most enduring goals in terms of the stakeholder expectations it is seeking to satisfy and the department's philosophy and values in pursuing these goals. Once its mission and philosophy are clear, an athletic department is ready to turn its attention to the environment in which it must pursue these goals. Covell et al. (2007) point out that even with a well-defined vision and mission, athletic department managers can get caught up in handling day-to-day issues and fail to recognize and respond to what's going on around them. Managers must recognize that their departments and programs do not operate in a vacuum, that it is critically important to monitor changes and trends in the environment and use their mission statements to guide their responses.

Analyzing departmental mission statements

How have intercollegiate athletic managers applied these tenets in the operation of their departments? To see how this process may differ within the three NCAA divisions, we will look at stated principles for D-I member the University of Notre Dame (Exhibit 4.2), the mission statement for D-II member California State University Chico (CSUC) (Exhibit 4.3), and the athletic philosophy statement for D-III member the University of the South (Exhibit 4.4).

| EXHIBIT | 4.2 | University of Notre Dame Statement of Principles for Intercollegiate Athletics. |

Throughout its long and proud history, the University of Notre Dame has embraced the philosophy that a well-rounded athletics program—including club, intramural and intercollegiate competition—comprises an integral part of Notre Dame's educational mission. This philosophy reflects the importance of operating an intercollegiate athletics program that fully comports with the University's aspirations as a Catholic institution. Notre Dame therefore dedicates itself to the pursuit of excellence in intercollegiate athletics within the framework of an academic community committed to the University's educational and religious objectives. Notre Dame also commits itself to the unquestioned integrity of its athletics programs. All individuals involved, directly or indirectly, in the athletics enterprise must maintain and foster the values and goals associated with the University's mission as a Catholic institution of higher education.

As a Catholic university, Notre Dame espouses Christian values and principles. These include the development of the human person—spirit as well as body—the pursuit of excellence in all endeavors, the nurturing of Christian character, and the call to personal integrity and responsibility. By providing a general description of the structures that support these endeavors, this document articulates the central values and expectations that guide Notre Dame's participation in intercollegiate athletics.

PRESIDENTIAL CONTROL

Notre Dame adheres to the principle of presidential control over intercollegiate athletics. The Director of Athletics reports to the President, who exercises ultimate responsibility for the conduct of the University's intercollegiate athletics program. The Faculty Board on Athletics serves as the principal advisory group to the President on educational issues related to intercollegiate athletics. The chair of the Faculty Board on Athletics also serves as the NCAA-mandated Faculty Athletics Representative.

Basic Principles:

1. The Faculty Board on Athletics nurtures Notre Dame's commitment to academic integrity within the athletics program, strives to ensure that the University's athletics program operates in consonance with Notre Dame's educational mission, and actively promotes the welfare and educational success of the University's student-athletes. The Board also functions as a formal liaison between the faculty and the athletics department. In carrying out its charge, the Board reviews policies, procedures and practices that affect the educational experience of student-athletes and advises the President of its findings and deliberations. The Board systematically ascertains the views and concerns of student-athletes. The Board reviews data on admissions of student-athletes and on their academic performance, progress towards a degree, and graduation rates. The Board assesses the effectiveness of institutional support for student-athletes. In addition, the Board sets guidelines for the approval of all student petitions for a fifth year of eligibility for athletics and votes on each such petition. The Board establishes guidelines for all intercollegiate athletics schedules and qualifications for captaincy of all University teams, and votes on all proposed schedules and captaincy nominations. The Board also assesses and revises procedures for resolving prospective conflicts between final examinations and post-season championship events. In its role as a liaison to the broader faculty, the Faculty Board disseminates appropriate, non-confidential information and initiates discussions on educational issues regarding intercollegiate athletics and the related concerns of the faculty and administration.

2. The Faculty Athletics Representative champions academic integrity, promotes the welfare of student-athletes, and helps ensure institutional control of intercollegiate athlet-

ics. More specifically, the Faculty Athletics Representative works with the President and the Director of Athletics to maintain appropriate University oversight of intercollegiate athletics; assists the President and Director of Athletics in determining institutional positions on proposed NCAA and conference legislation; serves on search committees for senior athletics administrators and head coaches; oversees decisions regarding eligibility of student-athletes; remains visible and available to student-athletes; and actively participates in all investigations and reports of possible NCAA violations.

ACADEMICS

Notre Dame dedicates itself to providing to all of its students an outstanding education. The University commits itself to developing in its students those disciplined habits of mind, body and spirit that characterize educated, skilled and free human beings. Notre Dame calls its students to pursue the wisdom of our culture and religious heritage, and to experience the human family's diversity and interdependence. To accomplish these objectives, the University provides to its students, on an equitable basis, ongoing opportunities to cultivate their moral, intellectual and physical well-being.

Basic Principles:

1. Any student hoping to succeed at the University needs a significant level of ability and preparation. Therefore, the Office of Undergraduate Admissions will accept into the University only those student-athletes who demonstrate, on the basis of the best available academic and character-based information, the capacity to complete a degree at Notre Dame.

2. Even for individuals manifestly well suited for Notre Dame, the adjustments to the rigors of academic and athletic life in a highly competitive university present difficulties. The University recognizes its responsibility to provide appropriate assistance to enable student-athletes to meet the demands of both academic and athletic competition. To this end, the University affords its student-athletes suitable academic counsel and support, primarily under the auspices of the Provost's Office. Other sources of support, both academic and personal, include the faculty, academic advisors, the residence-hall staff, coaches, athletics administrators and the Student Development Program.

3. The University strives to schedule practices and competitions so as to minimize conflicts with class periods and other academic assignments of student-athletes. In this regard, the rhythm of the academic year and the particular importance of final examinations warrant special attention. All playing schedules remain subject to the approval of the Faculty Board on Athletics.

4. Notre Dame expects its student-athletes to maintain the appropriate sequence and number of courses and the grade-point-average necessary to complete a degree within the usual time (normally four years), including summer classes when appropriate. Any exception to this policy remains subject to the approval of the Faculty Board on Athletics.

STUDENT LIFE

Like other students, student-athletes should have the opportunity to pursue fully the University's academic, cultural and spiritual resources. The University holds student-athletes not only to the same standard of conduct that applies to other students, but also to that higher level of behavior appropriate to their visibility.

(continued)

EXHIBIT   4.2   Continued.

Basic Principles:

1. Student-athletes must comply with all University rules and guidelines, including those set out in both the student handbook, *du Lac,* and in the Student-Athlete Handbook. The Office of Residence Life and Housing enforces the University-wide rules according to procedures applicable to all student disciplinary matters.

2. The University strives to integrate student-athletes into the student body so that all students may take full advantage of the educational and other opportunities afforded by campus and hall life. Given the centrality of residential life to the University's mission, student-athletes normally live in residence halls; exceptions to this policy remain subject to the approval of the Faculty Board on Athletics. Moreover, Notre Dame provides no separate residence halls or sections of residence halls for student-athletes.

3. The University lists among its primary concerns the physical and mental health of all members of the Notre Dame community. Because of the dangers inherent in athletic competition, the prevention of injuries and the provision of medical care for student-athletes demand particular concern and deserve constant attention. The appropriate sports-medicine and athletics-training personnel alone determine whether injury or illness precludes a student-athlete from practicing or competing.

4. Because of the harm illicit drug use causes and the pressure on student-athletes to use performance-enhancing drugs, drug-related education and counseling to student-athletes require particular emphasis. As a preventive measure, all student-athletes remain subject to regular, random, and unannounced drug testing according to the University's established drug-testing protocol. University Health Services decides the timing of drug tests, determines whom to test, and administers the tests. The drug-testing protocol prescribes the treatment of test results and the consequences of a positive test.

5. Notre Dame regularly provides chaplains for athletics teams. Chaplains' duties include pastoral care and liturgical services for student-athletes, coaches and staff.

COACHING STAFFS

The University strives to maintain a staff of coaches who represent the best in athletic instruction, who possess the ability to motivate and inspire, and who take responsibility for the full development of the student-athletes within their charge as students, athletes and persons. Coaches, who after all are primarily teachers, share with members of the faculty and other University personnel the obligation to educate, train and otherwise assist in the formation of students entrusted to them.

Furthermore, Notre Dame recognizes the important role each coach plays in the University's overall educational mission and makes this aspect an important part of both the coach's position description and periodic evaluation. Because of the public nature of their work, coaches represent Notre Dame in a highly visible manner. Their words and actions should therefore reflect the University's values and principles.

Basic Principles:

1. Notre Dame expects the personal and professional lives of its coaches to reflect the highest standards of behavior. Coaches' actions must demonstrate that athletic success may not jeopardize institutional or personal integrity or the welfare of student-athletes.

2. Notre Dame expects its coaches to appreciate the primacy of academic life at Notre Dame and to emphasize that primacy during the recruitment and education of student-athletes and their participation in intercollegiate athletics.

3. Notre Dame requires its coaches to adhere to the policies and procedures of the University, its conferences, and the NCAA. To that end, Notre Dame provides a comprehensive orientation to new coaches and suitable continuing education to other coaches. The University treats seriously all violations of University, conference or NCAA standards and reports such violations according to the applicable conference or NCAA procedures.

ADMINISTRATION OF THE DEPARTMENT OF ATHLETICS

The Director of Athletics and the other administrators in the department of athletics supervise all activities of the athletics program at the University. All aspects of the program must accord with the principles of justice and fairness. In addition, Notre Dame expects the personal and professional lives of its athletics administrators to reflect the highest standards of behavior. Athletics administrators also must adhere to the policies and procedures of the University, its conferences, and the NCAA.

The University treats all violations of such policies and procedures seriously.

Basic Principles:

1. The University maintains full and direct control of the financial operations of the athletics department, including all revenues. The operating budget and the ongoing financial activities of the athletics department remain subject to the same approval process as all other units of the University.

2. Historically, Notre Dame's athletics program has generated funds sufficient to cover its expenses, as well as to provide funds for the University's general operating budget. The generation of revenue must always take into consideration Notre Dame's integrity and priorities.

3. The University commits itself to the principle of racial, ethnic and gender diversity in the composition of its coaching and administrative staffs. Notre Dame will make every reasonable effort to promote this commitment as positions are created or vacated.

4. Consistent with its overall academic mission and program, its financial resources, and the athletic interests of its student body, the University will provide a full and stable athletics program for both sexes. Notre Dame embraces the principle of gender equity, and will continue to monitor its intercollegiate programs in accord with this principle.

5. In considering conference affiliations, the University will assess the extent to which the other institutions involved share Notre Dame's educational philosophies and goals, as well as its commitment to integrity in intercollegiate athletics.

CONCLUSION

Notre Dame endeavors to maintain a highly competitive athletics program consistent with its tradition, heritage, and overall mission as a Catholic university. It will attempt to excel in intercollegiate athletics, but always in conformity with its primary role as an educator and moral guide. Notre Dame will conduct its intercollegiate athletics program so as to support the University's commitment to education, as well as the letter and spirit of the policies and procedures of the University, its conferences, and the NCAA.

Source: Statement of Principles, 2006. These principles and mission statement are reviewed on a regular basis. Reprinted with permission.

| EXHIBIT | 4.3 | California State University, Chico Mission Statement. |

The mission of the Department of Intercollegiate Athletics and Recreational Sports at California State University, Chico, is to provide a competitive NCAA Division II intercollegiate athletics program and a broad-based recreational sports program. The department will strive to provide student-athletes with a quality intercollegiate athletic experience that encourages their intellectual, physical, social and emotional growth in an environment that promotes academic and competitive success, fair play, sportsmanship, gender equity and cultural diversity. The department will encourage participation in sport by offering a wide variety of intramural, club and recreational programming opportunities for the general student population. By achieving these fundamental purposes, the department enhances university life, contributes to the recruitment and retention of students, fosters pride in the university and strengthens university-community relations.

Intercollegiate Athletics—Core Values

1. Our mission must be consistent with the mission of the University.
2. We believe intercollegiate athletics prepares people for future challenges, endeavors, and life situations.
3. We believe in fostering an environment in which student-athletes become life-long participants in Wildcat Athletics.
4. We are committed to compliance with university policy, conference, and NCAA rules.
5. We are committed to promoting the principles of fair play, ethical conduct, sportsmanship and amateur athletic competition.
6. We are committed to gender equity and cultural diversity.
7. We will maintain a proper balance between athletics, academics, and student life.
8. We are committed to being a positive campus and community member and fostering relationships with all of our constituent groups.
9. Our student-athletes, coaches, and staff will be ambassadors locally and nationally.
10. Our student-athletes, coaches, and staff will uphold a high sense of character and honesty.

Source: Wildcats Athletics, 2006.

| EXHIBIT | 4.4 | University of the South Athletic Philosophy. |

The primary purpose of the athletic program at The University of the South is to make the most positive contribution possible to the present and future physical, emotional, and social well-being of students, faculty, and staff. This purpose stems not only from the belief that the mind functions better—intellectually, emotionally, and socially—in a stronger, healthier body, but from the knowledge that in a time of high medical costs, a healthy faculty and staff contribute to the economic strength of the University at large, and so directly serves the University's broader educational mission.

The secondary purpose of the athletic program is to make a positive contribution to the present and future physical, emotional, and social well-being of the Sewanee Community. The unique nature of this community requires the University to have an interest in the availability of recreational facilities for those living here who are not directly associated with the University. The facilities of the athletic department are intended to contribute to the community needs when such contribution does not interfere with the primary purpose stated above.

To that end of general well-being, the Director of Athletics and staff, under the direction of the Vice-Chancellor and Provost, shall provide clean, well-equipped, well-maintained facilities for general fitness and for specialized training to the widest possible University constituency. The Director of Athletics and staff shall provide supervision and expert teaching in every area of the program to maximize the safety, efficiency, and effectiveness of its goal.

Physical education, intramural sports, and general fitness programs (such as aerobics, weight training, lap swimming, and jogging), and recreational sports (squash, tennis) should take place under professional guidance and should aim to maximize the present and future well-being of students, faculty, and staff.

For varsity sports programs, the Director of Athletics, under the direction of the Vice-Chancellor and Provost, is distinctly charged to secure coaches of genuine excellence who understand the role of varsity athletics at the University of the South and within the guidelines for NCAA Division III and conference colleges and universities. Varsity sports exist to develop the athletic excellence of individuals and the spirit of teams that serve as a model to the entire community, and so to promote the end of general physical well-being. Coaches and athletes are further expected to represent the University and the ideal of civilized behavior.

To the greatest extent practicable, the place of the varsity athlete shall be undifferentiated from the place of any other student. Athletic opportunities for the non-varsity student shall be conducted on a footing of seriousness as close as possible to that of varsity sports, and the non-varsity opportunities (in club, intramural, instructional, and general fitness programs) shall be as wide and of as high a quality as University resources permit.

In admissions, academic advising, course selection, grading, living accommodations, and financial aid, the opportunities available for varsity athletes, actual or potential, shall be neither greater nor less than those available to any other student. Academic requirements, administered by the Deans of the College, shall be the same for all students.

The Athletic Department and its programs shall be controlled, financed, and staffed under the direction of the Vice-Chancellor and the Provost, through the same general procedures as other departments of the College, including periodic evaluations of staff performance, and of the success of the program in meeting its goals. The Athletic Department shall neither possess nor control any funds separate from those proceeding from the University's established budgetary procedures. A faculty-student committee, advisory to the Vice-Chancellor, shall contribute to the administration of the program.

The Director of Athletics, under the direction of the Vice-Chancellor and Provost, is distinctly charged to ensure that men's and women's varsity sports and programs receive fair and equal emphasis. At the varsity level fairness requires that both men's and women's teams find appropriate competitive opportunities with students from similar institutions, and at every level fairness requires facilities, coaching, and teaching of similar excellence for men and for women. The level of participant interest can be a factor in determining the level of support for a given program, but failure of interest can also be a factor in determining that a program is poorly supported or poorly managed.

In administering varsity sports, the Director of Athletics, under the direction of the Vice-Chancellor and Provost, is charged to give primary emphasis to in-season competition, but to encourage exceptional teams and individuals to engage in postseason championships.

Source: Athletic Philosophy, 2006.

The three statements represent the unique approaches of Divisions I, II, and III membership. In reviewing the statements, the first step for us to consider is how each statement meets the expectations of an effective mission statement. Does each summarize what each department does or seeks to do? Does each include a statement of its philosophy and values? Does each reveal the department's long-term vision to all stakeholders? How does the statement reflect its division membership?

Division I mission statement example. First, in the case of the University of Notre Dame, we are presented with an involved and detailed expression of ideas and concepts. This is not surprising, given the complex nature of Division I athletics, especially at a school that supports such high-profile programs. Notre Dame was one of the early leaders in the commercialization of intercollegiate athletics, and as a result has developed legions of fans, many of whom have no direct connection whatsoever with the school. They are fans of the school's teams, but neither they nor anyone they know may have actually attended the school. Such is the reality of stakeholder groups at many D-I institutions. In keeping with the divisional philosophy statement, the athletic program serves the needs of the general public and is expected to produce income sufficient to cover departmental expenses (an element reflected in the Notre Dame statement). This is done in large part through the school's football broadcasting agreement with NBC, which pays the school about $15 million a year (Sandomir, 2009).

One unique element of Notre Dame's mission statement conveys its status as a Catholic institution, with the statement that the school "espouses Christian values and principles. These include the development of the human person—spirit as well as body—the pursuit of excellence in all endeavors, the nurturing of Christian character, and the call to personal integrity and responsibility." In this case, the department is stating clearly that it is aligning its goals and principles with those expressed by the affiliated Congregatio a Sancta Cruce (C.S.C.) order of the Catholic Church that is responsible for operating the school. In pursuit of this part of the mission, the statement explains that the school provides chaplains for teams, whose duties include pastoral care and liturgical services for student-athletes, coaches and staff. From this statement it may seem that every student-athlete at Notre Dame is a willing and active Catholic, and this is probably not the case. One issue not included in the mission statement is how the needs of non-Catholics, non-Christians, or non-religious student-athletes are addressed in what seems to be an overtly Catholic environment.

The Notre Dame statement also outlines five key areas of focus that are critical to departmental management: presidential control, academics, student life, coaching staffs, and administration of the department, followed by a series of basic principles germane to each. Each key area and its related principles reflect Notre Dame's publicly expressed intent of how the school endeavors to operate its athletic programs. Each also addresses a facet of managing intercollegiate athletics that, for many D-I institutions, has often proven to be problematic. For example, the "Academics" section is crafted in response to critiques that student-athletes are less academically able or inclined than the student body at large, and that athletic departments often have little interest in educating, only in creating winning programs. The basic principles under this heading address issues relating to the academic preparedness of prospective student-athletes, the need to provide academic support for current student-athletes, and the expectation that student-athletes will maintain a minimum grade-point average and the course credits necessary for graduation.

The "Conclusion" statement reads that Notre Dame "endeavors to maintain a highly competitive athletics program consistent with its tradition, heritage, and overall mission as a Catholic university. It will attempt to excel in intercollegiate athletics, but always in conformity with its primary role as an educator and moral guide." This brief conclusion outlines the greatest sense of the future directions of the department. But at times does the need to be "highly competitive" conflict with the mission of a Catholic university? Might student-athletes or coaches be tempted to bend rules to win games in the highly competitive world of Division I athletics? Quite possibly, so Notre Dame athletic managers felt the need to remind all constituents that Catholic and Christian values (which, however, are outlined only briefly) must be used as guiding principles for all involved in Notre Dame athletics.

Division II mission statement example. The mission statement of California State University, Chico (CSUC), affords us an opportunity to review this approach from the perspective of a Division II institution. CSUC is a member of the 23-campus California state university system, established from schools mostly founded to promote teacher education. Nearly 15,000 undergraduates (98 percent of whom hail from California) are enrolled at CSUC, located 90 miles north of Sacramento and 174 miles northeast of San Francisco. The state-funded public school sponsors 13 varsity sports and is a member of the California Collegiate Athletic Association. In 2009, CSUC earned its sixth straight Top 25 ranking in the Learfield Division II Directors' Cup standings. This award is presented annually by the National Association of Collegiate Directors of Athletics (NACDA) to the best overall athletic programs in each NCAA division and the NAIA. The rankings are based on a point total accrued by a school's individual athletic programs in national competitions. CSUC has placed as high as third, back in 1904–05 (Wildcats Garner, 2009).

On first reading, the CSUC statement clearly is much shorter than Notre Dame's, but that doesn't mean it is less effective. True, the CSUC statement doesn't address specific areas such as presidential control and the role of Faculty Board of Athletics, but it does communicate the departmental mission, philosophy, and values, and its goals to the reader and stakeholders.

The CSUC statement addresses issues of education and social growth, as well as those pertaining to sportsmanship and "fostering relationships with all of our constituent groups." But does it have a clear statement that reflects the competitive nature of these programs? The statement does profess that the department aims to provide a "competitive NCAA Division II intercollegiate athletics program," as well as a "broad-based recreational sports program." Does the Notre Dame statement mention recreational sports? Should it? If recreational athletics are handled by a separate department, then no, the ND statement need not address any such issues. Actually, at ND such programs are referred to as "intramurals," and as such are operated under the auspices of the athletic department. At CSUC, the department is responsible for running such programs, so the mission correctly refers to it. The question raised from this coupling the management of a competitive Division II athletic program with the operation of a broad-based recreational sport program is whether CSUC can provide both to two very different stakeholder groups. So the question is: Can CSUC do both and do them both well? Maybe so, as CSUC aims only to field "competitive" teams, which may send the message to some that winning is not a high priority for the department. The success in the Directors' Cup standings, however, would seem to indicate otherwise.

Division III mission statement example. The Division III statement is from the University of the South (a.k.a., Sewanee). Sewanee is a private, liberal arts institution with an enrollment of 1,400, located between Chattanooga and Nashville in Sewanee, Tennessee (population 2,200). For a brief period in the 1920s, the school was a national football power, and formerly was a member of the Southeastern Conference (withdrawing in 1940). When asked about its former athletic department mission and goals, Mark Webb, Sewanee's AD, commented: "Over the past few decades we've kind of found our place. We're not in the entertainment business. We're about having programs that enhance the student experience. If a coach told a student-athlete [he or she] couldn't take a science class because of a practice, I'd hear from the professor" (Wolverton, 2009, p. A33).

Today, the school offers participation opportunities in 24 sports, including cheerleading and equestrian, which are not NCAA-sanctioned championship sports, and is a member of the Southern Collegiate Athletic Conference. The first read of the Sewanee statement reveals no specific delineation of core values like CSUC's, or basic purposes like Notre Dame's. What we find instead is a broadly written statement of purposes, which outlines the primary purpose "to make the most positive contribution possible to the present and future physical, emotional, and social well-being of students, faculty, and staff," with a secondary purpose to make similar contributions to the Sewanee community. The statement explains that these purposes will be pursued by providing general fitness facilities and programs.

Not until the fifth paragraph of the statement are varsity sports programs mentioned. Such programs, we read, "exist to develop the athletic excellence of individuals and the spirit of teams that serve as a model for the entire community," but we read in the next paragraph that "the place of the varsity athlete shall be undifferentiated from the place of any other student. Athletic opportunities for the non-varsity student shall be conducted on a footing of seriousness as close as possible to that of varsity sports." In closing, the statement charges that the Director of Athletics should "encourage exceptional teams and individuals to engage in postseason championships." So having read the full statement, what is your conclusion about the real mission of the Sewanee athletic department? How does it match up with the Division III philosophy statement? Does it seem more interested in the creation of "exceptional teams," or with securing the present and future physical, emotional, and social well-being of students, faculty, staff, and the Sewanee community? And, if it is less interested in creating competitive varsity programs, what message does it convey to stakeholders? In reviewing the Sewanee statement, it would seem that the school is trying to operate its athletic department to meet these varied goals and serve a range of stakeholders, which may be difficult to do successfully.

From our investigation, these statements seem to reflect accurately the basic elements of each school's respective divisional classification, and each statement seems to do in general what mission statements are intended to do: Explain to stakeholders what each department does or seeks to do. But does each include a statement of its philosophy and values and reveal the department's long-term vision to all stakeholders? Not all are clear on these points. A mission statement exists to provide direction for all stakeholders—what Peter Drucker defined as vision, the clear, shared sense of direction that allows organizations to achieve a common purpose. Drucker insisted that this vision makes possible the cooperation and commitment necessary for organizations to succeed. It is up to managers and stakeholders to agree on the direction, whatever it might be. The vision for Notre Dame is different from the visions of CSUC and Sewanee. And the vision of these three schools might vary widely from their own divisional counterparts. That's OK, as long as everyone at each school can agree on its unique vision, success can be achieved.

Envisioned future and BHAGs

A key element that seemed to be lacking in the statements we examined was what Collins and Porras (1998) called the envisioned future, which includes BHAGs, and a vivid description of what it will mean to achieve these BHAGs. In the case of departmental mission and goals, this sense of the envisioned future can be observed in the schools that take on the challenge of upgrading programs to move up in divisional classification, to become more competitive in certain programs, or to add programs in certain high-profile sports, or to develop intercollegiate athletic programs where none previously existed. Now we'll examine several cases and try to understand how these changes impact their departmental mission and goals. The questions following each case will reinforce your thinking about how the events reflect institutional vision, mission, and goals.

TRINITY COLLEGE MEN'S SQUASH   **case study** 4.A

Trinity College, a small (enrollment 2,200) private liberal arts school in Hartford, Connecticut, is home to the country's best squash team. In 2010 the team finished with a 23–0 mark and won its twelfth straight Dual Match Season title and its eleventh straight Collegiate Squash Association Team Championship title. The Bantams then owned a 225-match winning streak, giving the team the longest such streak in all of intercollegiate sports. During the 2010 season, the team's top players included Baset Chaudhry (Lahore, Pakistan), Randy Lim (Penang, Malaysia), Supreet Singh (Mumbai, India), Parth Sharma (Jaipur, India), and Andres Vargas (Bogota, Columbia).

Why does Trinity pursue excellence in squash? According to coaches, student-athletes, and administrators at Trinity, in the mid-1990s, former school president Evan Dobelle charged the then recently hired head coach Paul Assaiante with building a program good enough to take on then-dominant Ivy League programs like Harvard, Yale, and Princeton. Assaiante recalled the meeting with his president when the goal was made clear:

Evan called me into his office and he said, Coach, here's the deal. I noticed that the squash team plays the highest caliber of institutions in competition. You play Dartmouth and Pennsylvania and Yale, whereas your tennis team plays Williams and Middlebury and Bowdoin—and that's all great. But I need to be able to walk into boardrooms and raise money and get people excited, because I'm trying to give this school a facelift and a morale boost. And the fact that you're competing with those schools is very important to me. And my question to you is, how do we take it to the next level in that pond? Because if the tennis team wins the Division III national championship, that's great, and we can promote it. But if the squash team wins the national championship against a Princeton or a Harvard or a Yale, that's *very* [author's emphasis] compelling. (Lincoln, 2004, pp. 196–197)

As Dobelle alludes, the college squash world is different from the vast majority of American intercollegiate sports. The NCAA does not hold a squash championship (it is organized by the United States Squash Federation), and most collegiate programs are housed in a handful of highly selective Northeastern schools. This is why Trinity competes against Ivy League schools even though Trinity belongs to the Division III New England Small College Athletic Conference (NESCAC), whose membership consists of Amherst, Bowdoin, and eight other four-year institutions.

Assaiante, who grew up in the South Bronx section of New York City and didn't pick up a squash racquet until he was 27, was able to create a squash juggernaut by recruiting international players. He told Dobelle at that same meeting: "The best squash is not being played in this country. I coached the U.S. team in Cairo. We had our best finish in a decade: We finished seventeenth. So you've gotta let us begin looking in different ponds" (Lincoln, 2004, p. 197).

This approach was not new, as American intercollegiate squash has been dominated by foreign players for years, but Yale coach Dave Talbott questioned the academic merits of Trinity's players. Assaiante describes the reaction to his success by the squash community this way: "'Trinity? How the hell can it be Trinity? How dare you?'" (Beech, 2004, p. 30), even though the international players were stronger academically than the domestic players Trinity used to attract (Lincoln, 2004).

Trinity was able to attract good international players in part because Dobelle encouraged international recruiting trips by coaches, and he pushed squash prospects with demonstrated financial need to the top of the school's financial aid priority list. In addition to their travels, coaches worked hard to use alumni contacts and Dobelle himself in the recruiting process. Dobelle was able to convince Marcus Cowie, a player from England who had been rejected by Harvard, to come to Trinity by saying, "You know, Marcus, we don't really want to lose to Harvard anymore. You could be a big part of that." His first year, Cowie led the Bantams to a 6–3 win over the Crimson, the first-ever win for Trinity over Harvard. Now, according to one English player who attended Trinity: "There's huge pressure to go professional and play professionally. But going pro and going to school is impossible . . . so the U.S. offers a chance to do them together, and it makes more sense . . . [and] It's sort of known in England that if you wanted to play squash [in America], you go to Trinity" (Lincoln, 2004, pp. 203, 207–208). We will consider the departmental implications of reliance of international student-athletes in Chapter 5.

In the case of squash, Trinity has chosen a sport in which it can compete against the best programs in the country at the most prestigious schools, in part because there is far less competition for squash prospects than for those in say, football or basketball, where many more programs compete to attract the best players. Trinity, which as a Division III school is not allowed to provide athletically related aid, also can compete at this level against the Ivies, which under conference rules also do not provide such aid. Finally, Trinity seeks to measure itself against institutions such as the Ivies in terms of competing for faculty, students, and donations, so demonstrating the ability to compete against and to defeat the Ivies gives the appearance that Trinity is a peer of its more prestigious counterparts. But is all this reconcilable with Trinity's published athletic mission, which reads that the school "embraces intercollegiate athletics as an educational experience that is an integral component of the academic mission of the College" (Athletics Mission Statement, 2007, p. 1).

According to Wendy Bartlett, the Trinity women's squash coach, Dobelle made this part of his personal mission as well: "He made it clear he was not an academician. He came in as a visionary and a businessman and a politician, and did a tremendous amount for Trinity. People may have not liked the way he went about it, but he got an awful lot done. He was super at fundraising, . . . [and] he loved winning." Assaiante, whose job also includes some athletic fundraising, adds: "Dobelle was right. [He knew that] it makes [alumni] feel better knowing that their old alma mater is a winner . . . when I walk into their office and they take me down the hallway to meet the partner who was a soccer player at Princeton, and they grind each other for a few minutes" (Lincoln, 2004, pp. 197–198, 213).

Assaiante, who claims to have no recruiting budget, works the phones and the Internet to keep the pipeline open from Pakistan, India, Malaysia, Mexico, Sweden, and Zimbabwe. He is also the school's men's tennis coach, still drives the team van to away matches, shares a room with two players in $100-a-night motels, and hosts at his home during school breaks his international players who can't afford to travel home. "I love the guy. We play for him," says Chaudhry, the Bantams' number one player in 2010. Chaudhry is a former professional player who is eligible to play collegiately because he could prove he spent more in expenses that he earned in prize money (Bamberger, 2008, p. 64).

The squash team's level of success seems to be having an impact on other Trinity programs. The women's squash team finished third nationally in 2009. The 2008 baseball team went undefeated (37–0) during its regular and conference tournament season and won the D-III national title. The football program had a 34-game unbeaten streak which was snapped in 2006, but maintained its 35-game home winning streak though the end of 2009. The men's basketball team and men's ice hockey team qualified for NCAA tournament play in 2008, as did women's field hockey in 2009 (losing in the national quarterfinals). However, the program gained negative national attention at the end of 2010 season when squash co-captain Chaudhry, the top-ranked player in the country, was caught on video taunting Yale's Kenneth Chan at the end of the match that gave Trinity their twelfth national championship.

Other videos showed Chan taunting Chaudhry earlier in the match, but nonetheless Chaudhry withdrew from the National Singles Championship the next month (Trinity Squash Player Withdraws, 2010).

questions for you to consider

1. What environmental factors are impacting the management of Trinity's men's squash program?
2. Has the program realized any BHAGs? If so, what are they?
3. What might be the trade-offs in recruiting so many international student-athletes for Trinity's squash team?

FOOTBALL AT FLORIDA INTERNATIONAL UNIVERSITY

case study 4.B

Florida International University (FIU), located between strip malls and multi-lane highways on the west side of the burgeoning Miami metropolitan area, is a spread-out, 344-acre mix of concrete buildings ringed by huge parking lots (the school also has a 200-acre campus in northeast Miami-Dade County). Like many institutions in the area, FIU is a newcomer, a little over 30 years old. The student body of nearly 38,000 is mostly composed of commuters and part-time students, many of whom come from the area's widely diverse Latino population base. Its parking spaces far outnumber the dorm rooms on campus.

FIU is a Division I school, with memberships in the Sun Belt Conference and Conference USA, and had fielded strong programs in baseball, women's basketball, and men's soccer. But in football-mad Florida, Miami is a hotbed of youth and high school versions of the game. Tens of thousands of fans attend local high school games, the nearby University of Miami is a perennial top Division I Bowl Subdivision program, and neighboring Florida Atlantic University also recently added a football program. When other state-supported institutions to the north—the University of South Florida in Tampa, and the University of Central Florida in Orlando—made the jump to the Bowl Subdivision, former FIU AD Rick Mello saw

the same opportunity available for his school, especially because his stakeholders wanted football. Said Mello: "Couple that with the region, couple that with our vision for enhancing campus life, bringing back alumni, creating ties with the community. We have not been able to captivate the community's interest with other sports—not in the mass quantities football can offer" (Robertson, 2003, p. 1D). Mello named former Miami Dolphins quarterback Don Strock as the university's director of football operations in 1999 and head coach in 2000, after obtaining approval for the program from the Florida Board of Regents in May 2000.

Because FIU had budgetary issues, it decided to drop its men's soccer team and redirect the soccer-budgeted funds ($351,000) toward its new football program, which began play in 2002. The athletic department budget was $9.5 million, with $2.2 million earmarked for football. Said Mello: "Baseball and soccer and women's basketball have given us blips of attention, but in this marketplace, football has always been the force people gravitate to. That's where we see the opportunity for growth" (Robertson, 2003, p. 3D). At the announcement of commencement of the football program, FIU president Modesto "Mitch" Maldique cited the school's intent to build a 70,000-seat on-campus stadium and to move to I-A by 2006, affording FIU the chance of "going head to head with major public universities" (p. 3D). However, critics such as former University of North Carolina president and Knight Commission co-chair William Friday disapproved of the moves, commenting: "To disband a nationally significant soccer program because you've got to get more fans in the football stadium is a clear acknowledgement the institution has thrown itself into the entertainment business" (p. 3D).

The team finished 5–6 in its first year (2002), and attendance averaged just under 8,000 a game. Mello, however, was still sanguine about football, saying "Tradition takes time. The key is how long it will take to mature. But after one season, we have no doubt playing football was the right decision" (FIU Announces 2006 Football Schedule, 2005, p. 1). After facing external criticism, the decision to drop men's soccer was eventually rescinded. But right on schedule, the Golden Panthers moved to the Bowl Division in 2005, going 5–6, and in 2006 the team was set to take on in-state rival South Florida, cross-town rivals the University of Miami and Florida Atlantic University, as well as the University of Maryland and the University of Alabama. Said Strock: "They will all be big tests for this program. Our players, when they first got here, said that this is the kind of schedule they wanted to play. Now, we're going to see how they handle it" (FIU Announces 2006 Football Schedule, 2005, p. 1).

On initial review, one might have concluded that program failed to hold up under the initial scrutiny of the Bowl Subdivision limelight. On October 14, 2006, during a game with cross-town rival Miami in the Orange Bowl, which had been filled with trash-talking and taunting on both sides, a brawl between the team erupted after a Miami point-after-touchdown conversion. Players from both teams streamed onto the field to join the fray, with some kicking and stomping and others swinging helmets as weapons. Eight FIU players were ejected, and five from Miami were tossed. Much of the substantial post-melee coverage focused on the higher-profile Miami program, fueled by a public perception that the school did not punish its players sufficiently. And the local television commentator, a former Miami player, applauded the Hurricanes for the actions during the game. FIU and its conference, the Sun Belt, announced that two players were immediately dismissed from the team, and 18 players were suspended from the team's next game for their actions during the fight. The suspended players were required to complete 10 hours of anger management counseling and fulfill 50 hours of community service to help educate local youths on appropriate behavior at athletic competitions. After the incident, FIU's Strock told the media that such a melee would never be repeated, but before the end of the season, in which the Golden Panthers lost all 12 games, Strock resigned. In 2007, the program lost 11 more games in a row before winning its final game of the season, then went 5–7 in 2008, and 3–9 in 2009 (FIU Announces Disciplinary Actions, 2006; Reynolds, 2006).

questions for you to consider

1. If you were to asked to re-write the FIU athletic department mission statement following the football brawl with Miami, what factors would you include to assure that the incident would not be repeated?

2. What sorts of environmental factors may inhibit the future success of the FIU football program?

INAUGURATING AND AUGMENTING PROGRAMS AT JUNIOR COLLEGES

case study 4.C

Guilford Technical Community College, a two-year school in Jamestown, North Carolina, has 5,000 full-time and 4,800 part-time students. It is one of many two-year institutions seeking to develop intercollegiate athletic programs at schools where none previously existed. Under the leadership of its president, Donald Cameron, the school added women's volleyball (2007), women's basketball (2008), men's basketball (2007) and men's baseball (2008) in an effort to increase its enrollment of traditionally aged students, those 18 to 24 years old. According to Cameron, "Many young people are looking for experiences. Athletics is just one more way of offering extracurricular opportunities that make a whole student. Our bookstore manager will tell you that he cannot keep our sports paraphernalia in stock" (Ashburn, 2007, p. A30). North Carolina law forbids the community college from using state funds to pay for athletics, so the school must cover the approximately $200,000 budget from student fees, bookstore revenues, and donations.

Guilford Tech, along with Arkansas Baptist College (Little Rock), Coastal Bend College (Beeville, Texas), Little Big Horn College (Crow Agency, Montana), and Simmons College of Kentucky (Louisville), are among the 30 schools that have added programs and joined the National Junior College Athletic Association since 2003, boosting the association's membership to more than 500 schools, with much of the growth coming from public schools in the Midwest, Pennsylvania, North Carolina, and Virginia.

Robert Keys, president of Rockingham Community College in Wentworth, North Carolina, describes his school's decision to add programs: "We live in an athletics-minded world. A lot of people think that if you don't have an athletics program, you're not a real college" (Ashburn, 2007, p. A30). Keys identifies three critical issues that schools have to consider before adding programs: how to pay for the programs, whether to offer athletically related aid, and the strength of the programs. "If it's your goal to build a powerhouse and have a national championship, then you're going to have to recruit all over the country. But that exceeds what is typically the community-college mission, which is that local

kids have the opportunity to attend and play sports in their own backyard" (p. A31).

Iowa Central Community College in Fort Dodge is one school that is succeeding in attracting students from both near and far through athletics. With its nine men's and eight women's programs (including rodeo for both), the school has drawn in-state students as well as students from the bordering states of Minnesota, Nebraska, Wisconsin, and from more distant locales including Florida, Texas, and Kenya. According to head track coach Dee A. Brown, the programs are focused on growing the school's enrollment, noting that the track program brings the school about 60 students who otherwise would not have come to the 6,700-student school. Experts also expect these junior college programs to benefit from NCAA legislation passed in 2007 that changed the academic eligibility requirements for first-year students at Division I schools (see Chapter 9) (Ashburn, 2007).

questions for you to consider

1. How does the addition of intercollegiate athletic programs impact the mission and goals of junior colleges?

2. How might the mission statement of the athletic department at a school such as Iowa Central Community College read, based on the information outlined in this case study?

THE GROWTH OF WOMEN'S WRESTLING PROGRAMS

case study 4.D

In Chapter 11 we will learn about Title IX and the efforts of intercollegiate athletic programs to deal with gender equity issues. Much of the effort in pursuing gender equity has been in response to legal prodding or idealism, but not until recently has it been seen as a potential financial benefit. Officials at the following NAIA schools are looking to build programs to reach what they believe is an untapped group—female wrestlers: Missouri Baptist University (a private, Christian, four-year liberal arts school with 4,600 full-time undergraduates located in St. Louis), Menlo College (in Atherton, California, a former two-year school, now four-year school, with

900 students, the majority of whom are male and study business), Oklahoma City University (a private school with 2,100 undergraduates and member of the Sooner Athletic Conference, best known for producing 26 Miss Oklahoma pageant winners, three of whom went on to win Miss America titles), and Jamestown (North Dakota) College (a private, four-year Presbyterian liberal arts school with 1,000 undergrads and a member of the Dakota Athletic Conference).

One prompt for these actions is that 5,000 high school girls wrestled in the United States in 2006–07, a growth attributed in part to the inclusion of women's wrestling as an Olympic sport in 2004. So far, only eight schools offer women's wrestling. Pacific University, a private, four-year liberal arts school with 2,500 full-time undergraduates, offers the only women's wrestling program at an NCAA school; Menlo competes in NCAA and NAIA competitions; the University of Northern Michigan, a Division II school located in Marquette, Michigan, does not offer women's wrestling as a varsity sport but does host an Olympic developmental program overseen by the United State Olympic Committee (Thomas, 2008; Wilson, 2008).

Some schools have been reluctant to develop women's programs. According to Michael Burch, assistant men's wrestling coach at Brown University, a private school with 5,800 undergraduates located in Providence, Rhode Island, and a member of the Division I Ivy League, this is because "in general, there's this resistance to the personification of women as aggressive" (Thomas, 2008, p. A17). There are no such concerns, however, at schools where the additional students can make a significant financial difference. As we have seen in our reading from Chapter 1, the concept of using athletics to further institutional goals and objectives—in this case to improve the overall financial health of the institution—is well established in U.S. higher education. At Jamestown College, for example, the team has 17 women (including four from Hawaii, where, along with Texas and Washington, the sport has grown fastest). These students, according to wrestling coach Cisco Cole, would not have otherwise considered the school. Tani Ader, from Honolulu, Hawaii, a three-time state champion, came to Jamestown because, as she said, "I really want to wrestle, and wrestling in college is like the first step in going to the Olympics" (p. A17). Missouri Baptist hopes to garner attention for the school by attracting athletes such as Stephany Lee, who qualified for the Olympic wrestling trials for the 2008 Beijing Summer Games at 158.5 pounds (72 kg), and finished third. Says coach Brian Jackson, "It's not like Missouri Baptist is constantly throwing out Olympic-level athletes" (p. A17). Archie Randall, head coach at Oklahoma City, knew he could sell the program to administrators at the school, telling school AD James Abbott: "I can get you 30 girls, and you're gonna get a half million dollars" in tuition revenue (Wilson, 2008, p. A8). The school's women's team has a roster of 20, and awards eight grants-in-aid totaling $214,320.

questions for you to consider

1. Given the facts outlined in this case, are the mission and goals for the schools adding women's wrestling similar to or different from those of the junior colleges examined in Case Study 4.C?

2. Can you make the case that adding these programs at the schools in question might very well reinforce an athletic department's existing stated mission and goals?

CONCLUSION

The NCAA's separate three-tier divisional classification system, created in 1973, formally established separate classifications that acknowledged the differences in institutional mission and goals relating to intercollegiate athletics. The factors determining the direction of and differences in athletic programs relate to the philosophy statements for each division. Key elements of the Division I philosophy statement include striving for regional and national prominence, serving both the university and the general public, and striving to finance the athletic program through revenues generated. The Division II statement includes striving for broad participation and competitive excellence, encouraging sportsmanship, and permitting athletically related aid on a more modest basis than Division I. The Division III statement encourages participation, gives primary emphasis to in-season competition, and permits no athletically related financial aid.

Management expert Peter Drucker defines vision as the clear, shared sense of direction that allows organizations to achieve a common purpose, and insists that vision is the first contribution of management because a shared sense of direction makes possible the cooperation and commitment necessary for organizations to succeed. The most common way that organizations attempt to communicate this sense of purpose or direction is through a mission statement, is a summary of what an organization does or seeks to do, which often includes a statement of its philosophy and values. In the case of the University of Notre Dame, a Division I institution, the athletic department's mission statement is to serve the needs of the general public, and the department is expected to produce income sufficient to cover expenses while maintaining its Catholic tradition. The mission statement of Division II California State University, Chico (CSUC) addresses issues of education and social growth, along with sportsmanship and "fostering relationships with all our constituent groups," and it aims to provide a "competitive NCAA Division II athletic program" as well as a "broad-based recreational sports program." The statement for the Division III University of the South is a broadly written statement of purposes, that outlines as a primary purpose "to make the most positive contribution possible to the present and future physical, emotional, and social well-being of students, faculty, and staff," a secondary purpose to make similar contributions to the school community, and that "the place of the varsity athlete shall be undifferentiated from the place of any other student. Athletic opportunities for the non-varsity student shall be conducted on a footing of seriousness as close to that of varsity sports." Each of these statements reflects accurately the basic elements of the school's respective divisional classification, and each statement does in general what mission statements are intended to do.

One key element that seemed to be lacking from the mission statements in the case studies was the element of the envisioned future, which includes BHAGs, or "big, hairy, audacious goals." In the departmental mission and goals, this sense of BHAGs can be observed in the schools' taking on the challenge of upgrading programs to move up in divisional classification, to become more competitive in certain programs, to add programs in certain high-profile sports, or to boost enrollment by adding sports programs.

PRACTITIONER perspective:

THE FUTURE OF DIVISION III

In examining the three divisional philosophy statements, we identified characteristics of each classification that served to define the direction and goals of member institutions. However, there are other factors that make the process of divisional identity more complex. For example, we know that size of undergraduate population is not necessarily a distinguishing characteristic. So it has been determined that divisional identity is really based on the mission and goals of a school intercollegiate athletic program and how that chosen direction matches with the existing divisional structure.

But what if the division's structures and philosophies appear to be no longer sufficient to represent its members, or if membership in a divisional classification grows too large with members having supposedly disparate missions and goals? This seemed to be the case with Division III when consideration occurred to split the membership of this classification and to create a "Division IV." At issue here was the continued growth in Division III membership, which had swelled to over 400 by 2007 (with a projection that 60 more would seek to join by 2020), so much so that the Association had imposed a two-year moratorium on schools joining the division in 2006. This decision had some believing that such a large number of members had now brought varying perspectives on the mission and goals of their athletic programs that may not be in keeping with the Division III philosophy. John Fry, chair of the Division III Presidents Council and president of Franklin and Marshall College, a member of the Division III Centennial Conference, explained the exploration this way: "The status quo in Division III is not a workable option. We must have fundamental change in structure of the division" (Pennington, 2007, p. C12). Ronald Liebowicz, president of Division III NESCAC member Middlebury College, stated that he and some of his peer presidents were considering the move because of

the belief that the recent, rapid, and anticipated further growth in Division III, now with more than 420 member institutions, has altered, and will further alter, the character of D-III athletics. . . . The current concern is that with schools coming into D-III that have more lenient rules than NESCAC governing their athletic programs, the annual votes on rules changes taken at the NCAA Convention will . . . give our competitors on-field advantages that appear unfair. To counter this, a number of D-III member institutions are encouraging colleges that share our [and their] conference's philosophy on the balance between athletics and academics to support the proposal for a "Division IV." By establishing a new division or subdivision, schools would be grouped and compete with schools that share more similar philosophies on the role of athletics on their campuses. It would also allow the new division to introduce new and perhaps more stringent rules guiding athletics at their institutions. . . . It didn't seem right to me (or "fair") that some of our varsity teams compete against programs with student bodies that are two, three, and even five times the size of Middlebury's—programs that begin their seasons weeks ahead of our teams, with many more games/ contests under their belts, and with fewer restrictions on their recruiting, admissions and other areas. . . .

If colleges with philosophies that differ greatly from NESCAC began to dominate D-III rules, debates, and voting so there was a wider discrepancy in rules governing athletics between most D-III schools and NESCAC schools, what would happen if NESCAC teams began to get beaten and beaten badly in first-round NCAA tournaments as a result? . . . How much pressure would presidents of NESCAC schools begin to feel from student-athletes, coaches, athletic directors, alumni, parents, and others if our current success gave way to early tournament departures? (Liebowicz, 2008, pp. 26–27)

Liebowicz's comments refer to many of the same motivations for the formation of conferences (see Chapter 3) and the NCAA (see Chapter 1) and propose to govern intercollegiate athletic policy on individual campuses, the athletic managers on campus require the power and influence of regional or national governing bodies to enforce rules that govern the actions at their school, but also the actions of their competitors. His comments and campus interactions also reveal that athletics is a major part of life on his campus, and an influential factor in why students choose to attend a specific school.

The "Division IV" debate also involved factors relating to peer identity. Dick Rasmussen, chief executive of the University Athletic Association (UAA), an eight-school Division III conference whose membership includes Brandeis University (Waltham, Massachusetts), Carnegie Mellon University (Pittsburgh, Pennsylvania), the University of Chicago, and Washington University (St. Louis, Missouri), described the process for some as "a middle school dance where everyone is watching to see who moves from one end of the gym to the other first" (Pennington, 2007, C12).

Rasmussen's membership may wish to be aligned with certain schools that not only were believed to share their athletic philosophy but also those with whom it sought to be compared on academic grounds. Many saw the dispute as the presidents of the so-called "traditional" D-III members, private, selective, liberal arts schools (like those in the North Coast Athletic Conference, the Midwest Conference, the Iowa Intercollegiate Athletic Conference, along with the Centennial, NESCAC, and the UAA), looking to distance themselves from the likes of those in the WIAC and others. Douglas Bennett, president of Earlham College, a school of 1,200 undergrads in Richmond, Indiana, founded in 1847 by the Religious Society of Friends (Quakers), and a member of the North Coast Athletic Conference (which also includes schools such as Allegheny College [Meadville, Pennsylvania], Hiram [Ohio] College, and the College of Wooster [Ohio]), has been seen as a leader in pushing for D-IV.

Bennett (2007) has claimed that the "sheer size of Division III creates a host of problems," that "it is increasingly difficult to reach agreement in a common set of rules for organizing competition in a way that feels fair and appropriate to all," and that the philosophical difference among current D-III members "make life increasingly awkward." He notes that "we need (student-athletes) to be resident advisors, to be in the student productions. We want to keep athletics vital, but it's not the only thing students do. . . . Mutual frustrations have been building for many years. We will find harmony only if we divide Division III into two divisions or subdivisions, each able to make rules that accord with its own approach" (pp. 1, 3).

Dave Knobel, president of Denison University, a school of 2,100 undergrads in Granville, Ohio, and also a member of the North Coast Conference, summarized the D-IV rationale this way: "It doesn't make sense to have colleges that have varying athletic philosophies, and that have different needs based on whether they are enrollment driven or endowment driven, competing against each other" (Growing Pains, 2008, pp. 12–13). But such a move from the "traditionals" would mean a forfeiture of the chance to compete for national championships, which, according to Middlebury's Liebowicz, would not be popular on his campus and would damage the school's ability to recruit prospects. "My coaches have already told me, 'Forget it, it would be such a negative to be in a sub-division.' Personally, I doubt students would stop choosing Williams, Amherst or Middlebury because we're in Division IV. But I know others feel differently" (2008, p. 27). Said Acting Williams College AD Lisa Melendy, after hearing about the proposed split at the 2007 NCAA Convention:

> When the leadership started telling us about the inevitability of a split, we all looked around and said, "Who decided we had to split?" . . . At the convention there were people walking around saying, "I'll never join a Division IV." No one wants to be in Division IV. The name has such a substandard sound. It sounds like you've been demoted. (Pennington, 2007, p. C15)

Tom Calder, AD at Johns Hopkins University, a school with 4,400 undergrads in Baltimore, and a member of the Centennial Conference, which also sponsors a Division I men's lacrosse program, had other, more logistically focused concerns. He said, "My concern is, if I consider going to Division IV, what's it going to be? What kind of regulations would members support? There are a lot of unanswered questions" (Pennington, 2007, p. C15). It was also noted by many ADs that if colleges are unhappy with regulations being passed by the membership at the divisional level, they were always free to join conferences that set more restrictive policies. Earlham's Bennett dismissed this, commenting that "relying on conference standards alone is an imperfect solution; particularly in early season competition outside the conference, coaches and athletes want a level playing field and suffer when an opponent has practiced an extra week" (Growing pains, 2008, p. 8).

Initially, it was floated that the split would be based on a minimum sport-offering requirement, perhaps as many as 18, with restrictions on recruiting, length of playing seasons, and out-of-season practices—issues that were very much at the heart of the foundation of NESCAC in the early 1970s. Based on these factors, it would seem that the leaders of the so-called "traditionals" were looking toward national legislation to rein in athletic programs on their individual campuses. Others looked at the separation criteria as a financial issue. Amy Carlton, commissioner of the American Southwest Conference, a grouping of 16 colleges in Arkansas, Louisiana, Mississippi, and Texas, which includes schools such as Hardin-Simmons University, Mississippi College, University of the Ozarks, and Sul Ross State University, commented, "Don't these more restrictive proposals come down to how deep your pockets are? When you've got 600 students, how are you supposed to pay for the extra sports teams that are required?" (Pennington, 2007, p. C15).

John Dzik, AD at Piedmont College, a school of 2,000 undergraduates affiliated with the National Association of Congregational Christian Churches and the historically related United Church of Christ, with campuses in Demorest and Athens, Georgia, and a member of the Great South Athletic Conference, seconded the financial implications of the proposed split: "If the Division III leadership and the NCAA really want to put their money where their mouths are, they would restructure the division based on comparable resources." He noted that the schools that support some of Division III's most successful on-field programs are among the nation's wealthiest in terms of endowments (Dzik, 2007, p. 1).

In considering the possible split of the classification, the Division III Working Group on Membership Issues had been engaged since 2004 in studying legislative proposals considered by the Division III membership, noting that there had been be division on issues such as redshirting (to delay athletic participation to extend eligibility), practice time, and out-of-season participation, with some schools seeming to favor more restrictive rules relating to these areas. In response, Presidents Council chair Fry concluded, "You say to yourself, there are some issues here. There are two different ways of doing things, both of which are valid. Clearly, it's the case that Division III isn't broken, but it doesn't necessarily follow that if it's not broken, don't fix it" (Growing Pains, 2008, p. 5). Dan Dutcher, NCAA VP for Division III, indicated that any proposed split would need two-thirds support of the existing Division III membership, with any vote on the issue to come at the 2009 Convention at the earliest. No proposals would require schools to change, and 150 schools would have to agree to move to any new classification to be viable long-term.

As a result of these perspectives, in early 2008, the group sent a 75-question survey to all D-III members to collect data on perceptions of the proposed bifurcation. According to Rudy Keeling, chair of the committee and commissioner of the Eastern Collegiate Athletic Conference, the nation's largest athletic conference and only multi-divisional conference—321 member institutions ranging across 16 states from Maine to North Carolina and as far west as Illinois—the data collection process was in response to the fact that

> the diversity in size and mission of the institutions that comprise the division, concern has arisen as to the commonality of perspective on the role of intercollegiate athletics in the educational enterprise. Analysis for the Division III Working Group on recent closely contested legislative votes suggests there is a diversity of perspectives on the role of athletics in Division III. While such diversity is not surprising in such a large organization, there is reason to evaluate whether that diversity of opinion should best be served through structural change. Ultimately, the membership will have to decide the future of Division III. This survey will allow the division to move beyond speculation and analysis of past preferences and more directly address its future. (NCAA Division III Membership Survey, 2008, p. 3)

The survey was organized into sections to ascertain respondent perceptions of the current state of Division III in the areas of recruiting and initial eligibility, financial aid, sport sponsorship, academic performance and continuing eligibility, playing and practice seasons, presidential leadership, national championships, and for the consideration of structural issues and the components of a potential new grouping. In the latter section, respondents were asked directly to answer on a six-point scale ("strongly support," "support," "somewhat support," "somewhat oppose," "oppose," "strongly oppose") whether they wished to maintain the current Division III structure, to create subdivisions of Division III, or to create a new division altogether. For the questions in this latter section, intended to capture preferences on the composition and structure of a potential new divisional classification, respondents were asked whether they wished to be part of a new grouping that featured legislative standards less permissive than, more permissive than, or the same as those currently in place in Division III (NCAA Division III Membership Survey, 2008).

In April 2008, the committee released the findings of the study, to which 96 percent of the Division III membership contributed responses. Eighty-two percent indicated support or strong support for the maintaining of the current Division III structure, while only 15 percent supported or strongly supported creating a subdivision of Division III or creating of a new divisional classification. The reasons cited for the impetus to maintain the current structure were the potential break-up of existing conferences and the loss of traditional rivalries, increased travel, branding difficulties, and damage to the recruitment and retention of student-athletes. Members also cited the belief that the current structure worked well, and that a compelling case for structural change had not been made (with the acknowledgment that urgent claims of philosophical divides among members had been overstated). In addition, 86 percent of respondents indicated a preference for current D-III recruiting and initial eligibility standards, 88 percent either agreed or strongly agreed that schools should set their own standards for satisfactory academic progress, 81 percent indicated a preference for the current standards for maximum length of playing seasons, 52 percent indicated support for the 12-sport sponsorship standard, set to go into effect in 2012, and 97 percent either agreed or strongly agreed that D-III members should have the opportunity to qualify for participation in national championships.

In the final section, focused on divining respondent preferences for the composition and structure of a potential new divisional classification, no strongly supported trends emerged. However, almost half of the respondents indicated agreement or strong agreement that consideration of leadership in athletics (e.g., team captaincy) in awarding financial aid to students should be allowed, provided that it is consistent with the consideration of leadership in other student activities. In the opinion of Jack Copeland, writer for the *NCAA News*, a weekly journal published by the Association, the issue of leadership-based aid expressed in the survey "very well may uncover another philosophical fault line within the membership . . . (but) by supporting the current structure, most of the Division III membership indicated it can live with differences over philosophical issues—at least so long as those differences don't erode current membership standards" (p. 2; *NCAA Division III Membership Survey—Executive Summary*, 2008; *NCAA Division III Membership Survey*, 2008, p. 5).

In response to the conclusions from the survey data, working group chair Keeling said: "Our members are saying that despite our differences, they like being a part of Division III" (Copeland, 2008a, p. 1). The following comments collected by student researchers at Western New England College examining perspectives on the Division IV issue within the membership of the Division III Commonwealth Coast Conference, a grouping of 14 schools located in Maine, Massachusetts, New Hampshire, and Rhode Island, seemed to summarize the consensus of most D-III athletic administrators.

Lori Runksmeier, AD at New England College, a private school with 1,200 undergraduates located in Henniker, New Hampshire, stated, "I don't believe Division III is broken just because we don't have 100 percent agreement on philosophical issues. In fact, disagreement within an organization is healthy and leads to continued growth in thinking and positive change. If the issue is the size of Division III, then there are other avenues to explore besides the creation of a new division." Charlie Robert, AD and associate dean of students at Nichols College, a private school with just over a thousand undergraduates, located in Dudley, Massachusetts, added, "I am not in favor of a Division IV and am glad the discussion has been quieted for the time being. . . . Division

III, as it currently is [structured], has a healthy diversity of institutions. Division IV is not necessary" (Balinskas et al., 2008, p. 10).

However, it still appears that the question of Division IV is not dead. D-III VP Dutcher said, "The membership seems to be saying pretty clearly that structural change is not the way to go, but it's also clear that some pretty significant issues remain that need to be dealt with in some way" (Copeland, 2008b, p. 1). Fry, chair of the Presidents Council, is still involved in promoting the concept, and believes it still has life because, in his view, "one of the most important and significant accomplishments [concerning the issue] was the engagement we saw among presidents and chancellors" (Growing Pains, 2008, p. 1).

To take advantage of this newly established level of engagement, a subcommittee of the Presidents Council, chaired by James Harris, president of Widener College, a multi-campus private school with 6,500 undergraduates with its main campus in Chester, Pennsylvania, and a member of the Middle Atlantic Conference, was charged with issuing a series of "white papers" to investigate some of the issues identified by some above as contrary to the successful operation of Division III. The papers were shared with all D-III presidents in the Fall of 2008, and later posted on the NCAA's website. According to Harris, the papers were crafted to increase presidential involvement on an annual basis and to determine how presidents should be involved in future governance issues, to create a new philosophy statement and "brand identity" for the division that is "universally understood," and to develop a stronger commitment to the new philosophy (Copeland, 2008c, p.1).

The papers hoped to "articulate the characteristics that make Division III distinctive while simultaneously deciding how to best accommodate the future growth and diversity within the existing structural framework of the division" through the identification of nine key issues linked to the current philosophy statement and membership survey statement, and recommendations to the Presidents Council relating to each of the issues (Copeland, 2008b, p. 1). The key areas and selected recommendations are listed in Exhibit 4.5.

The response of the Division III membership to these proposals will determine whether Fry and the Presidents Council can move forward with their goal of creating a Division IV, whatever it might be.

| EXHIBIT 4.5 | Key areas of focus and recommendations from Presidents Council subcommittee white papers. |

1. Presidential leadership: Require a minimum of three presidents from each conference to attend the NCAA Convention every year; Consider the establishment of a separate process through which presidents can decide fundamental legislative issues.

2. Philosophy: Include in the philosophy statement a presidential expectation of active leadership of athletics programs at the institutional, conference, and national levels.

3. Financial aid: Mandatory "supermajority" for future revisions of applicable financial aid legislation.

4. Division II as a possible membership destination: Conduct periodic joint meetings of Divisions II and III.

5. Sport sponsorship and membership requirements: Review the current conditions and obligations of membership and determine whether activities or commitments should be added or removed.

6. Preference for current season standards: Engage in a more thorough review of the appropriate amount of competition permitted in the nontraditional playing season; Implement a mandatory "supermajority" vote to the amending process of key playing season legislation; Amend the philosophy statement to solidify the division's position on playing season length.

7. Academic considerations: No national initial or continuing eligibility standards will be considered; Encourage conferences to monitor and review initial and continuing academic progress of student-athletes versus the general student body.

8. Championships: Change access ratio policies to limit the championship field in team sports to 64.

9. Budget priority and dues: The Strategic Planning and Finance Committee should continue efforts to identify the needs of membership and develop strategies to meet those needs.

Source: Copeland, 2008c.

questions TO CONSIDER

1. Given your knowledge now of the NCAA's three-level divisional classification system, which best represents what you believe the mission of intercollegiate athletics should be?

2. In defining what it means to be a member of the NCAA's Division II, some find it hard to describe what membership in this classification means. If you were hired as a consultant to advise your school to switch to (or to remain in) Division II, what reasons would you cite to support this decision?

3. Take a look at the athletic department mission statement of your school. Does it accurately explain specific vision, mission, and goals? If not, how could it be changed so it would address these areas?

4. The cases in this chapter included schools adding new athletic programs. What program could your school add to meet both institutional and departmental goals?

5. The cases in this chapter included schools emphasizing the success of certain athletic programs. Does your school do this, and if so, what are the goals of taking this track?

references

Ashburn, E. (2007, July 6). To increase enrollment, community colleges add more sports. *Chronicle of Higher Education*, pp. A31–32.

Athletic Philosophy. (2006). University of the South. Accessed May 28, 2006, from: http://www.athletics.sewanee.edu/philosophy

Athletics Mission Statement. (2007). Trinity College. Accessed February 2, 2007, from: http://trincoll.edu/StudentLife/Athletics_mission

Balinskas, G., Cossar, K., DeKanchuk, M., & Wilcox, G. (2008). *Division IV Team Research Paper*. Unpublished manuscript, Western New England College.

Bamberger, M. (2008, February 11). The court supreme. *Sports Illustrated*, pp. 63–64.

Beech, M. (2004, March 1). A global racquet. *Sports Illustrated*, p. 30.

Bennett, D.C. (2007, June 8). Division III: Too big for its own good. *Chronicle of Higher Education*. Accessed September 23, 2008, from: http://0-find.galegroup.com

Bergofsky, E. (2002, October 14). Perpetual Panther power. *Sports Illustrated*, p. 14.

Carey, J. (2006, October 16). Miami-FIU melee ripples. *USA Today*, p. 11C.

Carlson-Thomas, C. (1992, February). Strategic vision or strategic con: Rhetoric or reality? *Long-Range Planning*, pp. 81–89.

Chen, A. (2000, November 27). A little goes a long way. *Sports Illustrated*, pp. 36–37.

Collins, J.C., & Porras, J.I. (1998). Building your company's vision. In *Harvard Business Review on change* (pp. 21–54). Boston: Harvard Business School Press.

Copeland, J. (2008a, April 9). News analysis: What's next in Division III? *NCAA News*. Accessed April 12, 2008, from: http://www.ncaa.orgwcm/connect/NCAA

Copeland, J. (2008b, August 8). Division III to study philosophy, beliefs. *NCAA News*. Accessed October 22, 2008, from: http://www.ncaa.orgwcm/connect/NCAA

Copeland, J. (2008c, September 23). Division III white papers offer basis for membership dialogue. *NCAA News*. Accessed October 22, 2008, from: http://www.ncaa.orgwcm/connect/NCAA

Covell, D., Walker, S., Siciliano, J., & Hess, P. (2007). *Managing sports organizations: Responsibility for performance*. Burlington, MA: Butterworth-Heinemann.

Dowling, W.C. (2007). *Confessions of a spoilsport: My life and hard times fighting sports corruption at an old Eastern university*. University Park: Pennsylvania State University Press.

Drucker, P. (1973). *Management: Tasks, responsibilities, practices*. New York: Harper & Row.

Dzik, J. (2007, July 13). Richer colleges, better teams. *Chronicle of Higher Education*. Accessed September 23, 2008, from: http://0-find.galegroup.com

FIU Announces 2006 Football Schedule. (2005, December 6). Accessed January 7, 2006, from: http://www.fiusports.com/football/releases/120605.htm

FIU Announces Disciplinary Actions. (2006, October). Accessed October 25, 2006, from: http://www.fiusports.com/ViewArticle.dbml.htm

Growing Pains. (2008, January 15). *Inside higher ed*. Accessed January 15, 2008, from: www.insidehighered.com/news

Kuharsky, P. (2003, September 14). Educators back Vandy reforms. *Tennessean*. Accessed September 18, 2003, from: http://cgi.tennessean.com

Liebowicz, R. (2008, Winter). Striking the balance. *Middlebury Magazine*, pp. 26–27.

Lincoln, C. (2004). *Playing the game: Inside athletic recruiting in the Ivy League*. White River Junction, VT: Nomad Press.

NCAA Division III Membership Survey. (2008). Indianapolis: NCAA.

NCAA Division III Membership Survey—Executive Summary. (2008). Indianapolis: NCAA.

Pennington, B. (2007, February 13). Division III seeks harmony between field and classroom. *New York Times*, pp. C12, C15.

Reynolds, T. (2006, October 16). Suspensions follow brawl. *Albuquerque Journal*, p. B3.

Robert, C. (2008, December 8). Personal communication.

Robertson, L. (2003, January 22). Footing the bill. *Miami Herald*, pp. 1D, 3D.

Sander, L. (2008, September 19). Athletics raises a college from the ground up. *Chronicle of Higher Education*. Accessed September 30, 2008, from: www.collegeathleticsclips.com

Sandomir, R. (2009, December 11). NBC still likes its Notre Dame strategy. *New York Times*, p. B15.

Statement of Principles for Intercollegiate Athletics. (2006). University of Notre Dame. Accessed May 28, 2006, from: http://und.cstv.com/school-bio/nd-ath-principles.html

Thomas, K. (2008, May 27). Women want to wrestle; small colleges oblige. *New York Times*, pp. A1, A17.

Tierney, M. (2009, December 16). A college's backbone. *New York Times*, pp. B12, B15.

Trinity Squash Player Withdraws From National Championship (2010, February 26). *Trinity College.* Accessed April 11, 2010 from: http://athletics.trincoll.edu/sports/msquash.

Wildcat Athletics Mission Statement. (2006). California State University, Chico. Accessed May 28, 2006, from: http://www.csuchico.edu/athletics/ad/missionstate.html

Wildcats Garner Sixth Straight Top 25 Finish in Directors' Cup. (2009, June 29). California State University, Chico. Accessed December 29, 2009, from: http://www.chico wildcats.com/news/2009/6/29

Wilson, R. (2008, April 4). Oklahoma hold 'em. *Chronicle of Higher Education*, p. A8.

Wolverton, B. (2009, September 4). One charter SEC member misses out on the money—but doesn't miss the league. *Chronicle of Higher Education*, p. A33.

Departmental organizational structure and human resource management

Key concepts to keep in mind as you read the chapter:

- The traditional models of organizational design, and how these models impact intercollegiate athletic management.

- The various components of individual school athletic departments.

- How individuals perform and function in each of the departmental roles, and how

these actions influence the management of departments.

- The challenges that are unique to the performance of athletic department personnel.

- The skills and requirements necessary to perform the roles required of each member of an athletic department.

Introduction

To understand the nature of intercollegiate athletic management as fully as possible, we now will consider organizational and structural issues at the individual athletic department level, with an additional focus on how departments hire and support personnel. Through this examination, we will gain insights into how many of the issues discussed throughout this text impact how individual institutions structure and organize their athletic departments to maximize efficiency and performance. As we will learn, the structure and operations at this level can be complex indeed. For instance, consider Ohio State University (OSU), a public school with more than 52,000 undergraduates, located in Columbus and a member of the Division I Big Ten Conference. The OSU athletic department employs 300, has oversight for 377 acres of fields and 16.9 million square feet in building space, sponsors 36 varsity sports for 926 varsity athletes, and pays for all this with an annual budget of $110 million (Wertheim, 2007). It is estimated that the program and its operations inject more than $100 million each year into the greater Columbus area (King, 2009). No one person can manage all aspects of such a program. It takes the coordinated efforts of many to enable a department to perform.

Much of our examinations thus far has looked at organizations from the top down, beginning with top managers such as school presidents, the president of the NCAA, conference commissioners, and athletic directors. We have yet to discuss in detail the roles and duties of other departmental personnel. Here we will focus on how personnel within an intercollegiate athletic department perform their duties, how departments seek to attract, train, and supervise the best personnel possible, and how departments are structured to enable personnel to perform well.

ELEMENTS OF ORGANIZATIONAL DESIGN

Two traditional models of organizational design are outlined in Exhibit 5.1.

EXHIBIT 5.1	Traditional models of organizational design.

Functional structure: A separate unit or department of specialists is created to perform each function essential for achieving the organization's goals; most commonly adopted by organizations producing a single product for a single market.

Divisional structure: The work of the organization is divided according to the kind of products or services provided, the type of customer served, or the geographic region in which the organization competes.

Source: Adapted from Covell et al., 2007.

Functional structure

Most intercollegiate athletic departments are part of a greater institutional organizational structure that is generally functional in nature. The athletic department is a separate unit within a college or university created to oversee intercollegiate athletic programs, as well as in some cases to teach physical education courses, and to organize and supervise club and intramural sports programs. As noted, each athletic department is then staffed by a director and several associate or assistant directors. The departments also are generally divided by specific task areas, with managers within the department having responsibilities for oversight of these areas (as outlined in their position descriptions). In some cases, an AD reports directly to the school president or chancellor, and in other cases the AD reports to a dean or vice-president responsible for student affairs.

Nonprofit foundation structure

In some circumstances, the athletic department is organized as a nonprofit foundation outside the traditional functional structure framework. For example, at the University of Florida, a public school with 35,000 undergraduates located in Gainesville and a member of the Division I Southeastern Conference, the department is organized as the nonprofit University Athletic Association (UAA), Inc., incorporated as such in March 1929. AD Jeremy Foley still reports directly to the president of the university, Dr. Bernie Machen, but the department is governed by a separate board of directors, which consists of no fewer than five members, composed of the school's president, vice-president, business manager, AD, and members of the school's Faculty Committee on Athletics. The UAA is empowered by state law to acquire resources and property, to manage investments, to borrow money, and to issue bonds for athletic purposes (*Articles of Incorporation*, 1929).

In keeping with its rules of incorporation, UAA has issued tax-exempt revenue bonds three times since 2001, raising a total of nearly $80 million for capital improvements for renovations and improvements to several athletic facilities, including club and luxury seating at Ben Hill Griffin Stadium, the school's football stadium (Management's Discussion, 2008).

Divisional structure

Some departments follow a divisional structure, in which programs are organized with separate male and female departments. One school that utilizes a divisional structure is the University of Tennessee (UT). Joan Cronan is the Women's Athletic Director at UT, a position she has held since 1983. In an interview for this book, when asked about the organization of the athletic department based on separation by gender, Cronan said the divisional model works well for the school:

> The benefits are that you can focus more on the separate departments. . . . [Men's AD] Mike Hamilton and I both wake up every day to figure out how to make UT athletics the best it can be. He has to focus on the men and I have to focus on the women, but there's not a day that goes by that we don't work together on a project. . . . The challenges are communication and to be sure you're all going the same

direction. I tell my staff all the time, if you can be efficient and effective, then you can be separate. As soon as we're not efficient and effective, then we're going to say, "Hey, what are we doing?" But as long as we're winning, as long as we're making money, as long as we're working together, it's the best program in the world. From the exit interviews that we do with student-athletes, the feedback is positive about the separate programs. We've worked extremely hard to combine the things from each side that are really positive. You have to be open to look at what is best for the overall [organization].

ORGANIZATIONAL RESTRUCTURING AT VANDERBILT UNIVERSITY

case study 5.A

While the vast majority of intercollegiate athletic departments at each divisional classification level follow a traditional functional structure with staffing and reporting lines as outlined, Vanderbilt University, a private school with 6,600 undergraduates located in Nashville, Tennessee, and a member of the Division I Southeastern Conference, has scrapped that model in favor of a different approach. In September 2003, then-school president Gordon Gee (now president at Ohio State) announced that he was eliminating the position of athletic director and folding the athletic department into the school's Office for Student Life and University Affairs. Gee made this move because the athletic department had become separated and segregated from the rest of the institution. "We have engaged in this arms race in athletics, and we've also engaged in this culture of separation," said Gee. "This is a different way of thinking" (Bechtol, 2003, p. 17).

This move might have been less surprising if Vanderbilt's athletic department had been mired in the type of scandal that occurred at other schools, but not one of the school's 14 programs had ever been on probation for NCAA rules infractions, and the graduation rate for the football program was 91 percent, third-best in the Bowl Subdivision. David Williams II, the school's vice chancellor for student life and university affairs, who would now serve as the de facto AD, described the change this way: "There was nothing broken, but we sat down and thought we could be even better" (Bechtol, 2003, p. 17).

An assistant vice chancellor would be responsible for day-to-day operations for the department's 14 varsity (since increased to 16) and 37 club sports, as well as intramural programs serving 1,000 participants. The school's central administration now would be responsible for financial, administrative, public relations, marketing, and facilities work. Gee also said that he did not expect to hire a traditional AD at any future date, and that current associate ADs would be retained. Academic support for student-athletes would be housed under control of the school's provost. The move did not come with a corresponding budgetary reduction. Gee believed the move could help athletics also benefit from the school's successful fundraising and marketing arms (Cass, 2003; Wolverton, 2007).

Todd Turner, AD at the school since 1996, was removed from his position but allowed to stay with the school as a special assistant. The move contributed to speculation that the lack of success of football and men's basketball during Turner's tenure led to the change, along with a botched hiring decision in 2002 involving a new women's basketball coach, which went afoul because a discrepancy on the coach's resume necessitated a $900,000 out-of-court settlement with the coach, after which Turner was forced to report to Williams. Earlier in 2003 Turner also was forced to cut $1.5 million from the department's budget because of shortfalls in fan support and fundraising. Also, the department did not receive its NCAA certification (see Chapter 2) after the 2003 review.

At the time of the announced changes, Gee understood that move would be questioned and met with resistance. "People are going to say, 'What does this mean for me?'" said Gee. "And we have to say to people, 'Trust us.'" Williams and Gee met with the school's Student-Athlete Advisory Council (SAAC, see p. 317) a few days after the announcement to address questions, and Williams told reporters that he assured the group, "there isn't going to be any deemphasizing. This is going to up the ante. We're going to beat people in recruiting because we're talking about something very special. We're going to give a recruit a great education and find a way for them to enjoy a way to partake in those other things at the university. . . . There will be some student-athletes who say, 'All I want to do is my sport.' That's their choice. We just want to make sure we show the athletes there is something more" (Cass, 2003, p. 2; Organ, 2003a, pp. 1–2; 2003b). In the immediate aftermath, most student-athletes saw the move as potentially positive. Chris Young, a receiver on the football team, commented, "There are a lot of students out there who just really don't understand how much we put in to what we've got going on. The more they see what we do, the better they will appreciate and understand it" (McClellan, 2003, p. 1).

Non-athlete students on the school's Nashville campus see the separation between them and intercollegiate athletes in other ways. Kuharsky (2003a, p.1) provides these quotes: "The only thing separating us is dinner," said a female sophomore. "I know the student-athletes get an amazing dinner over at [the athletic complex]. They always go over in a little cluster, and I'm jealous. The football players come home and talk about the great steak they just had and I just had another hamburger from (the dining hall)." Vensherrie Campbell, a women's track athlete who serves as the school's SAAC president, has heard these complaints as well. "It's one of those things people moan and groan about. I know they're never moaning when we get up at 6:30 and saying, 'I wish we had that.' It cuts both ways." Of the proposed plan, Campbell offered this opinion: "Sometimes it feels like we're cut off from academia. We surround ourselves with each other so much." Other non-athlete students on campus agreed with Campbell. One male sophomore, a member of a campus fraternity, added: "A lot of athletes are deterred from joining fraternities, and that's a big part of this campus. I don't think the university separated big teams on purpose, that's just the way it is, and I don't know that this will change it" (Kuharsky, 2003a, p. 1).

Many Vanderbilt coaches questioned the move, including Tom Corbin, head coach of the school's nationally ranked baseball team, which produced number one MLB draft picks David Price and Pedro Alvarez. When interviewed by ESPN's *Outside the Lines*, Corbin

said, "Your mind has a chance to go everywhere, and think, 'Oh my, I might be out of a job, we might be out of a program, we might be out of an athletic department.'" ADs at other schools also were skeptical, seeing the move as a precursor to a significant deemphasis of the school's intercollegiate athletic programs that may lead the school to change its divisional classification.

Although many national reform groups approved of Gee's actions, some individuals were more guarded in their praise, or were downright dismissive. Murray Sperber, former professor of English at Indiana University and a historian and longtime critic of the management and operation of Division I athletic programs, commented about the move:

> It could be a good way to disguise the financial losses and waste [by the] athletic department. It could be a good way of disguising the male/female athlete ratios and expenditures. It could be a good way of disguising coaches' inflated salaries by putting them on [as full-time employees] with the phys ed people. Nothing is simple in college sports, and Gordon Gee previously presided over questionable programs at Ohio State and Colorado. . . . The creative thing is to say, "We don't want to drop to Division III, but we want to get much more in line with academics, and the way to do it is to form a conference with schools that think like us [possibly Rice, Tulane, SMU, and the service academies]." That would attract a lot of attention and put athletics and academics closer together. It seems like a no-brainer. (Kuharsky, 2003b, p. 1)

In response to the significant levels of comments surrounding the decision, some in favor, some opposed, Gee offered some specific responses. Concerning Sperber's claim that the move was geared toward disguising financial losses and waste, Gee called such claims "hogwash" and explained:

> I and the university administration fully realize that if we called upon the athletic department to be totally self-supporting, then we will not be successful . . . so what we really believe is we need to come up with a financial model that says our revenue-producing sports need to produce revenue to support themselves, but we do not expect them to support the [other] sports. [Those programs] need to be supported through another mechanism, through the university's general [funds]. Then we don't get into this tension where everyone is driven to win to be able to survive. (Organ, 2003b, p. 2)

Concerning staffing issues, Gee said:

Whether we ultimately change their titles to something else, we haven't even thought about that. You have to understand, this is a macro-concept that will now require the people in the athletic program and within student life and within the chancellor's office to sit down and talk about this. I said this to the coaches the other day, "I'm not going to tell you this is the way everything is going to be because I need to hear from you." ... It's about us trying to come together with something that really makes some sense. (Organ, 2003b, p. 4)

Gee also noted that he didn't anticipate that many, if any, peer schools would follow Vanderbilt's lead (Organ, 2003b). On that score, Gee, who has since returned to Ohio State (he has often joked, "I've been president at half the universities in the country" [Wolverton, 2007, p. A24]), has been correct. In 2008, Vice Chancellor Williams told ESPN's *Outside the Lines* that no schools had contacted him with inquiries as to how to enact such a change. The evidence suggested success because, since the restructuring, Vanderbilt athletics began experiencing many positive outcomes (Bechtol, 2007). In 2007, 10 of 16 programs qualified for NCAA postseason play. The baseball program was ranked number one throughout most of the year, won its first SEC title (drawing 3,500 to weekend games, enabling scalpers to sell $10 tickets for $50). In 2008 the football team made its first bowl appearance since 1955, defeating Boston College, 16–14, in the Gaylord Hotels Music City Bowl. More student-athletes began taking part in student government, the school's honor council, and study-abroad programs, and the cumulative GPA of student-athletes rose from 2.8 to 3.1 (compared to the overall student body GPA of 3.25).

The change initiative reinforced an organizational design concept advanced by management historian Alfred Chandler. Based on his study of successful U. S. corporations, Chandler (1962) determined that successful organizations were designed by management to pursue specific strategies, and when they changed their strategies, they also changed their structures. Whether Gee and Williams knowingly applied these concepts at Vanderbilt, the new approach they elected to enact clearly was based in whole on a change in organizational structure. However, University of Mississippi AD Peter Boone, a critic of the move in 2003, told ESPN five years later: "Maybe we're all scared of change . . . (but) I'm not sure what changed. I'm not sure there was anything big about it other than there were reporting lines to a different place. If they're happy with it, and it works for them, then it's an absolute success" (Wolverton, 2007, p. A24).

questions for you to consider

1. Based on the issues outlined in the case, what factors can athletic managers and school administrators identify that indicate that the departmental restructuring has been beneficial to student-athletes specifically and the school in general?

2. If your school were to consider a similar restructuring move, what would be the major forces driving the motivation for the change, as well as the major forces that would restrain your school from making such a move?

OVERVIEW OF DEPARTMENTAL PERSONNEL COMPONENTS

As described by Covell et al. (2007), "People, in essence, are the organization. Their skills, knowledge, and abilities dramatically shape the organization and have a critical impact on the organization's ability to carry out its mission and achieve its goals." Academicians and sport industry experts consider management functions in the human resource area to be any sport organization's most important asset. With this in mind, Covell et al. further define human resource (HR) management as "the responsibility of management to establish and to maintain specific programs and systems needed to attract, to develop, and to support a high-performance workforce," and identify the important components of HR management as HR planning (including analyzing specific jobs to determine the characteristics required), staffing, training and development, compensation, employee wellness, and employee relations (pp. 307, 348). We will examine the various individuals who work in athletic departments and discuss the issues and responsibilities related to managing them or their managing of others.

Coaches

Article 11 of the *2008–09 NCAA Division I Manual,* which deals with the conduct and employment of athletics personnel, defines a head or assistant coach as "any coach who is designated to perform coaching duties and who serves in that capacity on a volunteer or paid basis" (p. 49). Although this definition may not be particularly enlightening, such definitions must be made when delineating who may perform certain duties in terms of recruiting, and in relation to other types of permitted coaches, specifically graduate assistants. With some exceptions, the general definition of a graduate assistant coach is one who is enrolled in at least 50 percent of an institution's minimum regular graduate program of studies. This coach may not receive compensation or remuneration in excess of the value of a full grant-in-aid for a full-time student, and may not serve as a graduate assistant for more than two years.

These definitions also are relevant because Bylaw 11.7 of the *Division I NCAA Manual* outlines limitations on the number of head coaches and assistant coaches, volunteer coaches, and student assistant coaches that each sport is permitted. Volunteer coaches are those who receive no compensation and are limited as to specific tasks they can perform. Student assistant coaches are undergraduates who have exhausted their eligibility or have been injured to the point at which they can never compete again. Volunteer and assistant coaches cannot receive compensation.

As an example of the NCAA's limitations on the number of coaches, Bowl Subdivision football programs are permitted one head coach, nine assistant coaches, and two graduate assistant coaches. These programs also are permitted to have an additional coach in the area of strength and conditioning, as long as that coach performs certain duties only prior to games and other organized activities. In addition, each program is limited in the number of coaches who are permitted (after certification of rules knowledge) to recruit off campus (see Chapter 7).

Covell et al. (2007) identify coaches as a critical component to intercollegiate athletic departments because of the unique abilities, personalities, and skills they possess and bring to their positions (p. 315). Because of their role in managing player talent and making critical game decisions, coaches are vital to program and department performance.

Position description

As outlined by Covell et al. (2007), a position description is a product of the job analysis process, to assess the critical skills necessary for a worker—in this case a coach—to carry out the goals and objectives of a sport organization. As a result, the position description then must provide a clear and concise summary of the skills, responsibilities, and tasks required in each job. The position description, therefore, provides the foundation on which much of the human resources (HR) management process is built, and also contributes to the shaping, staffing, training and development, performance evaluation, and compensation elements.

To understand the importance of position descriptions in advancing institutional goals, we use as examples position descriptions for head coaches at each of the NCAA's three divisional classifications posted in late 2008 from the Employment page of the NCAA's website, ncaa.org. The first is a posting for a head women's soccer coach at High Point (North Carolina) University, a private liberal arts school with 3,000 undergraduates and a member of the Division I Big South Conference (High Point, 2008). The position description outlines the responsibilities as recruiting, scheduling, skill/technique instruction, and budget management. The position requires coaching and recruiting experience, preferably at the Division I level, as well as a bachelor's degree (with a master's preferred).

The second example is a posting for a head women's volleyball coach at Anderson (South Carolina) University, a private Baptist-affiliated institution with 2,000 undergraduates and a member of the Division II Conference Carolinas (Anderson University, 2008). The posting for the position outlines that the head women's volleyball coach is responsible for all aspects of the administration of the program, all budgetary supervision and oversight, recruiting and monitoring academic progress of student-athletes, knowledge of all relevant NCAA regulations, scheduling, fundraising, and community development activities. A bachelor's degree from an accredited college or university is required, and candidates must have at least five years of coaching experience, and a proven ability to recruit successfully.

The third example is the head men's and women's swimming and diving coach position at Pomona (California) College, a member of the Claremont Colleges consortium (Pomona College, 2008). The schools have a combined enrollment of 2,350 students, and the athletic programs belong to the Division III Southern California Intercollegiate Athletic Conference. All coaches hired into the program also teach physical education courses, and as such are full members of the school's faculty. The position description requires that the chosen candidate have a master's degree in physical education or a related field, understand the NCAA Division III philosophy, appreciate the role of athletics in a school with rigorous academic demands, and have collegiate coaching and teaching experience. Although the description does not outline the specific duties to be performed once hired, the description does state that the department is particularly interested in candidates who have experience "working with students from diverse backgrounds and a demonstrated commitment to improving access to higher education for underrepresented students" (p. 1).

A comparison of these descriptions reveals similarities in the skills, responsibilities, and tasks for these positions, regardless of the sport or the posting school's divisional classification. What does differ in these cases, however, are the expectations beyond these basic duties that are unique to the institutional goals of each posting school. For example, the posting for the position at Pomona clearly states that any candidate would be a member of the school's teaching faculty and must be qualified to teach physical education courses, must understand that the school has "rigorous academic demands," and wants to attract students from "underrepresented" backgrounds, which in turn will impact the type of prospects the future coach will be able and encouraged to recruit. Neither the High Point nor the Anderson position descriptions focus on these issues and are crafted in such a way that would lead a candidate to conclude that the demands outlined for the Pomona job are not as important for those other positions, and that the job performance of coaches at High Point or Anderson would assess only the areas specifically outlined in the position description.

Coaches and the media

In Chapter 6 we discuss the lucrative components of media deals that many head football coaches have been able to secure. Here we discuss other types of interactions with the media that are expected of coaches, such as daily press conferences, weekly press briefings, and regular media interviews. These media-related tasks usually are handled by coaches in a rather perfunctory manner, with typical game-focused questions eliciting stock responses. This was not the case in 2007, however, when Mike Gundy, head football coach at Oklahoma State University (OSU), a public school with 23,000 undergraduates in Stillwater and a member of the Division I Big 12 Conference, responded to an article in a local newspaper. His 3-minute, 20-second rant in a post-game news conference (after a comeback win against conference rival Texas Tech University) criticized the article and its author. The article opened about why the team had changed starting quarterbacks and suggested that the OSU coaches were unhappy with the replaced QB's play and that he was unwilling to play through injuries. In his diatribe, Gundy verbally attacked the reporter, calling the QB in question "a good kid" and the article "fiction" and "garbage." He punctuated the tirade by claiming that the piece made him "want to puke," and rather than criticizing his player, he challenged the article's writer instead to "Come after me! I'm a man! I'm 40!" (Evans, 2007, C17).

Although the writer stood by her piece (as did her newspaper), and some coaches criticized Gundy for his emotional outburst, he explained his response this way: "I got louder as the rant went on because it continued to go through my mind that this player had been attacked through the media . . . , and that really disturbed me" (p. C17). Many OSU fans were supportive of Gundy. According to OSU's AD for media relations, Kevin Klintworth, fewer than 5 percent of the 3,000 e-mails the school received concerning the event were negative. Klintworth commented that many approved of Gundy's "standing up to the media." The publicity from the event was substantial. The video from the press conference was one of the most viewed on the website YouTube that month, and "I'm a man! I'm 40!" t-shirts were the rage in and around the Stillwater campus. Several recruits also were impressed with Gundy's public defense of his player. Said one: "I like that in a coach. He stood up for his players. He cares for them and not just himself" (p. C17). Even though Gundy may have damaged his relationship with segments of the local media, the outburst may have derived benefits with other stakeholder groups.

Graduate assistant coaches

Coaches face similarly demanding schedules as the time and energy commitments expected of student-athletes. But even more taxing schedules are demanded of graduate assistant coaches (a.k.a., grad assistants, or GAs), the young men and women trying to break into the profession as full-time employees. Consider the experiences of two grad assistant football coaches, Kevin Daft and Bert Watts, at the University of California, Berkeley (Cal), a public school with 25,000 undergraduates and a member of the Division I Pac-10 Conference. Daft played quarterback and majored in biology at the University of California, Davis, and was the third-string QB for the NFL's Tennessee Titans during its 1999 Super Bowl season. Watts, a Cal alumnus, was an American Studies major and a starting safety who led the team in tackles his senior year; he had been cut from the Oakland Raiders during the preseason training.

According to head coach Jeff Tedford, grad assistants "do so much behind-the-scenes work. It's not a glamorous job. It's a lot of hard work without a lot of recognition" (Whiteside, 2004, p. 1C). But it's a common step on the coaching ladder, as eight of Cal's 10 full-time football coaches began as grad assistants and a majority of the head coaches across the country did the same. Each got the post through his network of contacts as the positions never were advertised to outside applicants. Watts was a former player for Tedford, and Daft knew a previous Cal GA. As compensation, the graduate school tuition was paid for each.

So what do the GAs do during their 100-hour-a-week job? Unlike other schools, where GAs pick up a coach's coffee or dry cleaning, or wake up players so they make it to class, head coach Tedford says the GAs serve critical roles that can help them further their careers. Although not part of a written position description, the specific tasks for which Daft and Watts are responsible include the following (Whiteside, 2004):

- Give the equipment manager the uniform numbers of each week's opponents to prepare practice jerseys for scout teams.
- Revise the week's master game plan when changes are made (each plan goes through approximately 50 revisions each week; a typical offensive game plan at Cal includes 80 plays).
- Meet with groups of players three times each week to check on academic progress.
- Break down each opponent's game films and prepare charts listing tendencies and key personnel.
- Coach the scout teams in practice.
- During games, work with position coaches and coordinators to recognize defensive and offensive alignments.
- Help grade player performance after each game.
- Transport prospects to and from the airport during recruiting visits.
- Attend master's degree courses.

Like the full-time coaches, Daft and Watts usually sleep on air mattresses in their offices four nights a week, and because the football offices are in the same building as the game and practice facilities, they don't leave the building during the week. Says Watts, "We haven't had a day off in three months, but we're totally having fun" (Whiteside, 2004, p. 5C).

Athletic directors

Although we have discussed some of the roles, responsibilities, and perspectives of ADs thus far, here we will examine in greater detail the specific tasks, duties, and qualifications required of those who hold these positions, to understand more clearly the professional preparation and performance required of these managers.

Position description

As we learned above, the position description "plays a major role in shaping the staffing, training and development, performance evaluation, and compensation elements" of the HR management process (Covell et al., 2007, p. 320). In terms of job characteristics for an athletic director, each school and department must consider which characteristics are necessary for each position. Drew University, a private school of 1,700 students located in Madison, New Jersey, and a member of the recently founded Division III Landmark Conference, posted a vacancy for athletic director. Among the responsibilities listed for the job were the following (Drew University, 2008):

- Provide leadership to the school's 18 varsity sports teams.
- Responsible for strategic planning, program management, budgeting, personnel and student-athlete development, and staffing decisions.
- Supervise the Associate Director, the Assistant Director, and the Facilities Director, each of whom are also head coaches.
- Supervise 11 other head coaches (eight full-time, three part-time), two certified athletic trainers, an equipment manager, and an administrative assistant.
- Embrace leadership opportunities in the Landmark Conference.
- Work closely with the offices of student affairs, alumni and development, and admissions.

The skills and qualifications required of candidates included the following:

- The ability to articulate and to support an institutional philosophy that clearly demonstrates the integration of academics and athletics.
- A demonstrated commitment to the objectives of the Landmark Conference, including the centrality of the academic mission and the value of ethnic, cultural, and gender diversity.
- Master's degree in sport management, physical education, or a related field.
- Five years' experience in athletics administration, with preference given to candidates with Division III experience.
- Significant coaching experience at the college level a plus.
- Excellent interpersonal, leadership, and communications skills.

The above position description outlines the responsibilities, skills, and qualifications deemed vital at a Division III institution. At Division I and II schools, position descriptions vary to include other sorts of key responsibilities and skills.

A posting at Florida Gulf Coast University (FGCU), a public school with 9,500 undergraduates located in Fort Myers and a member of the Division I Atlantic Sun Conference, provides an example of skills and qualifications for a D-I AD at a program that made the move from Division II. The description states that the school is seeking "an energetic, visionary, and strong leader with proven strategic planning ability," who is also "both an innovator and an entrepreneur . . . who fully appreciates the concept of the student-athlete within a rising Division I context . . . and will continue to manage, build and promote a high-quality athletics program" (Florida Gulf Coast University, 2009).

The AD reports directly to the school president, and has direct oversight for all of the following departmental activities and functions: student-athlete recruiting; student-athlete health and academic performance; hiring, development and retention of coaches and staff. Specific duties include personnel and program administration, marketing, fundraising, budgeting, and public relations, as well as responsibilities in purchasing equipment and supplies, contest scheduling, and event management. The AD is also required to coordinate with nonathletic campus personnel in these areas as well. Minimum qualifications include a bachelor's degree and eight years of "successful" administrative experience in a collegiate or professional athletic organization, or a master's degree and six years of experience as outlined above (Florida Gulf Coast University, 2009).

Specific tasks and responsibilities for a Division II program are outlined in the posting for an athletic director at Armstrong Atlantic State University, a public school with 6,000 undergraduates located in Savannah, Georgia, and a member of the Peach Belt Conference. The posting, advertised on the job search page of the NCAA's website, stated that the AD position is responsible for the overall leadership, administration, and management of the 10-team intercollegiate athletic program, and reports directly to the school's president. Requirements for consideration include the following (Armstrong Atlantic, 2008):

- A minimum of a Master's degree in a related field.
- "Extensive, related and progressive" administrative experience.
- Working knowledge of applicable NCAA guidelines and federal regulations.
- Knowledge of the "opportunities and challenges" of administering a Division II program.
- A proven ability to "work and lead effectively and respectfully in a culturally diverse and ethnically rich environment."
- Proven record to fundraise successfully and "develop entrepreneurial involvement."
- Proven ability in the effective hiring, supervision, and evaluation of personnel, including a demonstrated commitment to equal employment opportunity and affirmative action.
- Administrative experience at the NCAA Division II level.

These descriptions detail what tasks ADs need to perform, and each also refers to the concept of providing leadership. Although a candidate can show the ability to prepare a budget and knowledge of NCAA guidelines, demonstrating the ability to lead can be more challenging. Still, the ability to lead and to provide vision are what most athletic departments are seeking above all.

Providing visionary leadership

In 2007, *Street & Smith's SportsBusiness Journal*, a respected trade publication covering issues pertinent to sport managers in all industry segments, tabbed Tom Jurich, vice president for athletics and director of athletics at the University of Louisville (Kentucky) (UL), a public school with 15,100 undergraduates and a member of the Division I Big East Conference, as its annual Athletic Director of the Year. According to UL's associate AD and senior woman administrator, Julie Hermann, Jurich is like a rock star around the city. "Going anywhere with Tom is a nightmare. He gets mobbed" (Nethery, 2007, p.1). Jim Patterson, a prominent Louisville businessman and founder of the Long John Silver's seafood restaurant chain and a major donor to UL athletics, commented that when Jurich came to the school in 1997, "The best thing that's ever happened to the University of Louisville is Tom Jurich" (p. 17).

Jurich had come to UL from a similar position at Colorado State University, a member of the Division I Mountain West Conference. Previous to his stint at Colorado State, Jurich had served for eight years as AD at Northern Arizona University, his alma mater, where he had been a first team All-American kicker on the football team. The school of 21,500 undergrads, located in Flagstaff, is a member of the Division I Big Sky Conference. Jurich had been named to the post at age 29, which at the time made him the youngest D-I AD. His contract runs through 2017, and pays $500,000 a year plus retention and performance bonuses (Nethery, 2007).

How did the AD position evolve so those in the position such as Jurich could achieve such status? The model for the contemporary AD as visionary leader has evolved over the last several decades, but many agree that the job template was first established by former University of Michigan AD Don Canham. He had been the school's men's track and field coach before taking over as AD in 1968, and at the time had built an eponymous company that sold video, athletic, and educational materials valued at $5 million. According to author Michael Rosenberg, Canham "loved unconventional marketing" and was "a born salesman," as evidenced by his entrepreneurial activities as a Michigan undergrad in the early 1940s, when he bought used sweatsocks for 8 cents a pair, then resold them for a quarter. As summarized by Rosenberg (2008), "a man who has sold used socks for a 200 percent profit tends to feel he can sell anything" (pp. 25–26).

To sell out the school's 1969 home game against Big Ten conference rival Ohio State (after the 1967 game had been played in front of 37,000 empty seats at 101,001-seat Michigan Stadium, Canham took out ads in Ohio newspapers to sell 25,000 tickets to Ohio State fans. He also understood the basic sport marketing precept that the results of games and game quality couldn't be guaranteed. "Until we start planting shrubs (in the stadium)," he said, "we're going to have to fill seats" (Rosenberg, 2008, p. 45). This was a particularly daunting challenge in the late 1960s, with an inventory of more than 100,000 seats and a less-than-stellar program under then new head coach Glenn Edward "Bo" Schembechler II. So Canham created advertising campaigns early in his tenure that emphasized the game day experience, including the at the time-novel concept of tailgating. And unlike most of his peers, Canham embraced the concept of televising football games and making the game broadcasts as appealing as possible to engage casual fans. This approach meshed well with the ideas of ABC Sports president Roone Arledge, who was seeking to do the same with college football broadcasts around the country. Arledge would go on to make groundbreaking efforts with the creation of the National Football League's "Monday Night Football," and with techniques implemented in numerous Olympic Games broadcasts (Rosenberg, 2008).

Canham brought creativity to facilities management as well, as evidenced by replacing the grass surface in Michigan Stadium with a new artificial playing surface called "Tartan Turf," a material then perceived to be superior to grass. The new surface did save $10,000 in annual maintenance costs, and Canham donated the old sod to a local Catholic church so he didn't have to pay to have it taken away. Canham was also one of the first ADs to capitalize on the nascent market for licensed products. After he had been on a track team road trip to the University of California, Los Angeles, he noticed that the UCLA bookstore was full of pennants, sweatshirts, and other apparel and products. He discovered that the bookstore, rather than the UCLA athletic department, had control of the licensing agreements and revenues (see Chapter 6). When he became AD at Michigan, he came up with several logos and word marks while sitting at his kitchen table, and he put the athletic department into the licensing business with exceptional returns.

Canham also worked with local media outlets to produce books and TV shows involving Schembechler to supplement the coach's compensation, as well as create additional publicity for the football program and the school. He also scheduled an NFL preseason game between the then-Baltimore Colts and the Detroit Lions at Michigan Stadium in August 1971. Through his efforts, the game drew a crowd of 92,000, netting the athletic department a $300,000 profit and allowing Canham to tap into a new market of potential ticket buyers for Michigan football. Canham also can be credited with renewing the practice of the guarantee game (which allows home teams to pay an opponent a set amount for appearing rather than a 50/50 split of all tickets sold), when he convinced University of Notre Dame AD Ed "Moose" Krause to renew the football series between the schools in 1978. The guarantee system allowed Canham to keep more revenue (Rosenberg, 2008). The guarantee system is now the norm, particularly for non-conference matchups.

Through Canham's efforts, by the mid-1970s, alumni gifts to the Michigan athletic department had gone from $46,000 annually to $300,000, the athletic department was making $100,000 a year from parking revenues alone, all home football games were sold out, and administrators from 28 other schools had contacted Canham for his advice on replicating his efforts on their campuses. During his tenure, Michigan's athletic department budget grew from $2 million in 1968 to $16 million in 1986. At his core, however, Canham was a fiscal realist who doubted the rationale of any school offering a full grant-in-aid for student-athletes in sports that generated no revenue, and he opposed the application of Title IX guidelines (see Chapter 11) on the same grounds. Canham was less than progressive in his approach to gender equity, but he was one of the first to envision the true financial power of cable television, as he was quoted in 1979—the same year that ESPN was launched—that "cable television has more potential than anyone has had a chance to think about" (Rosenberg, 2008, p. 310).

Canham was years ahead of his peers in terms of marketing, and he also knew the importance of staffing. When Canham hired Bo Schembechler away from Miami (Ohio) University to be his head football coach in 1968 (at a salary of $21,000), Canham liked the coach because he was a tireless worker and "a details man," with every assistant coach given specific responsibilities and every meeting beginning 5 minutes ahead of schedule. Canham also knew that his own future was tied to the success of the football program. He told Schembechler and his staff upon their appointments that they probably had five years to build a consistent winner, and if they didn't, all of them, Canham included, would be fired (Rosenberg, 2008).

Working with coaches

The AD position descriptions we looked at earlier reveal the importance placed on HR management for ADs at each of the NCAA divisional classification levels. Chief among the HR responsibilities are those involved in working with coaches.

Staffing. Many attribute the ability of the University of Louisville's Tom Jurich to establish an expectation of high performance to his efforts in HR planning and staffing, most notably in his ability to entice noted men's basketball coach Rick Pitino to come to UL in 2001. After the retirement of UL's longtime head men's basketball coach Denzil "Denny" Crum, Jurich publicly announced that Pitino was his choice to replace Crum. Pitino, who was watching the televised press conference at which Jurich made this announcement, said he was so surprised that "my wife and I almost fell off our couch" (Nethery, 2007, p. 17). Pitino had his doubts when he met with Jurich, stating, "This can't work . . . the (former) head coach of Kentucky can't become the head coach of Louisville." Pitino had served as the head men's hoop coach at UL's in-state rival from 1989 to 1997, winning the 1996 NCAA championship before leaving for an unsuccessful stint as head coach for the NBA's Boston Celtics. Jurich persisted, however, and convinced Pitino to visit the UL campus.

Crum had had a storied career, having been an assistant to the legendary John Wooden at UCLA in the 1960s. His 1979–80 and 1985–86 UL teams won the NCAA championship, he had compiled a career record of 675 wins and 295 losses, and he had been inducted into the Naismith Basketball Hall of Fame in 1994. Crum hadn't wanted to retire but was eased out of the job by Jurich and later publicly supported Pitino to replace him. Pitino agreed to take the job shortly thereafter, after turning down a similar offer from the University of Michigan. Of his facility with HR planning and staffing issues, associate AD Julie Hermann noted, "He has an amazing ability to assess people and to know which ones would be right for our needs" (Nethery, 2007, p. 23).

An incident involving Pitino, however, challenged Jurich's ability to manage staffing concerns. In 2009 Pitino was implicated in a salacious scandal in which he admitted to having had what he called "consensual sex" (extramarital nonetheless) with a woman in 2003 who later sought to extort $10 million from Pitino to keep quiet about the affair. Later it was revealed that Pitino gave the woman $3,000 after she claimed she was pregnant and was seeking an abortion. The woman later married the UL strength coach and alleged that Pitino pressured the coach into the marriage. They have since divorced. The scandal brought significant negative attention to the school and the program, which has been magnified by Pitino's very public avowal to the tenets of Catholicism. Indeed, a Catholic priest sits on the UL bench during games, even though UL is a public, non-denominational institution. In spite of the attention, Jurich stated publicly that he would not fire the coach and was behind Pitino "a million percent," but he acknowledged, "Right now there is a stain, no question about it" (Layden & Torre, 2009, p. 42).

Other staffing challenges that Jurich faced involved improving the football team. One of his first moves as AD was to fire head football coach Ron Cooper, who had gone 13–20 in three seasons. Jurich then hired John L. Smith, who took a program that had been 1–10 in the previous season and went 7–5 in his first year, starting a string of nine straight bowl appearances. When Smith left for Michigan

State University in 2003, Jurich hired Bobby Petrino, but Petrino left for the NFL's Atlanta Falcons after leading UL to a win in the 2007 Orange Bowl. Jurich knew he had to hire the right person to keep recruits and current players at the school, so he hired Steve Kragthorpe, whom Jurich had known from his time at Northern Arizona, where Kragthorpe had been an assistant football coach. Kragthorpe had turned around the program at the University of Tulsa (a member of Division I Conference USA) while he was head coach there. Kragthorpe regarded Jurich so highly that he said, "I would have gone to work for [him] if he had been athletic director at the University of Siberia" (Nethery, 2007, p. 24). However, Jurich fired Kragthorpe following the 2009 season after a three-season record of 15–21. Said Jurich of the move: "I don't think there was any one thing. . . . I thought we could get through the year and really build some momentum, but obviously that didn't happen" (Brown, 2009, p. 1). Jurich said the school would honor the remaining two years of Kragthorpe's contract, which was set to pay him about $1.2 million a year. Jurich then replaced Kragthorpe with former University of Florida defensive coordinator Charlie Strong.

In many cases, the staffing process for identifying and hiring coaches is aided through outside consultants, or "headhunters." One such consultant is Chuck Neinas, who has worked in various intercollegiate athletic management capacities, including former NCAA assistant executive director, commissioner of the Big 8 (now Big 12), and executive director of the now-defunct College Football Association, which negotiated TV contracts for several Division I conferences following dissolution of the NCAA's control over the awarding of college football TV broadcast rights (see Chapter 1). Neinas now serves as a middleman between ADs and college coaches, handling head football coach searches at Michigan State University, North Carolina State University, the University of Miami, and the University of North Carolina. He also ran searches that ended in the hiring of Mack Brown at the University of Texas, Bob Stoops at the University of Oklahoma, and Les Miles at both Oklahoma State and Louisiana State University (McCarthy, 2006).

Schools hire Neinas to find qualified candidates for an opening, and routinely pay between $30,000 and $40,000 (plus expenses) for his services. Once hired, Neinas asks the client AD to fill out a nine-part questionnaire to determine the type of candidate the school prefers. Neinas then contacts potential candidates on a confidential basis to gauge interest. He alerts his client verbally (never written), because he says the media are "too snoopy." This also protects Neinas from the open records laws in many states, which requires state-funded organizations, such as state universities, to make their documents available to any citizen who requests them, including representatives of the media (McCarthy, 2006, p. 3C).

Many ADs say that Neinas' working outside of such regulations accelerates the process and keeps it confidential, thereby allowing him to work behind the scenes and pursue the head coach of a conference foe. Once contacts have been made, ADs and presidents usually handle contract negotiations (with agents—see Chapter 6). However, a major criticism of using a headhunter like Neinas is that he is a part of the "old boy" network within intercollegiate athletics and has done little to advance minority candidates for positions (McCarthy, 2006; Thamel, 2008).

Compensation challenges. The next element that ADs must consider when hiring new coaches is often the compensation component of athletic HR management.

According to Covell et al. (2007), compensation ultimately is defined as "the re-wards individuals receive for performing the work of the organization" (p. 337). The salaries of coaches of D-I Bowl Subdivision programs will be examined closely in the next chapter. Although base salary and other cash bonuses are no doubt the most emphasized part of compensation packages, Covell et al. note that "the challenge for sport organizations is to design a total compensation system that allows the organization to attract and retain individuals with the skills and qualifications it needs to be successful, supports a high level of work performance for its members, and allows the organization to remain viable into the future" (p. 337).

In the next chapter we discuss some of the contract elements that Bowl Subdivision head coaches have been able to secure, and ADs have had to be innovative with compensation for other coaches as well. Consider the actions of Stanford University, a private school with 15,000 undergraduates located in Palo Alto, California, and member of the D-I Pac-10 Conference. In his efforts to entice top assistant coaches for the school's football program, AD Bob Bowlsby, who came to the school from the University of Iowa in 2006, was challenged by the sky-high housing prices in Palo Alto (which has the highest real estate prices of all the towns and cities in which Bowl Subdivision programs are located) and the surrounding San Francisco Bay area (Thamel, 2007).

When Scott Shafer came to interview for the football defensive coordinator's position, he was excited for the opportunity, then learned about home prices from his dejected wife, who had spent time viewing real estate. A house similar to the one the Shafers just built in Kalamazoo, Michigan (at a cost of $240,000), where Shafer worked as defensive coordinator for Western Michigan University, would run nearly $2 million in the Palo Alto area. To make the deal work, Stanford purchased a $2 million home for the Shafers 3 miles from the campus. The school did the same for David Shaw, the new offensive coordinator (coordinators receive about $200,000 in annual salary), and the rest of the football staff received a $3,000-a-month housing stipend. Under the initiative, backed in part by billionaire booster John Arrillaga, the school has purchased six residences and could buy as many as 40 homes and apartments so coaches can live close to campus and be able to spend less time commuting and more time with their families.

Bowlsby himself experienced similar sticker shock when he and his wife came from Iowa. Jack Harbaugh, whose son Jim is Stanford's head football coach, coached at Stanford in the 1980s, and the university helped pay his $200,000 mortgage. Bowlsby also commented that high real estate prices had been hurting the school's ability to attract and to retain coaches: "We found that people came here and didn't stay," he said, and "more often than not, they didn't come at all once they looked at housing" (Thamel, 2007, p. 8-7). Now able to afford housing in Palo Alto, coaches' families are able to take advantage of the benefits the community has to offer.

Termination. Every coaching hire by an athletic department means that a vacancy is being filled, usually because a coach has been terminated. Termination, which may occur for various reasons, is a decision that should be based on a job performance evaluation in light of a coach's position description. In some cases, the termination may result from a team's win-loss record, even though job descriptions rarely refer to such requirements in such specific terms. In other instances, the termination may come after a coach violates an NCAA bylaw in the course of his or her duties, often in the area of recruiting. Bylaw 11.2.1 of the *Division I Manual* stipulates that contract terms between coaches and institutions require that a coach found to be in violation of NCAA regulations "shall be subject to disciplinary or corrective action as set forth in the provisions of the NCAA enforcement procedures, including suspension without pay or termination of employment for significant or repetitive violations" (*2008–09 NCAA Division I Manual*, 2008, p. 51).

Such was the case at Indiana University (IU), a public school with 30,000 undergraduates located in Bloomington, and a member of the Division I Big Ten Conference, which accepted the resignation of head men's basketball coach Kelvin Sampson midway through the 2007–08 season. Sampson had been hired only two years before to replace Mike Davis, who had been an assistant to notorious former head coach Bob Knight. Knight was fired in September 2000 by then IU president (and former NCAA president) Myles Brand after a series of on- and off-court transgressions (none of which was related to NCAA rules violations).

Sampson had been head coach at Oklahoma since 1994, where his teams had averaged 23 wins a year but its graduation rate ranked 267th out of 317 schools. Sampson also had been penalized by the NCAA enforcement staff for making 577 impermissible phone calls between 2000 and 2004 while he was at Oklahoma. IU had hired Sampson with full knowledge of the violations and that the NCAA sanctions would follow him to Bloomington. Within two months of his hiring, Sampson was banned from recruiting off-campus and from making calls to recruits for one year. Many of IU's former players decried the move, including Kent Benson, the center on the 1975–76 team (the last D-I men's team to go through a season undefeated), who turned in his season tickets in protest. Other fans were less concerned, as evidenced by the posting on a popular Indiana basketball fan's website: "Graduation rates don't win basketball games" (Wertheim, 2008, p. 59).

In February 2008, IU received a letter from the NCAA enforcement staff detailing allegations of five major violations committed at IU by Sampson and his staff involving improper phone calls to recruits. Some of these included three-way calls involving recruits and an assistant coach on a cellphone issued to Sampson (which IU had self-reported the previous autumn). These offenses were the same in nature as those that Sampson committed while at Oklahoma, which were judged to be major in nature. IU AD Rick Greenspan said he had hoped that Sampson's latest actions would be judged as secondary (see Chapter 8) but nonetheless fired assistant coach Rob Senderoff, who had participated in the three-way calls. Sampson denied the latest violations, claiming that he didn't know he was being patched into the three-way calls. He also denied the claim that he lied to IU and NCAA staffers, stating: "I have never intentionally provided false or misleading information to the NCAA" (NCAA Report, 2008, p. 1). Nonetheless, IU president Michael McRobbie announced publicly that the school would enact its own investigation, and hired an Indianapolis law firm to conduct it, to decide on Sampson's future. The probe uncovered more than 100 additional impermissible calls, for which Sampson had agreed to forfeit a raise of $500,000. The school also self-penalized by forfeiting one basketball grant-in-aid for the 2008–09 season (Wertheim, 2008; Wieberg, 2008).

The situation was complicated because IU players threatened to quit if Sampson were fired. In addition, there were reports of player misconduct and marijuana use throughout the team, and the team's GPA had fallen to 2.13 during the previous semester—with an accumulated 19 grades of "F"—and players skipped classes regularly. On February 22, 2008, Sampson agreed to a $750,000 buyout of the five remaining years on his contract (which had a base salary of $550,000), in large part paid for by an anonymous booster donation of $550,000. As a condition of accepting the buyout, Sampson waived his right to sue IU for wrongful termination. In the aftermath, some were critical of the decision to hire Sampson given the infractions he had committed during his 12-year tenure at Oklahoma. IU trustee Phillip Eskew Jr. commented: "In retrospect, I think there should have been greater consideration" (Indiana's Sampson Agrees, 2008, p. 1). In response, Sampson released a written statement through the university that read in part: "While I'm saddened that I will not have the opportunity to coach these student-athletes, I feel that it is in the best interest of the program for me to step away at this time" (p. 1).

Assistant coach (and former IU guard) Dan Dakich took over to lead the then-15th-ranked Hoosiers for the rest of the season, even though all but five players (who had lobbied AD Greenspan to hire assistant Ray McCallum instead) boycotted Dakich's first practice. Dakich finished the year but was not named as the permanent replacement. Sampson reemerged as an assistant coach with the NBA's Milwaukee Bucks. IU used headhunter, and former D-I head men's basketball coach, Eddie Fogler to contact Tom Crean, head coach at Marquette University, a Catholic, Jesuit-affiliated school with 8,000 undergraduates located (ironically) in Milwaukee, Wisconsin, and a member of the D-I Big East Conference (Longman, 2008; Wahl, 2008). Crean took the job and said of his decision: "I didn't take this job for the immediate. . . . I look at this for where it's been and where it can possibly go" (Wertheim, 2008, p. 63).

As a result of Sampson's actions, the NCAA's Division I Committee on Infractions placed IU on probation for three years, stating that the school had exhibited a failure to monitor the men's basketball program, and instituted a five-year "show-cause order" for hiring Sampson. This means that any NCAA member school must get permission from the NCAA and would face recruiting restrictions through 2013. Senderoff, who subsequently was hired as an associate head coach at Kent (Ohio) State University, a public school with 30,000 undergraduates and a member of the Division I Mid-American Conference, received a three-year show-cause order. As a result of these developments, IU AD Greenspan announced his resignation in June 2008, effective at the end of the year (Wiedeman, 2008).

Diversity staffing

Previously we discussed the role and importance of coaches and athletic directors in promoting departmental and programmatic performance, and the issues pertaining to position descriptions and job qualifications. In many position descriptions the issue of gender, racial, and ethnic diversity is identified as important to candidate qualifications. But why is this a factor impacting HR management for intercollegiate athletic organizations? According to Covell et al. (2007), the American workforce and organizations are becoming more diverse and will continue on this trend, and that this growing diversity "represents a challenge as well as a special opportunity" (p. 71). Nonetheless, many sport organizations, including intercollegiate athletic departments, have been criticized for lack of commitment to diversity in hiring by staffing departments or coaching staffs that do not reflect team roster racial or sexual composition.

Consider the following data on diversity staffing in intercollegiate football programs:

- In 2006, of the 616 NCAA-affiliated football programs, only 16 (2.6 percent) had African-American head coaches, even though more than 32 percent of football student-athletes were African-American (Hohler, 2006).

- At the 120 Bowl Subdivision programs, where 50 percent of student-athletes were African-American, as of late 2009 only 12 head coaches were African-American, and one Division II head coach was African-American (Thamel, 2008; Wieberg, 2009).

- In 2008, only 9.2 percent of the ADs (and 2.5 percent of school presidents) at Bowl Subdivision schools were African-American (Thamel, 2008).

Additional issues involve hiring of same-sex coaches in certain women's sports, such as ice hockey, where data revealed that as more programs were added at colleges and universities (approaching 80) fewer and fewer of these teams (30 percent) had female head coaches (Matson, 2004). Also, there are stark differences in salaries for female head ice hockey coaches versus their male colleagues. At the University of Maine, a school with 10,000 undergraduates located in Orono, and a member of the D-I America East Conference (and Hockey East for men's and women's ice hockey, and the Colonial Athletic Association for football) the head women's coach was paid $39,128, while the second assistant for the men's team made $44,000, though both have the same years of experience (Matson, 2004). The diversity situation is as bleak for ADs. Data have revealed 10 African-American ADs, three Latino male ADs, and one female AD at schools with Bowl Subdivision football programs (Brady, 2006). By comparison, diversity hiring in D-I men's basketball has been more successful, where in 2008, 28.5 percent of programs were led by African-American head coaches (Thamel, 2008).

The continuing racial inequities in football hiring were highlighted in December 2008 when Auburn (Alabama) University, a public school with 20,000 undergraduates and a member of the Division I Southeastern Conference, accepted the resignation of head football coach Tommy Tuberville after his team completed a 5–7 season. Tuberville's mother told a local newspaper that her son was fired because he was tired of fighting against the significant influence of boosters in the athletic department. In response, the school gave him a buyout of $5.1 million, even though he had won nearly 90 games in 10 years (Glier, 2008).

The termination of Tuberville, a Caucasian, was surprising and unfortunate, but the hiring of his replacement, Gene Chizik, also a Caucasian, who was head coach at Iowa State University and a former defensive coordinator for Tuberville at Auburn, was what spurred national interest. The choice of Chizik became controversial because in his two years as head coach at Iowa State, his teams had won only 5 of 24 games and had lost 10 straight, including games to Kent State, the University of Toledo, and Championship Subdivision member the University of Northern Iowa. Many observers thought Auburn would turn to Turner Gill, former standout quarterback at the University of Nebraska (where he was 28–2 as a starter) and former head coach at the University at Buffalo (New York), a public school with 28,000 undergraduates and a member of the D-I Mid-American Conference. Before Gill, the Buffalo program had never won more than five games in a season and was 1–10 the year before Gill took over in 2006 after 13 years as an assistant at his alma mater—during which time the Cornhuskers team was national champion three times. Gill had just led the Bulls to an 8–5 record and to its first conference title and a birth in the International Bowl, the school's first ever bowl appearance. The school had turned down its only other bowl bid—to the Tangerine [now Capital One] Bowl in 1958—by a vote of the team because the leaseholder on the Orlando, Florida, facility in which the game was to be played banned interracial competitions and the team had two African-American players who would not have been able to play (Dupont, 2008).

Former NBA star and later TV commentator Charles Barkley (an Auburn alumnus) stated publicly that Gill should have been hired over Chizik based on a comparison of their records, and that Gill was not hired because he is African-American. Others speculated that Gill was passed over because his wife is Caucasian. Auburn AD Jay Jacobs defended the hiring of Chizik: "I was picking the best fit for Auburn. . . . I interviewed nine guys in seven days. I knew what I was looking for. . . . I played football here. I knew better than anyone else what we needed" (Glier, 2009, p. B10; Thamel, 2008, p. Y10). Chizik signed a five-year deal worth about $2 million a year (almost double his compensation at Iowa State). Barkley later reported that Gill, who had interviewed for the Auburn job, believed that it had been a courtesy interview and that Auburn had no real interest in hiring him (Chizik, 2008, p. C6; Glier, 2008; Smith, 2009).

Floyd Keith, executive director of Black Coaches & Administrators (BCA), a private nonprofit organization with a primary purpose "to foster the growth and development of ethnic minorities at all levels of sport both nationally and internationally" (About the Black Coaches, 2009, p. 1), described the hiring of Chizik this way: "When the door gets shut and the people who make the decisions are sitting around looking at each other, most of the time there's not a person sitting there who looks like me" (Thamel, 2008, p. Y10).

The NCAA and various conferences have developed programs to help prepare African-American assistants for head jobs, and several organizations are diligent in reporting the data on staffing, but these efforts have not yielded results. The data also show that the few African-American coaches who do get a chance at head positions will have precious little time to be successful, and they don't get another chance if they are fired. Said former Mississippi State University head football coach Sylvester Croom (the first African-American head football coach in the Southeastern Conference), who resigned in mid-season 2008: "I never anticipated getting but one shot. That's the reality of the times" (Thamel, 2008, p. Y10). Paul Hewitt, president of the BCA, suggested that recruits should consider diversity issues as part of the recruiting process: "If the top five defensive linemen and the top five offensive linemen in the country went to play for (African-American head coach) Randy Shannon at Miami and they won a national championship in two years, watch how fast this thing would change" (Smith, 2009, p. 14). Interestingly, heading into the 2009–10 academic year, the University of Buffalo is the only Division I Bowl Subdivision school with an African-American AD (Warde Manual), head men's basketball coach (Reggie Witherspoon), and head football coach (Gill). After these events, Buffalo gave Gill a raise and contract extension, but he left for a new head coaching job, at the University of Kansas, after the 2009 season.

Which human resource management techniques can intercollegiate athletic managers adopt to address the challenge of diversity staffing? Managers must be aware of Title VII of the Civil Rights Act of 1964, which forbids any organization from refusing to hire, train, promote, or transfer personnel based on sex, race, color, religion, or national origin. Thus, selections and all other employment-related decisions must be made on the basis of objective standards, such as actual requirements of the job indicated in a position description (Covell et al., 2007). When Auburn AD Jay Jacobs said that his new head football coach was "the best fit for Auburn," this statement would have to be defensible based on how the chosen candidate's qualifications matched those outlined in the position description.

In addition, Rice (1994) provides specific guidelines for promoting diversity in all organizations, including getting the CEO's commitment, setting specific diversity goals, adopting a plan for addressing the concerns of White men, and providing training in valuing diversity—carefully. In terms of CEO commitments, this refers to school presidents or chancellors. Presidents and ADs then could set diversity goals for staffing of future head and assistant coaching positions by a certain future date. If such a goal is set, however, current coaches, many of whom are probably Caucasian males based on the data outlined previously, likely will feel as if their positions will be threatened. As a result, presidents and ADs have to communicate to these threatened parties why diversity staffing makes sense for intercollegiate athletic departments, in part because diversity is seen as a special opportunity to help the athletic department staffing mirror the composition of the stakeholder base, allowing the department to meet more effectively the expectations of the groups that comprise the base, which in turn will promote organizational effectiveness. The final guideline—providing training in valuing diversity—can be difficult, as in some cases it seeks to allow staff members to experience what it is like to be a minority without seeming to point a finger of blame at non-minority participants.

Managing the impact of boosters on human resource management

We have learned that ADs are responsible for managing and evaluating athletic department personnel. Further, the significant interest in intercollegiate athletics by other stakeholder groups means that ADs must manage the actions of individuals outside of their departments. In the next chapter and in Chapter 11 we will discuss the impact of boosters and other interested parties in raising the funds necessary to operate intercollegiate athletic departments. Although the revenues generated from these sources are critical in promoting organizational performance, accepting gifts and donations has hidden costs. In the case of Oklahoma State University (OSU), this means that billionaire and longtime donor T. Boone Pickens is given a say in departmental coaching personnel decisions. In 2008, Pickens, who made his money in oil and later in investments, gave the school $165 million to be used for athletic facilities. The donation reportedly prompted the school's AD, Mike Holder, to pursue Bill Self, a former OSU hoops player who had just led conference rival University of Kansas to the NCAA Division I men's basketball title, to fill the vacant head coaching position at OSU. When asked about the OSU overture, Self, who decided to stay at Kansas, commented, "From the outside looking in, it appears they have great resources" (Brady, 2008b, p. 11). This caused reporters to break into laughter. When apprised of Self's comment, a spokesman for Pickens replied, also with a laugh, "I wonder who he was talking about."

Pickens himself had commented in 2006 that "with a gift like that, of course they're going to be respectful, and I'm going to be asked my opinion on things" (p. 11). In a follow-up to the Self comment, the Pickens spokesperson added, "It's very simple. Does Boone want the school to be competitive in athletics? Sure. Is he willing to help make that happen? Sure. . . . Does he exert undue influence? No" (p. 11).

Many expert opinions indicate that monetary donations come with a measure of power and influence. Sheldon Steinbach, former general council of the American Council on Education (ACE), a professional organization for college presidents and chancellors, described these types of situations: "It is not beyond any understanding that individual donors to an athletics program would be given greater than equal weight to their voice" (Brady, 2008a, p. 11). Gene Marsh, a law professor at the University of Alabama and member of the Division I Committee on Infractions (see Chapter 8), says that donors like Pickens are preferable to "the flatly illegal" actions of those who have given money directly to student-athletes, damaging their amateur status (p. 11). After Self turned down OSU, the school hired University of Massachusetts head coach Travis Ford to replace the fired Scott Sutton, who himself had been an OSU hoop standout as well as the son of longtime OSU head men's basketball coach Eddie Sutton.

Other critical AD tasks

Although much of this chapter has been devoted to the HR aspects of an athletic director's job, we know, from our introduction to Don Canham at Michigan and Tom Jurich at Louisville, and the position descriptions for other AD openings, at Armstrong Atlantic State University, Drew University, and Florida Gulf Coast University, that ADs must perform additional critical tasks. One example is provided by Jeremy Foley, AD at the University of Florida, who has had to contend with the challenges brought on by the competitive successes of his men's basketball and football teams. Foley has sought to continue this success through construction of a $28 million football office and weight training facility, and the addition of a women's lacrosse program, scheduled to begin play in 2010. Foley also has had to increase the salaries of two of his prominent coaches (Billy Donovan, head men's basketball, and Urban Meyer, head football) so they will remain in Gainesville. "There's a lot of pressure on academic success, and financial challenges with coaching salaries will always be there" (Catching Up, 2007, p. 22), says Foley, who was named 2006 Division I AD by *Street & Smith's SportsBusiness Journal*. "Everybody worries about costs, but we have a responsibility to gauge the market and act accordingly. In order to stay competitive, you have to respond to the market" (Q: What Is the Most Pressing Issue, 2007, p. 22).

Foley's activities identify two key issues that we will highlight in the next chapter: the financial implications of coaches' salaries, and facility construction and upgrades. These activities also have been on the agenda for University of Kansas (KU) AD Lew Perkins, who has been at the school since 2003, having moved from a similar post at the University of Connecticut. A main focus of the strategic plan that Perkins created upon his arrival was to upgrade athletic facilities in all sports to the level of those at its Big 12 rivals. In 2006, KU completed a $20 million renovation of its basketball venue, Allen Fieldhouse, and a $36 million football complex was completed before the 2008 season. The school also put $2 million into renovating its softball facility and improved both the track and field and women's soccer venues. During Perkins's watch, the KU athletic budget has more than doubled, growing to $54 million from $23 million (Catching Up, 2007).

Eric Hyman, who left his AD post at Texas Christian University to move to the University of South Carolina in 2005, and DeLoss Dodds, AD at the University of Texas, also have been directing their time and energy to upgrading facilities. According to Hyman, whose teams must compete against national powers in the Southeastern Conference, "the presentation of our facilities has to make a quantum leap forward, and we're working on that" (Q: What Is, 2007, p. 22). But both Hyman and Dodds cite academic issues as another key area of concern. Said Hyman: "The cultural issue we all face is academic reform. It's something that's not going away. I said that nine years ago, and it's still the same today" (p. 22).

Assistant and associate athletic directors

As indicated in the AD position descriptions, each intercollegiate athletic department generally has several other administrative positions that report to the AD. These mid-level positions, referred to as assistant ADs or associate ADs, usually have direct responsibilities for organizational functional areas such as media relations, compliance, or facilities. Consider the example of Millersville (Pennsylvania) University, a public school with 7,200 undergraduates and a member of the D-II Pennsylvania State Athletic Conference, which posted vacancies for two associate athletic directors. An advertisement in the *Chronicle of Higher Education*, a publication geared toward examining managerial issues that impact American colleges and universities, which also publishes position vacancies in all areas of higher education, outlined the duties, skills, and required qualifications for each.

The first position, Coordinator of Compliance, is responsible for overseeing that the athletic department is in compliance with all NCAA and conference rules and institutional policies. In meeting this charge, this associate AD has to educate coaches, boosters, student-athletes, and a staff about these rules, and document that all rules are followed. The other position, Coordinator for Academics, monitors the academic performance of student-athletes, serves as a liaison for the department to the admissions office, and supervises the school's SAAC (see Chapter 9). Both positions also have responsibilities in supervising on-campus athletic contests, scheduling, and organizing team travel arrangements. Candidates for both positions in the ad were required to have a bachelor's degree, with at least two years' experience in intercollegiate athletic administration (preferably in a Division II setting), and preferably a master's degree. Candidates also must demonstrate experience in working with student-athletes, and in operating NCAA compliance software is preferred.

Additional departmental personnel designations

Article 4 of the NCAA Constitution is dedicated to organization of the NCAA's legislative process. Under this article, several designations impact the organization and staffing of individual athletic departments, specifically, the positions of Faculty Athletics Representative and Institutional Senior Woman Administrator

Faculty Athletics Representative: A member of an institution's faculty or administrative staff (who holds faculty rank and shall not hold an administrative or coaching position in the athletic department) who is designated by the institution's president or chancellor or other appropriate entity to represent the institution and its faculty in the institution's relationship with the NCAA and its conferences. Duties shall be determined by the member institution.

Institutional Senior Woman Administrator: The highest ranking female involved in the management of an institution's intercollegiate athletics program. An institution with a female director of athletics may designate a different female involved in the management of the institution's program

Source: 2008–09 NCAA Division I Manual, 2008.

(SWA). Bylaws 4.02.4 and 6.1.3 offer definitions for each of these positions (presented in Exhibit 5.2), which have designated roles on many NCAA committees (see Chapter 2). For example, for the 20-member Committee on Competitive Safeguards and Medical Aspects of Sports, a general Association-wide committee, Bylaw 21.2.2.1 specifies that at least five positions be allotted for men, and at least five for women. Additional membership standards stipulate that one member must be a female AD or SWA, one woman must be from the field of medicine (a primary care physician or orthopedic specialist), and one woman has to be responsible for the total athletics training program at a member institution (*2008–09 NCAA Division I Manual,* 2008).

Faculty athletics representative

In 2008, the NCAA Faculty Athletics Representatives Association (FARA) developed a statement of purpose, in conjunction with NCAA public relations staffers, to be "the official faculty voice ensuring balance between academics and athletics for the benefit of student-athletes." According to FARA president Alan Hauser, an associate professor in the Northwestern University Feinberg School of Medicine, "there are a lot of entities at work within intercollegiate athletics.... As FARs, we feel we should be the ones who are ensuring that our student-athletes have strong balance between what they do in athletics and their academic responsibilities as a student" (Hosick, 2008, p. 1). Hauser suggested that this purpose can be achieved by monitoring for effectiveness and appropriateness of specific operations on campuses, including the student-athlete admissions process, and the academic eligibility support of student-athletes. Overall, the FARA is seeking to highlight the role of FARs and the ways in which each can contribute to a positive experience for student-athletes, regardless of the divisional classification of a school's athletic program (Hosick, 2008).

Senior woman administrator

The actions of the senior woman administrator can differ from institution to institution. At the University of Tennessee, Joan Cronan serves in the capacity as the

Women's Athletic Director. In an interview for this textbook, we learned that she has significant responsibilities concerning HR management. According to Cronan, "The human resource element of our jobs is probably the most important area we have to address. The most important thing I get to do is hire the right people and make them happy and able to do their job the best they can. My definition is that an athletic director's job is to make the coach's job the best it can be to make the athlete's experience the best it can be." In outlining the important skills she looks for in potential hires, she commented, "So as far as the right attitude and skills at Tennessee—in a recent interview with ESPN, I talked about the success of our program, and they wanted to know the reasons behind the success. I replied 'passion and pride.' You've got to have the ability to really have a passion about the area we're in and then be proud to wear the UT orange. The other factor is the ability to role up your sleeves and work hard. It's a career that's exciting, demanding, and is really rewarding. It's different than any other career you could probably get into. It's a lifestyle. It affords opportunities for people that no other profession does. And you have to be conscious of making your family a priority but still making your profession a priority."

And what are the challenges in finding good people to hire and training them once they are on board? According to Cronan, "We find the right people in lots of different places. We've been very fortunate that we have a strong sport management program here at Tennessee, and I've found a lot of people right here on campus through our graduate programs. Any good athletic director always has a list of people who are outstanding, and you're always looking for that right person that fits your program.

"Continuing education is important in whatever you're doing. The conference has done a good job of offering us programs which help us do our job. Administrators should always be looking for things that are going to help our staff get better both personally and professionally. For example, last year I had a local bank come in and talk about the retirement system at UT and things they can do. Anything that we can do that helps—anything we can share with our people helps."

As part of her tasks, Cronan also must coordinate with the HR staff of the university. "The athletic program is an integral part of the overall university," she noted. "We don't need to be a separate foundation. I've always described it that if a university is a home, athletics is the front porch. We are what people see first, and oftentimes the most, so our job is to keep the front porch appealing. So it's important that the university have all the major human resource benefit programs in place, such as retirement plans and insurance, to name a few. It's amazing that at many schools these things aren't a priority. For example, for years I've said the university has great healthcare. But it never clicked with me until a family member got sick how good our healthcare was. The university hospital covers everything our insurance doesn't pay. You can imagine what that meant to us as a family as we went through three years of major, major medical expenses. I walked away with no bills to pay. And that was something I had never paid attention to. What it did was raise my awareness to begin educating people on our staff about these benefits.

"Another example was with our apparel contract with Adidas. It's a huge contract, so obviously our department benefits from it. But what we also did was to sit down and give a personal—not UT-related—allotment to everybody within the department be it a head coach, an assistant coach, a secretary, a sports information assistant, so everybody's part of that team. Before, we were always looking around saying, 'I wonder where they got all this Adidas stuff?' Now, whether their daughter got it or their son got it—now they have that personal allotment."

CONCLUSION

In this chapter we considered the organizational and structural aspects of athletic department level, with an additional focus on how departments hire and evaluate personnel. The structure and operations at the individual athletic department level are varied and potentially complex, depending on the program's size, scope, and divisional classification and mission. Through the examples in the chapter, we learned that managing all aspects of any such program cannot be done by a single individual, and that coordinated efforts of many are required to ensure departmental performance.

The chapter begins with an examination of how organizational design influences departmental operations. Most intercollegiate athletic departments follow a traditional functional structure, which means that the athletic department is organized as a separate unit with a college or university. The department oversees intercollegiate athletic programs, and in some cases also teaches physical education courses, and organizes and supervises club and intramural sports programs.

The chapter also identified the specific personnel within an intercollegiate athletic department and described the nature of their duties, including coaches, administrators, and other associated personnel such as faculty athletic representatives. Issues that pertain to coaches include position descriptions and the demands of interacting with the media. Important aspects of athletic directors' jobs include the importance of hiring and maintaining qualified staff, and the impact of compensation, termination, and diversity on this process.

PRACTITIONER perspective:

E. GORDON GEE, President, The Ohio State University

At the beginning of the chapter we learned of the actions taken at Vanderbilt University to restructure the school's athletic department. In large part, this effort was initiated by former Vanderbilt president E. Gordon Gee, who is currently in his second stint as president of The Ohio State University. Gee served as chancellor of Vanderbilt from 2000 to 2007. Previously he was president of Brown University (1998–2000), Ohio State (1990–1997), the University of Colorado (1985–1990), and West Virginia University (1981–1985). Gee was born in Vernal, Utah, graduated from the University of Utah with an honors degree in history, and earned his J.D. and Ed.D. from Columbia University. He clerked under Chief Justice David Lewis of the U. S. 10th Circuit Court of Appeals before being named a judicial fellow and staff assistant to the U. S. Supreme Court, where he worked for Chief Justice Warren Burger on administrative and legal problems of the Court and federal judiciary. Gee returned to Utah as an associate professor and associate dean in the J. Reuben Clark Law School at Brigham Young University, eventually achieving the rank of full professor. In 1979 he was named dean of the West Virginia University Law School, and in 1981 was appointed to that university's presidency. President Gee agreed to be interviewed for this textbook to allow for the continued close consideration of departmental organization and structural issues, as well as his perspectives on issues highlighted throughout the chapter.

Q: *In the opening of the chapter, we outline the specific elements of the Ohio State athletic department and cite data that led a* Sports Illustrated *article to describe the department as "a medium-sized corporation." How do these data impact your perspectives on and involvement with the operations of your athletic department?*

A: It's the largest, most complex athletic department in the country, at more than $110 million in terms of annual expectations of revenues. But this is within the context of an institution that's the largest and most complex in the country, with a budget of well over $4 billion. So $110 million within a $4 billion budget is peanuts. OSU has 40,000 faculty and staff. We have 60,000 students, so the athletic department doesn't in any way feel like a medium-sized corporation. It feels like every other program within the institution—it's just very large. We have a College of Engineering that's the size of Bowling Green (Ohio) State University. We have a newly created College of Arts & Science that's bigger than most universities. So I try to keep it in perspective.

You have been president of several Division I institutions, including Ohio State once before. How much did you think athletics would be part of your job when you first became a president, and were your expectations accurate?

I was 36 when I became a university president at West Virginia University, and I think I understood its importance—I had never been to a college football game until I became a university president—and I think I understood its power. I understood the reaction of people at a certain level. But it was all fairly overwhelming to me. I didn't really understand the nature of intercollegiate athletics and the power that it has in terms of people's views of an institution. I started to figure that out at the University of Colorado—and, of course, we won the national championship in 1990 at Colorado in football. When I came to Ohio State, I really had it figured out, so I used their athletic program as a way to tell the story

of the university. I do it through interviews I have at halftime. I always focus on academic programs. At our football games we have 106,000 people in our stadium who have to sit there and listen to some of the things we're doing.

So the power of athletics as a power for good is one that you need to take advantage of. The power of athletics and the detriment to the institution can also be equally debilitating unless you manage it.

How is your relationship to and involvement with athletics at Ohio State different now than during your first presidential tenure?

I understand it much better. I went to Brown University in the Ivy League, and then went to Vanderbilt and did this thing of blowing up the athletic department and re-creating it. So I have a much more mature understanding. Of course, Ohio State's program is one of the best in the nation and we have good people doing good things. I hold everyone very responsible. I changed the title of our Athletic Director to Assistant Vice President and Athletic Director because I want everyone to understand he has a university responsibility. It's not only about athletics. I have a one university strategy, and I just tell everyone it's not the athletic department's money, it's not the hospital's money, it's our money, and we'll use it for the good of the institution. We're probably one of the few Division I schools that makes money and we're using the excess to support our Library System right now, as an example.

To those of us who study intercollegiate athletics, you're probably best known for your efforts to restructure the Vanderbilt athletic department while president there. What was the motivation for making the move, and do you believe the efforts have been successful in realizing your intentions?

The *New York Times* said this is one of the great stories of intercollegiate athletics in this country. When I started this process, my obituary was written in every major newspaper in the country, as was Vanderbilt's obituary as a member of the Southeastern Conference. Four years later, we went from 79th in the power rankings to 21st, which is probably one of the single biggest moves ever made by an athletic department over a short period of time, and became very competitive nationally in most of our sports. And the reason for it is this—the fact that I believe that the challenge of intercollegiate athletics is a very simple one: Most intercollegiate athletic programs are isolated, arrogant, and believe that there's only one way to salvation and it's their way.

At Vanderbilt we believed the very same thing, and it just wasn't working at that wonderful institution. So I said, I'm going to try a third way, which is to return to the old notion of intercollegiate athletics, which is a fully integrated model, not separate, not segregated, not isolated, and everyone is going to have a stake in its success—the provost, the vice president for finance, everyone else, and we're going to totally integrate it into the institution. And everyone said you can't do that because that's not the way athletics works. It's a business. We proved them all wrong. I think it's one of the greatest stories of intercollegiate athletics, and I take great pride in it.

At the time of the Vanderbilt restructuring, you were quoted as saying, "If I tried this at Ohio State or Colorado, I'd probably be pumping gas." Why was this restructuring possible at Vanderbilt, and would you attempt it at Ohio State or any other athletic program? If not, why?

For me, ultimately, it's not about the structure, it's about the philosophy. At Vanderbilt, I did the most radical restructuring—I got rid of the athletic department. There's no athletic department at Vanderbilt. It's all part of student life and fully integrated. But, to me, it's about the philosophy—about integration and not isolation, about programs working within the confines of the university, about making sure that the values of the university are totally aligned with the values of the athletic department. And what I've done since coming to Ohio State is I've made sure that the academic programs report to the provost, that the oversight structure is very much in place that has strong academic integrity to it. The athletic director is now a vice president signifying very clearly that he is first and foremost a university officer and not simply an athletic director. So, philosophically, I'm moving very much in that direction.

If you were advising a new president about the role of intercollegiate athletics in his or her job, what would you tell them?

There are three "third-rail" issues that can derail a university president from success. One is hospitals and the academic medical centers. The other, very often, is agriculture, if you're a land grant institution. And the third is athletics.

[Intercollegiate athletics] is a very dicey issue. What you've got to do is to take responsibility for it. You can't delegate responsibility and say "oh, I didn't know about it," because in the end the buck does stop with you and, therefore, you have to establish a very clear role and responsibility for athletics as part of the institution. You also have to establish that you will not tolerate misdeeds. When I came to Ohio State this time around, I just called in all the coaches and I told them two things—one, I don't want to be surprised, and I want to know the information. I don't want to read about it in the newspaper. If I do, you'll hear from me. A couple of times shortly after I got here, I read things in the newspaper. I get up very early in the morning, at 4:30, and I had these guys on the line at 4:30 in the morning [and I said] I don't want to read that again. The second thing I said to them is that I love intercollegiate athletics, I'm proud of it, I'm proud of what we can accomplish, but I'll fire you on the spot if you violate the rules of this institution. So just understand that I have this zero tolerance rule. And I think they believe that, because that's just the way that I am and the way I was for a long time.

The best advice for a university president is be in charge. Take responsibility, and don't let boards of trustees and others divert you from your given role, which is to make certain that the athletic departments are successful, but successful within the confines of the structure, function, and intellectual values of the university.

What lessons or advice would you give to future athletic administrators regarding presidential expectations on how an athletic director should manage an athletic department?

A significant number of athletic administrators, particularly athletic directors and sometimes football coaches, believe that they are above the law. What these athletic directors or coaches will try to do is try to put public pressure on the president to do what they want to do. The best advice I can give to an athletic administrator is, "Don't try that. You may try it, and you may be successful once, but you're going to run into a tough character like me and you'll be out pumping gas." A number [of administrators] have tested me on that issue, and I survived and they didn't. You have to be tough about that issue. Therefore, the advice to athletic administrators is live with the rules. Establish them definitively. Sit down with your president and at the very beginning work out a relationship that is one of mutuality and respect.

questions TO CONSIDER

1. Based on the traditional models of organizational design outlined above, explain which type of structure is most commonly adopted by intercollegiate athletic departments, and why this type of structure makes sense.

2. If your school were seeking to hire a new athletic director and you were asked to assist in the composition of a position description for the new AD, what are the most critical qualifications and duties that you would include so the school could hire the best possible candidate?

3. Identify and explain several key factors that would merit the termination of an athletic department coach or a staff member at your school. Then outline how the AD at the school should resolve the issue.

4. Based on what you have read, what do you need to do in the next five years educationally and professionally to position yourself for a career in intercollegiate athletic management?

references

About the Black Coaches & Administrators. (2009). Black Coaches & Administrators. Accessed January 16, 2009, from: http://bcasports.cstv.com/about/bca-about.html

Anderson University Head Coach of Women's Volleyball Position Description. (2008, December 22). National Collegiate Athletic Association. Accessed January 12, 2009, from: http://ncaamarket.org

Armstrong Atlantic State University Athletic Director Position Description. (2008, December 15). Accessed January 14, 2009, from: http://ncaamarket.ncaa.org/jobdetail.cfrm

Articles of Incorporation—University Athletic Association, Inc. (1929). Gainesville: University of Florida.

Bechtol, M. (2003, September 22). The Vanderbilt experiment. *Sports Illustrated*, p. 17.

Bechtol, M. (2007, June 11). A process of elimination. *Sports Illustrated*, p. 23.

Brady, E. (2008a, April 9). Booster won't enter search. *USA Today*, p. 11C.

Brady, E. (2008b, April 9). Pickens backs Okla. State at all costs. *USA Today*, p. 11C.

Brown, C.L. (2009, November 28). Steve Kragthorpe fired as Louisville football coach. *Louisville (Kentucky) Courier–Journal*. Accessed November 30, 2009, from: http://www.courier-journal.com/article/20091128/SPORTS02/911280335/-1/SPORTS0211/Steve+Kragthorpe+fired+as+Louisville+football+coach

Cass, M. (2003, September 9). Vandy reorganized athletics department. *Tennessean*. Accessed September 18, 2003, from: http://cgi.tennessean.com

Catching Up with Previous AD of the Year Winners (2007, June 4–10). *Street & Smith's SportsBusiness Journal*, pp. 20–22.

Chandler, A.D. (1962). Strategy and structure. Cambridge, MA: MIT Press.

Chizik, Auburn Eye Better Results. (2008, December 16). *Boston Globe*, p. C6.

Covell, D., Walker, S., Siciliano, J., & Hess, P. (2007). *Managing sports organizations* (2nd ed.). Burlington, MA: Butterworth-Heinemann.

Drew University Athletic Director Position Description. (2008, May 23). *Chronicle of Higher Education*, p. C24.

Dupont, K.P. (2008, December 31). Sour Tangerine. *Boston Globe*, pp. C1, C5.

Evans, T. (2007, October 19). A stand-up guy at Oklahoma State. *New York Times*, p. C17.

Evans, T., & Thamel, P. (2009, December 31). Leach is fired over treatment of player. *New York Times*, pp. B11–B12.

Florida Gulf Coast University Athletic Director Position Description. (2009, January 5). National Collegiate Athletic Association. Accessed January 12, 2009, from: http://ncaamarket.org

Glier, R. (2008, December 18). Race and football debated after Auburn picks a coach. *New York Times*, p. B18.

Glier, R. (2009, October 10). New Auburn coach wins over his critics with a 5–0 start. *New York Times*, p. B10.

High Point University Head Coach of Women's Soccer Position Description. (2008, December 18). National Collegiate Athletic Association. Accessed January 12, 2009, from: http://ncaamarket.org

Hohler, B. (2006, September 21). Few minorities get the reins in college football. *Boston Globe*, pp. A1, E8–E9.

Hosick, M.B. (2008, April 23). FARA sets mission. *NCAA News*. Accessed April 23, 2008, from: http://ncaa.org

Indiana's Sampson Agrees to a Buyout. (2008, February 23). *Washington Post*. Accessed February 25, 2008, from: http://0-www.lexisnexis.com.wildpac.wnec.edu

King, A. (2009, February 17). Putting the pieces together. *On Campus: Ohio State's Faculty Magazine*, pp. 1–3.

Kuharsky, P. (2003a, September 12). Athletes struggle to balance sports, campus life. *Tennessean*. Accessed September 18, 2003, from: http://cgi.tennessean.com

Kuharsky, P. (2003b, September 14). Educators back Vandy reforms. *Tennessean*. Accessed September 18, 2003, from: http://cgi.tennessean.com

Layden, T., & Torre, P.S. (2009, August 24). Surviving a scandal. *Sports Illustrated*, pp. 40–42.

Longman, J. (2008, February 23). Sampson forced out at Indiana. *New York Times*. Accessed February 25, 2008, from: http://0-www.lexisnexis.com.wildpac.wnec.edu

Management's Discussion and Analysis (2008, June 30). *University Athletic Association Annual Financial Statement*. Gainesville: University of Florida.

Matson, B. (2004, December 5). A growth sport is stunting female coaches. *Boston Globe*, p. E1, E18.

McCarthy, M. (2006, December 13). Big names are his game: Headhunter bags coaches. *USA Today*, p. 3C.

McClellan, B. (2003, September 12). Official: Vanderbilt athletics will improve. *Tennessean*. Accessed September 18, 2003, from: http://cgi.tennessean.com

NCAA Report Says Sampson Committed 5 Major Violations. (2008, February 14). *Washington Post*. Accessed February 25, 2008, from: http://0-www.lexisnexis.com.wildpac.wnec.edu

Nethery, R. (2007, June 4–10). The Cardinals' can-do man. *Street & Smith's SportsBusiness Journal*, pp. 1, 17–19, 23–24.

Organ, M. (2003a, September 11). It's business as usual for Vandy players. *Tennessean*. Accessed September 18, 2003, from: http://cgi.tennessean.com

Organ, M. (2003b, September 17). Gee says message misunderstood. *Tennessean*. Accessed September 18, 2003, from: http://cgi.tennessean.com

Pomona College Head Coach of Men's and Women's Swimming and Diving Position Description. (2008, December 29).

National Collegiate Athletic Association. Accessed January 12, 2009, from: http://ncaamarket.org

Q: What Is the Most Pressing Issue Facing Athletic Directors? (2007, June 4–10). *Street & Smith's SportsBusiness Journal*, p. 22.

Rice, F. (1994). How to make diversity pay. *Forbes*, pp. 79–86.

Rosenberg, M. (2008). *War as they knew it: Woody Hayes, Bo Schembechler, and America in a time of unrest*. New York: Grand Central Publishing.

Schmidt, R. (2007). *Shaping college football: The transformation of an American sport, 1919–1930*. Syracuse, NY: Syracuse University Press.

Smith, S.A. (2009, January 12). Up front. *ESPN Magazine*, p. 14.

Thamel, P. (2007, November 10). Attracting valuable coaches to the priciest college town. *New York Times*, p. 8-7.

Thamel, P. (2008, December 21). High interest but little opportunity. *New York Times*, pp. Y1, Y10.

2008–09 NCAA Division I Manual. (2008). Indianapolis: NCAA.

Wahl, G. (2008, March 3). Last call. *Sports Illustrated*, p. 47.

Wertheim, L.J. (2007, March 5). The program: Portrait of a powerhouse. *Sports Illustrated*, pp. 55–69.

Wertheim, L.J. (2008, November 3). Tom Crean's big red challenge. *Sports Illustrated*, pp. 55–63.

Whiteside, K. (2004, November 19). Long hours, little sleep and loving it. *USA Today*, pp. 1C, 5C.

Wieberg, S. (2008, February 19). NCAA enforcement rules tilt in coaches' favor, expert says. *USA Today*. Accessed February 25, 2008, from: http://0-lexisnexis.com. wildpac.wnec.edu

Wieberg, S. (2008, October 2). Division I sees unprecedented foreign influx. *USA Today*, p. 1C.

Wieberg, S. (2009, December 8).Minority coaches gaining traction in NCAA. *USA Today*, p. 1C.

Wiedeman, R. (2008, December 5). Indiana U. gets probation for violations in recruiting. *Chronicle of Higher Education*, p. A14.

Wolverton, B. (2007, July 20). Will Gee give the Buckeyes' huge sports program the Vanderbilt treatment? *Chronicle of Higher Education*, p. A24.

Finances

6

Key concepts to keep in mind as you read the chapter:

- How some intercollegiate athletic managers must deal with complex factors that impact revenue generation within the framework of a non-profit organization.

- The importance of NCAA-directed revenues to member institutions.

- The potential connections between on-field success and revenue generation, and how this competitive environment impacts departmental budgets.

- How divisional classification influences the nature of departmental budgets.

- The traditional and emerging revenue sources and expenditures that impact intercollegiate athletic departments.

Introduction

In 2006, the Ways and Means Committee of the U.S. House of Representatives, as part of an ongoing investigation of the finances of all nonprofit organizations, asked managers at several intercollegiate athletic departments and conferences, as well as NCAA officials, about their financial operations and whether their tax-exempt status is warranted. A change in status could cost intercollegiate athletics organizations hundreds of millions of dollars a year. Part of the committee's focus on finances was prompted as a result of spikes in athletic department spending—primarily on coaches' salaries and facility construction and renovations—in some cases at three times the rate of spending for the institutions in which they are housed, as well as increases in revenues, and whether these revenues were supporting legitimate educational purposes (Wolverton, 2006a).

This is one of a number of major questions relating to the financial operations of intercollegiate athletics organizations. This chapter continues with a primary theme throughout the text—how to meet key departmental objectives within the missions and goals of the unique higher education environments. Professional league and tour sport organizations have far fewer concerns than their intercollegiate counterparts on this score. Pro sport organizations exist solely to provide entertainment for their customers and to generate revenues and profits for their owners. This operational equation is much more difficult for intercollegiate athletics managers, and we will try to clarify the critical factors and variables here.

NONPROFIT STATUS AND REVENUE GENERATION

In Chapter 3, in the discussion of the roles of conferences and conference personnel, we discussed the efforts of commissioners such as the Big Ten's James Delany to bring in revenues for member institutions. But William Friday, former president of the University of North Carolina system and former longtime chair of the Knight Commission on Intercollegiate Athletics (see Chapter 12), exposed the problematic nature of such actions, commenting: "When you see conferences creating their own television networks, how you rationalize that into an educational function with a tax exemption is going to be very difficult to do—because it's strictly a business" (Wolverton, 2006a, p. A37). One such example is the Big Ten Network, which has been established as a for-profit company, meaning that any dividends the company earns will be taxed but the broadcast rights fees paid to the conference will not, because as Delany states, the money will go toward educational purposes such as financial aid. The network will also broadcast programming on academic issues, including information on how schools integrate athletic programs into an institution's academic environment. Delany offered no apologies in defending the revenues created by his conference: "The federal government and states say they want universities to be more entrepreneurial in the way they develop resources. We're trying not to be a burden on the taxpayers. Why shouldn't we do that?" (Wolverton, 2006a, p. A37).

Later that year, then-NCAA president Myles Brand responded to a letter from Representative Bill Thomas, a California Republican serving as chair of House Ways and Means committee, which questioned why federal taxpayers should subsidize what Rep. Thomas described as escalating coaches' salaries, costly chartered travel, and state-of-the-art athletics facilities through the maintenance of tax-exempt status. In his letter, Brand countered that the money brought in by the most successful football and men's basketball programs—estimated at $2.4 billion annually, part of an estimated $10 billion in revenue produced by all intercollegiate athletic programs—helps subsidize the participation opportunities for 380,000 athletes in all three divisions, and that "the lessons learned on the football field or the men's basketball court are no less in value or importance to those student-athletes than the ones learned on the hockey rink or the softball diamond—nor, for that matter, than those learned in theater, dance, music, journalism, or other non-classroom environments" (Wolverton, 2006b, p. A42).

In response to Rep. Thomas's specific criticisms, Brand noted that coaches' salaries are commensurate with those of other highly paid faculty members and within the range of reasonable compensation for federal tax purposes; chartered planes often cost less than commercial travel and help athletes miss fewer classes; schools often pay for facility upgrades with bonds or charitable contributions; and, like other nonprofit groups, athletic programs should be allowed to increase their visibility by building new facilities and recruiting the best employees. At the 2008 NCAA Convention, Brand also argued that schools have an "obligation" to help themselves by exploiting commercial opportunities (Wolverton, 2008, p. A23). Recall that (as discussed in Chapter 2) Brand also addressed the issue of tax-exempt status and its importance to the intercollegiate athletics enterprise.

At about the same time as Rep. Thomas's inquiry, the NCAA Presidential Task Force on the Future of Division I Athletics (2006) released a report, *The Second-Century Imperatives: Presidential Leadership—Institutional Accountability*. The task force, composed of current and former school presidents and chaired by former University of Arizona president Peter Likins, compiled the report in response to NCAA data indicating that intercollegiate athletics costs were indeed rising at a rate that, as Brand pointed to in the report's introduction, was not sustainable and was growing at a rate two to three times faster than the rest of higher education over the last decade. In addition, data showed that in spending to improve athletics facilities, many institutions held mortgages that represented, in Brand's words, "on average 20 percent of intercollegiate athletics spending. This factor puts institutions at risk over decades of time if the popularity of college sports wanes" (p. 4).

Although the report stated and restated numerous times that no financial crisis was imminent, these factors, admitted Brand, when combined with what he identified as "the popularity of intercollegiate athletics to media and marketing," as well as increased pressures to win and generate revenue, created an atmosphere in which "avid fans or trustees" interfered with presidential authority, and "the integration of athletics within the academy . . . and the primacy of education in the student-athlete experience have all been threatened" (p. 4). The ultimate goal of the report, Brand indicated in a speech to the National Press Club upon its release, was

> to moderate growth of athletics budgets so that institutional funds do not increasingly have to cover revenue shortfalls. We are not trying to reduce spending or even

cap it. Growth will, and *should* [author's emphasis] continue in athletic departments. For the vast majority of institutions, we simply must moderate the rate of growth so that participation opportunities are maximized without creating financial problems for campus resources. Budgetary growth in athletics budgets generally speaking, should resemble the growth for the campus as a whole. (Brand, 2006, p. 14)

We will learn more about the rest of this report and its impact on reform efforts in intercollegiate athletics in Chapter 12.

NCAA FINANCES

Because of its classification as a not-for-profit entity, and to maintain its tax-exempt status, the NCAA's annual budget must reflect the fact that revenues must equal expenses. Exhibit 6.1 shows revenues and expenses for the 2008–09 fiscal year, which indicated that revenues for the organization reached $564 million, up from $485.7 million two years earlier, an increase of more than 17 percent. What makes the NCAA's budget an important element in the discussion of intercollegiate finances is that the organization redistributes much of the revenue it generates to member institutions, the majority of which goes to Division I programs.

EXHIBIT 6.1	2008–09 NCAA budgeted expenses and revenues.	
ITEM	AMOUNT (IN MILLIONS)	PERCENTAGE OF TOTAL EXPENSES
EXPENSES		
Division I expenses and allocations	$451.20	68.25
Division II expenses and allocations	$28.80	4.37
Division III expenses and allocations	$21.00	3.18
Membership programs and services	$84.60	12.8
Administrative services	$27.80	4.2
Student-athlete welfare and youth programs and services	$21.20	3.2
Contingencies and reserves	$26.40	4
Total	$661.00	100%
REVENUES		
Television and marketing rights fees	$590.73	89.37
Championships revenue	$60.43	9.14
Investments, fees, and services	$8.83	1.34
Membership dues	$1.01	.15
Total	$661.00	100%

Source: NCAA Revised Budget, 2009.

Revenue

A closer examination of the association's revised budget for the fiscal year ending August 31, 2009, reveals greater detail concerning many of the items listed. For example, the lion's share of revenue is derived from television and marketing rights, which include the NCAA's corporate partnership program. The NCAA's emergence as a powerbroker was directly tied to its ability to control television appearances and revenues associated from football. That specific source of power was dissolved in 1984 when the U. S. Supreme Court ruled that the association could no longer limit the number of appearances a school could make in any given year. A decade later was however a watershed moment for procurement of its current most lucrative revenue stream when the NCAA signed an eight-year, $1.725 billion contract with the CBS network to broadcast championship events, most notably the men's Division I basketball tournament. The current deal to broadcast most championship events with CBS and Turner Broadcasting runs through 2024. This deal includes neither regular season games in any sport nor any Bowl Subdivision postseason football games; these are negotiated and paid to individual schools and conferences.

An additional component of NCAA's revenue is its "corporate champions" sponsorship program (which includes AT&T, Capital One, and Coca-Cola) and "corporate partners" sponsorship program (which includes Enterprise Rent-A-Car, The Hartford, Hershey's, LG, Lowe's, Kraft, and State Farm). These companies pay under this line item to associate their products and services with the NCAA and its sanctioned events as "official" partners.

As for the future of the Association and its ability to continue to develop current and new revenue streams, Greg Shaheen, the NCAA's senior vice-president for basketball and business strategies, notes that "a key factor is on broadening the awareness and exposure of our championships. . . . [D]iversification obviously also takes into account our ongoing work in making our expansive video library available to the public, or legendary photo collection, as well as our ticket and hospitality programs to provide fans a sanctioned means to access our events" (Top Official, 2008, p. A16). When asked whether the NCAA might start its own network, like the Big Ten and Mountain West Conferences, Shaheen responded: "The landscape of media outlets and distribution methods seems to grow by the day . . . A network approach is one of literally dozens of models we study on an ongoing basis" (p. A16).

Expenses

When examining more closely the specific expenses listed in the NCAA's budget, the most prominent is the $451.2 million comprising nearly 70 percent of the association's disbursements, the Division I expenses and allocations. In contrast are the modest disbursements to the Division II and III schools.

Disbursements to Division II and III schools

As dictated by Article 4 of the NCAA Constitution (Bylaw 4.01.2.1), the expenses and allocations to Division II and III schools are locked in at a set percentage of the annual expenses, 4.37 percent and 3.18 percent, respectively. While this allowance assures a fraction of the association's revenues are channeled to non-Division

I programs, the Association makes sure to return the majority of its revenue to the schools in the divisional classification through which it is generated.

Disbursements to Division I schools

As stated above, the most prominent expense category in the NCAA's budget is the Division I expenses and allocations. Of the amount funneled to D-I programs, more than $369 million consists of payouts to Division I athletic, conference, and student-athletes programs. More specifically, this revenue distribution plan has six main components, listed in Exhibit 6.2.

Broad-based distribution. The largest portion of this allocation is through broad-based distribution to all Division I schools. The broad-based distribution is made to institutions on the basis of the number of varsity sports sponsored (weighted one-third, totaling $51.6 million) and the number of athletics grants-in-aid awarded (weighted two-thirds, totaling $103.1 million) (see Chapter 7 for a full definition of grants-in-aid). An institution receives a unit (valued at $26,123) for each sport program it offers above the Division I minimum of 13. The grants-in-aid component is based on the number of athletic grants-in-aid awarded by each institution in sports in which NCAA championships are held and emerging sports for women (*2008–09 Revenue,* 2009). Exhibit 6.3 outlines the grant-in-aid valuation system. So, to apply this system, a school that awards 123 grants-in-aid would receive a check from the NCAA for $92,214.60 [(50 × $242.67) + (50 × $485.34) + (23 × $2426.70)].

Basketball fund. The next largest share of these allocations is distributed through the basketball fund. This line-item provides for money to be distributed to Division I conferences based on their performance in the men's basketball championship over a six-year rolling period. One unit is awarded to each institution participating in each game, except the championship game. In 2008–09, each unit was worth approximately $206,020. Independent schools receive a full unit share based on tournament participation over the same six-year period. The NCAA disperses the money directly to conferences, which are urged but not required to distribute the money equally to each conference member (*2008–09 Revenue,* 2009). This for-

---

EXHIBIT   6.2   Components of NCAA Division I expenses and allocations and amounts distributed.

COMPONENT	AMOUNT DISTRIBUTED (IN MILLIONS)
Broad-based distribution	$154.7
Basketball Fund	$143.2
Student-athlete Opportunity Fund (SAOF)	$31.3
Academic Enhancement Fund	$19.8
Special Assistance Fund for Student-athletes	$12.8
Conference grants	$7.2

Source: 2008–09 Revenue, 2009.

	Grant-in-aid fund valuation system.	EXHIBIT 6.3

NUMBER OF GRANTS	VALUATION POINTS	PER GRANT VALUE
1–50	1 point each x $242.67	$242.67
51–100	2 points each x $242.67	$485.34
101–150	10 points each x $242.67	$2426.70
151 and above	20 points each x $242.67	$4853.40

Source: 2008–09 Revenue, 2009.

mula was created in part to defray the distribution of all tournament revenue to one school based solely on how a specific team performs in a specific year.

Student-athlete Opportunity Fund (SAOF). This fund is the next largest line-item distribution, and it is based on the same formula as the broad-based fund. The SAOF, which is set to increase by 13 percent annually, is intended to provide direct benefits to student-athletes and their families who incur financial needs that arise in conjunction with participation in intercollegiate athletics, with enrollment in an academic curriculum, or through recognition of academic achievement, as determined by conference offices. All student-athletes are eligible for monies from the SAOF, regardless of whether they receive athletic or institutional financial aid. Conferences are required to report annually to the NCAA the fund recipients by sport and by gender, and the purpose and amount of each grant.

The Special Assistance Fund for Student-Athletes is intended for needs that are essential or emergency in nature for which financial assistance is otherwise unavailable. Eligibility for these funds is limited to student-athletes who have demonstrated financial need. Permissible uses of monies from this fund include clothing purchases and travel to and from home not to exceed $500, the cost of expendable academic course supplies (such as notebooks and pens), and medical costs not included in other health plans (such as hearing or vision therapy). Conferences are responsible for the oversight and administration of these funds as well.

Other distributions. The other components of the Division I revenue distribution plan include the Academic Enhancement Fund (intended to bolster academic support programs for student-athletes), and conference grants (from which payments of approximately $231,065 are made specifically to men's and women's basketball conferences to maintain programs for game officials in all sports, compliance and enforcement programs, and education and professional development opportunities for coaches, administrators, and student-athletes (*2008–09 Revenue, 2009*).

DEPARTMENTAL FINANCES

The NCAA has released periodic reports since 1969, examining the revenues and expenses of athletic departments at all member institutions. The most recent report, compiled by Daniel Fulks, professor of accounting and faculty athletics representative at Transylvania (Kentucky) University, shows relevant data from the 2005–06 fiscal year (*2005–06 NCAA Revenues,* 2008). Also, data regarding departmental finances reported annually to the federal government's Department of Education is available on that organization's website, www.ed.gov. We will first examine the aggregated data that provide a general picture of the increase in revenues and expenses of institutions and then we will examine schools at each classification level so we can continue to understand the specifics that influence the financial climate for athletic departments.

Increasing revenues and expenses of intercollegiate athletics

What, then, is really going on with athletic department budgets? All NCAA institutions spend approximately $7.75 billion a year on athletic programs, slightly less than the $7.8 billion in revenues generated. The 117 NCAA Bowl Subdivision football programs spent about $1 billion during 2004–05 ($74,000 per player), while the 326 Division I men's basketball programs spent about $789 million ($158,000 per player). The largest and fastest-growing expenses for Division I programs are the expenses for coaches and support staff salaries. The median salary for head football coaches grew 47 percent between 2004 and 2006, rising from $582,000 to $855,000, while the median salary for head men's basketball coaches rose 15 percent, to $611,900. Athletic aid and salaries combined for at least 50 percent of D-I expenses (Wolverton, 2006b, Kelderman, 2008a).

And what about the widely held belief that the revenues from these two sports help Division I programs cover all departmental expenses? For all but a handful of schools—17 of the 330 between 2004 and 2006—it doesn't happen. This is according to the 2008 semi-annual revenue and expenses report compiled for the NCAA by Daniel Fulks. The report noted that ticket sales and private donations accounted for half the revenue of D-I programs, and 16 of the 17 programs noted above were at schools that had Bowl Subdivision football programs. No specific data attributed to any one school were released in the report. Even at these "profitable" schools, the median amount of support from the college, defined as "allocated resources," those revenues not generated by athletic departments but, rather, given directly or indirectly to support these programs by their institutions, was 24 percent of the budget for athletics (Wolverton, 2006b; Kelderman, 2008a).

Specific information from other sources indicates the extent to which there is a significant gap in profits and revenues among D-I programs. According to data from the U. S. Department of Education based on the fiscal year ending June 30, 2006, the University of Notre Dame's athletic department's revenues exceeded expenses by $22.7 million, the largest departmental differential that year. The other most profitable programs were at the University of Georgia ($20.5 million), University of Central Florida ($19.5 million), and University of Michigan ($17.5 million). Schools that endured low revenues and either lost money or broke even included the Virginia Military Institute ($5.5 million in revenues, and a loss of $30,000), University of Louisiana–Monroe (which broke even on $7.2 million in revenue), and University of Louisiana–Lafayette ($8 million in revenue, also breaking even).

One such school facing significant potential budgetary shortfalls was the University of Arizona, the former employer of Presidential Task Force chair Peter Likins. According to former AD Jim Livingood, even though the men's basketball and football teams are a widely popular draw, the department was facing a potential $5 million deficit by 2011: "the perception is so much different from the reality. You look around and you have a hard time understanding how there could ever be a financial shortfall in something that is generating this kind of revenue. It would be impossible. You see the atmosphere, concessions, bookstore souvenirs, parking. But in fact, we are very close to a crisis . . . Costs are just growing too quickly" (Schoenfeld, 2006, p. 29; The Haves and Have-Nots," 2007).

The ultimate rationale behind these increases in expenditures? According to Todd Diacon, vice provost for academic operations and faculty athletics representative at the University of Tennessee, it's the concept that has schools thinking, "If you field a team, you ought to be able to compete to win," which has meant an increased pressure to spend heavily even on sports that don't generate revenue. "Even if we win the NCAA championship in swimming, that's not going to pay for the pool the school just built," said Diacon (Kelderman, 2008a, p. A15). The pool is only part of a construction binge on the Tennessee campus that includes a new softball stadium, a new soccer stadium, and plans for new facilities for golf, volleyball, and indoor track. As for other similar so-called "non-revenue" sports, across all Division I schools, the median amount of revenue generated by men's track and field teams in 2006 was $33,300, while median expenses were $584,000. During the same year, women's track and field programs' median revenues were $24,000, and median expenses were $761,000 (Kelderman, 2008a).

So athletic spending clearly is increasing, and it also may be true that while the *Second-Century Imperatives* report indicated that no crisis was imminent, there seems to be legitimate reason for concern. Schools apparently are willing to lose money on athletics programs because, as pointed out by Darin Spease, president of the College Athletic Business Management Association, there is increasing pressure to keep up with the spending of schools such as Tennessee, even at schools in other conferences and in the other divisional classifications. Said Spease, a senior associate AD at the University of North Carolina–Charlotte: "As long as there is an elite group of schools with generous alums, I don't see that it ends. I don't know how the rank-and-file schools compete" (Kelderman, 2008a, p. A15). Daniel Fulks, who compiled the NCAA report cited, agreed, noting that the escalating costs for recruiting and coaches salaries represented an "arms race" to attract the best players and coaches. Arizona's associate AD for business, John Perrin, echoed Fulks, stating, "Every time [the University of] Oklahoma gives [head football coach] Bob Stoops another raise [now to over $3 million a year], the rest of us just cringe," and Livingood added: "How are you going to tell [communities that support D-I programs like] a Gainesville, Florida, or a Knoxville, Tennessee, or an Ann Arbor, Michigan, or even a Tucson, Arizona, that smaller is better? You aren't. In fact, it's gone in the other direction" (Kelderman, 2008a, p. A15). Stephen Trachtenberg, president of George Washington University, defends such expansionary actions this way: "I think it's very hard to say you're committed to excellence if you're prepared to deny excellence in a very conspicuous and public aspect of your enterprise" (Schoenfeld, 2006, p. 29).

Some athletic administrators were critical of Fulks's report, citing that it did not allow them to count all revenue sources such as concessions, parking, and merchandise sales. University of Maryland AD Deborah Yow stated that her school received more than $2.7 million in such revenues, but that the report did not allow these monies to be credited toward the athletic department's bottom line. Although Yow agreed that athletic costs were rising too rapidly, she commented, "I just want the athletics programs to receive rightful credit for their revenues" (Kelderman, 2008b, p. A4). Other managers who also criticized the report included University of Texas associate AD for business, Ed Goble, who said it is nearly impossible for the NCAA to compile a report that compares costs fairly, in part because institutions vary in the ways they collect revenues and spend money, but also because Fulks's reporting forces them to make neat distinctions where none exist. In noting that students at Texas pay an optional fee of $70 to gain admittance to any athletic event—which generates $1.7 million a year—the report does not allow them to count it as generated revenue. Goble added, "There's a lot of gray in what appears to be black and white" (Kelderman, 2008b, p. A4). Mississippi State University AD Larry Templeton complained that the report did not allow his department to get credit for the 3,500 free seats—valued at $2 million if sold as other tickets—provided to students at the school's 10,500 home basketball venue.

Fulks responded to these criticisms by verifying some of these gray areas, commenting:

> On many, if not most, campuses, the parking areas are used at times other than athletic events, and the facilities are usually maintained by the institution. If the parking facility is strictly for athletic events and some or all of the revenues are retained by the institution, then I agree that the revenue should appear as generated revenue from athletics . . . but we have no way of determining this when we collect the data. (Kelderman, 2008b, p. A4)

So even if we are able to account for all the variables and gray areas in the revenue and expense data collection, and we still have situations in which athletic departments are losing money, is this such a bad thing? Why should intercollegiate athletic programs be expected to make money while other components of campus life—academic programs, the building and grounds division, the information technology office, the theater, dance, music, and journalism programs cited by Dr. Brand—are under no such set of demands? Former academician and intercollegiate athletics critic Murray Sperber identified the following as the problematic crux of the issue of athletic finance and budgets:

> If colleges were wonderfully wealthy institutions and could afford all sorts of amenities and doodads, then such financial losses would not be an issue. But higher education is in dire financial shape, rattling the tin cup in front of unsympathetic state legislators, taxpayers, and potential donors. The reality, which the NCAA now acknowledges, is that institutional subsidies for intercollegiate athletics usually comes out of funds that could go for academic purposes. . . . If I were paying tuition bills at Big Time U., and I read about its athletic department's red ink and subsidies, I would write to the president of the university and to the governing board to complain. (Sperber, 2008, p. A31)

In addition, Nathan Tublitz, a professor of neurobiology at the University of Oregon and co-chair of the Coalition on Intercollegiate Athletics, a reform group composed of faculty senate leaders at schools with Bowl Subdivision football programs (see Chapter 12), commented:

> What bothers me are the large amounts of money that are going to the athletic enterprise that really should be going to the academic side, because the academic side is more needy. . . . At the University of Oregon, we're finishing up a seven-year

fundraising campaign where over 40 percent of the fundraising has gone to athletics. And athletics is only 8 percent of the budget. Now, what does that tell you about the priority of our university president? (Colleges Slight Academic Prerequisites, 2008, p. 38)

In this context, Fulks himself has this to say:

There is some difference between athletics and chemistry. But still, if (athletics is) worth having, it's worth paying for. Just stop whining about athletics losing money unless you're going to start whining about the history department losing money. . . . We have to remember that what drives these decisions is not necessarily the financial aspect. There's an awful lot of ego involved—egos not only of the CEO and the AD but the board of trustees, boosters, and alumni. They're willing to pay for it. (Wieberg, 2003a, p. 11C; 2003b, p. 1C)

So we are presented with another paradoxical situation facing intercollegiate athletics managers: Some believe that intercollegiate athletics is not part of the educational experience and should not be drawing resources away from the institution. Therefore, intercollegiate athletics departments should be self-supporting and look to generate revenues in whatever way it can. But, as departments and programs begin to focus too extensively on profits, and the wins needed to generate them, they become further estranged from the institution as a whole. Therefore, others would argue that to integrate athletics into the institution, the institution must be prepared to pay for it. To address the corresponding aspects of the paradox, we will delve into the skeins of available data more deeply. In doing so, we will attempt to determine how intercollegiate athletic managers must understand them to make financial and budgetary decisions within the specific, not always rational environment of higher education, where all activities must be justified based on their connection with the educatory mission of the institution.

Division I schools with Bowl Subdivision football programs

For us to understand the factors that impact departmental budgets, we have to examine the specific revenues and expenses for each classification level. Let's begin with schools that sponsor Division I Bowl Subdivision football programs.

Revenue sources

Exhibit 6.4 lists the revenue sources and corresponding monies from these sources reported by 100 percent of the Division I schools with football programs (at the time, 117) that compete in the Bowl Subdivision (these schools comprise 11 percent of the total NCAA membership).

The "Other" category accounts for 22 percent—nearly a quarter—of all departmental revenues. This includes revenues from concessions ($522,000; 2 percent), radio and television broadcast payments ($2.8 million; 7 percent), and signage and sponsorships ($1.2 million; 4 percent) among others.

The continued reliance on the traditional revenue sources of tickets and other game-related revenues, and increases in expenses incurred by Division I athletic departments, has meant a concurrent increase in prices borne by consumers. Exhibit 6.5 lists the most costly football game attendance experience in each Bowl Subdivi-

EXHIBIT 6.4	Sources of total revenue—Division I schools with Bowl Subdivision football programs.

REVENUE CATEGORY	TOTAL FROM REVENUE SOURCE (IN THOUSANDS)	PERCENTAGE OF TOTAL REVENUES
Ticket sales	$7,854	27
Cash from alumni and others	$5,271	18
Institutional support	$3,029	10
NCAA and conference distribution	$2,641	9
Student activity fees	$1,854	6
Guarantees and options	$1,043	6
Postseason compensation	$898	3
Direct government support	$416	1
Other	$6,410	22
Total	$29,416	100%

Source: 2005–06 NCAA revenues and expenses of Divisions I and II intercollegiate athletic programs report, 2008.

sion Conference plus the University of Notre Dame (note that the "ordinary game" data are based on the least expensive single-game ticket available for any game during the 2008 season; the "marquee game" data are the least expensive for a top opponent or rivalry game; concession prices are for a standard hotdog and a large soda; the "Total" column includes marquee game ticket, hotdog, and large soda).

The Big 12 Conference had the highest average marquee game ticket price ($72.17), but these prices do not reflect the true cost of attending games, for if you were an Oklahoma State fan looking to purchase the cheapest ticket (in the upper area of an end zone) for the most expensive marquee game—against in-state rival University of Oklahoma—you would have to buy a full season ticket package at a cost of $294. Some experts also point out that the prices listed in Exhibit 6.5 are an underestimate because at some schools where demand is high, single-game tickets

EXHIBIT 6.5	Cost of attending football games at selected Division I Bowl Subdivision schools.

SCHOOL (CONFERENCE)	TICKET—ORDINARY GAME	TICKET—MARQUEE GAME	HOTDOG	SODA	TOTAL
Syracuse University (Big East)	$36	$57	$3.00	$4.00	$64.00
Clemson University (ACC)	$35	$60	$3.00	$3.50	$66.50
University of Notre Dame	$65	$65	$4.00	$3.50	$72.50
Michigan State University (Big Ten)	$46	$70	$3.00	$3.50	$76.50
University of Tennessee (SEC)	$40	$70	$5.00	$4.00	$79.00
University of Southern California (Pac-10)	$45	$75	$5.00	$6.00	$86.00
Oklahoma State University (Big 12)	$60	$100	$3.00	$5.00	$108.00

Source: Bachman, 2008b. Copyright 2008, The Chronicle of Higher Education. Reprinted with permission.

are sold out through season tickets and never go on sale to the general public, and at such schools a donation to the school's athletic fund is also required before an individual can even buy a season ticket.

For example, at the University of Florida, prospective season ticket buyers would need a minimum donation of $4,200 for the right to buy season tickets. Low season ticket demand drove the actions regarding season tickets at Oklahoma State. Fellow Big 12 member Iowa State University took a similar approach for tickets for its home game against in-state rival University of Iowa, which boosted its season ticket sales by 22 percent over 2007. "You leverage your best asset," said Steve Malchow, the school's senior associate AD. "It's not that complicated" (Bachman, 2008a, p. 2). Pac-10 member Oregon State University had the 12th highest cost of attendance in the subdivision, a level that was explained by AD Bob DeCarolis: "Nobody likes raising prices, believe me. But if you're going to pay the bills to continue to support the programs at the levels they are at, then that's a necessity" (p. 2).

Expenses

Exhibit 6.6 shows the averaged operating and total expenses for this same grouping of schools. As the data indicate, the difference between average revenues and expenses equals a loss of $758,000.

	Operating and total expenses—Division I schools with Bowl Subdivision football programs.	EXHIBIT 6.6

EXPENSE CATEGORY	TOTAL EXPENDITURE (IN THOUSANDS)	PERCENTAGE OF TOTAL EXPENDITURES
Salaries and benefits	$8,640	32
Grants-in-aid	$4,743	18
Team travel	$1,988	7
Contract services	$1,345	5
Guarantees and options	$1,181	4
Equipment/uniforms/supplies	$1,179	4
Recruiting	$541	2
Fundraising	$299	1
Game officials	$250	1
Sports camps	$235	1
Other	$6,792	25
Total operating expenses	$27,193	100%
Debt service	$1,438	
Capital expenditures	$1,544	
Total	$30,175	

Source: 2005–06 NCAA revenues and expenses of Divisions I and II intercollegiate athletic programs report, 2008.

Profitability

Further data compiled in the 2008 report shows the specific revenues and expenses for 22 varsity sports at schools with Bowl Subdivision football programs, some of which are presented in Exhibit 6.7. The data demonstrate that most programs fail to generate revenues that exceed expenses. As for these specific sports, 68 percent of football programs reported profits, with an average profit of $9.2 million, 28 percent reported deficits, with an average loss of just over $1 million, and 4 percent reported breaking even. Seventy percent of men's basketball programs reported profits (at an average of just over $3 million), while 26 reported deficits (an average of $400,000), and 4 percent broke even. Only 6 percent of women's basketball programs reported profits (at an average of $640,000), while 90 percent reported losses averaging $900,000, and 4 percent broke even.

According to a study conducted by *Forbes* magazine, 10 Bowl Subdivision football programs brought in at least $45 million in revenues in 2007. The study valued the football program at the University of Notre Dame at $101 million, based on what the program contributed to the institution for academic purposes (including grant-in-aid payments for football players—$21.1 million), the net profit generated by the football program that was retained by the athletic department, the distribution of bowl game revenue, and incurred spending in the school's home community around home games (estimated at $9.4 million in St. Joseph County, Indiana). A significant factor contributing to Notre Dame's financial value is the school's lack of conference affiliation in football, which allows the school to keep all of the $9 million payment it receives from NBC for the right to televise its home games. The study identified the University of Texas as the most profitable program at $46.2

EXHIBIT 6.7	Revenues and expenses for selected programs at Division I schools with Bowl Subdivision football programs.		
SPORT	**REVENUES (IN THOUSANDS)**	**EXPENSES (IN THOUSANDS)**	**DIFFERENCE (IN THOUSANDS)**
Football	$12,969	$7,046	$5,923
Field Hockey	$166	$535	-$369
Men's Basketball	$4,252	$2,227	$2,025
Women's Basketball	$506	$1,279	-$773
Men's Ice Hockey	$1,522	$1,169	$353
Women's Ice Hockey	$163	$593	-$430
Baseball	$367	$760	-$393
Softball	$151	$545	-$394
Men's Soccer	$130	$454	-$324
Women's Soccer	$156	$531	-$375

Source: 2005–06 NCAA revenues and expenses of Divisions I and II intercollegiate athletic programs report, 2008.

| Revenues and expenses at the University of Florida. | EXHIBIT | 6.8 |

- Operating revenue from football: $54,121,437
- Operating revenue from men's basketball: $8,769,101
- Operating revenue from sponsorships: $9,841,566
- Revenue from student fees: $2,578,306
- Contributions from boosters: $35,632,463
- Cash flow from tickets: $29,801,902
- Conference and NCAA receipts: $12,929,479
- Operating expenses from football: $14,645,758
- Operating expenses from men's basketball: $6,678,283
- Operating expenses from grants-in-aid: $7,705,076
- Total operating revenue: $89,911,319
- Total operating expenses: $85,564,564
- Operating income: $4,346,755

Source: University Athletic Association Annual Financial Statement, 2008.

million, of which $4.7 million went into academics. Texas merchandise royalties doubled to $8 million after the Longhorns won the 2006 BCS title, and premium and club seating at the school's home football venue generates $12 million a year (Schwartz, 2007).

Because of its status as a nonprofit organization, the University of Florida's University Athletic Association (UAA) is required to release a detailed annual budget delineating assets, liabilities, and operating revenues and expenses. Exhibit 6.8 outlines specific details from the UAA's 2008 financial statement, one example of the revenues and expenses for a Division I Bowl Subdivision program.

Division I schools with Championship Subdivision football programs

Revenue and expense data for 98 percent of Division I programs with Championship Subdivision football programs (which totaled at the time 122) is contained in Exhibit 6.9. When compared to schools with Bowl Subdivision football programs (which comprise 12 percent of the total NCAA membership), it is clear that these schools are far more dependent on institutional support—nearly half of claimed revenue—for the operation of their athletic programs, even though the amount of that support is approximately the same as that received by Bowl Subdivision schools. Other significant differences are found in the amount of revenue from broadcasting and cash from alumni and others.

Exhibit 6.10 shows expense data for D-I Championship Subdivision schools. Grants-in-aid account for a far higher percentage of the overall budget for Championship Subdivision schools, even though the total expenditure is more than $2 million less than Bowl Subdivision schools. Salaries and benefits are approximately

| EXHIBIT | 6.9 | Sources of total revenue—Division I schools with Championship Subdivision football programs. |

REVENUE CATEGORY	TOTAL FROM REVENUE SOURCE (IN THOUSANDS)	PERCENTAGE OF TOTAL REVENUES
Institutional support	$3,423	49
Student activity fees	$1,294	18
Cash from alumni and others	$540	8
Ticket sales	$451	6
NCAA and conference distribution	$297	4
Guarantees and options	$235	3
Direct government support	$188	3
Other	$541	8
Total	$6,999	100%

Source: 2005–06 NCAA revenues and expenses of Divisions I and II intercollegiate athletic programs report, 2008.

| EXHIBIT | 6.10 | Operating and total expenses—Division I schools with Championship Subdivision football programs. |

EXPENSE CATEGORY	TOTAL EXPENDITURE (IN THOUSANDS)	PERCENTAGE OF TOTAL EXPENDITURES
Salaries and benefits	$2,569	35
Grants-in-aid	$2,393	32
Team travel	$673	9
Equipment/uniforms/supplies	$343	5
Recruiting	$164	2
Contract services	$124	2
Game officials	$102	1
Sports camps	$67	1
Guarantees and options	$66	1
Fundraising	$46	1
Other	$849	11
Total operating expenses	$7,396	100%
Debt service	$53	
Capital expenditures	$98	
Total	$7,547	

Source: 2005–06 NCAA revenues and expenses of Divisions I and II intercollegiate athletic programs report, 2008.

	REVENUES (IN THOUSANDS)	EXPENSES (IN THOUSANDS)	DIFFERENCE (IN THOUSANDS)
SPORT			
Football	$1,070	$1,483	-$413
Field Hockey	$171	$288	-$117
Men's Basketball	$746	$793	-$47
Women's Basketball	$337	$591	-$254
Men's Ice Hockey	$936	$781	$155
Women's Ice Hockey	$357	$492	-$135
Baseball	$193	$327	-$134
Softball	$151	$264	-$113
Men's Soccer	$175	$286	-$111
Women's Soccer	$155	$277	-$122

EXHIBIT 6.11 Revenues and expenses for selected programs at Division I schools with Championship Subdivision football programs.

Source: 2005–06 NCAA revenues and expenses of Divisions I and II intercollegiate athletic programs report, 2008.

the same in terms of overall percentage of expenditures, but Championship Subdivision schools pay approximately $6 million less in this category. These data also show that Championship Subdivision schools also operate on average at a deficit of $923,000, approximately $165,000 more than that at Bowl Subdivision schools, on revenues that are significantly lower.

The final comparison between D-I departments can be assessed by examining the revenues and expenses in individual programs at Championship Subdivision schools, as shown in Exhibit 6.11. At the Championship Subdivision level, football and men's basketball generate neither the revenues nor the profits accrued at the Bowl Subdivision schools, but because most other sports run lower average deficits, the average overall departmental deficit difference is mitigated. Only 25 percent of Championship Subdivision programs reported a profit (at an average of $450,000), with 64 percent losing an average of $810,000 and 11 percent breaking even. At this level, 33 percent of men's basketball programs reported an average profit of $440,000, while 59 percent reported an average loss of $330,000, and 9 percent broke even.

An example of the revenues and expenses of an individual program with a Championship Subdivision football program is seen with the 2008–09 budget figures from the University of Maine, in Exhibit 6.12.

Division II schools with football programs

Revenue and expense data for 100 percent of Division II institutions with football programs (at the time, 151) are outlined in Exhibits 6.13 and 6.14. These schools comprise 15 percent of the total NCAA membership. The data show an increased

EXHIBIT 6.12   University of Maine 2008–09 athletics budget.

REVENUE

- Institutional support: $5.6 million
- University benefits: $1.8 million
- Ticket sales: $1.75 million
- NCAA revenue sharing: $675,000
- Summer camps: $659,000
- Guarantees: $600,000
- Corporate sponsorships: $475,000
- Merchandise sales: $415,000
- Fundraising: $320,000

EXPENSES

- Grants-in-aid: $5.4 million
- Sport operating funds: $5.1 million
- Administration: $3.5 million
- Summer camps: $525,000
- Medical services $500,000

Source: University of Maine (2009).

reliance on internal revenue sources, constituting 72 percent of all such institutions' athletic funding, as well as similar budgetary proportions for most all expenditures as D-I schools with Championship Subdivision football programs. The data also show that these D-II programs run an average annual deficit, specifically $271,000, which is less than D-I schools but more significant when compared to the levels of revenue generated. At Division II schools without football programs, the average annual revenues are $1.6 million and annual average total expenses equal $1.91 million, for an annual average deficit of $310,000, higher than that at schools with football programs.

EXHIBIT 6.13   Sources of total revenue — Division II schools with football programs.

REVENUE CATEGORY	TOTAL FROM REVENUE SOURCE (IN THOUSANDS)	PERCENTAGE OF TOTAL REVENUES
Institutional support	$1,457	57
Student activity fees	$380	15
Cash from alumni and others	$209	8
Ticket sales	$122	5
Direct government support	$122	5
Guarantees and options	$17	1
NCAA and conference distribution	$12	0
Postseason compensation	$8	0
Other	$229	9
Total	$2,559	100%

Source: 2005–06 NCAA revenues and expenses of Divisions I and II intercollegiate athletic programs report, 2008.

EXPENSE CATEGORY	TOTAL EXPENDITURE (IN THOUSANDS)	PERCENTAGE OF TOTAL EXPENDITURES
Salaries and benefits	$1,072	39
Grants-in-aid	$849	31
Team travel	$260	9
Equipment/uniforms/supplies	$155	6
Contract services	$51	2
Recruiting	$43	2
Sports camps	$43	2
Game officials	$38	1
Fundraising	$29	1
Guarantees and options	$12	0
Other	$197	7
Total operating expenses	$2,748	100%
Debt service	$9	
Capital expenditures	$73	
Total	$2,830	

Operating and total expenses—Division II schools with football programs.   **EXHIBIT   6.14**

Source: 2005–06 NCAA revenues and expenses of Divisions I and II intercollegiate athletic programs report, 2008.

Exhibit 6.15 provides data regarding revenues and expenses for specific sports programs at D-II schools that sponsor football. All sports shown, other than men's ice hockey, reported an aggregated average annual deficit. Twenty-nine percent of D-II football programs reported a profit (at an average of $107,000), 63 percent reported deficits (at an average of $286,000), and 8 percent reported breaking even. Thirty percent of D-II men's basketball programs reported a profit (at an average of $48,000), 63 percent reported deficits (at an average of $115,000), and 7 percent broke even. Similarly, 30 percent of women's basketball programs reported profits (albeit at a lower annual average of $30,000), 62 percent reported deficits (also at a lower annual average, $105,000), and 8 percent broke even.

Division III schools

The most recent data were collected from Division III schools (41 percent of the overall NCAA membership), also compiled by Daniel Fulks for the NCAA from information from 916 institutions (89 percent of the division at the time). The report containing the data draws comparisons between schools that support football programs and those that do not. At schools with football, the average total operating expenses were $1.57 million (an increase of 26 percent from two years earlier). At schools without football the total was $900,000 (an increase of 34

EXHIBIT **6.15**   Revenues and expenses for selected programs at Division II schools with football programs.

SPORT	REVENUES (IN THOUSANDS)	EXPENSES (IN THOUSANDS)	DIFFERENCE (IN THOUSANDS)
Football	$465	$604	-$139
Field Hockey	$110	$124	-$14
Men's Basketball	$200	$258	-$58
Women's Basketball	$174	$231	-$57
Men's Ice Hockey	$785	$617	$168
Women's Ice Hockey	$361	$524	-$163
Baseball	$106	$135	-$29
Softball	$83	$110	-$27
Men's Soccer	$92	$124	-$32
Women's Soccer	$81	$116	-$35

Source: 2005–06 NCAA revenues and expenses of Divisions I and II intercollegiate athletic programs report, 2008.

percent from two years earlier). The average expense per student at schools with football equaled $3,400 (up from $3,000 two years earlier), and at schools without football, the total was $3,700 per student (up from $3,100 two years previous). Exhibits 6.16 and 6.17 show revenues and expenses, respectively, for several sports at schools in the division that offer football (note that direct game expenses include team travel, game officials, equipment, uniforms, and supplies).

EXHIBIT **6.16**   Revenues for selected programs at Division III schools with football programs.

SPORT	FUNDRAISING	INSTITUTIONAL SUPPORT	ALL OTHER REVENUES	TOTAL REVENUES
Baseball	$11,400	$46,000	$9,700	$67,000
Softball	$7,100	$31,300	$16,700	$55,100
Men's Basketball	$6,800	$61,000	$7,000	$74,000
Women's Basketball	$5,300	$51,400	$13,600	$70,300
Field Hockey	$3,000	$35,800	$11,200	$50,100
Football	$16,400	$182,000	$13,600	$212,000
Men's Golf	$3,300	$16,700	$6,400	$26,400
Women's Golf	$1,300	$13,300	$5,500	$20,100
Men's Soccer	$3,400	$40,800	$5,500	$49,700
Women's Soccer	$3,100	$33,400	$12,200	$48,800

Source: 2002–03 NCAA revenues and expenses of Division III intercollegiate athletic programs report, 2005.

	DIRECT GAME EXPENSES	RECRUITING	SALARIES	ALL OTHER EXPENSES	TOTAL OPERATING EXPENSES
Expenses for selected programs at Division III schools with football programs.					EXHIBIT 6.17
SPORT					
Baseball	$26,300	$1,400	$32,000	$6,700	$66,800
Softball	$20,200	$1,100	$25,500	$4,900	$51,700
Men's Basketball	$26,000	$3,600	$48,000	$7,000	$85,000
Women's Basketball	$23,800	$2,200	$41,500	$7,000	$74,000
Field Hockey	$15,800	$1,000	$31,900	$3,300	$52,000
Football	$60,600	$9,900	$131,100	$24,200	$225,900
Men's Golf	$8,200	$500	$11,900	$2,800	$23,200
Women's Golf	$6,100	$300	$11,200	$1,900	$19,500
Men's Soccer	$17,700	$1,800	$26,200	$8,100	$53,800
Women's Soccer	$16,400	$1,600	$24,100	$7,600	$49,700

Source: 2002–03 NCAA revenues and expenses of Division III intercollegiate athletic programs report, 2005.

Comparison of the four types of schools

Although the available data for Division III do not afford an exact match with the data for Divisions I and II, these data are still meaningful enough for us to think about how budgets and finance impact each type of school. Exhibit 6.18 shows overall aggregated average departmental revenue and expense data for each type of school examined in this section.

The comparative data suggest that revenues and expenses are higher based on the level at which schools choose to compete in football, and that competing in the Division I Bowl Subdivision in football does not guarantee that an athletic department will balance its books. Also, clearly, schools that compete at the other levels are not assured of breaking even.

TYPE OF SCHOOL	REVENUES	EXPENSES	DIFFERENCE
Aggregated average revenues and expenses with Division I, II, and III schools football programs.		EXHIBIT 6.18	
Division I Bowl Subdivision	$29.41M	$30.17M	-$76,000
Division I Championship Subdivision	$6.99M	$7.54M	-$55,000
Division II with football	$2.55M	$2.83M	-$28,000
Division III with football	N/A	$1.57M	N/A

Source: 2002–03 NCAA revenues and expenses of Division III intercollegiate athletic programs report, 2005; 2005–06 NCAA revenues and expenses of Divisions I and II intercollegiate athletic programs report, 2008.

SIGNIFICANT DEPARTMENT REVENUES

The data shown thus far have given us a good overall picture of financial and budget issues across intercollegiate athletics. Now we will look more in depth at the nature of specific revenues impacting departmental bottom lines that often are overlooked but are important nonetheless.

Fundraising

As noted by several current athletic managers and school presidents, and supported by NCAA research, athletic department fundraising efforts are critically important to the financial well-being of athletic departments. The data show that fundraising from alumni, boosters, and others accounts for 18 percent ($5.27 million) of the annual aggregate average Division I Bowl Subdivision athletic budget, making it the second most important revenue source for these departments. The annual aggregate average for Championship Subdivision schools from this source is $540,000—8 percent of departmental budgets—and also 8 percent ($290,000) at Division II schools with football programs. One study showed that athletics gifts accounted for 26 percent of total giving at Bowl Subdivision schools. Exhibits 6.19 and 6.20 present past and more recent data outlining the importance and components of fundraising programs at several Division I institutions. In all, the top 54 athletic fundraising programs brought in more than $1 billion in cash gifts in 2008 (Wolverton, 2009).

Donations

The swimming program at the University of Arizona is both successful in the water and on solid financial footing because of donations. Coach Frank Busch knows this

EXHIBIT 6.19	Athletic donations data at selected Division I schools.			
SCHOOL	ATHLETIC DONATIONS IN 2006	AMOUNT RAISED IN CAPITAL CAMPAIGNS FOR ATHLETICS IN PAST 5 YEARS	GOAL OF CURRENT CAPITAL CAMPAIGN FOR ATHLETICS	NUMBER OF FULL-TIME ATHLETICS FUNDRAISERS
University of North Carolina	$51M	$230M	N/A	20
University of Virginia	$45.24M	$188M	N/A	19
Ohio State University	$39M	N/A	$100M	9
University of Florida	$37.4M	N/A	N/A	11
University of Georgia	$36.6M	$64M	N/A	8
University of Tennessee	$35.8M	N/A	$210M	8
Louisiana State University	$35M	N/A	$100M	6
U. of California at Berkeley	$34.1M	$100M	$125M	12
Texas A&M University	$32.1M	$95M	N/A	18
University of Louisville	$30.6M	$53M	N/A	9

Source: Fund Raising, 2007. Copyright 2007, *The Chronicle of Higher Education.* Reprinted with permission.

| | Totals and elements of athletic fundraising at selected Division I schools, 2007–08. | EXHIBIT | 6.20 |

INSTITUTION	ATHLETIC DONATIONS IN 2007–08	GIFTS FOR PRIORITY SEATING	GIFTS FOR LUXURY SEATING	GIFTS FOR FACILITIES	GIFTS FOR ENDOWMENT
University of Texas	$45.9M	$17.6M	$16.9M	$11.4M	$0
University of Florida	$45.6M	$23.4M	$11.6M	$10.3M	$100,000
University of Tennessee	$38.4M	$13.3M	$6M	$14.6M	$2.5M
University of Virginia	$36.3M	—	$4M	$16.5M	$3M
University of Georgia	$36.1M	$29.9M	$3.2M	$1.2M	$4.5M
University of Kansas	$34.7M	—	$1.3M	$9.6M	$463,791
University of Oklahoma	$33.6M	$15.8M	$3M	$12.5M	$2M
Ohio State University	$32.4M	$6.8M	$1.6M	$4.5M	$2.9M
University of North Carolina	$31.6M	$8.5M	$0	$9.3M	$9.2M
Louisiana State University	$30.4M	$4.5M	$11.8M	$7.3M	$2.1M

Source: Fund Raising, 2009. Copyright 2009, *The Chronicle of Higher Education.* Reprinted with permission.

is not because of any revenues his program generates; it is because of the efforts of one donor—William Hillenbrand, a former swimmer at the school—who gave enough money to renovate the pool and put a substantial percentage of his fortune ("a staggering amount of money," according to Busch) in a trust that went to Arizona swimming upon his death. Says Busch: "Our sport has one of those guys . . . you don't (remember) who graduated from your program 25 years ago and hit it big with a dot.com and now has more money than he knows what do to with. And one day he says, 'Here's $5 million for a new facility'" (Schoenfeld, 2006, p. 32). The school won both the men's and the women's NCAA D-I swimming championship in 2008, the first ever for both programs. Busch knows he's lucky, because at many other Division I schools, coaches and student-athletes in the so-called non-revenue sports are forced to work to raise money on their own to cover team expenses.

Perhaps no school may be more influenced by fundraising than the University of Oregon, a public school with 20,000 undergrads, located in Eugene and a member of the Division I Pac-10 Conference. Donations helped pay for $160 million in renovations to the school's main athletic center and $100 million to renovate the school's football stadium. Much of the monies donated to Oregon athletics has come from two main donors: former insurance executive Patrick Kilkenny (who served as the school's AD from 2007 to 2009, donated his $500,000 annual salary back to the institution), and Nike co-founder and chairman Phil Knight (a former track athlete at the school, whose estimated personal worth is $8 billion). Knight made a recent gift of $100 million, earmarked for athletics, to the school's ongoing capital campaign (which raised $717 million, 40 percent to go to athletics). His gift creates a "legacy fund" to protect against future budget shortfalls, especially important because the school plans to construct a new $200 million home basketball facility (intended to be paid for by issuing state bonds).

Among many Oregon faculty members who have criticized these risky expenditures is Nathan Tublitz, co-chair of the Coalition on Intercollegiate Athletics. He stated: "They're potentially mortgaging the academic future of the university to build an ultraopulent facility" (Fain, 2007, p. A39). Neal Zoumboukas, a former assistant football coach at the school hired as an emissary to the rest of the institution, was surprised by the reaction to the department's efforts to become self-sustaining through fundraising: "We shouldn't be chastised for what we're doing. We should be complimented." In all, nine of the school's 40 full-time fundraisers work for athletics, and they brought in $12.5 million in 2006 (Fain, 2007, p. A39).

Others at Oregon view the monetary contributions that benefit athletics as also aiding the institution as a whole. Then-school president David Frohnmeyer noted, "That single 'O' [part of the school's athletic trademarks] is now a world-recognized brand. We actually see a pour-over effect helping the academic side," and a law school professor believes that athletic success puts Oregon on an equal footing with Pac-10 foes Stanford University and the University of California. He stated, "I think success in athletics helps sustain, in the public's eye, that we're a quality institution" (Fain, 2007, p. A40). It can be argued that this was the case for donors such as alumnus David Petrone, chairman of the Housing Capital Company, a company based in the San Francisco Bay area. A big supporter of Ducks athletics, Petrone began writing $1,000 checks 15 years ago, bringing him "closer to the university." He has given more than $5 million to the school, more than half of which have gone to academic programs (Fain, 2007).

Donor access and influence. With these extensive donations, questions of access and influence are inevitable. Phil Knight regularly talks with university officials and coaches, dons a headset at football games to listen to coaches' play-calling, and is allowed to roam the sidelines. He clashed with former Oregon AD Bill Moos, which many say led to Moos's subsequent firing after the school joined an anti-sweatshop group, the Workers Rights Consortium. Knight and Nike have been oft-criticized for their low pay and poor working conditions for workers in Asia. Said Knight: "Bill Moos had ten chances to make the right decision . . . and missed every one of them" (Fain, 2007, p. A41). And in what some called a fit of pique over the issue, Knight gave $105 million to rival Stanford's Graduate School of Business, which he attended after his undergrad time at Oregon.

Former AD Kilkenny, who helped pay Moos a $2 million severance package before assuming the position, was reportedly hired in part because he is a close personal friend of Knight, despite never having earned even an undergraduate degree (having dropped out of Oregon in the early 1970s). Then-school president Frohnmeyer claims he informed Knight of the Kilkenny hire only after it had been made. Kilkenny also had resigned from the school's board of trustees in 2006 over the Workers Rights Consortium issue. In an interview on ESPN's *Outside the Lines* program in 2008, Kilkenny called the move "a statement of support for Phil" and described his relationship with Knight as one "based on professional respect. . . . He's an amazing human being, and I'd like to call him a friend." Kilkenny admitted that he would consult with Knight and other donors when making personnel decisions.

The question of access and influence is not limited to Oregon. R. Gerald Turner, president of Southern Methodist University (a school familiar with the dark side of booster involvement) and co-chair of the Knight Commission on Intercollegiate

Athletics, warns: "There's just so much money around athletics programs. When there's all that money, you have to worry about people who care nothing about the institution but are absolutely devoted to that program's winning. If you're not vigilant, it can quickly get out of control" (Wolverton, 2007a, p. A40). Former Auburn University president, William Muse, who battled over these issues while at the school, said: "When people contribute big bucks, sometimes they expect to provide not only advice, but direction. I suspect it's human nature to feel if you've given a whole bunch of money, you not only want to be listened to, but want whatever suggestions you've made to be implemented" (p. A40).

Impact of financial markets on donations. Even well-heeled donors are not immune to feeling the pain of fluctuating financial markets, which in turn can impact their willingness to give to athletic departments. In 2008, when the global economy endured a significant downturn, the $165 million donated to the Oklahoma State University (OSU) athletic department to improve facilities by billionaire oilman T. Boone Pickens, which had been invested along with $37 million from other donors into a hedge fund controlled by Pickens, lost a considerable percentage of its value. At that point, OSU AD Mike Holder said all projects related to the funds would be put on hold until the fund recovered. A spokesman for Pickens said, "Unfortunately, the economic downturn has hit everyone hard, and Boone is not immune. . . . Hopefully, the markets will improve soon and Boone can get back to the business of giving serious money. Boone likes making money, and he likes to give it away" (Drape & Evans, 2008, p. B17). Donors to athletic departments at the universities of Oklahoma and Kansas were also on shaky ground, threatening the prospects of projects at those schools as well.

Student-athlete efforts

At Pennsylvania State University, a public school with 38,000 undergrads located in University Park and a member of the Division I Big Ten Conference, members of the school's fencing team spend the morning after home football games cleaning trash out of the 107,000-seat stadium. This job earns the team money to take an overseas trip once every four years. At Butler University, a private school with 4,400 undergraduates in Indianapolis, Indiana, and a member of the Horizon League, the softball team does the same after home football and basketball games, as the sport is responsible for raising money to cover 15 percent of its budgeted expenses.

At the University of Utah, a public school with 29,000 undergraduates located in Salt Lake City and a member of the Division I Mountain West Conference, male and female swimmers work on similar projects to raise money. Said Utah swimmer Andrew Brown: "I'm just happy we still have a swimming team, because a lot of Division I teams are being cut. It's unfair that we have to put in extra work because our sport might not be as fun to watch, but it's fair that the school is giving us the chance to work to keep the program around" (Kider, 2007, p. A16).

Endowments

As the data indicate, fundraising is a much more significant component in athletic department revenues than just to keep the fencing team in foils and sabres. Several Division I programs, therefore, are seeking to build an athletic department endowment close to that of Stanford University, which topped $500 million in 2008 and generates $25 million a year to cover expenses for grants-in-aid and other programmatic needs as institutional support resources dwindle. In all, a study (Fund Raising, 2009) reported that more than two dozen athletic departments are involved in or planning endowment campaigns, with the combined goal of money to be raised totaling $2.3 billion. These efforts are seeking money to endow (meaning that the revenue generated from the gift would pay for a specific expenditure) salaries (which would cost $1 million for a volleyball coach at the University of Virginia), team expenses ($8 million for the golf program at the University of Georgia), and grants-in-aid ($32 million for 284 student-athletes at Ohio State). Endowment efforts have raised endowments to $55 million at Penn State, $51 million at Georgia, and $43 million at Florida State; and Cal is looking to boost its athletic endowment fund from $45 million to $450 million by 2014, and to $1 billion by 2030 (Keller, 2009; Wolverton, 2009). Exhibit 6.21 lists changes in athletic endowments at several other Division I institutions.

Licensing

Licensed products—items of clothing or products bearing the name or logo of a popular collegiate or professional sport team—have been around for a comparatively short time and comprise a specialized subset of the sporting goods industry. Both of these areas produce revenues in the billions of dollars worldwide and are the third-highest source of domestic revenue for major sports properties (Adams, 2003).

The manufacturers of licensed products, the *licensees*, include well-known sport-product companies such as Nike, Under Armour, and Adidas; prominent electronics manufacturers Nintendo, Sega, and Sony; and smaller firms such as Artcarved (jewelry), Mead (stationery), and Pinnacle (trading cards and memorabilia). Licensees pay sport organizations, the *licensors*, for the right to manufacture products bearing team and school names, nicknames, colors, and logos. If these names and logos are registered with the U.S. Patent and Trademark Office, they are called *trademarks*. A trademark is defined under the Federal Trademark Act of 1946, commonly referred to as the Lanham Act, as "any word, name, symbol, or

EXHIBIT 6.21 Athletic endowment values at selected Division I institutions.

INSTITUTION	ENDOWMENT VALUE, 2003	ENDOWMENT VALUE, 2008
University of North Carolina	$94M	$212M
Duke University	$68.5M	$150.7M
Georgia Institute of Technology	$48.6M	$80M
University of Virginia	$36.7M	$61.8M
University of Washington	$30M	$56M
University of Connecticut	$28.9M	$48M
Indiana University	$27.3M	$42.3M

Source: Fund Raising, 2009. Copyright 2009, *The Chronicle of Higher Education.* Reprinted with permission.

device or combination thereof adopted and used by a manufacturer or merchant to identify his goods and distinguish them from those manufactured or sold by others." The law defines *trademark infringement* as the reproduction, counterfeiting, copying, or imitation, in commerce of a registered mark, and bars companies that do not pay for the right to use these trademarks from manufacturing products bearing those marks (Lanham Act, 15 U.S.C. § 1051–1127, 1946).

Benefits of licensing

Licensing enables schools and teams to generate brand recognition and interest and to increase revenues with little financial risk. Licensees assume the risk by manufacturing the product and then paying a fee to the licensor, called a *royalty*, for the use of specific trademarks on specific products. Royalty fees generally range from 4 percent (for toys and games) to 20 percent (for trading cards and video games) and are based on gross sales at wholesale costs. Apparel royalties range from 11 percent for on-field items to 15 percent for player identified items (Adams, 2003). *Wholesale costs* are those paid by the retailer, not the price paid by consumers. Licensees use the established images and popularity of sport teams to boost their sales.

Over the course of the 20th century, intercollegiate athletic organizations gradually realized the financial potential of such connections. In 1924, while walking down Fifth Avenue in Manhattan, sportswriter Francis Wallace observed the shops' displays and neckties in colors of what he termed the "aristocracy of the gridiron" (Army, Harvard, Notre Dame, Princeton, and Yale), but none was licensed. In 1947, University of Oregon Athletic Director Leo Harris and famed filmmaker Walt Disney reached an agreement to allow Oregon to use Disney's Donald Duck image for the university's mascot. These were some early steps toward development of licensable properties, and the University of California, Los Angeles (UCLA) is generally credited with being the first school to enter into a licensing agreement in 1973, when its school bookstore granted a license to a watch manufacturer.

The NCAA formed its properties division to license championship merchandise in 1975, but it does not administer licensing programs for member schools. Significant revenue growth began in the late 1980s, when the University of Notre Dame, which began its licensing program in 1983, experienced growth of 375 percent between 1988 and 1989. Collegiate licensed product sales totaled $100 million in the early 1980s. In 1995, sales reached $2.5 billion. The peak for licensed sales for major college and pro licensed products was 1996, with sales of $13.8 billion. That figure had slipped to $11.8 billion by 2001 (Sperber, 1993; Nichols, 1995; Plata, 1996; Hiestand, 2002).

Some NCAA Division I-A schools administer their own licensing programs. The benefit of self-maintenance is that schools can retain a greater portion of sales revenues. The remainder of Division I Bowl Subdivision schools, like the smaller pro leagues and many Championship Subdivision schools, enlist the services of independent licensing companies to manage their programs. The Collegiate Licensing Company (CLC), formed in 1981, was purchased by sport marketing company IMG and is now part of its IMG College division. It articulates licensing agreements on behalf of approximately 200 colleges and universities, bowls, conferences, the Heisman Trophy and the NCAA as its independent licensing company. Client colleges pay a portion of the royalties to CLC for their efforts. We will learn more about CLC and IMG College in the Practitioner Perspective at the end of the chapter.

The importance of protecting trademarks for revenue and brand identity

The financial implications of protecting an intercollegiate athletic department's trademarks are significant, as was seen when the Georgia Institute of Technology, a public school with 13,000 undergraduates in Atlanta and a member of the Division I Atlantic Coast Conference, spent $800,000 to win a $600,000 settlement in a copyright infringement case with the Salt Lake City Buzz, a Class AAA minor league baseball team. Georgia Tech claimed that the team infringed on its Yellow Jacket mascot, named "Buzz." The claimed financial amount at risk was about $300,000 in annual licensing revenues that Tech used to pay for athletic aid and other athletic expenses. Said a Tech spokesperson: "The issue all along was not just financial. Licensing is a little more than selling t-shirts. It's brand awareness. Buzz . . . is one of Georgia Tech's biggest symbols." As part of the settlement, the Salt Lake City team opted to change its nickname to the "Stingers" (O'Toole, 2001, p. 1C).

Another case in which an intercollegiate athletic program sought to defend its trademark involved Texas A&M University and the NFL's Seattle Seahawks. Texas A&M, a public school with 38,000 undergraduates located in College Station and a member of the Division I Big 12 Conference, sought to keep the Seahawks from using the phrase "12th Man" (sometimes written "Twelfth Man"), which it claimed it owned under a common law trademark under Texas law, and to which it held registered trademark rights as granted by the U.S. Patent and Trademark Office. According to the school, the phrase refers to a game against then-powerhouse Centre College in 1922, when the Texas A&M team was running short of reserve players. Legend has it that former Aggies player E. King Gill was called to the sideline from the press box by head coach Dana X. Bible to suit up in case Gill was needed. (He wasn't; the Aggies won 22–14.) But Gill's willingness to play, even though he would be ineligible by today's standards, and serve his alma mater evolved into one of the school's most cherished traditions. Gill himself is memorialized with a statue on campus, donated by the Class of 1980. This story is related to all incoming first-year students during orientation, and the student body stands for the duration of home games as a symbolic gesture to signify their readiness to play. More recent head coaches have built on the tradition by utilizing non-athletic-aid recipient walk-on players (sometimes wearing a number 12 jersey), and the school has named its athletic fundraising arm the "12th Man Foundation" (Brown, Zuefle, & Bastista, 2007).

The Seahawks' use of the phrase came from a ceremony in which the team retired the number 12 jersey in 1984 to pay tribute to fan ardor that made its then-home venue, the Kingdome, the loudest in the league and, therefore, difficult for opposing offenses to hear snap counts. Upon moving into its new home venue in 2002, the team began to utilize the term more actively, selling team jerseys with the number 12 and "Fan" for the name on the back, along with other licensed products and merchandise, and using former players and celebrities to raise the "12th Man" banner during pre-game ceremonies. After the team's appearance in the 2006 Super Bowl, when these and other activities intensified, Texas A&M moved to protect its trademark (Brown, Zuefle, & Bastista, 2007).

Texas A&M stated that the Seahawks had ignored letters asking the team to cease use of the phrase, but the Seahawks responded that it the fans, not the club, were promoting the phrase, and that the team sold merchandise and raised banners only with the number 12. Texas A&M disagreed, claiming that the club had sold 12th man merchandise and created a 12th Man Club. The case was settled out of court in 2006. Texas A&M allowed the Seahawks to use the phrase in the northwestern United States and continue all current use of the phrase in merchandise sales and activities in exchange for a one-time licensing fee payment of $100,000 and an annual royalty of $5,000, and also state publicly, each time it is used, that the phrase is owned by the school (Brown, Zuefle, & Bastista, 2007).

These cases indicate that the schools placed high value on protecting their image and marks because they established a strong sense of brand identity with, and loyalty and commitment from, their fans and community members, which these schools had worked for decades to develop and strengthen. Protected images and marks are an important source of revenue, generated directly through fees and royalties paid for their use, and indirectly by strengthening the loyalty of a paying fan base.

Bowl games

Recall that the first American intercollegiate athletic events were two boat races between Harvard and Yale. A railroad company wanted to accustom vacationers to travel on its line by providing an event to attract them. Does this sound like any contemporary intercollegiate athletic event that takes place annually, say in December and January? If you thought of bowl games, you're on to something.

From our reading in this chapter, we know that Division I football competition is segmented based on the type of program that schools offer, and that the amount of revenue an athletic department can generate is directly connected to its football program's competitive classification. In 2004, the Fox network secured broadcast rights for the Fiesta, Orange, and Sugar Bowls, and three so-called "national championship" games between 2007 and 2010 for approximately $330 million ($82.5 million annually). In 2008, ESPN finalized an agreement to carry the Bowl Championship Series from January 2011 through January 2014, paying nearly $125 million annually ($495 million in total) for the Fiesta, Orange, and Sugar Bowls, and the so-called "national championship" game. ABC, ESPN's corporate partner, has rights to the Rose Bowl at $30 million a year through 2014, but this game also could migrate to ESPN at some point. The new deal, too, gives ESPN radio and digital rights, which includes operation of the official BCS website and simulcasting of games online and for mobile devices.

Fox, unhappy with the decision of the commissioners of the BCS-member conferences and member-school presidents, released a statement that read, "Unfortunately, [they] were not satisfied [with our bid], and they've decided to take their jewel events to pay television." Fox Sports president Bob Thompson put it this way: "We put together what we thought was a very competitive bid [Fox offered $395 million over four years, and had a chance to match ESPN's offer—and declined]. . . . Given the current economic condition, we went as far as we could. And we lost" (Smith & Ourand, 2008, p. 36). ESPN's Sean Bratches, executive vice-president of sales and marketing, justified the outlay this way: "With the robust college football schedule we have across multiple platforms, our ability to package the BCS will drive some incremental revenue to our company" (McDonell, 2008, p. 12; Weir & Hiestand, 2008). In the case of media-based revenue, bowl games rights fees clearly make a significant difference to the schools that belong to BCS-member conferences (Sandomir, 2004).

So how are the bowl games able to generate other revenues so they may entice schools to participate? Consider the case of the Outback Bowl, played each New Year's Day at Raymond James Stadium in Tampa, Florida, matching up teams from the Southeastern Conference and the Big Ten Conference. The game was moved to Tampa from Birmingham, Alabama, in 1986, and has been played as the "All-American" and "Hall of Fame" bowls. In the 2005 game, the University of Georgia defeated the University of Wisconsin, 24–21, and each school brought home $2.75 million. How is this bowl, which lacks the panache of the BCS games (which pay participants $11 million to $14 million) or the tradition of others such as the Cotton Bowl, able to generate this revenue? It happened, according to Jim McVay, president and CEO of the Outback Bowl (the national Australian-themed steakhouse restaurant chain, headquartered in Tampa, became title sponsor in 1996), because "We've worked hard . . . and positioned ourselves as one of the top bowl games in the country in terms of the teams we select and what we pay" (Sandomir, 2006, p. C12). The Outback Bowl, which is shown on ESPN during a late-morning slot, generated a 4.5 rating in 2006 (or 4 million households nationwide), the second-highest rated bowl for the network (after the Holiday Bowl).

ESPN's "Bowl Week," when 20 of the 28 bowls that year were shown, is the network's highest rated week of the year. The 2009 Outback Bowl game (in which Iowa defeated South Carolina, 31–10) also drew just over 4 million viewers (a 10 percent drop from the previous year), ranking it 17th of the 34 games that year (Sports Wrap, 2009). In the 2010 game, Auburn defeated Northwestern in overtime, 38–35, drawing nearly 50,000 spectators, with a per-school payout of $3.3 million (Auburn's Field Goal, 2010).

The Outback Bowl is run by the nonprofit Tampa Bay Bowl Association (similar in organization to most other bowls), which in 2006 generated revenues of $8.8 million (up 75 percent from 1997) and an excess of $604,126. Of that $8.8 million in revenue, $3.4 million came from ticket sales, $2.1 million from ESPN's broadcast rights payment, and $1 million from Outback for naming rights. Most of the revenues that year went to the participating schools (University of Florida and University of Iowa, $2.65 million each). Game-day expenses totaled $443,055, and advertising costs were $169,435. CEO McVay earned a salary of close to $500,000, making him the highest paid bowl executive in the country. McVay's main tasks are to negotiate TV and sponsorship deals, which saves the bowl the approximately $450,000 it would have cost to have an outside company such as IMG College or ISP Sports for the service (Sandomir, 2006).

What does all this mean for the host city and surrounding communities? Is the motivation the same now as it was at Lake Winnespesaukee in 1852? According to Sandomir (2006), bowl games today are "civic enterprises designed to put the best face on the cities where they are played" (p. C13). Beginning the previous summer, the Outback Bowl sponsors 20 promotional events, including parades, festivals, pageants, golf and tennis tournaments, team outings, and other events. Says McVay, "Our mission statement is simple. We're out to create an economic impact in the Tampa Bay area and to positively showcase our community nationally and internationally" (p. C13).

Sound familiar? We know that back in 1852, the Harvard and Yale teams received two weeks of fun at the expense of the railroad company for their efforts, and the winning Harvard crew won a pair of silver-tipped black walnut oars. A nice gesture, but not quite $14 million, or even $2.75 million, even when adjusting for inflation. But even today, bowl participants don't go home empty-handed. NCAA bylaws allow bowl game participants to receive up to $500 in gifts from bowl organizers (in addition to the $350 in gifts that schools can provide their own participants). For the 2010 Outback Bowl, participants received gift cards from Best Buy and Outback, a Pro-Swiss watch, a Jostens ring, and a commemorative hat. Other examples of bowl swag include HD camcorders (Gaylord Hotels Music City, GMAC, R&L Carriers New Orleans, Papajohns.com), TVs/LCD monitors (AutoZone Liberty, Pacific Life Holiday, Rose Bowl, San Diego County Credit Union Poinsettia), and other sundry electronics such as iPods (Valero Alamo, Meineke Car Care) and a Garmin GPS (Allstate Sugar) (Broughton, 2009).

Another way that schools seek to maximize revenues from bowl games is through the selection of participating schools, often made so bowls can generate as much revenue as possible. For example, in 2007, when the Chick-fil-A Bowl leadership was determining which schools would be invited to play, it made its decision in large part based on the number of tickets each team would sell. The bowl has an agreement that allows it the first choice of schools from the Atlantic Coast Conference (ACC) after the conference gets its BCS entry, and usually the second choice from the Southeastern Conference (SEC) after its BCS entry. The alliances with these conferences have benefited the bowl in terms of ticket sales. The game, played on New Year's Eve in Atlanta's Georgia Dome, has sold out 12 years in a row, ranks first in attendance for non-BCS games, and drew more than 75,000 fans to the 2006 game (a 31–24 Georgia win over Virginia Tech). In 2007, sixth-ranked Virginia Tech won the ACC title game, defeating 11th-ranked Boston College (BC) 30–16 in Jacksonville, Florida.

By rights, you would think that BC would get the Chick-fil-A bid as league runner-up, but BC brought a scant number of fans (fewer than 5,000) to Jacksonville, which Chick-fil-A Bowl president Gary Stokan noticed. "It's not good. . . . We have to protect our ticket," he said (Schlabach, 2007, p. 7). If Virginia Tech had lost, it would have received the bid to go to Atlanta, but Stokan was concerned about selecting a school like BC that might not sell its allotment of 17,500 tickets. The bowl selected the University of Miami in 2004 and 2005, which sold fewer than 10,000 tickets each year. Because of this concern, Stokan selected Clemson University over BC, even though BC had beaten Clemson during the ACC season. "The city really depends on us because we're one of the top 10 conventions. We have an obligation to hotels, restaurants and retailers" (p. 7). The decision proved to address Stokan's concerns, as Clemson sold all of its 17,500 tickets in 24 hours, and the game again was a sellout.

SIGNIFICANT DEPARTMENT EXPENSES

The second half of the budgetary equation for athletic departments is managing expenses. We will examine some of the most significant expenses that departmental managers must consider when attempting to balance their budgets or attain profitability.

Coaches' compensation

As we learned from the expense data outlined above, salaries and benefits are the most significant expenses for intercollegiate athletic departments. Also, many school presidents and ADs are concerned about the trend of escalating costs associated with the enterprise, and nowhere is this seen more substantially than in the recent increases in salaries and benefits for head coaches in football and men's basketball.

Football

Consider that, as of the 2009 season, several Division I Bowl Subdivision head football coaches (Mack Brown, Texas, $5 million; Pete Carroll, Southern California, $4.4 million; Bob Stoops, Oklahoma, $4.3 million; Urban Meyer, Florida, $4 million) earned $4 million a year or more in salary alone. Six more made at least $3 million, and another 16 earned at least $2 million, slightly double the number of two years before, with the average pay for the 120 head coaches rising to $1.36 million. Alabama's Nick Saban's annual estimated total compensation was close to $5 million a year (on a salary of $4.1 million). Making on or about the 2009 total salary average were Bobby Petrino (Arkansas) and Jeff Tedford (California). The head coach who earned the least in total compensation? Charlie Weatherbie of the University of Louisiana-Monroe, at just under $160,000 (not including maximum potential bonuses of $30,000) (Behind the Salary Numbers, 2009).

Top assistants made considerably less, with defensive coordinators averaging $200,000 in total compensation, and offensive coordinators earning $193,000, but Monte Kiffin, former defensive coordinator at Tennessee (father of former UT head coach Lane Kiffin) made $1.2 million a year (plus a $300,000 bonus if he stayed through the end of the regular season). Kiffin's nine assistants at UT earned an average of $369,000. In all, 66 assistants, including more than two dozen in the Southeastern Conference, make $300,000 or more a year. By comparison, head coaches in the conference average $2.64 million a year in salary. In all, the staffs at Alabama, Louisiana State, and Oklahoma earn more than $6 million in salaries. At the University of Missouri, head coach Gary Pinkel's pay has increased from $585,000 in 2000 to $2.52 million guaranteed (an increase of 331 percent), and his assistant's pay grew 130 percent, from $885,000 to $2.1 million guaranteed. NCAA bylaws require that all coaches are contractually obligated to provide a written detailed account annually to the school president for all athletically related income and benefits from all sources outside the institution (Burke, 2008; Pinkel's Deals, 2009; Wieberg, 2009; Wieberg et al., 2009). The lowest paid assistants, at $30,000 a year, were Louisiana-Monroe's Marty Humphrey and New Mexico State University's defensive backs coach Mike Rutenberg, who puts in 112 hours a week during the season, making his hourly compensation $5.58 an hour—nearly two dollars less than New Mexico's state minimum wage (Perez, 2009).

Oklahoma AD Joe Castiglione makes no apologies for paying $4.3 million to his head coach, Bob Stoops. Before hiring him in 1998, the school's storied program had been foundering. Since Stoops' arrival at the Norman campus, his 2000 team won the national championship and his teams have won close to 100 games and posted several top-10 poll finishes. Athletics revenues grew from $26.1 million in 1999, the year before his arrival, to $64.6 million in 2006, with football accounting for more than half of that total. Without football revenue, the athletic department would have shown a deficit of more than $19 million. In addition, donations to athletics have quadrupled, from $4.2 million to $17.1 million, and the athletic department has turned more than $2.5 million back to the institution for non-athletic "academic enhancement."

Said Castilgione in an interview, pausing for effect after each word: "Bob . . . Stoops . . . is . . . worth . . . every . . . penny . . . he . . . gets" (Wieberg, 2006, p. 16C). Stoops' deal runs through 2011, and he collected a $3 million "anniversary benefit" in 2008, his tenth year at the school. By comparison, school president David Boren makes only $312,000, and the average salary for presidents at schools similar to Oklahoma is just under $400,000; full professors make an average of $95,650 (Wieberg, 2006; Wieberg & Upton, 2007). Oklahoma's head of the faculty senate, chemistry professor Roger Frech, does not begrudge Stoops his income, saying,

> I suppose eyebrows are arched and raised from time to time. . . . I think faculty, in general, recognize there are significant differences in the market costs for individuals in different disciplines. . . . You may not personally put the same value on the football program that someone else might. But I think that's sort of the real world. (Wieberg, 2006, p. 16C)

At Alabama, administrators justify the compensation of head football coach Nick Saban because of the program's profitability—estimated at $32 million in 2007, with football revenues accounting for 77 percent of all departmental funds. The profits were earmarked to pay off the $130 million in departmental debt incurred for capital improvements. Alabama president Robert Witt, described as "decidedly pro-football" by *Forbes* magazine writer Monte Burke (2008, p. 2), also highlighted Saban's influence in aiding the school's $500 million capital campaign, noting, "We had 100,000 donors in that campaign, and a major reason they support us is football. . . . Why do Ivy League schools even bother to field teams that are never going to win a bowl game? It keeps the alumni money flowing. That's how you pay for the English department" (p. 2). Witt also notes that none of Saban's salary comes from either student fees or state funds, coming instead from departmentally generated revenue sources. While Witt's claim about the relation between winning teams and donations to academic programs has been echoed by many school presidents and administrators, scholar (and former Notre Dame football player) Michael Oriard points out that the evidence to support this claim is largely missing. He cites the work of Cornell University economist Robert Frank, whose research showed that the documented evidence for donations to academic programs based on athletic success were "meager and inconclusive" (Oriard, 2009, p. 245).

Occasionally coaches themselves have been questioned about the propriety of their salaries in relation to other salaries and expenditures at their schools. In one such case, in 2009, University of Connecticut men's basketball coach Jim Calhoun was questioned at a post-game press conference about the appropriateness of his $1.6 million salary—qualifying him as the highest-paid state employee—in light of Connecticut's recent $2 billion budget deficit. When asked by journalist and political activist Ken Krayeske whether he was considering giving any money back to help close the deficit, Calhoun responded that he makes "a lot more than that" and said he would return

> not a dime. I'd like to be able to retire someday. . . . Quite frankly, [the men's basketball program] brings in $12 million to the university [later reports put the figure at $7.3 million, of which the program spent $6.1 million] . . . nothing to do with state funds. . . . Get some facts and come back and see me. . . . My advice to you is, shut up. (Anthony, 2009a, p. 1)

Connecticut governor M. Jodi Rell called Calhoun's remarks "an embarrassing display" (Nocera, 2009, p. 2), and members of the state legislature called for Calhoun to be reprimanded. Calhoun later complained that the school didn't support him during the post-tirade media attention: "I would have liked to have had maybe a statement come out of our athletic department . . . simply saying that 'Coach may have been a little too harsh . . . but he's our guy'" (Amid Slump, 2009, p. 4C; Anthony, 2009b, p. 1; Lawmakers, 2009).

U. S. Senator Charles Grassley (R-Iowa) also spoke out against the high salaries earned by Texas's Mack Brown and Football Bowl Subdivision (FBC) head coaching colleagues, commenting: "There always seems to be money for million-dollar salaries (for coaches) . . . even with staff salary freezes and tuition increases" (Berkowitz & Wieberg, 2009, p. 10C). Exhibit 6.22 provides the aggregated average salary and benefit expenditures at Division I and II schools with football.

Basketball

High salaries also are paid to select Division I men's basketball coaches. Heading into the 2008–09 season, University of Tennessee head coach Bruce Pearl earned $1.1 million a year in base salary, endorsements, and other compensation, through 2012. In justifying the contract, which includes a buyout clause if the school chooses to terminate it, and a penalty clause if Pearl leaves for another job before it expires, school president Dr. John Peterson commented: "Not only is Coach Pearl one of the very best coaches in the nation, but more importantly, he had become a great ambassador for our university" (UT Gives Pearl Pay Raise, 2006, p. 1).

Even select men's assistant basketball coaches can cash in. An example is Kansas State University's Dalonte Hill, who became associate head coach of the program in 2007 at an annual salary of $150,000 and an additional $270,000 from media appearances and other services. Hill came to the school along with then head coach Bob Huggins, but when Huggins left to take the head job at West Virginia University, top assistant Frank Martin took over for Huggins and Hill was promoted in kind. Hill is known for his recruiting expertise and was responsible for attracting now-NBA star Michael Beasley to Kansas State. The reform group the Coalition on Intercollegiate Athletics noted that Hill's salary exceeds that of Kansas State president Jon Wefald, and referred to the salary boost as a reward for recruiting Beasley, even though it seemed clear that he would leave after one year for the NBA. Kansas State AD Bob Krause took exception to the Coalition's characterization of the salary boost, noting that Hill's compensation included responsibilities for game preparation, recruitment, and bench coaching. "[Hill's] a rising star," noted Wefald, "and I can tell you now he's turned down job offers that were equal to or greater than his current situation" (Wieberg, 2008b, p. 6C).

EXHIBIT 6.22 Aggregated average salary and benefit expenditures at Division I and II schools with football.

TYPE OF SCHOOL	AVERAGE SALARY AND BENEFIT EXPENDITURE	PERCENT OF TOTAL EXPENDITURES
Division I Bowl Subdivision Football	$8,640,000	32
Division I Championship Subdivision Football	$2,569,000	35
Division II with football	$1,072,000	39

Source: 2005–06 NCAA revenues and expenses of Divisions I and II intercollegiate athletic programs report, 2008.

Tennessee boasts the highest paid female coach. Pat Summitt is the longtime head coach of the Vols' women's basketball program and all-time winningest basketball coach (men or women) in NCAA history. Summit topped the $1 million mark in 2006, and was set to make an average of $1.3 million through 2011 (Women's Basketball Coach, 2006).

Other sports

Salaries for head coaches in other sports are far below these levels. A few Division I head baseball coaches (Augie Garrido of Texas, Jim Morris of Miami [Florida]) earn as much as $600,000 per year in base pay. Bob Todd, head baseball coach at Ohio State, made almost $331,000 in 2008, more than twice as much as the average Big Ten head baseball coach. In 2008, John Markell, head men's ice hockey coach at Ohio State, earned $227,500 in base pay, less than the average salary of $365,000 made by coaches at other Big Ten schools. Blaise MacDonald, head ice hockey coach at the University of Massachusetts Lowell, made $178,000. Other 2008 salaries at Ohio State include head field hockey coach Anne Wilkinson ($105,000 versus Big Ten average $92,500), head softball coach Linda Kalafatis (just under $100,000 versus Big Ten average about $111,000), head men's soccer coach John Bluem ($156,000), and Andrew Teitelbaum, head rowing coach ($91,400 versus Big Ten average $79,100) (Kobritz, 2007; Bush, 2009; Estes, 2009).

Comparison data on coaches' salaries

The picture in Division III is vastly different from the high earnings and plush perks enjoyed by Division I football and men's basketball coaches. Exhibit 6.23 outlines the aggregated average salary expenditures for head and assistant coaches in selected Division III sports programs.

			EXHIBIT 6.23
Aggregate average salaries of coaches in selected sports at Division III schools with football programs.			
SPORT	**HEAD COACHES' SALARIES**	**ASSISTANT COACHES' SALARIES**	**NUMBER OF ASSISTANTS**
Baseball	$21,700	$7,000	1.89
Softball	$17,000	$5,200	1.60
Men's Basketball	$32,100	$9,700	1.85
Women's Basketball	$27,400	$8,000	1.76
Field Hockey	$20,800	$7,000	1.40
Football	$44,000	$63,700	7.19
Men's Golf	$9,500	$3,500	1.08
Women's Golf	$8,900	$4,600	1.07
Men's Soccer	$18,400	$4,900	1.49
Women's Soccer	$16,200	$4,900	1.45

Source: 2002–03 NCAA revenues and expenses of Division III intercollegiate athletic programs report, 2005.

Additional data from a study by the *Chronicle of Higher Education* lists the aggregate salary data for all coaches and other mid-level athletic department personnel regardless of NCAA division, as well as listing by institutional type. See Appendix A.6 for a summary of those data.

Although these data reflect significant differences in compensation compared to the high-profile D-I football and men's basketball coaches, what isn't revealed is that many head and assistant coaches at the D-III level have additional coaching or administrative responsibilities, that their coaching duties reflect only a portion of their overall salary, and that some head and assistant coaches in certain sports also are part-time hires with no other departmental responsibilities.

Pressure for increasing salaries

What are the factors that contribute to rising coaching salaries for head coaches and the significant differences in market costs?

Revenue potential. Successful football teams can generate significant revenue potential, as indicated in the case of Bob Stoops at Oklahoma. And the revenues that can come from success have led to competition among schools to hire coaches when vacancies arise. Consider the following chain of events in 2007, when Michigan State University (MSU) fired head football coach John L. Smith, whom the school had hired away from the University of Louisville in 2003. Smith went 4–8 in 2006 and was fired with two years left on his contract. He had been making $1.5 million guaranteed his last year, and he received a buyout of $4.3 million (the amount due to him in the remaining years of his contract).

MSU turned to Mark Dantonio, who had just completed an 8–5 year at the University of Cincinnati. Dantonio had a guaranteed income of just under a half-million dollars at Cincinnati but got a deal of $1.15 million guaranteed annually on a five-year rollover contract at MSU. Dantonio also had to pay $100,000 to buy out his Cincinnati contract. To fill its vacancy, Cincinnati tapped Brian Kelly, who had been the head coach at Central Michigan University, which was coming off a conference championship and 10–4 season. Kelly also had won two Division II national championships as head coach at Grand Valley State. Kelly's guaranteed income at Central Michigan was just under $190,000, but bumped up to $800,000 at Cincinnati (with a $100,000 signing bonus for his five-year deal—62 percent more than Cincinnati was paying Dantoni). Kelly paid $175,000 as part of his contract buyout. Central Michigan then hired Butch Jones, who had been an assistant at West Virginia University (after previously serving as an assistant at Central Michigan) to replace Kelly at $265,850 a year on a four-year deal (a 44 percent increase over Kelly's deal) (Wieberg & Upton, 2007). These universities all saw that to attract top revenue-generating coaches, they would have to increase their current salaries for this position.

Counteroffers. Pressure to increase salaries also intensifies when coaches are thinking about leaving schools for other jobs and institutions must make counteroffers to keep the coach. When University of Michigan head coach Lloyd Carr resigned after 13 seasons in 2007 (in part because of his team's noteworthy loss to Appalachian State), several coaches, including Brian Kelly—who went 9–3 his first year at Cincinnati (with the team earning its highest end-of-season ranking ever), and Les Miles of Louisiana State, that year's Bowl Subdivision national champion—were rumored to be on Michigan's list to replace Carr. Kelly used the interest from Michigan to begin discussions about a raise and for facility upgrades at Cincinnati for new practice facilities and seating expansion at the school's 35,000-seat home game venue. In response, Cincinnati president Nancy Zimpher said she would give him "every consideration within our means, but not beyond them" (Wieberg & Upton, 2007, p. 2A). Cincinnati couldn't keep Kelly, however. After he led the Bearcats to a 34–6 record during his time and two BCS bowl appearances, Kelly left the school in 2009 to take over as head coach at the University of Notre Dame. But the departure meant that in light of the terms of his contract, Kelly had to pay Cincinnati $1 million. Ironically, Cincinnati hired Butch Jones—who had replaced Kelly after he left Central Michigan—to replace Kelly again (Kelly Takes Rich Resume, 2009; Thamel, 2009).

To replace Carr, after Michigan AD Bill Martin got permission to speak with Miles, who had played and served as an assistant at Michigan, LSU AD Skip Bertman took a more munificent stance with Miles, bumping his guaranteed money from $10 million over five years to $15 million, noting that the boost likely would cause an increase in football ticket prices and preferred-seat licenses. Miles's contract had several built-in clauses that guaranteed raises based on wins and increases in other coaches' salaries. Bertman, LSU's former head baseball coach, defended the move, stating: "There was a time when we were content to be 4–4 in the (conference) and win three other games and go to a bowl. But evidently we're not content to do that anymore. And we have to pay" (Wieberg & Upton, 2007, p. 2A).

Michigan eventually hired former West Virginia head coach Rich Rodriguez and, after threats of lawsuits and countersuits, the school paid West Virginia the majority of his $4 million buyout for the privilege of whisking him away. In summarizing these bids and bluffs, University of Mississippi AD Pete Boone, who fired head coach Ed Orgeron and replaced him with recently fired University of Arkansas head coach Houston Nutt (at double the rate but Orgeron was getting; don't feel too bad for Orgeron—he was promptly hired as an assistant at Tennessee at $650,000 per year), noted that when playing along in the coaching shuffle, "The price of poker has gone up" (Wieberg & Upton, 2007, p. 2A; Wieberg, 2009).

The buyout clause in the case of Michigan and Rich Rodriguez indicates the importance of contractual language that spells out the financial obligations of coaches and institutions alike if a coach leaves or is terminated. Occasionally, the pressure to hire a new coach leads to shoddy procedures. Ohio State president Gordon Gee (featured in the Practitioner Perspective in Chapter 5) explains part of this problem: "What I think happens is the fact that, gosh, we lost our coach, and so we've got to get someone the next day, and so we panic" (Wieberg & Upton, 2007, p. 2A). Raymond Cotton, a lawyer specializing in compensation cases for university presidents, agrees, noting: "The panic leads to overpaying and lack of adequate negotiations. It leaves the university exposed" (p. 2A). What occurs then is that contracts seldom contain specific enough language to explain the obligations of each side in the event a coach is fired or leaves before the contract expires.

One example involves former University of Kentucky head men's basketball coach, Billy Gillespie. When he was fired in 2009 with five years remaining on a seven-year contract, he claimed in a suit against Kentucky that because of a memorandum of agreement (MOA) between him and the school, he was owed $1.5 million annually for up to four years if fired without cause. Often, coaches are fired "with cause," meaning that they have violated a specific term of the contract; win/loss records usually are not included as specific cause). Kentucky countered that the MOA was not a contract (referring to it as "an agreement to agree") and, therefore, was not enforceable, even though the school sent no fewer than six offers of written contracts to Gillespie's lawyers over the 20 months before his termination (according to Kentucky, each was met with a counteroffer from Gillespie's lawyers) (Sander & Fain, 2009, p. A23).

Impact of agents. A final and related element that has contributed to the salary growth for head coaches is the ability of agents, within the context of this highly competitive market, to structure contracts that reflect favorable salary increases and other benefits for their clients. Although the impact of agents across Division I is a relatively new phenomenon, the model can be traced to the 1920s, when sportswriter Christy Walsh served as an agent for legendary Notre Dame head football coach Knute Rockne. Much like C.C. Pyle did for University of Illinois star running back Harold "Red" Grange, Walsh negotiated endorsement deals and motivational speaking engagements for Rockne, and helped the coach use job offers from Columbia, Loyola Marymount, and USC to leverage salary boosts and commitments for facility upgrades from Notre Dame. As a result, at the height of his career, before his death in a plane crash in 1931 (en route to California to make a film of his life story for which he was to be paid $50,000), Walsh helped Rockne earn $75,000 a year. This equates to just over $1 million in today's dollars but also was more valuable because of lower income tax rates). Not until the early 1970s would other coaches earn as much as $75,000 a year (Sperber, 1993; Sahr, 2007).

Agents usually take 3 to 5 percent of these deals as their commission and are generally unapologetic for the increases their efforts have generated. Says Jimmy Sexton, who represents Steve Spurrier of the University of South Carolina and Frank Beamer of Virginia Tech: "We're responsible for driving up prices. What else are we supposed to do? Drive them down?" (McCarthy & Wieberg, 2006, p. 15C). Coaches such as Iowa's Kirk Ferentz say they need the expertise of agents like Sexton and Neil Cornrich (who represents Ferentz and Bob Stoops). Ferentz relies on his agent's expertise because "all I know is football. . . . I have zero knowledge when it comes to the business aspect of things" (p. 15C). Lawyer Raymond Cotton, however, says coaches "are much more business-oriented than the schools," are in search of "cold, hard cash," and "that attitude is paying off for them" (Sander & Fain, 2009, p. A24). Says Cornrich of the efforts of agents: "Clearly, knowing the market leads to a fair result to both sides" (p. A24).

Perks

Beyond salaries, coaches' contracts usually provide for other perks as well. In the case of LSU head football coach Les Miles, his agent, George Bass, had negotiated escalator clauses. These provide the coach with salary increases based on the salaries of other coaches. In Miles's contract, LSU was required to make Miles at least the fifth-highest paid coach in the Southeastern Conference if his team won 10 games in a season, third-highest if the Tigers won the SEC championship, and third-highest in the nation if LSU won the Bowl Subdivision national championship. When he was hired by Alabama in 2007, Nick Saban (who had coached previously at Michigan State, LSU, and the NFL's Miami Dolphins) and his agent, Jimmy Sexton, were able to ink an eight-year, $32 million deal. The contract includes 25 hours of use of the school's private jet, two cars, a country club membership, total control of the football program in the areas of recruiting and hiring, and the agreement that Saban could leave the school at any time without incurring a financial penalty (Wieberg, 2006; Wieberg & Upton, 2007; Burke, 2008).

An insight into what exactly a contract might entail is indicated in the contract between Ohio State and Jim Tressel, outlined in Exhibit 6.24. The deal, which he signed in 2006 and ran through January 31, 2013, was extended through the 2014 season in March 2010.

Media deals

While the compensation for duties for Tressel and others of his more highly paid colleagues is indeed lucrative, you may have noticed that one of the forms of income for these coaches is from a less traditional source and has little to do with running practices or breaking down opponents' game films. It is income from so-called "media deals," in which coaches are paid to appear on weekly radio and TV shows, and taped or live pre- and post-game radio, TV and online interviews. This income often dwarfs these coaches' actual cash salary from their institutional

Terms of contract between head football coach Jim Tressel and The Ohio State University.	EXHIBIT 6.24

- Base salary: 2009, $525,000; 2010, $550,000; 2011, $575,000; 2012, $600,000.
- Signing bonus: $500,000.
- Bonus for participating in BCS championship or "other similar Division I national championship game if the BCS system is no longer in existence": $200,000.
- Annual contribution to retirement plan: $40,000.
- Apparel, shoe, and equipment contracts (Tressel must work as consultant to Nike on product design and performance, and as an instructor or lecturer at Nike camps and events): $429,000 in 2006, increasing to $725,000 in 2012.
- Longevity bonuses (if still coaching at OSU on January 31 of each year): 2007: $400,000; 2008, 2009, 2010: $425,000; 2011 and 2012: $450,000; 2013: $925,000.
- Compensation for media, promotions, and public relations: $524,000 in 2006, increasing to $800,000 in 2012.
- Academic achievement bonuses: If team graduation rate is 60 percent, $30,000; if 70 percent, $50,000; if 80 percent, $100,000. Grant-in-aid players with cumulative GPAs of 3.0 or higher at the end of each non-summer quarter: 40 percent, $20,000; 50 percent, $30,000; 60 percent, $50,000.
- Tickets: 40 per game, ten press passes, four parking passes per home game, plus four for each home basketball game. Tickets may not be resold.
- Air transportation: Private jet flights for all recruiting visits if destination is 200 miles from campus. Also ten hours of private jet use per year, not to exceed $225,000 per year.
- Automobiles: One vehicle each for Tressel and his wife, plus all insurance costs.
- Golf course membership and dues at an area course.
- Total salary in 2010: $3.472 million; 2011: $3.602 million; 2012–2014: $3.727 million a year.

Source: Special Report, 2006; Gordon, 2010.

employers. For Jim Tressel, these activities, combined with other required personal promotional appearances, totaled $524,000 in 2006, and were set to increase to $800,000 in 2012. To earn this money, the specific responsibilities for Tressel include those listed in Exhibit 6.25.

Although coaches unquestionably value the income these media agreements bring, other benefits are derived as well. Tommy Tuberville, head coach at Texas Tech University, who grew up watching University of Arkansas head coach Frank Broyles's coaches show Sunday afternoons during the football season, described his show while head coach at Auburn University, *The Auburn Football Review*. He said it was less of a highlight show and "more of a promotional film to get your program out to recruits and parents . . . . All the TV shows go directly toward selling your program" (McCarthy, 2006, p. 1C). Several companies such as Action Media Sports (clients include Alabama, Oklahoma State, and South Carolina), IMG College (clients include Arizona, Florida, and Kentucky), and ISP Sports (clients include Boston College, Pittsburgh, and Washington) specialize in producing these shows as part of media rights broadcasting deals for all sports, although football is the most valuable piece of these deals at the vast majority of schools.

As part of ISP's deal with Auburn, the school is guaranteed $5.7 million annually, allowing Auburn AD Jay Jacobs to funnel much of that money to his coaching staff. "It's a win-win for everybody," says Jacobs (McCarthy, 2006, p. 2C). These companies make their money back by selling advertising and sponsorships, and some agreements between companies and schools call for less upfront in rights fees and more from a share of ads and sponsorship sales, which many schools used to do on their own.

Some of the other most lucrative such deals include the University of Florida's 10-year, $80 million deal with Sun Sports (with Sun Sports paying for the right to sell radio, signage, Internet, corporate partner rights along with purchasing TV broadcast rights). The University of Nebraska has a similar deal with IMG College, which pays the school $100 million over 13 years; and the University of Connecticut recently inked a comparable deal with IMG College reported to be worth $80 million over 10 years (Jones, 2008; Smith, 2008). So while coaches' pay is still a

---

EXHIBIT 6.25 Specific contractual media-related responsibilities for Ohio State head football coach Jim Tressel.

- Live weekly radio show
- Five-minute taped interviews for daily radio show
- 15-minute live or taped interviews for pre-game radio show
- 15-minute live interview for post-game radio show (for which an assistant may stand in)
- Participate in Ohio State's football website and other programs and appearances at a mutually agreed upon time
- Personal appearances on a half-hour television show the Sunday after each game
- Last segment personal appearances on half-hour television highlight show

Source: Special Report, 2006.

significant expense for these D-I athletic departments, schools are subsidizing only a portion of the payouts through transitional salary payments.

Guarantees

In the mid-1970s, University of Michigan AD Don Canham negotiated a deal with University of Notre Dame AD "Moose" Krause to play a series of football games in which the teams would not split evenly the ticket revenues from their respective home games but, rather, pay the other school a flat fee. This agreement gave renewed life to the concept of the guarantee. In reviewing specific line items on the revenue-and-expense report, guarantees and options constituted 6 percent of the aggregate average of the departmental revenues of Division I schools with Bowl Subdivision football programs. Even though it may be only 6 percent, that amount equaled on average about $1.043 million for each program. For these same schools this item also appears as an expense equaling 4 percent—$1.18 million—of the aggregate average departmental total.

The Fulks report (*2005–06 NCAA Revenues,* 2008) also shows that for D-I schools with Championship Subdivision football programs, "guarantees and options" appears as a revenue item, accounting for 3 percent—$235,000 on average—of departmental revenues. Now, even though these items account for a small percentage of departmental revenues and expenses, only 25 percent of Championship Subdivision programs reported a profit (at an average of $450,000), 64 percent lost an average of $810,000, and 11 percent broke even. In this context, the revenues from guarantees and options can make the difference in terms of profitability.

Certain games each year are scheduled in which longshot BCS or Championship Subdivision schools will travel to play against upper-echelon BCS programs on their home turf. Why schedule such a game when the chances for victory are slim? Exceptions are Appalachian State University's win at the University of Michigan in 2007—the most noteworthy of the occasional exceptions—along with the University of Maine downing Mississippi State University in 2004, and the University of New Hampshire defeating Northwestern University in 2006 and the United States Military Academy in 2008. The answer, of course, is money. Schools schedule these games because the home teams are willing to pay them, and the amount for the guaranteed payouts is rising. In 2009, the U. S. Naval Academy—a Bowl Subdivision team that plays an independent schedule—received $1.4 million to travel to Columbus and take on Ohio State. OSU AD Gene Smith calls the payout a "special situation," because another school pulled out, leaving a hole in the Buckeyes' schedule, but also because "we've always wanted to play a service academy (which includes the U. S. Military Academy and the U. S. Air Force Academy). This is our opportunity . . . and we can afford it"(O'Toole, 2008, p. 1C).

Other Bowl Subdivision schools are ratcheting up their guarantees as well, including the University of Wisconsin, which paid about $1 million for each of its two games against Championship Subdivision foe the University of Northern Illinois in 2008 and 2009; the University of Texas, paying Florida Atlantic University $900,000 for a game in 2008; and the University of Arkansas, paying $850,000 to the University of Tulsa for its 2008 game. Western Kentucky pocketed $2.4 million in four guarantee games in 2008—losses at Alabama, Indiana, Kentucky, and Virginia Tech by a combined score of 140–36. Duke University AD Kevin White attributes the payout inflation to the recent schedule expansion to 12 games, which allows schools to generate more revenues from an additional home game and give them an additional win that can count toward boosting their profile for bowl placement. "I think it's just subject to whatever the market will bear," said White, formerly AD at the University of Notre Dame (O'Toole, 2008, p. 1C). For the privilege of traveling to Michigan and beating the Wolverines in what some have called the greatest upset in college football history, Appalachian State returned to campus $400,000 richer (Thamel, 2007; Wieberg, 2008a).

Travel

A challenge to the profitability of guarantee games is the increased cost of travel. When Ohio State traveled to Los Angeles to play USC in a non-conference football matchup in 2008, the cost for the school's two charter airplanes totaled $346,000, which included a fuel surcharge of $24,000. If the team had taken a commercial flight, it would have been hit with extra baggage fees at check-in—new and unbudgeted-for expenses for large teams with lots of equipment. These new costs may put the scheduling of future such games in doubt, because, according to Ben Jay, Ohio State AD for finance and operations, "for each and every one of these trips, you have to make a decision on whether it's cost-efficient or not and whether it's worthy" (Abrams, 2008, p. C19).

Although guarantee games at least allow for the opportunity for a program to gain revenue from a road game, the majority of travel costs constitute an expense that must be borne directly from departmental budgeted expenditures. Consider the plight of the University of Alaska–Anchorage (UAA), a school with approximately 20,000 undergraduates and a member of the Division II Great Northwest Athletic Conference (GNAC), which also sponsors a men's ice hockey program as a member of the Division I Western Collegiate Hockey Association (WCHA). At UAA, all road trips for all sports require a flight, and its shortest trip, to the University of Alaska–Fairbanks, clocks in at 310 miles. Other trips include GNAC road games in Idaho, Oregon, Montana, and Washington, and trips to WCHA road games in Colorado, Michigan, Minnesota, and Wisconsin. As a result of these scheduling obligations, the average UAA student-athlete logs 25,000 travel miles each season, and the school's travel budget rose to $1.7 million in 2008–09. Dr. Steve Cobb, UAA's AD, reckons that his men's ice hockey team could pay as much as $20,000 to check playing equipment, and requested the school's board of regents for a one-time allotment of $225,000 to close the budget gap. He said, "Our conference schedule is always made in advance. We don't have much room to adjust to current market prices" (Abrams, 2008, p. C19). High travel costs also make it difficult for the school to schedule non-conference home games.

Increasing travel costs also are felt by other related organizations. In 2008, the NCAA increased the minimum distance for plane travel for Division I championships from 350 miles to 400 miles and is considering allotting more time between the announcement of tournament brackets and competitions so teams can find less costly transportation, and rescheduling contests from heavy-volume travel times such as holidays. Division III schools, which tend to travel far shorter distances to contests, are also feeling the pinch. At Wheaton (Illinois) College, a private Christian liberal arts school with 2,400 undergrads and a member of the Collegiate Conference of Illinois and Wisconsin, the travel budget increased from $260,761 in 2007–08 and to $334,901 the next year. Each of the school's 22 teams usually takes one out-of-region trip each year. For example, the softball team was scheduled to play five doubleheaders in California in early March 2009, and men's tennis scheduled two matches in Orlando during the same period. Wheaton's AD, Dr. Tony Ladd, offered several solutions to keep these trips as a part of each team's schedule: have the baseball team make its spring trip to Florida instead of Arizona (because the cheapest ticket to Phoenix was $600), have the men's and women's basketball teams travel together in a chartered bus, and cut back on the number of contests. "But that would be one of the last things (we would do)," says Ladd. "It's sort of swallow hard and try to find more money in the budget elsewhere" (Abrams, 2008, p. C19).

Facility construction

Although much of this chapter has been devoted to issues that affect mostly Division I programs, we know, from the data presented, that growth in expenses for Division III schools also has been a concern for managers at these institutions. One expense that has been growing as fast at D-III schools as at D-I schools has been athletic facility construction. While major D-I conferences have raised nearly $4 billion for new buildings and plan to raise $2.5 billion more in the coming years, similar efforts are going on in D-III. Exhibit 6.26 provides an overview of significant completed or planned athletics facility construction projects at schools in the Centennial Conference, an 11-member D-III grouping in the mid-Atlantic region.

These projects are part of a greater trend in Division III over the past five years, in which 10 similar facilities have been built at an average cost of $20 million. The project at Gettysburg got off the ground after a $2 million gift from Robert Ortenzio, a Class of 1979 alumnus who wrestled while at the school. The Board of Trustees committed to borrowing any money necessary to complete the project, and the school was considering a new student fee of $150 annually, beginning in 2010–11, to offset the estimated $360,000 in annual facility utilities and maintenance costs (Kelderman, 2008c).

Athletic facility construction projects at Centennial Conference schools.	EXHIBIT 6.26

- Franklin & Marshall College (Lancaster, Pennsylvania): $2.5 million athletic field on the site of a former scrap yard. The school plans to move all varsity athletic facilities away from the center of campus to the site of a former factory.
- Gettysburg (Pennsylvania) College: $25-million, 55,000-square-foot facility with an eight-lane pool, four-lane warm-up pool, and state-of-the-art hydrotherapy spa.
- Haverford (Pennsylvania) College: $28-million athletic building with three competition-level basketball courts and a fitness room with nearly 100 aerobic and strength-training machines.
- McDaniel College (Westminster, Maryland): $4-million fitness center, with 9,000 square feet for exercise equipment, weights, and dance and aerobics classes.
- Ursinus College (Collegeville, Pennsylvania): $13-million fieldhouse big enough for two batting cages, four basketball courts, three tennis courts, a volleyball court, and a six-lane 200-meter track.

Source: Kelderman, 2008c. Copyright 2008, *The Chronicle of Higher Education.* Reprinted with permission.

Why is all this building going on now? Adam Hertz, AD at Swarthmore (Pennsylvania) College, another member of the Centennial Conference, says it is because of the expectations of prospective student-athletes and non-athletes alike, as a result of their experiences coming from the best high schools in the country. Said Hertz: "Thirty years ago, you could throw a stack of weights in a room and call it a fitness center. . . . I don't think any one of us doesn't look enviously at another institution and wonder if [a new sports facility] is going to impact recruiting" (Kelderman, 2008c, p. A10). Gettysburg alum Ortenzio supported this notion when he explained the motivation for his gift: "To be able to attract students and their parents . . . you've got to have places like this where health and athletics . . . really become a big part. And if you don't have it, I think you're at a competitive disadvantage" (p. A10).

Other motivations include efforts to keep successful coaches from leaving because they think they are losing recruits to schools with better facilities. Franklin & Marshall president John Fry expressed concern in the Division III building spate, characterizing the trend as "an arms race. . . . You see a lot more spending on athletics, and you wonder if that's the highest and best use of those dollars" (Kelderman, 2008c, p. A11). Regardless of Fry's concern, Franklin & Marshall swimmer Thomas Grabiak turned down Gettysburg because its existing pool was "terrible" and he was "blown away" by the facilities at Franklin & Marshall (Kelderman, 2008c, p. A11).

THE FINANCIAL OUTLOOK AT INDIVIDUAL INSTITUTIONS

We will examine cases from several specific Division I athletic programs, going beyond the numbers to gauge the importance and implications of the financial figures and how certain sport programs are expected to produce wins so they also may generate significant revenue.

THE OHIO STATE UNIVERSITY

case study 6.A

The athletic department at The Ohio State University (OSU) can be characterized as a medium-sized corporation. In 2006, it had a budget of $110 million, with 3,000 employees, oversight for 377 acres of fields, and 16.9 million square feet in building space. It sponsored 36 varsity sports for 926 varsity athletes. It also generated $104.7 million in revenue (more than $60 million from football, which itself turned a $28.4 million profit), an overall departmental profit of $2.9 million. How did Ohio State grow to its current size? One advantage relates to geography as OSU is located in Columbus, a large and growing city, which itself is in the heart of the state, easily accessible via interstate highways. Although

the state has several other Division I programs, including Bowling Green University, the University of Dayton, and Miami University, these programs are part of the so-called "mid-major" conference level and lack the national interest garnered by OSU and its peer institutions. In addition, OSU's membership in the Big Ten has allowed it to benefit from the aggressively entrepreneurial efforts of Commissioner James Delany in developing the Big Ten Network and other avenues for more revenue for member schools. All of these factors provide OSU with significant revenue-generating advantages (Wertheim, 2007).

These market advantages are not lost on sponsors like Huntington Bank, a Columbus-based bank with more than $36 billion in assets and 380 branches in Indiana, Kentucky, Michigan, Ohio, and West Virginia. While OSU's home basketball court displays signage from Value City (a department store) and 22 other sponsors around the perimeter, Huntington Bank's multimillion dollar deal includes signage, in-arena ATMs, and suite-level naming rights at the basketball and football venues. To leverage this sponsorship to reach students and other fans, the bank created the Buckeye Banking premium, in which customers receive checks and ATM cards with the Buckeyes logo, which also affords them discounts at school merchandise stores. Reportedly, more fans join the program and spend more when Buckeye teams—especially football—win. Jim Kunk (OSU Class of 1975), the bank's president for Central Ohio, says the partnership makes sense for Huntington because, "at the end of the day, [OSU has] a great brand and a great following" (Wertheim, 2007, p. 67).

This brand equity and a sizable following also allow OSU to curry favor with donors such as Steve Milligan, Class of 1985, who is CFO of Western Digital, one of the world's largest suppliers of computer hard drives. Several years ago, Milligan made a one-time donation of $50,000 to the school's general fund, and a year later an athletic department fundraiser called him to ask about endowing a grant-in-aid for an OSU student-athlete, to the tune of $100,000. Through the Stephen D. Milligan Family Scholarship, first awarded to 2006 Heisman Trophy winner Troy Smith, Milligan joined more than 100 other donors—including former Buckeye athletic standout golfer Jack Nicklaus, wide receiver Joey Galloway, and hoopster Jim Jackson—who have contributed $36 million toward the endowment program. Without these donations, the athletic department would not be self-supporting. Along with a tax benefit, the gift allowed Milligan to upgrade his football season tickets. (OSU, like most programs, institutes a point system for donors to allow for such benefits.) Although he lives in California, Milligan comes to at least five home games a season to sit in his seat 10 rows from the field at the 45-yard line (Wertheim, 2007).

Regarding the finances of OSU athletics, president Gordon Gee stated flatly that he is "president of the university with the largest, most-powerful athletic program in the country," but that the school is "looking very carefully to make sure our cost structures are in line, that we're not just simply building to build or we're not simply paying to pay but, rather, that we have a systematic approach to what we're trying to do and that is part of the overall planning and strategic positioning of the university" (Fain, 2008, p. A24). Having made this comment, however, Gee admitted that if head football coach Jim Tressel were to leave the school, "I'm stepping down with him. . . . Folks leak that they're talking to someone, and then all of a sudden they get a huge bump in their own salary. . . . I hope I don't have to deal with that" (p. A24).

questions for you to consider

1. If the OSU athletic department can be accurately described as a small business, what sorts of skills are required of its departmental managers to operate it successfully?

2. What are the factors that contribute to the development of OSU's brand equity, and what must departmental managers do to maintain it?

THE UNIVERSITY OF ARIZONA — case study 6.B

University of Arizona's then-AD Jim Livingood was far less sanguine about the financial state of his athletic department than those concerning Ohio State in Case Study 6.A. Through the example of the University of Arizona, a public school with 29,000 undergraduates located in Tucson and a member of the Division I Pac-10 Conference, we see the direct pressures to generate enough revenues through football ($14 million) and men's basketball ($17 million) to keep the Wildcats out of the red. Says Livingood of this phenomenon, "We talk about other revenue streams, but far and away the one that could help more than the others put together is to win at football" (Schoenfeld, 2006, p. 29). Softball coach Mike Candrea—who also coached the U.S. Olympic team and has led the Wildcats to eight NCAA championships—understands the environment as well: "The way you help softball . . . is to buy season tickets for football" (p. 32). The department's marketing director, James Francis, would like to help softball generate more fans but says: "We have to put our resources in the area where we'll get the biggest return. . . . We have to take everything and allocate it to football" (p. 32).

What is the cause of these budgetary concerns at Arizona? First, unlike many programs that receive allocated funds from its host institution and through student fees, Arizona gets nothing from these sources (but neither does the department have to pay the school for grant-in-aid awards, as some other schools are required to do). The department is forbidden from soliciting signage from beer and alcohol companies because the campus is "dry;" alcohol is not permitted on the grounds. This restriction, according to athletic department personnel, costs the school $1 million annually. In addition, only 18 percent of the venue revenue at the school's home basketball venue goes to athletics. The rest goes to the student union,

and athletics gets none of the parking revenues. And the department gets none of the revenue from the sale of licensed products. Even if the Wildcats succeeds in men's basketball by winning another national championship, they likely will not see much additional revenue and more than likely will begin to lose money if the team struggles. Companies such as Alltel pay upwards of $500,000 for signage at the McKale Center (the team's home basketball venue), but only because the program is one of the best in D-I. "If you're not on TV anymore," said former associate AD Chris del Conte, "it's difficult to justify" that kind of expenditure (Schoenfeld, 2006, p. 33). Any money generated by any sport at Arizona goes into a general fund for the AD to apportion. Softball might be able to generate some revenue from signage at its home field, but the donor who gave the money to build it wanted the venue to stay free from such advertising. "We have to respect his wishes," says Candrea (p. 33).

questions for you to consider

1. Based on the Arizona and Ohio State cases, which department is operating under conditions that would allow it to generate more revenue?
2. What factors contribute to the differences?

DEALING WITH SEVERE BUDGET CUTS IN CALIFORNIA PUBLIC COLLEGES AND UNIVERSITIES   case study 6.C

In 2009, because of the global economic meltdown fueled in large part by imprudent actions by multinational banking concerns, the state of California was facing a crippling budget crisis, and state-funded education programs had to endure $8.1 billion in budget cuts, with even stiffer cuts scheduled for 2010. As a result, athletic departments in the University of California (10 campuses and nearly a quarter-million students, faculty, and staff) and California State University systems (with 23 campuses and nearly half a million students, faculty, and staff) have had to reduce expenses and increase fundraising. Coaches and admin-

istrators have taken furloughs and pay cuts, programs have been dropped, and overall expenses have been reduced. For example, the football team at Cal Berkeley took busses to their game at UCLA rather than flying, a savings of nearly $30,000. UCLA head football coach Rick Neuheisel took a voluntary 10 percent pay cut, amounting to $25,000 and Cal Berkeley head coach Jeff Tedford took a similar voluntary cut. For coaches in the Cal State system, the 10 percent pay cuts are mandatory, and must be taken in the form of furlough days; coaches must not show up for work or take work home. Most coaches work anyway. Keith West, the head women's soccer coach at Cal Berkeley State Northridge (23,000 full-time undergrads and a member of the Division I Big West Conference), assessed the situation this way: "What are they going to do? Take away our keys? . . . When you want to be great, you have to put in the extra work" (Witz, 2009, p. B12).

The economic recession also limited the ability of schools to derive income from revenues. Football attendance was down at Fresno State (23,000 full-time undergrads and a member of the Division I Western Athletic Conference), where the team played before its smallest crowd in 23 years; and there were more than 2,000 empty seats at UCLA's famed Pauley Pavilion when the UCLA men's team took on top-ranked Kansas. Also, referendums to increase funding for athletics were rejected at Northridge, Fullerton, and Long Beach, in large part because tuition was set to rise by 32 percent the following year. At Fullerton (28,000 full-time undergrads and member of the Division I Big West Conference), both the equally successful wrestling and women's gymnastics programs were on the verge of being dropped to save the school a combined $150,000, but the head coaches, Dan (wrestling) and Jill (gymnas-tics) Hicks (who are married), whose salaries also were cut 10 percent, mapped out a fundraising plan to save their respective sports. Both programs were saved for the time being. USA Gymnastics contributed $75,000 to the gymnastics program, and the team ran a joint fundraising exhibition with the UCLA team, netting $30,000. Wrestling ran a money-making invitational tournament and curried a $14,000 donation from a local doctor. USA Gymnastics chairman Peter Vidmar sees only more fundraising in the future for gymnastics coaches and is creating seminars for coaches to help them learn how to do it (Witz, 2009).

questions for you to consider

1. Based on the tasks that coaches have to perform, how much fundraising should they realistically be expected to do while maintaining the rest of their responsibilities?

2. How can departmental administrators and school fundraising officials aid coaches in fundraising responsibilities?

CONCLUSION

Managers associated with intercollegiate athletics have expressed varying concerns regarding the growing expenses associated with their programs, and critics of the enterprise have questioned the value of these expenditures in relation to the educational missions of the sponsoring institutions. NCAA data indicate the level of revenue it generates and how that revenue is distributed to member institutions. The data on athletic departmental revenues and expenses at all three divisional levels show that in the aggregate, athletic department revenues do not cover expenses at any of the three Division classifications. Revenues indeed are higher at D-I schools that have Bowl Subdivision football programs, but so are the expenses incurred to maintain programs at these schools, with significant differences in how individual sport programs at these schools are supported. The range of revenues and expenses include fundraising, licensing, bowl games, guarantees, coaches' compensation, travel, and facility construction. The specific characteristics and situations at several schools illustrate how athletic departments are allocating resources, and the impact of these decisions on how athletic departments are choosing to pursue their stated missions.

PRACTITIONER perspective:

PAT BATTLE, Senior Corporate Vice President, IMG College

IMG made a significant foray into intercollegiate athletics in 2007 when the company acquired The Collegiate Licensing Company (CLC), the largest collegiate trademark licensing agency in the United States. Based in Atlanta, Georgia, CLC is a full-service licensing and marketing company that assists collegiate institutions with a wide array of licensing and administration services, helping to protect, develop, and manage their brands in the $3 billion collegiate merchandise marketplace. Under the agreement, CLC operates as a freestanding unit within IMG's Sports and Entertainment Group, overseen by Group president George Pyne. CLC founder and chairman Bill Battle will continue to help lead the company he founded, alongside Pat Battle. (IMG to Acquire, 2007, p. 1).

In making the announcement, Ted Forstmann, IMG's chairman and CEO, said, "This acquisition provides IMG and CLC's clients with a significant new opportunity for growth. The combination of IMG's expertise and resources will not only allow CLC to continue its leadership position in collegiate licensing but, more importantly, to grow into other areas of collegiate sports as well." Forstmann continued, "In its 25-year history, Bill and Pat Battle and their talented leadership team have built CLC into collegiate sports' preeminent licensing company. I'm delighted IMG's unmatched portfolio of sports, entertainment and media assets will now include the dynamic college sports segment." Added Pat Battle, "This is an innovative opportunity for us to try to move our clients' licensing programs much further, much faster in the future. Our great team of people in Atlanta will now have access to IMG's resources and unique way of building brands that can really help to shift the collegiate licensing paradigm in the future" (p. 1).

Throughout the chapter we have focused on the full range of revenues and expenses for intercollegiate athletic programs. Pat Battle agreed to be interviewed for this textbook so we could learn more about licensing and how to boost departmental revenues.

Q: *Before becoming part of IMG, you helped create and operate The Collegiate Licensing Company (CLC). Outline the background and development of this company, and its impact on the growth of intercollegiate athletics.*

A: Collegiate Licensing Company, formerly Golden Eagle Enterprises (GEE), was started by my dad, Bill, in 1981 to address enforcement and compliance issues that were arising at the time because state-of-the-art screen printing had made it very easy for anyone to enter the business of printing and selling t-shirts. In 1981, with the retail market for collegiate merchandise estimated to be $100 million (the majority of sales taking place through campus bookstores), GEE started the licensing program for the University of Alabama. At the time, the primary goal at Alabama (and the handful of other pioneer schools that started programs that same year) was to ensure that the university marks were used properly, and that they were using the marks on products of an acceptable nature and quality. The branding and financial objectives for licensing didn't materialize until the mid-1980s.

In 2008, the retail market for collegiate merchandise has grown to more than $3.5 billion in annual sales, with less than 20 percent of the sales now taking place on college campuses. Retail distribution of college products spans virtually every channel of distribution, from mass, to mid-tier, to sports specialty, to upscale department store, to online, and many more. The market has also expanded outside the United States, with nearly 50 schools involved in a global licensing program aimed at expanding distribution into Europe, Asia, and many other areas around the world.

Of the $3.5 billion in retail sales, apparel accounts for approximately 62 percent, with Nike leading the way. Non-apparel, which continues to close the gap each year, is led by the college market's number one licensee Electronic Arts (EA). The EA Sports NCAA Football video game has become the number-two selling sports game in North America, generating eight figures in annual royalties for the schools, the NCAA, and other properties who are in the game. While a large proportion of college sales have been and continue to be driven by athletics, we are seeing a growing trend toward "college" being marketed as a lifestyle brand.

With that as background, CLC today serves as the exclusive licensing agent for more than 200 college properties, including colleges, universities, bowls, conferences, and the NCAA. The properties represented by CLC (which include the University of Michigan, Notre Dame, University of Texas, and University of North Carolina, among others) represent approximately 80 percent of the overall market for college products. In representing its clients, CLC performs administrative, enforcement, and marketing functions on a turn-key basis. CLC's primary objective is to continue to expand the market for collegiate merchandise to ensure that college students, alumni, and fans have easy access to a diverse mixture of quality products through multiple channels of distribution.

Why did it make sense for both parties for IMG to acquire CLC? What were the advantages you contemplated for CLC when you were thinking about this acquisition?

IMG is the global leader in marketing golf, tennis, and fashion. The company was founded by Mark McCormack 40 years ago. McCormack pioneered the business of sport marketing. When McCormack passed away a few years ago, Ted Forstmann bought the company. Forstmann believed that IMG had an opportunity to expand its golf, tennis, and fashion business into other sports and entertainment categories. One of the areas Forstmann and IMG president George Pyne identified was intercollegiate athletics. The goal was to use the media, marketing, and licensing infrastructure of IMG to bring professionalism and expertise into the very fragmented collegiate marketplace.

As IMG explored a way to enter college sports, the firm decided to pursue acquisition of CLC as the cornerstone of its intercollegiate athletics strategy. IMG's interest in CLC was threefold: first was the fact that CLC was a licensing company, an area that Forstmann and Pyne both believed was an area of future growth for the company; second was the fact that CLC was focused on the collegiate "space," a highly fragmented, undervalued market in which a vertical operation such as IMG could have a profound impact; and third was the fact that CLC enjoyed long-term, longstanding relationships with more than 200 collegiate properties.

From CLC's perspective, IMG was the perfect fit to not only help CLC grow its core licensing business but also to provide the resources necessary to expand into the collegiate media and marketing businesses. IMG as a company sold more than $600 million in global sponsorships in 2007. IMG produced more than 10,000 hours of media programming (mostly in sports) in 2007. To bring the vast infrastructure, resources, and relationships of IMG into the highly fragmented and undervalued collegiate marketplace was the impetus for the acquisition. And, since the acquisition of CLC in May 2007, IMG College acquired Host Communications in November 2007 to enter the multimedia rights and marketing areas as well.

Much of this chapter focuses on how schools generate revenue through ticket sales, media rights fees, and donations. How important are licensing revenues to schools within each divisional classification level and how do these differ across divisions?

It is important to note that collegiate licensing programs began in the early 1980s for the primary purpose of protecting the marks of the institution. As the market for collegiate merchandise grew beyond campus and into mainstream retail, so, too, did the revenue-generation opportunities. With nearly $4 billion in annual retail sales of collegiate merchandise today, nearly $150 million in annual royalties are generated on behalf of colleges and universities with licensing programs. In 2007 alone, 32 CLC schools each generated in excess of $1 million in gross royalties from licensing. So, while the primary objective for most institutions remains to protect their trademarks and goodwill, the incremental revenues provided have become an added benefit. Most institutions divide revenues in some portion between the athletic department and other departments on campus and use these revenues for some combination of academic and/or athletically related financial aid.

What is the difference between working with colleges and universities in licensing and working with professional leagues? How do their expectations differ and/or vary?

While consumers likely view collegiate licensing as very similar to the professional leagues (because pro and collegiate products are sold by many of the same licensees, displayed in the same retail stores, and marketed in a similar fashion), there are definitely some differences. Where the primary objective of the pro leagues would center on profit, colleges and universities are primarily concerned with protecting their trademarks and ensuring that the institution is represented in the market in a proper and positive light. Also, a major difference stems from the fact that most of the licensed products for the pro leagues revolve around the star athletes (like trading cards, jerseys, video games, and other player related memorabilia), where collegiate licensing programs, due to NCAA regulations restricting commercialism around student-athletes, would never feature a product using the name or likeness of an NCAA student-athlete. We like to say that the collegiate market is about the name on the front of the jersey (meaning the school), which is one of the many characteristics that makes collegiate licensing so unique, and so popular, rather than the name on the back of the jersey.

Why do some schools like The Ohio State University choose to administer their licensing programs in-house?

Over the past decade or so in the collegiate licensing business, there has been a significant movement to outsourcing. The trend toward outsourcing is consistent with what is generally taking place in other parts of a university campus, such as bookstores, and athletic marketing rights. There seems to be a philosophy on college campuses to focus on the core mission of the university (defined as education), and bringing in experts in various fields to administer non-core activities in a more effective and cost-efficient manner. As it specifically relates to licensing, many institutions over the past decade (the above CLC clients, plus Cal Berkeley, University of Minnesota, Rutgers University, and many more) have decided to outsource. The rationale behind this decision is that they will receive greater services and more net revenues by bringing in a professional management company.

For the schools that continue to manage their programs internally, the number-one reason given would be control. While I would argue (and do so every day) that a university with CLC has more control over its marketing, branding, and enforcement activities, the perception of losing control seems to concern many schools. For the nearly 200 colleges and universities represented by CLC, the university makes the ultimate decision related to any and all product, design, and licensee approvals, as well as any changes in licensing policies.

What can athletic departments and schools do to increase their licensing revenues?

The easy answer to the question is to win, as there is a clear relationship between winning and increased licensed product sales. Beyond winning, though, there are definitely some things a school can do to expand sales and associated royalties. We find that the most successful licensing programs are the ones that incorporate licensing thinking into every aspect of their business operations. For many years, licensing played second fiddle to media and marketing initiatives on campus and within athletic departments. Today on college campuses, consistent with what is happening in the sports and entertainment business in general, there is a convergence of the media, marketing, and licensing worlds. For the universities who recognize this and choose to integrate the three disciplines, there are real opportunities for growth. Companies like Nike, adidas, EA Sports, Wilson, Russell, and many others are university licensees who are also investing in university marketing and media programs. Also, many traditional sponsors and advertisers are beginning to activate in the marketplace by running licensed promotions incorporating the marks of the schools that they sponsor. This coordinated approach begins with a mindset from the decision makers in intercollegiate athletic management that will then permeate throughout the business operations of the schools and the athletic department.

What are the skill sets and educational training you look for when bringing someone to work within CLC?

Even as the licensing industry has grown dramatically in the United States and abroad, there are still very few educational programs centered on the discipline of licensing. At CLC, because we are involved in the dynamic world of intercollegiate athletics, we have been fortunate over the years to have attracted great people with a real passion for what they do. The qualities that we look for in a prospective employee have nothing to do with licensing expertise and everything to do with qualities such as a commitment to customer service, teamwork, a strong work ethic, creativity, and a passion for intercollegiate athletics. It is a combination of those traits that would be found in the executive team at CLC, all of whom began in entry-level positions within the company and rose through the ranks over time. We believe in promoting from within, and are proud of the fact that such a large percentage of our staff has been with the company for a decade or more. The licensing knowledge and expertise will be learned on the job, but it is the other intangibles that determine the rate and the route each individual will take.

questions TO CONSIDER

1. If you were a Division I AD responsible for creating more revenues for your athletic department, what are some of the factors that make this charge more challenging for your organization as opposed to a professional league or tour sport organization?

2. Identify and explain the key components of the NCAA's revenue distribution plan, and how this plan impacts athletic departments differently depending on a school's divisional classification.

3. The AD at your school has been asked to make a presentation to the school's president and board of trustees about departmental expenses and possible ways to cut expenditures. Your AD has asked you to present a summary and recommendations for this presentation. Outline the five major expenses for your school's athletic program, and how the department might cut back on expenses by 10 percent.

4. Let's consider a scenario in which developments within your school's conference have made it apparent that your school must have a new indoor athletic training center for its intercollegiate programs. Based on what you have read in this chapter, provide a basic plan as to how your school would pay for such a facility, and what this facility might cost.

5. Having read the Practitioner Perspective featuring Pat Battle, provide an outline as to how your school could increase its licensing revenues.

references

Abrams, J. (2008, October 3). College teams feeling pinch from fuel costs. *New York Times*, p. C19.

Adams, R. (2003, July 7–13). Leagues favor fewer deals, higher quality. *Street & Smith's SportsBusiness Journal*, pp. 21–22.

Amid Slump, ACC Alters Tournament Ticket Sales. (2009, February 25). *USA Today*, p. 4C.

Anthony, M. (2009a, February 22). Calhoun, activist go one-on-one after UConn win. *Hartford (CT) Courant*. Accessed February 23, 2009, from: http://www.courant.com/sports/husky/men/hc-ucmennotes

Anthony, M. (2009b, February 28). Lack of support hurts UConn's Calhoun. *Hartford (CT) Courant*. Accessed March 4, 2009, from: http://www.courant.com/sports/college/husky/men/hc-calhoun

Auburn's Field Goal in OT Holds Up as Northwestern's Trick Play Fails. (2010, January 2). *ESPN.com*. Accessed January 5, 2010, from: http://scores.espn.go.com/ncf/recap?gameId=300010002

Bachman, R. (2008a, August 22). Sticker shock at the stadium. *Oregonian*. Accessed December 3, 2008, from: http://www.oregonlive.com

Bachman, R. (2008b, August 22). What's it cost to see your college football team? *The Oregonian*. Accessed December 3, 2008, from: http://www.oregonlive.com

Behind the Salary Numbers (2009, November 10). *USA Today*, p. 5C.

Berkowitz, S., & Wieberg, S. (2009, December 11). Brown's deal gets attention. *USA Today*, p. 10C.

Brand, M. (2006, October 30). Speech before the National Press Club, Washington, DC.

Broughton, D. (2009, December 7–13). Bowls roll out the "gift suite" for athletes. *Street & Smith's SportsBusiness Journal*, pp. 32–33.

Brown, M.T., Zuefle, D.M., & Batista, P.J. (2007). Will the real 12th man stand up? Texas A&M and Seattle Seahawks settle dispute over right to identify fans as "12th Man." *Sport Marketing Quarterly*, 16(2), pp. 115–177.

Burke, M. (2008, September 1). The most powerful coach in sports. *Forbes*. Accessed December 3, 2008, from: http://www.forbes.com

Bush, B. (2009). One price of OSU winning: Higher salaries for coaches. *The Columbus (OH) Dispatch*. Accessed July 16, 2009, from: http://msn.foxsports.com/cbk/story/9451322/One-price-of-OSU-winning:-higher-salaries-for-coaches

Colleges Slight Academic Programs to Fuel Athletics. (2008, September 22–28). *Street and Smith's SportsBusiness Journal*, p. 38.

Drape, J., and Evans, T. (2008, October 21). Financial straits of big boosters hit athletic departments. *New York Times*, pp. B14, B17.

Dubner, S. (2007, September 3). Color this graduate impressed. *New York Times*, p. D8.

Estes, A. (2009, February 11). UMass employees top list of highest-paid state workers. *Boston Globe*. Accessed July 16, 2009, from: http://www.boston.com/news/education/higher/articles/2009/02/11

Fain, P. (2007, October 26). Oregon debates role of big sports donors. *Chronicle of Higher Education*, pp. A38–A41.

Fain, P. (2008, January 11). Buckeyes' leader believes presidents should help contain spending. *The Chronicle of Higher Education*, p. A24.

Fund Raising for Athletics in 6 Major Conferences. (2007, October 5). *Chronicle of Higher Education*, p. A35.

Fund Raising for Athletics in 6 Major Conferences. (2009, January 23). *Chronicle of Higher Education*. Accessed January 21, 2009, from: http://0-chronicle.com.htm

Gordon, K. (2000, March 17). Tressel re-ups for two more. *Columbus Dispatch*. Accessed April 2, 2010 from: http://dispatch.com/live/content/sports/stories/2010/03/17.html.

Hiestand, M. (2002, August 19). Sports gear so out of style it's in style. *USA Today*, p. 3C.

IMG to Acquire Collegiate Licensing Company. (2007, May 1). Accessed January 25, 2009, from: http://www.imgworld.com

Jones, D. (2008, July 15). Florida's marketing deal pegged at $80M. *USA Today*, p. 12C.

June, A.W. (2007, May 18). After costly foray into big-time sports, a college returns to its roots. *Chronicle of Higher Education*, pp. A33–34.

Kelderman, E. (2008a, May 23). New data show many colleges footing large share of athletic expenses. *Chronicle of Higher Education*, p. A15.

Kelderman, E. (2008b, May 30). Athletic directors cry foul over NCAA's data. *Chronicle of Higher Education*, p. A4.

Kelderman, E. (2008c, July 11). Small colleges sweat over sports facilities. *Chronicle of Higher Education*, pp. A1, A10–A11.

Keller, J. (2009, January 23). For Berkeley's sports endowment, a goal of $1-Billion. *Chronicle of Higher Education*, pp. A13, A16.

Kelly Takes Rich Resume to Notre Dame. (2009, December 11). *USA Today*, p. 10C.

Kider, T. (2007, August 24). Bake sales and trash pickup help college teams stay afloat. *New York Times*, pp. A1, A16.

Kobritz, J.I. (2007, September 13). Salaries for college baseball coaches mirrors popularity. *The Biz of Baseball*. Accessed July 16, 2009, from: http://www.bizofbaseball.com

Lanham Act, 15 U.S.C. § 1051–1127 (1946).

Lawmakers Want Calhoun Reprimanded. (2009, February 17). *Boston Globe*, p. C2.

McCarthy, M. (2006, November 17). Media deals turn into cash machines. *USA Today*, pp. 1C–2C.

McCarthy, M. & Wieberg, S. (2006, November 17). Reviled or loved, agents get results. *USA Today*, p. 15C.

McDonell, T. (2008, December 1). Ka-ching! Ka-ching! *Sports Illustrated*, p. 12.

Median salaries of midlevel administrative workers by job category and type of institution, 2007–08. (2008, March 28). *Chronicle of Higher Education*, p. A18.

NCAA Presidential Task Force on the Future of Division I Athletics. (2006). *The second-century imperatives: Presidential leadership—institutional accountability*. Indianapolis: National Collegiate Athletic Association.

NCAA Revised Budget for Fiscal Year Ended August 31, 2009. Accessed July 11, 2009, from: http://www.ncaa.org

Nichols, M.A. (1995, April). A look at some of the issues affecting collegiate licensing. *Team Licensing Business*, 7(4), p. 18.

Nocera, J. (2009, February 23). Jim Calhoun defends his salary. *New York Times*. Accessed February 23, 2009, from: http://executivesuite.blogs.nytimes.com

Oriard, M. (2009). *Bowled over: Big-time college football from the Sixties to the BCS era*. Chapel Hill: University of North Carolina Press.

O'Toole, T. (2001, October 3). Copyright case over 'Buzz' costly to Georgia Tech. *USA Today*, p.1C.

O'Toole, T. (2008, June 12). Money talks with college football guarantees. *USA Today*, p. 1C.

Perez, A.J. (2009, November 12). New Mexico State's Rutenberg pays dues to chase dream. *USA Today*. Accessed November 18, 2009, from: http://usatoday.com

Pinkel's Deals: By the numbers. (2009, November 11). *USA Today*, p. 2C.

Plata, C. (1996, September/October). Ducks & dollars. *Team Licensing Business*, 8(6), p. 38.

Posnanski, J. (2009, December 26). The running back and the cheerleader and what came after the greatest college football game ever. *Sports Illustrated*, pp. 58–64.

Sahr, R.C. (2007). Currency conversion factors, 1700 to estimated 2012. Unpublished manuscript, Oregon State University.

Sander, L., & Fain, P. (2009, June 12). Coaches' contracts are fertile ground for conflict. *Chronicle of Higher Education*, pp. A1, A23, A24.

Sandomir, R. (2004, November 23). Fox secures rights to college football bowls. *New York Times*, p. C17.

Sandomir, R. (2006, December 17). College bowl scene flush with corporate dollars. *New York Times*, pp. C12–C13.

Schlabach, M. (2007, December 5). Team selection an extended process for Chick-fil-A Bowl. Accessed December 14, 2007, from: http://sports.espn.go.com/espn/print?id=31426112&type=story

Schoenfeld, B. (2006, June 19–25). Tough times in Tucson. *Street & Smith's SportsBusiness Journal*, pp. 1, 29–33.

Schwartz, P.J. (2007, November 20). The most valuable college football teams. *Forbes*. Accessed December 3, 2008, from: http://www.forbes.com

Smith, M. (2007, September 10–16). Schools hesitate to make the leap. *Street & Smith's SportsBusiness Journal*, pp. 24–26.

Smith, M. (2008, September 22–28). IMG's campus crusade adds UConn in $80 million deal. *Street & Smith's Sports-Business Journal*, p. 3.

Smith, M., & Ourand, J. (2008, November 24–30). How ESPN bid bowled over BCS. *Street & Smith's SportsBusiness Journal*, pp. 1, 36.

Special Report: Coaching Agreement Creates a Jet-Set Career. (2006, November 17). *USA Today*, p. 14C.

Sperber, M. (1993). *Shake down the thunder: The creation of Notre Dame football*. New York: Henry Holt.

Sperber, M. (2008, May 23). Stop hiding the financial truth about college athletics. *Chronicle of Higher Education*, p. A31.

Sports Wrap: College Football Bowls Over Audiences (2009, January 9). Accessed January 25, 2009, from: http://blog.nielsen.com

Thamel, P. (2007, September 9). Upset in the books, focus now shifts to a coach's future. *New York Times*, pp. D1, D8.

Thamel, P. (2009, December 31). Cincinnati's next test is keeping its gains. *New York Times*, pp. B11–B12.

The Haves and Have-Nots. (2007, March 5). *Sports Illustrated*, p. 59.

Top Official Says NCAA Should Seek Revenue Sources Beyond Basketball. (2008, March 21). *Chronicle of Higher Education*, p. A16.

2002–03 NCAA Revenues and Expenses of Division III Intercollegiate Athletic Programs Report. (2005). Indianapolis: NCAA.

2005–06 NCAA Revenues and Expenses of Divisions I and II Intercollegiate Athletic Programs Report. (2008). Indianapolis. Indianapolis: NCAA.

2008–09 NCAA Division I Manual. (2008). Indianapolis, NCAA.

2008–09 Revenue Distribution Plan. (2009). Accessed on July 11, 2009, from: http://www.ncaa.org/wps/wcm/connect/NCAA/About+The+NCAA/Budget+and+Finances/Budget

University Athletic Association Annual Financial Statement. (2008, June 30). Gainesville: University of Florida.

University of Maine Athletics Budget Breakdown. (2009). Orono: University of Maine.

UT Gives Pearl Pay Raise, Contract Extension. (2006, March 8). Accessed October 29, 2008, from: www.wate.com

Weir, T., & Hiestand, M. (2008, November 17). BCS officially headed to ESPN starting in 2011. Accessed November 19, 2008, from: http://usatoday.com

Wertheim, L.J. (2007, March 5). The program: Portrait of a powerhouse. *Sports Illustrated*, pp. 55–69.

Wieberg, S, (2003a, August 5). Brand: Athletics pricey, worthy. *USA Today*, p. 11C.

Wieberg, S, (2003b, August 15). NCAA's Brand: Fiscal fitness up to schools. *USA Today*, p. 1C.

Wieberg, S. (2006, November 17). To Oklahoma, Stoops worth more than his weight in gold. *USA Today*, p 16C.

Wieberg, S. (2008a, October 6). A Western Kentucky, a calculated move up. *USA Today*, pp. 1C–2C.

Wieberg, S. (2008b, October 22). Coach's pay draws ire. *USA Today*, p. 6C.

Wieberg, S. (2009, November 10). Top assistants command big pay. *USA Today*, p. 1C.

Wieberg, S., & Upton, J. (2007, December 5). The money game. *USA Today*, pp. 1A–2A.

Wieberg, S., Upton, J., Perez, A.J., & Berkowitz, S. (2009, November 10). Pay booms in hard times. *USA Today*, pp. 1A–2A.

Witz, B. (2009, December 28). In California colleges, coaches face furloughs and fund-raising. *New York Times*, pp. D1–D2.

Wolverton, B. (2006a, September 22). Congress broadens an investigation of college sports. *Chronicle of Higher Education*, pp. A36–A37.

Wolverton, B. (2006b, November 24). NCAA defends tax-exempt status as Congressional scrutiny of colleges increase. *Chronicle of Higher Education*, p. A42.

Wolverton, B. (2007a, October 26). As athletics donations go up, some leaders fret over booster influence. *Chronicle of Higher Education*, p. A40.

Wolverton, B. (2007b, October 26). For small programs, fund raising can be ticket to the big time. *Chronicle of Higher Education*, p. A41.

Wolverton, B. (2008, January 25). Athletes' hours renew debate over college sports. *Chronicle of Higher Education*, pp. A1, A23.

Wolverton, B. (2009, January 23). For athletics, a billion-dollar goal line. *Chronicle of Higher Education*. Accessed January 21, 2009, from: http://0-chronicle.com.htm

Women's Basketball Coach Hits the $1 Million Mark. (2006, May 22). *The Chronicle of Higher Education*. Accessed July 16, 2009, from: http://chronicle.com/news/article/470/womens-basketball-coach-hits-the-1-million-mark.

Recruiting

7

Key concepts to keep in mind as you read the chapter:

- The importance of recruiting as a component of resources acquisition for athletic departments.

- The battery of specific rules and restrictions that govern the recruiting process.

- Specifics pertaining to permissible financial assistance available to student-athletes.

- The multiple environmental factors that influence recruiting.

Introduction

The recruiting process is the culmination of years of effort by prospects and their families as they participate in school and youth sports teams chasing the dream of an athletically related aid to subsidize their college educations, one that will be realized by only approximately one of every 81 high school senior girls and one of 93 senior boys annually. The average award? Just over $10,000—which could be as little as 20 percent of the cost of attendance at some schools. The competition among those seeking the total $1.4 billion annually awarded grants-in-aid is stiff, as 7.3 million boys and girls are competing in high school sports, but NCAA student-athletes number just under 400,000, and only 123,000 receive athletic aid (Pennington, 2008a).

In analyzing the recruiting process and its impact on prospects, a study of nearly 300 student-athletes on 17 teams in the Division I Mid-American Conference (whose full membership is composed of 12 public schools in Illinois, Indiana, Ohio, Michigan, and New York), performed by the *Chronicle of Higher Education*, found that student-athletes generally thought their schools were portrayed to them fairly during the recruiting process. However, some respondents expressed dissatisfaction. Said one: "Coaches can tell you whatever they want, pretty much what you want to hear. But once you sign your name on the dotted line, they can do whatever they want, and you're stuck there" (Sander, 2008c, p. A1). Other respondents indicated that the process was "very overwhelming and stressful, and not always having a clear idea of what I wanted made it more difficult," and "it's hard to know what you're going to want in a school and make such a huge life choice" (p. A17). In the study, 54 percent of respondents reported that coaches initiated contact with them, 46 percent took only one official visit, and during campus visits only 27 percent met with a professor or sat in on a class. Thirty-seven percent indicated they made a verbal commitment to their school of choice before the beginning of their senior year in high school (Pennington, 2008a).

The risks in the recruiting processes are felt at the Division III level as well, if the following comments of an anonymous father, a college professor, are credible:

It is hard to put into words the frustration and distress that our daughter has experienced because her coach and her college were not truthful about the recruiting process. . . . After doing all she was asked, including attending summer and preseason camps and working tirelessly in practice, she and several other members of the team, who were part of an overflowing roster, were informed early in the season that they would not be active players in varsity games, might not even dress for games. They would play on a reserve team instead. . . . One day a former high school teammate, friend, and walk-on player at another college [contacted our daughter and expressed] her excitement about [her] and her team in a forthcoming varsity contest. Dejectedly, our daughter wrote back to say that she would not dress for the game and most likely would not be able to see her friend because she would be at a reserve team practice on another field. As a result of her experience, she had decided to transfer to another college. (An Ugly Game, 2008, p. B20)

In this context, we have to understand what these activities mean and how they are defined.

DEFINITION AND NATURE OF RECRUITING

The applicable definition of the term "recruiting" is "any solicitation of a prospective student-athlete or a prospective student-athlete's relatives [or legal guardian(s)] by an institutional staff member or by a representative of the institution's athletic interests for the purposes of securing the prospective student-athlete's enrollment and ultimate participation in the institution's inter-collegiate athletics program" (*2008–09 NCAA Division I Manual*, 2008, p. 79). With this basic understanding of the concept of recruiting, we will learn the details on how it impacts the management of intercollegiate athletics programs. This includes the nature of recruiting, its rules, practices, and impact on intercollegiate athletics stakeholders.

Recruiting as resource acquisition

In a very real sense, it can be argued that recruiting is about resource acquisition. Student-athletes are one of the basic resources necessary to maintain winning programs, and recruiting is the process through which programs obtain these vital resources. Former NCAA president Myles Brand himself verified this concept in a 2006 speech before the National Press Club in Washington, DC, when he told his audience: "The ability to compete successfully is tied to recruiting incoming student-athletes" (National Collegiate Athletic Association, 2006, p. 1).

Correlation of winning to coaches' employment and earnings

For coaches at all levels, the ability to recruit has a direct correlation to how much a team can win, how long coaches can keep their jobs, and how much they can earn as a result of their success. Consider the case of Seton Hall University (SHU), a member of the Division I Big East Conference founded by the Catholic Arch-diocese of Newark, located in South Orange, New Jersey, with an undergraduate enrollment of just over 5,000. SHU has had the most success in its men's basketball program, with a team reaching the finals of the NCAA Division I tournament in 1989 under head coach P.J. Carlesimo (later a throat-choked foe of notorious former NBA player Latrell Sprewell). But the Pirates have not approached that level since then, and in 2006 the school fired head coach Louis Orr, former standout at Syracuse University and NBA player, even though Orr led SHU to the NCAA tournament the previous season.

SHU turned the reins over to Bobby Gonzalez, who for the previous seven years had served as head coach at nearby Manhattan College (Riverdale, New York), a similarly sized Catholic school. Gonzalez led the Jaspers, member of the Division I Metro Atlantic Athletic Conference (MAAC), to two NCAA tournament appearances, in large part based on his ability to recruit players from the talent-rich metropolitan New York City area. Joe Quinlan, SHU's AD, said the move to hire Gonzalez was to recruit this region. Gonzalez knew he was hired in large part because of his recruiting resume: "If you can't get players, you've got no chance" (Finley, 2006, p. C19).

Lots of other schools are located in the metro New York City area, including SHU's Garden State neighbor and fellow Big East member Rutgers University. These schools are looking for local talent—as are hundreds of other schools outside the area. Gonzalez's replacement at Manhattan, former University of Pittsburgh assistant and Brooklyn native Barry Rohrssen, came to the school with a strong recruiting resume as well, having served as the conduit to woo NYC talent to Western Pennsylvania. SHU's Gonzalez knew all about the competition from the schools looking to sign the players they believe would help them win. For Rohrssen at MAAC-member Manhattan, the challenge was to identify the "sleepers," talented players who for various reasons were overlooked by his power conference neighbors. If he doesn't find them, he knows he won't be there for long.

Such was the case with Gonzalez, who was fired from SHU at the end of the 2009–10 season (after signing a contract extension through 2015), in part because of team performance (a record of 66–59 with no NCAA tournament appearances), in part because of Gonzalez's behavior on and off the court (he was assessed seven technical fouls in 2009–2010 and was universally disliked by athletics department personnel because of "unprofessional" and "selfish" behavior [Vescey, 2010, p. B15]), as well as that of his players (one player, Robert Mitchell, dismissed from the team by Gonzalez for comments critical of the coach, was charged with kidnapping, robbery, burglary, and possession of a firearm; another, Herb Pope, punched a Texas Tech University player in the groin during a nationally televised National Invitation Tournament postseason game) (Thamel & Schmidt, 2010). As for the next hire, school president Monsignor Robert Sheeran had this to say: "I said this to Louis Orr, I said this to Bobby, and I'll probably say this to the next coach: Give us wins with a lot of fun" (Vescey, 2010, p. B13). The next coach? Former Iona College head coach Kevin Willard, another local MAAC product, at $1 million a year for five years (Thamel, 2010).

Example: A summer camp showcase

What exactly are coaches looking for in their recruits? What qualities must recruits possess for coaches to pursue them? Consider the following scenario, as related by noted writer John McPhee, who helped us understand the classic ideal of the student-athlete with the example of Bill Bradley in Chapter 1. McPhee traveled to the campus of the University of Maryland in College Park to observe a summer camp geared toward recruiting rising high school senior boy's lacrosse prospects. This camp, which began in 1989 as the Top 205—so-called because it initially hoped to attract that number—has two overlapping sessions (each three nights and four days), and draws more than 800 high school players recommended by their coaches. NCAA recruiting Bylaw 13.12.1.2 dictates that camps must be open to "any and all entrants (limited only by number, age, grade level and/or gender" (*2008–09 NCAA Division I Manual*, 2008, p. 118), so the camp is filled on a first-come, first-served basis. According to McPhee (2009), "players want to come because they know who is going to be watching" (pp. 39–40). The camp costs $595, and parents often are waiting outside the fields before and after sessions to hand to attending coaches DVDs highlighting their sons' exploits.

At the session observed by McPhee, coaches from the following schools (among others) were present: Birmingham–Southern, Brown, Bucknell, Colgate, Cornell, Dartmouth, Denver, Franklin & Marshall, Harvard, Hobart, Hofstra, Holy Cross, John Hopkins, Loyola, Maryland, Massachusetts, Michigan, North Carolina, Ohio State, Rensselaer Polytechnic Institute, Princeton, Syracuse, Towson, U.S. Air Force Academy, U.S. Military Academy, Washington and Lee, and Yale—altogether approximately 200 in number, mostly from schools located in the country's traditional lacrosse cradles: New England, Long Island and upstate New York, Baltimore, and Washington, DC.

The coaches are there in their personal folding chairs, placed in a narrow strip between two playing fields. The action on the field begins with one-on-one drills, then half-field scrimmages, then full-field scrimmages run by the camp's staff, usually assistant coaches at Maryland, Towson, or Princeton, the three schools that run the camp. The camp's coaches then draft 20 teams, 22 players per team. University of Denver head coach Bill Tierney calls the camp "one-stop shopping for coaches" (McPhee, 2009, p. 39).

The coaches watch, make notes, and chat among themselves, as evidenced by these exchanges overheard by McPhee about a specific player:

Coach 7 to Coach 8: He has pretty good skills, but he needs serious work in the weight room.

Coach 8: He can't play.

Coach 9: He's probably not going to get it done for us.

Coach 10: I don't think he can play for us, either.

Coach 11: He needs some work stickwise. He's pretty athletic, though. He's tough.

McPhee describes the interchanges as "like being in a barn at a quarter-horse auction" (p. 39).

Much of the evaluation of players, however, is a private matter to coaches, and consists of the notes they make while observing the action. When one player picks up a ground ball with one hand and moves at a leisurely pace toward the goal crease and then throws a bad pass, McPhee notes that "fifty coaches write 'lazy' or something less flattering" (p. 39). Denver head coach Tierney, who took over the Pioneers program in 2009 after 22 years at Princeton, having led the Tigers to 14 Ivy League and six NCAA championships, made the following notes on certain players at the camp. For goalies: "Good poise good position; quick hands; not bad stopper; oversteps w/ right foot; drops hands on right shot; smart talks too much." On players' defensive skills: "Very big, athletic, lazy on D; overaggressive; tall thin good slide fast tough; smallish good stick sees field no hustle on D; bad feet; good feet; no feet too much stick; slapper." And on players' offensive skills: "Loves to shoot; dumb shooter; just catch & finish, no dodge; skinny feeder gets in the way no move; black hole, not aware; slick in traffic, dances; chucker" (p. 40).

Tierney writes "NTB" because parents are often looking over his shoulder at the camp, and he hopes they think this means "not too bad." In reality, it means "not too bright." It has nothing to do with the player's grades or test scores but, rather, how he plays. Tierney generally attempts to assess size, speed, and skills, recognizing four speeds: slow, average, fast, and burner. He says, "A kid can be small if he's fast, but not if he isn't." Size categories include dumpy, gross, huge, meatball, midget, stocky, and thick-ass dodger. The skills refer to stickwork and include three simple ratings: bad, average, and great. Says Tierney of a prospect's rating: "Size, speed, skills—you need to have two out of three. You can improve stick [skills], but not the other two." Echoing the comments of other coaches and managers, Tierney believes that "recruiting is a long-term investment," and at any given time he is in contact with 600 prospects—"kids who write us, and kids we write to" (McPhee, 2009, p. 40).

From the coaches' perspective, the highlight of the camp is the night of Day Three, when 44 of the top players in camp play in an All-Star game. In this matchup, eight are from the Baltimore/DC area and six are from Long Island. Coaches, mostly standing on the endlines of the field, outnumber players three to one. The rest of the campers not chosen for the game sit in the stands, watching, along with parents and siblings. Given the skills of the players chosen, the game is a joy to watch, with McPhee reporting: "Goal answering goal. Fast. Full of isododging, inside rolls, two-on-ones, and Gilman clears" (p. 40). While McPhee notes that many of the coaches are far enough along in the recruiting process with certain prospects "that they have come to regard them as theirs," Tierney is particularly focused on one player, Forest Sonnefeldt, who is 6' 6", 240 pounds and plays attack, an offensive position. He is from Manhattan and attends the Fieldston School in the Bronx, where he scored 83 goals and had 50 assists his junior year. "A first-rate player from New York City is something very rare," says Tierney. Sonnenfeldt is playing well, scoring goals. Tierney's assessment: "Finisher big target RH shooter good skills" (p. 40). Sonnenfeldt was offered admission to Princeton before Tierney left for Denver, and the player accepted, saying: "I visited a bunch of schools. I really liked the (Princeton) campus and I really liked the coach. It's a great team, great organization. It's a real homey feeling. After I visited the school, I felt it was the best place for me" (Staszewski, 2009, p. 1).

There are plenty of other top players on the field as well, and this game ends in a tie and is settled in overtime. Maryland coach Dave Cottle, one of the five winningest men's active coaches, is also watching the action closely. During the action, one player cradles the ball right-handed, goes into a rocker step, does an inside roll, sprints left, and while diving headlong toward the goal, shoots and scores. Someone asked Cottle, "Is he one of yours?" "Not yet," Cottle replied (McPhee, 2009, p. 40).

HISTORICAL PERSPECTIVES

ow did recruiting become such a critical part of any intercollegiate athletic program? To answer this question, we will look at the history of these practices.

Concurrent with the creation of intercollegiate athletic competition was the emerging desire for on-field success. This desire led to the development of methods for securing talented student-athletes, some of whom schools would soon deem improper. As we learned in Chapter 1, student-run organizations operated athletic programs well into the early 20th century. In the 1860s and 1870s, faculties began to impose their will on athletic programs when they perceived that athletic matters were infringing on students' academic activities, and additional concerns were raised regarding professional coaches and payment of student-athletes. A specific concern with recruiting prospects—at the time often referred to under the religiously tinged term "proselytizing"—was raised in the 1880s, when Harvard president Charles Eliot appointed a committee of faculty, students, and alumni to examine the practice of providing "financial inducements" to promising football players (Smith, 1988, p. 129).

Later, under the leadership of head coach Bill Reid, Harvard football benefited from Reid's efforts to set up Harvard Clubs at the elite prep schools that fed athletes to the major Eastern schools. He invited star prep athletes to campus to watch games, and spoke at various alumni group events and schools in an effort to "spread the gospel" of Crimson football. Other schools cultivated contacts at prep schools through coaches and alumni, some of whom directed promising prospects to schools for seasoning. One such case involved James Hogan, who entered Phillips Exeter Academy, a New Hampshire private secondary school, at age 23, and went on to Yale four years later, where the star football player was given the lucrative franchise of selling American Tobacco Company products on the New Haven campus. Princeton benefited from the efforts of booster and zealous alumnus Charles Patterson, who pestered promising prospects at Phillips Exeter and Phillips Academy (a private secondary school in Andover, Massachusetts), to take Princeton's entrance exam regardless of their year of study (Smith, 1994). When the head of the Andover school asked one of the younger students why he took the exam (which he passed), he said, "At the top of the paper I wrote my weight—205 pounds. I guess I'll pass all right. Patterson said I would" (Watterson, 2000, p. 57).

Over time, efforts to woo valuable prospects emerged at other schools. In the 1920s, reports emerged of highly evolved systems of subsidies and support for football stars, where an "uhlan" (a student with a car) would fraternize with promising high school players to sell them on his school, while other students would work to find easy classes, cushy on-campus jobs, and alumni-funded aid for players. Northwestern University, a Big Ten member whose on-field performance was lagging in the 1920s, changed its fortunes through a network of 50 alumni scouts and alumni grants to cover first-year expenses. At Louisiana State University (LSU) in the 1930s, then-Louisiana governor Huey Long suggested that LSU obtain the services of a talented Tulane University quarterback by offering his father a highly coveted state job.

Other southern schools worked actively to obtain talent by paying travel expenses to bring recruits to campus for tryouts, and eventually approving outright "scholarships" for football players. In addition, the Big Ten's Michigan State University created athletic grants for prospects regardless of financial need after a local insurance salesman died and willed the school half a million dollars. Recipients were required to maintain a "C" average to retain the funding. The system of subsidization was so entrenched at the University of Pittsburgh that players actually went on strike in 1939 after the school's president tried to curtail allotments of payments and campus jobs. These techniques were employed on the West Coast as well, as evidenced by the efforts of alumni to direct prospects to their alma maters (Shapiro, 1983; Watterson, 2000).

As we read in Chapter 3, concerns over recruiting and subsidies led to dissolution of Pacific Coast Conference (PCC) in the 1950s. Until 1940, alumni often scouted and paid the tuition for promising athletes throughout the PCC, and coaches often were not involved in the recruiting process at all. At Stanford, former star players induced several players to attend their alma mater, especially those from the talent-rich Southern California area. A decade before, when star player Woody Strode, one of the first African-Americans to suit up in the league, matriculated at

UCLA, he noted that the school funneled him more than $100 a month, and that he and others were expected to work off the money doing campus maintenance. "A lot of great athletes were janitors; they scrubbed toilets. [I] used to walk around campus with a stick picking up papers, and we did a little gardening, too," said Strode (Johnson, 2006, p. 85).

In the 1950s, additional inducements to recruits, mostly in football, indicated that work-study jobs were only part of the financial outlay to student-athletes at many schools. In addition to the issues in the PCC, at Arizona State a booster group known as the Sun Angels Foundation paid nearly $80,000 to football players, an action for which the school earned NCAA sanctions. At Michigan State, the Spartan Foundation boosters made payments of $55,000 to football players between 1949 and 1952, enabling the school to build a national championship team. Similar practices continued at Michigan State well into the 1960s, with head football coach Duffy Daugherty creating a system whereby boosters would disburse money to players for tuition payments. In 1956, the NCAA passed legislation outlining specific recruiting guidelines, including limits on official visits, timeframes, and procedures for using booster club funds to subsidize student-athletes (Shapiro, 1983; Watterson, 2000).

The impact of these events notwithstanding, many experts noted that additional revenues from television prompted schools to continue to up their antes in seeking to secure talented prospects. The most egregious case of improper recruiting and subsidy occurred in the football program at Southern Methodist University in the 1970s and 1980s (see Chapter 8).

FINANCIAL AID AND THE RECRUITING PROCESS

As the history of recruitment shows, the amount of financial aid a student receives has been a key, and often contentious, element in the recruiting process. This aid is commonly referred to as an "athletic scholarship." In 1956, the NCAA membership approved the athletics grant-in-aid (GIA), or athletic "scholarship," which meant that any prospect could receive tuition, fees, room and board, books, and $15 a month for the school year (Byers, 1995).

What a GIA refers to is the amount of aid awarded to a prospective student-athlete based on his or her athletic ability. As defined in NCAA legislation, financial aid includes all institutional sources of funding, as well as funding from other sources. Exhibit 7.1 outlines these sources.

The full-grant-in-aid consists of money to cover the cost of tuition and fees, room and board, and required course-related books. Student-athletes may receive financial aid up to the full cost of attending their institution (which includes supplies, transportation, and other expenses related to attendance), with exceptions for monies received from a Pell Grant (supplied to needy students by the federal government). Room-and-board funds may be used to cover off-campus housing and board. Student-athletes also may receive financial aid to cover the cost of summer courses, provided that the student-athlete has been in residence at least one term prior to the summer. If a student-athlete receives any aid in which athletic ability is a determining criterion, the aid is awarded for a period of no more than one academic year; there is no such thing as a four-year "full ride." Aid is tabulated and awarded on an annual basis, with all awards made on or before July 1 prior to the academic year in which it is to be effective (*2008–09 NCAA Division I Manual*, 2008).

| Permissible sources of financial aid. | EXHIBIT | 7.1 |

INSTITUTIONAL SOURCES OF FINANCIAL AID

- Scholarships
- Grants
- Tuition waivers
- Employee-dependent tuition benefits
- Loans
- Aid from government or private sources for which the institution is responsible for selecting the recipient or determining the amount of aid
- Aid awarded through an established outside program in which athletics participation may be a major criterion

OTHER PERMISSIBLE FINANCIAL AID

- Financial aid received from anyone upon whom the student-athlete is naturally or legally dependent
- Financial aid awarded solely on the bases of having no relationship to athletic ability
- Financial aid awarded through an established continuing outside program (e.g., National Merit Scholar) in which athletics participation is not the major criterion

Source: 2008–09 NCAA Division I Manual, 2008, pp. 170-171.

Division I limits

Under Division I regulations, each sport is limited in the number of students on each roster who can receive aid in which athletic ability is a determining criterion. Sports are categorized as either "head-count" or "equivalency."

Head-count sports

In the head count sports, listed in Exhibit 7.2, each student-athlete who receives athletically related aid in any amount counts toward the maximum allowable number of students receiving such aid. For example, the women's gymnastics sport

| Head count sports and limits—Division I. | EXHIBIT | 7.2 |

Football (Bowl Division): 85 (with a limit of 25 of those on aid for the first time)

Football (Championship Division): 63 (with a limit of 30 of those on aid for the first time)

Women's Basketball: 15

Men's Basketball: 13

Women's Gymnastics: 12

Women's Volleyball: 12

Women's Tennis: 8

Source: 2008–09 NCAA Division I Manual, 2008.

is allowed 12 counters, and each student-athlete receiving athletically related aid counts toward that total, whether she is receiving aid that meets the full amount permissible or whether she receives any amount less than that.

Equivalency sports

All other Division I sports are classified as equivalency sports; that is, there is a limit on the value of the financial aid awards that an institution may provide in any academic year to participants in these sports. For example, the limit for wrestling is 9.9, meaning that a school may provide aid not to exceed the maximum amount allowed to a single student-athlete multiplied by 9.9. So, if the maximum amount of the full grant-in-aid allowed at the school is $30,000, the athletic department cannot distribute more than $297,000 ($30,000 × 9.9) to its wrestlers. The school determines how the aid can be distributed. The school can opt to give full grants to nine wrestlers ($30,000 each) and an additional partial grant of $27,000 to a tenth wrestler, or split the money any number of ways (full grants to two wrestlers and partial grants to the rest of the team, or equal partial grants to each, or some combination thereof), as long as the total amount does not exceed $297,000. Ice hockey is excepted from this format, with a maximum equivalency limit of 18, and a limit of 30 who may receive athletic aid.

Exhibit 7.3 outlines the maximum equivalency limits in the remainder of the NCAA Division I sports. One noteworthy restriction in awarding aid occurs in baseball, when in 2007 the membership passed legislation (effective for the 2009–10 academic year) limiting baseball squad sizes to 35, with no more than 27 permitted to receive aid, and no player allowed to receive less than 25 percent of a full GIA (Chapter 9 provides a more thorough discussion on baseball exceptions) (Thomas, 2008).

| EXHIBIT 7.3 | Maximum equivalency limits–Division I. |

MEN'S SPORTS

Baseball: 11.7	Lacrosse: 12.6	Tennis: 4.5
Cross Country/Track and Field: 12.6	Rifle: 3.6	Volleyball: 4.5
Fencing: 4.5	Skiing: 6.3	Water Polo: 4.5
Golf: 4.5	Soccer: 9.9	
Gymnastics: 6.3	Swimming and Diving: 9.9	

WOMEN'S SPORTS

Archery: 5	Golf: 6	Squash: 12
Badminton: 6	Lacrosse: 12	Swimming and Diving: 14
Bowling: 5	Rowing: 20	Synchronized Swimming: 5
Cross Country/Track and Field: 18	Rugby: 12	Team Handball: 10
Equestrian: 15	Skiing: 7	Water Polo: 8
Fencing: 5	Soccer: 12	
Field Hockey: 12	Softball: 12	

Source: 2008–09 NCAA Division I Manual, 2008, p. 183.

	EXHIBIT	7.4

Maximum equivalency limits–Division II.

MEN'S SPORTS

Baseball: 9.0

Basketball: 10.0

Cross Country/Track and Field: 12.6

Fencing: 4.5

Football: 36.0

Golf: 3.6

Gymnastics: 5.4

Ice Hockey: 13.5

Lacrosse: 10.8

Rifle: 3.6

Skiing: 6.3

Soccer: 9.0

Swimming and Diving: 8.1

Tennis: 4.5

Volleyball: 4.5

Water Polo: 4.5

Wrestling: 9.0

WOMEN'S SPORTS

Archery: 9.0

Badminton: 10.0

Basketball: 10.0

Bowling: 5.0

Cross Country/Track and Field: 12.6

Equestrian: 15.0

Fencing: 4.5

Field Hockey: 6.3

Golf: 5.4

Gymnastics: 6.0

Ice Hockey: 18.0

Lacrosse: 9.9

Rowing: 20.0

Rugby: 12.0

Skiing: 6.3

Soccer: 9.9

Softball: 7.2

Squash: 9.0

Swimming and Diving: 8.1

Synchronized Swimming: 5.0

Team Handball: 12.0

Tennis: 6.0

Volleyball: 8.0

Water Polo: 8.0

Source: 2008–09 NCAA Division II Manual, 2008, p. 148.

Division II limits

Some Division II programs have limits that differ from those in Division I, as listed in Exhibit 7.4. All Division II sports are classified as equivalency sports. Not counting those awarded in football and basketball, a school cannot provide more than a total of 60 equivalencies in men's sports in any academic year (*2008–09 NCAA Division II Manual*, 2008, p. 148).

Impact of the limits

According to research published in 2008, the impact of these limits means that the average athletic aid award totals $10,409. But in some sports, the award could be as low as $2,000. Exhibit 7.5 shows participant and award data for several sports (including both Division I and II participants).

The information in this exhibit shows that few prospects can expect to have their entire college costs covered through athletically related aid.

EXHIBIT 7.5	Grant-in-aid participant and award data.					
	TOTAL H.S. PARTICIPANTS	**AWARDS AVAILABLE**	**STUDENTS RECEIVING AID**	**TOTAL GIA $ (IN MILLIONS)**	**AVERAGE % OF FULL GIAs**	**YEARLY VALUE PER PARTICIPANT**
Men's Ice Hockey	32,166	1,089	1,369	$29.8	80	$21,755
Women's Ice Hockey	4,245	423	529	$10.9	80	$20,540
Women's Gymnastics	21,620	411	512	$8.4	80	$16,478
Football	1,025,762	19,549	29,299	$367.3	69	$12,980
Women's Rowing	2,359	958	2,295	$22.3	42	$9,723
Wrestling	239,105	789	2,160	$14.5	37	$6,703
Baseball	451,701	3,983	12,272	$71.3	36	$6,338

THE MECHANICS OF RECRUITING AND THE RULES THAT GOVERN THEM

As we know, recruiting is a crucial function in producing winning intercollegiate teams. But how does this process actually occur? We will review some of the basic rules governing recruiting activities and illustrate how some of these rules impact actual recruiting methods and actions, as conveyed by Bruce Feldman. He spent a year observing and documenting the recruiting efforts of the University of Mississippi's football staff, led by (now former) head coach Ed Orgeron (pronounced OH-zhur-on), now an assistant coach at the University of Southern California. The public school (a.k.a., "Ole Miss") located in Oxford, has an undergrad population of 17,000 and is a member of the Division I Southeastern Conference.

Prospect eligibility for recruitment

According to Bylaw 13.02.11 of the *2008–09 NCAA Division I Manual*, a prospective student-athlete is one who has started ninth-grade classes; that status is retained until he or she enrolls in any four-year collegiate institution, including summer classes. All applicable recruiting bylaws are imposed beginning with ninth-grade classes. Orgeron (a.k.a., Coach O), who came to the school in 2004 after serving as defensive line coach, was a highly successful head recruiter at both the University of Miami and the University of Southern California. University of Mississippi chancellor Robert Khayat identified Orgeron's recruiting skill as the key in his hiring: "The teams that are the most successful have the really good athletes, and they keep replenishing them. We felt we needed to recruit better, and I think Coach Orgeron has shown that he will be able to do this on a consistent basis" (Feldman, 2007, p. 177).

Orgeron tutored the coaches at Mississippi that if they were to land the desired players, they had to identify them early. That meant being the first to find and contact not only prospects who would be signing that year, but also promising high school juniors and sophomores. The key deadline the coaches were working under was the first Wednesday in February, the first date on which prospects could sign letters of intent signifying their commitment to accept grant-in-aid offers. To get to the limit of 25, staffs have to begin with a list of up to 1,000 names of potential candidates. At 8 A.M. every Wednesday, Orgeron and his staff met to go over the state of their recruiting, reviewing film, assessing scouting reports, prioritizing their needs, and trying to figure out what competitor schools they had to beat out to land their choices.

In May 2006, not only was the Rebels staff working on the Class of 2007 prospects (of whom the staff had already broken down 200 evaluation tapes by the 2006 National Signing Day), but Orgeron also was demanding that they produce lists of all promising Class of 2008 candidates, and lists of all the prospects who would be attending the Ole Miss camp the next month, along with names of their coaches. In all, Orgeron estimated that he and his staff devoted 15 percent of their jobs to recruiting, knowing that premier programs like Southern California and LSU didn't have to recruit as hard to stay on top, because, as noted by Feldman, "blue-chippers sought them out."

According to one Ole Miss assistant, "I used to think recruiting was August to January and then you go hard for a month in the spring. Not [Orgeron]. He's persistent, and it's all the time" (Feldman, 2007, pp. 146, 148). As evidence of this notion, to view most completely Mississippi junior college prospects near the end of their season, Orgeron chartered a plane for him and some of his staff to see games in Jackson, while other staff members drove to games elsewhere. The trips would last no more than 18 hours, because the coaches had to get back to campus to prepare for their game against conference rival Auburn later that week. Orgeron's emphasis on making contact with potential recruits as early as possible shows that eligibility rules are important to both prospects and coaches.

Permissible recruiting personnel

As noted, alumni were among the earliest sources of recruiting information and contacts for intercollegiate athletic programs. While alumni and other such "representatives of athletics interests" certainly have not experienced a diminution in their ardor for wins (and in some cases, their activities enacted to achieve such wins), the evolution of NCAA rules has limited the extent to which these groups may influence the recruiting process. Such "representatives" are often called "boosters." Bylaw 13.02.13 specifically defines a representative as "an individual, independent agency, corporate entity or other organization who is known (or should have been known) by a member of institution's executive or athletics administration" to be involved in promoting the institution's athletic interests, to have donated money to an athletic department, or to have provided benefits to a prospect or his or her family (*2008–09 NCAA Division I Manual*, 2008, p. 80).

The general rule governing permissible recruiters, covered in Bylaw 13.02.5.1, is that, except for some specific exceptions, all contacts are to be made only by "authorized institutional staff members," and that off-campus recruiting can be performed only by those who are "certified on an annual basis as to knowledge of applicable recruiting rules." To become certified, personnel must pass a "standardized national test developed by the NCAA national office" formulated to assess an understanding of recruiting and freshman eligibility legislation. Individual member conferences are responsible for administering and correcting the tests. Institutional staff members such as faculty are allowed to contact prospects only on campus or within 30 miles of campus during a prospect's official visit, a step discussed later in more detail (*2008–09 NCAA Division I Manual*, 2008, pp. 79, 81, 82).

For other types of contacts such as telephone calls, only coaches and some specific institutional staff members (such as academic advisors) may initiate calls to prospects. Others, such as enrolled student-athletes, may receive but not initiate calls from prospects after July 1 of the prospect's junior year (*2008–09 NCAA Division I Manual*, 2008, pp. 85–86).

Permissible telephone calls

The timing and number of permissible calls varies by sport and gender, as follows:

- Football: may receive one call between April 15 and May 31 of the prospect's junior year
- Men's basketball: one call not before June 15, two in August
- Women's basketball: calls beginning as early as April 15
- All other sports: a prospect and his or her family or legal guardian(s) may not be contacted by a recruiter before July 1 following the completion of his or her junior year

After these dates, schools are allowed only one call per week outside of a contact period (see below). All electronically transmitted human voice exchanges (including video conferencing and video phones) are considered to be telephone calls (*2008–09 NCAA Division I Manual*, 2008, pp. 83–85).

At Ole Miss, at the first big recruiting meeting of 2006, all the coaches were making calls to recruits from their "war room," which they would repeat every Monday night from that point on. The room became a hive of activity, with all the Rebels assistant coaches on cell phones talking to or text-messaging recruits. "Here, I'm going to let you talk to Coach O," says one, giving the recruit's name to Orgeron as he hands him his cellphone. According to Feldman (2007), "at some point during each call, Orgeron will hold the phone in the air, and on cue everyone in the room . . . will belt out the Rebel Yell, a primal howl that is an indecipherable jumble of 'GO REBELS!' and 'OLE MISS REBELS!' and the kid's first name" (pp. 26–27). Later in the process, Orgeron required all coaches to make 30 minutes of phone calls to coaches of desired underclassman prospects as well, the number of which is not subject to NCAA limitations.

But the rules are often tested, either by accident or on purpose. While recruiting wide receiver prospect Carl Moore, University of Florida head football coach Urban Meyer called Moore's girlfriend, a gymnast, who was being recruited by the Gators' gymnastics program. Such a call violates the permissible callers rule (Bylaw 13.1.3.4.1), which specifies that only coaches in the sport for which prospects are being recruited may call them, and would be classified as a minor violation.

In another improper call involving Moore, Coach Meyer encouraged Gators QB Tim Tebow to call Moore immediately after Tebow won the Heisman Trophy in December 2007. Bylaw 13.1.3.5.1.1 of the *2008–09 NCAA Division I Manual* explicitly forbids coaches from directing current student-athletes to make calls to prospects, but the school and NCAA investigation found no violations in the recruitment of Moore. One Internet recruiting expert had this to say: "Most coaches use whatever tactics they can—that are legal—to attract recruits. You recruit the girlfriend, the mom, the grandma, the little league coach" (Jones, 2008, p. 7C).

Face-to-face contacts

As outlined in the *Division I Manual*, the recruiting process of coaches is dictated by the types of contacts they can have with prospects. A "contact" is defined as "any face-to-face encounter between a prospective student-athlete or the prospective student athlete's parents, relatives, or legal guardian(s) and an institutional staff member or athletics representative during which any dialogue occurs in excess of a greeting" (*2008–09 NCAA Division I Manual*, 2008, p. 78).

Recruiting periods for face-to-face contacts

Bylaw 13.02.04 delineates specifically what activities can occur during which period of the year, as outlined in Exhibit 7.6. Only football and men's and women's basketball are subject to each of these periods. The recruiting calendars of all other Division I sports are delineated as either contact or dead periods.

Permissible off-campus contacts

In most Division I sports, off-campus contacts with a prospect and his or her family or legal guardian(s) cannot occur until on or after July 1 following the prospect's completion of his or her junior year in high school. The exceptions are men's and women's basketball, which do not allow such contact until a prospect begins senior-year classes, and women's gymnastics, which does not allow contact before July 15 following a prospect's junior year. In addition for most Division I sports, each

---

NCAA Division I recruiting periods.   EXHIBIT   7.6

Contact Period: Authorized athletics department staff members may make in-person, off-campus recruiting contacts and evaluations during this period.

Evaluation Period: Authorized athletics department staff members may be involved in off-campus activities designed to assess the academic qualifications and playing ability of prospective student-athletes. No in-person, off-campus recruiting contacts can occur during this period.

Quiet Period: In-person recruiting contacts can be made only on the member institution's campus. No in-person, off-campus recruiting contacts can occur during this period.

Dead Period: No in-person recruiting contacts or evaluations are allowed, either on- or off-campus.

Source: 2008–09 NCAA Division I Manual, 2008.

institution is limited to seven recruiting opportunities (contacts and evaluations combined) per prospective student-athlete. The exceptions to this rule are football (six), men's basketball (seven, but not more than three in-person, off-campus), and women's basketball (five combined). Exceptions also are permitted for the U.S. service academies (Air Force, Coast Guard, Merchant Marine, Military, Naval), where authorized recruiters are permitted to make in-person, telephone, and off-campus contacts during a prospect's junior year.

Contacts with prospects and families. During football's two designated contact periods, coaches are allowed to meet with each prospect and his family once a week. Before the Ole Miss staff headed out for one such period, Orgeron dictated his requirements: "I expect you out of the hotel by 7:00. No sleeping in 'til 9:00. I wanna hear, 'That coach told me he was going to be here at 8 o'clock and he was here at 7:50'" (Feldman, 2007, p. 230). Other guidelines included getting transcripts from a prospect's counselor, wearing Ole Miss gear, stopping by to chat up local high school coaches, and knowing as much as possible about the prospects and their families. Said Orgeron: "When you go inside the home, it's no 'Hi, howya doin?' bullshit. Address the parents by their first names: 'Hello, Mary,' and 'Good to see you, Dan.' Don't try to get by with 'Ma'am' and 'Sir.' Get a personal relationship going" (p. 231).

One issue that continues to dog Ole Miss in recruiting battles is the school's obstructionist approach to integration in the 1960s. When questioned about this by the cousin of one recruit during a home visit, Orgeron addressed it head on: "I heard about that when I first got here. But it's just not that way anymore. It's not. One of my coaches . . . is African-American, and he doesn't feel that way. If he did, he wouldn't be sending his son to Ole Miss" (p. 233).

Evaluation contacts. An evaluation is defined under Bylaw 13.02.6 of the *2008–09 Division I NCAA Manual* as "any off-campus activity designed to assess the academic qualifications or athletics ability of a prospective student-athlete" and may not include "personal contact with a prospect" (p. 79). One challenge endemic to the evaluation process and period is that, unlike in other sports, where top prospects spend their summers at camps and tournaments, enabling recruiters to gauge how they measure them against each other, football recruiters must rely almost solely on evaluations done by individual coaches or on game films sent by high schools, usually showing prospects against inferior opponents.

To deal with this challenge, Orgeron and his staff decided to record games and practices on their own, a practice permitted under current NCAA recruiting bylaws (although some rival schools called the move an invasion of prospects' privacy). Orgeron was convinced that the move would allow them to fine-tune the recruiting process, and after the Rebels' four-person video staff had edited the videos (eliminating blurry sequences), the entire staff then could see the position-specific movements of prospects at weekly meetings, enabling GIA decisions on something more than the word of a single coach. This also was very much in line with one of the recruiting philosophies of Coach O, who believed, as noted by Feldman, "with every fiber of his being, that you can never, *never* [author's emphasis], watch too much game tape" (2007, p. 106).

Another method of evaluating prospects is the on-campus camp, where players hoping to catch the eyes of college coaches travel for hours to take part in NFL

Combine-type drills (vertical jump, 40-yard dash, shuttle run, bench press) and a team's personal coaching drills over the course of six hours. According to Feldman (2007), "Ask any coach in college football: summer camp is the best mechanism that college programs have for finding players. Video is essential, but most coaches will tell you there's nothing that beats direct observation. Especially direct, *hands-on* observation" (p. 120). The drawback is that these camps still don't provide true game conditions in which prospects can be evaluated. Ole Miss holds five such sessions each summer, one each dedicated to specific offensive and defensive positions. Such camps allow the Rebels staff not only to observe prospects up close but also to sell the merits of their program and facilities to those they are hoping to sign.

Orgeron also uses the camp as a way to sell his method of coaching and to see if the recruits can respond to hard coaching. At Ole Miss's linemen camp, Orgeron addresses the entire group this way: "Everyone give me your eyes. This is *not* a recruiting camp. You will be coached here just like an Ole Miss Rebel. Nobody talks back to a coach, and nobody's bending over or taking a knee on our fields. We do *not* [author's emphasis] show any signs of discomfort here. Got that?" (p. 124). To prove this point, offensive and defensive line prospects matched up in nearly full-contact one-on-one pass rushing drills, even though the players were wearing just shorts and t-shirts, with the losing side doing 10 push-ups (coaches included) for each lost contest. When one prized offensive line recruit defeated the camp's best D-line prospect, Ole Miss offensive line coach Frank Wilson rushed in and jumped on the recruit's back, followed immediately by the rest of the O-line prospects. Just 24 hours after the camp had ended, Orgeron met with his staff members to drive home the point that they had to build on the contacts they had made immediately to land their targets (Feldman, 2007).

Coaches' limits on contacts and evaluations. Under Division I legislation, coaches for the following sports are limited in the number of days (as measured 12:01 A.M. to midnight) they may recruit off-campus: Championship Division football (42), softball (50), women's volleyball (80), women's basketball (85), men's basketball (130). If two coaches are off-campus on the same day, this is counted as two days toward the sport total. In addition, permissible off-campus recruiters are limited in the number of contacts and evaluations, defined as recruiting opportunities, per recruited prospect. For sports other than football and basketball, the total permissible off-campus recruiting opportunities per prospect during the academic year is seven, of which no more than three may be contacts. Off-campus football recruiters are limited to three evaluations, only one of which may be used in the fall, and women's basketball recruiters are limited to five recruiting opportunities during the academic year (*2008–09 NCAA Division I Manual*, 2008).

At Ole Miss, all the coaches, including Orgeron, are on the road during the four-week spring recruiting period. During the first week, Orgeron started in northern Mississippi and worked his way throughout the state over five days, covering 1,800 miles, with 21 stops, ending in New Orleans. In the second week, he was back in Mississippi, then on to Tennessee, Alabama, Arkansas, and Georgia, returning to Mississippi to speak at a high school coaches' clinic. Weeks three and four were spent in Louisiana, Alabama, and Florida. Orgeron also considered as a key task to get his assistants as fired up about recruiting as he was, and he gave a $100 prize to the one who came back to campus with the most visitor passes from high schools (Feldman, 2007).

Campus visits and noteworthy limits

Along with coaches evaluating and contacting prospects off-campus, prospects may travel to campuses. In an official visit, a prospect visit is financed in whole or in part by the visited school. A visit is deemed unofficial when the prospect pays for the visit at his or her own expense. Certain sports can offer only a certain number of official visits. These include football (56), basketball (12), and baseball (25). Schools may provide only one official visit to a prospect, and prospects are limited to five total official visits, none of which may occur before the opening day of classes for their senior year, and may not be before prospects have submitted their standardized test scores to the institution visited. Visits are limited to 48 hours, beginning at the time the prospect steps on campus. After the 48-hour period, the prospect must exit the campus immediately (*2008–09 NCAA Division I Manual*, 2008, pp. 80, 104–109).

Many of the strictures in the NCAA manuals may seem arcane—for example, the limitations on permissible activities relating to official visits. The general restriction for transportation on official visits (Bylaw 13.5.2.1) reads:

> A member institution may pay the prospective student-athlete's actual round-trip transportation costs for his or her official visit to campus from any location, provided the prospective student-athlete returns to the original point of departure, or if return transportation is provided to the prospective student-athlete's home, educational institution or site of competition, the cost does not exceed round-trip expenses from the prospective student-athlete's original point of departure. Use of a limousine or helicopter for such transportation is prohibited.

Bylaw 13.5.2.3 continues to specify limit on permissible air transportation: "An institution providing air transportation to a prospective student-athlete to and from an official campus visit must use commercial transportation at coach-class airfare." Bylaw 13.5.2.3.1 continues the limitations: "An institution may not arrange payment of the airline ticket to allow a prospective student-athlete [or a prospective student-athlete's relatives, friends or legal guardian(s)] to take advantage of ticket bonuses, rebates, refunds, upgrades or other benefits connected with the purchase of the ticket."

Later in the official visit section, under Bylaw 13.6.7.9, institutions are notified that certain "miscellaneous, personalized recruiting aids," which can include "any decorative items and special additions to any location the prospective student-athlete will visit (e.g., hotel room, locker room, coach's office, conference room, arena) regardless of whether or not items include the prospective student-athlete's name or picture" may not be arranged. Such items also include personalized jerseys, personalized audio/visual scoreboard presentations, and allowing prospects to run on the field with a team during pre-game introductions (*2008–09 NCAA Division I Manual*, 2008, pp. 103, 109).

As noted, Division I Bowl Subdivision schools are limited to 56 official visits per year, which usually begin on the Friday of a home football weekend and end the following Sunday morning. One Ole Miss recruit's Saturday began with an 8:15 A.M. wakeup call and a 9 A.M. breakfast meeting with academic counselors, followed by a tour of the strength and conditioning facilities. Then the recruit took a campus tour with a department ambassador—one of the dozen or so attractive female Ole Miss students "decked out in snug dresses and stilettos" (Feldman, 2007).

The hostess usually is briefed on the recruit's background and interests, and as part of the tour the hostess ushers the recruit to the Grove, an oval-shaped, 10-acre wooded park in the middle of campus where Rebels fans congregate for an elaborate tailgating ritual using U-Hauls to truck in tables and linens, crystalware and candelabras, rugs, tents, and La-Z-Boy recliners, making the Grove appear to be, in the words of one witness, "a kind of Kentucky Derby without the horses. . . . The first Bloody Mary is poured before nine (A.M.)" (St. John, 2004, pp. 162, 164).

The high point of the campus visit is attending the game. In or after one game, in which Ole Miss defeated conference rival Vanderbilt University, 17–10, all the recruits joined the team in its locker room, then a key recruit of the weekend had dinner with Orgeron, his player host, and a few other Rebel coaches. Although much of the dinner conversation was not focused on football, Orgeron tried to use the time to gauge how much the recruit liked football. The next morning, when the recruit left campus, Orgeron summed up the visit: "I really liked him. And I really think he liked it here and liked us. I just don't know if he's coming" (Feldman, 2007, p. 198).

THE COURTING OF DARRELL AND JAMARKUS — case study 7.A

Consider the case of a blue-chip football recruit, Darrell Scott, a highly touted running back from Oxnard, California. He chose the University of Colorado in 2008 over the University of Texas, UCLA, and Louisiana State. Two days before the National Letter of Intent signing day, Scott sat down with his mother to make his decision. He eliminated LSU first because it was too far away from his hometown and the coaches there had not spent enough time recruiting him. UCLA was the only local school he was considering, but because of a change in head coaches, the school had entered the hunt late. Scott then focused on Texas. Initially he said of the school: "I like the area. I like the atmosphere, the fans, everything . . . the coaching staff," and spoke favorably of the program's national prominence and commitment to running the ball (Evans, 2008a, p. C13). But when Texas changed running backs coach, it gave Scott pause, and then considerations turned to Colorado, in large part because of Scott's two-year relationship with Darian Hagan, a former Buffaloes standout and the team's current running backs coach. Also, Scott's uncle, Josh Smith, was a receiver there. Scott liked Colorado head coach Dan Hawkins and the Buffaloes' rush-oriented offense, was a bit put-off by the frosty Rocky Mountain climate in Boulder, but was assuaged with the program's indoor practice facility.

After opting for Colorado, Scott called Texas to inform the coach of his decision. The Texas coach tried to change his mind, but Scott rebuffed him. Before the Wednesday announcement, though, Scott was still receiving text messages and phone calls from current Texas players, and one from then-Southern California quarterback Mark Sanchez (not permitted under NCAA recruiting rules, as discussed earlier). Also, there were rumors that Scott had chosen Colorado because his mother had been offered a bank job there, which his mother denied (Evans, 2008a). After all that, however, Scott left Colorado during his sophomore year, seeking to transfer to a school closer to home (Sports Log, 2009).

Texas also lost another prized recruit, Jamarkus McFarland, a 6' 3", 290-pound defensive tackle prospect, to Big 12 rival University of Oklahoma later that same year. McFarland, from the east Texas town of Lufkin, opted for Oklahoma because of the school's recruiting efforts, which included school president David Boren promising McFarland a spot in the leadership class he teaches for selected academically gifted first-year students. Interestingly, McFarland's mother initially preferred Texas because she thought it had a stronger academic profile than Oklahoma. McFarland chose Oklahoma in part because of an experience at a party in Dallas hosted by Texas fans after the Longhorns had defeated Oklahoma. "Alcohol was all you can drink; money wasn't an option," McFarland wrote in an assignment for his English class his senior year at Lufkin High School. "Girls were acting wild by taking off their tops and pulling down their pants. Girls were also romancing each other" (Evans, 2008b, p. B8). In the same paper, McFarland compared the Dallas party to one he attended at a sorority house during his recruiting visit to Oklahoma: "Some people were tipsy, but in control of themselves. . . . Some people who attend the University of Oklahoma seem to represent different values than some people who attend the University of Texas" (p. B8).

questions for you to consider

1. Identify and explain the risks involved with some of the practices that schools utilize to attract top prospects.

2. Identify and explain the factors that influenced Scott and McFarland in making their respective decisions, and how recruiters can seek to understand the nature of these key factors.

KEY ISSUES IN MANAGING RECRUITING

As stated, athletic recruiting is really resource acquisition for intercollegiate athletics programs. Without the requisite talent, no program can achieve the much sought-after game success. We will review some of the key recent and emerging issues that impact recruiting practices.

Recruiting expenditures

In his book *The Blind Side: Evolution of a Game*, author Michael Lewis chronicles the emergence of Michael Oher (pronounced "Oar"), an outstanding offensive lineman prospect attending a small private Christian high school in Tennessee. The 6'6", 345-pound, exceptionally strong and athletic Oher overcame a troubled childhood to become the one of the country's most sough-after recruits. Oher eventually narrowed his college choices to three: LSU, Tennessee, and Mississippi. Tennessee had become a player for Oher after the school made an offer to Oher's high school coach to join its staff. When Tennessee traveled through Memphis en route to a road game at Mississippi, then-head coach Phil Fulmer took his entire team to practice at Oher's school, with a plan to roll up to the field in the team busses, and, offensive lineman leading the charge, have the entire team surround Oher and give him a cheer. Unfortunately for Fulmer, the busses got stuck in traffic and missed Oher, who had left campus minutes before to make his official visit to Mississippi. After four years at Ole Miss, Oher was selected in the first round of the 2009 NFL Draft (23rd overall) by the Baltimore Ravens.

Maybe if Fulmer had used a helicopter, he might have beaten the traffic, landed Oher, and still have his job at Tennessee. Silly, you say? Consider that, though private planes have long been used by coaches to cross the country, the use of helicopters, while impermissible for transporting recruits, has become fashionable for head coaches. Helicopters help coaches like UCLA's Rick Neuheisel get to four or five games on a Friday night and avoid Los Angeles' notoriously snarled traffic. This transportation is provided courtesy of the grandson of bandleader and composer Lawrence Welk (ask your grandparents about him), and it also provides an undeniable buzz factor when coaches swoop in and land.

When Notre Dame head coach Brian Kelly was at the University of Cincinnati in 2009, he attended five games across the city of Cincinnati on one Friday night and had assistant coaches at each site to make sure the games would not be at half-time, to ensure maximum attention. Said Kelly of the decision to use the helicopter, the cost of which ($1,500 an hour) was paid for by a booster: "We're using it to get to games, but if by chance you make it a big event, so be it" (Thamel & Evans, 2009a, p. B11). One school's student section responded to his arrival by chanting "Brian Kelly" and clapping rhythmically. Even rolling up in a Hummer is unlikely to elicit such a response, let alone a school-owned mini-van.

The point here is that some schools are willing to commit seemingly unlimited resources to certain programs in an effort to win games. In 2006–07, Tennessee spent close to $1 million on football recruiting alone, and another $1 million on recruiting for other sports (Feldman, 2007; Sander, 2008b). Although this is nothing new, the Division I membership has tried to limit the resources devoted to these activities so more schools might be able to be competitive.

At least one Division III school has made an effort to limit recruitment resources, even though schools in this division already spend far less on recruiting than do those at the other classification levels. At Amherst (Massachusetts) College, a private liberal arts school with 1,700 undergraduates and a member of the New England Small College Athletic Conference, AD Suzanne Coffey has asked her coaches to send fewer bulk mailings to recruits, to e-mail rather than to make telephone calls, and is looking to rely on its alumni more to monitor local newspapers and academic honor roll reports to identify potential recruits, and who can meet through conference calls with coaches to discuss their findings (Viera, 2009).

Nonetheless, a study released by the *Chronicle of Higher Education* in 2008 noted that 48 percent of Division I athletic programs at least doubled their recruiting budgets over the previous decade, with the University of Maryland (277 percent), Kansas State University (267 percent), and LSU (248 percent) leading the charge. In all, 21 D-I schools spent more than $1 million for recruiting in 2007, a total that does not include salaries for recruiting coordinators or the construction of new facilities built in part to lure prospects.

Exhibit 7.7 lists data for the highest spending schools at each division level. Note that some of the data for high-spending Division II and III schools is skewed because the schools listed sponsor Division I programs in certain sports.

Travel

Much of the cost increases are attributed to travel costs, as coaches cast their nets over broader geographic territory to find talent. Tennessee's athletics CFO Bill Myers explained the growth in expense this way: "If (coaches have) to spend an extra thousand dollars to see a kid somewhere who can make a difference in our program, we want them to do it. Recruiting is an area we want to invest in. . . . A typical per-coach week is around $3,000 to $4,000" (Sander, 2008b, p. A1). Former Maryland athletics CFO Larry Leckonby, now AD at the Citadel, explained Maryland's increase this way: "Kids who 20 years ago wouldn't dream of leaving the mid-Atlantic area, they're getting scholarship offers from around the country. And West Coast kids who would stay in the Pac-10 think nothing of coming East to Duke or Maryland" (p. A11). Geography poses a financial challenge at Kansas

| EXHIBIT | 7.7 | Schools with highest recruiting expenditures by division. |

	2007 EXPENSES	2002 EXPENSES	1997 EXPENSES
Division I (Bowl Subdivision)			
University of Tennessee	$2,005,700	$1,419,400	$915,000
University of Notre Dame	$1,758,300	$1,014,600	$674,000
University of Florida	$1,451,400	$1,097,300	$665,000
Auburn University	$1,374,900	$1,228,900	$646,000
Kansas State University	$1,316,700	$626,600	$359,000
Median for all D-I BS	$632,600	$499,000	$371,500
Division I (Champ. Subdivision)			
Princeton University	$941,000	$624,800	$282,000
Harvard University	$851,900	$712,400	$485,000
Columbia University	$778,000	$477,000	$328,000
Dartmouth College	$774,700	$708,000	$464,000
Brown University	$757,200	$708,000	$534,000
Median for all D-I CS	$195,600	$126,300	$93,000
Division I (no football)			
Marquette University	$521,600	$130,600	$139,000
Xavier University (OH)	$482,400	$387,200	$185,000
Boston University	$447,900	$367,800	$266,000
University of Denver	$426,400	$343,600	N/A
St. John's University (NY)	$412,600	$153,900	$188,000
Median for all D-I no football	$143,700	$107,200	$74,000
Division II			
University of North Dakota	$272,900	$180,700	
Minnesota State at Mankato	$210,400	$155,400	
St. Cloud State University	$164,700	$210,700	
University of Central Missouri	$148,600	$49,000	
University of Minnesota at Duluth	$139,700	$116,900	
Median for all D-II	$28,000	$19,100	
Division III			
New York University	$181,400	$197,700	
St. Lawrence University	$156,700	$135,200	
Rensselaer Polytechnic Institute	$155,600	$91,300	
Hobart and William Smith Colleges	$135,500	$66,000	
Union College (NY)	$119,600	$95,800	
Median for all D-III	$19,700	$11,900	

Source: Sander, 2008b. Copyright 2008 *The Chronicle of Higher Education.* Reprinted with permission.

State, where 54 percent of the school's 350 student-athletes are from out of state. The nearest major airport is in Kansas City, two hours away, so the school expected to spend nearly a half-million dollars on private jet travel for coaches' recruiting trips in 2008 (Sander, 2008b).

Travel costs, however, are beginning to have a greater impact on recruiting activities. Colorado College, a private school of 1,900 undergraduates located in Colorado Springs and a member of the Division I Western Collegiate Hockey Association (although a member of the Division III Southern Collegiate Athletic Conference in all other sports), traditionally has stocked its men's ice hockey program with players from the Northeast U.S. and Canada. In the past, coaches typically have gone to the Northeast around Christmastime to watch prep school tournaments, and made five trips to Canada, each trip lasting up to five days. Now head coach Scott Owens says he has skipped the Northeast trip and makes one fewer trip to Canada (Viera, 2009).

And travel costs also influence student-athletes and parents in the recruiting decision-making process. Some recruiting experts think that attending a school closer to home will enable the parents to get to more games to see their kids play, and this may force schools to recruit prospects closer to their campus. Tom Lemming, a national football recruiting analyst, says that the most prominent Bowl Subdivision programs probably will not be affected by this phenomenon, but "for most of the country, it will be more regionalized" (Viera, 2009, p. B12). Even so, Marion Moses, mother of Morgan Moses, a highly touted offensive lineman prospect from Richmond, Virginia, who was looking at schools in 2009, said that her family's ability to see Morgan play would "make a big impact on the decision." She added, "I can tell you already, I'm not going to be able to make every game if he would go to California" (Viera, 2009, B12). After receiving grant-in-aid offers from Alabama, Ohio State, Tennessee, the University of Virginia, and Virginia Polytechnic Institute, Moses chose Virginia—the school located closest to his hometown.

Direct mail programs

An additional major expense relates to the cost and frequency of mailings that schools send to prospects to curry interest and favor. This is particularly questionable based on the dubious effectiveness of many such mailings. *Sports Illustrated* writer George Dohrmann tracked the recruiting correspondence received by Roberto Nelson over the course of his recruiting beginning in his sophomore year. Nelson, a top-rated 6'3" guard prospect from Santa Barbara (California) High School who graduated in 2009, saved every piece of mail he received from schools—2,161 pieces in all, from 56 different schools. Of the numerous school mailings (the University of Kentucky alone sent him 295 pieces), only 18 schools sent Nelson any personalized mailings. In all, he opened only 387 pieces of the total he received (17.9 percent) (Dohrmann, 2009). One Pac-10 recruiter explained why the mailings have continued even if recruits did not seem to be reading them: "Everyone else is doing it, so no one wants to be the one not to" (p. 61).

NCAA bylaws (13.4.1) have been amended to limit most recruiting mailing to prospects until the June 15 previous to men's basketball and men's ice hockey prospects' sophomore year (all other prospects cannot receive materials until September 1 of their sophomore year) (Dohrmann, 2009; *2008–09 NCAA Division I Manual*, 2008). Some schools also are beginning to rethink the use of mailings and printings based on associated costs in addition to their dubious effectiveness. Many schools have ceased printing the longtime staple multi-page media guides, because now most are simply uploading files to school websites. And the impact of such moves? Consider that although Nelson eventually received GIA offers from more than a dozen Division I programs, including UCLA, Florida State, and Ohio State, he ultimately chose to attend Oregon State University after four phone calls and a home visit from newly hired head coach Craig Robinson (brother-in-law of President Barack Obama). And the number of mailings sent from Oregon State? None (Dohrmann, 2009).

Technology and the pressure to stay in touch

As noted in the preceding examples, Division I coaches must hit the road to attend camps and tournaments across the country during the contact and evaluation periods, with hundreds in attendance, all hoping to snag one of the handful of blue-chip prospects. On September 1, the competition intensifies with a barrage of mailing, both snail and electronic. A symptom of this escalation is the advent of text-messaging. Ceal Barry, former head women's basketball coach at the University of Colorado, notes that the rise in expectations for program success has ratcheted up the demands of the recruiting trail. For example, in the 1970s, women's basketball recruiting consisted of spring on-campus tryout days (with the cost incurred by the families of recruits). At the end of the day, coaches would select a half-dozen girls and invite them and their parents for a campus tour. That was it. But because of the pressures to compete, Barry explains how text-massaging evolved into a crucial recruiting tool:

> How do we get the recruits to notice us? Mail them a fancy brochure? Too slow. Send them an e-mail? They never check it. Ah, send them a text message. Text them in the morning before school. Text them during chemistry. Text them during their free periods. Heck, text them during practice that afternoon. . . . And after you text them, encourage them to send instant messages at any time: during meetings, at dinner, late at night, whenever they feel the urge, you make sure you're available! And just to make sure you aren't shirking responsibility, assign your assistant coaches the task of keeping their computers on at night, within whispering distance of their sleeping quarters, in case a West Coast prospect happens to want to chat at midnight. (Barry, 2005, p. 8-7)

As a result of this brave new world, the Ivy League proposed a complete ban on all text messaging in Division I, which was approved by the divisions Board of Directors in April 2007. Like Barry, the ban was favored by many coaches as well. In addition, the measure was strongly supported by NCAA's Division I Student-Athlete Advisory Council (SAAC), which cited the extensive intrusion and cost to prospects (anywhere from 10 to 50 cents per message on some plans) caused by excessive texting. Said Anna Chappell, a former student-athlete at the University of Arizona and chair of the Division I SAAC: "It's intruding on their lives and creating inappropriate relationships with coaches. . . . student-athletes as a whole said they wanted the elimination of text-messaging" (Wolverton, 2007, p. A46). Shane Lyons, Atlantic Coast Conference associate commissioner, noted that eliminating texting also would eliminate a loophole that allowed coaches to use texting to prod prospects to initiate telephone calls that a coach could not (Hosick, 2007).

Others argued against the ban, citing that students could block certain messages and were not required to give their numbers to coaches. The American Football Coaches Association, the national professional organization serving football coaches at all levels and lobbying the NCAA on legislative issues it believes have an impact on its membership, had argued for a delay in the ban vote and instead had preferred to set limits on texting, similar to those placed on phone calls. In light of these conflicting opinions, the Division I Board of Directors (composed of 18 school presidents) reported that it was open to future legislation that would allow restricted texting, but a move to repeal the ban at the 2008 NCAA Convention failed when 79 percent (240) of the 306 members represented voted to keep it in place (Thomas, 2008).

The Internet and fan and booster involvement

The advent of Internet fan sites such as Rivals.com and Scout.com that keep score of the relative success of the recruiting battles between schools turned an already challenging process into a major source of fan and booster involvement with their favorite programs. According to Feldman (2007): "With the possible exceptions of auctions and porn, no other business is better suited to the Internet than college football recruiting" (p. 8). For example, for $9.95 a month, Rivals.com provides subscribers with information about which prospects their schools are recruiting, including relevant data such as 40-yard dash time and high school GPA on each (although many prospects lie about these numbers to make their dossiers look better). These sites also give feedback from prospects on their official visits and video highlights. Rivals.com and Scout.com serve as hubs to hundreds of school-focused satellite sites including, among others, BamaOnLine.com (Alabama), IrishEyes.com (Notre Dame), GatorBait.net (Florida), and OMSpirit.com (Ole Miss). On Signing Day 2007, Rivals.com claimed 74.5 million page views—almost five times the number MSNBC.com had drawn on its 2006 Election Night coverage. Although most coaches dismiss the ability of these sites to evaluate players, they know the impact these sites can have on swaying recruits.

In addition, recruits managing their own blogs and pages on social networking sites often become the target of fan and booster ardor. For example, in 2006, when QB prospect Steven Garcia penned a blog on the website of the *Tampa (Florida) Tribune* newspaper, much of the traffic on the blog (the tenth most visited page on the site) came from University of South Carolina fans and boosters eager to convince Garcia to come to Columbia. One poster read: "Man, Stephen, we need you in Columbia. We are gonna win championships, and you're gonna help us win them. If you commit to [Florida], you're just gonna be in the shadow of Tim Tebow your whole career, but if you come to South Carolina, you have a chance to become a hero" (Feldman, 2007, p. 75). According to Feldman, "Garcia was amused about the following he was developing online. . . . He said that he got a kick out of the crazy comments and added that 'fan base will play a pretty big role' in his decision-making process" (p. 76).

Negative recruiting

In pursuit of high-caliber prospects who will help a program win games, conference titles, and national championships, some recruiters inevitably take a "by any means necessary" approach to convince a prospect to matriculate. In one case involving the women's basketball program at Louisiana State, the abrupt resignation of former head coach Pokey Chatman at the end of the 2007 regular season led to incidents of negative recruiting by LSU's competitors. Chatman, a former standout player at the school, was asked to resign by LSU officials in response to allegations that she had inappropriate sexual relationships with former players (Longman, 2007a).

While the issues were being addressed and litigated in the immediate aftermath of the scandal at LSU, Gail Goestenkors, head women's basketball coach at the University of Texas, opined on the recruiting implications of the case: "I think there are coaches who may try to use this against any female coaches who aren't married and just make innuendo, to put fear in some players' minds or parents' minds" (p. C15). However, Geno Auriemma, head coach of the University of Connecticut women's cagers, says such negative recruiting can backfire: "What if the kid you're recruiting is gay and you don't know it? You bring the topic up and the kid says, 'I'm not playing for this guy; this guy's got problems'" (p. C17). Nora Lynn Finch, senior women's associate AD at North Carolina State University, notes that inappropriate sexual relationships are not restricted to female coaches: "My experience is that there have been more issues with male coaches and male staff than female coaches and staff" (p. C17). More than 30 percent of Division I women's basketball programs have male head coaches, now including LSU, which replaced Chatman with Van Chancellor, former successful head coach at Mississippi and for the WNBA's Houston Comets.

Negative recruiting can stem from hard feelings between schools when a prospect spurns one school for another. In 2008, after losing a recruit to rival University of Michigan and new head coach Rich Rodriguez, then-Purdue University head football coach Joe Tiller complained that Rodriguez was "a guy in a wizard hat selling snake oil to get a guy at the last minute." Of the lost prospect, Tiller said: "I can say this: We won't go back (to that school to recruit) again, and we won't be the only institution not to" (O'Toole, 2008, p. 5C). Other common recruiting conflict barbs are related to the perception of varying admissions standards between competing institutions. In 2008, University of Arizona head football coach Mike Stoops described rival Arizona State University (ASU) as a "j.c.," as in junior college, prompting an ASU official to respond: "Our academic standards are as high as Arizona's. . . . The academic profile of our incoming freshman class is the same as the University of Arizona's" (p. 5C). Stoops later issued an apology for the remark.

Criminal behavior of prospects

The challenge to attract quality prospects often leads coaches to recruit individuals who have committed crimes and acted inappropriately in other off-field situations. Consider the 2007 case of football recruit Dennis Godfrey, who matriculated at Wake Forest University, located in Winston-Salem, North Carolina, and a member of the Division I Atlantic Coast Conference. Initially the school had deferred Godfrey's admission after it was learned that he had been charged with kidnapping and raping a 16-year-old girl in October 2005. In January 2007, the felony charges were dropped in exchange for a no-contest plea to simple assault and obstruction of justice. Godfrey did not admit guilt but was placed on probation for a year and was required to perform community service.

Wake Forest, coming off its best season ever in 2006, winning the ACC football title and playing in the Orange Bowl as the conference's representative in the Bowl Championship Series, is not alone in recruiting prospects with legal issues. The University of Hawaii, the University of Louisville (where football player Nate Harris was charged with armed robbery as a 19-year-old), the University of Miami (with the notable case of former football player Willie Williams, who was arrested 11 times before enrolling), the University of Oregon, and the University of Southern Mississippi all have enrolled players with similar backgrounds. Wake Forest president Nathan Hatch defended the school's decision to enroll Godfrey (although he never spoke to Godfrey directly during the process), stating, "We would not admit someone we deem to be a threat to other students" (Carey, 2007, p. 3C). But there were still criticisms of the enrollment from within the Wake Forest community. A professor at the school said: "If Godfrey weren't a football player, he wouldn't be getting a second chance. They don't give these kinds of second chances to kids who want to come play the piano" (p. 3C).

To deal with these types of recruiting challenges, University of Oklahoma AD Joe Castiglione notes that most schools have stated policies relating to recruiting athletes with legal issues. OU has instituted a program to check the background of all recruits before signing a letter of intent. At the 2007 NCAA Convention, Richard Ashby, a police detective in California for 14 years, spoke during a seminar on the issue of student-athletes and crime. "If you can't afford to have someone looking after these kids at all times," he said, "if you don't have people who are like them in a place they can trust, don't recruit them" (Dohrmann, 2007, p. 64). Other schools heed this advice and state publicly that they opt not to recruit such players. University of Georgia president Michael Adams noted that "we have refused to recruit and we have refused to admit certain people who have had character issues" (Carey, 2007, p. 3C).

In an effort to avoid these issues at Ole Miss, Ed Orgeron and his staff composed a list of "character questions" (e.g., Has he ever been arrested? Does he have any children?) to give them a clearer picture of the person being recruited. One Ole Miss assistant instantly dropped a recruit when he got this voice mail greeting: "If you're not my mom or a hot girl or tryin' to give me money, don't even bother leavin' a message" (Feldman, 2007, p. 210).

Challenges of the equivalency system

We'll learn in Chapter 10 about the challenges facing Division I student-athletes in balancing the time and effort demands of athletics with the rest of college life. In sports that are part of the equivalency system of grants-in-aid, another factor that complicates the life of a student-athlete is something that writer Bill Pennington calls "scholarship envy." Coaches negotiate grant packages with student-athletes behind closed doors, with awards kept secret. But word eventually gets out, according to Jillian Loyden, goalkeeper on the women's soccer team at Villanova University: "If someone has a few really poor games, you hear girls during the bus ride saying, 'And she's on 75 percent scholarship. What is the coach thinking?'" (Pennington, 2008b, p. C18). Villanova head women's field hockey coach, Joanie Milhous, tries to keep the issue under wraps. "We ask (our players) to avoid the subject," she says, "but we have a lot of girls who are roommates. It's a long year—how many things do you keep from your roommate?" (p. C18). Many coaches also note that parents also get wind of awards and compare them. Stephanie Campbell, who received $19,000 a year toward the $40,000 Villanova tariff, dislikes the inequities of the equivalency system but also sees it as a source of personal motivation: "There were girls on the team doing the same work as me—driving themselves to exhaustion—and I know they weren't getting a lot of money. I had so much respect for them. I thought, 'Well, I can't let up'" (Pennington, 2008b, p. C18).

Division III challenges

Even at Division III programs, the pressure to recruit and to convince prospects to matriculate exists, along with increased expectations from prospects and their families. Consider Haverford College, a private school with 1,200 undergraduates and a member of the Centennial Conference, located near Philadelphia, where nearly 40 percent of students participate in varsity sports and recruited athletes comprise about 15 percent of each incoming class. Athletic Director Greg Kannerstein (who also has served as acting Dean of Admissions at the school), said, "The nature of the process gets more organized every year. The parents are more savvy, the athletes are more polished, the institutions more meticulous" (Pennington, 2006, p. 8-1).

Haverford's women's volleyball coach Amy Bergin, related her approach to the process:

> Of 1,000 I contacted, about half will reply. About half that reply will be academically qualified. About half of them will be truly interested in Haverford. About half of them will be actually good enough to play volleyball for us. About half of that group will apply for admission. About half of them will get accepted. And about half of them will decide to come here. If that happens, that's a really good year. That's almost eight girls. (Pennington, 2006, p. 8-6)

To achieve this goal, Bergin spends her summer evenings calling prospects and seldom travels anywhere without a three-ring binder containing her contact list database printout. Each time she contacts a prospect—some of whom she has called five times—she notes the date of the conversation and what was discussed in the prospect's file so as not to repeat herself. Speaking about her conversations, Bergin relates: "There are the girls who say, 'I'm a Division I talent.' And I think, 'Forget it. I don't need the attitude.'" And of the game videos sent to her by prospects (some done by for-profit recruiting services): "You just laugh at some of the professional videos I get with their Hollywood special effects. It's so unnecessary. . . . I've seen enough girls hitting balls as 'Eye of the Tiger' plays in the background to last a lifetime" (Pennington, 2006, p. 8-6).

In 2006, ESPN, the sports and entertainment network responsible in large part for revolutionizing the broadcasting and media coverage of intercollegiate athletics, partnered with Texas Tech University (TTU) and its then-head men's basketball coach Bob Knight to produce a television reality show. The program, called "Knight School," selected 16 current TTU male students and allowed them to compete, under the tutelage of Knight and his coaching staff, for one spot on TTU's varsity roster for the 2006–07 season. "This isn't a dream, it's fantasy," said one prospect of the tryout opportunity. "Who wouldn't want to play for Bobby Knight? He's a legend" (Bickelhaupt, 2006, p. 1). On the first day, Knight, known for his tough talk, resolutely expressed opinions, and occasionally bullying behavior, stated: "I told these kids at the beginning that I was going to work with them and coach them as though they were on our team, not as though they were kids that are involved in a television show" (p. 1).

Gerald Myers, TTU's athletic director, said the 16 participants had to meet the same standard of test scores and grade-point averages as any other student-athlete, and show a satisfactory rate of progress toward a degree. "The N.C.A.A. wanted to make sure that they had to be qualified, and they couldn't be recruited," he said (Sandomir, 2005, p. 1). Tyler Hoffmeister, the program's survivor, made little significant contribution to the Red Raiders' on-court fortunes. Hoffmeister played in four games for a total of 10 minutes, scoring two points on his sole field goal attempt of the season in a blowout win against the University of Arkansas-Little Rock.

Why would Knight go through all this to find a player who warmed the last spot on the Red Raider bench instead of preparing his key contributing players for the rigors of the upcoming season? In the days before the airing of the first show, Knight, who that year would become Division I men's basketball's all-time winningest head coach, was asked by an *ESPN Magazine* reporter about another possible edge the show might give—in the recruiting wars against Big 12 foes such as the University of Texas, Texas A&M, Oklahoma State, and the University of Kansas. In response to the query, Knight was characteristically dismissive: "People who ask that kind of question don't know anything about recruiting. Players are looking for a school close to home where they can get some playing time" (Knight Time, 2006, p. 18).

It's hard to argue with the observations of a coach who has recruited talent sufficient enough to win more than 900 games at three different schools (before TTU, Knight was head coach at the U. S. Military Academy and at Indiana University—where he was fired by school president and former NCAA President Myles Brand for on- and off-court behavioral transgressions). Some data support Knight's proximity claim, as evidenced by a study published by *Sports Illustrated*. The magazine tracked football recruits at the six Bowl Championship conferences (Atlantic Coast, Big East, Big Ten, Big 12, Pac-10, Southeastern) from 2004 to 2008 and found that the vast majority of recruits for schools in each conference came from the states in which member schools were located (Hot and Heavy, 2009).

Former NFL quarterback Jay Fiedler offered these more illustrative insights from a student-athlete's perspective as to what the recruiting and the subsequent decision-making process meant for him:

> Dartmouth was the only school that offered me everything: a great engineering school, a campus I loved, students who felt right for me, a winning football tradition, and a good track program. It was also the only school that recruited me by having both the head football coach and the head track coach visit my home. It may have been a little thing, but the fact that the football coach had taken the time and effort to learn about how much competing in track and field meant to me spoke volumes about how much he wanted me in the football program. (Lincoln, 2004, pp. ix–xi)

Additional insights into the decision-making process is provided in a study of Division III student-athletes by Lemoi, Pelosi, and Covell (2008), who noted that family influence, athletic communications materials, relative strength of the athletic program, and availability of desired major are especially important in influencing final choices.

So are Knight, who retired in 2008 as the winningest D-I men's hoops coach of all time, Fiedler, a former starting QB with the NFL's Miami Dolphins, and the study cited above that far apart in their perspectives? They're probably closer than we might have imagined. What these examples indicate is that the influences and variables that impact the recruiting processes for intercollegiate athletes are clearly highly personal and idiosyncratic, and are dependent on the unique characteristics of the schools, coaches, and prospects involved.

questions for you to consider

1. Based on the comments of the case, if Knight is correct in his identification of the reasons why a prospect chooses a certain school, why do you think he took the time to participate in the *Knight School* program (other than payment from ESPN)?

2. Based on his recollection of his recruiting and subsequent decision to attend Dartmouth, do you think Jay Fiedler's experience is representative of most high school prospects? Why or why not?

CONCLUSION

Recruiting is defined by the NCAA as the solicitation of a prospective student-athlete or a prospective student-athlete's relatives [or legal guardian(s)] by an institutional staff member or by a representative of the institution's athletic interests for the purposes of securing the prospective student-athlete's enrollment and ultimate participation in the institution's intercollegiate athletics program. Concurrent with the creation of intercollegiate athletic competition was the emergence of the desire for on-field success. This desire led to the development of methods for securing talented student-athletes, some of which would soon be deemed improper by schools. In the 1860s and 1870s, faculties began to impose their will on athletic programs when they perceived that athletic matters were infringing upon students' academic activities. Additional concerns related to professional coaches' recruitment and payment of student-athletes. Over the next several decades, practices relating to these areas became both more established and more systematic at schools throughout the country, culminating with the NCAA passing legislation that outlined specific recruiting guidelines, including limits on official visit timeframes and procedures for using booster club funds to subsidize student-athletes, as well as formal approval of the athletics grant-in-aid, or athletic "scholarship."

As defined in NCAA legislation, financial aid includes all institutional sources of funding such as scholarships, grants, and tuition waivers, as well as funding from other sources such as financial aid awarded with no relationship to athletic ability. The full grant-in-aid consists of money to cover the cost of tuition and fees, room and board, and required course-related books. Student-athletes may receive financial aid up to the full cost of attending the institution. Aid is tabulated and awarded on an annual basis with all awards made on or before July 1 prior to the academic year in which it is to be effective.

Under Division I regulations, each sport is limited in the number of students on each roster who can receive aid in which athletic ability is a determining criterion. Sports are categorized as either "head-count" or "equivalency." In head-count sports, each student-athlete who receives athletically related aid in any amount counts toward the maximum allowable number of students receiving such aid. Equivalency sports place a limit on the value of the financial aid awards that an institution may provide in any academic year to team participants. All Division II sports are classified as equivalency sports.

A prospective student-athlete is one who has started classes for the ninth grade, and that status is retained until he or she enrolls in any four-year collegiate institutions, including summer classes. All applicable recruiting bylaws are imposed at the point of beginning ninth-grade classes. The recruiting process for coaches is dictated by the types of contacts they can have with prospects. A "contact" is defined as any face-to-face encounter between a prospective student-athlete or the prospective student-athlete's parents, relatives, or legal guardian(s) and an institutional staff member or athletics representative during which any dialogue occurs in excess of a greeting. The Division I recruiting calendar for football and basketball is divided into four periods: Contact, Evaluation, Quiet, and Dead. The recruiting calendars of all other Division I sports are delineated as either contact or dead periods. Key current issues in recruiting include advances in and controls on uses of communications technologies, how schools deal with the past criminal behavior of prospects, and negative recruiting among coaches at competing schools.

PRACTITIONER perspective:

STEFANIE PEMPER, head women's basketball coach, U. S. Naval Academy

In 2008, Stefanie Pemper made a big career move. At the time the fourth all-time winningest coach in NCAA Division III history, Pemper took the job as head women's basketball coach at the U. S. Naval Academy (Navy), a national service academy with 4,400 undergrads located in Annapolis, Maryland, and a member of the Division I Patriot League. Over the previous decade, Pemper had compiled a record of 235–48 at Bowdoin College, a private liberal arts school with 1,600 undergraduates located in Brunswick, Maine, and a member of the New England Small College Athletic Conference. She had led the Polar Bears program to nine NCAA Tournament appearances, including five Elite Eight appearances and an appearance in the NCAA championship game in 2004. After that season, Pemper was honored as the Women Basketball Coaches Association Division III National Coach of the Year.

Pemper grew up in California, and attended Idaho State University, a public school with 13,800 undergraduates located in Pocatello and a member of the Division I Big Sky Conference, where she was a two-time All–Conference team selection. She started her coaching career at the University of Alaska–Anchorage in 1993 as a graduate assistant, before moving back to Idaho State as a full-time assistant (1994–95), and then to an assistant post at Harvard (1996–98). While she was at Harvard, the women's program won three straight Ivy League titles and set a league record by winning 32 straight conference games. In 1998, Harvard became the first men's or women's Number 16 seed to win a Division I NCAA Tournament game when the Crimson upset Number 1 tournament seed Stanford.

Pemper came to Annapolis to replace Tom Marryott, who had been the head coach for five years and whose final team had a 7–23 record. Of her decision to take the Navy job, she said, "I'm excited for the challenge and looking forward to being part of the (Navy) community. The young women who choose Navy are special. It'll be a collective effort. I'm confident our staff will have great integrity and work ethic, but in the end it's the players who have four years to determine what kind of experience they have. I'm really looking forward to guiding that process." In her first two years, the team went 16–15 and 17–14

(8–6 in conference both years) and lost in the semifinal of the Patriot League tournament.

Pemper agreed to be interviewed for this book so we could learn from her recruiting experiences from multiple perspectives: prospect, student-athlete, graduate assistant coach, full-time assistant coach, Division III head coach, and Division I head coach.

Q: *Thinking back to your experiences as a recruited prospect, describe what you recall from that time.*

A: My dream to play college basketball included four things: Get a full grant-in-aid, to a Division I school, in a state outside my home state of California, in a location that I could tolerate. Just to get away from home. Nothing more than that. Just kind of an adventure.

Idaho State brought me up in the spring and made me an offer. It turned out to be my only offer. Cal State–Los Angeles was interested but was Division II. Central Arizona College—a juco powerhouse (located in Coolidge, Arizona)—was interested in me for basketball and softball. My last option was Golden West College, a juco in my hometown (Huntington Beach), also for basketball and softball.

Idaho State was the first school that met all those criteria, so I accepted. I distinctly remember not wanting to screw around and lose the offer even though the program wasn't successful. My parents never spoke to a coach at ISU, not because either party wasn't friendly but because assistant coach Nancy Graziano would ask for me when she called and my mom didn't think it was her place to butt in. My dad didn't live with us, but he never called a college coach regarding recruitment of me. It never occurred to me to tell my parents about the ISU offer, but after I called Coach Graziano to accept, I immediately told my parents.

I was likely the last of a breed. I didn't play AAU because at the time there was only one AAU team in the Orange County, California, area. My only true chance to be "seen" in the ways that girls are recruited today was at the Blue Star West Camp, held at Pepperdine University the year I went. Back then, Blue Star offered just three "invite only" camps: West, Midwest, and East. Anyone who was anyone attended. It was a four-day camp, but unbeknownst to me, the college coaches were in attendance only one night, the first night. After dividing all the campers into teams, we played games all night. It was my first and last experience feeling like I was in a "meat market." I had three major problems in terms of getting noticed: A post player on our team was Natalie Williams, who would go on to play basketball and volleyball at

UCLA and later in the Olympics and WNBA. The second problem was Martha Richards, a sharp-shooter who ended up playing basketball and golf at Stanford and is now the women's golf coach at Texas. The third problem: a point guard who knew that Natalie and Martha were her tickets to stardom more than I was.

Idaho State first saw me in December of my senior year at a holiday tournament at Marina High School in Huntington Beach, when I hit a 30-foot shot to win a game by one. At the time, I thought I tied the game—the three-point line was new that year—and wondered why my teammates were mobbing me. Coach Graziano was at the tournament looking for late talent; ISU wasn't in a position to get many early looks. She had previously coached at Alemany High School in Mission Hills, California. She was home for the holidays and knew the good local tournaments.

How did your own personal experiences as a recruit influence your approach to recruiting today?

Maybe not in a good way, because I think it influences it, in that I keep it simple—"simple" meaning that I think with some coaches there's such an age gap between most Division I head coaches and high schoolers that the phone calls are really cold. I would describe them as very nuts-and-bolts, almost just informational—and I think boring for the kids in some sense. I think kids can also feel a lack of connection. You'll hear that word from me a lot—connection. There are probably some people who, no matter what age they are, connect well with other people, with young people, and some who don't.

But at the same time, you have very winning programs that recruit that way. Take any famous coaches. They pick up the phone and they're interested in you, and a lot of times that's what your relationship is going to be with them. And there's nothing wrong with that. I actually overheard a phone call recently after a young recruiting coordinator came into a head coach's office and said, "I've got to get a commitment out of this kid today." This isn't how we do business. My assistant doesn't come in and say that to me.

And there's something about it that I also respect, which is: At the end of the day, what do we need to know? "What does your transcript say? This is what we do. This is what we're about. Do you like it?" Someone like me believes in trying to start that relationship right then and there, and probe around and get to know them in a way that tries to see that they're the right fit. I do look at it as a relationship that is oftentimes for the rest of your life. I try to approach it that way, and I want it to be special. I don't want us just to represent a community well and be successful on the court. I want it to be very healthy all around. To me, that starts in the recruiting process, and it starts with trying to get the right people.

Nancy Graziano connects with people well. She's totally that woman who, when you go back to Idaho State, you look her up. She's in administration now at ISU. You would never think of going to that town without saying "hi" to her. She connects well with people. She connected with me—a very caring person, and was that way my whole career. But not the head coach. I didn't connect with him at all. I didn't when I played. A very similar dynamic in recruiting happened when you played, and even when you graduated. You have a zero relationship with a kid. I would consider those kids to be really low maintenance. They just come here and play.

Sometimes I think that's the good way—the more personal approach. I think it makes me a little less patient with what I would call "needy" kids and "needy" parents, because my parents were both very involved in my life, very loving parents, but at the same time, they said "It's Stefanie's situation, and Stefanie worked hard growing up."

We didn't necessarily devote a ton of resources (to basketball). I can remember coming to my mom when I was a freshman in high school, so nervous, and explaining that Billy Moore, the UCLA coach, and [former UCLA standout] Ann Meyers, one of the first players I looked up to, were running an overnight camp. I said "I've never done one of those. Can I go?" and "This is how much it cost—I can raise the money!" and "Can I go? Will you let me go?" And she let me go. Times have just changed.

I had two older brothers who were both recruited. One of them ended up playing at Biola University (a private evangelical Christian school with 4,000 undergraduates in La Mirada, California, and a member of the NAIA's Golden State Athletic Conference). He was 6'11". He played only a year, and he dropped out. He had trouble with the coach. And my other brother, who was 6'7" and very athletic, was an even better athlete. But he got into a wrong crowd and ended up getting a volleyball scholarship to Long Beach (California) State. He picked up volleyball his senior year in high school. And he actually left after a year, too. Their recruiting process was really similar to mine. It was very random. You think: What if I hadn't made that 30-foot shot? Would Nancy Graziano have been as enamored with me? Where would my life have gone?

What else is different about recruiting now, compared to when you were a prospect and from your early experiences as a recruiter?

Ten years ago I would have fought the idea that I would have had to recruit parents. Now I agree with it. Part of a healthy program, broadly defined, is having parents who feel good about the program and feel like they know me and have a connection to me. Of course, at the end of the day, I can understand why parents have concerns. I try to let them see enough of me so they can say, "You know what? She's a good person. She's a normal person."

The second thing that can be good [about parental involvement], is that I do think a lot of kids are like their parents in some ways. They would never admit it at that age, but they're going to be like them—so familiarize yourself with that. The apple doesn't fall far from the tree.

The other thing [parental involvement can do] is that I'm a big believer in the mental side of the game, and when you see what parents are like and how they treat their kids, how they talk to them, what kind of expectations they put on them, it can help you as you then work with them. If their parents are always telling them they're great at something, or not good at something, that's going to be in their head, and as a coach you're going to have to work through that.

Having said that, for most of the players I coach now at Navy, the parents don't know me. They could walk in right now and I wouldn't even know what they look like. We have a couple of parents who never came to a game this year. One of our better players at Bowdoin always talked about her father in really great ways, and the man literally said only one thing to me in four years, and it was a very polite thing, but that was it. He never tried to charm me; he never tried small talk. And I think that player—who is now an assistant at Bowdoin—always showed tremendous maturity, initiative, ownership—the stuff you really want.

Are parents overly involved in the decision-making process for prospects?

I don't think so. And even some of the (parents) you think might be, I really believe them when they say, "We're not going to make this decision for her." I think if parents have a really good relationship with their kid, they can stay out of it, but the kid's going to want to please them. And that's not bad, and some of that directs the decisions to play close to home. I think you see that a lot—this idea of staying close to home.

Former head coach Bob Knight said that kids want to go to a school close to home where they can get some playing time. Is that really all there is to this process?

He has to admit it's too simple to say it that way. That's definitely true for some kids, but there's much more to it. The academic side of things being one of those—the success of the program—certainly for men now, the ability to get noticed and maybe get to play at the next level. Probably even for women. That's not exclusive for men anymore. You know that there are D-I women's programs that brag about the players they've sent to the WNBA, absolutely.

What are the similarities and differences in the recruiting situations you faced at the different schools at which you have worked?

There was a level of "sophistication"—that's the word you would use on a good day; on a bad day you'd use "entitlement"—with the Harvard recruits and families versus other schools. At Bowdoin, I really tried to tap into in-state players. Those are some wonderfully unentitled people. I had two "horror stories" at Bowdoin in ten years that I recruited—very educated, wealthy families, and just ugly stuff. I had what I would call my first and only "Ivy League" recruit at Bowdoin, and I'll just leave it that it was not a good experience. It was just entitlement, the meddling. On the front end, the unrealistic feelings about the daughter and her skill set, lying about what other coaches felt about the daughter. And then the daughter getting there and (the parents') overreactions to what was happening with her playing time. And then they started picking at other things I was doing, all a reflection of frustration. And then, ultimately, the daughter choosing not to play.

It's part of why I left (Bowdoin). I tell people the two reasons I left are that, first, I didn't want to stay in that (winter) climate the rest of my professional life and, second, I wanted to work with a different kind of kid than I had the last 13 years. I feel like there was a community I was immersed in over that 13 years—I don't want this to come off sounding harsh—but there was a community of people who think that everyone cares what they think.

So what are the similarities and differences you have seen thus far at Navy?

The difference at Navy is that it's a simpler process: "Here's what we're saying. This is actually the truth. This is what we mean." For example, one thing I do is tell recruits how many official visits we've already offered, to give them a perspective. There's less name-dropping, less of a feeling of bragging about someone's abilities.

It's just simpler. When I call, a parent says, "You want to talk to my daughter? All right—here she is."

I would say 20 percent have some connection to the military. Oddly enough, when you look at some of the best players, they have a connection. Our second-team all-league player: one sister graduated from West Point and one is at Air Force. Her brother is here. Her dad was in the Air Force. There is something neat here, too. Some of the athletes have a little bit of a chip on their shoulder that they weren't recruited higher. You definitely hear that on our football team, which is great to work with.

My point is that, much like at Bowdoin or Harvard, you end up with the kids who want to be here the most. And most schools might say, "Well, we're all that way." Well, here we have that whole third piece. We have academics, we have athletics, and then we have that whole other military piece. So our goal is to educate people, and then if we throw out the hook and if they take that bait, a lot of times they're the people who are going to end up on our team. And we like that, because the whole adage of "choose the school based on what if athletics wasn't part of the picture," to some degree we're still doing that here.

The prospects you are recruiting—in general, where else are they looking?

To be honest, we were recruiting some kids last year who weren't getting a lot of D-I looks. Now we're recruiting more people who are getting more D-I looks. If you were talking to my peers, they feel like it's so random. Sometimes we recruit against the Ivies. We recruit against the Big East sometimes, and the Big Ten. Sometimes you can't steal a kid away from Winthrop University. The one thing is that we can recruit nationwide, but we probably have our geographic pocket as well. On our current roster we have Indiana, New Mexico, California, New Jersey, Texas, Oklahoma, Delaware, New York, Connecticut, North Carolina.

When you're looking at your recruiting for the upcoming year, how many prospects are you actively recruiting?

About 70. It's hard to know (what the initial pool size was). When you say "actively recruiting," I mean calling. There are still probably 40 other people we're mailing information to. Of course we're waiting for some questionnaires to come back. We have a prep school (the Naval Academy Preparatory School, in Newport, Rhode Island), which muddies the water a bit. In any given year, we're looking to bring in five, when you factor in the prep school.

I like working at schools like this and Bowdoin and Harvard, where kids can quit (basketball) and still get a great diploma. I tell the story that when the University of Maine interviewed me back in 2005. I sat down with the two graduating senior captains, I knew them both and had seen their careers. They were terrific. We walked into the locker room, we sat down, and one looked at me and said, "You coach Division III? You must work with kids who really love it." And I didn't expect such a star at that level to say that, because what she then got into is that not everyone here loves it like she loved it. And at these schools, kids like that can quit. And the reality is that we all over-recruit anyway. If you're not trying to get better in recruiting, you're not doing what's best for the program. So if we're doing that, why shouldn't kids have a mechanism for getting out of that but still getting their diploma?

What skills, abilities, and qualities are you looking for in the prospects you're recruiting?

"Intangibles" is probably at the top of the list—toughness, playing the game with aggression, risk, and confidence. And then athleticism would probably be next. Academically, they all have to be at a certain level. I was trying to dig out whether there was a (success) correlation between really sharp kids academically, between kids who were getting a 1400 SAT versus a 1200. I would love anyone's research on that. There are some kids in that 1400 or higher range, and they're kind of stress-balls. There are other kids who are just awesome kids, and really calm and really smart, and those are the ones I think you do want. You'll hear some coaches say, "I don't want a 1400 SAT kid." Baloney. There are some terrific 1400 kids out there.

Do you think coaches, in their recruiting, are looking for prospects who replicate the skills, abilities, and mindset they possessed?

I've thought about that, and the only thing that I've been recruiting is "competitiveness." That's at the top of that list of intangibles. Whenever I hear, in the recruiting process, kids or their parents call them competitive, it makes me hesitate. Because I think that people who are competitive, especially at a young age, don't say it; they just show it. I want to be the person who describes you that way. So to be honest with you, it wasn't until five years ago that I really realized in my own life that I'm competitive. We all recruit kids who are a little too short and a little too slow because they're wicked competitors, and that often means they're really smart and savvy on the court. They know how to communicate with their teammates. They're motivated.

I was a really good passer. I passed to the post position really well. I led the (Big Sky) conference in assists two years in a row, but our teams (now) don't pass the post very well. So I don't think I've done a good job at that.

We try to recruit the typical "New England Patriots" type of player. When you think about the Patriots, they have Tom Brady, maybe Randy Moss, and a bunch of "Patriot" players. And that's essentially what we try to do here. But it's very common for your neediest players—even at this level—to be your best players. And it doesn't have to be bad; it can be stuff from a kid's past, immature things like temper. It doesn't have to be that the kid's selfish or a bad kid.

I really do think that the kids who are the most receptive and the most responsible in the process often get better looks—if they have their transcript ready, if they send it when a coach asks them to send it. I'm surprised at how unreliable some kids are, and how that absolutely affects how much we go after them. We'll sometimes say, "If I call and leave a message and the kid doesn't call back, cross them off." Not all coaches will say that. There's a coach here at the Naval Academy—it's hilarious—doesn't bother with questionnaires, doesn't send out mailings. This guy believes, "Get the kid on the phone. Get the coach on the phone. 'Let's talk business. Let's get you (on campus).'" On the other hand, we're over at admissions all the time, hauling boxes of mailings over. And I think the mailings make a difference. This coach, he's a terrific coach, and I really respect him. I think you can make yourself crazy as a coach if you try to figure out that there's always a great way to do it. And I've never been like that. It's a lot like X's and O's. If you try to be someone else, you may not be successful.

What's the biggest challenge you face recruiting at Navy?

I think just the size—how big of a net we have to cast. Just the effort, but fortunately we have four full-time assistants. We feel like—it's hard to admit this, and it may not even be true all the time—but there's a feeling that you're going to lose a lot of the top kids if they get a call from a school they're going to be more interested in. (We lose them because) people say to them, "You don't want to be in the Navy for five years" or, "Why go to a college that makes you wake up early and wear uniforms and not go off-campus, and you get to do what you want and drink the way you want to drink?" Especially if there's no financial need in the family.

You hear some people say this—I don't say this, and I don't like to hear it—that at (Navy) you can be recruiting someone for five months and then a coach from another university calls and she's gone. That happens at a lot of schools, not just service academies. And it happens at different levels. So that's why we cast a big net, so we can find that "diamond in the rough."

I was just talking to an assistant coach at Penn State who used to be an assistant here for three years. Her back-up point guard at Penn State, she said, nobody wanted. She was from a small town. She said to me, "Stefanie, the gal wasn't recruited." And good for them, because a lot of schools will say, "Oh, no interest. She must not be very good." And the coach said, "She's not an amazing player, but we love her. Great passer, great with recruits." It happens even at the highest levels where you fish someone out.

What percentage of your job is recruiting?

I would say probably 35 to 40 percent, because we have such a big staff. At Bowdoin that was a different percentage, a much higher percentage. I didn't allow my assistant to make phone calls, to send mailings, to write notes, because we had a position that wasn't well-funded, and I thought I'd have basically a 22-year-old for one year every year, and I didn't want to give such a big responsibility to a person who isn't as good as I am at recruiting. It came back to bite me, because it turns out that Julie Veilleux stayed with me at Bowdoin for three years, and then I hired her here and she had no recruiting experience, but she's learned quickly.

Is recruiting the most important part of your job?

No, I don't think so. It's the most important part of a couple of my assistants' jobs. I lead my program, and I manage my staff. That's a huge part of what I do. I still think that the actual practices, the actual games, the actual meetings—team and individual, the mentoring—are the most important part of a coach's job. And being a respectable member of the community, buying in to the college's philosophical goals.

If there was something you could change about the recruiting process that would make it a better experience for coaches and prospects, what would it be?

I think home visits should be legal in March (of a prospect's junior year) for everyone in Division I. They are currently legal for service academies. Because what's happening now in D-I is that kids aren't making as many informed decisions, and this is leading to more transferring. D-II coaches love it because they think they know their recruits so well. Now they're asking for some re-

strictions because they hate to recruit year-round. D-III is the same way, but the pressure isn't on D-III coaches as much as D-II to recruit year-round. So it's a funny balance: They want more restrictions, but they love it that they know their recruits so well.

We did about 20 home visits this past March. We can call prospects their whole junior year. And of those 70 kids, we still have six or seven in the mix that we did a home visit with in March. We feel like the home visit was very valuable. That was interesting. We were the first "foot in the door," if you will. It's interesting. I don't know that we need a head start (in recruiting), but we need time. I remember (a woman) who used to be an assistant here who's now the head coach at Merrimack College (a private Catholic school with 2,000 undergraduates located in North Andover, Massachusetts, and a member of the Division II Northeast-10 Conference in all sports except men's ice hockey), saying, "My home visits [while at Navy] were three-and-a-half hours at least." We have so many myths to dispel; we have so much to teach them. They hear things, they hear stories. And it was true. I did them in March, and the shortest one was three hours.

It's funny, when I applied (for the job) here, one of the first things I wanted to know about was how women are treated, the climate for them. And I've got to tell you, talking to everyone and being here a year, it's not really much of an issue. Media perceptions are that it's an issue, so those were my perceptions. Twenty percent of the student body is female, which is the most of the service academies.

But transferring is becoming an issue. A friend of mine is the women's basketball coach at Umpqua Community College (a two-year school with 3,000 full-time students located in Roseburg, Oregon, and a member of the Northwest Athletic Association of Community Colleges). He had a shooter this year—a great shooter, an unbelievable three-point shooter. [A very successful Big East school] throughout the winter was recruiting his shooter. And they admitted to him that they were recruiting her—as a junior at (the school)—to essentially get rid of a current sophomore shooter they had, a kid they had recruited out of high school. And at the end of the spring, they literally said to my friend, "You know what? This sophomore kid for us ended up having a good NCAA tournament. We're going to keep her. We don't need your kid."

I'm sorry, but I thought transferring had a little bit more to do with the kid saying, "Coach, can I meet with you? I'm really struggling about my role. I'm not sure that I'm good enough. You're not really using me." This felt more like, "You're not good enough. We're running you off. We're bringing in a juco kid." I think that stinks.

questions TO CONSIDER

1. Identify and explain the importance of recruiting highly skilled prospects who have demonstrated solid citizenship.
2. Based on what we have read, what remedies can you suggest to curtail the significant pressures that schools face in trying to attract top prospects?
3. Among the skills necessary to be an intercollegiate coach, where does the ability to recruit rank?
4. Can the case be made that current recruiting bylaws are too restrictive, and that schools and coaches should be able to expend whatever resources they wish to attract top prospects?
5. Are current recruiting restrictions more advantageous for prospects, or for schools and coaches?

references

An Ugly Game. (2008, December 12). *Chronicle Review*, p. B20.

Barry, C. (2005, March 23). A coach's farewell message. *New York Times*, p. 8-7.

Bickelhaupt, S. (2006, February 17). Reality check: "Knight School" makes the cut. *Boston Globe*. Accessed April 7, 2007 from: www.boston.com/sports/colleges/mens_basketball/articles/2006/02/17/reality_check_knight_school_makes_the_cut/

Byers, W., with Hammer, C. (1995). *Unsportsmanlike conduct: Exploiting college athletes*. Ann Arbor: University of Michigan Press.

Carey, J. (2007, January 29). Legal woes big challenge in recruiting. *USA Today*, p. 3C.

Dohrmann, G. (2007, August 13). Trouble in paradise. *Sports Illustrated*, pp. 60–64.

Dohrmann, G. (2009, August 3). You've got *(too much)* mail. *Sports Illustrated*, pp. 57–61.

Evans, T. (2008a, February 7). A prize recruit's thinking cap. *New York Times*, pp. C13–C14.

Evans, T. (2008b, December 26). And the winner is. . . . *New York Times*, pp. B7–B8.

Feldman, B. (2007). *Meat market: Inside the smash-mouth world of college football recruiting*. New York: ESPN Books.

Finley, B. (2006, November 8). Recruiting becomes a highly sought coaching skill. *New York Times*, p. C19.

Glier, R. (2009, December 18). Kiffin says Tennessee's recruiting was legal. *New York Times*, p. B11.

Hosick, M.B. (2007, April 23). Division I gives thumbs down to text messaging. *NCAA News*. Accessed April 30, 2007, from: http:www.ncaa.org/wps/wcm/connect/NCAA/NCAA+News+Online/2007/Text/

Hot and Heavy. (2009, January 26). *Sports Illustrated*, pp. 52–53.

Johnson, J.W. (2006). *The wow boys: A coach, a team, and a turning point in college football*. Lincoln: University of Nebraska Press.

Jones, D. (2008, February 6). Coaches push the envelope. *USA Today*, p. 7C.

Knight Time. (2006, February 6). *ESPN Magazine*, p. 18.

Lemoi, J., Pelosi, M., & Covell, D. (2008). *Joining the team: Identifying and assessing critical factors influencing student-athlete matriculation*. Paper presented at the meeting of the North American Society for Sport Management. Toronto, Ont. Canada.

Lewis, M. (2006). *The blind side: Evolution of a game*. New York: W.W. Norton.

Lincoln, C. (2004). *Playing the game: Inside athletic recruiting in the Ivy League*. White River Junction, VT: Nomad Press.

Longman, J. (2007a, April 19). In recruiting season, mistrust is raised. *New York Times*, pp. C15, C17.

McPhee, J. (2009, May 25). One-stop shopping. *New Yorker*, pp. 38–40.

National Collegiate Athletic Association. (2006). *The second-century imperatives: Presidential leadership—Institutional accountability*. Indianapolis: NCAA.

O'Toole, T. (2008, February 8). Recruiting season sparks some fights. *USA Today*, p. 5C.

Pennington, B. (2005, September 11). Even at the smaller colleges, recruiting is a big-time endeavor. *New York Times*, pp. 8-1, 8-6.

Pennington, B. (2006, May 21). Results can be jarring as recruiting carousel stops. *New York Times*, pp. 8-1, 8-6.

Pennington, B. (2008a, March 10). College athletic scholarships: Expectations lose out to reality. *New York Times*, pp. A1, A15.

Pennington, B. (2008b, March 12). Divvying scholarship dollars can divide a team. *New York Times*, p. C18.

Sander, L. (2008a, May 9). For coaches, a race with no finish line. *Chronicle of Higher Education*, pp. A1, A18–A19, A21.

Sander, L. (2008b, August 1). Have money, will travel: The quest for top athletes. *Chronicle of Higher Education*, pp. A1, A9–A11.

Sander, L. (2008c, December 19). For college athletes, recruiting is a fair (but flawed) game. *Chronicle of Higher Education*, pp. A1, A17–A18.

Sandomir, R. (2005, August 9). Coming soon: Bob Knight the reality star. *New York Times* [on-line]. Accessed March 3, 2007, from: www.nytimes.com/2005/08/09/sports/ncaabasketball/09sandomir.html

Shapiro, B.J. (1983, Winter). John Hannah and the growth of big-time intercollegiate athletics at Michigan State University. *Journal of Sport History*, 10(3), pp. 33–55.

Smith, R.A. (1988). *Sports and freedom: The rise of big-time college athletics*. New York: Oxford University Press.

Smith, R.A. (Ed.). (1994). *Big time football at Harvard, 1905: The diary of coach Bill Reid*. Urbana: University of Illinois Press.

Sports Log: Tailback Scott Leaving Colorado Squad. (2009, November 4). *Boston Globe*, p. C2.

St. John, W. (2004). *Rammer jammer yellow hammer: A journey into the heart of fan mania*. New York: Crown Publishing.

Staszewski, J. (2009, April 24). Unselfish Sonnenfeldt betters teammates, Fieldston. Accessed June 24, 2009 from: http:www.fiveborougsports.com

Thamel, P. (2010, March 29). Seton Hall hires coach from Iona. *New York Times*, p. D3.

Thamel, P., & Evans, T. (2009a, October 17). Helicopter's clatter carries powerful recruiting message. *New York Times*, pp. B10–11.

Thamel, P., and Evans, T. (2009b, December 10). Vols pledge cooperation with N.C.A.A. in inquiry. *New York Times*, p. B15.

Thamel, P., & Schmidt, M.S. (2010, March 18). Seton Hall, in turmoil, fires Gonzalez. *New York Times*, pp. B13, B15.

Thomas, K. (2008, January 13). N.C.A.A. ban on text-messaging as recruiting tool will remain. *New York Times*, p. 7-6.

2008–09 NCAA Division I Manual. (2008). Indianapolis: NCAA.

Vescey, G. (2010, March 18). In the end, conduct counts above all else. *New York Times*, pp. B13, B15.

Viera, M. (2009, January 14). Tighter budgets affect recruiting. *New York Times*, p. B12.

Watterson, J.S. (2000). *College football: History, spectacle, controversy*. Baltimore: Johns Hopkins University Press.

Wolverton, B. (2007, May 4). NCAA bans text messaging, frustrating some coaches and relieving others. *Chronicle of Higher Education*, p. A46.

Compliance and enforcement

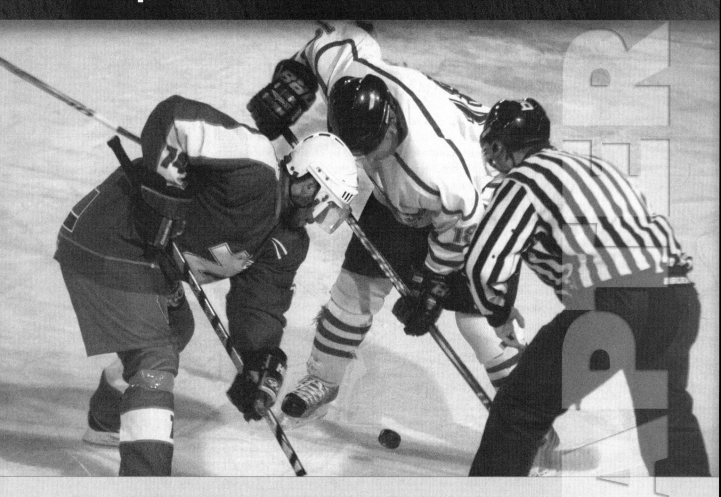

Key concepts to keep in mind while you read the chapter:

- How the current systems of rules governing the operation of intercollegiate athletic departments impact how departments are managed.

- How the current systems of enforcing the rules impact the management of intercollegiate athletic departments.

- Why the dual-focused system of compliance and enforcement is seen as a critical component in the operation of athletic departments, conferences, and national governing bodies such as the NCAA.

Introduction

Two areas that have great importance in intercollegiate athletic management are the related areas of rules compliance and enforcement. As we have learned, recruiting is a critical resource acquisition component for intercollegiate athletic departments. Because of its critical role in acquiring talent for athletic programs, recruiting (and the companion area of academic eligibility, upon which we will focus in the next chapter) is of particular importance to the compliance and enforcement dyad. These factors are so important that in 2004, Vanderbilt University Vice Chancellor for Student Affairs, David Williams II, told members of the U.S. Congress in a hearing investigating issues pertaining to intercollegiate athletics that

> while many colleges have clean recruiting programs and would never ever think of, or allow something illegal [by NCAA standards] or unethical to take place, there are others that either condone questionable behavior or look the other way so as not to see the questionable behavior. . . . The coaches feel that pressure and realize that great athletes make great teams and great teams make successful seasons. So, in order to get those great athletes, they must be recruited and the saga begins. If University A is following the rules and recruiting legally and ethically while University B is doing it just the other way, does this not give University B a leg up in the process? (Recruiting, 2004)

What Williams is referring to in his congressional testimony is a critical concept introduced in Chapter 1—that of the level playing field, in which the rules and guidelines enacted by governing bodies create a system of fairness in the methods by which intercollegiate athletics is managed. The area of recruiting is where maintaining the level playing field is most often tested. Through efforts to ensure compliance with conference and nationally instituted rules, and a system to penalize institutions that choose to ignore enforcement, intercollegiate athletic governing bodies seek to maintain the concept of a level playing field.

DEFINITIONS

The term "compliance" refers to the extent to which schools follow the rules specified by their governing bodies such as their conference or the NCAA. This concept is explained in detail under one of the NCAA's 16 principles for conduct of intercollegiate athletics—institutional control and responsibility. This principle contains Bylaw 2.1.1—the responsibility for control—which reads that "it is the responsibility of each member institution to control its intercollegiate athletics program in compliance with the rules and regulations of the Association." If this should fail to occur, the process of enforcement begins. The *2008–09 NCAA Division I Manual* (2008) conveys that the approved mission of NCAA enforcement programs is to "eliminate violations of NCAA rules and impose the appropriate penalties should violations occur." If the need for an NCAA investigation arises, schools are bound to assist with any such process under the responsibility to cooperate (pp. 3, 295). Exhibit 8.1 contains the full text for each these key terms.

| Definitions of key terms—compliance and enforcement. | EXHIBIT | 8.1 |

Mission of NCAA Enforcement Program (Bylaw 19.01.01):

It shall be the mission of the NCAA enforcement program to eliminate violations of NCAA rules and impose appropriate penalties should violations occur. The program is committed to fairness of procedures and the timely and equitable resolution of infractions cases. The achievement of these objectives is essential to the conduct of a viable and effective enforcement program. Further, an important consideration in imposing penalties is to provide fairness to uninvolved student-athletes, coaches, administrators, competitors and other institutions.

Responsibility to Cooperate (Bylaw 19.01.03):

All representatives of member institutions shall cooperate fully with the NCAA enforcement staff, Committee on Infractions, Infractions Appeal Committee and Management Council to further the objectives of the Association and its enforcement program. The enforcement policies and procedures are an essential part of the intercollegiate athletics program of each member institution and require full and complete disclosure by all institutional representatives of any relevant information requested by the NCAA enforcement staff, Committee on Infractions or Infractions Appeals Committee during the course of an inquiry.

Source: 2008–09 NCAA Division I Manual, 2008, p. 295.

HISTORICAL PERSPECTIVES

The rapid rise in popularity of intercollegiate athletics, especially football, with stakeholders groups—students, alumni, the general public—meant increased concern over the wins and losses of individual programs, and the need for competing schools to cooperate in forming common sets of rules to govern play on the field as well as the operation of individual programs, specifically in the areas of recruiting and student-athlete eligibility. Conferences were the first to take on the roles of compliance and enforcement, but the NCAA assumed these roles gradually over the course of the 20th century.

In Chapter 1 we mentioned the impact of repeated violations in recruiting and amateurism at Southern Methodist University (SMU), which resulted in the NCAA forcing the school to shut down its football program. SMU is certainly not the only case of rules violations to influence managing intercollegiate athletics. Others include cash payments to recruits and their families at California–Berkeley, Kentucky, and Mississippi, and the falsifying of prospect transcripts by men's basketball coaches at the University of New Mexico in the mid-1970s and, later, similar academic malfeasance involving student-athletes and administrators at the University of Georgia (twice) and the University of Minnesota. However, the resulting sanctions imposed on SMU—often referred to as the "death penalty"—have impacted significantly all subsequent NCAA enforcement actions.

SMU, located in Dallas and founded in 1911, turned to football early to develop ties with the community and potential financial backers. SMU had been suspended (and barely avoided expulsion) from the Southwest Conference for a year in 1922 because of illegal cash subsidies to football players. The issue led to nominal faculty control over athletics, but boosters, through the school's board of trustees, never fully disengaged from influencing the football program. As a result, SMU gained national prominence in football during the 1930s and 1940s, topped by the exploits of Heisman Trophy winner Doak Walker, and built a football stadium on campus with borrowed funds before it had the money to complete its library (Watterson, 2000). During this time in Texas, a state described by author and native Gary Cartwright (2006) as one with "a largely rural, largely homogenous society," college football:

> . . . shaped our world and gave us stature. . . . It would be hard to exaggerate the excitement that the first kiss of autumn generated at all levels of Texas society. . . . Thanks to the Humble Radio Network, the nation's first broadcast network, you couldn't visit a drugstore or barbershop or even walk along a sidewalk without hearing the roar of the crowd and the boom of the marching bands at (Texas A&M's) Kyle Field or the Cotton Bowl (in Dallas). . . . You didn't have to be college educated to have a favorite team. Service stations operated by Humble Oil & Refining Company [now Exxon], which also owned the radio network, gave out pennant-shaped window decals, each with the colors and name of a conference school. Bank presidents with degrees from SMU and pipe fitters who hadn't finished third grade displayed their choices on the rear windows of their cars. Millions of Texans from Beaumont to Laredo to Amarillo never saw a game but lived and died from Saturday to Saturday with the [Texas Christian Horned] Frogs, the [SMU] Mustangs, the [Baylor] Bears, the [Texas] Longhorns, the [Texas A&M] Aggies, the [Rice University] Owls, the [University of Arkansas] Hogs—and later the [Texas Tech] Red Raiders and the [University of Houston] Cougars. In our division of loyalty, we discovered unity: Everyone loved the Southwest Conference. (pp. 37–38)

Given this highly charged environment, when SMU's football fortunes faded in the 1960s, and, combined with the emergence of the NFL's Cowboys nearby, the local businessmen/boosters on the school's board grew tired of the ribbing they were getting from Texas, Texas A&M, and Oklahoma alums at their local country clubs. So the board moved into action by again providing cash and gifts to lure and to keep prized players. For these actions, the NCAA penalized SMU in 1973 with probation and a ban on postseason and television appearances for two years. According to some recruits, SMU often offered less money than other schools, but Head Coach Ron Meyer's flash and salesmanship often served to seal the deal. Meyer left SMU for the NFL's New England Patriots following the 1981 season, ahead of another round of NCAA investigations. At the height of the payments, boosters had amassed a slush fund totaling $400,000. But SMU was not alone among its conference foes in these efforts to attract prospects.

Author Gary Cartwright joked that when the conference dissolved in 1995, "at least one of its schools was usually on probation and the majority of players free on bond" (Cartwright, 2006, p. 36). Indeed, beginning in the mid-1980s, along with SMU, Texas Christian University (in Fort Worth), Texas A&M, Texas Tech, Texas, and the University of Houston were found to have committed violations and were placed on probation (Watterson, 2000,).

But the system was working on the field for SMU. In the first six years of the 1980s, the Mustangs won 61 games, won or shared three SWC championships, and peaked with an undefeated season in 1982, along with a number two national ranking. Although the protracted cycle of booster payments to recruits and players was significant enough to earn NCAA penalties, what made the SMU case so remarkable was that the boosters involved were often members of the school's board of trustees. The trustees often undercut the ability of school administrators to address the issues, and when the school faced charges from NCAA investigators, the trustees fought these charges vehemently. When Bobby Collins was hired to replace Meyer and refused to work with the boosters, who were used to having access to locker rooms, sidelines, and team flights, they circumvented Collins and continued the payment system through assistant coaches. When SMU president L. Donald Shields belatedly demanded that the booster payments stop, board of trustees chair Bill Clements told him to stay out of it and "go run the university."

When faced with another NCAA investigation in 1984, Clements sought to phase out the payment system to keep players from revealing the violations to investigators, but these covert actions did not stop the NCAA from imposing a three-year probation the next year. In 1986, the situation spiraled out of control as the Mustangs lost several lopsided games, including a 69–7 defeat by Notre Dame, and two players broke into an assistant coach's office to steal the team's monthly payroll. When confronted, the players refused to give back the money, and the team, fearful of public disclosure, failed to suspend the players for the act. A booster replaced the money. The system was no secret on campus, as no one passing by the football practice facility could fail to notice the sports cars parked outside (Watterson, 2000; Drape, 2009).

In the face of these events, Shields, once a public proponent of SMU football, considered shutting down the program himself, but the board rejected the action. Shields resigned that November. The board chose faculty athletics representative Lonny Kliever, a theology professor, to head an internal investigation to avoid the possibility of an NCAA-imposed "death penalty," which would have applied, as SMU had incurred its second set of major violations within five years. Even after the school's report, however, sanctions required that the school shut down the program for 1987 and 1988. Although the NCAA had urged SMU to come clean sooner, the process had been confrontational for years. A school-sponsored post-scandal report characterized the school's approach this way: "SMU's consistent position with the NCAA was: 'You have made your allegations, now let's see you prove them.' SMU's attitude communicated to coaches, staff and players was: 'Never volunteer anything, never give an inch. You are on the SMU team, and the SMU team sticks together'" (Byers, 1995, pp. 24–25). Former board chair Clements, who later served as governor of Texas, typified this approach when he initially denied his involvement with the payment system. When asked why he had lied, he said, "Well, there wasn't a Bible in the room. . . . " (Cartwright, 2006, p. 43).

Within two days of the "death penalty" edict, the New York Times reported that 130 coaches from 80 schools (the University of Alabama alone sent six) descended on Dallas to entice SMU players to transfer (Watterson, 2000). In the aftermath, SMU's football program languished for nearly three decades. From its return in 1989, the team went 62–163–3. From 1980 to 1986, 28 SMU players were drafted by the NFL; since then, only seven have been drafted. The program operated without a full complement of GIAs until 1992. In 2009, the team qualified for its first bowl game since the shutdown and defeated the University of Nevada 45–10 in the Sheraton Hawaii Bowl on Christmas Eve in Honolulu. In the interim, the school sought to improve its academic profile and built a 32,000 on-campus football facility to help bring the program back. Of the program's subsequent success, current SMU AD Steve Orsini put it succinctly: "It proves there is life after death" (Drape, 2009, p. B11).

As a result of the SMU case and others in the 1970s and 1980s, the NCAA's investigatory process was seen by some as all-powerful, nitpicking, and overzealous, which made it an easy target for fans and critics. Tricia Bork, who worked for the Association as vice president of championships until 2000, spoke of this phenomenon during her NCAA tenure: "When I'm on an airplane . . . I'll do anything to keep from telling him that I work for the NCAA. Because more often than not, he'll start talking about the enforcement staff and how we whacked his favorite team" (Rushin, 1997, p. 2). Steve Mallonee, who helped members interpret rules as part of the NCAA's Division I Membership Services, found the job all-consuming: "The first four or five years here, I couldn't watch games or commercials around games [on TV] without saying, 'There's a violation, there's a violation'" (Rushin, 1997, p.10).

THE PROCESS TODAY

To handle allegations of rule violations, each divisional Management Council is empowered to appoint a Committee on Infractions. This body is responsible for administration of the NCAA enforcement program and is composed of 10 members, seven of whom must be present or former staff members at NCAA institutions or member conferences, and no fewer than two of whom shall not be associated with college, conference, or similar sport organization. The committee is charged with hearing complaints regarding rules compliance, has the right to conduct necessary investigations, determine the facts relating to alleged violations and find violations of NCAA rules and requirements, and to impose disciplinary and corrective actions other than suspension or termination of NCAA membership (*2008–09 NCAA Division I Manual*, 2008).

Infractions cases

As prescribed in the NCAA bylaws, the NCAA enforcement staff, which numbers 29 members, each of whom works on no more than three cases at a time, follows a specific procedure in all investigative actions.

1. In the first step, the preliminary review of information, enforcement staff members receive information that an institution is, has been, or may have been in violation of NCAA legislation. The enforcement staff works on referrals of alleged violations from various sources: coaches, boosters, athletic directors, students, parents, reporters. According to NCAA's David Berst, the Association's former enforcement head: "We're always trying to figure out who has an ax to grind. But you can have an ax to grind and still be telling the truth. [We operate] on the kind of information upon which reasonably prudent persons would rely in the conduct of serious affairs" (Rushin, 1997, pp. 8–9).

2. If the information is deemed reasonably substantial, staff members notify the institution that a preliminary investigation will be conducted.

3. If violations are confirmed, and are believed to be major in nature, the institution and enforcement staff enter the summary disposition process, in which the institution determines its position regarding possible violations and a report is written and accepted by all involved parties and forwarded to the Committee on Infractions.

4. If the Committee accepts the findings and penalties proposed in the report, an infractions report is released, and the process is complete. If the Committee does not accept the findings or the penalties, however, additional steps are required before the case ends.

As you might expect, not all parties investigated see the process as fair. In the 1990s, members of the Florida State football team took part in a free-sneaker spree at a local Foot Locker store and were involved in signing with agents. The program received a year's probation and was banned from postseason play and from television appearance for one year. Then-school president Sandy D'Alemberte, who previously had served as the head of the American Bar Association, complained of the NCAA's 11-month investigation: "I thought there were some terrible due-process violations . . . and I thought some evil got done: Some very good people here were slandered by a bad person, an outside witness" (Rushin, 1997, p. 9). Nonetheless, the incident gave Steve Spurrier, then head coach of rival University of Florida, the opportunity to deem the school "FSU: Free Shoes University."

Types of violations

As defined in the *NCAA Division I Manual*, any school that violates a stated rule is subject to one of two types of penalties depending on the type of violation.

- Of *secondary* violations, the NCAA's David Berst admitted, "This is the area where people say, 'The rules are too complex; you need a manual to understand them.' And we generally agree" (Rushin, 1997, p. 8); and
- Berst describes *major* violations as "the kind in which you don't need a manual to understand that you did something wrong" (p. 8).

Exhibit 8.2 further distinguishes between the types of violations.

Example of secondary violation

While major violations have a greater negative impact on athletic departments, secondary violations, when coupled with other secondary violations, or as part of a series of other violations both major and minor, are also problematic. Consider the case of Lincoln University, a Division II state-funded institution with nearly 3,000

Types of NCAA violations.　**EXHIBIT　8.2**

Secondary: A violation that is isolated or inadvertent in nature, provides or is intended to provide only a minimal recruiting, competitive, or other advantage and does not include any significant recruiting inducement or extra benefit. Multiple secondary violations by a member institution may collectively be considered as a major violation.

Major: All other violations other than secondary, specifically including those that provide an extensive recruiting or competitive advantage.

Source: 2008–09 NCAA Division I Manual, 2008, p. 296.

undergraduates located in Jefferson City, Missouri, founded after the Civil War for the benefit of African-Americans. (This is a separate institution from the Lincoln University referenced in Chapter 1.) Officials from Lincoln appeared before the D-II Committee on Infractions, the university's first major infractions case, on December 10, 2004, to address allegations of violations in the institution's athletics program. The issues and findings in the case, which included both major and secondary violations, are excerpted below:

> The majority of the violations were found to have occurred in the football and men's basketball programs, although violations were also found in the women's track and men's golf programs. The violations mainly involved the participation of ineligible student-athletes and occurred as a result of the institution failing to maintain proper control over its athletics program. Because of the substantial competitive advantage gained by the institution in allowing the ineligible student-athletes to compete and the fact that the violations were not isolated, this case is classified as major in nature.
>
> The committee was concerned that this case is part of a growing trend in which Division II institutions, either through inadvertence or ignorance, are failing to devote the resources necessary to effectively operate a Division II athletics program. . . . Lincoln was ill-equipped to handle the addition of football when it was reinstated as a varsity sport in 2000. . . .
>
> Following the addition of football, the compliance coordinator mistakenly applied eligibility rules and was unable to keep track of the large influx of student-athletes, in large part due to the institution's failure to ensure that he was adequately trained and that a comprehensive compliance system involving other campus departments was in place. This case should serve as a cautionary tale to other institutions similarly situated that they must devote adequate resources to the administration of their athletics programs so as to ensure that all obligations under the rules of NCAA membership are being met. Failure to do so will not excuse future violations should they occur. The institution is to be commended for its full cooperation during the investigation and the improvements it has made to its compliance program since the inception of this case. (*Lincoln University Public Infractions Report*, 2005, p. 1)

As part of the series of major violations, the Committee on Infractions cited several violations, secondary in nature, including the following:

> ALLOWING NONQUALIFIERS TO PARTICIPATE. [NCAA Bylaws 14.3.2.2.1.1, 14.3.2.4 and 14.3.4 (*2000–01 NCAA Division II Manual*)] During the spring semester of the 2001–02 academic year, the university allowed two freshman student-athletes (henceforth, "student-athletes 11 and 12," respectively) who were NCAA nonqualifiers out of high school, to participate in the football program's out-of-season conditioning and spring football practice sessions.
>
> **Committee Rationale**
> The enforcement staff and the university were in agreement with the facts set forth in this finding and that violations of NCAA legislation occurred. The committee concurred. While this violation standing alone may be secondary, the committee determined it to be major as it is part of the cumulative case. (*Lincoln University Public Infractions Report*, 2005, p. 3)

Note that the term "nonqualifier" refers to students who were not academically eligible to participate under NCAA bylaws.

Examples of major violations

The extended issues concerning payments to football players at Southern Methodist University constituted the most major of violations in NCAA history. A more recent example of a major violation at the Division I level—which involved violations in academic fraud—occurred at Saint Bonaventure University in 2002–03, a school of 1,900 undergraduates located in Olean, New York, affiliated with the Franciscan order of the Catholic Church and a member of the Atlantic 10 Conference. The school had allowed men's basketball player Jamil Terrell to enroll and deemed him immediately eligible for competition even though Terrell transferred to the school from Coastal Georgia Community College with a certificate in welding and not the required associate's degree. But the action was not a simple case of misinterpreting NCAA rules. According to the investigation, school president Dr. Robert Wickenheiser, whose son was an assistant coach for the men's basketball program, overruled the rules interpretations of Gothard Lane, the school's athletic director, and declared Terrell eligible. In addition, when Terrell later encountered problems in his coursework, Wickenheiser intervened with the school's academic administrators to have Terrell dropped from several classes after the school's advertised deadline so that Terrell would not receive "F's" on his official transcript (One Year Later, 2004).

While Terrell was suiting up and contributing for the Bonnies, AD Lane went to the school's board of trustees president, William Swan, to alert him of Wickenheiser's actions. Swan put Layne off. Once the school alerted the NCAA of Terrell's status, he was deemed ineligible, forcing the Bonnies to forfeit all but one of its victories during the 2002–03 season. The Atlantic 10 banned the team from its postseason tournament. In protest, the team boycotted its last two games, costing the school more than $120,000 in league fines. Once the board began to examine the issue and Wickenheiser's involvement, it accepted the resignations of Wickenheiser, Lane, and the basketball coaching staff. Swan, an alumnus and former school mascot, eventually was overcome by his culpability in the scandal and committed suicide, hanging himself at his home in August 2003. The NCAA deemed the violations major in nature and placed the school on probation through 2007 (Gardiner, 2003; One Year Later, 2004). Although this is an extreme case, it shows that serious consequences with far-reaching stakeholder implications can stem from infractions.

Major violations are not found solely at the Division I level. In 2007, the Division III Committee on Infractions handed down penalties to the University of Southern Maine (USM), a public school with 11,000 undergraduates on campuses located in Lewiston, Gorham, and Portland. A member of the Little East Conference, USM had reported a series of infractions relating to improper work-study payments to 37 student-athletes (out of 175 working in the school's athletic facilities), totaling more than $10,000. Two athletic department personnel allowed workers who were employed as part of their financial aid packages to be paid without performing their duties, to overstate the numbers of hours worked, and to work additional hours, having punched in under assumed names. One student collected $3,300 under the improper system.

In response to the violations, deemed major in nature, the Committee on Infractions placed USM on two years' probation. USM also has acted in advance of the sanctions by suspending the two staffers a week each without pay; five coaches received written reprimands; and the student-athletes involved were suspended from competition when department managers learned of the fraud. In response to the penalties, reported to the NCAA by USM in 2004, Athletic Director Al Bean stated, "We're both embarrassed that this took place and disappointed. We take great pride in our program. Certainly, in this particular area, we fell down. We didn't live up to expectations" (Thomas, 2007, p. 1). The 13 sports in which the 37 student-athletes played remained on probation until February 2009.

At the time the USM penalties were announced, 37 other schools were serving a probationary period, including three schools (Baylor University, for violations in men's basketball and football; Cal State, Fresno, for violations in men's basketball; Florida A&M, for violations in 13 sports) with probation not to conclude until 2010. Along with USM, two other Division III schools were on probation: Mac-Murray College (Jacksonville, Illinois) through May 2009, for violations in men's tennis; Ohio Northern University (Ada, Ohio) through September 2007, for violations in football.

Penalties

After any investigation is complete (the average processing of a case is approximately nine months) (Wieberg, 2007), the Committee on Infractions can decide

- that the actions in question warrant no penalties,
- that penalties enacted by the school or conference are sufficient, or
- may impose specific penalties as prescribed in the *NCAA Manual*.

Exhibit 8.3 lists a sampling of the penalties that may be imposed for both secondary and major violations.

Appeals process

All schools, student-athletes, and institutional staff members facing major violations as a result of the enforcement process have the right to appeal the findings or penalties, or both. An infractions appeal committee is charged with hearing the appeal. The committee is composed of five members, at least one of whom is not connected to a collegiate institution or a professional or similar sport organization, and the remaining members are required to be current or former staff members at member institutions. According to NCAA bylaws, this committee is empowered to hear and act upon the findings of major violations, and also may establish or amend enforcement policies and procedures. This committee may set aside penalties

- if they are deemed excessive or inappropriate based on all the evidence and circumstances,
- if the Committee on Infractions findings were clearly contrary to the evidence presented, or
- if a procedural error affected the reliability of the information that was utilized to support the findings.

The appeals committee acts on a simple majority vote to either accept the Committee on Infractions finding and penalty or alter either or both. If new evidence is presented as part of the appeal, the case is referred back to the Committee on Infractions for further review (*2008–09 NCAA Division I Manual*, 2008).

| Sampling of penalties resulting from NCAA rules infractions. | EXHIBIT | 8.3 |

PENALTIES FOR SECONDARY VIOLATIONS

- Termination of the recruitment of a prospective student-athlete by the institution.
- Permanent ineligibility of a student-athlete to represent the institution in intercollegiate competition.
- Forfeit/vacate contests in which an ineligible student-athlete participated.
- An institutional fine for each violation, with the monetary penalty ranging in total from $500 to $5,000, except when an ineligible student-athlete participates in an NCAA championship or other postseason competition, in which case the $5,000 limit shall not apply.
- A limited reduction in the number of financial aid awards that may be awarded during a specific period in the sport involved to the maximum extent of 20 percent of the maximum number of awards normally permissible in that sport.
- Suspension of head coach or other staff members for one or more competitions.

PENALTIES FOR MAJOR VIOLATIONS

- A two-year probationary period.
- Reduction in the number of expense-paid recruiting visits to the institution in the involved sport for one recruiting year.
- A requirement that all institutional staff members determined by the committee knowingly to have engaged in or condoned a major violation be subject to termination of employment, or suspension without pay for at least one year.
- A reduction in the number of financial aid awards.
- Sanction precluding postseason competition in the sport.
- Ineligibility for any television programs involving coverage of the institution's intercollegiate athletics team or teams in the sport or sports in which the violations occurred.

Source: 2008–09 NCAA Division I Manual, 2008, pp. 298–299.

KEY MANAGEMENT ISSUES IN ENFORCEMENT

While conference and NCAA rules attempt to be as specific as possible in terms of outlining how intercollegiate athletics programs must operate their programs to be in compliance, there is no shortage of newly emerging developments and resulting impacts that influence how departments are managed. The following examples outline how various environmental factors have influenced the compliance and enforcement processes.

The impact of infractions on coaches

As we saw with SMU football, NCAA sanctions can cripple a program for years on end. Coaches who are implicated in investigations, however, are also liable to receive punitive measures that could impact negatively their own personal careers. Such was the case with Todd Bozeman, former head men's basketball coach at Cal–Berkeley. In 1993, then 29-year-old Bozeman's team, led by guard Jason Kidd, upset defending champion Duke in the NCAA Division I tournament. In an effort to replace Kidd after he left Cal for the NBA, Bozeman admitted to paying $30,000 to the parents of point guard recruit Jelani Gardner. When Gardner's parents became upset with

Bozeman because of a perceived lack of playing time, they contacted NCAA investigators about the payment. Bozeman was fired in 1996, and the NCAA imposed an eight-year show-cause ban, which meant that any school that considered hiring Bozeman would have to show just cause why he should be hired. For a decade, Bozeman remained out of college coaching, at times selling pharmaceuticals, and later serving as an advance scout for the NBA's Toronto Raptors (Longman, 2007).

But in 2006, a decade after his firing from Cal, Bozeman was hired at Morgan State University, a public, historically Black college with 6,000 undergraduates located in Baltimore, Maryland, and a member of the Division I Mideastern Athletic Conference. The program there had garnered few wins over the many years since winning a Division II national championship in 1974. Of the hire, Bozeman commented that he felt he eventually would get another chance to coach but lamented the years it took to get it. Morgan State chose Bozeman in part because he was a native of nearby Washington, DC and thought he could use his contacts there for beneficial recruiting connections (Longman, 2007).

Bozeman was up-front with administrators and players about his past at Cal, which to Morgan State player Jerrell Green means: "You can relate to him. He made a mistake. You know that if you did something wrong, he's not going to look down on you" (Longman, 2007, p. C19). Bozeman said he had been heckled about his past only once since returning, when fans at nearby American University chanted, "Thirty thousand!" Bozeman claimed it didn't bother him, laughing: "I thought, hey, they did their homework" (Longman, 2007, p. C19). But in reflecting about his actions at Cal, Bozeman was more serious, noting: "I didn't appreciate what I had at the time. If I did, I would have thought more about the consequences of the decisions I made" (p. C19).

Limitations on investigative and enforcement power

Many critics of NCAA's enforcement process have labeled the organization as an omnipresent, all-powerful police force waiting to pounce on schools for the slightest of errors in departmental management. The truth of the matter is that the enforcement process is often hampered by procedural limitations by which the NCAA must operate. The NCAA is not an arm of local or federal law enforcement and cannot force testimony from any source.

A case involving former USC and later NFL running back Reggie Bush underscored these procedural shortcomings. Investigators were following up on allegations that Bush and his family received money and rent-free housing from a would-be agent (with whom Bush ultimately did not sign) during Bush's senior season at Southern Cal. If true, such actions would have violated NCAA amateurism legislation and USC would have had to forfeit any games in which the ineligible Bush would have played. But when Bush became ensconced in the NFL and under no threat of direct penalty from NCAA sanctions, neither he nor his family agreed to speak to NCAA investigators about the matter. David Price, NCAA's vice president of enforcement services, describes the process this way: "We have the ability to require certain people to talk to us or face an unethical-conduct charge . . . primarily school personnel, people who are directly under our jurisdiction. But when you go outside that group, . . . if they refuse to cooperate, there's not a whole lot more we can do about it" (Yaeger, 2008, p. 221).

A former investigator says that incidents like the Bush case have a significant impact on rules compliance "because the chance that (a violator) can really be held accountable for going outside the rules is probably decreasing as a result" (Wieberg, 2007, p. 8C). Price also admits that the only way they could ever get Bush to testify would be "through [USC]. We do not have any direct authority or jurisdiction over the former student-athlete. . . . We have certainly gone to institutions many times and asked them for their cooperation in trying to get their former student-athletes to talk to us. Sometimes we're successful and sometimes we're not" (Yaeger, 2008, p. 222).

In December 2009, a California state appellate court ruled that Bush and former USC head coach Pete Carroll could be questioned about whether the running back received cash and gifts while playing for the Trojans. See Chapter 12 for more information about this case.

The role of the Internet in tracking potential violations

The proliferation of fan-focused Internet communities and message boards has added an element of populist vigilante justice to the enforcement process. One noteworthy example occurred in January 2006, when a user named "aggiegrant06" posted a thread on the popular fan site TexAgs.com that his girlfriend, who worked at a car dealership in Norman, Oklahoma, had been distributing paychecks to people who turned out to be football players at Texas A&M's Big 12 conference rival, University of Oklahoma. The Oklahoma players later were dismissed from the team for their involvement with the no-show jobs, but the dismissals were not enough to avoid having to forfeit the games in which the players participated, including all the team's wins in 2005. Aggiegrant06's posting was pulled from the site soon after it appeared, according to Brandon Jones, the site's owner, because the comments lacked sufficient evidence, even though they proved to be true. Jones added: "It's rare when we see something that is blatantly dishonest. . . . And I'd say it was about three years ago when we started to cross into the realm of legitimacy" (Roberts, 2007, p. 8-9). The site attracts more than 200,000 unique visitors each month (including former Texas A&M president and later-U.S. Secretary of Defense Robert Gates—user name "ranger65") and allows fans to chat about all things Texas A&M football, including coaching decisions and team uniforms.

Postings reporting alleged transgressions on other sites include the late-night revels of former Iowa State University head men's basketball coach Larry Eustachy, the Division I men's basketball pool betting activities of UCLA head football coach Rick Neuheisel (while at the University of Washington), and on "canesport.com," a site operated by the University of Miami (Florida), potential infractions in contacting recruits by University of Alabama head football coach Nick Saban. Of the posting, Saban, former head coach at LSU who left the NFL's Miami Dolphins to return to the college ranks at Alabama in 2007, said, "I think it's funny it came from Miami," intimating that the poster had some sort of agenda against him (Roberts, 2007, p. 8-9).

Unfortunately, technological advances also have allowed overzealous fans to harass student-athletes in a public setting, as when former University of Florida quarterback Tim Tebow was asked to pose for a picture with a cellphone camera with a female fan at a RadioShack store, only to find that the women tried to take off her shirt for the shoot. "It happened four or five times," said a beleaguered Tebow. "Most of the time I just dive out of the picture. Some people can just be crazy" (Thamel & Evans, 2009, p. A1). Potentially more damaging is the posting of false information that has harmed student-athletes. Such an incident occurred in 2008 when James Conradt, a University of Nebraska fan, posted a bogus story on the Internet message board hosted by an Oklahoma City newspaper, claiming that University of Oklahoma quarterbacks Sam Bradford and Landry Jones had been arrested on cocaine-distribution charges. The posting later was reported as fact by at least two Texas radio stations. Conradt apologized publicly, but the father of one of the Oklahoma QBs threatened legal action. Oklahoma associate AD Kenny Mossman commented that the hoax was part of a problematic trend: "The Internet has enabled a lot of this kind of thing to happen, and it's really disappointing" (Bogus Story, 2008, p. 6C).

SELF-REPORTING OF VIOLATIONS AND THE USE OF OUTSIDE COUNSEL

case study 8.A

In 2006, incidents of payments to student-athletes and academic fraud at the University of Kansas (KU) were revealed. This revelation was not from an investigation by NCAA staffers but, rather, from a 700-page report generated by a private law firm, Bond, Schoeneck & King, hired by KU and staffed by former NCAA investigators led by Rick Evrard. The report also suggested penalties for these actions, including probation and reduction in scholarships. In October of that year, as part of the summary disposition process, the NCAA accepted most of the recommended sanctions and agreed not to impose postseason bans on the football team and men's and women's basketball teams. The study took two years to complete and cost Kansas nearly half a million dollars, far less than the money the school might have lost had the Committee on Infractions recommended the postseason play ban and the subsequent loss in related revenue (Drape, 2007).

Incidents of self-reporting NCAA violations is a growing trend. Bond, Schoeneck & King was involved with several other cases, first serving in that capacity for the University of Minnesota in 1999, when the school was dealing with the repercussions of academic fraud in its men's basketball program (earning the firm $920,000), and later working on behalf of Ohio State University, from 2003 to 2006, investigating various violations and accusations of academic misconduct by former star running back Maurice Clarett (earning the firm nearly $511,000 in the process). Several other such firms also specialize in these practices. An example is Ice Miller of Indianapo-

lis (which also has former NCAA investigators on staff), which worked with officials at the University of Oklahoma to navigate and negotiate the school through major violations in men's basketball that resulted in two-years' probation (earning the firm $336,000) (Drape, 2007).

A more recent case of self-punishment for NCAA violations involved the University of Southern California (USC), which enacted sanctions for actions surrounding its men's basketball program and the recruitment of O.J. Mayo, who played at the school for only one season (2008–09) before leaving for the NBA. The school reported that Mayo was involved with a booster who helped steer him to the school, and that former head coach Tim Floyd (who resigned in 2009 to take an assistant job with the NBA's New Orleans Hornets and then returned to take over as head coach at the University of Texas–El Paso) gave the booster $1,000 to funnel to Mayo. Others have alleged that the booster funneled hundreds of thousands of dollars to Mayo on behalf of a sport agency firm. As a result, USC announced that it would not participate in any postseason tournaments in 2010, would reduce GIAs and off-campus recruiting by coaches through 2011, would return to the NCAA money earned through its 2008 Division I tournament appearance, and would vacate all 21 victories earned while Mayo was on the squad. In 2010 the NCAA was still investigating the USC program for amateurism violations connected with former running back Reggie Bush (U.S.C. Announces Penalties, 2010), and some skeptics believed that the program took such action against the men's basketball program to lessen potential sanctions that might be imposed against its high-profile football program (especially since the investigation uncovered connections between Mayo and a local businessman who had provided a car to USC football running back Joe McKnight (Pugmire, 2010).

Writer Bill Plaschke of the *Los Angeles Times* put it this way: "It was as if [USC athletic administrators] were spanking the basketball team with one hand while wildly pointing at the football team with the other . . . *Whack! See how we can deal with Joe McKnight? Whack! See how mad we are at Reggie Bush? Whack! Could you just leave us alone now?* [author's italics] (Holmes, 2010, p. 1). Members of the 2009–10 men's squad called the sanctions "unfair," as evidenced by comments of senior guard Dwight Lewis: "We did feel like we had a chance to be in the NCAA tournament. . . . To have that taken away, it was hard." Forward Kasey Cunningham, out because of a season-ending knee injury, succinctly summarized the team's perspective: "This sucks" (pp. 1–2). After the sanctions were announced, Mayo's agent denied that the player had received any gifts or money during his recruitment by or playing for USC. Floyd also denied any wrongdoing (Pugmire, 2010).

A former athletic administrator at Marshall University, a public school with 17,000 undergrads located in Huntington, West Virginia, and a member of Division I Conference USA, criticized NCAA staffer tactics, as well as the consulting firms:

> I've seen [NCAA staffers] threaten people's careers, badger them to get the answers they want, belittle them and make people cry. . . . [These consulting law firms] are very adept at how to satisfy the [Committee on Infractions] to minimize the damage to their high-paying clients. They have no problem advising their clients to sacrifice someone lower on the totem

pole. You never see a high-profile coach or administrator losing their job. There's a lot of doubt about whose interests are actually being represented. Many of these lawyers have personal relationships with NCAA staffers and decision makers. They are lobbying and doing what they can to manipulate the system. (Drape, 2007, p. 20)

Regardless of these criticisms, KU AD Lew Perkins justifies the use of these firms and the expenditure:

> We get anonymous calls 10 to 15 times a year about one thing or another our kids are doing wrong. Ninety-nine percent of the time, it is inaccurate. But we follow it up and report it to the NCAA. . . . I'd rather have [the law firm] tell me our problems than someone from the NCAA. (Drape, 2007, p. 20)

The evolution of this booming legal cottage industry can be traced directly to the impact of the SMU "death penalty" case of the late 1980s that shut down the university's football program. Schools today are loath to risk the heavy potential costs that can come from being on the wrong side of the enforcement process, so they act to self-punish in advance of anticipated heavier sanctions from NCAA investigators.

questions for you to consider

1. If you were an athletic director at your school and had discovered secondary violations in your program, would you consider hiring an outside firm to self-report the violations? What is the reasoning behind your decision?

2. What if the violations were major in nature? What would your decision be then, and how would you justify it?

CONCLUSION

Compliance refers to the extent to which schools follow the rules specified by their governing bodies, such as their conference or the NCAA. The principle of responsibility for control is defined as the duty of each member institution to control its intercollegiate athletics program in compliance with the rules and regulations of the Association. If this fails to occur, the process of enforcement begins.

The NCAA became a significant regulatory entity within intercollegiate athletics when it assumed the ability to pass and, more important, to enforce rules governing the operation and management of individual schools and their athletic programs. Repeated violations pertaining to recruiting and amateurism at Southern Methodist resulted in the NCAA forcing SMU to shut down its football program. This action, called the "death penalty," has significantly impacted all subsequent NCAA enforcement actions.

To handle allegations of rule violations, each divisional Management Council is empowered to appoint a Committee on Infractions. This body is responsible for administering the NCAA enforcement program and is composed of 10 members. The committee is charged with hearing complaints regarding rules compliance, has the right to conduct necessary investigations, to determine the facts relating to alleged violations and find violations of NCAA rules and requirements, and to impose disciplinary and corrective actions other than suspension or termination of NCAA membership. The 29-member NCAA enforcement staff follows a specific procedure in all investigative actions. Any school that violates a stated rule is subject to one of two types of penalties: secondary (one that is isolated or inadvertent in nature, provides or is intended to provide only a minimal recruiting, competitive, or other advantage), and major (all violations other than secondary, specifically including those that provide an extensive recruiting or competitive advantage).

After any investigation is completed, the Committee on Infractions can decide that the actions in question warrant no penalties, that penalties enacted by the school or conference are sufficient, or may impose specific penalties. Penalties for secondary violations include termination of the recruitment of a prospective student-athlete by the institution, permanent ineligibility of a student-athlete to represent the institution in intercollegiate competition, and forfeiture of contests in which an ineligible student-athlete participated. Penalties for major violations include a two-year probationary period, a reduction in the number of financial aid awards, and sanctions precluding postseason competition. All schools, student-athletes, and institutional staff members facing major violations as a result of the enforcement process have the right to appeal the findings or penalties, or both. Technological advances, specifically the proliferation of fan-focused Internet chatrooms and message boards, have enabled virtually anyone to contribute to the enforcement process, although such contributions may lead and have led to unfounded accusations of wrongdoing.

PRACTITIONER perspective:

JOSEPHINE POTUTO, Chair of NCAA Division I Infractions Committee and the Richard H. Larson Professor of Constitutional Law, Nebraska College of Law

Josephine Potuto joined the faculty at the Nebraska College of Law, affiliated with the University of Nebraska, in 1974. She has a B.A. in Journalism from Douglass College of Rutgers University, an M.A. in English Literature from Seton Hall University, and a J.D. from the Rutgers University Law College. Professor Potuto is the Faculty Athletics Representative for the University of Nebraska at Lincoln, represents the university on NCAA committees, and is a member of the governance group of the Big 12 Conference. She is also a past chair of the Big 12 Conference and a member of the NCAA Men's Gymnastics Championship Committee. Professor Potuto agreed to be interviewed to allow for continued consideration of the role of the Infractions Committee.

Q: *You're a professor of constitutional law and Faculty Athletics Representative (FAR) at the University of Nebraska. How do these two positions impact your role as Chair of the Committee on Infractions?*

A: The faculty on campus, whether it's teaching constitutional law or teaching in the college of education, is enormously helpful on the Committee on Infractions in a number of ways; primarily it gives one a very good feel for how campuses operate. On campus, the FAR in some ways is a translator between the athletic side of the enterprise and the academic side, because these two sides don't talk the same language and they don't have the same instincts about things. For many years, given that athletic departments were pushed to be able to fund their programs and get into fundraising independent of the university, they became kind of a satellite operation that in many ways is separate from the rest of the campus. Those in the athletic department don't have a good feel for how campus committees and how campus structures operate. And that's not unique to them because I think faculty, in their own ways, are characters.

In relation to the Committee on Infractions, understanding the academic world and how those who teach and those who do research and those who are academic administrators approach things is extremely helpful. It's also helpful to have an understanding of the processes. For example, we had a case once where the issue was the protocol in regard to exams. Those who teach know that in every academic discipline there are requirements that you retain exams for a period of time. That's not something that is routinely known by those who aren't on the faculty. All kinds of things like that come up.

My legal training is enormously helpful on the Committee, in part simply to be sure that we keep track of the record in the case and to be sure that the procedural issues are handled. The Committee couldn't operate if it didn't have lawyers on it. And then constitutional law on top of that—you deal with due process issues and what constitutes a fair process, and that turns out to be very helpful, too. It's helpful in an odd way because there's a notion among lawyers—particularly those who appear before the Committee whose training comes from traditional court model and that adjunctive model—that whatever goes on in that model automatically should apply in infractions hearings. The "alternative" in alternative dispute resolution means it is an alternative to the way things are typically handled in a court proceeding or a trial. And if one wanted to do it exactly the way it's done in a court proceeding or trial, one wouldn't set up an alternative process. One would have to start with how this process is set up as the way to resolve issues and to conduct proceedings, and we need to live within that world because that's the world that the member

institutions have chosen to hear and resolve these infractions issues. They didn't set up a process where you go to court and have a trial. So it's within that process that we need to operate.

Teaching constitutional law is helpful in remembering that it's an alternative process. Within the process, we need to be careful that people are treated fairly and that there's adequate notice and they're given an adequate opportunity to respond, and all those things that constitute due process of law.

Many fans and observers of intercollegiate athletics are often critical of the NCAA's enforcement efforts. What are some of the criticisms, and are they warranted?

One criticism is that enforcement staff gives big schools a pass and goes after the little guys. A second criticism is that there are major cases out there and the enforcement staff doesn't do anything about them. A third criticism is that, particularly when former NCAA staff are on the staff of a university, there is too close a relationship with the university and they can't maintain objectivity. Another criticism is that they are prone to favor the schools and treat the coaches or individuals at risk differently.

All of those criticisms spring from the ways in which NCAA enforcement operates. One is that enforcement staffers do not see themselves—and the way the structure currently is set up, they're not supposed to see themselves—as prosecuting student-athletes, investigating the way police would investigate or prosecuting the way a prosecutor would—that is, in a strictly adversarial role. NCAA staffers see themselves—and under the structure they're supposed to see themselves—as working cooperatively with institutions to uncover violations that may have occurred and then to put a case together for the infractions committee to consider. And, in fact, there are bylaws they need to provide refuting information, and the enforcement case summary will summarize some of the positions of the school and the coaches.

That process inevitably gives rise to some of the complaints that they are too close to the schools, or that they favor some schools over other schools because they know somebody at the school. I believe the process would be better served if we stopped claiming that they were supposed to cooperate with the schools and it became strictly adversarial.

Partly, some of these criticisms come from the fact that the enforcement processes are confidential and infractions hearings are confidential, so there's not a good feel of what occurs, like the extent to which the committee puts the staff on the line and inquires how they did the investigation, or when the committee will drop an allegation completely or change something from a major to a secondary violation. Recently, we had a case where we dismissed the whole thing after we heard it. The fact that none of that is really available to the public feeds into their perception.

The fact that the NCAA has no subpoena power and that everything depends on the principle of cooperation drives a lot of the public perception as well. A case will occur, and there will be information out there that somebody said he gave a player money while he was in college, and there's all this stuff in the newspapers about it, and the NCAA is doing nothing. The fact that it's a former player and you have no subpoena power to put a case together is, at best, extremely difficult. What feeds into it are the public stories out there that may or may not be true. There may be assertions by people with no evidence to support. And yet, in the public eye, here's a case against a big school and there's all this information and the NCAA does nothing.

How has the NCAA refined the infractions process over the last 10 years, and what do you think are the most difficult issues the infractions process faces in the years ahead?

The main thing that has occurred with establishment of the infractions appeals committee—at least in the first few years of that committee—was a really close, productive look at how the infractions process worked. But more than that, the fact that you know that somebody is going to be reviewing what you did has a positive effect on the care you take in doing your job and writing the reports. The work of the appeals committee has clearly meant that infractions reports are much more informative as to what occurred, and how the committee sees it and how the penalties were imposed and are the way they are. And I think that has had a very positive effect, both on the committee and on institutions and others who would be looking at reports in compliance, and how they should view conduct on campus.

Another area that's changed—in my view, it hasn't changed enough yet—is a push by committee to have the enforcement staff reflect better in a case in which there's the university but there's also a coach. For example, if the only entity in a case is the university, if the university self-reports and says "yes, we did all these things and we admit every one of them," there's not much the enforcement staff needs to do except to say, "here are the violations that the university agrees to." Now I say, not much, as compared to saying nothing. I think the enforcement staff still has an obligation to look into the case to

be sure there aren't other things that the university has missed, or maybe someone is hiding because there's a responsibility to all the other schools, which makes this process different from other kinds of adjudicative processes because there's a need to try to maintain an even playing field through enforcement and infractions. The fact that a university agrees to everything I don't think means that enforcement can just tie a ribbon and say this case is done—in part, it does.

But once you have a coach involved, you have now a triangle. The fact that the university will fall on its sword and say, "yes, we did everything," when in fact the allegedly culpable actor is a coach sets up a different dynamic that there may be reasons why the university is willing to agree to everything because of maybe potential litigation or because the coach is no longer at the school and they think penalties will run to the coach, and if he's not there, they will affect the severity of the tentative penalties for the school. So when there's a coach—and when I say "coach," it could be another staff member at risk—when that dynamic is in play, the staff has to be sensitive to the extent to which it can accept some of the university's admissions as to what occurred and what the coach did. I think the staff has been doing more with that over the years, but I still think, from my perspective anyway, they're not there and they still need to adjust to the number of times there's a coach in the room also and what fairness means to the coach.

Other ways that this comes up are, under the cooperative principle, and the way investigations are currently done, the staff works with cooperative schools in investigating and coming to a conclusion as to the scope of the case. That said, when the staff puts the case together and the interviews are done, that's the point at which coaches should have an opportunity to do their own investigations. Sometimes they're able to do them earlier but it's really once the case is pretty much put together and the staff thinks they understand what's happened from working with the school. At that point, a coach may want to do additional interviews or challenge some of the ways the case is put together. I think the staff has been a little resistant to it, not because they're unwilling to be fair to the coach, but they now have a picture of what happened in the case and they may believe the coach is still trying to influence people to change the information that they provided or simply try to slow down the process and make it inefficient. I don't think they've reached a point where the coach's interests in this—I guess you'd call it a triangle—are really being reflected entirely adequately.

Talking about the other part of the question—what would I change and what are the problems going forward? I think that still needs to be resolved. There are certainly times when the enforcement staff and the Infractions Committee have a different view on all the allegations that should have been charged and that makes it very difficult. The Committee has the authority to add findings if it thinks the case warrants it, but it is very inefficient and very time-consuming. The staff has to do its job of putting a case together, and again it may relate to working with the school and of getting a little too much of an "insider look." When you see yourself as cooperating and working from the inside, sometimes it's a little hard to step outside and see how others might look at it.

Penalties—going forward, I think the committee is clearly taking a look at penalties. I think the committee is going to be imposing penalties, at least in certain kinds of cases. The committee will be looking at cooperation not so much as a plus as a minus if an institution or coach fails to cooperate. I think we're going to be looking at different kinds of penalties from what has been improved on in the past. The Baylor case from a few years ago is a good example of where they took Baylor out of conference competition I think, as a way to get at the violation.

If the Infractions Committee had the authority to pass legislation, what would you enact immediately, and why?

I would say clearly that an obligation of NCAA membership is to cooperate in an investigation, and there's no credit given for your meeting your obligation of membership with regards to penalty. We'd need legislation there because the Infractions Committee has been pushing for quite a while that we need to give credit for cooperation. Although I'm in a decided minority on the Committee on this point, I would get rid of the term limits for Infractions Committee members. It takes quite a while to really understand the process. I would allow people to continue to serve. I would require them to rotate off at least for a couple years. I would also open up a little more to talking to media—not about facts in particular cases, but a little more with regard to how things are done. We did that recently in a case, and we need to do more with that.

I'm not so sure I would do nominations from conferences. The current nomination process through the conferences has changed how people are brought forward for service on the committee. We need to be really careful about it because some of the committee members have substantial academic records, and this is one of the elements that gives the committee credibility.

There should be legislation that says clearly that you have to have direct responsibility to serve on the committee. For example, a member can't be an assistant athletics director; he or she has to be an athletic director. One can't be an assistant commissioner; one has to be a commissioner. One can't be an assistant professor but, rather, a full professor. The face of the Committee needs to be at a really high level in terms of perception: You deal with university presidents and high-powered lawyers, some of whom are going to push and push for a hearing unless someone stops them. They are less likely to push if the public face and stature of the Committee is at a high level. And then, in litigation, when judges look at the Committee, they're going to have a very different look depending on the background and reputation and experience level and status of Committee members. I would do something to assure that you had to have that level of a person on the Committee.

In this chapter we note the trend of schools' self-investigating and self-imposing penalties rather than waiting to hear from the Committee on Infractions. Why has this trend developed, and how does it impact the efforts of the Committee and the outcome for the institutions?

The cooperative principle requires that institutions self-investigate and self-report. If there is reason to believe that there's something going on on your campus, under NCAA bylaws you have the obligation to do it. I don't know that this is occurring more than it did, and I don't know what the data are. It may be that when a school does its own investigation, it can do things that are less disruptive to the everyday activities on campus, in part because people aren't going to say "oh no, the NCAA is here," and that buzz won't be there. It's also less disruptive because school officials are there on campus all the time and can work around academic schedules and team trips in ways that the enforcement staff can't. The staff is going to come to a campus, and they're going to have to get it done when they're there.

Whether this is an increased perception, I can't answer, but certainly an institution believes that to the extent it has done the investigation and has ferreted out what happened and has cooperated fully, that puts the school in a better posture before the Committee on Infractions. And to the extent that the Appeals Committee credits cooperation in some way, or requires that the committee acknowledge publicly that we're crediting it, the perception may be true.

With regard to penalties in particular, it's sensible to impose penalties and start divvying them up because the enforcement infractions process can take a few years before it gets to the full committee. At first, if you want to have the penalties apply most directly to the people who were involved at the time of the violations, the faster you put them in place, the better. Second, even from a tiny perspective in terms of deterrents and acknowledging the seriousness of the crime, if a kid has done something, you don't say a week from now, "We're going to punish you for this." You're going to try to get it done as close as possible to the crime, to note how important it is and also for the deterrent effect. On occasion, it may be that an institution wants to avoid a particular penalty. To the extent it structured penalties and has them in place, it may believe that will direct the committee one way, and away from a different penalty. And that's true to an extent. Ultimately, it's the committee that decides what the penalties should be in a case, and while we're informed of what the institution has done, we can't permit the institution to substitute its judgment.

In the text we discuss how the NCAA gradually assumed its current legislative and enforcement authority. If all of it were taken away tomorrow, what do you think would happen to intercollegiate athletics?

In enforcement, whether it's criminal, or whether it's NCAA or the Securities and Exchange Commission, there's an element of the process that's achieved by the fact that you have rules in place. In other words, there are at least some actors who wouldn't put on a seatbelt but will do it if there's a law that says you have to put on a seatbelt. The very fact of the law or the regulation will modify their behavior. There's also an element of having rules that state what the standard is and, therefore, it says this is something our group disapproves of or finds to be unethical, even if the rule or the law is not regularly enforced. There's also an element in the NCAA processes that allows the schools that want to be rules-abiding but need some structure to assure them that they're not going to be at a competitive disadvantage for doing it.

Those three elements occur without regard to how effective the process is in getting at most or all of major violations that are being committed. If the rules were erased, the elements would be lost. Most schools still would like to be rules-abiding, but there will be different versions of the minimum standard of what rules-abiding should be. And then, some coaches think, on some rules, "now it's open season," and will go out and make contact with prospects all the time and who will make phone calls. There would be a huge increase in that sort of conduct, which would have a negative impact, not only on driving everyone to the lowest common denominator, but have a negative impact on prospects. Those rules are in place not only to maintain a level playing field, but they're in place to protect prospects while they're in high school to have some semblance of a normal high school life.

The public outcry from the media and others would be serious—that the NCAA doesn't care about people who violate rules. The reaction would be, "this is what we knew all the time," that all the NCAA is interested in is exploiting student-athletes and commercializing it and making as much money for institutions as they can so we can pay huge coaches' salaries, and any other interests aren't important to them.

questions TO CONSIDER

1. Many observers of intercollegiate athletics have been quite vocal in their criticisms of the NCAA's compliance and enforcement procedures. Explain why these critics express this type of concern and whether you agree with such a critique.

2. Based on what you have read in the chapter, can the argument be made that current compliance and enforcement procedures are ineffective and should be strengthened?

3. Based on your knowledge of the material in the chapter, has the landmark SMU case served to significantly deter other programs and departments from breaking mandated rules? Why or why not?

4. Are coaches and administrators being held substantially accountable for their actions in the violations noted in the chapter, or are other measures necessary to deter future violations?

references

Bogus Story Angers Family. (2008, July 11). *USA Today*, p. 6C.

Byers, W., with Hammer, C. (1995). *Unsportsmanlike conduct: Exploiting college athletes.* Ann Arbor: University of Michigan Press.

Carey, J. (2007, January 29). Legal woes big challenge in recruiting. *USA Today*, p. 3C.

Cartwright, G. (2006). 0:00 to go. In P. King (Ed.), *Great football writing* (pp. 36–43). New York: Sports Illustrated Books.

Dohrmann, G. (2007, August 13). Trouble in paradise. *Sports Illustrated*, pp. 60–64.

Drape, J. (2007, March 4). Facing N.C.A.A., the best defense is a legal team. *New York Times*, pp. 1, 20.

Drape, J. (2009, December 24). New life at S.M.U. with a bowl to play. *New York Times*, p. B11.

Gardiner, A. (2003, April 18). St. Bonaventure fires coach after trustees find violations. *USA Today*, p. 7C.

Holmes, B. (2010, January 5). Somber Trojans try to carry on after sanctions. *Los Angeles Times*. Accessed January 5, 2010, from: http://www.latimes.com/sports/college/basketball/la-sp-usc-basketball5-2010jan05,0,4415152.story

Jones, D. (2008, February 6). Coaches push the envelope. *USA Today*, p. 7C.

Lincoln University Public Infractions Report. (2005, January 26). Accessed April 7, 2007, from: https://goomer.ncaa.org/wdbctx/LSDBi/LSDBi/html

Longman, J. (2007, December 28). Road to redemption winds slowly. *New York Times*, pp. C15, C19.

One Year Later. (2004, June 15). *USA Today*, p. 3C.

Plaschke, B. (2010, January 4). USC takes action on basketball, waits to see reaction. *Los Angeles Times*. Accessed January 5, 2010, from: http://www.latimes.com/sports/college/basketball/la-sp-plaschke4-2010jan04,0,3432202.column

Pugmire, L. (2010, January 7). Mayo's agent denies player accepted cash of gifts for play at USC. *Los Angeles Times*. Accessed January 8, 2010, from: http://www.latimes.com/sports/college/basketball/la-sp-oj-mayo-usc7-2010jan07,0,3855281.story

Recruiting of College Student Athletes: Hearing before the Subcommittee on Commerce, Trade, and Consumer Protection of the Committee on Energy and Commerce, House of Representatives, 114th Cong, 1st Sess. 2004. Accessed April 3, 2008, from: http://0-web.lexisnexis.com.wildpac.wnec.edu/

Roberts, S. (2007, July 15). Internet whistleblowers go where N.C.A.A. fears to tread. *New York Times*, p. 8-1, 9.

Rushin, S. (1997, March 3). Inside the moat. *Sports Illustrated*. Accessed August 7, 2008, from: http://find.galegroup.com/itx

Thamel, P., & Evans, T. (2009, September 17). College stars run for cover from fans' hidden cameras. *New York Times*, pp. A1, A4.

Thomas, K. (2007, February 23). USM accepts NCAA findings. *Portland (Maine) Press Herald*. Accessed March 3, 2007, from: http://sports.mainetoday.com/college/stories/070223usm.html

2008–09NCAA Division I Manual (2008). Indianapolis, NCAA.

U. S. C. Announces Penalties for Men's Basketball Team. (2010, January 4). *New York Times*, p. D6.

Watterson, J.S. (2000). *College football: History, spectacle, controversy.* Baltimore: Johns Hopkins University Press.

Wharton, D. (2009, December 29). Court ruling in Reggie Bush case could lead to depositions. *Los Angeles Times*. Accessed January 8, 2010, from: http://www.latimes.com/sports/college/usc/la-sp-usc-reggie-bush29-2009dec29,0,1337276.story

Wieberg, S. (2007, April 23). NCAA enforcement power in flux. *USA Today*, p. 8C.

Yaeger, D., with Henry, J. (2008). *Tarnished Heisman: Did Reggie Bush turn his final college season into a six-figure job?* New York: Pocket Books.

Academic standards

Key concepts to keep in mind as you read the chapter:

- The factors that have motivated national governing bodies such as the NCAA to develop academic standards that apply to all member institutions.

- Environmental factors and stakeholder input that influenced the development of association-wide standards.

- The distinction between initial and continuing academic eligibility.

- The specific elements that are used to determine eligibility in both areas, and the challenges faced in how these elements are collected and analyzed.

Introduction

For the first century or so of intercollegiate athletic competition, most colleges and universities maintained a separate admissions standard for athletes, choosing to admit any athlete without abiding by the school's stated admissions policies. Ever since the NCAA's formal inception in 1905, a constant struggle has been waged to come to grips with the thorny issue of academic eligibility, usually through the organization's legislative mechanisms, at various times pitting against each other myriad combinations of member institutions, coaches, athletes, school presidents, politicians, and social critics. The twin goals of this arduous process are to determine

1. what exactly the appropriate level of academic achievement should be required of prospective student-athletes, and
2. how these factors should be assessed first in the admissions process, and again as student-athletes pursued their studies once enrolled.

These dual factors eventually would become known as initial (pre-enrollment) and continuing (post-enrollment) eligibility.

As we have read, the NCAA assumed piecemeal the role of arbiter for initial eligibility academic requirements. But the ensuing standardization as the NCAA attempted to level the playing field runs counter to trends in American higher education. As intercollegiate athletics historian John Thelin (1996) observed, higher education "is remarkable for its decentralized arrangement characterized by institutional autonomy, voluntary association, and relatively little government regulation" (p. 10). The constant friction over what constitutes acceptable benchmarks by which student-athletes are to be deemed eligible has led to an ever-evolving set of evaluative criteria, with an ever-changing corresponding degree of effectiveness in assuring that the young men and women who participate in athletics are not merely athletes, but also truly students. Intercollegiate athletics are legitimized through eligibility rules, which as noted by Helman (1989), provide "standards that tether commercial athletics to the educational purposes of higher education" (p. 237).

EARLY STAGES OF NCAA-MANDATED ACADEMIC STANDARDS

Intercollegiate athletics historian Ronald A. Smith pointed out that "from an early period in American intercollegiate athletic history, there was pressure to bring in athletes with little regard for academic considerations" (Smith, 1988, p. 175). Why? Because once games between schools began to be played, the outcome of these games—who won and who lost—became the focal point of competition. As a result, conflicts developed concerning the participation of freshman, graduate, and non-degree "special" students, student residency requirements, and students transferring solely for athletic purposes. All of these issues eventually would precipitate and impact the growth and development of the NCAA, for as intercollegiate football historian Colonel Alexander Weyland wrote, before the NCAA, "there was no authorative body that could take the necessary action" to control the issue (Falla, 1981, p. 11).

In light of the decentralized nature of American higher education, intercollegiate athletics would come to serve as a point of contact between institutions where none had previously existed. "Institutions that had never found it advisable to consult on matters of curriculum," wrote Rudolph (1990), "now sought means of regulating their athletic relations" (p. 374). Even so, student and alumni organizers—the managers of early intercollegiate athletics—were unable to deal with these problems, as evidenced by the 1889 Intercollegiate Football Association postgraduate eligibility controversy, which saw Harvard University withdraw from the league after disputing the eligibility of several Princeton University players. This dispute offered Yale University's football coach, Walter Camp, the opportunity to proffer an early definition of a "bona fide" student-athlete: one who matriculated for the full academic year and pursued a regular course of study (at least five lectures or recitations per week) (Smith, 1988).

To deal with these types of conflicts, some conferences, school presidents, and faculties began to exhibit greater control over athletics, eventually usurping student and alumni control entirely, taking actions on their own to deal with academic eligibility issues. As noted in Chapter 3, some early examples include: the 1895 "Chicago Conference," attended by faculty representatives from the seven schools that later founded what would become the Big Ten Conference, and the 1898 "Brown Conference," attended by students, faculty, and alumni delegates from all except one of the schools of the present-day Ivy League. The subsequent report from the Chicago Conference sought to "'weed out' a 'student who has entered the university for athletic purposes only'" (Smith, 1988, p. 140) and as part of its 20 rules for reform, the report recommended that "only students in good academic standing would be eligible to participate," and that "no student admitted without passing the university entrance examination, or convincing governing authorities that he was capable of doing a full year's work, would be eligible for athletics" (p. 140). Other actions included Harvard banning frosh participation in 1903. In 1906, Wesleyan University and Williams College opted to ban frosh from athletic participation if they were deficient in high school Carnegie units. In 1921, the newly formed Southern Conference (now the Atlantic Coast Conference) banned frosh participation for students with fewer than 15 Carnegie units (*Academic Standards,* 1994; Smith, 1988).

In 1906, the first convention of the IAAUS (the nascent NCAA), adopted a policy concerning academic eligibility. The first constitution of the IAAUS stated that intercollegiate sport should be "maintained on an ethical plane in keeping with the dignity and high purpose of education," and that "no student shall represent a college or university in any intercollegiate game or contest who is not taking a full schedule of work as prescribed in the catalogue of the institution" (Falla, 1981, pp. 21, 144). Although lofty and, to most, right-minded, the membership chose not to give the IAAUS any powers to enforce these dicta.

Smith (1988) points out that the group was formed on "the principle of individual (institutional) autonomy," and that "home rule dominated the NCAA for the first half-century of its existence. The individual colleges agreed collectively to act individually" (p. 207). Enforcement was left to the unlikely scenario of individual student-athletes voluntarily reporting any possible infractions, contingent on the requirement to fill out, sign, and date a 15-question eligibility card that concluded with the following provision: "On my honor I state that the above answers contain the whole truth, without any mental reservation" (Falla, 1981, p. 25). But at the 1908 Convention, Palmer Pierce reiterated the self-policing principles: "The immediate control is now left to the colleges and universities themselves. Local associations are encouraged for the purpose of securing such government and uniformity in, and enforcement of, eligibility rules as may bring about the best results. . . . The fellow . . . who lies about his eligibility status will be ostracized. Hard, honest, honorable playing of any game, win or lose, is what this association desires" (Mott, 1995, p. 10).

INITIAL ELIGIBILITY

As noted, the determination of academic eligibility for student-athletes has two components: initial (pre-enrollment) and continuing (post-enrollment). Initial eligibility refers to determination of the appropriate level of academic achievement for incoming prospects. We will review how managers and stakeholders identified the need for such standards, and how the standards have evolved. A summary of the standards is provided in Exhibit 9.1.

EXHIBIT **9.1**	The evolution of initial eligibility standards.

- **The Sanity Code, 1946:** Athletes must have academic credentials similar to the rest of the student body. Athletes are allowed to receive need-based scholarships, and non-need-based scholarships if they ranked in the top 25 of high school class or maintain a college B average.

- **1.600 Rule, 1965:** Incoming college athletes must achieve a predicted first-year college GPA of at least 1.600 (of 4.000) before receiving athletically related aid. Became the NCAA's first national academic standard.

- **2.0 Rule, 1973:** Athletes must graduate from high school with a 2.0 or a C+ average, regardless of coursework, to be eligible for participation and athletically related aid.

- **Proposition 48, 1983:** Athletes must graduate from high scool with a 2.0 or a C+ average in 11 core academic courses, in addition to scoring a combined 700 on the SAT or a 15 composite on the ACT, to be eligible for participation and athletically related aid. In 1986, the standards were lowered to 1.9 GPA, 680 SAT, and 14 ACT.

- **Proposition 42, 1988:** Athletes must meet all standards of Proposition 48, without exception. This closed the partial qualifier loophole, in which athletes who had the GPA but not the test scores were still allowed to receive athletically related aid in exchange for losing one year of athletic eligibility.

- **Current standards:** In 1992, the core courses requirement was raised to 13 courses, and the test score floor was changed to a sliding format, meaning that the higher the GPA, the lower the required test score. Since 2003, Division I athletes must graduate from high school with a GPA of 3.550 in 16 core courses and score at least a combined 400 on the SAT I and II or 37 on the ACT. Division II athletes must graduate from high school with a 2.0 GPA, and 820 SAT I and II or 68 ACT. Division III does not have across-the-board standards.

Early methods of defining and enforcing initial eligibility

By the early 1920s, most major conferences had adopted a freshman ineligibility policy: All first-year students were ineligible to compete with and against upperclassmen, leaving them to compete on frosh-only squads. Many dismantled these limit rules in conjunction with the manpower shortages that accompanied World War II and the Korean War, but some reestablished them soon thereafter. Even though frosh were ineligible at certain schools, they were still eligible to receive athletically related aid. The frosh eligibility issue endured until 1972, when the NCAA approved first-year participation in all sports (Mott, 1995; Sack & Staurowsky, 1998).

Most of the efforts to set eligibility policy that attained even the most modest levels of success were achieved at the conference level. Even so, what is clear from these early efforts is that no school was willing to institute rules that may cause it to face a competitive disadvantage if other schools against which it competed were unwilling to adopt such changes, and that no overarching entity existed to impose rules that would be applied equally to all schools. In 1922, the NCAA supported this reliance on conference oversight by adopting a 10-point code that emphasized Association principles pertaining to eligibility and amateurism. The code encouraged schools to join regional conferences and stressed that these conferences should act as the primary enforcement body, given that the proximity of local rivals and retention of autonomy would act as a stronger influence toward maintaining stated goals.

In 1939, the NCAA inched toward the creation of an Association-wide standard by establishing eligibility rules for National Collegiate championships. These rules were made more specific in 1946, stating that only those student-athletes admitted to their schools under the same admissions standards as all others would be eligible, and at the time of participation, all student-athletes must be enrolled in a full course of study as defined by the school (Falla, 1981). As with all NCAA rules, however, these were not backed with any enforcement mechanisms; hence, their impact was negligible.

The "Sanity Code"

The NCAA took the first step in coupling rules with an enforcement mechanism soon after the 1946 National Championship rules clarification. At a so-called "conference of conferences" in Chicago that same year, school presidents and faculty members crafted a set of principles to deal with what they perceived as an acceleration of unsavory recruiting practices and athletic subsidies. These recommendations were sent to the NCAA membership for consideration (Helman, 1989). The principles came to be known as the "Sanity Code" because supporters believed that "adherence to such principles (was) necessary to restore sanity to the conduct of intercollegiate athletics" (Falla, 1981, pp. 132–133). According to Sperber (1998), the code was created as an effort by these established conferences to stem the rising tide of competition for recruited athletes, and that the title "Sanity Code" was a revised version of the original "Purity Code" title, which was dismissed as sanctimonious by scornful members of the press.

Whatever the title, the terms of the code required that athletes possess academic credentials similar to the rest of the student body. In other words, student-athletes had to be admitted under the admission standards applicable to all students at the school. The principles were brought to the membership for approval at the 1947 Convention in New York. Article III, the Principle of Sound Academic Standards, demanded that institutions "shall see to it that an athlete is admitted to college on the same basis as any other student and observes and maintains the same academic standards." Article IV, "the Principles Governing Financial Aid to athletes," required that student-athletes receive only need-based financial aid.

Longtime NCAA executive director Walter Byers (1995) summarized the Code's impact on initial eligibility:

> A student-athlete could receive tuition and fees if he showed financial need and met the school's ordinary entrance requirements. . . . He could receive a scholarship exceeding tuition and fees *regardless* [author's italics] of need if he ranked in the upper 25 percent of his high school graduating class or maintained a B average in college. (p. 67)

To be a scholarship athlete, the NCAA and the Sanity Code's backers now stated, you must be, at the very least, a student capable of admittance regardless of athletic ability. The Code did not dictate what players a school could admit, or which frosh student-athletes could be eligible to compete, but it did take an unprecedented step in the next most influential area—how schools could spend their athletic financial aid dollars.

Adoption of the Sanity Code as Article III of the NCAA Constitution at the 1948 Convention represented the NCAA's first attempt to couple the rules on amateurism, financial aid, and eligibility with an enforcement mechanism. To uphold the Code, a three-member Constitutional Compliance Committee was created to hear cases and make rulings on infractions, as well as committees to investigate complaints. However, the only penalty the NCAA could impose was expulsion from the Association, an extreme measure indeed.

The Code met with significant opposition before adoption, which continued until its removal. Southern schools thought that traditionally stronger academic and athletic programs in the North would gain competitive advantages because of the code. Several schools, including the University of Virginia, flatly refused to comply. Virginia and six other schools (Boston College, University of Maryland, Citadel, Villanova University, Virginia Military Institute, and Virginia Polytechnic Institute) were cited for violations of the code and actually were expelled by the Compliance Committee, but were retained after a 111–93 vote before the entire membership failed to secure the necessary two-thirds majority (Lawrence, 1987).

The Compliance Committee continued its investigations through 1950, finding Clemson University, the University of South Carolina, and four others in violation. The schools vowed non-compliance, which led to a battle over the merits of the Code at the 1951 Convention. Large Northern schools and schools from the South lobbied successfully, by a vote of 130–60, to eviscerate the Code through adoption of "Amendment D," which deleted Section 4 (Lawrence, 1987).

The Sanity Code ultimately failed for lack of enforcement, and in its place the NCAA convention substituted a constitutional provision requiring that student-athletes make "nominal progress" toward a degree (Lawrence, 1987). This elastic standard, subject to local interpretation with limited impact, was something to which all members could subscribe.

1.600 Rule

On the heels of the demise of the Sanity Code followed establishment of formal athletic scholarships as well as point-shaving scandals in basketball programs across the country and cheating on tests by football players at the U.S. Military Academy. These events renewed the concern about the role of athletics within higher education. Sack and Staurowsky (1998) addressed this point, stating that "with an athletic scholarship system in place, it became absolutely imperative for the NCAA to establish a minimum academic level for awarding scholarships. To not do so would have fueled public cynicism that already surrounded professionalized college sports" (p. 96). Fans of intercollegiate athletics demanded not only exciting and well-played games but also preservation of the idealized notion of the student-athlete—that the participants in games were also fully integrated in and engaged with pursuit of a degree. The bulk of NCAA legislation over the next decade dealt with recruiting and athletic aid issues, and conferences again were left to create and enforce academic standards. In 1959, however, the NCAA did strengthen academic eligibility standards for championship competitions, requiring that student-athletes be enrolled in a full course of study of no fewer than 12 semester or quarter hours (Falla, 1981).

After a proposal in 1962 to study eligibility issues, in 1965 the NCAA created a national standard. This required an incoming college athlete to achieve a predicted first-year college GPA of at least 1.600 (on a 4.0 scale) before the prospect could receive athletically related aid. The concept of the predictor scale was not new. The Big Ten Conference had developed and instituted a "1.7" model in 1961—the same year the conference approved a full grant-in-aid program for athletes. The requirements had cut frosh student-athlete attrition significantly at several schools. The prospect's standardized test scores on either the SAT or the ACT test were also utilized in determining eligibility, which, according to Byers (1995), "provided an essential national comparative standard" (p. 158).

Opposition to the 1.600 Rule was not surprising, as many schools saw the rule as a threat to their competitiveness. But criticism and defiance came from unexpected sources as well—namely, members of the Ivy League. The schools in the conference were unwilling to submit to NCAA control over their admissions processes and academic autonomy, and they chose to denounce the measure. Another criticism of the rule, as outlined by Fleisher et al. (1992), was that schools with higher academic admissions standards were more likely to benefit from strict eligibility rules. These schools would benefit from higher standards, putting pressure on other schools with lower standards. Thus, the schools with the higher standards would be more successful athletically because they no longer would have to compete for student-athletes they were unwilling to admit.

2.0 Rule

The NCAA would be sued several times in conjunction with efforts to overturn the 1.600 Rule, albeit unsuccessfully. The result of passage of the measure, however, was that the academic caliber of student-athletes improved considerably nationally. Nonetheless, attempts to weaken the 1.600 Rule were defeated at almost every convention until 1973 (New Triple Option, 1978).

At the 1973 Convention, critics cited racial discrimination and loss of institutional autonomy as the rationale to dismantle the 1.600 Rule. Brubacher and Rudy (1976) point out that the Civil Rights Act of 1964 required that no college receiving federal funds may practice racial discrimination. Subsequent "affirmative action" programs placed schools under pressure to admit students of color, many of whom were unable to gain eligibility under the 1.6 standards. As a result, a new system was proposed, one that would merely require an athlete to have graduated from high school with a 2.0 or "C+" average in any course of study, not necessarily a course focusing on preparing a student to enter and succeed in a traditional undergraduate program. The membership voted to repeal the 1.600 Rule, and then opted to replace it with a weaker version, the "2.0 Rule." The new rule, proposed by athletic directors and coaches who wanted to make recruiting easier, required that student-athletes who graduated from high school with a 2.0 accumulative six-, seven-, or eight-semester GPA (based on a maximum 4.0 scale), regardless of course content and test scores, be deemed eligible for participation and athletically related aid. This requirement weakened the academic standards of its athletes because it didn't require students to take more challenging college prep courses.

The retreat from Rule 1.600, combined with the declaration of freshman eligibility in all Division I sports in 1972, led to many of the rules violations and abuses of the 1980s. University of Delaware AD David Nelson declared that "this academic regression was a recruiter's dream," and Walter Byers claimed that the rule change led to "a decade of mediocre academic values and free-handed recruiting" (Byers, 1995, p. 297). That decade would culminate with a renewed proposal for minimum academic standards for prospective student-athletes.

Proposition 48

The relaxing of standards resulting from replacing Rule 1.600 with Rule 2.0 led to renewed criticisms of athlete educational exploitation by certain schools. Said Dick Bestwick, head football coach at the University of Virginia: "Many scholarship players are attending college for one purpose—to play college football and try to make it to the pros. They don't care about academics and neither do the coaches. I've found that more and more college athletes are getting accepted to play college football who couldn't get into school before" (Opinions Out Loud, 1977, p. 2).

Not only were more athletes being admitted with poor academic qualifications, but an NCAA study conducted from 1975 through 1980 discovered that only 42.9 percent of Division I-A (now the Bowl Subdivision) football players graduated. A similar study conducted by The Sporting News found that 45 percent earned degrees, including a high of 100 percent in the Ivy League, to a low of 16.7 percent in the infamous now-defunct Southwest Conference (Morris, 1992). The concern over low graduation rates and star athletes who could neither read not write would gradually push schools to reconsider the issue of initial eligibility standards.

At this point, school presidents began to take a leadership role concerning the issue. In 1982, the Ad Hoc Committee on the Problems of Major Intercollegiate Athletic Programs of the American Council on Education (ACE), chaired by Harvard president Derek Bok, cited the lack of control by presidents and trustees and suggested that colleges opt to pay athletes in football and basketball. Under one scenario proposed, blue-chip athletes "would be paid a market wage rather than the artificially constrained 'grant-in-aid.' . . . Ideally, the athletes need not be students, as to avoid all the admissions and eligibility questions" (Pay for College Athletes, 1982, p. D22).

This proposal showed a limited grasp of the realities of the intercollegiate athletics enterprise, but a more substantive and realistic proposal put forth by the committee at the 1983 NCAA Convention dealt with initial eligibility requirements. This proposal retained the concept of the 2.0 GPA Division I eligibility floor but stipulated that the GPA would be computed from coursework in a core curriculum of at least 11 academic courses, including at least three in English, two in mathematics, two in social science, and two in natural or physical science (including as least one laboratory class, if offered by the high school), as well as a 700 combined score on the SAT verbal and math sections or a 15 composite on the ACT (Proceedings, 1983, p. A-35).

The key sticking point to this new plan—which would become known as Proposal (or Proposition) No. 48, its numeration in the Convention's voting agenda—was its reliance on standardized test scores. Much of the dispute was based on race, and much of the criticism for the plan came from presidents of historically Black colleges and universities (HBCUs) and many coaches. At the convention, Joseph B. Johnson, president of Grambling State University, stated, "The ACE proposal blames the victim. . . . The committee's proposal, ladies and gentlemen, discriminates against student-athletes from low-income and minority group families by introducing arbitrary SAT and ACT cutoff scores as academic criteria for eligibility" (Proceedings, 1983, p. 103).

Johnson's fear that Blacks would be disproportionately harmed by No. 48 was well-founded. Forty-nine percent of black male students failed to achieve at least a combined 700 score on the SAT in 1981—as compared to 14 percent of Whites and 27 percent of other minorities. Many coaches also opposed Proposition 48 because the new rules clearly would raise the stakes in the already cutthroat world of recruiting. The competition for athletically able bodies would be intensified as more stringent academic requirements were imposed. Fewer prospects would meet both sets of criteria, with just as many programs seeking to engage their services—an unpleasant prospect for college recruiters (Proceedings, 1983).

Despite these concerns, No. 48 was passed, along with a measure to allow the awarding of athletically related aid to prospects who met either the test score or GPA minimum (termed a "partial qualifier"), to take effect in August 1986 with the incoming class of 1990. However, when additional studies revealed the significant and disproportionate impact that No. 48 would have on African-American prospects, legislation passed at the 1986 Convention lowered the floor standards to 1.900 GPA, 680 SAT, and 14 ACT for the following year (Proceedings, 1983).

Proposition 42

With every piece of approved NCAA legislation, there have been loopholes, many of which are not readily apparent when the measure is approved. Some schools thought the partial qualifier was a loophole because the partial qualifier exception enabled prospects who underperformed in high school to still qualify for athletically related aid, at the cost of a lost year of athletic eligibility, thereby undercutting the impact and intent of initial eligibility legislation. The call to eliminate the perceived partial qualifier loophole came from the schools of the Southeastern Conference (SEC), which had opted on their own to eliminate the awarding of funding to partial qualifiers by 1993 in the wake of an academic scandal at the University of Georgia, where an academic affairs administrator ordered a remedial studies teacher to change the grades of student-athletes—including football players who were then eligible to compete in the 1982 Sugar Bowl. Georgia coaches and officials, fearing recruiting and, subsequently, competitive disadvantages, convinced the rest of the SEC membership to ban nonqualifiers conference-wide in 1988. Then the SEC had to impress this approach on the rest of the Division I membership, for if they continued to offer athletically related aid to partial qualifiers, the SEC schools believed that as a whole they would be put at a recruiting and, subsequently, a competitive disadvantage.

The SEC's proposal, Proposition 42, did away with the partial qualifier exception for receiving athletically related aid. The new proposed legislation restricted athletically related aid to qualifiers only, those who met both the GPA and test score standards, beginning in August 1990. The SEC lobbied hard for it after the move failed once, and it passed by a slim margin (163 to 154, with two abstentions) (*1989 NCAA Convention Proceedings*, 1989; Oberlander, 1989).

The most vociferous detractors of the change were two African-American head coaches of prominent Division I men's basketball programs: John Chaney of Temple, and John Thompson II of Georgetown. The day after passage, Chaney, who had five ineligible frosh, tore into the vote, stating, "They've gone far beyond what I figured anybody who considered themselves interested in education would go," and suggested that schools with African-American players leave the NCAA and form a new association (Wieberg, 1989, p. 1C). Chaney also blamed "racist coaches [and] racist presidents" for conspiring to pass the legislation (Thompson to Walk, 1989, p. 69).

Two days after the passage of Proposition 42, Thompson announced that he would not be on the bench for third-ranked Georgetown's game against Boston College on January 14. Thompson devised the protest to draw attention to the "tremendous tragedy" that Proposition 42 would cause, and that he would not be on the bench during a game "until I am satisfied that something has been done to provide these student-athletes with appropriate opportunity and hope for access to a college education." Georgetown president Reverend Timothy Healy backed Thompson and called Proposition 42 "unwarranted and unacceptable . . . an intrusion in the college's business" (Weaver, 1989, p. 45). Thompson's protest did not end following the Hoyas' 86–60 victory over BC, as he did not accompany his team to Rhode Island for its game with Providence College on January 18 (Schuster, 1989).

The next day, Thompson, Healy, and Georgetown AD Francis Rienzo met with SEC Commissioner Harvey Schiller and NCAA Executive Director Richard Schultz to discuss Proposition 42. Following the summit, members of the NCAA's Presidents' Council stated that they would recommend postponing implementation of Proposition 42 in the form of proposed legislation at the 1990 Convention ('90 Convention, 1989). Thompson then announced he would end his boycott "based on the fact that I think there's a sincere effort on the part of the people in the N.C.A.A. . . . to make a sincere commitment to take this thing back before the convention and re-evaluate what has happened" (Rhoden, 1989, p. A23).

At the 1990 Convention, Proposition 42 was rescinded through passage of Proposition 26, which reinstated the partial qualifier. But it state did that a partial qualifier could receive institutional aid based on demonstrated financial need only and not from an athletics source.

Subsequent actions and initial eligibility today

Once the financial aid issues relating to initial eligibility were more or less settled to the satisfaction of most, later adjustments in qualification related to the actual academic performance of prospects. At the 1992 Convention, a measure brought forth by the NCAA's Presidents Commission and the NCAA Council called for an increase in core courses from 11 to 13 (with the additional two courses to be in the areas of English, mathematics, or natural or physical sciences), and an adjustment of the existing standardized test score floor (criticized by many as deleterious to many minority groups) to a sliding scale format. Under this new system, the higher a prospect's GPA, the lower one's test scores could be and still be eligible. Both measures passed easily and took effect in August 1995.

Today, the system finalized in 1992 is very much in place, with some slight alterations. A prospect with a GPA of 3.55 or above could score as low as a combined 400 on the SAT I and II, or 37 on the ACT, and gain first-year eligibility. Refer back to Exhibit 9.1 for eligibility standards.

Standards for Division I

As for core courses, in 2003 the Division I Board of Directors approved another adjustment, effective for first-year prospects in August 2008, requiring that the core course GPA be tabulated from a total of 16 core courses in these areas, as shown in Exhibit 9.2.

Standards for Divisions II and III

In determining initial eligibility, Division II schools have retained the benchmarks associated with the original Division I standards. To be defined as a qualifier and to be eligible to compete as a first-year student at a D-II institution, prospects must

Required core courses for first year students, effective August 1, 2008.	EXHIBIT 9.2
English	4 years
Mathematics (at the level of Algebra I or higher)	3 years
Natural or physical sciences (including at least one laboratory course if offered by the high school)	2 years
Social science	2 years
Additional course in English, mathematics, or natural or physical sciences	1 year
Additional courses in any of the above areas (as well as foreign language, philosophy, or nondoctrinal religion)	4 years

Source: 2008–09 NCAA Division I Manual, 2008, p. 143.

have achieved a minimum 2.000 GPA (based on a 4.000 system) in the prescribed number of core courses, and a minimum combined score of 820 on the SAT or 68 on the ACT. D-III has no unilateral first-year initial-eligibility standards. Each school determines its own initial eligibility standard (*2008–09 NCAA Division II Manual*, 2008; *2008–09 NCAA Division III Manual*, 2008).

CONTINUING ELIGIBILITY

As noted in the Introduction, the goal in determining what constitutes the proper mix of athletic and academic endeavors for intercollegiate competitors has been to determine these measures before the prospect matriculates (initial eligibility), and then periodically after student-athletes have enrolled (continuing eligibility).

Major rules

The major rules governing post-enrollment Division I academic eligibility for students who enrolled after August 1, 2003, often referred to as progress-toward-degree requirements (minus some specific exceptions) are summarized and listed in Exhibit 9.3.

Student-athletes are also limited to four seasons of competition in any one sport, and these four seasons must be completed in five calendar years from the semester or quarter in which the student-athlete first enrolled for a minimum full-time program of studies at a collegiate institution.

Transfer regulations

The general principle governing eligibility of students transferring to Division I and Division II institutions (Bylaw 14.5.1) is that a student is required to complete one full academic year of residence before being eligible to compete, unless he or she satisfies one of a number of requirements or qualifies for one of a number of exceptions or waivers. The bylaw defines a transfer student as an individual who transfers from a collegiate institution after having met any one of a number of conditions at the original institution, most of which pertain to the student's status relative to full-time enrollment.

If a student-athlete is transferring to a D-I Bowl Subdivision football, basketball, or ice hockey program, he or she qualifies for the one-time transfer exception (Bylaw 14.5.5.2.10), which affords immediate eligibility provided that the student-athlete has not previously transferred from another school, is in good academic standing, and has been given written certification from his or her previous school that the school approves of the transfer. At Division III schools, a student-athlete may transfer and be eligible immediately if he or she has never practiced or used a season of eligibility at his or her previous institution, or if he or she is transferring from a four-year school and if the student-athlete had been eligible to compete at the previous school (*2008–09 NCAA Division I Manual*, 2008; *2008–09 NCAA Division II Manual*, 2008; *2008–09 NCAA Division III Manual*, 2008).

| Major rules governing post-enrollment Division I academic eligibility. | **EXHIBIT** | **9.3** |

Full-time status (Bylaw 14.1.8.2):

To be eligible for competition, student-athletes must be enrolled in at least a minimum full-time program of studies leading to a baccalaureate or equivalent degree as defined by the institution, which shall be not less than 12 semester or quarter hours.

Fulfillment of credit-hour requirements (Bylaw 14.4.3.1):

An enrolled student-athlete must have completed successfully six-semester or quarter credit hours during the preceding regular academic term, and 24-semester or 36-quarter hours prior to his or her second year of collegiate enrollment.

Hours earned during the regular academic year (Bylaw 14.4.3.1.3):

A student-athlete shall earn at least 75 percent of the minimum semester or quarter hours required for progress toward a degree during the regular academic year, with no more than 25 percent allowed taken during summer terms.

Designation of degree program (Bylaw 14.4.3.1.4):

A student-athlete shall designate a program of studies leading toward a specific baccalaureate degree by the beginning of the third year (fifth semester or seventh quarter) of enrollment.

Fulfillment of percentage of degree requirements (Bylaw 14.4.3.2):

A student-athlete entering his or her third year of collegiate enrollment shall have completed successfully at least 40 percent of the course requirements in the student's specific degree program, at least 60 percent of the course requirements entering his or her fourth year, and at least 80 percent entering his or her fifth year.

Fulfillment of minimum grade-point average requirements (Bylaw 14.4.3.3):

A student-athlete entering his or her second year of collegiate enrollment shall present a cumulative minimum grade-point average (based on a maximum of 4.000) that equals at least 90 percent of the minimum GPA required for graduation (e.g., if a 2.000 GPA is required for graduation, student-athletes must have at least a 1.900 GPA). Entering his or her third year, a GPA equaling 95 percent is required (a 1.950 if a 2.000 is required), and entering his or her fourth and subsequent year, a GPA equaling 100 percent is required (a 2.000 if a 2.000 is required).

Source: 2008–09 NCAA Division I Manual, 2008.

Students transferring from two-year schools to Division I and II schools must complete an academic year of residence before being eligible to compete, unless he or she had been met the terms of initial eligibility outlined above, and earned at least a GPA of 2.000 and has satisfactorily completed at least an average of 12 semester credits acceptable toward a baccalaureate degree at his or her new school for each term enrolled at the two-year school. In this case, the student is deemed eligible immediately. A two-year transfer student who did not qualify under initial eligibility requirements can still be immediately eligible at his or her new school if he or she has graduated from the two-year school and has a 2.000 GPA with a minimum of 48 credits applicable toward a baccalaureate program at the new school. A student transferring from a Bowl Subdivision to a Championship Subdivision football program may also use the one-time exception (*2008–09 NCAA Division I Manual*, 2008; *2008–09 NCAA Division II Manual*, 2008).

KEY DEVELOPMENTS IMPACTING ACADEMIC ELIGIBILITY

The above information outlines the many factors that have influenced the establishment and maintenance of academic eligibility rules. Now we will examine some of the many environmental factors and stakeholder interests that continue to shape the form of these standards.

Attempts to measure student-athletes' academic performance

As we have discussed throughout this chapter, the issue of academic performance of student-athletes has been talked about and debated almost since the day Harvard beat Yale in that crew race in New Hampshire back in 1852. As a result, several ways have been developed to measure academic performance, including graduation rates, academic progress rate, and coaches' graduation rate.

Graduation rates

In recent years, the main data relied upon for gauging student-athlete academic performance has been the rate at which they graduated from college. Data released by the NCAA in 2008 indicated that 72 percent of Division I student-athletes who enrolled between 1998 and 2001 graduated within six years of initial matriculation. This, according to the Association, was a five-point increase over data released in 1999 (Sander, 2008).

Exhibit 9.4 lists the graduation rates for student-athletes in specific sports, noting that the NCAA's data differ from that reported by the U. S. Department of

EXHIBIT 9.4	Individual sport Division I graduation rates.		
SPORT		**NCAA GRADUATION RATE**	**U.S. DEPT. OF EDUCATION RATE**
Women's Skiing		96	73
Women's Gymnastics		95	85
Women's Lacrosse		94	84
Men's Lacrosse		88	74
Women's Golf		87	71
Men's Ice Hockey		83	64
Women's Basketball		82	64
Men's Soccer		79	58
Baseball		68	74
Football (Bowl Subdivision)		67	55
Football (Championship Subdivision)		65	54
Men's Basketball		62	46

Source: Sander, 2008. Copyright 2008, *The Chronicle of Higher Education.* Reprinted with permission.

Education, as the NCAA does not figure in students who transfer to other schools as long as they are in good academic standing when they leave. These data reveal a range in performance based on the sport, with baseball, men's basketball and football student-athletes graduating at a lower rate than the others. Six men's basketball programs (University of Arizona, Clemson, University of Connecticut, University of Georgia, University of Maryland, University of Texas) graduated a third or fewer of their players. In response to these numbers, former NCAA president Myles Brand commented: "While we know there is room for growth in a few sports, we are seeing notable improvement. The numbers are moving in the right direction" (Sander, 2008, p. A22).

Academic progress rate

Although the Association has sought to promote academic performance, we know from the previous chapter that enforcement—the combination of rules and the penalties for running afoul of them—is a critical component in keeping the competitive playing field level and promoting organizational mission and goals. We saw this above with the establishment of initial and continuing eligibility rules, but these rules tended to penalize individual student-athletes for their lack of academic performance, not the schools themselves. In 2004, the Association and its members made a significant move to ratchet up penalties on schools for low academic performance, when the NCAA Division I Board of Directors initiated a system that would build on the formulas of initial and continuing eligibility and determine which programs at which schools were failing in their educatory missions, and penalize them accordingly with a loss of GIAs and bans on post season play.

The tool to measure classroom achievement, known as the Academic Progress Rate (APR), is a formula that measures how long a student-athlete remains at a specific school, and the progress the student-athlete makes toward a degree. According to the formula, a program will receive points when an athlete receiving athletically related aid remains eligible and makes progress toward a degree each semester. Each of these student-athletes can receive two points per semester, one for being academically eligible during the season and one for returning as eligible for the next semester (those who earned no points based on this system are now known as "0-for-2's").

A team's overall score is calculated by dividing the number of points its players earn by the highest number it could have earned, and that percentage is assessed a point total by multiplying by a thousand. For example, a 12-person basketball squad with two players leaving during the first semester would receive only 40 of a possible 48 points, earning a score of 833 (40/48 × 1000) for the year. Programs scoring below 925, which, based on comparative data, translates to a projected graduation rate of 50 percent, was to be subject to penalties beginning in 2007 (based on a two-year average of scores). Ultimately, the ratings were to be based on a four-year average (Bombardieri & Blaudschun, 2005; Wieberg, 2005c, 2007b).

When the measure was introduced, former NCAA President Brand said the measure would "mark a time when we held not only our students but our athletic teams and our institutions accountable for having student athletes progress academically in a timely way" (Pennington, 2004, p. C17). The system has its critics nonetheless, including some faculty members such as Linda Bensel-Meyers, a professor of English at the University of Denver and later president of the Drake Group, an association of professors and administrators seeking to reform intercollegiate athletics. Recall that Bensel-Meyers left the University of Tennessee when she discovered that incidents of plagiarism had been ignored and multiple favorable grade changes had been filed for many of the school's football players. She said the plan would "increase cheating because it increases the pressure on faculty to pass students who cannot do the work" (Pennington, 2004, p. C17).

Some coaches, however, praised the plan. Jim Haney, executive director of the National Association of Basketball Coaches, the national professional organization that serves basketball coaches at all levels and lobbies the NCAA on legislative issues it believes impacts its membership, supported the system, stating, "For the coaches, it's going to be easier to focus on what you have to do. It's right there. . . . If you focus on that, I don't see what the problem will be (Pennington, 2004, p. C18).

Others within athletic departments complained about the methods used to compute the ratings. University of Louisville head men's basketball coach Rick Pitino, whose team's rating (833) fell below the established benchmark in 2005, said: "We don't look good because of one year. Once we found out what was being done [with the APR], we changed our mindset in recruiting" (Wieberg, 2005c, p. 7C). University of Connecticut AD Jeff Hathaway, whose men's basketball team also rated poorly, commented that the system should consider the impact of exceptional situations: "Transfers, fifth-year student-athletes who remain at the institution to complete their degrees after having exhausted their athletic eligibility, student-athletes who elect to leave school prior to the completion of a semester for entry into professional sports—may be better reflected in data collection and reporting" (Wieberg, 2005c, p. 7C).

Early reports on the APR system. In 2005, the NCAA reported the initial findings of the APR system. In Division I institutions, 56 percent (183 of 326 programs, 411 programs of a total of 5,720 programs) had at least one program that fell below the projected graduation rate of 50 percent. These data were issued to inform schools of their status, and did not yet carry any associated penalties.

In 2007, the NCAA released its third annual report of D-I annual progress data, indicating that a greater percentage of programs in the problem sports (44 percent of men's basketball teams, 40 percent of football teams, and 35 percent of baseball teams) posted scores low enough to cost them GIAs. As a result, 49 teams at 35 different schools were subject to immediate penalties based on continuing poor academic ratings, including football programs at the University of Arizona (docked four GIAs), Florida International University (nine), San Jose State (seven), and eight other programs. Men's basketball programs at Iowa State (two) and the University of Cincinnati (one) also lost GIAs, as did nine other programs.

Future penalties for programs that continue to underperform (by posting APR scores below 900) could include limits on weekly practice time in 2008, and bans on participation in NCAA post-season championships in 2009. GIA losses are capped at 10 percent of allowable slots.

At Texas Southern University, a public historically Black school with 9,500 undergraduates located in Houston and a member of the Southwestern Athletic Conference, five of 18 programs (men's basketball and tennis, women's soccer, golf, and softball) were flagged (down from 11 in 2005). Texas Southern AD Alois Blackwell claimed the deficiencies were a function of a limited budget: "It's money-driven. If you have more money, you can hire more academic advisors. . . . And you can have the tutors you need" (Wieberg, 2007a, p. 12C).

Texas Southern was not alone: Nine other HBCUs were cited for underperforming programs, and none of the 49 programs cited was at a school from the Atlantic Coast, Big East, Big Ten, Big 12, Pacific-10, or Southeastern—the conferences that generate more revenue for academic support services. In response, the NCAA made $1.6 million available to "limited resource institutions" such as Texas Southern to help bolster academic support programs.

The problem was not restricted to HBCUs. When the 2008 APR report was released, the football program at San Jose State, a public school with 23,000 undergraduates and a member of the Western Athletic Conference, lost nine more GIAs because of continuing low performance and was slated to have four hours of practice time reduced per week (Carey, 2007; Thamel, 2007b, 2008; Wieberg, 2005a, 2005b). Head coach Dick Tomey, who took over the program in 2005 after stints as head coach at the University of Hawaii (1977–86) and University of Arizona (1987–2000), and as a defensive assistant for the 2004 BCS champion University of Texas, explained that the poor performance was a result of lack of funds for an adequate academic support program, what he called "class warfare" between the programs affiliated with the BCS and those like his: "There's such a difference between the B.C.S. schools and those that are not" (Wieberg, 2007a, p. 12C). Karl Benson, commissioner of the Western Athletic Conference, said of his membership: "I know we may have not had the same resources that others have had" (p. 12C).

The 2008 report also cited continuing poor performance in the football program at Temple University, and men's basketball programs at Centenary College (Louisiana), East Carolina University, and New Mexico State University. If performance in these programs continues to lag, the schools were warned they could be barred from post-season play in 2009–2010. Even though Temple lost an additional two GIAs, AD Bill Bradshaw and head coach Al Golden were upbeat about the team's academic performance. Bradshaw said the university had invested nearly a half-million dollars in a "complete overhaul" of the program's athletic support system, and that the program's two subsequent recruiting classes had APR scores of 980 and 975, well above the 925 threshold. Golden was quoted in a released statement that "we inherited a liability and in just a short 29 months made it our single greatest asset" (Thamel, 2008, p. C18).

Transfer rules and the APR system. One change to the transfer rules, enacted in August 2007, was related to the new APR system. This transfer measure required that to be deemed eligible for athletically related aid at his or her new school, any student-athlete transferring to a Division I institution must have been academically eligible to compete at his or her former school. The rule does not impact those transferring to Division II institutions.

NCAA vice president for member services, Kevin Lennon, who oversees the APR program, explained that the system was to limit transfers based on poor academic performance. Syracuse University head men's basketball coach, Jim Boeheim, agreed, claiming that a student-athlete considering transferring from Syracuse reconsidered because of the new legislation. Of the student-athlete in question, Boeheim said, "It's possible a kid may rethink and say, 'It's not so bad here.' To me, it's absolutely a great rule, and not just because of the impact on the APR, because of the overall welfare of the kid, too" (Wieberg, 2007b, p. 2C).

Earning back GIAs. One way that schools can earn GIAs back under the APR system is to assist former student-athletes who failed to gain their degrees before their athletic eligibility was exhausted to earn their diplomas later. Consider the case of C.J. Masters, a former defensive back at Kansas State, who left school six classes shy of his degree in criminology in 1993 to pursue a career in pro football. When Masters's dream of pro football stardom came up short, he bounced from job to job, eventually finding a niche working with children with developmental disabilities, but later found he couldn't advance in his new career because he lacked his undergraduate degree.

Under the APR system, returning students can qualify for NCAA grants or tuition assistance. From 2002 to 2005, 38 percent of D-I football programs had at least one former player return to finish his degree, with 45 returning to complete at the University of Nebraska, and 33 at the University of Tennessee. One school, Marshall University, actively courted former players by searching a school database for all who had left school early during the past decade and needed fewer than a year's credits to graduate. The search actually identified 12 former players who were already degree-eligible, one of whom simply had to pay $100 in parking tickets. For those who needed credits, the school initiated a program in which eligible former players could work in the Marshall athletic department in exchange for tuition and living expenses.

Other schools, such as Southern Utah University, a public school with 6,500 undergraduates located in Cedar City and a member of the Summit League, have focused more on securing a fifth year of non-athletic aid for student-athletes. And Kansas State helped C.J. Masters obtain a $2,000 grant through the NCAA and allowed him to take several online courses and transfer several others from a community college in Arizona (McCormack, 2006).

Coaches' graduation rate

Although many see the APR system as a significant achievement in improving the academic performance of certain student-athletes, others have suggested different systems. One such alternative was put forth by Gerald Gurney, senior associate AD for academics and student life at the University of Oklahoma, and Jerome Weber, a professor at the school, who suggested that the APR be supplanted by what they call the coaches' graduation rate, or CGR. Under this system, every prospect recruited by a coach would be afforded six years in which to graduate, and the success rate of each recruit would be tied to the recruiting coach rather than the school at which the coach worked. Although the CGR proposes no penalties for underperformance, the model is believed to be a better system than the APR because such a measure "could support hiring or salary decisions based at least in part on the academic performance and graduation rate attributable to an individual head coach's recruiting activities" (Gurney & Weber, 2008, p. A32).

case study 9.A

BASEBALL—THE SURPRISE PROBLEM

Issues of academic progress and graduation rates for high-profile Division I men's sports such as football and basketball have been examined with extreme scrutiny for decades. The emergence of the APR system has shown that in the sport of baseball, academic problems are also an issue. While 44 (out of a divisional total of 336, 13.1 percent) basketball and 40 (out of combined subdivisional total of 241, 16.6 percent) football programs were cited as underperforming, 35 (out of a total of 293, 11.9 percent) baseball programs were similarly identified.

One contributing component to low academic performance in baseball is that, unlike some sports, baseball student-athletes have been allowed to transfer and be eligible to play immediately at their new school without first having a year's residency. Another factor is that, because baseball is an equivalency sport (11.7 full grants—see Chapter 7), few baseball student-athletes receive a full GIA, and this makes transferring for reasons of greater aid more attractive (Carey, 2007). Other issues include the high number of missed classes because of game times (many occurring mid-week) and compactness of the spring season schedule, the fact that hundreds of players are selected each June in the Major League Baseball draft before their intercollegiate eligibility is exhausted, and also because many baseball players play in competitive leagues far from campus in the summer, limiting their ability to enroll in summer courses.

Dave Keilitz, executive director of the American Baseball Coaches Association, the national professional organization that serves baseball coaches at all levels and lobbies the NCAA on legislative issues it thinks impacts its membership, theorized that the problem had to do with baseball's being poorly funded in terms of GIAs per participant. Keilitz cited that the average roster size was 27, and that "most Division I players still think pro baseball is in their future. If they're not playing as a freshman, they immediately start to think they should maybe look at somewhere else" (Carey, 2006, p. 7C).

In response to these issues, the NCAA Division I Board of Directors threatened a draconian act, an across-the-board reduction in the length of playing seasons. Instead, the NCAA Executive Committee formed the Baseball Academic Enhancement Committee, in 2006. The purpose was to study the causes and generate potential remedies, which included possible increases in GIA equivalencies to 15 full-grants or to 25 half-grants. In 2007, the newly formed committee proposed a four-pronged package to address the conclusion that the sport's APR was below standard. The following measures suggested by the baseball committee were adopted by the Board of Directors, to take effect August 1, 2008:

- Baseball student-athletes must be academically certified for the fall term to be eligible to play in the following spring.
- Baseball student-athletes must now have a year in residence before they are eligible to compete if they transfer from one school to another.
- Each student-athlete receiving athletically related aid must receive at least the equivalent of 33 percent of a full grant-in-aid, with the maximum number receiving athletically related aid capped at 27 (previously there was no limit).
- Teams that fall below a 900 APR score will have their playing seasons reduced by 10 percent (current limit is 56 games) to 50 games.

The financial aid rules were enacted to combat the notion that less aid and less restrictive transfer rules made it more attractive for baseball players to jump from school to school seeking more aid and playing time, and hindering a school's tabulation of graduation rates. The rules also discontinued the "tryout scholarship," where for as little as $400 in athletic aid, prospects would be encouraged to matriculate to go through fall practices, then awarded more aid if they made the team.

According to Villanova University head coach Joe Godri: "If some coach brings in four guys at $400 and gets one keeper, that has been viewed as a good deal. He got a good player for $1,600" (Pennington, 2008, p. C14). Under the old rules, the players cut would then be able to transfer without a losing immediate eligibility, which is no longer the case. Longtime Mississippi State University head coach Ron Polk dislikes the measures: "We're the only partial schol- arship sport that has to have its athletes eligible two consecutive semesters and that has restrictions on how to distribute our [GIAs]," said Polk, who had sent an 18-page letter to various college presidents and NCAA officials outlining his displeasure (Carey, 2007, p. 11C).

questions for you to consider

1. Based on this case, is there a better solution to the academic progress problem in baseball?
2. Should these same measures be applied to other sports in which academic progress rates have been lagging? Why or why not?

Expenses associated with academic support

Among the numerous financial issues and challenges facing intercollegiate athletic managers are pressures to build new or renovate existing athletic facilities. These pressures are emerging in relation to other athletic department tasks, including academic support. Consider the following recently completed or planned academic support building projects at Division I schools (Wolverton, 2008):

- Indiana University: A $3 million academic facility for student-athletes inside its existing football stadium, which will be seven times as big as the athletic department's existing academic services space.

- University of Oregon: A 34,000-square-foot academic facility for student- athletes scheduled for completion in 2010. Phil Knight, billionaire co-founder of Nike, is covering the construction cost, controlling all details of the project and requiring that the university spend $1 million in computer equipment and annual upkeep. Non-athletes can use the facility, too, as long as space is not being used by student-athletes.

- University of Southern California: Broke ground in 2008 for a $13.5 million academic facility for student-athletes.

- University of Texas: Opened a 25,000-square-foot academic center in the fall of 2008, which was part of a major renovation to its football stadium.

Also, consider the 2007 budgetary expenses and staff dedicated to academic sup- port services at the 10 top-spending Division I schools shown in Exhibit 9.5. And, according to Wolverton (2008), four Division I schools reported increasing their spending on academic support by more than 300 percent since 1997: St. John's University (New York), 911 percent; Wake Forest University, 766 percent; Clemson University, 367 percent; and University of Oregon, 330 percent.

Several factors have contributed to these building projects and other academi- cally related expenses. The sliding scale for initial eligibility has meant that more prospects have been able to compete as first-year students, and existing continuing eligibility standards mean that some of these academically at-risk student-athletes are requiring more support to meet these expectations. In addition, the estab- lishment of the APR system means that programs are now penalized if their student-athletes are not graduating. At the University of Oklahoma, for example, senior associate AD Gerald Gurney notes that 60 percent of admitted student-

| | Financial data for academic support services at Division I schools. | EXHIBIT | 9.5 |

INSTITUTION	BUDGET	FULL-TIME EMPLOYEES	FACILITY SQUARE FOOTAGE
University of Oklahoma	$2,920,000	13	25,000
University of Texas	$2,000,000	18	25,000
University of California, Los Angeles	$1,855,000	N/A	N/A
University of Tennessee	$1,750,000	18	33,000
University of Kentucky	$1,700,000	11	20,000
Ohio State University	$1,600,000	21	8,000
University of Florida	$1,525,971	N/A	15,000
Auburn University	$1,500,000	14	33,000
Texas A&M University	$1,422,762	13	28,000
Pennsylvania State University	$1,414,947	16	27,970

Source: Wolverton, 2008. Copyright 2008, *The Chronicle of Higher Eduction*. Reprinted with permission.

athletes are so-called "special admits," which means that they did not meet the university's admission requirements.

One study performed at the University of Indiana found that colleges and universities across the country are admitting more non-athlete students with remedial academic needs. Nathan Tublitz, a biology professor at the University of Oregon and co-chair of the Coalition on Intercollegiate Athletics, a faculty-led reform group, is critical of the move toward admitting less prepared prospects, and that, "more schools are accepting students that are further and further away from the average student at the institution" (Wolverton, 2008, p. A22).

To meet the goal of making sure that student-athletes succeed academically, schools must not only spend money on lavish facilities and equipment but also have to create systems and hire qualified personnel. In Chapter 7 we learned that former University of Mississippi head football coach Ed Orgeron and his staff struggled with the idea of recruiting prospects who were marginal academically. In response to the issue of assisting such prospects, Ole Miss tripled its operating budget and staff size after 2003, when it began to 50 tutoring sessions a week. Five years later, the number of tutoring sessions reached 800. Ole Miss now has four full-time "learning specialists," and their annual salaries total $175,000. But the role and tasks of such personnel can be problematic. From 1998 to 2008, 25 institutions committed major violations involving academic fraud, including incidents in which personnel wrote papers or took tests for student-athletes, or school personnel gave course credit to student-athletes who did not perform course work or attend class.

To combat some of these abuses, many athletic departments employ "class checkers" to make sure that student-athletes are attending class. Texas A&M spent nearly $50,000 on this program in 2008. The University of Tennessee keeps track of how much time its student-athletes spend at their 33,000-square-foot academic support center by having them swipe their student ID at the door as they enter. To make sure that tutors aren't establishing unprofessional connections and activities with student-athletes, Michigan State, a public university with 36,000 undergraduates located in East Lansing and a member of the Division I Big Ten Conference, which had five tutors in 1996, now has 120, and a two-year limit on tutor tenure. The rules and procedures are in place, according to Jim Pignataro, the school's director of student-athlete support services, to make sure tutors don't get too close to student-athletes, because, "the minute you lose your academic integrity, you lose everything" (Wolverton, 2008, p. A23).

High school diploma mills

Upon an initial review, University High School (UHS) in Miami, Florida, would appear to be a reputable American high school. It certainly has a distinguished group of alumni, many of whom are enrolled at major colleges and universities across the country. It must have a decent athletic program, too, when considering that many of these alums are Division I college football players at schools such as Arizona State, Auburn, Florida State, and the University of Tennessee. But upon a closer look, things appear questionable at UHS. The school holds no classes and has no educational accreditation, and it advertised itself as "the easiest, fastest way to become a high school graduate." Diplomas can be earned in four to six weeks at a cost of $399. Its founder, Stanley Simmons, previously served 10 months in federal prison after pleading guilty to committing mail fraud from his involvement with a similar school in Arizona. Simmons sold the school in 2004 to Michael Kinney, a 27-year-old arrested for marijuana possession charges in 2003. The school consists of two small rooms on the third floor of an office building located between an animal hospital and a Starbuck's coffee shop (Thamel & Wilson, 2005; Thamel, 2006a).

UHS is not a singular phenomenon. In the last few years, similar institutions have sprouted up across America: Lutheran Christian Academy and Rise Academy in Philadelphia; Boys to Men Academy in Chicago; God's Academy in Irving, Texas; One Christian Academy in Mendenhall, Mississippi; and Stoneridge Prep in Simi Valley, California, among others. These "schools," none of which has been accredited by the appropriate state education oversight organizations, do differ somewhat from UHS: Some, though not all, have actual classes, albeit often for only two hours a day, but their students in most cases are African-American male basketball players looking to become eligible to play in college. So why don't these players stay at home and attend their local schools? Because, based on their previous academic performance, they will be deemed academically eligible by the NCAA to compete in college, and these "schools" allow them to do so with little or no work in bogus courses. At least 200 players have done so in the last decade by enrolling in such "schools" (Thamel & Wilson, 2005; Thamel, 2006a).

According to college recruiters, Lutheran Christian, housed in a red-brick community center on North 17th Street in Philadelphia, has become a running joke. At Lutheran, all 30 students at the school are basketball players who were not required to go to classes. Their only teacher was the head basketball coach, Darryl Schofield. "What we were told when we first got there was, 'How you perform on the basketball court, that's what you do for your grades,'" said Roosevelt Lee, a former student. After a month at Lutheran, he said he received credit for five courses, earning all "B's," although he never took a test, attended a class, or received instruction (Thamel, 2006a, p. B18). In 2005, Lutheran sent at least 11 players to Division I schools, including two each to Mississippi State and the University of Texas–El Paso, and others to Georgetown, Temple, and Washington State (Thamel & Wilson, 2005).

The future of such organizations is not bright, as evidenced in late December 2005, when University High School announced that it was going out of business. The local state attorney's office was awaiting returns from subpoenas in its investigation of the school over possible criminal fraud charges, and the NCAA had requested that the school respond to questions regarding its curriculum. In announcing the closing, founder Stanley Simmons said the school had been "totally mismanaged—probably more than mismanaged. There is no way I would consider remaining in the business" (Wilson, 2005, p. B15). Questions remained as to whether students who obtained credits and degrees from University High and the other diploma mills would remain eligible at their current colleges.

NCAA list of academically ineligible schools

In the summer of 2006, the NCAA released a list of 16 schools from which it would not accept graduated students as academically eligible, and another 22 that would be subject to ongoing review. Lutheran Christian, along with others mentioned above and additional well-known boys' prep hoop powers such as Fork Union Military Academy and Oak Hill Academy in Virginia, and Bridgton Academy in Maine, were among the schools identified. Said Oak Hill coach Steve Smith: "I'm embarrassed to be on the list with some of those schools," and Kevin Lennon, NCAA vice president for membership services (responsible for issues dealing with bylaws and interpretations), responded: "We know some places have shut down, and I'd imagine we've discouraged others from opening" (Thamel, 2006b, p. C18).

In 2008, the Association's High School Review Committee denied approval for Charis Prep, located in Wilson, North Carolina, after reviewing the school's curriculum and visiting the site. The committee cited concerns over a lack of quality control or organized curriculum structure. The ruling means that Charis graduates cannot use core courses earned at the school, grades, or completion of its course of study to meet initial eligibility requirements (NCAA Rules, 2008).

NCAA legislation on core courses for initial eligibility

In a related action in 2007, described by some as its most significant in dealing with these types of schools, the NCAA Division I Board of Directors passed legislation that limited to one the number of core courses that could be counted toward the required initial eligibility total after a prospect's fourth year after entering high school. The move was seen as closing the loophole in current bylaws that permitted prospects from moving from school to school seeking an easy path toward certification. NCAA VP Lennon assessed the change this way: "If you've been a prep school focused on simply getting kids eligible that are not high school graduates, this (new rule) is going to be problematic for you. . . . The part that was really distasteful was that some of our college coaches were encouraging the behavior" (Thamel, 2007a, p. A29; Wolverton, 2007, p. A48).

Much like the criticisms that followed passage of Propositions 42 and 48 more than two decades ago, many (mostly Division I men's basketball coaches) decried these new measures as limiting opportunities for poor prospects from weak public schools. Paul Hewitt of Georgia Tech commented, "We're slowly but surely taking away the opportunity to overcome a bad start. That's a shame" (Thamel, 2007a, p. A29). Prep schools with accredited programs also denounced the move, and some predicted a flood of lawsuits for students facing ineligibility based on the new rules, especially those who enter schools and repeat a grade. The NCAA's Lennon addressed these concerns, noting that a waiver process would be in place to deal with such cases. "We're not shutting out opportunity," he said, "we're encouraging better behavior. . . . Legitimate prep schools in the business of preparing students for college and wanting to improve their academic portfolio will continue" (Thamel, 2007a, p. A29).

Initial eligibility and junior college transfers

Many who are familiar with the NCAA's legislation on core courses and initial eligibility noted that junior college programs would benefit from the new rules outlined above, citing that many such programs had lacked talent over the past decade as students pursued fifth, sixth, or even seventh years in high school to obtain a Division I grant-in-aid offer contingent on their initial eligibility certification, and not lose two years of Division I eligibility. Observers cite that the total number of juco athletes has stayed the same over the past decade, but more elite athletes have bypassed jucos for prep schools. Steve Miller, football recruiting coordinator at Northwest Mississippi Community College in Senatobia, Mississippi, observed: "We miss out on a lot of kids who should be in the junior-college system because they're encouraged by big-time programs to go to prep schools" (Ashburn, 2007, p. A31).

One prep school coach complained that the rule allowed junior college coaches to go "from eating Caesar salad to prime rib," but Steve Green, head men's basketball coach at South Plains College, a junior college in Levelland, Texas, explained, "This puts the focus back on junior college again where our people are prepared to help these kids" (Powell, 2007, p. 26). Greg Heinz, AD at Blinn College in Brenham, Texas, stated plainly that the role of jucos is to "provide an opportunity for those kids who don't meet NCAA academic requirements. . . . A lot of them wouldn't go to college if athletic opportunities weren't available to them" (Thamel, 2007a, p. A29). Art Becker, AD at Scottsdale (Arizona) Community College, and president of the NJCAA, agreed: "One of our missions is to deal with students who have problems in high school. . . . I feel [this] is the place where students should go for redemption" (Wolverton, 2007, p. A48). Wayne Baker, the NJCAA's former executive director, concurred in part: "I'm not sure it will send more athletes in terms of numbers, but I think the quality will improve" (p. A48).

As noted, a major component of athletics at junior college programs is to prepare student-athletes for recruitment to play at four-year institutions. Often, student-athletes who matriculate at two-year schools have done so because they have failed to meet Division I and II initial eligibility requirements. The general current transfer bylaws state that student-athletes transferring from a two-year school to a four-year school must complete a full year in residence at that institution, unless they have been deemed a qualifier (see above), have spent at least a semester in residence at the two-year school, and have earned at least a 2.0 GPA in at least 12 credits that will transfer toward any degree program at the four-year school. Transfer students who were not a qualifier must first graduate from their two-year school with a GPA of 2.0 to be eligible for athletic aid and to compete without first completing a year of residence at the four-year school (*2008–09 NCAA Division I Manual*, 2008).

However, the competitive impact of junior college transfers among Division I schools continued to grow, as 6,000 were counted at Division I in 2006–07—one in every 19—especially in baseball and men's basketball (one in six) and the football Bowl Subdivision (one in 13). The academic eligibility challenge that accompanies these transfers is that these student-athletes are more likely to become academically ineligible at their new schools, which in turn lowers the school's APR score. Temple and San Jose State, two of the football programs suffering penalties from low APRs, have relied heavily on juco transfers.

As a result, the NCAA's Academic Cabinet, a new panel chaired by Oklahoma AD Joe Castiglione, is reviewing possible bylaw changes that would require all academically risky juco transfers to sit out a year at their new schools, because, according to Castiglione, "they are not necessarily any more prepared than they were coming out of high school" (Wieberg, 2008, p. 6C). NJCAA head Wayne Baker called the proposed move an "unfair requirement," and San Jose State AD Tom Bowens agreed, responding, "You have certain (junior college coaches) who get their kids lined up and get all their remedial (classes) taken, and (the players) can transfer and walk in anywhere in the United States. Those are really solid kids. I think it's very dangerous to start making sweeping generalizations" (Wieberg, 2008, p. 6C).

CONCLUSION

n the initial period of intercollegiate athletics, most institutions maintained separate admissions standards for athletes, choosing to admit any athlete without abiding by the school's stated admissions policies. As a result, institutions, conferences, and the NCAA were forced to determine dual factors that would eventually become known as initial (pre-enrollment) and continuing (post-enrollment) eligibility. The primary goal of this system was to assure that all institutions would use the same academic criteria to screen prospective student-athletes, offer admittance based on student performance, and, in some cases, offer financial aid based on that student's athletic ability.

The NCAA's first step in coupling rules with an enforcement mechanism was the membership's adoption of the "Sanity Code" in 1947, which required that athletes possess similar academic credentials as the rest of the student body, and that student-athletes receive not only need-based financial aid but could also receive funds exceeding tuition and fees if they ranked in the upper 25 percent of their high school graduating class or maintained a "B" average in college.

In 1965, the NCAA established its first-ever minimum academic standards for awarding athletically related financial aid through creation of a national standard requiring prospective student-athletes to achieve a predicted first-year college GPA of at least 1.6 (on a 4.0 scale) before they could receive athletically related aid. In 1973, the membership voted to repeal the 1.600 Rule, and then opted to replace it with a weaker version, the 2.0 Rule, which required that student-athletes who have graduated from high school with a 2.0 accumulative sixth-, seventh-, or eighth-semester GPA (based on a maximum 4.0 scale), regardless of course content and test scores, be deemed eligible for participation and athletically related aid.

The relaxing of standards led to renewed criticisms of athlete educational exploitation by certain schools. Concerns over low graduation rates motivated school presidents to take a leadership role in the issue. In 1983, the membership passed Proposition 48, which retained the concept of the 2.0 GPA eligibility floor but stipulated that the GPA would be computed from coursework in a core curriculum of at least 11 academic courses, as well as a 700 combined score on the SAT verbal and math sections or a 15 composite on the ACT. Many critics decried the plan because it was feared that the system would disproportionately harm African-American prospects.

At present, the major rules governing post-enrollment Division I academic eligibility include that student-athletes must be enrolled in at least a minimum full-time program of studies leading to a baccalaureate or equivalent degree as defined by the institution, which shall be not less than 12 semester or quarter hours, that a student-athlete shall earn at least 75 percent of the minimum semester or quarter hours required for progress toward a degree during the regular academic year, with no more than 25 percent allowed to be taken during summer terms, and that upon entering his or her third year, a GPA equaling 95 percent is required (a 1.95 if a 2.0 is required), and entering his or her fourth and subsequent year, a GPA equaling 100 percent is required (a 2.0 if a 2.0 is required). The general principle governing eligibility of students transferring to Division I and Division II institutions is that a student is required to complete one full academic year of residence before being eligible to compete, unless he or she satisfies one of a number of requirements or qualifies for one of a number of exceptions or waivers.

A key recent development relating to academic issues is the NCAA's creation of the Academic Progress Rate system, which determines which programs at which schools have been failing in their educatory missions, and penalizes them accordingly with a loss of GIAs and bans on post-season play.

An additional development has been the emergence of dozens of academically bogus "schools" that have not been accredited by the appropriate state education oversight organizations. Players have chosen to attend these schools so they will be deemed academically eligible to compete in college, as these "schools" allow them to do so with little or no work, in bogus courses. In 2007, the NCAA Division I Board passed legislation limiting to one the number of core courses that could be counted toward the required initial eligibility total after a prospect's fourth year after entering high school. Many who are familiar with this legislation note that junior college programs will benefit from the new rules. They noted that many such programs had lacked talent over the past decade as students pursued additional years in high school to obtain a Division I grant-in-aid offer contingent on their initial eligibility certification, and not lose two years of Division I eligibility.

PRACTITIONER perspective:

PHYLLIS LABAW, Associate Director of Athletics–Student Services,
Georgia Tech Athletic Association

Phyllis LaBaw oversees the academic support services and Total Person Program for the more than 350 student-athletes at Georgia Tech. She was named Georgia Tech's Associate Director of Athletics in April 2005 after working at the University of South Florida, where she served as Associate Athletic Director for Academic Support and Student-Athlete Development. She had been a member of the athletics staff at South Florida since 1994, where she oversaw academic support services for more than 400 student-athletes in 18 NCAA-sponsored sports and was involved in numerous other administrative duties. In 2000, LaBaw was awarded the Lan Hewlett Award from the National Association of Academic Advisors for Athletics, recognizing outstanding service in academic advising and athletics administration. LaBaw earned degrees in Finance and Psychology from the University of South Florida and is pursuing a Ph.D. in Psychology.

LaBaw is also responsible for managing efforts at Georgia Tech's Hearn Academic Center, where the staff is vested with the responsibility of monitoring, supporting, and assisting student-athletes through their pursuit of degree programs. The academic advisors are responsible for overall coordination of internal policies for study hall and tutoring. The student-athletes are responsible for course selection, registration, and satisfactory progress toward a degree. An Academic Coaching Program provides an additional layer of educational support and structure to student-athletes by establishing methods and techniques for managing their studies. The services offered are designed to aid student-athletes during their transition from high school to college.

The authors interviewed Ms. LaBaw to learn more about the role of academic support within a Division I athletic department. Cindy Moore, who previously served as Associate Director of Academics at Georgia Tech, also contributed to the content of these responses.

Q: *In the late 1980s, the NCAA passed initial academic eligibility legislation for financial aid, practice, and competition. Are such rules governing freshmen eligibility still necessary?*

A: Freshmen eligibility requirements continue to be necessary today to regulate the college preparatory curriculums for prospective student-athletes and to ensure that the courses they take will potentially prepare them for university-level coursework. However, future efforts may need to continue to focus on verifying the rigors of course content among high school and prep schools, as well as those who are home-schooled. The NCAA has historically taken a strong stance on evaluating the transcripts and approving courses and graduation requirements of international prospective student-athletes, and for the same reason, our domestic transcripts and secondary school curriculum may have to come under greater and equivalent purview. With the increase in the "high school powerhouses" (with Nike sponsorships to match), the NCAA Eligibility Center may have to review and reevaluate the standards of evaluating domestic academic courses and graduation requirements for prospective student-athletes.

Occasionally some critics of initial eligibility legislation propose that instead of the current system, all first-year student-athletes should be barred from competition while they adjust to the academic demands of college life. What's your reaction to such a proposal?

I adamantly oppose the suggestion that first-year student-athletes should be barred from competition while adjusting to the academic demands of college life. Creating a "cookie cutter" college experience for student-athletes is an inherent problem facing many institutions. By this, I mean that each student-athlete, as well as each sport, cannot dictate a "one size fits all" model to academics and adjustments. Instead, individual student-athletes and each sport must be administered uniquely. Making mass generalizations regarding the student-athlete population is problematic on many levels. Halting athletic participation simply delays an inevitable situation for student-athletes who must learn to balance academics and athletic participation.

In this chapter we discuss some of the NCAA's most recent legislative efforts to deal with low graduation rates in some sports. What is noteworthy of these efforts, and do you expect that these moves will facilitate the intended result?

The most noteworthy of the legislative efforts to deal with graduation rates is that of the APR. It is positive in that a real-time rate of retention and eligibility has been brought to the forefront. However, most coaches and administration are more concerned about the short-term impact, that of scholarship reduction versus "best practices" for truly increasing graduation among their teams. I strongly recommend that member institutions formulate an APR Support staff whose mission is to educate academic services staff, student-athletes, coaches, and administrators. Programs should also instill a "professional athlete" preparation program into their APR Support efforts, whose goal is to guide this group in maintaining eligibility as well as providing a host of additional resources, such as dealing with finances, communications, agents, and so on.

This APR Support staff would serve as an ombudsman and focus much of its time on those individuals who are significantly likely to continue in professional athletic careers (baseball, basketball, football) and educate this population on financial planning, agents, and degree completion. Likewise, a member of the APR staff could also educate and mentor those who are post-eligibility status and likewise need guidance and attention regarding degree completion, career networking, and career placement. These functions, of course, would extend beyond that offered through most life skills programs.

Some faculty critics of these new graduation-rate rules comment that they will be subject to pressure to give better grades to student-athletes. There have been cases of such pressures at several schools in the recent past. How would you address this concern on your campus?

The concern of pressuring faculty as it relates to grades is an institutional issue that must first be addressed within athletic department academic support units. Generally, such "pressures" are initiated through support staff seeking "information" on student statuses. Educating and professionalizing the academic staff on compiling information and serving as an advocate for the athlete with integrity and within ethical boundaries must be core to the mission of the academic and athletic unit. In addition, enlisting support and opening lines of communication in conjunction with the Faculty Athletic Representative, as well as eliminating any communication between coaching staffs, graduate assistants, and other representatives from the department to faculty, is critical. Professional representatives from the academic support staff should be the only individuals who communicate with faculty regarding academic progress and referral. Continuous and comprehensive education for the academic staff regarding expectations and procedures should also take place, particularly with new advising, study hall, and tutorial changes each semester.

Another criticism of student-athlete academic performance is that many are encouraged to enroll in course and degree programs that are viewed as less than rigorous. How does one in your position deal with the temptations for the Georgia Tech athletic department to act in a similar manner?

Dealing with the criticisms surrounding courses or degree programs that are "less rigorous" involves several strategies. First, every course offering, as well as every degree program, must promote and maintain the high academic standards that reflect the overall mission of the institution. This strategy extends beyond the efforts of academic support units. Secondly, the students (as well as critics of such) must be educated on what can be reasonably attained given the academic history of the student and the athletic demands of the sport. For example, some majors require extensive lab time, studio time, rotation and/or rotation time in hospital or clinics. Many of the requirements take place in the afternoon and directly conflict with practice and competition schedules.

Like all students, student-athletes must consider all of the program requirements and choose what is feasible given all of their interests. For academic staffs, it should not be their role to persuade a student-athlete with regard to degree programs. Instead, requiring the student-athlete to visit with academic program directors and advisors so program requirements and pre-requisites can be outlined is critical to allowing the student-athlete to make an informed decision as it relates to degree interest.

If you were empowered to change any aspect of the student-athlete experience at Georgia Tech that would substantially improve their academic performance, what would you do?

Several initiatives could be employed to enhance the academic experience and performance of student-athletes. First, lobbying for NCAA legislative change with regard to full-time enrollment during the season of competition should be considered. Given the amount of time required both athletically and academically compromises the student-athletes' college experience and creates an environment that promotes negative outcomes such as depression, academic dishonesty, and apathy.

Second, continuous efforts to mainstream student-athletes with the general student population are also critical to their preparedness for their lives after college and after athletics.

Third, student-athletes who have graduated from their institutions, yet still have a season of eligibility remaining, should have the opportunity to enroll in a full-time community service hours or full-time internship hours related to their degree if they opt not to pursue graduate studies or a second degree program. This would benefit the institutional and neighboring communities and/or prepare them for work upon completion of their athletic eligibility and avoid the unintended reality of enrolling in and being financially liable for courses in which there is no interest.

Fourth, athletic departments should enhance positive ways to reinforce academic successes (large and small) for all student-athletes. Under the premise that "no one outgrows the need for positive reinforcement," departments may want to look at a shift from focusing too heavily on the punitive stance of dishonesty and missed classes, and spend at least equal time positively reinforcing the large percentage of student-athletes who meet their academic challenges daily.

questions TO CONSIDER

1. Are the factors that influenced the formation and evolution of initial eligibility still an issue for athletic departments? Why or why not?

2. How about for continuing eligibility? Why or why not?

3. Based on your responses to the previous two questions, how might you suggest changes to the processes that assess both initial and continuing eligibility that would serve to improve the system?

4. Should the NCAA take a greater role in controlling the admissions processes of individual schools to ensure more uniformity in the academic preparedness of intercollegiate athletics participants? Why or why not?

references

Academic Standards time-line, 1890–1994. (1994). Overland Park, KS: NCAA.

Ashburn, E. (2007, July 6). To increase enrollment, community colleges add more sports. *Chronicle of Higher Education*, pp. A31–32.

Bok, D. (1985). Presidents need power within the NCAA to preserve academic standards and institutional integrity. In D. Chu, J.O. Savage, & B.J. Becker (Eds.), *Sport and higher education* (pp. 207–210). Champaign, IL: Human Kinetics.

Bombardieri, M., & Blaudschun, M. (2005, March 1). NCAA teams may face sanctions. *Boston Globe*, pp. A1, A9.

Brubacher, J.S., & Rudy, W. (1976). *Higher education in transition: A history of American colleges and universities 1636–1976.* New York: Harper and Row.

Byers, W., with Hammer, C. (1995). *Unsportsmanlike conduct: Exploiting college athletes.* Ann Arbor, University of Michigan Press.

Carey, J. (2006, June 28). Baseball's academics scrutinized. *USA Today*, p. 7C.

Carey, J. (2007, April 27). NCAA targets academic in baseball. *USA Today*, p. 11C.

Falla, J. (1981). *NCAA: Voice of college sports.* Shawnee Mission, KS: National Collegiate Athletic Association.

Fleisher, A.A., Goff, B.L., & Tollison, R.D. (1992). *The National Collegiate Athletic Association: A study in cartel behavior.* Chicago: University of Chicago Press.

Gurney, G.S., & Weber, J.C. (2008, October 24). A better way to measure coaches' wins and losses. *Chronicle of Higher Education*, p. A34.

Helman, J.W. (1989). *A history of American intercollegiate academic eligibility: Educational compromises to competitive interests.* Unpublished doctoral dissertation, Pennsylvania State University.

Lawrence, P.L. (1987). *Unsportsmanlike conduct: The National Collegiate Athletic Association and the business of college football.* New York: Praeger Publishers.

McCormack, E. (2006, July 7). A classroom comeback. *Chronicle of Higher Education*, pp. A37, A39.

Morris, W. (1992). *The courting of Marcus Dupree* (Rev. ed.). Jackson, University of Mississippi Press.

Mott, R.D. (1995, January 4). The 100-year debate. *NCAA News supplement: 89th convention issue*, pp. 1, 10–11.

NCAA Rules Against North Carolina Prep School. (2008, September 15). Associated Press.

New "triple option" may be submitted. (1978, June 1), *NCAA News*, p. 4. Accessed September 17, 2008, from: http://nbcsports.msnbc.com.

'90 Convention will get Legislation to Postpone Initial-Eligibility Changes. (1989, January 25). *NCAA News*, pp. 1–2.

1989 NCAA Convention Proceedings. (1989). Mission, KS: NCAA.

Oberlander, S. (1989, January 25). New NCAA rule on aid stirs emotional protest; repeal seen possible. *Chronicle of Higher Education*, pp. A1, A36.

Opinions Out Loud. (1977, May 15). *NCAA News*, 14 (7), p. 2.

Pay for College Athletes Proposed by Educators. (1982, June 9). *New York Times*, p. D22.

Pennington, B. (2004, April 29). N.C.A.A. set to put teeth in academic guidelines. *New York Times*, pp. C17-18.

Pennington, B. (2008, March 11). Baseball's tryout process is threatened by new rules. *New York Times*, p. C14.

Powell, R.A. (2007, April 22). Tennis in a parking lot. *New York Times Education Life*, pp. 4A-26–28.

Proceedings of the 77th annual convention of the National Collegiate Athletic Association (1983). Mission, KS: National Collegiate Athletic Association.

Rhoden, W.C. (1989, January 21). Thompson returns as N.C.A.A. acts to delay rule. *New York Times*, p. A23.

Rudolph, F. (1990). *The American College and University: A History*. Athens, GA: University of Georgia Press.

Sack, A.L., & Staurowsky, E.J. (1998). *College athletes for hire: The evolution and legacy of the NCAA's amateur myth*. Westport, CT: Praeger.

Sander, L. (2008, October 24). Athletes' graduation rates are higher than ever, NCAA data show. *Chronicle of Higher Education*, p. A22.

Schmidt, R. (2007). *Shaping college football: The transformation of an American sport*. Syracuse, NY: Syracuse University Press.

Schuster, R. (1989, January 18). Thompson won't budge; NCAA could. *USA Today*, p. 1C.

Smith, R.A. (1988). *Sports and freedom: The rise of big-time college athletics*. New York: Oxford University Press.

Sperber, M. (1998). *Onward to victory: The crises that shaped college sports*. New York: Henry Holt.

Thamel, P. (2006a, February 26). Schools, with few classes, build hoop dreams. *New York Times*, pp. A1, B18–19.

Thamel, P. (2006b, July 6). Oak Hill officials upset with N.C.A.A. listing. *New York Times*, p. C18.

Thamel, P. (2007a, May 1). Some prep schools believe N.C.A.A. rules go too far. *New York Times*, p. A29.

Thamel, P. (2007b, May 3). N.C.A.A. looking ahead on poor academic progress. *New York Times*, p. C18.

Thamel, P. (2008, May 7). Smaller programs hit hard in N.C.A.A. academic report. *New York Times*, p. C18.

Thamel, P. & Wilson, D. (2005, November 27). Poor grades aside, top athletes get to college on $399 diploma. *New York Times*, pp. A1, A9.

Thelin, J. (1996). *Games colleges play: Scandal and reform in intercollegiate athletics*. Baltimore, Johns Hopkins University Press.

Thompson to walk in protest of NCAA. (1989, January 14). *Boston Herald*, p. 69.

2007–2008 NCAA Division I Manual. (2007). Indianapolis: NCAA.

2007–2008 NCAA Division II Manual. (2007). Indianapolis: NCAA.

2007–2008 NCAA Division III Manual. (2007). Indianapolis: NCAA.

2008–2009 NCAA Division I Manual. (2008). Indianapolis, IN: National Collegiate Athletic Association.

2008–2009 NCAA Division II Manual. (2008). Indianapolis, IN: National Collegiate Athletic Association.

2008–2009 NCAA Division III Manual. (2008). Indianapolis, IN: National Collegiate Athletic Association.

Weaver, Jr., W. (1989, January 14). Thompson to leave bench in protest on scholarships. *New York Times*, p. 45.

Wieberg, S. (1989, October 19). Schultz: Prop 42 to change. *USA Today*, p. 5C.

Wieberg, S. (2005a, January 5). New academic rules challenge programs. *USA Today*, p. 6C.

Wieberg, S. (2005b, March 1). Academic progress rates analyzed. *USA Today*, p. 7C.

Wieberg, S. (2005c, March 1). Administrators, coaches absorb results, take aim at new standard. *USA Today*, p. 7C.

Wieberg, S. (2007a, May 3). Poor-grade penalties stiff. *USA Today*, p. 12C.

Wieberg, S. (2007b, May 22). NCAA tightens rules over player transfers. *USA Today*, p. 2C.

Wieberg, S. (2008, November 12). Transfers' academics on radar for NCAA. *USA Today*, p. 6C.

Wilson, D. (2005, December 24). School that gave easy grades to athletes is closing. *New York Times*, pp. B15, B17.

Wolverton, B. (2007, May 11). NCAA ruling on preparatory schools could send more athletes to junior colleges. *Chronicle of Higher Education*, p. A48.

Wolverton, B. (2008, September 5). Spending plenty so athletes can make the grade. *Chronicle of Higher Education*, pp. A1, A19–A23.

Student-athlete well-being

10

Key concepts to keep in mind as you read the chapter:

- The factors that define student-athlete status.

- The key issues that impact the student-athlete experience.

- Structure and role of the Student-Athlete Advisory Committee at the institutional and national levels.

Introduction

We learned in Chapter 2 that the NAIA's purpose is "to promote the education and development of students through intercollegiate athletic participation" (About the NAIA, 2005, p. 1). We also learned that one of the purposes of the NCAA is "to initiate, stimulate and improve intercollegiate athletics programs for student-athletes and to promote and develop educational leadership, physical fitness, athletics excellence and athletics participation as a recreational pursuit" (*2008–09 NCAA Division I Manual*, 2008, p. 1). These associations clearly are stating that intercollegiate athletic programs should be operated for the benefit of participating student-athletes. As a result, it stands to reason that intercollegiate athletic managers should be mindful of what is best for their student-athletes when performing their duties.

STUDENT-ATHLETE DEFINED

What about this term "student-athlete"? The NCAA created the term in the 1950s to convey the message that college athletes were not solely focused on athletic pursuits. Economist Andrew Zimbalist (1999) wrote that former NCAA Executive Director Walter Byers coined the term to assist NCAA member schools in their fight against workers' compensation insurance claims against injured football players. Others found the term to be specious. Former University of Maryland basketball standout and former U.S. Congressman Tom McMillan commented, "We do not hear equivalent terms such as student-artist or student-musician because art and music do not rival athletics for control of our institutions of learning" (Rushin, 2007, p. 4). This broaches again the familiar topic of what constitutes the appropriate role of intercollegiate athletics on American campuses. At all levels in all associations, approximately half a million student-athletes are participating in intercollegiate athletics.

What qualifies a student to become a student-athlete? To be eligible in Division I and II, prospects must meet certain academic criteria to compete both as a first-year student and as they continue through school (see Chapter 9). Academic requirements for student-athletes at other levels are somewhat less proscribed, and individual schools are allowed to set some criteria. In addition, the NCAA requires that student-athletes be amateurs. Under Bylaw 12.02.3 of the *Division I Manual*, a professional athlete is defined as "one who receives any kind of payment, directly or indirectly, for athletics participation except as permitted by governing legislation of the Association" (*2008–09 NCAA Division I Manual*, 2008, p. 61). A basic purpose of the NCAA is to maintain a clear demarcation between intercollegiate athletics and professional sport. In support of this premise, NCAA legislation dictates that student-athletes lose their amateur status and are deemed ineligible in a sport if they take part in any of the actions listed in Exhibit 10.1.

| Actions leading to loss of amateur status under Bylaw 12.1.2. | EXHIBIT | 10.1 |

- Uses athletic skill (directly or indirectly) for pay in any form in that sport.
- Accepts a promise for pay even if such pay is to be received following completion of intercollegiate athletics participation.
- Signs a contract or commitment of any kind to play professional athletics, regardless of its legal enforceability or any consideration received.
- Receives, directly or indirectly, a salary, reimbursement or expenses or any other form of financial assistance from a professional sports organization based on athletics skill or participation, except as permitted by NCAA rules and regulations.
- Competes on any professional athletics team, even if no pay or remuneration for expenses was received.
- After full-time collegiate enrollment, enters into a professional draft.
- Enters into an agreement with an agent.

Source: 2008–09 NCAA Division I Manual, 2008, pp. 62–63.

Much of the remainder of amateurism legislation in the *Division I Manual* outlines the many prohibited forms of pay and related professional activities, and the allowable exceptions to these strictures, including grants from the U. S. Olympic Committee, and tryouts for professional teams under certain conditions. The bylaw also delineates the proper use of agents, which has often been a source of conflict for student-athletes and intercollegiate athletic managers. Further the bylaw states how athletic departments can use properly the images and likenesses of student-athletes in promotional and media materials so as to preserve amateur status—another thorny issue (*2008–09 NCAA Division I Manual*, 2008).

Even though the Association attempts to clarify the rules and rationale related to professionalism and amateurism, these interpretations have been tested in several instances. For example, amateurism legislation does not permit student-athletes to sign endorsement deals even though student-athletes are allowed to turn pro in one sport and receive a salary for it, and can remain an amateur and compete intercollegiately in another sport. In 1998, however, the NCAA permitted Tim Dwight, who later played in the NFL for several teams, to sign several endorsement deals before returning to the University of Iowa to compete in track in 1999.

The most notable case of late involved Jeremy Bloom, a professional moguls skier and erstwhile University of Colorado (CU) football player. In 2004, after a three-year dispute, the NCAA ruled that Bloom could not play football at Colorado because he had signed an endorsement deal that was apparently based on his skiing prowess. Bloom had finished ninth in the 2002 Salt Lake City Winter Olympics, after which he matriculated at Colorado and performed as the Buffaloes' top punter returner. In February 2004, Bloom had signed an endorsement deal with Equinox Fitness Clubs, a national chain of fitness clubs, as well as manufacturer of skiing equipment—in an effort, some argued, to dare the NCAA to rule him ineligible for football.

A CU spokesperson said the school supported Bloom's dispute with the NCAA because he was seeking funds to train for the 2006 Torino Winter Olympics, and because "skiers don't get (a salary) to cover their expenses. They have to do it through endorsement deals" (Klein, 2004, p. 1). A year earlier, Bloom had actively lobbied for states to pass laws similar to one approved in Nebraska in 2003 that permitted student-athletes to receive payments (Suggs, 2004a, 2004b).

After losing his initial NCAA appeal in May 2004, Bloom asked the Colorado District Court, and then the Colorado Court of Appeals, for a preliminary injunction to keep the NCAA from enforcing its endorsement ban, but the courts denied his request. On Bloom's behalf, CU then appealed to the NCAA's Student-Athlete Reinstatement Committee for redress, which was again denied. Chair of the panel, Carolayne Henry, associate commissioner of the Division I Mountain West Conference, explained in a written statement:

> Amateurism is the principle that separates college sports from professional sports. . . . The Bloom case is one of the few cases where the severity of the violation, the importance of the amateurism bylaw, and the level of culpability are so significant that reinstatement would have violated [the principle of amateurism]. (Suggs, 2004b, pp. 1–2)

Bloom qualified for and competed at the 2006 Winter Olympics, and won two World Cup season titles, but was later cut from the Philadelphia Eagles, which had selected him in the fifth round of the 2006 National Football League draft. In 2008, Bloom made another bid to make the NFL with the Pittsburgh Steelers but was cut in preseason. In 2009, he founded a charitable organization, Wish of a Lifetime, which provides services to low-income senior citizens (Former World Cup, 2008; Roberts, 2009).

MANAGEMENT ISSUES AND STUDENT-ATHLETES

What is clear from the Bloom decision is that the NCAA is adamant about preserving the amateur status of student-athletes. Because of this, the potential for paying student-athletes is equally unlikely. But other elements that impact the lives of student-athletes are potentially more important for intercollegiate athletic managers to understand. We will highlight a few key issues that influence student-athletes, and how these issues impact the management of intercollegiate athletic departments.

Time demands

Consider the daily schedule of Stephanie Campbell, a field hockey player at Villanova University, a private Catholic institution with just over 6,000 undergraduates located in suburban Philadelphia, and member of the Division I Big East conference. She began classes at 7 A.M. each day so she could be in the locker room by noon for four hours of weightlifting and on-field practice. Travel to away games forced her to miss classes and exams, and most evenings she had mandatory team meetings, study halls, and weekend practices. She spent weekend nights in her room trying to catch up on sleep.

During her first year, Campbell struggled with the time demands, until her mother put the experience in perspective, telling her: "Villanova costs more than $40,000 a year to attend. They're paying you $19,000 to play field hockey. At your age, there's no one out there anywhere who is going to pay you that kind of money to do anything. And that's how you have to look at this: It's a job, but it's a great job" (Pennington, 2008a, pp. C15, C18). Campbell kept at it for four years, became a team captain as a senior, majored in marketing, and graduated in 2008. The spring of her senior year, she admitted: "Receiving an athletic scholarship is a wonderful thing, but most of us only know what we're getting, not what we're getting into. . . . I know a lot of people who would have loved to trade places with me. But I'd still say Division I athletics is not meant for everybody. Nobody tells you that" (Pennington, 2008a, pp. C15, C18).

Tim Poydenis, a baseball player at Villanova, echoed Campbell's sentiments:

> You know, maybe if you're a scholarship football player at Oklahoma, everything is taken care of for you. But most of us are non-revenue-sport athletes who have to do our own fundraising just to pay for basics like sweat pants and batting gloves. . . . We love what we do, and it is worth it, but everyone thinks every college athlete is on a pampered full ride. The truth is a lot of us are getting $4,000 and working our butts off for it. (Pennington, 2008a, pp. C15, C18)

These experiences are the rule, not the exception. Most D-I student-athletes report that they devote at least four hours a day to their sport, not counting injury treatment, games or travel, and classes scheduled in the mornings to leave time each afternoon for practices and games. Then there are often team dinners and mandatory meetings and study halls after that. Joe Taylor, a Villanova soccer player, describes the problems faced next: "You come back to your dorm room ready to crash, but you've got homework or maybe a test the next morning. The rest of the dorm is starting to get a little rowdy because those guys have all finished their homework. They might be getting ready to go out. A lot of them took a nap in the afternoon" (Pennington, 2008a, p. C18).

An NCAA study of 21,000 student-athletes supports these individual observations, with one in five noting that their sport participation has prevented them from choosing the academic major they wanted (Wolverton, 2008c). Division I football players reported spending almost 45 hours a week on activities related to their sport, with golfers, baseball players, and softball players reporting similar time spent, even though NCAA bylaws permit only 20 hours a week to be spent on in-season activities. Some school presidents and athletic managers admitted abuses in time demands. John Roush, president of Centre College, a private school with 1,200 undergraduates located in Danville, Kentucky, and a member of the Division III Southern Collegiate Athletic Conference said, "It's not just the time but the command of experience these coaches have. They dictate what kids do on their breaks, in the summer. In Division I sports, the time of these young men and women is owned by the coach who is under such pressure to win that it goes against reason" (Wolverton, 2008c, p. A23).

In response to these observations and findings, the NCAA's Committee on Academic Performance, which created the Academic Performance Rating system, has expressed an intent to look at the effect of time demands on student-athletes and whether student-athletes are clustering in certain majors. Whatever the findings of future studies, clearly for many student-athletes, participating in intercollegiate athletics means being a full-time student and a full-time athlete.

For some, the demands of participation that serve as a precursor to intercollegiate athletics can prove to be too much, as was the case with Elena DelleDonne, a top recruit for the women's basketball team at the University of Connecticut (UConn), a public school with 20,000 undergraduates located in Storrs, and a member of the Division I Big East Conference. The 6'5" DelleDonne was the most sought-after recruit in the nation coming out of high school in 2008 (she had received her first grant-in-aid offer when she was in 7th grade). DelleDonne was one of the finest high school athletes ever in the state of Delaware. She led her high school to four state basketball titles and one state volleyball championship, set the all-time state high school girls scoring record with 2,818 points, and established a national record for free-throw accuracy by converting 80 straight at one point. She was a five-time All-State basketball player, was named the 2007–08 National Player of the Year by the Naismith, McDonald's, and Gatorade foundations and *USA Today*, and was a two-time selection to the *Parade* All-American team (Former High School, 2009).

DelleDonne began taking classes at UConn in June 2008, but after only two days, she realized she was burned out on basketball, left UConn, and later transferred to the University of Delaware, a public school with 15,000 undergrads located in Newark (near her home) and a member of the Division I Colonial Athletic Association. There, she played volleyball, a sport she had played for the first time as a senior in high school (Longman, 2008). DelleDonne had initially set a goal to be the best female basketball player in the country and trained manically with this outcome in mind. She had been making strides to this end, with many calling her the next Candace Parker (the former University of Tennessee and later WNBA star). In explaining her decision to leave basketball, DelleDonne said, "I was sick of being unhappy. . . . It wasn't fun. It was like a job, and it was a job I wasn't getting paid for" (p. Y12). DelleDonne said she felt excited about volleyball games in a way she no longer did with basketball, and has noted new challenges with her current sport that she relishes (Longman, 2008).

There was also speculation that DelleDonne missed the connection with her older sister, Elizabeth, who was born deaf and blind and has cerebral palsy. Her father wondered whether Elena's decision to attend Delaware had less to do with basketball burnout than with homesickness, particularly the separation from Elizabeth. Comments from other coaches supported this notion, including the following from Stefanie Pemper, head women's hoop coach at the U. S. Naval Academy: "That was really the primary reason. When she talked about homesick, it was that. It was having that person out of her life. They have a great relationship, and I don't think Elena realized how much she would miss that relationship."

But after a year off from basketball and playing volleyball at Delaware, and after earning conference All-Rookie honors and leading the team in blocks (.96 per game) in that sport, the school announced that DelleDonne would join the school's hoop team. DelleDonne said: "I'm looking forward to playing again and joining my new teammates this upcoming season. I'm extremely excited to be competing in my home state and for Coach [Tim] Martin. I really enjoyed playing volleyball this past fall but found myself missing basketball. Basketball has been an important part of my life, and I realized that it's my first love and my passion" (Former High School, 2009, p. 1). Her return to basketball was auspicious, as she averaged 26.7 points and 8.8 rebounds a game and was named all-conference player of the year.

But some student-athletes don't start or even receive much, if any, playing time. What do they get out of the intercollegiate athletic experience? They work just as hard, get up just as early, and deal with all the same time demands. Consider the case of Stephen Duckett and Joe Hughes, former members of the perennially strong men's basketball team at Xavier University, a private Catholic, Jesuit-affiliated school with 4,000 undergrads located in Cincinnati, Ohio, and a member of the Division I Atlantic 10 Conference. Both Duckett and Hughes had been good high school players, but neither received any Division I grant-in-aid offers, so they became "walk-ons" at Xavier, meaning that they received no athletically related aid. And from their first practice at Xavier, they knew why. Said Duckett: "Physically, there was no comparison. It was like, wow, I couldn't believe their speed and size. I'm looking at myself, 6-foot-4, 190 pounds. I'm like, What am *I* gonna do?" [author's emphasis] (Wolverton, 2008d, pp. A1, A7). What they do is serve as subjects to prepare their teammates for games and spend time watching game films of opponents and trying to mimic them in practice. "You have to know your role," said Duckett. "You can't come in here thinking you're gonna be a big shot."

During games, their job is simple. "Keep morale high," said Hughes. "Make some noise." At timeouts they're the first off the bench to encourage teammates, and scream and cheer throughout the game. They get to play only when, according to Hughes, "we're beating the crap out of some team" (Wolverton, 2008d, pp. A1, A7). And for this privilege, they still have the same time demands and expectations as their more celebrated teammates. But there is some small measure of glory for Duckett and Hughes. Late in games, if Xavier has a big lead, fans will chant their names, hoping they will get into the game, and erupt in cheers when they do. And if they don't get in the game? It's OK, says Hughes. "We had the best seats in the house" (p. A7).

Academic impacts

The time demands inherent in intercollegiate athletics significantly influence the undergraduate experiences of student-athletes. Consider the efforts facing football student-athletes at Rutgers University, a public school with 39,000 undergraduates located in New Brunswick, New Jersey, and a member of the Division I Big East Conference. They had to travel to Florida during their fall semester exam period to take on the University of Central Florida in the St. Petersburg Bowl, and they had to take their exams on the road while preparing for the game—played on December 19, only two weeks after Rutgers' last regular season game. Rutgers head coach Greg Schiano expressed disappointment about the bowl appearance, in large part because the team would have less practice time. Although some players expressed frustration about the timing of the game and the increased pressure of taking exams and practicing, frosh wide receiver Mark Harrison put it this way: "I knew what I was getting into when I came here. You've got to be self-disciplined. Lot of late nights" (Caldwell, 2009, p. B14).

Also, for many Division I student-athletes, intercollegiate athletic participation influences their choice of academic major. According to former Student Athletic Advisory Council head Dylan Malagrino of Syracuse University, "Coaches and academic administrators in the athletic department might be strongly encouraging students to take easier majors or to choose a major and never switch" (Upton & Novak, 2008, p. 1). Also multiple sources have suggested that the NCAA's new Academic Progress Rate system of assessing student-athletes' progress toward a degree, which penalizes programs with low scores, has served to encourage coaches and academic advisors to push student-athletes toward less demanding major programs.

Data collected by multiple sources seem to support Malagrino's claim. Researchers state that if more than 25 percent of a team is in the same major, it constitutes a non-random cluster, regardless of the size of the team. One study published in *USA Today* (Degrees of Responsibility, 2008) reviewed the rosters of nearly 600 Division I teams and determined that 83 percent of the teams had at least one cluster, one-third of the 235 clusters included at least 50 percent of the team's roster, and one-third of the schools had two or more teams clustering in the same major program. For example, in 2007–08, at 17 of the top 25-ranked Bowl Subdivision football teams, at least 25 percent of the juniors and seniors receiving athletic aid had clustered in the same major, including:

- University of Michigan: 75.6 percent in general studies
- Virginia Polytechnic Institute: 63.3 percent in apparel, housing, and resource management
- University of Southern California: 57.9 percent in sociology
- West Virginia University: 40.5 percent in athletic coaching education
- University of Cincinnati: 35.9 percent in criminal justice
- Louisiana State University: 33.3 percent majoring in interdisciplinary studies
- University of Missouri: 31.7 percent in hotel and restaurant management

But is this clustering a concern? According to Walter Harrison, president of the University of Hartford and chair of the Division I Committee on Academic performance—not necessarily. *USA Today*'s study revealed two clusters of softball players in rigorous biology programs, which is rare given that such programs demand lab courses that can infringe on practice time. Harrison believes that the 25 percent threshold may be too low and suggests that 40 to 50 percent would be "significant, in my opinion" (Steeg, Upton, Bohn, & Berkowitz, 2008, p. 1A), and that monitoring the appropriateness of a major is an issue for the school's accrediting agency.

The feedback from individual student-athletes seems to support Central Florida's Harrison. Steven Cline, a two-year starting defensive lineman at Kansas State University, a public school with 19,000 undergraduates located in Manhattan and a member of the Division I Big 12 Conference, graduated in 2008 with credits toward a master's degree in college student personnel. This major according to the school, is designed to prepare students to work at "college student affairs agencies." Cline had this to say about his academic experience:

> The whole time I was at Kansas State, I felt stuck—stuck in football, stuck in my major. . . . The athletics academic advisor said, "This is what everybody is doing. It's the easiest major." . . . Now I look back and say, "Well, what did I really go to college for? Crap classes you won't use for the rest of your life?" . . . I was majoring in football. . . . It was a stupid effort on my part. I wouldn't advise any other athlete to do that. I'd tell them to choose a career—a real career for their life after football and work toward it. (Steeg, Upton, Bohn, and Berkowitz, 2008, p. 2A)

After graduation, Cline chose not to pursue the master's program in which he had earned credits but, instead, to work in construction to save money to return to school and study to become a veterinarian (Steeg, Upton, Bohn, & Berkowitz, 2008).

Another perspective is offered by C.J. Schlatter, a former All-American wrestler at the University of Minnesota, a public school with 29,000 undergraduates located in Minneapolis and a member of the Division I Big Ten Conference. Schlatter majored in nursing even though he claims that some of his coaches suggested that he take an "easier" major so he could "breeze through" to an undergraduate degree. Minnesota wrestling coach J Robinson defends this approach, noting that the "athletic door is open only a certain time" (McCarthy & Berkowitz, 2008, p. 7C). Schlatter, who graduated in 2008, was kidded by teammates for his choice of major, but upon graduation took a nursing job at a Minnesota hospital at a annual salary of $55,000. Some of his former teammates were in shock, says Schlatter. "Some of them are scrambling, he said. They have a four-year degree, but no job, nothing to do with it" (McCarthy & Berkowitz, 2008, p. 7C).

Some have voiced concerns that the creation of "sport-focused" majors such as sport management, leisure studies, and athletic administration has been in part to create easy academic havens for student-athletes. But Scott Kretchmar, a professor of exercise and sport science at Pennsylvania State University, disputes this, noting: "To me, a career related to sports is very viable, just like in music. . . . I think there's a lot of bias against so-called non-intellectual majors—theater, music, dance (physical education), kinesiology—majors that don't rely so much on words and numbers" (McCarthy & Berkowitz, 2008, p. 7C). Ultimately, individual schools decide what programs and degrees to offer, and administrators at these schools are responsible for gauging the academic rigor and professional utility of these programs to best serve all their students.

Disputes with coaches

Many athletes who have participated in interscholastic or intercollegiate athletics have had an instance in which they and their coach didn't see eye-to-eye on an issue. Maybe it was play-calling, playing time, the expectations of their parents, or some other topic. In most cases, coaches and players can resolve such conflicts. When a resolution is not forthcoming, however, some student-athletes choose to leave a team and terminate their participation. In some instances, however, student-athletes claim that they are forced off teams by coaches.

Such a situation was alleged in 2008, when Andrew Giuliani, son of former New York City mayor and past presidential hopeful Rudy Giuliani, filed a lawsuit in federal court accusing Duke University, a private school with 6,200 undergraduates located in Durham, North Carolina, and a member of the Division I Atlantic Coast Conference, of bad faith by recruiting him to play golf at the school and then taking steps to remove him from the team (Cowan, 2008). In his suit, Giuliani asked for damages and the right to use the school's state-of-the-art golf training center for the rest of his life—something he claims was promised to him during the recruiting process by the school's longtime former coach, Rod Myers, who died of cancer in 2007. Giuliani also admits in the suit that he may have misbehaved early in the year when, during an argument, he threw an apple in the face of a teammate, threw two clubs (breaking one), and drove his car dangerously in a parking lot. While admitting these actions, he claimed they were nothing when compared to the "bizarre" treatment he received from the school's new golf coach, O.D. Vincent III, who previously had been head coach at UCLA.

The lawsuit describes "mind games" and a lack of due process, because after the above incidents, he was told he was no longer eligible to play, and claims that the only way he would be able to stay on the team was if he were to persuade each of his teammates to write to the coach to indicate and explain their willingness to keep Giuliani on the team. Giuliani claimed this demand was impossible, as Vincent planned to shrink the size of the team, which, as a result, pitted one teammate against another in competition for a spot. Five of his teammates e-mailed Giuliani and told him they did not want him on the team. In six rounds during the previous season, Giuliani averaged a score of 74.5 per round, putting him in the bottom half of the 14-man squad. After being cut, Giuliani did not choose to transfer from Duke to another school. In response, school administrators released a brief statement that read: "Duke's coaches and student athletes are held to the highest standards. . . . We intend to vigorously defend this lawsuit" (Cowan, 2008, p. C11).

In December 2008, halfway through his second season as head coach, Vincent resigned and took a position as senior associate athletic director at the University of Washington, his alma mater. Vincent and Duke officials claimed that the move had "nothing to do with the lawsuit" (p. 1). In May 2009, a federal magistrate judge in North Carolina found no evidence that any of the above alleged promises constituted a legally binding contract, and recommended dismissal of the case, which later occurred.

An additional example of the types of disputes between coaches and players occurred in 2006 at New Mexico State University, a public school with 13,400 undergraduates located in Las Cruces, and a member of the Division I Western Athletic Conference. Dismissed members of the football team brought a discrimination lawsuit against the school's president and board of trustees. The suit alleged that the three players, who were Muslim, were made to "feel like outcasts" by then head coach Hal Mumme, and were eventually kicked off the team because of their religious beliefs. The actions, the plaintiffs claimed, violated their constitutional rights, specifically the First Amendment and the Equal Protection Clause of the 14th Amendment and Title VI of the Civil Rights Act of 1964. The players, recruited by Mumme's predecessor, reported that when Mumme was hired in 2005 (after stints as head coach at Kentucky, Valdosta [Georgia] State, and Southeastern Louisiana), the coach "initiated a practice of having the players lead the Lord's Prayer after each practice and before each game" (Henig, 2006, p. A37). The claim also alleges that once Mumme found out about the players' religious affiliation, he treated them differently, banning two from attending a team event and repeatedly questioning the third about his thoughts about the terrorist group Al Qaeda. One player, Mu-Ammar Ali, had been a starting running back but was then demoted to fifth-string.

The players were eventually dismissed, according to the school, because they were "troublemakers," and the decision was based on performance and team rule violations. The New Mexico chapter of the American Civil Liberties Union filed the suit on behalf of the players. Peter Simonson, the chapter's executive director, stated that the case was "about a few university officials who took it upon themselves to assert . . . their narrow range of religious beliefs over the players" (Henig, 2006, p. A37). The case was settled in 2007, just days before it was scheduled to go to trial, with a cash settlement of $165,000 going to the players. The school did not admit to any wrongdoing, but Mumme was fired at the end of the 2008 season after compiling a four-year record of 11–38 (4–28 in conference games) (New Mexico, 2008).

case study 10.A

In 2009 Texas Tech University (TTU), a public school with 24,000 undergraduates located in Lubbock and a member of the Division I Big 12 Conference, suspended head football coach Mike Leach while it investigated complaints from a player and his family over how Leach treated player Adam James, son of former Southern Methodist and NFL standout Craig James, after a concussion. The case soon devolved into a dispute that seemed to be based on efforts by Leach to discipline James for behavioral issues, and the attempts by his father to influence the TTU coaching staff to get his son more playing time.

According to media reports, James was injured December 16. The next day, he was diagnosed with a concussion by team doctors. That day, James said Leach told trainers to put him in "the darkest place you can find," so he was sent to an equipment shed near the practice field, where a member of the athletic staff checked on James to make sure he did not lean against anything or sit on the floor. According to a media report, James spent two hours in the shed (the size of a one-car garage) filled with coolers, and that James was "caught" sitting down on one. All the coolers were removed, and the door to the shed was closed with James inside. James said Leach told him that if he came out, he would be kicked off the team.

Media reports indicated that Craig James called university officials to report the allegations on December 19. A university attorney interviewed him and his son the next day. Leach was then questioned, as were trainers, student trainers, and the doctor who examined Adam James. Leach was "begged to work something out to avoid a confrontation." The school's attorney then told Leach's attorney that the university required a letter of apology by noon December 28, but Leach did not submit one. One media report cited the comments of a person with knowledge of the investigation: "That's when they made the decision to suspend [Leach], thinking that would bring him to his senses" (Schad, 2009, p. 1). According to Leach's lawyer, a doctor who examined James supported Leach's actions. "He was not hurt by what happened in the equipment room," the lawyer said. "And [Leach] did not do anything to worsen the

situations, in fact, he put him in a safer environment by being inside" (Blaney, 2009, p. 1).

Leach's contract called for him to receive an $800,000 bonus if he were TTU's head coach on December 31, 2009, but also he would receive $400,000 a year per year left on the contract if fired without cause (through 2013). School officials questioned whether the bonus would be paid given the suspension (Blaney, 2009; Schad, 2009). The James family issued a public statement criticizing the school and the program for "actions and treatments not consistent with common sense rules for safety and health" (Texas Tech, 2009, p. B11). Leach's lawyer referred to Craig James as a "helicopter parent" who called his son's position coaches and was disgruntled about his son's playing time. One media report cited a person close to the events who claimed that James promised to compliment the coaches on the air if his son were to play more. ESPN reporters later obtained an e-mail in which TTU's inside wide receivers coach Lincoln Riley referred to James as "unusually lazy and entitled," and Riley said he had been worried about James's effect on the rest of the receivers because of "his weak and conceited attitude." In a separate e-mail to TTU AD Gerald Myers, Riley wrote: "Two practices before Adam James claimed he had a concussion, Coach Leach and I were forced to discipline him for poor effort from the previous practice and poor effort during the early drills of that day. This has been a common theme about Adam's work ethic and attitude during his entire career" (Schad, 2009, p. 1). In another media report, Leach and his staff warned the player that they would play voicemails left by James's father lobbying for more playing time in front of the entire team (Evans & Thamel, 2009).

Leach's attorney sought a temporary restraining order seeking to bar TTU from keeping him from coaching the team in its Valero Alamo Bowl matchup against Michigan State on January 2, 2010, in San Antonio. But minutes prior to the hearing on December 30 (scheduled for a courthouse in Lubbock that was packed with fans there to support Leach), TTU officials handed a letter to Leach's attorney, informing him that Leach was "terminated with cause effective immediately," because, in the school's judgment, he had "meant to demean, humiliate and punish the player" and "continuous acts of insubordination" (Leach Fired, 2009, p. 1; Evans & Thamel, 2009, p. B11). Leach claimed he was fired as a result of lingering anger on the part of the school relating to his contract negotiation earlier in the year, and stated that he planned to sue TTU for wrongful termination. Leach's record as head coach was 84–43, and he is the all-time winningest head coach at the school (Evans & Thamel, 2009).

questions for you to consider

1. There has been significant recent attention given to the issue of concussions at all levels of football. Why was this issue not part of the case outlined above?
2. Given that the TTU athletic department had hoped to avoid negative publicity in dealing with this case, how do you think the case will have resolved?

Injuries

Although injuries are an unavoidable part of any physical activity, treating them and paying for the costs associated with treatment can be problematic.

Medical coverage

You might assume that if an intercollegiate participant is injured during a game or contest, the costs associated with the treatment of and rehabilitation from the injury would naturally be paid for by the school providing the program. In 2005, the NCAA required member institutions to verify that all participants had health insurance before they were allowed to compete. In the wake of this action, some schools opted to pick up the costs of initial treating of all injuries, but others refuse to take on any costs for care and treatment. Many student-athletes have medical insurance through their parents' policies, but these plans often exclude varsity sports injuries, limit out-of-state treatment, or do not cover entire costs. Some colleges buy secondary policies to fill the gaps, although even these plans have holes. Only players who are hurt severely enough to require extensive care can opt for the NCAA's catastrophic insurance, but the coverage carries a $90,000 deductible (Peterson, 2009).

Some colleges provide medical cost coverage for their athletes. An example is Middlebury (Vermont) College, a private liberal arts school with 2,400 undergraduates and a member of the Division III New England Small College Athletic Conference, where all varsity athletes and students in club sports have accident insurance paid for by the college. Spalding University, a private Catholic school with 1,700 undergraduates located in Louisville, Kentucky, and a member of the Division III St. Louis Intercollegiate Athletic Conference, also pays for secondary coverage for athletes. "These young men and young women are representing your institution," said Charlie Just, Spalding's compliance director. "Ethically, I think it's the right thing to do" (Peterson, 2009, p. 1).

Some Division I schools also provide comprehensive coverage. The University of Iowa, a public school with 21,000 undergraduates located in Iowa City and a member of the Division I Big Ten Conference, provides among the most comprehensive coverage for varsity student-athletes. The school received 4,200 medical bills for student-athletes in 2008, paying $776,454, according to documents obtained through an Iowa Public Records Law request. The university has also begun paying for uninsured full-GIA student-athletes to enroll in the student health care offered on campus (Peterson, 2009).

Other students, however, are not so fortunate. Erin Knauer, a walk-on crew student-athlete at Colgate University (a private school with 2,750 undergraduates located in Hamilton, New York, and member of the Division I Patriot League), accrued $80,000 in medical bills after injuring her back and legs during training during her freshman year in 2007. Her symptoms were later diagnosed as postviral myositis, a muscular inflammation that can cause weakness and pain. Because Colgate officials deemed the condition an illness—not an athletic injury—they said financial responsibility fell to Knauer. According to Steve Chouinard, Colgate assistant athletic director, "There has to be some direct line from the injury to what she's being treated for" (Peterson, 2009, p. 1). Because of the way her condition was diagnosed, Knauer's insurance covered less than a third of the cost.

If Knauer had been treated the same way under the university's athletic insurance, she would have had full coverage after a $1,000 deductible. Instead, she had to use her student health policy, leaving her $55,000 in debt on the original $80,000 in bills. Knauer had some financial assistance and additional coverage from her family, but her father, a chemical engineer, twice lost his job and the accompanying insurance. As a result, Knauer worked two jobs to help meet her minimum monthly payments of $200 to $250. Even after paying off some of the debt and negotiating reduced fees with the hospital, she was still facing $7,000 to $8,000 in bills (Peterson, 2009).

In response to the above information, which appeared in the *New York Times* on July 15, 2009, Colgate AD David Roach wrote to the paper seeking to dispel the impression that his school didn't take care of its student-athletes:

> All injuries are handled by certified athletic trainers in Colgate's sports medicine office and are referred to medical specialists as needed. In addition to general health insurance required of all Colgate students, student-athletes are covered by a policy, paid for by the university, that ensures coverage of expenses incurred during participation in athletic events like a game, team practice, conditioning or weight training. (In-box, 2009, p.1)

Diagnosis and treatment

The risks of failing to diagnose injuries correctly and to provide the proper level of care can be costly for schools and athletic departments, as evidenced by the 2009 decision by LaSalle University, a private Catholic school in Philadelphia with 4,700 undergraduates and a member of the Division I Atlantic 10 Conference, to settle a lawsuit brought by Preston Pleveretes, a former football player. He claimed he had been improperly treated by the school's medical staff. After sustaining a concussion during a practice, Pleveretes was cleared to play, and he suffered a subsequent injury in a game against Duquesne University. The injury occurred when he lost consciousness momentarily after a hard block on a punt return. He regained consciousness, then collapsed into a coma from swelling of the brain, leaving him with speech impediments, memory loss, and other issues requiring 24-hour care.

LaSalle paid Pleveretes $7.5 million, but admitted no wrongdoing. The suit alleged that most of the immediate care and medical advice that Pleveretes received was from a student-health nurse rather than a trained expert in concussions, and that no proper neuropsychological testing was administered. LaSalle argued that Pleveretes hid his symptoms from school medical personnel and that he was treated by methods that were standard for the time. The NCAA requires no specific protocol for schools to follow regarding concussion management, although the NCAA's Committee on Competitive Sports recommended in 2009 that any student-athlete who loses consciousness or shows symptoms related to concussions refrain from participation for the rest of the day in which the symptoms occurred, and that participants remain on the sidelines until cleared by a doctor. LaSalle has since dropped its football program for reasons the school says were unrelated to this case (Schwarz, 2009a, 2009b; The N.C.A.A., 2009).

Club sports and the student-athlete experience

Nearly every topic and perspective discussed in this book relates to intercollegiate varsity-status athletics, but we cannot ignore the rapid proliferation of club-level programs on campuses across the country. For example, 20 years ago, a national club volleyball championship drew 20 teams and 206 male athletes; in 2008, the same championship hosted 258 teams and 2,806 participants in four men's divisions and two women's divisions. A national club soccer championship started in 1994 grew from 15 teams and 252 participants to 75 teams and 1,380 participants in 2008. A similar tennis tournament that began in 2000 with 11 teams and 80 participants drew 64 teams and 523 participants in 2008.

Club teams are also competing for championships in bass fishing, ballroom dancing, and Brazilian martial arts. In all, an estimated two million college students are participating in competitive club sports, and some programs are so popular that there are tryouts and waiting lists. This compares with 430,000 participants in programs governed by the NCAA and NAIA. One common explanation given for the boom in club sports is that, as a result of organized sports at the youth and school levels—involving 40 million at any given time—more students are leaving high school with extensive athletic interest and experience, but only 5 percent are good enough to make varsity college teams (Pennington, 2008b).

Most club team programs are overseen by campus student activities boards, but some are supervised by intercollegiate departments. Institutional funding may be as little as $500 or as much as $20,000, but typically amounts to a few thousand dollars. This requires participants to pay a fee, maybe as much as $1,000 for a sport such as ice hockey, and fundraising is common. Each sport has a national governing body that assists with functions such as scheduling and hosts a national tournament, and many require participants to maintain a 2.0 grade-point average (Pennington, 2008b).

Some club athletes also are a bit envious of the benefits that come with varsity competition, but are able to understand the positives that come from their more hardscrabble experiences. Said Betsy Pantazelos, a recent captain of the alpine ski team at Boston (Massachusetts) University, a private school with 17,000 undergraduates and a member of the Division I America East Conference: "It's easy to be jealous when you're watching the varsity kids board a nice coach bus as someone loads their equipment on for them" (Pennington, 2008b, p. B19).

What draws participants to these activities, since no financial aid accompanies participation, there are no crowds, and most of the organizing and funding is done by the participants themselves? David Gerstle, player-coach of Yale University's club water polo team, explains it this way: "I think it's a more collegial experience than the varsity team model. . . . It's a ton of work, but we do it because we take ownership of our team. . . . It's also sport for the love of sport" (In-box, 2008, p. 8-8). Yale had sponsored a varsity water polo team until 1991, when it dropped the sport, but student participants in other club sports at Yale criticize the school for what they call financial support that is

> worse than meager: Despite an endowment totaling more than $20 billion, Yale's Club Sports Office does not receive enough money to provide players with facilities, proper equipment, medical care, or safe transportation. . . . Women's and men's rugby spent the first days of their spring season picking shards of glass off their field that remained from the previous fall's varsity football tailgates. (In-box, 2008, p. 8-8)

Jim Giunta, executive director of the National Collegiate Wrestling Association, which hosted 70 club teams at its latest championship (up from 17 a decade ago), noted that this growth occurred after many schools dropped varsity wrestling programs in response to issues pertaining to gender equity (Pennington, 2008b). Eric Pearson, chairman of the College Sports Council, a national coalition of coaches, athletes, parents, and fans, underscores this point:

> The single biggest factor in the growth of club sports in college may be the stringent enforcement of Title IX. . . . The vast majority of college club teams consist of male athletes. . . . The sad truth is that, because of Title IX's gender quota restrictions, men's club teams that apply to become varsity are shut out. . . . In the Big 12 Conference, to cite one example, men's club soccer teams have been denied varsity status at every university, while their female counterparts enjoy full varsity sponsorship status. (In-box, 2008, p. 8-8)

Giunta adds this insight into club sport athlete: "They do it because they love their sport. . . . We don't have the prima donnas you see at the highest levels of college athletics" (Pennington, 2008b, pp. B11–B12).

Many club team athletes are also finding that the level fits their college experience well. Tiffany Villalba, a member of the Villanova women's club soccer team, which won the open division at the sport's national championship in 2007, describes it this way: "The club team fills a big gap between [varsity and intramurals]. It's not demanding, but it's not trivial" (Pennington, 2008b, p. B11).

Although varsity sport athletic departments usually have little oversight of club teams, they often must coordinate the shared use of practice and competition space. Nonetheless, Tim Selgo, AD at Grand Valley State University, a public school with 20,000 undergraduates located in Allendale, Michigan, and a member of the Division II Great Lakes Intercollegiate Athletic Conference, is a fan of club sports: "Hey, our women's rugby team beat Michigan State. That's a great source of pride" (Pennington, 2008b, p. B12).

The development of a club football program at the University of Vermont (UVM) a public school with an undergraduate population of about 10,000, located in Burlington and a member of the Division I America East Conference, outlines the managerial experiences to be gained by students involved in the endeavor. UVM dropped varsity football in 1974 because of issues of competitiveness with foes that comprised the now-defunct Yankee Conference. But when

Doug DeLuca came to the school in 2006, he wanted a chance to continue his career, so he approached school administrators about starting a club program. He got their permission to use the school's name and logo, and then had to raise about $35,000 for equipment, negotiate a million-dollar insurance policy, and to find opponents, a coach, and a place to play and practice. Then he could go about getting players. Robert Corran, UVM AD, thought the process would be difficult: "I remember somebody asking me if we had any football equipment left. And I said: 'Not anything you'd want. They don't use single-bar face masks anymore'" (Pennington, 2008c, p. B12).

DeLuca got his team together in large part because he used technology—a website, Facebook, e-mail, texting. He also did it through old-time sales techniques by going to club and intramural games on campus to recruit participants who might have played high school football and would want to give it another go. He also appealed to the campus student government and contacted UVM football alums and created a booster club for financial support. He got $11,000 from the student government, and $18,000 from alumni. Each player had to pay $175 for equipment. DeLuca worked through the athletic department to use the school's rugby field for practice and for the necessary insurance, and found two UVM alums who would provide medical staffing for the games. A local high school agreed to let the team use its field on Sundays for home games. The team didn't have a locker room, so players brought their gear to class and dressed in the midst of trees adjacent to the field. The sidelines along the practice field were usually littered with street clothes and textbooks, and one player's dog was leashed to a nearby tree. Every few days, someone would spy the practice, inquire, and join up (Pennington, 2008c).

After all this, in September 2007, the UVM club team, 50 strong and wearing uniforms much like those worn by the varsity back in 1974, took the field in front of 2,000 fans, and defeated a local semi-pro team. The players had gone door to door at campus housing, handing out fliers about the team and its first game, and arranged shuttle bus service from campus to the field. "We tell people who ask us, 'We're not the club football team on campus; we're the only football team on campus,'" said tight end Tim Snow (Pennington, 2008c, p. B12). The team went 6–4 that first year, and in 2008, the team took on semi-pro teams and junior varsity teams from Bates College, Dartmouth College, and Williams College, winning two of seven. The team started looking for a site that would enable it to play on Saturdays, although this would effectively shut out the team from playing college sub-varsity teams. Dartmouth coach Buddy Teevens was so impressed with the UVM team that he promised to send extra equipment and blocking sleds. Teevens hoped the UVM program would inspire other schools in the region that once had football, and other smaller schools, to develop club programs. "They could form their own little league and I would play every one of them," he said (Pennington, 2008c, p. B12).

School administrators said the program would never be a stepping stone to re-establish a varsity program, but AD Corran was laudatory nonetheless: "It's filled a void and been a service to the student body. We can't do anything but applaud their efforts" (Pennington, 2008c, p. B12). DeLuca, scheduled to graduate in 2010, appointed four underclassmen players to pick up his managerial duties. DeLuca liked Dartmouth's Teevens' notion of a new league. "That would be perfect," he said. "I could come back for a homecoming game" (Pennington, 2008c, p. B12).

Student-Athlete Advisory Committee

To address concerns of student-athletes' input into issues that impact their participation, the membership at the 1989 NCAA Convention approved the formation of an Association-wide Student-Athlete Advisory Committee (SAAC), which was created primarily to review and offer student-athlete input on NCAA activities and proposed legislation affecting the student-athlete experience. In addition, in 1995 the Association passed legislation (Bylaw 6.1.4) requiring each individual institution to establish its own SAAC, with the composition and duties to be determined at the campus level (*2008–09 NCAA Division I Manual*, 2008; Student-Athlete Advisory Committees, 2004).

The initial national committee included 28 student-athletes from all membership divisions, but when the Association restructured in 1997, three separate national divisional SAACs were created, with a total of 79 members serving. The mission of the national divisional SAACs is "to enhance the total student-athlete experience by promoting opportunity, protecting student-athlete welfare and fostering a positive student-athlete image." Each national SAAC is composed of male and female members, and each conference in the division is represented. The SAACs have the responsibility of representing the voice of their colleagues by assisting in the review of NCAA proposed legislation. SAAC members fulfill this charge by soliciting responses to proposed legislation from their peers, and by communicating with their respective divisional management councils.

The Division I SAAC consists of one student-athlete from each of the 31 D-I conferences, with each member serving a two-year term, and two D-I SAAC members participate as non-voting members of the D-I Management Council. The Division II SAAC consists of one student-athlete representative from each of the D-II multi-sport conferences, one student-athlete representative of independent institutions, and student-athlete at-large positions. Divisions II and III SAACs are allowed to speak to legislative issues at annual conventions, but no SAACs are permitted to vote on legislative issues. No member may serve more than two years, and can serve on the committee for up to one year after completing his or her intercollegiate athletic eligibility (Student-Athlete Advisory Committees, 2004, p. 2; *2008–09 NCAA Division I Manual*, 2008; NCAA Student-Athlete Advisory Committees, 2008).

In 2008, the national Division III SAAC—the largest committee in the Division III governance structure and representing two appointments on the Division III Management Council—was composed of 24 members (16 of whom were chosen from each of the four D-III regions, and eight selected as at-large members). In addition to its representative role, the D-III SAAC has been charged with implementation and oversight of the initiatives specific to the SAAC from the Division III Strategic Plan. The D-III SAAC meets three times annually (in January, July, and November), and participates in an April telephone conference.

NCAA bylaws require that each member school and conference also have SAACs. Campus SAACs are responsible for discussing issues that affect student-athletes on individual campuses and forwarding that information to the conference SAAC. The conference SAACs are responsible for collecting feedback from member campuses, forming a conference perspective, and forwarding that perspective to the national SAAC. Conference SAACs also are encouraged to form their own strategic plans (as are campus SAACs) in relation to the NCAA's mission, their division's philosophy, and individual conference and school missions. Such plans are expected to enable SAACs to establish priorities in focusing efforts and to use resources most effectively (*NCAA Division III Student-Athlete Advisory Committee Manual 2006–07*, 2006).

Campus and conference SAACs are encouraged to create a diverse membership by recruiting members that equitably represent gender, ethnicity, sport, academic class, and academic major, and to create constitutions that address mission, administrative, and procedural issues. For example, the constitution of the New England Small College Athletic Conference SAAC requires the committee to have a male and female member from each of the 11 member schools, and committee members are to be appointed by October 1 of each year for a minimum term of one year. The committee is to meet at least once a year, and be overseen by a chair (who must be a junior or senior at his or her school), vice-chair, and alternate. Eleven members must be present to conduct committee business. To endorse a measure or proposal, a three-quarters majority must be achieved.

But the impact of SAACs at the conference and campus level can take a variety of forms. The SAAC of the Alleghany Mountain Collegiate Conference (AMCC), which consists of 10 schools in Maryland, Ohio, and Pennsylvania, has coordinated collection efforts at four member campuses (Frostburg State College, La Roche College, Pennsylvania State University–Behrend, and University of Pittsburgh–Bradford) to collect athletic equipment and supplies for schools in New Orleans that have struggled to rebound after the devastation inflicted by Hurricane Katrina in 2005. Also, at Denison University, a private liberal arts school with 2,100 undergrads located in Granville, Ohio, and a member of the Division III North Coast Athletic Conference, the school's SAAC teamed up with the local Salvation Army to assist in the Adopt-A-Family program, which matches impoverished families with groups to provide for their needs during the holidays; it collected nearly $2,000 to purchase gifts for 40 local children (DSAAC Providing Chirstmas, 2007; AMCC Student-Athlete Advisory Committee, 2008). The activities of most school SAACs are coordinated in conjunction with an athletic department manager, usually an assistant or associate AD.

FOREIGN STUDENT-ATHLETES

The success of the nearly all foreign-born squash team at Trinity College discussed in Chapter 4 is not an isolated phenomenon. Consider the 2007–08 rosters and student-athletes at programs at some other schools (Wolverton, 2008a):

- Women's swimming at Southern Methodist University, one of the top 20 Division I programs over the past decade, fields a squad with nine foreign nationals: Belgium, Czech Republic, England, Mexico, Slovenia (two), Slovakia, South Africa, Spain (with an assistant coach from Switzerland).

- Women's basketball at St. Mary's College of California, a Roman Catholic school with 2,500 undergraduates located in Moraga, and a member of the Division I Big West Conference, broke into the Top 25 with four players from Australia.

- Women's golf at Arizona State University, which has appeared in 15 consecutive Division I NCAA tournaments, has four foreign starters (one each from Argentina, Columbia, Spain, and Sweden) in its starting five.

- Men's Cross Country at the University of Texas-El Paso (UTEP), whose head coach is a former gold-medal distance runner from Kenya, a country well-known for its long-distance runners, has a roster filled entirely with Kenyans on full grant-in-aid (compared to a student body of which 80 percent hails from the county in which the school is located). The track team also has 40 international students from 12 countries.

- Men's soccer at the University of California, Santa Barbara, a public school with 17,700 undergraduates and a member of the Division I Big West Conference, went from 2–17 with all native players in 1999 to a national championship in 2006 with nearly half of its starting lineup foreign-born (Canada, England, Ireland, Jamaica, Ghana, Mexico, New Zealand).

- Jovan Bubonja, a native of Belgrade, Serbia, turned down an offer to play goal for the national team of his native country to accept a full grant-in-aid to play for the men's soccer team at the University of Illinois at Chicago, a public school of 25,000 undergraduates and member of the Division I Horizon League. The school has five other foreign-born players on its roster as well.

Scott Drew, head men's basketball coach at Baylor University, a private, Baptist-affiliated school with 12,000 undergraduates located in Waco, Texas, and a member of the Division I Big 12 Conference, credits the international growth of basketball to more foreign-born student-athletes playing in his sport: "The NBA does such a great job of promoting basketball. You look at the interest coming off the Olympics and how certain countries just really embrace basketball" (Wieberg, 2008a, p. 10C).

To illustrate that point, consider the actions of John Calipari, head men's basketball coach at the University of Kentucky, a public school with 15,000 undergraduates located in Lexington and a member of Division I Southeastern Conference. Calipari practices Mandarin for half an hour a day with an assistant coach who hails from China, and while head coach at the University of Memphis, took his team to Beijing in the spring of 2008. Why? "I'd love to get a basketball player from there," says Calipari, "one preferably with professional potential" (Wilson and Wolverton, 2008, p. A27). Calipari says he doesn't want a team consisting entirely of Chinese players but has a vision in which he establishes contacts with China so top players from the country will be able to play intercollegiately in the United States. Then the NCAA could broadcast the Division I men's basketball tournament there, gaining revenues from rights fees. "If we can start changing the culture of what they do with their young players, it can help us all" (Wilson & Wolverton, 2008, p. A29).

The NCAA's 2008 data revealed that since the 1999–2000 academic year, the number of foreign-born Division I student-athletes grew from 3,625 to 10,023 in 27 men's and women's sports, and accounts for 6.2 percent of all Division I student-athletes (compared to 2.4 percent in 1999–2000, and 2 percent of the general undergraduate populations at these schools). Fifty percent of women's ice hockey and women's tennis players hail from outside the United States, as well as 31 percent of men's ice hockey players, 30 percent of men's tennis players, 14 percent of women's golfers, 13 percent of all skiers, and 10 percent of men's soccer players. The numbers are also growing in basketball, gymnastics, swimming, and track. One expert believes that these numbers will grow until foreign-born athletes are the majority (Wieberg, 2008b).

Reasons for the increase in recruitment

Why are all these foreign-born athletes competing in the United States? And why are coaches like Calipari looking to bring over even more? Doesn't the United States have enough basketball players? According to coaches and administrators, the need to win is driving the growth in international student-athletes. In sports such as golf, soccer, and tennis, more American youths are turning professional out of high school. Billy Pate, head men's tennis coach at the University of Alabama, a public school with 23,000 undergraduates located in Tuscaloosa and a member of the Division I Southeastern Conference, where six of his 12 players are foreign nationals, describes the numbers: "Only 40 or 50 guys are impact players in American tennis, and by the time the Dukes and Stanfords get their pick, you've got no choice but to go international" (Wilson & Wolverton, 2008, p. A27).

Other coaches suggest that foreign-born players are less pampered and easier to coach. Jeff Jones, head men's basketball coach at American University, a private Methodist-affiliated school with 6,000 undergraduates located in Washington, DC, and a member of the Division I Patriot League, has traveled to Hungary, Lithuania, and Slovenia to recruit. He concluded: "In so many countries in Eastern Europe, the economy is such that it is very hard for them to go to college. They are very grateful for the opportunity to come to the United States and get three meals a day and live in a nice dorm and be able to play basketball and get a free education" (Wilson & Wolverton, 2008, p. A27). Part of this foreign influx has come from the expansion of domestic sports schools in the United States, where many foreign athletes come to train and earn an American high school diploma, and international scouts who, for a fee, work with foreign athletes to help them establish contacts with U.S. coaches (Wieberg, 2008a, 2008b).

But some U. S. coaches think that bringing in foreign-born recruits takes away participation opportunities for American students. University of Colorado track-and-field coach Mark Wetmore believes he might win more meets with international athletes but chooses not to recruit them because, "As a state institution, we have a responsibility to Colorado and U.S. taxpayers to make sure their sons and daughters have first priority. Imagine if after 18 years of paying taxes in the state of Colorado, or Maine, or Florida, your daughter has been able to throw the shot put 42 feet but your state institution does not make an athletic scholarship available to her because they can get someone from Iceland who can throw 43 feet" (Wilson & Wolverton, 2008, p. A27). But Constantine Ananiadis, head women's tennis coach at Oberlin (Ohio) College, a private liberal arts school with 2,850 undergraduates and a member of the Division III North Coast Conference, disagrees. Ananiadis, who came to the United States from Greece to play tennis at Stetson University, a private institution with 2,300 undergraduates located in Deland, Florida, and a member of the Division I Atlantic Sun conference, believes that "international kids should have just as much opportunity to compete as American players. Isn't this the land of opportunity?" (Wilson, 2008, p. A31).

At Texas–El Paso, no one appears to be concerned that the men's cross-country team is all Kenyan. Darla Smith, the school's faculty athletic representative, noted that "the fact that these athletes are good students is what matters" (Wilson, 2008, p. A31). The runners have a cumulative GPA of 3.16. All of the Kenyan runners came to the school because they wanted an American education, and they knew that running, the national pastime of their country, was the only way they could pay for it. Most grew up on farms in remote areas with six or seven siblings. Japeth Ng'Ojoy grew up on a farm that grows corn and tea. He is majoring in biology and hopes to go to medical school, because in Kenya, he says, "we need a lot of doctors." Ultimately, however, the Kenyans are at UTEP because they are good and can help the program win. Head coach Paul Ereng, whose Olympic medal made him well-known back home, rebuilt the flagging program with Kenyans because, as he says, "the success and life of this team has come from international students" (Wilson, 2008, p. A31).

Eligibility issues

Winning with international players has raised the issue of these athletes' eligibility. In response to these concerns, the NCAA began to regulate eligibility for international athletes, a task that fell previously to individual schools. According to the NCAA's director of amateur certification, Bill Saum, that means "gathering legitimate information from more than 200 countries" (Wieberg, 2008a, p. 10C). Saum reports that there were 472 amateurism violations involving foreign student-athletes in the two years after the Association began reviewing cases—46 in men's and women's basketball, 108 in men's soccer, and 135 in men's and women's tennis—accounting for 87 percent of all violation cases (Wieberg, 2008a). As a result, international prospects must answer questions relating to amateurism rules, such as:

- In any sport, have you ever authorized anyone (other than your parent, legal guardian, or coach) to market your athletic skill or reputation?
- Before attending classes full time at any college, have you ever competed in an event and accepted prize money?
- Before attending classes full time at any college, have you ever competed on a team where anyone received more than their expenses to play on the team? (Wolverton, 2008b)

The challenge for athletic managers is that in attempting to enforce its amateurism bylaws on foreign student-athletes, many who formerly were approved for competition by schools will now be sidelined. For example, in 2007, two high-profile German men's basketball recruits—Lucca Staiger, who had committed to Iowa State University, and Fabian Bocke, recruited to attend Washington State University—had to forgo a year of eligibility because they had played in a nonprofit, German government–sponsored league in which two teammates had been paid $200 a month. NCAA personnel admit that the transition to the new system has been less than seamless, that they were not prepared for the large number of foreign student applications and that foreign coaches and teams are reluctant to provide details about prospects for fear of their eligibility being threatened. Washington State associate AD for compliance, Steve Robertello, expressed his displeasure with the system: "That's the frustrating thing. It's hard to look at your student-athlete and say 'you can't play,' when other guys from the same league have qualified before. . . . You'll be hard pressed to find many club teams in Europe that will not be defined as professional" (Wolverton, 2008b, p. A32).

As a result, the NCAA's amateurism cabinet considered relaxing some of its current amateurism legislation involving foreign-born student-athletes, specifically those who had played on a professional team, suggesting "the current definition of a professional team is too broad and unfairly penalizes prospective student-athletes who never intended to professionalize themselves" (Wieberg, 2008a, p. 10C).

CONCLUSION

The NCAA coined the term "student-athlete" to convey that college athletes were not solely focused on sports. To qualify as a student-athlete, an individual most meet specific requirements relating to academics and his or her status as an amateur athlete. The NCAA dictates the criteria for loss of amateur status. Much of the amateur legislation in the *Division I Manual* outlines prohibited forms of pay and related professional activities and the allowable exceptions within those activities.

To operate an intercollegiate athletics program, athletic managers must be aware of the well-being of their student-athletes. Challenges to that well-being include the restrictions that come with maintaining amateur status, balancing the demands of their sport with the rest of their lives in college, pressures related to their choice of academic major, the growth of club sports on some campuses, and the role of Student Athlete Advisory Councils (SAACs) at the campus and national levels.

A relatively new phenomenon in intercollegiate athletics is the increase in recruitment of foreign-born athletes. Not surprisingly, this trend has presented new challenges for departments, including the costs of recruiting them and eligibility issues related to their amateur status.

PRACTITIONER perspective:

FOUR DIVISION III MEN'S ICE HOCKEY PLAYERS

Throughout this chapter we have read about specific experiences of student-athletes across the spectrum of intercollegiate athletics. For this practitioner perspective, the authors interviewed four men's ice hockey student-athletes attending an NCAA Division III school. The four are all upperclassmen, hail from different parts of the United States, play different positions, and garner various levels of playing time. They have weathered some trying times throughout their careers—specifically, consistently losing seasons and a change of head coaches leading into the season in which they were interviewed. Often, such interviews focus on the achievements and successes of student-athletes and programs. The authors sought to learn more about the experiences of student-athletes in programs that struggle to win games, and what motivates them to keep playing in spite of a lack of obvious success. The four were inter- viewed together toward the end of the 2009–10 season and are identified only as Players A, B, C, and D.

Q: *Describe your decision to come to the school.*

A: **Player A:** A lot was comfort. Playing sports was very high up there, and comfort level—being able to do it or not, definitely seeing that a D-III team was more of the skill set for me.

I live 15 minutes away, and I kind of like that aspect, being able to go home when I need to. I applied to nine schools, including Quinnipiac, Merrimack, Fitchburg State, Elmira, Sacred Heart, UConn, and a couple of other schools as well. I compared them all, and [this school] was pretty low, budget-wise, compared to the other schools. They did a lot better job with financial aid. So probably the biggest components were hockey, expenses, and comfort.

Player B: I transferred here mainly because of hockey. When I got cut at [another school], I looked at [this school] and Suffolk as two schools to transfer to. Suffolk was more in the city, and I wanted an actual campus—which this school had—and I knew the program was kind of rebuilding. At prep school my program was rebuilding there, and I was a part of that, and they went on to win the league two years ago, so it was something cool to be around. My freshman year I stayed home, and from 10th to 12th grade I went to prep school in New Hampshire.

It's just the feel [here]. People are cool. I liked [the former coach] when I was visiting, and the sport management academic program was also a key factor in deciding to come here.

Player C: I actually had a couple of kids from my high school come here. One of them played [hockey], one of them didn't. Just them talking about it and everything. I looked at only three or four schools, and [this school] was the only one that had sport management and had D-III hockey. The others had club teams, and I didn't want to play club. It's just not as good hockey. It doesn't mean as much in some places.

Player D: I took the alternate route—I played junior hockey for two years. I came out to the East Coast to play for [a nearby junior team], and I had a pretty good experience. We won our league my first year and went to Nationals, and did all right at Nationals. The next year wasn't the greatest experience. I was getting recruited by five or six Division III teams in the New England and New York area. What I based my decision on was the coach—how I thought the coach would be, whether he's a decent guy, a decent human being, because I had problems with other coaches—and how his game plan was, what kind of systems he was playing. I had a list of questions I was asking coaches.

I liked [the former coach at this school] a lot from that. I was asking, where do I fit in in the program, what am I going to be doing, and what's his plans for the years upcoming—is he moving on, is he going to go somewhere, is he using this as a stepping stone? He told me he wasn't, but he ended up leaving [for a head coaching job at another Division III school]. He said he was going to be here for all my four years, that he wanted to see his first recruiting class go through. I knew the situation with the team being for years and years not as competitive as they were in the early 1990s. I wanted to play right away, too, so that was big. And, also, I thought the school's [academic] degree held more weight than the other schools that were recruiting me.

Was it your sense in the recruiting process that coaches were telling you what you wanted to hear?

Player D: Yeah—most of the coaches. I thought [the former coach at this school] was pretty honest and straightforward compared to the other ones. The Buffalo State coach, for instance—you'd ask him a question and he kind of wouldn't answer it, or answer it with something else. With playing time, he'd be like, "Right now I have you slotted as a second-pairing defense and possible power play, and a little bit of penalty kill." And then you talk to him later down the road and he'd say, "Right now I see you probably third set of defense, maybe a little penalty kill." It probably depended on who he was getting in and talking to, too. The [former coach at this school] was pretty straightforward with anything I asked him. He answered it right away, no pauses. He really didn't have to think about it.

I hurt my knee my first year in junior hockey. In the preseason I was getting contacted by a Sacred Heart assistant coach and a Mercyhurst assistant coach, a UConn assistant coach. And when they found out I hurt my knee, they kind of shut down the conversation. That was a little bit of a blow. I really didn't know what I was going to do. After I had the surgery and rehabbed and everything and came back, I was having a good time. We weren't doing that well—coaching trouble—and I didn't know for sure if I was going to continue to play hockey.

Describe your experience playing hockey at this school.

Player A: The experience with being part of a team has been amazing. Being at college and on a team has been one of the most rewarding experiences I've had. Just the feeling that you always have a place, you always have a buddy, you always have a friend somewhere.

In regard to the experience of playing hockey—it puts a lot more on your plate, but it also makes you more active. The idea of your GPA going up during hockey season is true for me. It makes it so you're a lot less lazy. Overall I wouldn't want to change the experience. I wouldn't want to go to college without playing, for sure. It's been positive for the most part. It's a little bit of an emotional rollercoaster, in a sense. We deal with winning and losing with the idea that you're always representing your team, whether something good happens, whether something bad happens. At college, things are out there—grades, getting in trouble—anything good or bad. You're under a microscope in that aspect. Like I said, it's kind of like a rollercoaster—when things are going well, a lot more is going well; when things are going bad, it gets exponentially bad.

Player B: I would never change anything. I wanted to play college hockey ever since I was a kid. So doing that and being with the guys—you're with them every day. Most of our team lives with guys on the team, so it's like a big family. You deal with stuff outside the rink, and you deal with stuff inside the rink, on the ice. It's been the best thing that could ever happen. Playing has its ups and downs. Our team hasn't done so well the past couple years, but with the new coach, he's getting things in the right direction.

Player C: You learn a lot from having to deal with different types of people on the team. Not everyone on the team is the same kind of person. There's a lot of characters. I don't have to like everyone but I have to get along with them. You can put me in the room with anybody on the team and I'm not going to rip their eyes out, but . . . .

Player B: You have to deal with [teammates] for practices and games, but if you don't want to be with them outside of that time, as long as you get along with them during the time you're with them, it should make things run smoothly.

Player D: I've changed my perspective on college athletic life. I went from focusing solely on hockey when I first came in to now focusing on my grades and trying to move on. It's been tough. I knew it was going to be tough coming in with a program like this, but it's turned into almost a chore in a sense. You have to show up and play and work. It's not as much fun as it was my freshman year. Our freshman year we weren't good. No talent on our team at all. We were awful. The kids on our team shouldn't have been playing college hockey. But that was our most successful season with wins. We were a team—we played together, we liked to be around each other, we hung out together. And last year that kind of went down, this year it kind of went down, and now it's picking back up toward the end.

Describe the situation in having a change of coaches this year.

Player C: It's like you're a freshman again. You've got to make sure you do the right things. Everything you did with the last coach, everything he knows about you— maybe he tells the new coach a few things, but they're two different people. They're not going to have the same views on everything. People's roles change to what the new coach wants you to do.

Player D: At the beginning, I thought things would be changing a lot, and it turned out to be the same thing. Everything that was said in the beginning of the season was said two seasons in a row. Nothing turned out the way it should have. I know with [the former coach] he would always say, "No one's buying in to the systems." Maybe that's true, maybe it wasn't, but no one's buying into the systems now. We started off ok, and then it just went downhill. I feel like our coach doesn't know what to do sometimes. He's flipping out. Everyone's flipping out.

Player A: Tensions are a lot higher right now. The fact is that we've had a couple seasons like this, that everything will snap. I know with me personally, you can see it. You can see it in other people—coaches, fans even. Tensions are high. Every small mistake is magnified. That's what happens with the kind of losing culture we've had, and that's something we're trying to get over. Changing coaches, getting better recruiting classes, whatever, but we haven't actually found that thing that will actually do it.

What are the biggest reasons that the program hasn't been successful in winning games?

Player A: That's a loaded question.

Player D: There's a few things, one being the history of the program. I think [the former coach] was the first full-time coach, so I can see previously the history of the program not being able to recruit people they could have possibly recruited because a part-time coach can't go out on the road all the time to focus on that.

Player B: There's also the fact that this school's pretty expensive for some families. That's mainly why the state schools have better recruiting access, because if you live in-state, you can go to some schools for less than $10,000.

Player D: I talked to [the former head coach] about the recruiting process over the past two years, and he was saying he tried to hammer into kids' minds that you can take out loans, that it's ok to do, especially now in this economy, with some schools not giving out aid the way they used to. But it's a major issue. Plus [the town in which the school is located] isn't the most desirable place to go to college. We're out of the area that you don't want to be in, so it's not too bad. My freshman year—a lot of people left to go home on the weekends. Now it's kind of turning where people stay on campus on the weekends. There's still a decent amount of commuters, so some people go home on the weekends, so it's kind of hard to get people in the stands at games.

What about the facility in which you play?

Player C: It would be really nice if it were on campus.

Player A: A lack of success has hurt recruiting, but the facility is pretty tough. We're in a locker room that's freezing cold.

Player C: It's actually a garage that was turned into a locker room my freshman year.

Player A: We have to walk across a rink to get to the showers and bathroom. So that's not that desirable. It's hard to put a nice spin on that, especially when you're looking at another school that's cheaper, had a couple more wins the other season, and the locker rooms are a lot nicer.

A lot of kids come in and think, this is college hockey, this is a big step up. For me, my high school locker room was better, and our facilities were a lot better. I think it was probably the same for the other three guys here, which definitely hurts recruiting. Even the fan base, which is a small thing, but it factors in with people when deciding.

Player D: The facility . . .

Player B: And tuition . . .

Player D: Those are probably the two biggest things that hurt recruiting. It almost doesn't matter whose coaching, or what kind of degree you can get. When you're coming out of high school or junior hockey, you think you could possibly one day play minor league hockey. People really think that, even though it's not that viable an option. They'll notice it once they start playing D-III hockey. Equipment is a big thing, too. We get equipment from school, which is really nice. The equipment that we get, though, isn't that high-quality. Next year our stuff is going to be nice; they ordered higher-quality gloves, pants, helmets, sticks. Our first two years here we had the lowest-end of hockey equipment. The gloves cost $30 a piece, and they fall apart. They try to refurbish them, and we get them back the next year, and they're really bad. The new gloves will be top-of-the-line; they won't get ripped-up or fall apart.

So what has to happen to make the program successful?

Player A: It might sound cliché, but the only thing that comes to mind is getting everyone on the same page, going in the same direction. Whatever that is—whether it's to be in the best shape, whether it's to be the most

talented, getting the most freshmen, whatever it is. Whatever the system is, whoever the coach is, just do the same thing. We experienced a lot of people going at each other—going at a coach, going at teammates—just not agreeing. Half the people doing one thing, everyone not committed. So whatever it would take to get that. If you're asking what it would take to get that?

Is it a system issue, like how to run the power play?

Player C: Everybody's got to want the same thing. Not everyone wants the same thing. Some people are point-driven. Some people are here to wear the jacket hoping they can get girls. Everyone needs to want the same thing.

Player B: Coach has gotten into our heads that it's our "need to" skills, not our "want to" skills. He puts into perspective—you need to block a shot to save a goal, or you need to finish a check so we get the puck, and you need to do certain things during the game, off the ice, everywhere in order to be successful.

Player C: He says, "You can't be a boy. You've got to be a man. Boys do what they want to do. Men do what they need to do." It makes a lot of sense.

So what's been the problem in getting that? Why has it been so hard getting that commitment?

Player D: Different attitudes in the people we're recruiting. That's what it comes down to.

Player C: Coach is going to know recruiting now—what types of people he needs to recruit. We have many different types of people on the team. Some people would cut off their foot for the team. Some people would rather skate off the ice and get the hell off the ice as fast as possible if it means someone is going to do harm to them.

Is that hard to determine in the recruiting process?

Player C: You can kind of tell with some people. They also watch them play. They'll go watch someone play, and they can tell right away if he's going to be the kid who doesn't play defense and just skates around center ice waiting for that home run pass. That's not somebody he's going to want on his team.

Player D: I think what would have helped this school if this would have happened was to get an experienced coach. From my understanding from what I've heard is that our current coach is highly paid compared to other Division III coaches. I thought that they would have gone with someone with experience, especially from [this state]. I know there were a number of coaches who were older and had college hockey head coaching experience and knew this area. They need to know this recruiting area. If you go to [another state], the kids there are going to go to a state school at the Division III level, so [recruits] really need to come from this area. I think it would have helped the school turn into a better program in the long run. If you get a guy that's going to stay around, who has family roots here. I feel like that's what should have happened instead of another young coach. The last three coaches have all been young, all first-time head coaches. I think if they're spending the money they supposedly are spending, they should have picked somebody with experience. And I know there were plenty of options out there for that. So I was a little disappointed in that aspect.

Do you talk with any recruits when they come to campus and, if so, what do you tell them about coming to the school?

Player A: I would tell them a lot of the reasons that I came. I'd talk to them about hockey more than school. What I'd say with that is trying to make a winning program and that whole idea. People who are coming out of high school who are getting recruited think they're really good, whatever level it is. Every freshman we get, they think they're the best freshman. And you say to them, "Do you want to be part of something special?" other than just being another player at another school that gets 14 recruits.

You just tell them that they have a chance—a chance—to have a lot of playing time and be a part of something where we take it to the next level. That's what I was told (in the recruiting process). I walked on, but I talked to the coach a little bit before, and that was his mindset. So I tell recruits that, and you'd be surprised how many people want to make a difference. They want to make an impact. They don't just want to go through the motions.

Given where the program is, can you honestly recommend to a recruit that he come here?

Player B: I feel that with [the new coach], he's striving to make an impact on this campus with the hockey program, and the actions that he's taken this year with some guys, you know he's not going to tolerate any off-ice stuff. That's been a problem more this year. I would tell them that if they come here, they'd be making a good decision based on hockey, because Coach is really looking to change things around.

Player D: I've met with a few recruits this year and last year. I told them, "Don't listen to me, don't take my word for it, but this is what I'm going to tell you—Pick a school that you're going to want to go to, that you're going to like. Pick a school not based on the coach, because he might leave. We had one that already left." And I told them, "Ask as many questions as you can. Find out about the coach, what his intentions are for everything. Just keep asking questions. You're not going to play professional hockey, so the bottom line here is you want to get a degree that you like in a field where you want to work. You're going to have to make the decision yourself. I can tell you what you want to hear, but really base it on your education. This is Division III hockey."

Do you think negatively about your college experience overall because the hockey program hasn't been very successful?

Player C: I'm not going to look negatively on it. There's always something you could do to make something better. I'm sure I'm going to be done with school—and I'm sure these three guys will agree—that we could sit here and say, "Wow, if we just did a few more things to make ourselves better, we could have had two more wins this year." But I enjoyed playing hockey here a lot. I enjoy the people around me. I wouldn't want to go 0–25 every year, but if we did, I'd still have a great time doing it.

question TO CONSIDER

1. Based on the issues faced by student-athletes, which one is most encountered by student-athletes on your campus, and how should athletic department managers address it to improve student-athletes' experiences?

references

About the NAIA. (2005). National Association of Intercollegiate Athletics. Accessed July 8, 2008, from: http://naia.cstv.com/member-services/about.htm

AMCC Student-Athlete Advisory Committee (2008). Alleghany Mountain Collegiate Conference. Accessed September 8, 2008, from: http://www.amcconf.org/SAAC.htm

Blaney, B. (2009, December 29). Leach's attorney says coach did no wrong. *Lubbock (TX) Avalanche-Journal.* Accessed December 29, 2009, from: http://ap.lubbockonline.com/pstories/sports/college/20091229/540699264.shtml

Brady, E. (2006, February 28). Buffalo busts racial barriers. *USA Today*, pp. 1C–2C.

Caldwell, D. (2009, December 17). Finals for Rutgers,on paper and in pads. *New York Times*, p. B14.

Cowan, A.L. (2008, July 25). Forced off Duke's golf team, Giuliani's son sues. *New York Times*, p. C11.

Cowan, A.L. (2009, May 21). Judge calls lawsuit "far from the fairway." *New York Times*, p. A24.

Degrees of Responsibility. (2008, November 19). *USA Today*, p. 7C.

DSAAC Providing Christmas for Area Children. (2007, December 21). Denison University. Accessed September 17, 2008, from: http://www.denison.edu/athletics/dsaa

Evans, T., & Thamel, P. (2009, December 31). Leach is fired over treatment of player. *New York Times*, pp. B11–B12.

Former High School All-American Elena DelleDonne to play Women's Basketball at University of Delaware This Winter. (2009, June 2). Accessed from: http://www.bluehens.com/sportsinfo/womens_basketball/wbb10-delledonnejoin.html

Former World Cup, Olympic Skier Jeremy Bloom cut by Steelers. (2008, August 26). *Times Leader.* Accessed September 3, 2008, from: http://www.printthis.clickability.com

Henig, S. (2006, September 8). Muslim former players sue New Mexico State U. *Chronicle of Higher Education*, p. A37.

In-box: Burress, Guns, Crime and Punishment. (2008, December 7). *New York Times*, p. 8-8.

In-box: Letters to the Editor. (2009, July 26). *New York Times.* Accessed August 9, 2009, from: http://www.nytimes.com/2009/07/26/sports/26inbox.html

Indiana's Sampson Agrees to a Buyout. (2008, February 23). *Washington Post.* Accessed February 25, 2008, from: http://0-www.lexisnexis.com.wildpac.wnec.edu

Klein, A. (2004, February 20). 2-sport athlete escalates challenge to NCAA by signing a deal to appear in fitness ads. *Chronicle of Higher Education.* Accessed August 7, 2008, from: http://find.galegroup.com/itx

Leach Fired Short of Tech's Bowl Game. (2009, December 30). Accessed December 30, 2009, from: http://sports.espn.go.com/ncf/bowls09/news/story?id=4781981

Longman, J. (2008, October 19). Walking away. *New York Times*, pp. Y1, Y12.

McCarthy, M., & Berkowitz, S. (2008, November 19). Minnesota task force aimed at student-athletes. *USA Today*, p. 7C.

NCAA *Division III Student-Athlete Advisory Committee Manual 2006–07.* Indianapolis: NCAA.

[The] N.C.A.A. Re-evaluates Concussions. (2009, December 16). *New York Times*, p. B15.

NCAA Student-Athlete Advisory Committees. (2008). National Collegiate Athletic Association. Accessed September 8, 2008, from: http://www1.ncaa.org/membership/membership_svcs/saac/campus-conf-div.html

New Mexico State Fires Mumme. (2008, December 2). *SI.com.* Accessed January 10, 2009, from: http://si.printthis.clickabilitu.com

Pennington, B. (2008a, March 12). It's not just an adventure, it's a job. *New York Times*, pp. C15, C18.

Pennington, B. (2008b, December 2). Rapid rise on college club teams creates a whole new level of success. *New York Times*, pp. B11–B12.

Pennington, B. (2008c, December 3). A year of toil and sweat, then they played a game. *New York Times*, pp. B11–B12.

Peterson, K. (2009, July 16). College athletes stuck with the bill after injuries. *New York Times.* Accessed August 9, 2009, from: http://www.nytimes.com/2009/07/16/sports/16athletes.html

Roberts, S. (2009, December 28). Special senior moments. *Sports Illustrated*, p. 88.

Rushin, S. (2007, March 3). Inside the moat. *Sports Illustrated.* Accessed August 7, 2008, from: http://find.galegroup.com/itx

Schad, J. (2009, December 30). Sources: Leach anticipates firing soon. Accessed December 30, 2009, from: http://sports.espn.go.com/ncf/bowls09/news/story?id=4779341

Schwarz, A. (2009a, November 18). N.C.A.A lets colleges decide on protocol. *New York Times*, p. B13.

Schwarz, A. (2009b, December 1). LaSalle will pay ex-player $7.5 million. *New York Times*, p. B14.

Steeg, J.L., Upton, J., Bohn, P., & Berkowitz, S. (2008, November 19). Athletes guided toward "beating the system." *USA Today*, pp. 1A–2A.

Student-Athlete Advisory Committees. (2004). National Collegiate Athletic Association. Accessed August 7, 2008, from: http://www.ncaa.org/wcm/connect/NCAA/Academics+and+Athletes/SAAC/index

Suggs, W. (2004a, May 21). U. of Colorado athlete loses a round in court in battle with NCAA. *Chronicle of Higher Education.* Accessed August 7, 2008, from: http://find.galegroup.com/itx

Suggs, W. (2004b, September 3). NCAA declares skier ineligible for football. *Chronicle of Higher Education*. Accessed August 7, 2008, from: http://find.galegroup.com/itx

Texas Tech Suspends Its Coach. (2009, December 29). *New York Times*, p. B11.

2008–09 NCAA Division I Manual. (2008). Indianapolis: National Collegiate Athletic Association.

Upton, J., & Novak, K. (2008, November 18). College athletes cluster in majors at most schools. *USA Today*. Accessed November 19, 2008, from: http://usatoday.com

Wieberg, S. (2008a, October 2). Division I sees unprecedented foreign influx. *USA Today*, p. 1C.

Wieberg, S. (2008b, October 2). Foreigners fill 6.2% of D-I roster spots. *USA Today*, p. 10C.

Wilson, R. (2008, January 11). A Texas team loads up on All-American talent, with no Americans. *Chronicle of Higher Education*, pp. A30–31.

Wilson, R., & Wolverton, B. (2008, January 11). The new face of college sports. *Chronicle of Higher Education*, pp. A27–A29.

Wolverton, B. (2008a, January 11). A Serbian star spurns professional offers in favor of an American education. *Chronicle of Higher Education*, p. A33.

Wolverton, B. (2008b, January 11). Controversy surrounds NCAA's certification of international athletes. *Chronicle of Higher Education*, p. A33.

Wolverton, B. (2008c, January 25). Athletes' hours renew debate over college sports. *Chronicle of Higher Education*, pp. A1, A23.

Wolverton, B. (2008d, March 14). The joy of benchwarming. *Chronicle of Higher Education*, pp. A1, A7.

Zimbalist, A. (1999). *Unpaid professionals: Commercialism* Princeton University Press.

Title IX and gender equity

Key concepts to keep in mind as you read the chapter:

- Historical developments that influenced the need for gender equity legislation.

- The distinction between the terms "Title IX" and "gender equity," and what each means.

- Key court cases that shaped the nature of gender equity legislation and enforcement.

- The standards used to gauge whether intercollegiate athletic programs are in compliance with current gender equity standards and requirements.

- Developments that have continued to shape gender equity standards and requirements.

Introduction

On June 23, 1972, President Richard Nixon signed into law Title IX of the Education Amendments of 1972. The landscape of collegiate athletics was forever changed that day, as the legislation would greatly influence collegiate sport participation and beyond for decades to come. One of the initial impacts of the Title IX federal legislation was an increase in the number of females participating in collegiate athletics. In the 1971–72 academic year, before passage of Title IX, the number of female athletes participating in college athletics totaled 29,977 compared to 170,384 male athletes. In comparison, in 2005–06 there were 168,583 female athletes and 224,926 male athletes participating in college athletics, an increase of 468 percent in female participation since 1971–72 compared to an increase of 32 percent in male participation over the same time period. This increase in number of participation opportunities is a result of the growth of sport teams and sport offerings for females across institutions. In 2005–06 there were 9,150 female college sport teams, compared to 4,279 female sport teams in 1981–82. Over the same time period, the number of men's sport teams increased from 6,746 in 1981–82 to 8,137 in 2005–06 (National Collegiate Athletic Association, 2008b).

One of the ways that compliance with Title IX is gauged at institutions is by comparing the percentage of male and female student-athletes to the general student body composition. As a result, many institutions offer more female sport teams than male sport teams to offset the large roster sizes of football teams to comply with Title IX. The scope of Title IX has been broadened with subsequent court decisions, adding to the areas of applicability and the protection provided under this federal legislation. Collegiate athletic administrators have to be knowledgeable about this statute and its application to college athletics.

DEFINITION AND HISTORY OF TITLE IX

Title IX of the Education Amendments of 1972 states: "No person in the United States shall, on the basis of sex, be excluded from participation in, be denied the benefits of, or be subjected to discrimination under any education program or activity receiving federal financial assistance" (20 U.S.C. § 1681). *Gender equity* is another term that has been used to address a comparison between the benefits and opportunities provided to both sexes within college (and high school) athletic programs. The NCAA Gender Equity Task Force defines gender equity: "No individual should be discriminated against on the basis of gender, institutionally or nationally, in intercollegiate athletics" (National Collegiate Athletic Association, 2008a, p. 3). The Task Force further states, "An athletics program can be considered gender equitable when the participants in both the men's and women's sports programs would accept as fair and equitable the overall program of the other gender" (p. 3).

Since the time when Title IX was signed into law in 1972, enforcement and compliance of this legislation has followed many paths. With the initial passage of this legislation came much debate as to whether Title IX would apply to college athletic departments. Language within the legislation was not specific, referring only to application within education programs or activities receiving federal financial assistance. Various groups and individuals such as Senator John Tower from Texas and the NCAA itself used a variety of approaches to argue against Title IX's applicability to college athletics. As such, when Title IX was first passed, numerous athletic directors and college presidents did not believe that athletics was included within the purview of Title IX and, therefore, they did not have to comply with the legislation.

Department of Health, Education and Welfare oversight

In 1972, the Department of Health, Education, and Welfare (HEW) was the government agency responsible for overseeing enforcement of Title IX. In 1974, while HEW was preparing to finish its first draft of regulations to assist institutions in interpreting and applying Title IX, Senator John Tower of Texas proposed an amendment that would have exempted "revenue-producing sports" from being counted when determining Title IX compliance. Tower argued that collegiate athletic departments relied on the revenue-producing sports of football and men's basketball to fund sport programs and opportunities within the whole department. He worried that the HEW rules would undercut revenue-producing sport programs, damaging the overall sports program of the institution. In his words, "Were HEW . . . to promulgate rules which damaged the financial base of intercollegiate sports, it will have thrown the baby out with the bath water" (Suggs, 2005, p. 68).

When HEW released the final Title IX regulations in 1975, revenue-producing sports were not excluded, and institutions were provided with guidelines to follow to determine whether equal athletic opportunities for members of both sexes were being provided. Although these 1975 Title IX regulations helped lay the groundwork in terms of applicability of Title IX to college athletics, there was still much confusion among athletic administrators in what they were required to do to maintain compliance with Title IX. Athletic administrators moved slowly, if at all, in making changes to more fully accommodate female student-athletes. As a result, in 1979 HEW released Title IX policy interpretations to explain more clearly how the law would be applied within college athletics. These policy interpretations address three areas:

- the provision of athletic scholarships,
- the effective accommodation of student athletic interests and abilities (i.e., sport participation), the benefits, and
- opportunities provided to each sex (e.g., equipment, facilities, schedule).

The interpretations are still in place today and have guided enforcement efforts surrounding Title IX compliance.

With the Title IX regulations and policy interpretations in place as of 1979, college athletic administrators could now take measures, such as performing internal Title IX compliance audits, to determine how closely their athletic departments were complying with Title IX. It is important to note that Title IX is a federal statute, and failure to comply ultimately leads to penalties institutions such as withdrawal of federal funding.

In 1980, HEW separated into two departments, with the Office for Civil Rights (OCR) within the newly organized Department of Education taking on the role of Title IX enforcement. As with any new regulations or policy interpretations, athletic administrators and even the Office for Civil Rights investigators themselves were confused in interpreting policy and in determining Title IX compliance.

Grove City College v. Bell

A larger blow that limited Title IX's application to college athletics came with the 1984 Supreme Court decision in the *Grove City College v. Bell* (1984) case.

In 1977, Grove City (Pennsylvania) College, a private college founded in 1876 to promote Christian values (with a full-time undergraduate enrollment of 2,500 and a member of the Division III Presidents' Athletic Conference), refused to produce a gender-equity plan as required by the Department of Health, Education and Welfare. HEW determined that the college received federal money through a financial aid program for students, the Basic Educational Opportunity Grants (BEOGs) program, and therefore had to comply with Title IX. The school took the position that it did not have to comply with Title IX, as it was a private institution. As such, HEW initiated plans to cut off the federal financial aid provided to these students. Grove City College and four of its students sued (Wong, 2002).

The U.S. Supreme Court ruled in 1984 that only those programs receiving direct federal funding had to comply with Title IX (often referred to as the "programmatic approach"). At Grove City College, this meant that only the financial aid program, which received federal funding to support the BEOG program, had to comply with Title IX. No other department on campus, including athletics, had to comply with Title IX. This ruling effectively took all the enforcement muscle out of Title IX's application to college athletic departments, for athletic departments do not receive *direct* federal funding but, rather, receive indirect funding via allocation within their institutions. As a result, the OCR dropped numerous active Title IX investigations against athletic departments because it could not be established that the athletic department received direct federal funding. Once again, athletic administrators found themselves in a confusing position regarding how to determine the applicability of Title IX to college athletics.

Civil Rights Restoration Act of 1987

The limitation on enforcement of Title IX lasted for four years until passage of the Civil Rights Restoration Act in 1987. This Act served "to restore the broad scope of coverage and clarify the application of Title IX of the Education Amendments of 1972 (Civil Rights Restoration Act of 1987, 1988). This was referred to as an "institutional approach" to Title IX enforcement, meaning that if any department or program within an institution received federal funds, all programs (including athletics) at the institution had to comply with Title IX. The OCR's enforcement muscle to investigate Title IX violations and complaints was restored, as now all programs and activities within a college or institution receiving any sort of federal funding, even if the institution itself saw itself as private, were subject to Title IX compliance.

Franklin v. Gwinnett County Public Schools

Additional support encouraging institutions to comply with Title IX was provided in 1992 when the U.S. Supreme Court found in *Franklin v. Gwinnett County Public Schools* (1992) that victims of discrimination under Title IX could receive monetary damages. A large increase in Title IX cases resulted because student-athletes could now pay for private attorneys and other legal bills with the knowledge that if successful, they would receive monetary damages (Wong, 2002). This ruling by the Supreme Court escalated the penalties associated with non-compliance of Title IX, which led institutions to take the law's requirements more seriously and implement compliance studies and compliance plans.

Application to sexual harassment

The application of Title IX within college athletics has evolved over the years beyond its increased impact on female participation in college sports. Two areas within athletics that have seen litigation involving Title IX include sexual harassment and retaliation discrimination. In 1997, the Office for Civil Rights, the governmental agency responsible for enforcing Title IX, acknowledged that sexual harassment is actionable under Title IX guidance.

These OCR guidelines were revised further in 2001, helping to clarify the types of claims that fall within Title IX's protection in a publication titled, *Gender Equity in Intercollegiate Athletics* (National Collegiate Athletic Association, 2008a). This application came to light in 2001 when two women who alleged they were raped by University of Colorado football players or recruits filed a federal lawsuit under Title IX, *Simpson et al. v. University of Colorado* (2007). Within the area of retaliation discrimination, the Supreme Court found, in its ruling in *Jackson v. Birmingham Board of Education* (2005), that Title IX protects retaliation directed toward teachers and students of either sex because he or she has complained of sexual discrimination against another group in violation of Title IX.

Commission on Opportunity in Athletics

Title IX received additional scrutiny in 2002 when then-Secretary of Education Rod Paige formed the Commission on Opportunity in Athletics, a federal advisory panel created to study the law. The Commission was composed of members from Division I athletic programs, athletic conference offices, women's groups, and former and current athletes. The Commission was charged with studying Title IX, including collection of information by the OCR during investigations, analysis of issues surrounding Title IX, and topics of debate with Title IX enforcement, and to solicit public input with the goal of improving the application of current federal standards for measuring equal opportunity under Title IX (Secretary's Commission, 2003). From June 2002 until January 2003, the Commission held six public meetings across the United States, hearing testimony and gathering information and data from various constituency groups representing a variety of viewpoints on Title IX. On February 2003, the Commission released its report, *Open to All: Title IX at Thirty* (Secretary's Commission, 2003). In this report the Commission developed 23 key recommendations, 15 of which were unanimously approved by members of the Commission. Overall, the Commission found strong and broad support for the original intent of Title IX while also hearing a great deal of confusion and debate about how the law should be enforced.

Many of the recommendations put forth by the Commission met with opposition from two of its members, Donna de Varona and Julie Foudy, who submitted a minority report expressing their concern. This report summarized the concern that most of the recommendations put forth by the Commission would weaken Title IX standards and enforcement procedures, which, it was feared, would lead to reduced opportunities for women and girls in sport (de Varona & Foudy, 2003). However, in July 2003, the administration of then President George W. Bush endorsed Title IX as it currently existed, serving to eliminate any significant changes made to the enforcement methods used for compliance (U.S. Department of Education, Office for Civil Rights, 2003).

NCAA INVOLVEMENT WITH TITLE IX

When Title IX was first introduced and started to impact intercollegiate athletics, the NCAA did not warmly embrace the federal statute. The Association brought the first legal challenge to Title IX in the mid-1970s, in *NCAA v. Califano* (1980) (Joseph Califano was the Secretary of the U.S. Department of Health, Education and Welfare). The NCAA asserted that HEW, in issuing the regulations,

- exceeded its authority under Title IX;
- had some regulations that were arbitrary and capricious under the Administrative Procedure Act;
- had some regulations that were unconstitutionally vague; and
- had some regulations that created a sex-based quota system in violation of Title IX and the Fifth Amendment.

The NCAA stated that enforcement of the Title IX regulations would injure the NCAA and its members (*NCAA v. Califano*, 1980). The lawsuit eventually died in 1980 when the U. S. Court of Appeals for the Tenth Circuit ruled that, as an independent association, the NCAA did not have legal standing to sue HEW.

After passage of the Civil Rights Restoration Act in 1987 and the enforcement muscle of the OCR in regard to Title IX was restored, the NCAA, as the governing body for intercollegiate athletics, decided that it had to take a more proactive approach. In 1991, the NCAA found disturbing results after surveying member institutions regarding expenditures for women's and men's athletic programs. Through that survey, the NCAA found that although undergraduate enrollment was roughly 50 percent male and 50 percent female, men comprised 69.5 percent of the participants in intercollegiate athletics and their sport programs received approximately 70 percent of the athletic scholarship funds, 77 percent of the operating budgets, and 83 percent of the recruiting money (NCAA, 1993).

In the spring of 1992, NCAA Executive Director (the position now called President) Richard Schultz formed the Gender Equity Task Force and charged it with defining gender equity, examining NCAA policies to evaluate their impact on gender equity, and recommending a path toward measuring and realizing gender equity in intercollegiate athletics (NCAA, 1993). One of the key issues the Task Force faced was what to do about the sport of football and its large roster sizes, equipment budgets, operating and recruiting budgets, and personnel (Suggs, 2005).

In July 1993, the Task Force released its findings and recommendations, and the NCAA endorsed the "Principle of Gender Equity," which now states: "It is the responsibility of each member institution to comply with federal and state laws regarding gender equity" and "The Association . . . should adopt legislation to enhance member institutions' compliance with applicable gender-equity laws" *(2008–09 NCAA Division I Manual,* 2008, p. 4). The Task Force also recommended adopting a system of "emerging sports" for women, identified as sports that were not NCAA championship sports yet, but sports for women that had a chance to grow. These sports included crew, ice hockey, team handball, water polo, synchronized swimming, archery, badminton, bowling, and squash. Since 1993, crew/rowing and ice hockey have become popular sports for women, with 144 rowing teams and 79 women's ice hockey teams sponsored by intercollegiate athletic departments in 2006–07 (NCAA, 2008b). Women's crew is a popular sport because of its large roster size. The average squad size in 2006–07 was 50 student-athletes, which helps to compensate for the large roster size of football.

Another recommendation coming from the Gender-Equity Task Force was the creation of a gender-equity source book for member institutions. As a result, in 1994 the NCAA first published *Gender Equity in Intercollegiate Athletics: A Practical Guide for Colleges and Universities.* This manual was written to provide "practical advice and real-life examples to assist the membership in its efforts to alleviate inequalities in its intercollegiate programs" (NCAA, 2008a, p. 6), and has been updated regularly since its initial publication. Some of the topics include the history and sources of the law, a step-by-step guide for understanding Title IX compliance, harassment and employment issues facing colleges and universities, and relevant case law. The NCAA has also conducted numerous gender-equity seminars and has created a women's resource center at the NCAA national office.

On a number of occasions and during various speaking events, former NCAA president Myles Brand endorsed the federal requirements for Title IX. While speaking at a meeting of the National Wrestling Coaches Association in May 2004, Brand told the group that Title IX has been used as an excuse to eliminate sport programs. Title IX should not be seen, though, as the cause. Instead, these decisions are made at the institutional level, and while the number of wrestling programs at NCAA schools over the past two decades dropped from 363 to 222, the number of football teams increased from 497 to 619 (Brand Defends Title IX, 2004).

APPLICATION AND ENFORCEMENT
IN INTERCOLLEGIATE ATHLETICS

s stated, the Department of Education's Office for Civil Rights is responsible for enforcing several federal civil rights laws including Title IX. The OCR employs several enforcement methods, including pursuing investigations brought by a complaint from an individual or organization, as well as selecting schools at random to undergo a compliance review. If an institution is found to be in violation of Title IX, the penalty that the OCR can assess is to withdraw federal funding to that institution. The magnitude of this potential penalty is enormous, as the large majority of public institutions could not operate without federal funding. Private institutions would also be impacted through withdrawal of financial assistance programs supported by the federal government, so some students could not afford to attend that institution.

The OCR uses a non-confrontational or proactive approach in investigating potential Title IX violations. If an investigation by the OCR determines that a violation of Title IX has occurred, the OCR attempts to obtain voluntary compliance by working with the institution and negotiating remedies along with a timeline to fulfill these remedies (U. S. Department of Education, 1998). In an effort to assist institutions with interpreting Title IX, the OCR also offers a technical assistance program that is "designed to provide education officials with the skills and knowledge necessary to apply the laws to their own circumstances and thereby facilitate voluntary compliance" (U. S. Department of Education, 1991). The OCR has yet to institute the withdrawal of federal funding penalty.

In 1990, the OCR published the *Title IX Athletics Investigator's Manual* (U. S. Department of Education, 1990) to provide guidance to OCR investigators when pursuing a Title IX complaint or investigation. This manual has also been helpful to athletic administrators and consultants in understanding the requirements of Title IX and how investigations are performed, as well as conducting internal Title IX audits. The manual lists 13 program components:

1. the accommodation of interests and abilities
2. athletic financial assistance
3. equipment and supplies
4. scheduling of games and practice times
5. travel and per diem allowances
6. tutoring
7. coaching
8. locker rooms
9. practice and competitive facilities
10. medical and training facilities and services
11. housing and dining facilities and services
12. publicity, support services (administrative support, and office space)
13. recruitment of student-athletes

These component areas are grouped into three primary areas of investigation first established as part of the 1979 HEW policy interpretation: athletic financial assistance (athletic scholarships), accommodation of student athletic interests and abilities, and benefits and opportunities.

Financial assistance

The athletic financial assistance area investigates whether athletic scholarship aid provided for male and female student-athletes is awarded on a substantially proportional basis. In determining compliance, the OCR looks at the proportion of athletic scholarship dollars provided to male and female student-athletes and compares this to the respective proportion of athletes who are male and female. The 1990 *Investigator's Manual* does not provide an actual allowable proportion requirement, but the OCR further clarified this component area through a July 1998 policy interpretation stating that this proportional analysis should be within one percentage point (U. S. Department of Education, 1998). In other words, if the percentage of female student-athletes within the athletic department is 50 percent, the percentage of athletic scholarship aid provided to these female student-athletes should be within 1 percent, or not less than 49 percent of the total aid allocated.

It is important to note that a difference beyond the one percentage point allowable discrepancy should not be viewed automatically as a Title IX violation. Within an investigation of each of the three Title IX component areas the OCR has identified certain nondiscriminatory factors—differences that "appear to be on the basis of sex and thus, are apparent disparities [but] may actually be permissible differences" (U. S. Department of Education, 1990, p. 10). Nondiscriminatory factors include:

- unique aspects of a particular sport such as the rules of play,
- nature/replacement of equipment, and
- unique facilities needed for a particular sport that are allowable differences that justify an apparent sex discrimination disparity.

Within each component area section of the *Title IX Athletics Investigator's Manual* is a section called "Caution," which lists several examples within that component area of differences in benefits provided to men and women that may be the result of nondiscriminatory reasons and therefore are allowed. Two possible nondiscriminatory factors identified for the financial assistance area are (a) higher costs of tuition for out-of-state students that in some years may be unevenly distributed between men's and women's sport programs; and (b) a disproportional allocation of scholarship aid in a given year as a result of a sport program's development, including spreading athletic scholarship aid distribution over four years when starting a new sport program, to ensure a more consistent influx of student-athletes being recruited to that team.

Student athletic interests and abilities

The second component area of Title IX compliance is the accommodation of students' interests and abilities. This area addresses the extent to which the institution has met the interests and abilities of male and female students and determines compliance based on a "three-prong" test (U. S. Department of Education, 1990):

1. whether intercollegiate participation opportunities for male and female students are provided in numbers substantially proportionate to their respective enrollment;
2. where members of one sex are underrepresented (failure to meet Prong 1), whether the institution can show a history and continuing practice of program expansion that is responsive to the developing interests and abilities of the underrepresented sex; and

3. where the members of one sex are underrepresented and the institution cannot show a continuing practice of program expansion (failure to meet Prong 1 or Prong 2), whether the institution can demonstrate that the interests and abilities of the members of the underrepresented sex have been fully and effectively accommodated by the present athletic program in place.

Meeting Prong 1

When applying the three-prong test to investigation of the accommodation of student interests and abilities, the OCR will first compare the ratio of male and female athletes to the ratio of male and female undergraduate students (Prong 1). For example, if the athletic department at a college or university had a total of 200 student-athletes of which 100 were male and 100 were female, this university would have a 50 percent male and 50 percent female student-to-athlete ratio. If the undergraduate student body at the school is 500 males and 500 females for a total of 1,000 students, the ratio of students by sex would also be 50 percent male and 50 percent female. This school would be found to have met Prong 1 based on the equal male and female ratios (both 50 percent) of both the athletic department and the undergraduate student body. It is important to note that Prong 1 does not require equal ratios but, rather, that the requirement is "substantially proportionate." The OCR, though, has not set a statistical requirement for allowable discrepancy between these percentages and, therefore, has not clarified what "substantially proportionate" means. Instead, Prong 1 is investigated on an institution-by-institution basis because undergraduate student bodies and size of athletic departments vary significantly across institutions.

If an institution fails to meet Prong 1, meaning that the OCR has determined that the ratio of male and female student-athletes when compared to the ratio of male and female students at the institution is not substantially proportionate, the athletic department can still be found in compliance with Title IX's component area of effective accommodation of student interests and abilities by meeting one of the remaining two prongs.

Meeting Prong 2

Prong 2 looks at the history of the athletic department to determine if the institution has made progress, and investigates whether the institution can show continued progress toward compliance with future steps to be taken at the institution. An institution can show a history of program expansion by (U. S. Department of Education, 1996):

1. adding intercollegiate teams or upgrading teams to intercollegiate status;
2. increasing the number of participants in intercollegiate athletics who are members of the underrepresented sex; and
3. providing an affirmative response to requests by students or others for addition or elevation of a sport team.

An institution can show continued progress toward compliance by demonstrating that it is implementing a plan that will include program expansion (the addition of varsity teams or upgrade of club teams) for the underrepresented sex.

Syracuse (New York) University, a private school with 12,500 undergraduates and a member of the Division I Big East Conference, was one of the first institutions to meet Title IX compliance in this component area by satisfying Prong 2. In May 1995, members of the university's female club lacrosse and softball teams filed suit alleging that the school was discriminating against female students. At the time, female students comprised 50 percent of Syracuse's undergraduate student body, but only 32.4 percent of the student-athlete population was female (Barr, 1999). Although at the time of the lawsuit the percentage of female student-athletes was low in comparison to the female student body, the courts (district and appeals court) found that Syracuse had a plan to add three new women's varsity sports in the near future. Syracuse was able to satisfy Prong 2 through its plan to add these varsity teams (*Boucher v. Syracuse,*1999).

Meeting Prong 3

If both Prong 1 and Prong 2 can not be met by an institution, compliance with this component area within Title IX can still be met if the institution can demonstrate that the interests and abilities of the underrepresented sex have been fully and effectively accommodated by the athletic department (sport team and participation opportunities) that is in place. In investigating this area, the OCR will look at (U.S. Department of Education, 1996):

1. whether there is unmet interest in a particular sport;
2. sufficient ability to sustain a team in that sport; and
3. a reasonable expectation of competition for the team.

In other words, if an institution had recently discontinued a varsity team for females and/or has a female club team in a sport that isn't offered for women at the varsity level, the OCR will usually find that there is unmet interest and will work with the institution to bring back the discontinued team, or raise the club team to varsity status.

Many institutions, in an effort to comply with Title IX's component area of effective accommodation of student interests and abilities by meeting Prong 3, have used questionnaires or surveys of current and prospective students to try to measure student interests in athletic participation. In March 2005, the OCR issued an Additional Clarification letter to institutions to provide guidance in regards to meeting Prong 3. This clarification letter included a web-based model survey instrument to help measure student interest in participating in intercollegiate varsity athletics (U.S. Department of Education, 2005). The efficacy of this survey instrument was much debated, and in 2010 the DOE withdrew the instrument. At the core of the debate over the survey was the issue of whether a survey instrument can accurately capture potential student interests in athletic participation. The survey is web-based and e-mailed to current students at an institution.

One of the arguments of concern with this survey instrument is that, by surveying students currently at the institution, you are potentially missing out on a contingent of students who chose not to attend that institution because they did not offer a particular sport program (Brady, 2005). Another concern is that the survey methodology calls for interpreting a non-response as non-interest in participation. For example, if a student at an institution does not reply to the survey instrument, the institution can interpret this as the student's lack of interest in participating in intercollegiate varsity sports. This debate over the efficacy of the survey instrument to measure effective accommodation of student's interests in abilities in intercollegiate varsity athletic participation is sure to stay until brought before a court as a means used by an institution to meet Title IX compliance. To date, such a court case has yet to happen.

Benefits and opportunities for student-athletes

The third major area of Title IX consists of the benefits and opportunities provided to male and female student-athletes. This component area is usually referred to as the "laundry list" of areas that are investigated by the OCR and is provided in Exhibit 11.1.

The goal of Title IX within this component area is that the benefits and opportunities provided to the male student-athletes are comparable to the benefits and opportunities provided to the female student-athletes.

Once again, nondiscriminatory factors may be involved in justifying any discrepancy that on the surface may be interpreted as sex discrimination. For example, the overall equipment budget of the male student-athletes may be substantially more than that provided to the female student-athletes. This discrepancy is allowable if it can be attributable to certain sport programs, primarily on the men's side, that require equipment that is more expensive, or more equipment is needed because of roster sizes (e.g., football rosters are larger and participation in the sport requires more and more costly equipment than, say, women's soccer or women's volleyball). Title IX is not violated as long as the male and female student-athletes are receiving comparable treatment; that is, as long as the women's soccer and volleyball teams are receiving the same treatment as the men's soccer and volleyball teams.

We emphasize that Title IX does not require a sport-by-sport analysis. For example, when investigating a potential Title IX violation, the OCR collects information and conducts interviews within each sport program. But a comparison between men's and women's individual sport teams, such as comparing the men's basketball team to the women's basketball team, is not performed. Instead, Title IX

EXHIBIT 11.1   The "laundry list" of areas investigated by the OCR.

Equipment and supplies

Scheduling of games and practice time

Travel and per diem allowance

Opportunity to receive coaching and academic tutoring

Assignment and compensation of coaches and tutors

Locker rooms

Practice and competitive facilities

Medical and training facilities and services

Housing and dining facilities and services

Publicity

Support services

Recruitment of student-athletes

Source: U.S. Department of Education, 1990.

uses an overall program assessment and compares what the male student-athletes receive overall versus the female student-athletes. This approach allows institutions to make strategic decisions in terms of sport programs they want to support to a greater extent than others. It provides institutions with latitude to make these types of strategic decisions regarding resource allocation and support to individual sport programs as long as male and female student-athletes receive comparable treatment and funding on an overall athletic department level.

LEGAL ARGUMENTS AND CHALLENGES TO TITLE IX

ince Title IX was passed in 1972, the subsequent decades have seen a great deal of evolution in the federal statutes' application and the policy guidelines provided to institutions to assist in interpretation and compliance. The OCR website (www.ed.gov/about/offices/list/ocr/index.html) provides links to Title IX publications and documents, including nine "Dear Colleague" letters or Memorandums issued from the Office for Civil Rights to institutions to provide additional clarification and guidelines relative to Title IX (U. S. Department of Education, 2008).

The evolution of Title IX's application and enforcement has also played out in the courts through various lawsuits that have been argued and decided. The discussion of history in this chapter provided information on two important landmark cases, the Supreme Court decisions in *Grove City College v. Bell* (1984), which restored the institutional approach to the enforcement method of Title IX, and *Franklin v. Gwinnett County Public Schools* (1992), which allowed victims of Title IX discrimination to receive monetary damages. The additional lawsuits discussed next show the broadened scope of Title IX's application, calling on collegiate athletic administrators to become ever more aware and knowledgeable about this statute and its application to college athletics.

Effective accommodation of student interests and abilities challenges

A landmark case in Title IX's history is the First Circuit Court of Appeals decision in *Cohen v. Brown University* (1996). In 1991, as a result of financial constraints brought on by a university-wide cost-cutting directive, Brown University, a member of the Division I Ivy League, demoted from university-funded varsity status to donor-funded varsity status the women's gymnastics and volleyball teams, as well as the men's water polo and golf teams. Female student-athletes brought a class-action lawsuit against Brown, claiming that the school discriminated against women in operation of the athletic program. At issue was the effective accommodation of student interests and abilities component area of Title IX.

In 1993–94, Brown University funded 32 intercollegiate varsity teams, 16 for men and 16 for women, of which 25 were university-funded (12 for men, 13 for women). Overall, the student-athlete population was composed of 62 percent men and 38 percent women, and the composition among university-funded sports was 61 percent men and 39 percent women, in comparison to the student undergraduate composition of 49 percent men and 51 percent women (*Cohen v. Brown University*, D.R.I. 1995). These statistics show that Brown University did not meet the requirements of Prong 1.

This case is important because of two key arguments used by the university on appeal, ones used often by opponents of Title IX. The first argument is that the three-prong test effectively renders Title IX as an affirmative action statute that mandates imposing quotas. The First Circuit Court of Appeals dismissed these arguments, stating first that Title IX does not mandate a finding of discrimination based solely upon a gender-based statistical disparity. A second argument used by Brown was that there is a difference in the level of interest in sports between the sexes in general and, therefore, significant disparities in athletic opportunities should be allowed.

The Court of Appeals responded in that Title IX was enacted to remedy historical discrimination experienced by girls and women, and that women's lower rate of participation reflects women's historical lack of opportunities to participate in sports (*Cohen v. Brown University*, 1996). Brown University appealed to the U.S. Supreme Court, which refused to hear the case.

Discrimination challenges

Another Title IX case of note is *Mercer v. Duke University* (1999), in which Heather Sue Mercer, an all-state kicker during high school, was put on the Duke University football roster during the 1995 season but then was informed that she was off the team at the start of the 1996 football season. Mercer alleged that during the 1995–96 school year, in which she was listed on the fall team roster and participated in the spring 1996 team conditioning drills, she was the subject of discriminatory treatment by the university and the football coach.

At the trial court level, the case was dismissed, with the court reasoning that Title IX provided a blanket exemption for contact sports. Schools are allowed to prohibit females from competing on contact sport teams. However, the Fourth Circuit Court of Appeals overturned the decision, finding that once Duke University allowed Mercer to try out for the football team, it voluntarily opened the team to members of both sexes and therefore Title IX and its regulations regarding discrimination based on gender were applicable. Duke University was found to have violated Title IX by cutting Mercer from the football team because she was a woman (*Mercer v. Duke University*, 1999).

Reverse discrimination concerns

One of the primary concerns of organizations such as the National Wrestling Coaches Association and the College Sports Council is that men's varsity sport teams are being dropped by schools in an effort to comply with Title IX. Although men's teams in Division I decreased during the 1980s, men's teams in all divisions increased overall during this time period. Also, since 1988–89, there was a net gain of 202 men's teams, as well as 2,292 women's teams in the NCAA. Since 1988–89 the men's sport team with the greatest net loss of teams was the sport of wrestling (101 teams) (NCAA, 2008b).

The National Wrestling Coaches Association filed a lawsuit against the Department of Education, arguing that male student-athletes were being discriminated against because the enforcement standards directly caused a reduction in the number of men's sport teams. The U.S. District Court judge dismissed the case on the grounds that the wrestlers failed to show that Title IX caused their teams to be dropped and that even if Title IX were to be altered the wrestling teams would not be reinstated (*National Coaches Wrestling Association v. United States Department of Education*, 2003). The case was appealed to the U. S. Court of Appeals for the District of Columbia. The court affirmed the District Court's ruling, finding that the wrestlers did not have standing to sue the Department of Education, as their injuries (cutting their sport teams) were caused by the decisions of specific universities (*National Coaches Wrestling Association v. United States Department of Education*, 2004). The U. S. Supreme Court refused to hear the case on appeal.

Some schools have been seeking other ways to address the participation concerns associated with men's sports. Consider the decision by Brigham Young University (BYU), a private school with 30,000 undergraduates located in Provo, Utah, and owned by the Church of Jesus Christ of Latter Day Saints (the Mormon Church), involving its club-level men's soccer program. As we learned earlier, the rise in club sport programs is connected to dropping certain men's sports programs because of proportionality concerns. At BYU, the club men's soccer program has been especially successful, winning six National Intramural-Recreational Sports Association championships. But as a result of proportionality concerns (BYU's full-time undergraduate population is 51 percent female), the school has refused to re-elevate the program to Division I varsity status. Perviously, the school sponsored a D-I program (from 1983 to 1987) but dropped it, according to school officials, because of poor performance. In the latter situation, the move to D-I varsity status would require adding a comparable women's program, and the school does not have the resources to do so (Longman, 2003).

In 2003, however, the school decided to spend $40,000 (provided by donors, including some players' parents and the Mormon Church) to purchase a franchise in the Premier Development League (PDL). This is a minor-league soccer circuit consisting of 68 teams that play from May to August. The PDL allows high-school and college-aged players to play more games and to maintain their amateur status. According to the BYU program's website, the PDL provides competition that is "considered higher than NCAA soccer in the pyramid of U. S. soccer development" (BYU Soccer, 2008). Although BYU's players would not receive grants-in-aid (to do so would cost the school an estimated $500,000), the program expected to make money in its new league, where budgets run from $60,000 to $150,000. Shoe and apparel maker adidas agreed to sponsor the team for $20,000 a year, and the program would charge $5 for game admission, with attendance expected to average 3,000 a game. The school was to provide up to $40,000 a year in support, used to maintain playing fields and a coaching stipend.

Program head coach Chris Watkins noted that gender equity laws have hurt the development of men's soccer in the United States, but gender equity advocates viewed the move with suspicion, fearing that the action would be a way to circumvent existing laws, which, they note, would also apply to club teams and intramural and recreational programs. Some BYU female students had been lobbying school officials to form club teams in ice hockey, field hockey, and water polo. School officials, however, say BYU was not seeking to skirt the laws, noting that the number of athletes was not being increased, and that a men's soccer program was going to exist in some form regardless. University vice-president Fred Skousen explained the move as an opportunity to "give our soccer players a chance to compete at a high level without having to significantly increase our funding" (Longman, 2003, p.2). The team finished fourth in the PDL's Southwest Division in 2009, with a 7–5–4 record.

Retaliation discrimination challenges

More recently, Title IX has been a legal theory used in claims of retaliation discrimination. In *Jackson v. Birmingham Board of Education* (2005), a male teacher who coached the girls' high school basketball team filed a lawsuit after receiving unfavorable evaluations leading to his removal as the team's coach for complaining that the girls' team received unequal funding and access to the school's equipment and facilities. The Supreme Court found that when a person is being retaliated against because he or she complains of sex discrimination, this constitutes intentional discrimination on the basis of sex in violation of Title IX. In the settlement agreement in this case, the male coach was reinstated as girls' basketball coach and the Board of Education promised to take necessary steps to provide the female athletes with comparable facilities as those used by the male athletes (Brumback, 2006).

Sexual harassment challenges

In *Simpson et al. v. University of Colorado* (2007) female students at the University of Colorado filed a lawsuit alleging that they were sexually harassed at a party by university football players and recruits, in violation of Title IX. The Tenth Circuit Court of Appeals found that the alleged sexual assaults were caused by CU's failure to provide adequate supervision and guidance relative to its recruiting program and the use of player-hosts chosen to show the football recruits a "good time." In 2008, this lawsuit was settled out of court, with Lisa Simpson receiving $2.5 million and requiring the university to create a new position in the Office of Victim Assistance and hire an independent adviser to monitor the school's compliance with federal sex discrimination laws (AAUW LAF, 2008).

THE EVOLUTION OF TITLE IX ENFORCEMENT   **case study 11.A**

The standards used by the Department of Education's Office for Civil Rights to determine compliance have evolved over the course of both legal challenges and OCR investigations. Under Prong 1 of the OCR's three-prong test of the investigation of the accommodation of student interests and abilities, the OCR first compares the ratio of male and female athletes to the ratio of male and female undergraduate students. Prong 1 does not require equal ratios but, rather, that the requirement is "substantially proportionate," and that the OCR has not set a statistical requirement for allowable discrepancy between these percentages. Instead, Prong 1 is investigated on an institution-by-institution basis because undergraduate student bodies and size of athletic departments vary significantly across institutions.

In many cases, the unofficial benchmark for substantial proportionality has been determined to be 5 percent; that is, if participation of the underrepresented sex is within 5 percent of the total full-time undergraduate enrollment of that sex, an athletic department has been deemed to be in compliance. For example, if the number of female student-athletes at your school totaled 40 percent of the student-athlete population, and females accounted for 45 percent of the total full-time undergraduate population, your school would have been viewed as in compliance.

However, a 2009 case involving three female club sport student-athletes at the University of California, Davis (UCD), a public school with 24,000 undergraduates and a member of the Division I Big West Conference, seemed to change this 5 percent benchmark. At UCD in

2007–08, women comprised 56 percent of the total full-time undergraduate enrollment and 50 percent of the student-athlete population. In the settlement between the school and the plaintiffs, the agreement called for the UCD athletic department to achieve substantial proportionality of 1.5 percent within 10 years. The school would do this in part by adding varsity field hockey in the Fall of 2009, and to contribute $110,000 to a fund to develop additional club sports. The agreement also allowed UCD to trim the rosters of men's teams to bring the program into compliance.

UCD AD Greg Warzecka commented that his school had "a solid history of commitment to its female athletes and coaches and to expanding opportunities for women in college sports" (Thomas, 2009, p. B11), but Marcia Greenberger, co-president of the National Women's Law Center, an advocacy group often involved in such cases, stated: "It is a boost in the momentum toward the real goal of equality of opportunity, and not a goal of approximate equality, but real equality" (p. B11). Noreen Farrell, the lead lawyer for the plaintiffs, expects more cases such as these to go to trial in the next few years, as many schools face difficult budget decisions and female enrollments continue to increase. "The question now is," said Farrell, "how do we make sure that women aren't disproportionately impacted by the budget cuts and shrinking athletic budgets?" (p. B11).

question for you to consider

1. If you were advising Greg Warzecka in how to meet the 1.5 percent benchmark set in the settlement, how would you recommend he meet this goal—adding women's teams, cutting men's teams, or limiting the rosters of men's teams? Outline the impact of your decision in terms of budgets and how they will impact the student-athlete experience.

CONCLUSION

Since the passage of Title IX as part of the Educational Amendments Act of 1972, the positive impact of this law has become evident, as many new doors of opportunity have been opened for women and girls in athletics. Athletic administrators, though, face the task of understanding the requirements of Title IX and also managing their own strategic approach to complying with this federal statute, given their institution's unique population and financial resources. A number of resources are available to help administrators, as well as student-athletes, coaches, and parents, understand Title IX and assist them with methods of compliance.

The political debate surrounding Title IX continues as organizations such as the National Women's Law Center, Women's Sports Foundation, and National Organization for Women, among others, argue the merits of Title IX and the appropriate enforcement methods. In contrast, the National Wrestling Coaches Association and the College Sports Council have questioned the appropriateness of certain compliance standards—in particular the proportionality test. These groups have sparred over the use of surveys to gauge women's interests in athletics.

The Office for Civil Rights website can be a first point of contact to explore programs and initiatives, as well as frequently asked questions and answers. The NCAA website also provides a multitude of links and resources. Other associations, such as the Women's Sports Foundation, can be of assistance in understanding and navigating this federal statute aimed at eliminating sex discrimination in educational programs and activities, including intercollegiate athletics.

PRACTITIONER perspective:

EDWARD "TED" LELAND, V.P. for Advancement at the University of the Pacific, Co-chair of the 2003 Commission on Opportunity in Athletics

Throughout the chapter we have focused on the impact of Title IX and gender equity on intercollegiate athletic programs. To help us understand these concepts from the perspective of departmental practitioners, the authors sought the insights of Dr. Edward "Ted" Leland. He served as AD at Stanford for 14 years, during which time Stanford teams won 50 national team championships. In 2000, the National Association of Collegiate Directors of Athletics honored him as its Athletic Director of the Year, and he has been named one of the "10 most influential persons in college athletics" by *Street & Smith's Sports Business Journal*. During Leland's tenure, Stanford's athletic program raised more than $270 million in private donations, invested some $185 million in building and renovating athletics and recreation facilities, and increased its athletics endowment to $375 million. Leland also chaired the NCAA Division I Management Council (1999–2001), and served on the executive committee of the Bay Area Sports Organizing Committee (1996–2002), a group that sought to attract the 2012 Olympic Games to San Francisco.

In 2006, Leland accepted the position of Vice President for University Advancement at the University of the Pacific, his alma mater. Leland oversees fundraising and alumni relations on all three of the university's campuses. He earned his bachelor's degree in 1970 and his master's degree in 1972 from the University of the Pacific. He played football and coached at the school before returning as the director of athletics from 1989 to 1991. Leland also served as AD at Dartmouth College from 1983 to 1989.

Q: *Looking back on your time in intercollegiate athletics, what are your recollections of the political landscape surrounding the legislative passage of Title IX?*

A: In the 1970s, people had an idea that women ought to be treated equally and have equal opportunity, and yet they didn't have any idea how that looked and what it was going to mean. I can remember in those days how horrified everybody was that we actually might have females in the training room. Now it's commonplace. You couldn't find a training room today without females as athletes, doctors, trainers, and physical therapists. Most training rooms are now fully integrated. That's a sociological change.

There has also been significant change in the understanding of Title IX. When the law was passed in 1972, there was no real direction given to anybody on how to comply. This didn't occur until the late 1970s with the release of the Policy Interpretations. When that 1979 interpretation came out, it took another couple of years for people to figure out what Title IX was all about, what it meant, and how it was going to be enforced. As a result, the enforcement has become more complex and more confused since then.

You were a co-chair of the 15-person President Bush–appointed Commission on Opportunity in Athletics that convened in 2003. What was your role on the Commission, what was its charge, and was the Commission successful in meeting this charge?

There were really two major questions asked of the commission. The first was how Title IX was servicing the public. Our answer, based on the testimony we heard and the documents we received, was that Title IX is a huge success. The American people support Title IX. This is one of the most popular pieces of civil rights legislation that we have. The second question we were asked was whether there was a better way to administer Title IX, other than the 1979 HEW Policy Interpretations. Our commission concluded that there really wasn't a better way. We supported the 1979 interpretation, although there were a number of recommendations that suggested slight changes in certain areas. We suggested tightening up enforcement, making the penalties easier to levy, making interpretations clearer across the country, making Prongs 2 and 3—the interest and abilities test—more understandable. But in general, our commission supported the 1979 interpretation, which was a big step.

At the time, there was a great deal of question as to whether the 1979 interpretations were appropriate. Our commission said they are the best we've got.

Some of the women's advocacy groups thought we were a huge threat to Title IX, with some apocalyptic comments about returning women to the "Stone Age." None of that happened. If our commission did anything, it strengthened Title IX.

In 2005, the Department of Education issued a statement that it would allow intercollegiate athletic departments to utilize periodic surveys to gauge interest in women's athletics. Why did some Title IX advocates criticize this action?

This idea of an omnibus interest test was discussed by the commission and was not supported—nor do I support it. It was not in keeping with the recommendations of the commission. It was sort of beaten down so hard when it was first released that I don't know of anybody who's using surveys. I happen to like the fact that we use ratios, and I believe it has really helped women's athletics. I like the fact that we use a system based on the number of women participating, but I can see the other side of the argument. In my experience at Northwestern, Pacific, Dartmouth, and Stanford, there was always an interest by women to participate in sports. When we added a sport, women showed up to play—skilled women, committed women. My direct experience as a practitioner was that women were always interested.

In their book, Playing with the Boys: Why Separate Is Not Equal in Sports, *authors Eileen McDonagh and Laura Pappano argue that financial equity can be accomplished by scaling back expenditures on football and men's basketball, which they describe as "hardly suitable for educational institutions." What's your reaction to this statement?*

I have two reactions. First, on the question as to whether the expenditures in football that are disproportionate, that are opulent and are hardly suitable for educational institutions, my answer is "yes." I would say that's also true of women's basketball and men's basketball and some other sports. Football isn't alone. The bigger point is that women's advocacy groups, for different reasons, have seen football as the enemy. And part of it is because this sport throws ratios off, part of it is because of the opulent spending, part of it is because there's no equivalent women's sport. That's what leads to this distrust or outright hostility toward intercollegiate football.

My experience is exactly the opposite. Football is the woman athletes' best friend. If I were a woman athlete growing up in Stockton, California, and I wanted a chance to be a female athlete at the University of the Pacific, the best thing that could happen for me would be for Pacific to bring football back [football was discontinued at Pacific in 1995]. This would achieve the following: It would require that Pacific add more opportunities for women, and it would probably bring a lot of resources to the program that would make my experience as a student, and my chance for a scholarship, even better.

In 1991, when I became AD at Stanford, we had 650 athletes—450 men and 200 women. When I left, we had added 200 women's opportunities in seven women's sports and not dropped any men's teams. We were now up to 400 women athletes with an additional seven women's sports in the department. The question is whether we would have done that if we didn't have football. Anybody who watched our metamorphosis at Stanford would say no—we wouldn't have 400 women athletes if we didn't have football.

Who would have the best women's teams? The answer is schools with big-time football. At the Division I NCAA Softball World Series, the NCAA Division I Women's Basketball Final Four, the NCAA Division I women's swimming championships, the top 10 are all schools with football. The great women athletes are going to the football schools. We can sit in a law office somewhere and say that's a bad deal, but the women athletes who want a great experience, who have the talent, are going to the football schools—and that's really the BCS schools. I would summarize it this way: If one thinks his or her obligation to provide equal opportunity is to manage the ratio between men and women, then he or she doesn't like football. If one thinks his or her obligation to provide equal opportunity for women involves providing as many opportunities for women as one can, one supports football. It's just the way you look at what equal opportunity means.

Sure, there's the issue surrounding the salaries being paid to football coaches, and there's the issue surrounding the number of coaches in a football program, and there's the issue surrounding the expense of football teams spending Friday nights in the hotel even for home games. I understand these issues, and I don't support all those things. You can see by my track record that I never bought into the high salaries, but at the same time, some of this angst is misplaced. If I were a women head coach at any school, I'd be out there supporting football because if they drop football, the whole athletic program is going to take a step backwards. The number of trainers, strength coaches, facilities, the number of dollars for scholarships, and everything else, will decrease.

Why do many believe that the federal government's current method of measuring compliance with Title IX is not fair to all intercollegiate student-athletes?

The one thing you can say about our commission is that it was the most extensive, fairest, and open discussion of Title IX ever. We had exhaustive testimony from a variety of sources take place before our commission. We had 400 people testify, and everyone but one said something to the effect that they were fully in agreement with equal opportunity for women, but they had some little way they thought Title IX could be administered in a better way. And the biggest concern that people had was that some schools are still not in compliance with Title IX. There's still work to be done, so one one could say our method is still not fair because we haven't reached equality yet.

But, on the other hand, the question is: What are those inequities? One is the difference in grants-in-aid (GIAs) between men's and women's teams in the same sport. For example, women's tennis has eight GIAs while men's tennis receives 4.5. Yet they wear the same uniforms, they have the same-size locker rooms, and they compete with the same schedule. Why is that? Tennis people on the men's side don't understand that, and who

would expect them to? Another glowing example is in rowing. Men's rowing goes without GIAs and women's rowing has them, yet they work out in the same boathouse, they sometimes have the same coaches, they use the same equipment, they keep the same hours, and they train next to each other. But the women are on athletic aid and the men aren't. So people rebel.

There is also the message we're hearing from the wrestlers. The first people who testified in open hearings before our commission were three wrestlers from Marquette University who had their sport dropped and were told their sport was dropped because of Title IX. These three young men drove all the way to Atlanta to tell their story. It was a sad story. Anyone who loves athletics and believes in athletics like I do, it brought tears to my eyes. This wasn't a good deal. Nobody was happy that Marquette had to drop this sport. The reality is that there has been a drop in wrestling programs. And at times that's been blamed on Title IX. That's why people sometimes don't like the way the government is measuring compliance with Title IX. On the one hand, people aren't in compliance, and on other hand, there are these micro inequities that are affecting different sports and male athletes. Overall, the public good has been served tremendously well by Title IX, but it's a significant social change in America that hasn't been without some bumps along the way.

questions TO CONSIDER

1. Based on the history and evolution of Title IX and gender equity enforcement, explain the need for such laws when the law was initially passed, and whether the need for such rules are still valid today.

2. Based on the three-prong test established by the Department of Education's Office for Civil Rights, determine whether your school's athletic program is in compliance with each prong.

3. This chapter includes several court cases that impacted significantly the ways in which gender equity laws have been enforced. Identify and explain which case you think was the most influential in influencing gender equity enforcement.

4. Examine the rosters of intercollegiate athletic programs at your school, and compare the number of participants in male and female programs. If there are equal numbers of teams but more male than female student-athletes, explain why your athletic department might still be out of compliance with gender equity laws.

5. Based on the data you gathered in the previous question, outline the options that departmental managers have in order to comply with the established equity benchmarks.

references

AAUW LAF Plaintiff Settles Discrimination Suit with University of Colorado at Boulder for $2.5 Million. (2008, January 4). Accessed August 22, 2008, from: http://www.aauw.org/About/newsroom/pressreleases/010708_Simpson.cfm

Barr, C. (1999, October). Still afloat. *Athletic Business*, pp. 26, 28.

Boucher v. Syracuse University, 164 F.3d 113 (2d Cir. 1999).

Brady, E. (2005, May 16). Women's groups, OCR spar over Title IX surveys. *USA Today*. Accessed July 30, 2008, from: http://www.usatoday.com/sports/2005-05-16-title-ix_x.htm

Brand Defends Title IX. (2004, May 20). *USA Today*. Accessed August 22, 2008, from: http://www.usatoday.com/sports/college/2004-05-20-brand-title-ix_x.htm

Brumback, K. (2006, November 29). Alabama coach settles Title IX case. *Boston Globe*. Accessed August 22, 2008, from: http//www.boston.com/news/nation/articles/2006/11/29/Alabama_coach_settles_title_ix_case

BYU Soccer—History. (2008). Accessed December 29, 2009, from: http://www.byusoccer.com/history/php

Civil Rights Restoration Act of 1987, Public Law 100-259, March 22, 1988.

Cohen v. Brown University, 879 F.Supp. 185 (D.R.I. 1995).

Cohen v. Brown University, 101 F.3d 155 1st Cir. (1996).

de Varona, D., & Foudy, J. (2003). Minority views on the Report of the Commission on Opportunity in Athletics. Accessed July 30, 2008, from: http://www.womenssportsfoundation.org/binary-data/WSF_ARTICLE/pdf_file/944.pdf\

Franklin v. Gwinnett County Public Schools, 503 U.S. 60 (1992).

Grove City College v. Bell, 5 U.S. 555 (1984).

Jackson v. Birmingham Board of Education, 125 U.S. 14987 (2005).

Longman, J. (2003, March 7). B.Y.U. soccer finds novel alternative to N.C.A.A. *New York Times*. Accessed December 7, 2009, from http://www.nytimes.com

Mercer v. Duke University, 190 F.3d 643 (4th Cir. 1999).

National Coaches Wrestling Association v. United States Department of Education, 263 F.Supp 2d 82 (D.D.C. 2003).

National Coaches Wrestling Association v. United States Department of Education, 366 F.3d 930 (D.D.C. 2004).

NCAA. (1993, July 26). *NCAA gender-equity task force report.* Accessed August 22, 2008, from: http://ncaa/org/gender_equity/resource_materials/Historical/Task_Force_Reportpdf

NCAA. (2008a). *Gender equity in intercollegiate athletics: A practical guide for colleges and universities.* Accessed July 23, 2009, from: http://www.ncaa.org/library/general/gender_equity/gender_equity_manual.pdf

NCAA. (2008b). *NCAA sports sponsorship and participation rates report 1981-82 – 2006-07.* Accessed August 22, 2008, from: http://www.ncaapublications.com/Uploads/PDF/ParticipationRates20084232c5b7-6441-412c-80fl-7d85f3536a51.pdf

NCAA v. Califano, 444 F.Supp. 425 (D. Kan. 1978) and 622 F.2d 1382 (10th Cir. 1980).

Secretary's Commission on Opportunity in Athletics. (2003). *Open to all: Title IX at thirty.* Washington, DC: U.S. Department of Education.

Simpson et al. v. University of Colorado, 500 F.3d 1170 (10th Cir. 2007).

Suggs, W. (2005). *A place on the team*. Princeton, NJ: Princeton University Press.

Thomas, K. (2009, June 10). Title IX ruling could lead to more strict standards. *New York Times,* p. B11.

2008–09 NCAA Division I Manual. (2008). Indianapolis: NCAA.

U.S. Department of Education, Office for Civil Rights. (1990). Title IX athletics investigator's manual. Accessed June 24, 2008, from: http://www.eric/ed.gov/ERICDocs/data/ericdocs2sql/content_storage_01/0000019b/80/14/cl/26.pdf

U.S. Department of Education, Office for Civil Rights. (1991). *Equal opportunity in intercollegiate athletic. Requirements under Title IX of the Education Amendments of 1972.* Accessed June 24, 2008, from: http://www.ed.gov/about/offices/list/ocr/docs/interath.html

U.S. Department of Education, Office for Civil Rights. (1996, January 16). *Clarification of intercollegiate athletics policy guidance: The three-part test.* Accessed July 30, 2008, from: http://www.ed.gov/about/offices/list/ocr/docs/clarific.html

U.S. Department of Education, Office for Civil Rights. (1998). *Title IX and sex discrimination.* Accessed June 24, 2008, from: http://www.ed.gov/about/offices/list/ocr/docs/tix_dis.html

U.S. Department of Education, Office for Civil Rights. (2003). *Further clarification of intercollegiate athletics policy guidance regarding Title IX compliance.* Accessed July 30, 2008, from http://www.ed.gov/about/offices/list/ocr/titleqguidanceFinal.html

U.S. Department of Education, Office for Civil Rights. (2005, March 17). *Additional clarification of intercollegiate athletics policy: Three-part test—part Three.* Accessed July 30, 2008, from: http:/www.ed.gov/about/offices/list/ocr/docs/title9guidanceadditional.html

U.S. Department of Education, Office for Civil Rights. (2008). *Reading room.* Accessed August 22, 2008, from: http://www.ed.gov/about/offices/list/ocr/publications/html

Women's Sports Foundation. *Title IX Myth-Fact.* (2008). Accessed August 21, 2008, from: http://www.womenssportsfoundation.org/Content/Articles/Issues/Title-IX/T/Title-IX-MythFact.aspx#

Wong, G. (2002). *Essentials of sports law* (3rd ed.). Westport, CT: Greenwood Publishing Group.

Reform efforts and ethical concerns

12

Key concepts to keep in mind as you read the chapter:

- The factors that influenced organizations and individuals to embark upon reform efforts throughout the history of intercollegiate athletics.

- The factors that influenced organizations and individuals to initiate more recent reform efforts.

- The nature of recent developments impacting the ethical management of intercollegiate athletic departments.

Introduction

We have learned about the unique nature of the U.S. intercollegiate athletic enterprise and how this uniqueness impacts organizational mission and goals, as well as operational areas such as departmental and institutional finances and budgets. We also have learned how the influences of outside and affiliated organizations such as conferences, the NCAA, and other governing bodies impact internal policies and procedures of departments and institutions.

Problematic issues and conflicts have emerged as a result of the distinct nature of the enterprise. Managers have attempted to maintain what they believe is the proper and acceptable role of intercollegiate athletics programs within the specific setting of higher education.

Consider the challenges faced by two different presidents of the University of Alabama. Several years ago, when overseeing the management of his school's football program, former president Andrew Sorensen expressed frustration in comprehending the expectations of certain rabid fans. After the team lost an early season home game to Louisiana Tech, which fans had expected Alabama to win, Alabama then upset conference foe the University of Florida on the road. Sorensen then observed: "After the Tech game, I heard from three thousand people who wanted [the head coach] fired, and after the Florida game, I heard from three thousand people who wanted me to give him a contract extension. What still puzzles me—they were the same three thousand people" (St. John, 2004, p. 154). We also know, as discussed in Chapter 6, that current Alabama president Robert Witt identified football as a significant factor in aiding the school's recent $500 million capital campaign.

Sorensen's and Witt's observations are illustrative of the culture and expectations at Alabama, and also underscore the complexities surrounding the challenges faced by school administrators and athletic managers. Sorensen, Witt, and their colleagues might not like listening to these rabid fans, courting them at school events, and using athletics to generate the funds for other programs, but, given the nature of their jobs, they have no choice.

Even with some of the best efforts to deal with the varied stakeholder interests inherent to the enterprise, real and perceived flaws in managing this unique enterprise persist. What we are left to consider in this chapter are some of the principal ethical issues that contemporary intercollegiate managers face, and the means that managers and stakeholders alike have employed to operate their programs effectively and responsibly. First, to gain a historical perspective, we will review several of the major efforts undertaken by schools and managers to examine how to operate athletic programs within the ethical rubrics of higher education.

REFORM EFFORTS PAST AND PRESENT

Efforts to deal with how the operational areas of intercollegiate athletics impact the stated mission and goals of the higher education environment have existed for nearly as long as intercollegiate athletic competitions. Several of the most significant efforts undertaken to review these challenges and to reform the enterprise are explored next.

The Carnegie Report

Back in Chapter 1, we discussed the issues and events that led to the formation of what was to become the NCAA. The negative trends in intercollegiate sport continued, however, as chronicled in a report on intercollegiate athletics released in October 1929. The study, *American College Athletics*, commonly referred to as the "Carnegie Report," was the third such inquiry devoted to athletics authorized by the Carnegie Foundation for the Advancement of Teaching. The report was written by Dr. Howard Savage, a former teacher at Bryn Mawr College and member of the Carnegie Foundation staff. The intent of the inquiry, initiated in 1926 in response to requests from the NCAA and from numerous college groups, including many college presidents, was

> to ascertain the significant facts concerning college athletics in the United States and Canada, to analyze these facts in relation to American college and university life, . . . and to present a summary of American college athletics, their merits and their defects, together with such suggestions looking to their improvement. (Thelin, 1996, p. 3)

The report was compiled after visits to 112 U.S. colleges and universities, and interviews with presidents, administrators, and other personnel. Areas of focus included amateurism, administrative control, recruiting, values in athletics, the role of coaches, and the role of the press. Savage (1929) found that "Whatever the reason, it is certain that the seriousness with which college athletics are nowadays taken has driven certain well-recognized abuses under cover, but at the same time has propagated and intensified them" (p. 32). In the "Administrative Control" section of the report, Savage found that "very few [schools] appear to operate upon a consistent or complete educational policy that includes athletics," and

> that many university or college presidents have left the shaping of athletic policies to conferences, committees, or specialists in physical education, who represent not so much the welfare of the institution and its undergraduates as special interests of one sort or another, all of which apparently feel that material prosperity, their own prestige, or professional standing must be served before other ends can be considered. (pp. 79–80)

Savage cited numerous cases at schools such as the University of Alabama, Boston College, the University of Iowa, and Stanford University, where presidents, trustees, and alumni intervened to press for admittance of unqualified student-athletes. Also uncovered were cases in which athletes were allowed to pass examinations "under circumstances that were, to say the least, unusual." In a review of the academic records of 2,787 student-athletes at 52 institutions, Savage concluded:

> It cannot be said that in general athletes are greater idlers than non-athletes. . . . Grades of athletes seem to average slightly lower than those of non-athletes. . . . It takes the athlete about half a college year longer, on the whole, to obtain his degree. . . . [Athletes] possess about the same or slightly better intellectual capacity than non-athletes [based on a specially administered standardized test at thirteen schools in Pennsylvania]. (pp. 124–126)

Savage vividly summarized his report's findings by stating:

> Faculties, trustees, and even college presidents are not yet united as respects the maintenance of strict requirements in the face of the supposed benefits that can be wrung from winning teams. The fact that all of these supposed advantages are tinged at one point or another with the color of money casts over every relaxation of standards a mercenary shadow. (pp. 118–119)

Savage fixed the blame for much of these developments on college presidents, because "often, the shaping of (athletic) policy has depended upon satisfying as many special claims as possible without due regard to the best interests of the undergraduates" (p. 83), and school presidents, he believed, could best effect reform.

The findings of the report proved to be an invaluable resource for data on the state of intercollegiate athletics at a specific point in time, and in many ways highlight how many of the issues that challenge intercollegiate athletic managers today are much the same as those of nearly a century ago. Still, it ultimately did little to effect reform. According to Thelin (1996), the report "triggered refutations and denials by college presidents. . . . One ritual was for a college official to endorse the Carnegie study in principle, with the specific disclaimer that its charges did not describe the athletic program at his own campus" (pp. 27–28). Athletic administrators were generally quick to dismiss the report. Big Ten commissioner John Griffith grumbled:

> I think that I am better informed of Big Ten athletic conditions than any investigator for the Carnegie Foundation. And I honestly believe that [our programs] are cleaner . . . than are any other ten universities anyone can name. When the Carnegie report relies on the facts uncovered by an agent in a twenty-four hour visit to a university, it seems to me that it is evident that the report cannot be always fair to the institution. (Thelin, 1996, p. 29)

Interviews of students on campuses at the time found little concern with the report, while many periodicals questioned the objectivity of the report. However, the general reaction to the report was typified by the comments of Fordham University football coach Frank Cavanaugh: "Why get excited? The report only tells what everyone already knew" (Schmidt, 2007, p. 233).

Savage later responded that no critic was able to refute the conditions the report described, but the factors that rendered the report's recommendations were, as described by Thelin (1996), both nostalgic and naïve. The report recommended that control of intercollegiate athletics be returned to students, to be run by and for students, as if the issues plaguing the enterprise had emerged only after paid coaches and institutional personnel had taken over management duties. Such a proposal was viewed as no more realistic then as it would be today.

The Graham Plan

We have discussed some of the actions dealing with questions of student-athlete academic eligibility, and the subsequent evolution of rules governing this issue. The NCAA's first attempt in this area emerged with the short-lived "Sanity Code" in the mid-1940s. Earlier, some schools and athletic managers had attempted to institute similar reform on a broader scale. In 1935, Southern Conference presidents, led by University of North Carolina president Frank Graham, recommended an end to remuneration for athletic ability and for all financial aid to be awarded by a faculty committee. In response to the so-called Graham Plan, Graham was warned by a friend that "If your policy is adopted and as a result of same the University of North Carolina has a third or fourth rate football team . . . the alumni are going to rise up in their wrath" (Sack & Staurowsky, 1998, p. 41).

Graham and his colleagues were to find little support for the plan, which, though adopted in 1936, was abandoned just two years later. The regulations, said Graham, "cut too deeply into entrenched practice. . . . I am shocked to find that college presidents for this reason and that reason do not want to stand [in] back of the . . . regulations" (p. 41). Clearly, from the response to the plan, any serious reform efforts would require a national scope as well as mechanisms for enforcement and punishment.

Knight Foundation Commission on Intercollegiate Athletics

School presidents took a leadership role in establishing more rigorous academic eligibility standards in the mid-1980s. And in the early 1990s, presidents reestablished an active voice in calls for reform following the advent of the Knight Foundation Commission on Intercollegiate Athletics. The "Knight Commission" was formed in 1989 in response to renewed presidential concerns that the academic integrity of higher education was being threatened by abuses in intercollegiate athletics. Having identified rampant commercialism and public distrust after a year of conducting interviews with school and athletic administrators, the Commission recommended that only presidents could effect real reforms. They could achieve these changes in part by controlling the NCAA through attendance at the annual convention and overseeing athletic affairs more closely (Knight Foundation, 1991).

Knight Commission member John DiBiaggio, then president of Michigan State, wrote of his personal observations concerning the issues to be addressed by the Commission (DiBiaggio, 1991):

> Very frankly, higher education has suffered in the marketplace—the marketplace of public opinion, not the broadcast ratings—because we have been seen as tolerating behaviors inimical to our stated institutional values . . . I believe strongly that more presidents and chancellors should, like [Theodore Roosevelt], who led athletic reform early in this century, use their bully pulpits to advocate for reform. . . . We have been too ambiguous and too timid in our advocacy for reform. (pp. 21–22)

He summed up this approach subsequently in saying: "Accountability cannot be achieved unless the presidents are in charge of intercollegiate athletics" (DiBiaggio, 1992, p. 28). In response to evidence of weak academic qualifications of Division I men's basketball and football student-athletes, DiBiaggio remarked, "You can't tell me that a student with that type of preparation can play a sport, take a full load of classes, and perform at acceptable levels" (Naughton, 1997, p. A43). DiBiaggio's experiences were underscored in 1989 by Miami (Ohio) University president Paul Pearson: "If you want to be the president at one of those big football institutions . . . you know you have to compromise your ethics. . . . At some schools if the president tries to turn things around, he's fired" (Telander, 1989, p. 58).

Today, the Knight Commission has 22 members (seven of whom are currently school presidents), and is headed by Amy Perko, a former NCAA legislative assistant and enforcement representative and associate AD at the University of Kansas.

Its co-chairs are William Kirwan, chancellor at the University of Maryland system, and R. Gerald Turner, president of Southern Methodist. The organization continues to facilitate the study of issues that impact intercollegiate athletic management. *Keeping Faith with the Student-Athlete: A New Model for Intercollegiate Athletics* (Knight Foundation, 1991) served as an influential trigger to subsequent related reform efforts within the NCAA and remains its most significant contribution.

Keeping Faith with the Student-Athlete

Much like Howard Savage with the Carnegie Report decades before, members of the Knight Commission spent more than a year interviewing intercollegiate athletics stakeholders. In response to the data collection, the organization issued its first report, *Keeping Faith with the Student-Athlete: A New Model for Intercollegiate Athletics*, released in 1991.

The need for reform. In Chapter 1, entitled "The Need for Reform," the report opined (Knight Foundation, 1991):

- that problems are most apparent within major athletics programs and are concentrated in the sports that can lead to a professional career,
- that recruiting is the most frequent cause of punitive action by the NCAA, that big-time athletics programs have taken on all of the trappings of a major entertainment enterprise (sacrificing traditional rivalries, rescheduling the dates and start times of games to satisfy broadcast preferences), and
- that three out of four Americans believe that television dollars, not athletic and school administrators, control intercollegiate athletics.

The chapter predicted three possible futures for intercollegiate athletics: (1) Higher education will put its athletics house in order from within; (2) order will be imposed from without, with the enterprise regulated by the government; or (3) if unchecked, existing abuses will spread, destroying the intrinsic value of athletics.

The new model. In Chapter 2, "The New Model: 'One-Plus-Three,'" the report seeks to offer practical solutions to the challenges outlined above, in what is termed the "one-plus-three" model. The "one"—presidential control—directed toward the "three" elements critical to effective intercollegiate athletic management, identified as (1) academic integrity, (2) financial integrity, and (3) accountability through certification (similar to the process since adopted by the NCAA—see Chapter 2). Exhibit 12.1 depicts these elements.

This model is necessary, the report claims, because ADs, coaches, or athletic department personnel are unable to accomplish reform of intercollegiate athletics. Reform, therefore, relies on school presidents, who control the institution as a whole.

The report suggested that this model can work if trustees endorse presidential authority in all matters of athletic governance, if presidents seek to control conferences by exercising voting power within the conferences, if presidents exhibit greater influence and control in the NCAA by attending and voting at annual conventions (a process that has since changed, see Chapter 2), if presidents commit their institutions to equity, and if presidents attempt to control their institution's involvement with commercial television (Knight Foundation, 1991).

One-plus-three model for the reform of intercollegiate athletics.   **EXHIBIT   12.1**

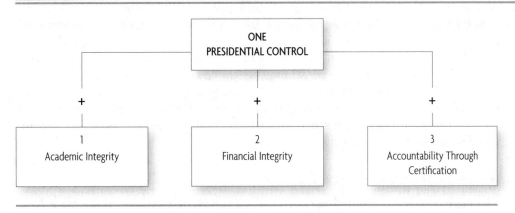

In terms of "academic integrity," the report recommends that student-athletes undertake the same courses of study offered to other students and that student-athlete academic performance be measured by the same criteria applied to other students. Further, to achieve these goals, the NCAA should strengthen initial eligibility requirements, grants-in-aid should be offered for a five-year period (to compensate for time demands placed on athletes), student-athletes should retain their eligibility by showing progress toward a degree each semester, and graduation rates of student-athletes should be equal to that of the general student body.

In attempting to achieve "financial integrity," the chapter recommended that

- athletics costs should be reduced through a reduction in the size of coaching staffs, and in number of grants-in-aid awarded;
- grants-in-aid should be expanded for low-income athletes to cover personal and miscellaneous expenses;
- athletic fundraising should go through the university's financial system to curb the independence of booster clubs;
- the NCAA television revenue-sharing plan should be revised to put less value on payouts based on wins in the men's basketball tournament;
- all athletics-related coaches' income should be reviewed and approved by the hiring institution;
- coaches should be offered long-term contracts as greater security for coaches takes off pressure that causes recruiting violations; and
- institutional funds should be available to help fund the athletic department to reduce the pressure on revenue sports to support the entire athletic program.

The final component, "accountability of certification," outlined a process, overseen by the NCAA, that should compare student-athletes to the rest of the student body in terms of admissions, academic progress, and graduation rates, as well as processes wherein schools undertake audits on financial issues, academic issues, and athletic governance. The report also recommended that institutions agree to schedule only those colleges and universities that have passed all aspects of the certification process (Knight Foundation, 1991).

A Solid Start

A year later, the Commission (Knight Foundation, 1992) released a second report, *A Solid Start*, which indicated that the reform movement seemed to be under way. Actions that had been done included passage of increased academic standards at the 1992 NCAA Convention, specifically in the area of continuing eligibility. This included legislation requiring percentage benchmarks of credits toward progress to a specific degree, as well as minimum grade-point average requirements needed in those courses. This second report also indicated that many governing boards and higher education associations had given their public endorsement to the recommendations in the first report.

A New Beginning for a New Century

The next year, the Commission issued a third report, *A New Beginning for a New Century* (Knight Foundation, 1993), citing additional progress in convincing stakeholders of its reform efforts. The report included data indicating that in 1989, nearly two-thirds of Americans believed that state or national legislation was needed to control intercollegiate sports, but that less than half felt that way four years later. This third report also declared that problematic issues associated with the three key areas identified in the 1991 report were being addressed successfully. Specifically, academic integrity was being restored through higher academic and satisfactory progress degree requirements; and financial integrity was being restored through a reduction in number of grants-in-aid and in the numbers of coaches on staff, by a review of athletic budgets as part of the NCAA certification program, and by requiring coaches to have written approval from their presidents for all athletically related outside income. The report also identified the certification process as the capstone of the reform movement, involving the entire campus community in a detailed examination of athletics policy issues. It suggested that regular self-examination reviewed by outside peers should curb abuse before it starts instead of after the damage has been done. At that point in time, it was expected that the Commission would disband, even though the report warned that two main issues continued to weigh heavily on intercollegiate athletics policy discussions: cost containment and gender equity.

Future directions

The Knight Commission marked its 20th anniversary in 2009. Big Ten Commissioner James Delany said, "In 1989, their voice was needed," but now the role of the group must evolve. Peter Likins, former president at Arizona and former Commission member, noted that it still has a job to do, but that "there are very serious challenges in doing it, because what has to happen now cannot be accomplished by NCAA rules" (Sander, 2009, p. A17). Founding co-chair Friday says the group must be more active than ever, noting, "We've come to a critical moment. Not to carry the fight on now would be to admit that . . . commercialism has snowballed so big that you can't control it anymore" (Sander, 2009, p. A17). In response, in 2009, the Commission released a survey of 95 Bowl Subdivision school presidents, which indicated that they are concerned about growing coaches salaries and expenses, yet they feel powerless to curb them. However, current co-chairs Kirwan and Turner admitted that they had no vision of the form for a successful reform agenda (Thomas, 2009).

The Coalition on Intercollegiate Athletics

Another reform group working outside the framework of national governing bodies and intercollegiate athletics management to provide the perspectives of faculty members is the Coalition on Intercollegiate Athletics (COIA), chartered in 2003. In its charter, the group is described as advocating for the reform of intercollegiate athletics through the efforts of faculty senate leaders at schools with Bowl Subdivision football programs. As of 2008, it had members from 55 of the 115 total of these schools, with a purpose "to articulate a broad national faculty voice in support of reform efforts and to contribute ideas toward a successful long-term strategy for reform, and to work with other groups committed to ensuring that athletics enhances rather than undermines the academic mission" (Charter of the Coalition on Intercollegiate Athletics, 2003, p. 1).

The goal of the COIA is to work toward "the adoption of an acceptable, comprehensive program of staged reform by the NCAA or by some alternative emerging structure" (p. 1). COIA co-chair Nathan Tublitz, a professor of neurobiology at the University of Oregon, noted the main objective of the organization:

> To put back the student into the student athlete and put the student athletes' education first. . . . We're getting to the point where we're realizing that there's a divergence of the interests and backgrounds of and performances of many of the student-athletes and the rest of their peers at the university. . . . The academic enterprise is not a service industry; it is not a corporate entity. It has the goal of educating the young people of our country. That's a very different type of mission than a for-profit business. (Colleges Slight Academic Programs, 2008, p. 38)

In June 2007, COIA released *Framing the Future: Reforming Intercollegiate Athletics,* in response to the notion that "intercollegiate athletics, while providing positive benefits to athletes, the campus and the broader community, at times clashes with the educational goals and mission of our institutions" (Coalition on Intercollegiate Athletics, 2007, p. 1). The report contained 28 proposals in four areas: academic integrity and equality, student-athlete welfare, campus governance of intercollegiate athletics, and fiscal responsibility. These areas closely mirror the areas of inquiry formed by the NCAA's Presidential Task Force on the Future of Division I Intercollegiate Athletics (see below). The stated goal of the COIA is that each of these 28 proposals be accepted as standard working policies and practices. Some of the specific recommendations of the report are given in Exhibit 12.2.

Although many of these recommendations seem reasonable, some run counter to how we know athletic departments operate. For example, as we learned earlier, there are very specific guidelines as to the academic qualifications of prospective Division I and II student-athletes. For non-athletes, however, schools may admit any students they wish, based on whatever criteria they believe to be valid. Therefore, it could be argued that in most cases, schools would oppose the application of such standards to their entire applicant pool because it would give these schools far less latitude in composing each entering class.

| EXHIBIT | 12.2 | Recommendations from *Framing the Future*. |

- Financial incentives for winning should be removed from coaches' contracts.
- The use of long-term or three- to five-year rolling contract for coaches should be provided to ensure security to prioritize student development over winning.
- Presidents should have an increased role in negotiating commercial contractual arrangements at the local and conference level.
- Conference participation need not be limited to athletics, and presidents should improve academic interactions between institutions in a conference. Future conference configurations should thus be designed on the basis of academic, athletic, and geographic considerations, which should enhance both the athletic and academic programs.
- The institutional officers responsible for budgetary decisions about athletics should include, in addition to the president and the athletic director, the chief academic officer of the institution and the chief financial officer.
- In admissions and in the living and academic conditions of campus life, athletes should be viewed and treated as much as possible like other students with extracurricular commitments.
- General admissions policies should be the same for all athletes and non-athletes. Campus administrators and faculty governance bodies should work together to develop these policies.

Source: Coalition on Intercollegiate Athletics, 2007.

The NCAA's Presidential Task Force on the Future of Division I Intercollegiate Athletics

As noted in our discussion of finances and as highlighted by the 1993 Knight Commission's valedictory report, there has been significant concern on the part of school presidents concerning ever-increasing athletic department expenditures. This was expressed through the report from the NCAA's Presidential Task Force on the Future of Division I Intercollegiate Athletics (2006), entitled *The Second Century Imperatives: Presidential Leadership—Institutional Accountability*. The 48-member task force, which included several school presidents featured throughout this text (specifically, Ohio State president Gordon Gee, Robert Khayat of the University of Mississippi, and R. Gerald Turner of Southern Methodist), was convened by former NCAA president Myles Brand in January 2005, with the charge to address "perplexing and difficult issues and to develop an agenda of action for the future" (p. 4). The report gave significant attention to financial issues and also attempted to react to concerns that task force chair Peter Likins, former president of the University of Arizona, called "the danger of cultural isolation of student-athletes from the intellectual purposes and academic values of our universities" (p. 5). As a result of these concerns, the task force was divided into four subcommittees: (1) fiscal responsibility, (2) implications of academic values and standards, (3) presidential leadership of internal and external constituencies, and (4) student-athlete well-being.

The introduction to the report underscores the premise of the committee, which was to deal with issues at the core of successful intercollegiate athletic management. Echoing many of the crucial themes discussed through this text, the report stated flatly that if intercollegiate athletics is to continue as a fixture of higher education into the future, if it is to be sustained as an important educational component of the college and university campus, if it is to be fully integrated into the mission of the academy, there are two important imperatives for the second century [of the NCAA]. There must be presidential leadership that begins at the campus level, and there must be institutional accountability for the conduct of the enterprise . . . the Task Force understands that athletic reform must now emphasize—both in scale and consequence—the local campus level. There will always be a need for national leadership in the forming and reforming of athletics within higher education . . . [but] it is time to take athletics reform home again. (p. 8)

The above quote notes the well-evolved power of the NCAA to elicit reform, much of which was in response to ineffectual efforts focused on the school and conference levels, in instances such as dealing with injuries and deaths in football, and numerous conflicts related to academic standards, recruiting, and amateurism. It is a trend that the report identifies as "the dependency on national policy to arbitrate local behavior [which] has desensitized the need at critical moments for each member campus to exercise good judgment" (p. 10).

In the case of initial academic eligibility, we have learned how school presidents took a greater role in managing national standards. The creation of new management councils as a result of the NCAA's restructuring in the late 1990s (see Chapter 2) bolstered those efforts. Since that time, school presidents have continued to seek more influence in athletic management. The above statement, written by school presidents, serves as a formalized call to their colleagues to advance the issues of reform in a broadened range of areas. It also recalls the charge offered by the 1991 Knight Commission report that school presidents are the key to successful reform, even though the 2006 Presidential Task Force report admits that many school presidents "rise to their positions without exposure to the governance of intercollegiate athletics" (p. 11). The challenge in such a charge, as we have seen, is the problem of instituting measures and policies on one campus that then may be perceived as serving to hinder on-field competitiveness. This, as we have learned, is what created the need for the NCAA to serve as a national arbiter concerning such control measures.

The *Second Century Imperatives* report attempts to confront potential on-campus pushback by making clear that the goal of intercollegiate athletic programs "to maximize the number of students who benefit from competing as part of their total educational experience . . . is jeopardized as the collegiate model drifts toward the professional approach" (p. 9). In further defining the key problems facing intercollegiate athletic managers, the report identifies "the need for ensuring the financial integrity of college sports," as evidenced by ever-increasing salaries of head coaches in Division I football and men's basketball and the accelerated growth rate of athletic expenditures.

In response, the report recommends that the component of the Division I philosophy statement that expects D-I athletic departments "to finance its athletics programs insofar as possible from revenues generated by the program itself" be eliminated, because "the effect has been an unrealistic expectation for athletics to meet its own bottom line in a manner that has pushed the enterprise away from the university . . . and in some cases activated a level of commercial collaboration outside the values of higher education" (p. 11). To further bridge the perceived gap between athletics and the rest of the academy, the report recommends that ADs "should be elevated to the equivalent of deans and vice presidents. They should sit on the president's council or cabinet and participate fully in providing advice to that office and setting policy for the campus" (p. 14). The body of the report outlines issues and other key recommendations of the four subcommittees.

Fiscal responsibility

The chapter written by the Fiscal Responsibility group, entitled "Leadership's Bottom Line," restates the concerns regarding increasing athletic expenditures and notes that the most rapidly growing revenue category for departments is "allocated funds," which are those monies coming from state or local governments and the institutions themselves that also allocate funds for educational purposes. The committee does not suggest that the NCAA should attempt to cap expenditures through legislation arising from federal antitrust concerns. Nor does it suggest that the NCAA seek to curry an exemption to these laws. Instead, the subcommittee recommended to the Task Force that "the only feasible approach to fiscal responsibility [is] a process that calls on campus leadership exercised by the president and supported by clearly defined and comparatively transparent financial data" (NCAA Presidential Task Force, 2006, p. 22).

To meet this charge, the subcommittee recommended that the Division I Board of Directors "monitor and conduct a regular analysis of the trends in intercollegiate athletics financing and provide those data to appropriate constituencies," and that "all Division I institutions shall be required to submit operating and capital financing data annually as part of the requirement for NCAA membership (NCAA Presidential Task Force, 2006, p. 24). Key data to be provided are listed in Exhibit 12.3. Committee member David Hardesty, Jr., president of West Virginia University, provided a summary of the need for this data sharing and the need for presidents to act on financial matters: "Having clear and comparable data is an effective self-policing mechanism for the marketplace. . . . Policy-making, presidential leadership, board governance, realistic expectations and faculty expectations are all tied up in actually knowing what's going on" (p. 27).

EXHIBIT 12.3   Key financial data to be submitted by Division I athletic departments.

- Athletics expenditures as a percent of institutional expenditures
- Total athletics revenues and percent change from the previous year
- Allocated revenues as a percent of total athletics revenues
- Allocated revenue increase as a percent of institutional revenue increase
- Athletics debt service as a percent of total athletics expenditures
- Athletics expenditures for salary and benefits, participation and game expenses, facility and administrative support, and debt service as a percent of total expenditures

Source: NCAA Presidential Task Force, 2006, pp. 26–27.

Academic values and standards

Chapter 2 of the report, entitled "The Value of Integration," contains recommendations from the Academic Values and Standards Subcommittee. The group attempts to address a key question—specifically, what does it mean for athletics to be fully integrated with the academic mission of an institution? The group stated that, "like all other parts of the campus, the mission of intercollegiate athletics is to educate" (NCAA Presidential Task Force, 2006, p. 32), but that integration between athletics and academics has been strained over the past three decades as athletic departments were asked to become more self-sufficient financially. To reconnect athletic departments with the rest of its host institutions, the subcommittee recommended that faculty members become more involved in athletic programs, with the faculty athletics representatives (FAR), to play a key role in this process. "The FAR is the person best equipped, both in terms of knowledge and time commitment, to monitor the successful integration of athletics and academics" (p. 33). The Coalition on Intercollegiate Athletics is also identified as a potential partner in managing this reconnection.

Regarding specific structural recommendations, the group suggested that athletic department rules compliance personnel report directly to managers outside of the athletic department, such as the registrar, admissions director, and financial aid director. Finally, in an effort to bridge the gap engendered through athletic department self-sufficiency, the subcommittee recommended eliminating the clause in the Division I philosophy statement requiring this independent status. In support of this notion, subcommittee member Michael Adams, president of the University of Georgia (and also a member of the Knight Commission), said:

> College sports should look like a collegiate enterprise. At the venue itself, there should be a limited number of commercial intrusions. . . . A University of Georgia game is a different experience than an NBA game, and I want that difference to be clear. . . . I don't think any of us want our uniforms to look like South American soccer jerseys or NASCAR drivers' suits. The standard is a clear distinction between a for-profit enterprise and a nonprofit activity that supports the mission of the academic institution. (p. 37)

The recommendations of the Internal and External Constituencies Subcommittee are outlined in Chapter 3, "The Roles of Governing Boards and Athletic Clubs." The importance of administrative leadership is highlighted through the subcommittee's charge that "unequivocally, the principle of institutional control puts responsibility over all aspects of an athletics program in the hands of the chief executive officer" because, as we have learned throughout the text, "at one pole are those who want athletics to be successful at any price and at the other there are those who would rein in athletics to little more than intramural status" (pp. 41–42). It is therefore up to presidents and chancellors, the subcommittee concludes, to facilitate intercollegiate athletics into the greater institutional community, to be "the keepers of the collegiate model" (p. 43). To aid in achieving this end, the report suggests that school governing boards must develop a "constructive understanding with regards to athletics," and that this can be attained through an orienteering process for all new board members, and by the school president acting as "the individual charged with ensuring sound communication and coordination among all the constituencies about the broad direction in which the athletics program is heading" (pp. 44–45).

The subcommittee also proposes that the presidential leadership be reviewed as part of the NCAA's athletic certification process. This can be facilitated by including more school presidents on certification review committees, and should include a requirement that "institutions provide materials containing rules education and policies and procedures to organized athletics groups and representatives of the institution's athletics interests (i.e., boosters)" (p. 47).

Student-athlete well-being

The work of the Student-Athlete Well-being Subcommittee is contained in the final chapter of the report, "Celebrating the Student-Athlete." The chapter admits that "from a national perspective, legislative proposals often have unintended—or at times even intended—consequences on student-athlete well-being." Because of this, the group cited the need for "a collaborative effort to set a legislative agenda that enhances student-athlete well-being in many areas of the educational experience—from financial aid to eligibility standards to playing and practice seasons" (NCAA Presidential Task Force, 2006, p. 50). The agenda considerations compiled by the subcommittee include the "assimilation of student-athletes into campus life, an examination of financial aid practices, methods of ensuring student-athlete academic success, a discussion of health and safety issues, and an assessment of competition opportunities and possible enhancements" (p. 50).

To address these agenda items, the subcommittee proposed that the Division I governance structure establish a data-based definition of prospects with "at-risk" academic profiles to evaluate the level of academic and life-skills support needed to ensure success. The group also noted that financial aid policies should be reviewed to assess whether student-athletes have adequate opportunities to receive non-athletically related aid, to strengthen legislation requiring a hearing for cancelled or reduced athletically related aid, to consider whether such aid should be renewed automatically based on established criteria, or awarded for more than one year, and to reexamine whether the current head-count and equivalency allocations are appropriate. In addressing the status of student-athlete eligibility, the group suggested that the Division I membership consider legislation providing for a fifth season of eligibility as a standard, or whether it should have to be earned based on certain academic criteria, and allowing student-athletes in all sports the option of transferring after their first year and be immediately eligible to compete.

Bringing reform home

In the report's summation, even while many of the suggested reforms occur through the NCAA legislative process, it reemphasized that the NCAA

> must shift from a reform agenda carved out by national Association legislative mandate to change influenced by individual presidential leadership. It is time to take athletics reform home. . . . Each president must exercise *local* leadership to ensure the continued conformance of athletics with academic mission (authors' emphasis). (NCAA Presidential Task Force, 2006, p. 57)

The report further asserts that presidents can meet this charge only with the cooperation of a "well-informed faculty," athletic administrators who are "working with the institution the university to solve institutional problems, rather than expanding departmental autonomy," governing boards that are not "so engulfed within their relationships with coaches or athletic directors that they become a barrier to effective presidential leadership," and boosters and fans "who put winning above all else" (p. 57). What remains to be seen is whether the charge to "bring reform home" will have the support of the others living in the house so that the desired renovations can be undertaken.

KEY ETHICAL ISSUES IMPACTING THE MANAGEMENT OF INTERCOLLEGIATE ATHLETICS TODAY

While the above organizations are acting to deal with issues believed to be harmful to the management of intercollegiate athletics, many more issues are still to be addressed. The remainder of this chapter will examine several of these key issues and their impact on all related stakeholder groups.

Hazing

Studies have indicated that nearly four out of five NCAA student-athletes have been subjected to hazing as part of a team initiation process, many of whom endured illegal activities and forced drinking of alcohol. In several cases, these activities have led to injuries, extreme alcohol poisoning, and even fatalities. One of these studies defines hazing as "any activity expected of someone joining a group that humiliates, degrades, abuses, or endangers, regardless of that person's willingness to participate" (Duffy, 2000, p. D17). While athletic departments are concerned about protecting their student-athletes from physical and emotional harm, there is also the very real consideration of potential lawsuits and other deleterious effects. Coaches, too, are potentially liable for any injuries and criminal actions related to hazing if it is proven that they knew of the activity but did nothing to stop it (Brady & Libit, 2006; Sandomir, 2006; Oppenhuizen, 2008).

Perhaps the most notorious and impactful hazing case that led to these unwanted outcomes involved men's ice hockey players at the University of Vermont. In October 1999, at an off-campus house rented by team captain Kevin Karlander, nine first-year players were subjected to a range of degrading activities, including performing nude pushups over glasses of beer into which they dipped their genitalia, and doing the "elephant walk," which involved parading around the house while holding the genitals of the person ahead of him in line. Although some of the players did not publicly object to the proceedings (said one, "We were all given the option beforehand to opt out, and nobody did" [Duffy, 2000, p. D17]), one later did. Corey LaTulippe was a backup goaltender who left school after the incident and filed suit against the school and seven players, alleging that his civil rights and privacy were violated, and that he was a victim of assault and battery. According to former teammates, however, LaTulippe brought the case because he was cut from the team.

Initially, the players on the team conspired to cover up the incident. As a result, the Vermont State Attorney General criticized the school for laxity in investigating the claims, and school officials opted to cancel the team's final 15 games. LaTulippe later admitted under oath in a deposition that some allegations in the lawsuit were false, after which he and the school settled the lawsuit for $80,000 and entered into an agreement that did not contain any admission of wrongdoing by the school or its employees (Duffy, 2000; Gardiner, 2001). Joe Flammia, an upperclassman on the team, reacted to the situation this way:

> If I didn't regret everything that happened, I'd have to be crazy. We lost our season. I wish we didn't do it, but by the same token, I went through it, and nothing happened. Nobody likes doing it—I didn't enjoy it [as a freshman]. But we all went through it. There was a sense of pressure that we had to do it. [As freshmen], we were told, "Guys, we don't want to do it, but we have to. You'll have to do it, too. It brings us together." . . . I've gotten e-mails from players as far away as Alaska, people I don't even know asking me for details of what we did because they've done the same things and don't want to get into trouble. I think what we did was excessive, but I've heard from other players saying they've done a lot worse. (Duffy, 2000, p. D17)

After the program was reinstated the following season, then-Vermont governor Howard Dean, who had spurred the state attorney general's investigation into the hazing and was a vocal critic of the university's handling of the crisis, had this to say: "I was very upset and angry when it happened because I thought the university was trying to sweep it under the rug. But they've done a great job of turning this around" (Gardiner, 2001, p. 1).

Many associated with the Vermont case hoped the publicity surrounding the case would curtail future activities (even in the face of the qualified regret expressed by players like Flammia). Nearly every state has passed some form of anti-hazing laws, and most schools have instituted anti-hazing policies and informed their students of penalties and repercussions. But hazing still persists.

Another incident occurred at Salve Regina University, a private Catholic liberal arts institution with an undergraduate enrollment of 2,000, located in Newport, Rhode Island, and a member of the Division III Commonwealth Coast Conference. The school suspended five members of the men's soccer team from school and also required the forfeiture of five games as a result of a hazing incident that led to a confrontation with and an assault by non-team members. The incident occurred early on the morning of September 23, 2007, when witnesses at a local bar told police they had seen three team members and several others involved in a fight over a racial slur that had been written on the back of one of the player's t-shirts. According to police, the player did not know of the writing on his shirt, which had been placed there while the players were drinking at a party earlier that evening. When the players were confronted about the slur, one was punched in the face and kicked in the head after he fell to the sidewalk.

The attacker was charged with simple assault. In response, a school spokesperson stated that "we do believe a hazing incident took place," and that the school "has an ongoing investigation" concerning the actions of "a number of students" with regard to "a number of incidents at different times and different dates. . . . It's not the men's soccer team as a whole," but the forfeiture makes "a strong statement about the men's soccer coach," Craig O'Rourke II (Macris, 2007, p. 1). A spokesperson at an NCAA website dedicated to exposing hazing (NCAAHazing.com) noted that the men's soccer incident marked the third hazing event at the school in the past two years, and the second involving the men's soccer team.

Posting compromising material on social networking sites

In the numerous other cases that have followed the Vermont incident, much of the evidence demonstrating the hazing activities is actually provided by the participants, through their own websites or those of others. In 2006, the website badjocks.com posted photographs, accessed via a file-sharing system used by students to upload the images, showing hazing activities at various universities and colleges. Women's soccer team members at Northwestern University were shown blindfolded and dressed in their underwear with their hands tied behind their back, and two players were shown doing lap dances for members of the school's men's soccer team. Members of the women's lacrosse team at Catholic University of America were shown in sexually suggestive poses with a male stripper. Kenyon College baseball team members were shown shaving heads, drinking, and with one player's back marked by an obscene phrase proposing anal sex. The website included additional photos of similar activities at more than a dozen other schools. Said Christine Plonsky, director of Women's Athletics at the University of Texas: "None of us is immune. You hope none of these things go on, but you might find out they do" (Wolverton, 2006b, p. A37).

Most schools have instituted anti-hazing policies and informed their students of penalties and repercussions, and also recommended that their student-athletes cleanse their pages on social-networking websites, such as Facebook and MySpace, of compromising photos and references. One school, Loyola University, a private Jesuit-affiliated institution with a total enrollment of 15,000, located in Chicago, and a member of the Division I Horizon League, has gone one step further and banned student-athletes from maintaining such pages altogether. Loyola AD John Planek said he wasn't concerned with the school's image but, rather, protecting student-athletes from gamblers, agents, and sexual predators, and, in some cases, from rabid fans. "I know it's not a popular decision, said Planek. "This is a safety issue and a well-being issue. . . . I think we may be ahead of the curve (and that other schools will follow suit)" (Sandomir, 2006, p. C18).

Bruce Madej, associate AD at the University of Michigan, believes that schools could not legally bar student-athletes from posting such pictures on social-networking websites: "There is no silver bullet to tell them what they can or can't do. You have to tell them they not only represent the university but their families" (Sandomir, 2006, p. C18). However, an expert in campus free-speech issues, Kermit Hall, president of the University at Albany (New York), believes that what Loyola is doing is permissible legally: "There are team rules on curfews and other things, and if one of those rules is you can't be on Facebook—or if you are, that you present yourself in a way that shows the values of your university—I think schools can do it" (Brady & Libit, 2006, p. 2C). Hall also noted that student-athlete codes of conduct are generally both comprehensive and vague so schools can regulate and oversee the sites.

Other schools, such as Auburn University, the University of Iowa, Ohio State University, and the University of North Carolina, do not ban students from maintaining pages on such sites but warn them that they will be monitored and cannot contain content that might be damaging to the schools. In its student-athlete handbook, Ohio State administrators warn student-athletes that they "shall not post or contribute any content to any social networking or other Internet site that reflect negatively . . . on yourself, [or] your team" (Oppenhuizen, 2008, p. 9C). Coaches are also potentially liable for any injuries and criminal actions related to hazing if it is proven that they knew of the activities but did nothing to stop it.

In this light, Mark Titus, a former team manager and walk-on backup forward for Ohio State's men's basketball team, maintains a blog site—clubtrillion. blogspot.com (the term "trillion" refers to what seldom-used players call their line in the game box scores—all zeros for minutes played, points, etc., for all 12 statistical categories—with 12 zeros referring to the amount equaled in the number representing a trillion). This site has been visited by close to two million people since he began it in 2008. Titus has nearly 6,000 followers on Twitter, and has the maximum number of 5,000 friends on Facebook. An eccentric jokester who missed only one question on the math section of the SAT, Titus had scored three points in his career heading into the 2009–10 season. He writes a little about basketball, but most of his postings make fun of the Buckeyes' star player Evan Turner, who admits that Titus is the team's most popular player because of his blog.

ESPN writer Bill Simmons opines that the popularity of the blog site relates to Titus's self-depreciating humor and his ability to bring readers into a world to which they have no other access. Titus credits head coach Thad Motta for allowing him to maintain the site but has been asked by school officials to take down certain information, such as a teammates' GPA. Motta credits Titus for keeping the team loose, as he did before the 2007 NCAA championship game, when right before the game Titus—who was almost assuredly not going to see a second of playing time unless the game outcome was decided—told Motta, "I've got five fouls to give. I'll be [at the end of the bench] if you need me." Motta recalls cracking up laughing in response, and the tension of the moment was temporarily relieved (Thamel, 2009, pp. 8–9). Titus also used the site to sell "Club Trillion" t-shirts to raise money for a charity focused on helping children deal with life-threatening illnesses.

Student-athlete criminal behavior

Throughout the text we have discussed issues having to do with inappropriate student-athlete behavior. Although not all instances rise to the level of criminal offenses, athletic departments with increasing frequency are facing challenges in monitoring these behaviors as a result of several cases including:

- the 2006 on-field brawl between Florida International University and the University of Miami football teams,
- concerns over criminal behavior of recruiting prospects encountered by Wake Forest University and others,
- the hyper-publicized interactions between Duke University men's lacrosse players and strippers hired to perform at an off-campus player residence in 2006, which led to ill-informed allegations of rape (later proven to be false).

Instances of student-athlete behavior have been especially problematic at Montana State University (MSU), a public school with approximately 12,000 undergraduates located in Bozeman, and a member of the Division I Big Sky Conference (with a Championship Subdivision football program). In May 2007, former wide receiver Rick Gatewood was charged with running a drug ring that had imported 11 pounds of cocaine to the area over a 23-month period. Gatewood allegedly used cash from his grant-in-aid award to finance the operation, and later pled guilty to charges. Six months earlier, two other former MSU student-athletes were alleged to have murdered a local man believed to be a cocaine dealer.

In addition, in 2005, a former men's basketball point guard served 90 days in jail for raping a 15-year-old girl, and, in 2004, an assistant football coach was sentenced to four years in jail for dealing methamphetamines. Another complaint against the athletic programs, which rely heavily on recruiting junior college transfer students, is the poor academic performance of the student-athletes. The six-year graduation rates for the men's basketball program was 21 percent for football (2 percent for transfers), and 33 percent for men's basketball (13 percent for transfers), in the most recent available data (Dohrman, 2007).

For many in Bozeman (population approximately 35,000) and the surrounding Gallatin County area (in the southwestern section of the state), the school's athletic programs have served as a rallying point. The actions outlined above, however, brought criticism from residents and the media alike. One local sportswriter opined: "Murder. Kidnapping. Cocaine. Here. In Paradise. It's all so incongruous, so spiritually bankrupt, so very wrong." A local woman wrote in a letter to a local newspaper: "Shame on us as a community for not being more outspoken, for not holding the school accountable long ago" (Dohrman, 2007, p. 61). Others point out that many of the actions have been perpetrated by African-American males who hail from urban locales in California and Florida, far from bucolic Gallatin County. Some locals complain that slots should be given to locals only, and others go so far as to suggest that the school make all former Bobcat student-athletes leave town (which is 95 percent White) after their careers. But MSU coaches have been able to compete and to succeed by recruiting players from all over the United States, including those with less than stellar academic profiles. According to one former MSU gridder: "There were players who would brag how they could have gone to a Pac-10 school if they had had the grades, which makes you wonder how they got in [here]. And everyone on the team knew who the guys were who had been in trouble with the law" (p. 63).

School administrators have responded to the criminal actions and public criticism. School president Geoff Gamble, who played defensive back at Fresno State University for a year, acknowledged the issue of the profiles of some student-athletes, and that the school should not have pursued at-risk prospects. To underscore this point, a panel of independent investigators hired by the school found that the football program had almost total autonomy in admitting recruits. In addition, head football coach Mike Kramer, who arrived in 2000 and had led the Bobcats to three Big Sky Conference titles and a 19–10 upset over the University of Colorado in 2006, was fired in 2007 after school administrators cited a "crisis in leadership." Kramer promptly sued the school, with his lawyer stating that "[the firing] was done by people who were covering their own backsides." As to the suggestion that all former non-resident student-athletes vacate the region after competing, Gamble replied, "There are some folks who say if we just brought in Montana kids, none of this would happen. But you can't isolate yourself" (Dohrman, 2007, p. 64). New head football coach Rob Ash concurs, saying that to be competitive, the program must recruit nationally and admit transfers.

Gender identity

In Chapter 11 we discussed the many legal issues pertaining to Title IX law and the pursuit of gender equity. An issue that has been somewhat prominent in Olympic sport but less so in intercollegiate athletics is that of athletes changing gender and its impact on competitive equity. In their study of women's sport participation opportunities, McDonagh and Pappano (2008) note an accepted belief that men are superior to women in all forms of athletic competition. As a result, for decades prior to the 2000 Summer Olympics, the International Olympic Committee (IOC) performed various tests to gauge whether males were attempting to pass as females to gain a competitive advantage, whether certain females benefited from genetic chromosomal abnormalities, and later, whether women were utilizing performance-enhancing substances such as testosterone.

The concept of identifying an athlete's sex has become more complicated with the advent of transsexual athletes. As McDonagh and Pappano point out: "Debate about allowing transsexuals to compete is ostensibly aimed at ensuring fair play but challenges our understanding of male and female. When, exactly, is a person male? And when does that actually bestow an advantage?" (p. 47). The authors also note that sports organizations do not agree on the participation of transsexual athletes, but that before the 2004 Summer Olympics, the IOC decided to allow transsexual athletes to compete in their postsurgical sex category if they met certain criteria, including verifiable hormonal treatments. The IOC also stipulated that athletes must wait two years after surgery to compete in their new gender.

This issue is beginning to emerge for consideration in American intercollegiate athletics, as evidenced by the case of Keelin (nee Kelly) Godsey, a student-athlete at Bates College, a private liberal arts school with an enrollment of 1,700, located in Lewiston, Maine, and member of the Division III New England Small College Athletic Conference. Before her senior year, Godsey, who had developed into one of the greatest female student-athletes in school history (an 11-time All-American in the hammer throw, shot put, and discus), changed her name to Keelin and asked to be referred to using the male pronoun "he." Godsey had endured considerable abuse in high school for her androgynous appearance and had attempted suicide several times because of it. Bates athletic administrators consulted with NCAA officials to determine Godsey's eligibility, which defines a student-athlete's sex as it is classified by state law (Grossfeld, 2006). Bates determined that Godsey would be allowed to compete as a woman even though she would now be referred to as "he," as long as Godsey delayed hormone therapy and possible sexual reassignment surgery. The school released a statement that read:

> At Bates, we understand this to mean that an individual who is physically and physiologically female may compete in intercollegiate athletic competition with females . . . since he will not have changed his physiology to male, he will meet the criteria required to compete in women's sports. . . . College should be a safe place—physically, emotionally, and intellectually—where students can learn about themselves and their world. One's gender identity is part of that learning. (p. C10)

Said Godsey of the decision:

> There are no rules being broken. I am not doing anything illegal, anything wrong. I'm not doing anything other than going by a different pronoun and a different

name. . . . Why now? I've hid who I am for my entire life. It's hard to live what you see as a lie. . . . For me to be in a fair competition, I have to compete as a female. I couldn't compete versus men. (p. C10)

Jeff Ward, AD at conference rival Bowdoin College, expressed no problem with the actions: "It's not an issue. There's no hormone replacement, how she chooses to identify herself, that doesn't have anything to do with what we do. She's not breaking any rules; those are her decisions, not ours" (p. C10). Bates officials confirm that Godsey had not tested positive for any male hormone supplements. Godsey's wish to be referred to as a man provided no competitive advantage, and the decision to allow him to continue to compete against women clearly was made in the spirit of maintaining fair competition for all involved.

Monetary compensation of student-athletes

Colleges and universities are not exempt from claims of athlete exploitation. Many of the claims come from individuals who have direct experience with the enterprise. NFL receiver Anthony Gonzalez, a former standout at Ohio State, commented: "We basically have a job that generates millions and millions and millions of dollars, and at the end of the day, we don't really see any of it" (Wertheim, 2007, p. 67). Some in government agree, including longtime Nebraska state senator Ernie Chambers, who has supported legislation to pay a stipend to student-athletes in his state. Said Chambers: "In big-time college athletics, not just football, there are no amateurs. Whenever you get something of value [like fees, books, tuition and so forth] for performing athletically, you're a professional" (Whiteside, 2004, p. 5C).

And none other than former NCAA head Walter Byers expressed after his retirement in 1987 that "dramatic changes" are required in the "oppressive" laws of the "self-righteous" NCAA, particularly to spread the wealth to student-athletes. "Collegiate amateurism is not a moral issue," Byers wrote. "It is an economic camouflage for monopoly practices" (Rushin, 1997, p. 4).

Others might argue in response that what Gonzalez and his student-athlete colleagues receiving athletic aid are getting for their revenue-generating efforts is an opportunity for a college education, which, depending on the institution, may be worth upwards of $200,000. However, noted author Michael Lewis, who chronicled the recruiting efforts of former University of Mississippi offensive lineman Michael Oher, agrees with Gonzalez:

> Everyone associated with [college football] is getting rich except the people whose labor creates the value. . . . The arrangement sounds like simple theft; but up close, inside the university, it apparently feels like high principle. That principle, as stated by the N.C.A.A., is that college sports should never be commercialized. But it's too late for that. College football is already commercialized, for everyone except the people who play it. (Lewis, 2007, p. 1–11)

Licensing

As Lewis (2007) points out, the precipitate of many financial activities and relationships between athletic departments and outside corporations and interests are instances in which athletic departments and institutions are criticized for using student-athletes for free in situations in which others would usually be compensated. For example, the University of Texas and Nike have an equipment and apparel deal (much like that between many other athletic departments and suppliers) in which all coaches and athletes (except swimmers and divers, who wear Speedo suits) are outfitted head to toe in Nike apparel and footwear in practices, competitions, and official appearances. So important is this blanket coverage for Nike that publications and media relations staffers monitor photos and interviews to ensure that competing manufacturers' apparel doesn't slip into departmental publications. Nike keeps vigil as well, as reported by Christine Plonsky, Texas' director of women's athletics. "If TV coverage shows one of our athletes stepping off a team bus with a cap that's not Nike's," she says, "they'll call it to our attention" (Brenner, 2003, p. 21).

Behavior of licensees. An additional factor that can potentially complicate such apparel agreements is the behavior of licensees, specifically in the manufacturing of products in factories that have poor working conditions. Recognizing the importance of licensed products in terms of revenues and branding, schools can incur negative reactions from consumers and interest groups if the companies into which they enter licensing agreements have a history of exploiting workers. Because of the mission and nature of education environments, colleges and universities have been particularly vulnerable to criticism on this score, especially from student-run groups on their own campuses.

The United Students Against Sweatshops, a national coalition of students critical of sweatshop factory conditions, lobbied to convince 96 schools (Columbia, Michigan, North Carolina, and Stanford, among others) to end or suspend licensing agreements—some as valuable as $1 million in sales—with Russell Athletic (owned by parent company Fruit of the Loom) after the company closed a factory in Honduras when its workers unionized, leaving 1,200 jobless. As a result of the actions, Russell agreed to rehire the workers and not to fight unionization efforts in its seven other Honduran factories. In response, Mel Tenen, who oversees licensing agreements at the University of Miami (Florida)—the first school to end its agreement with Russell—commented, "It's not often that a major licensee will take such a necessary and drastic step to correct the injustices that affected its workers" (Greenhouse, 2009, p. B4).

The victory for the movement came after a decade of convincing multiple schools to adopt codes of conduct for their licensees. Scott Nova, executive director of the Workers Rights Consortium, to which more than 170 schools belong, sees the move as a "maturation of the universities' codes of conduct," and that schools now could exercise their ability to influence the actions of companies and licensees (p. B4). The union president at the plant in Honduras that had been closed praised the actions of the student groups, stating, "For us, it was very important to receive the support of the universities. We are impressed by the social consciousness of the students in the United States" (p. B4).

Student-athletes' names to sell licensed products. Using student-athletes' names to sell products directly without compensation has been used in more devious ways. For example, in 2004, the University of Connecticut (UConn) licensed and sold jerseys (for $49.99) and hats ($26.99) bearing the numbers of star hoop players Ben Gordon, Emeka Okafor, and Diana Taurasi at the campus bookstore, online, and through local retail outlets such as Bob's Stores. NCAA regulations passed in 1992 bar schools from using player names and likenesses to sell products, and also ban student-athletes from promoting commercial ventures. The UConn bookstore website, however, touted one of the "favorite player hats" as honoring "the team player who wears the #3 UConn jersey for women's basketball," a.k.a., Taurasi.

Critics of these practices, such as former UCLA football player Ramogi Huma, head of the Collegiate Athletes Coalition, a California-based organization he founded to advocate for better living conditions for student-athletes, argue that UConn and other schools are acting unethically and contradictory to the spirit of the NCAA rules in licensing and selling these products. Huma says college athletes such as Gordon, Okafor, and Taurasi should share in the proceeds from sales of the apparel. "The reason (the products) are being sold . . . is that these are famous players," Huma claims. "If a player gets a cut of the sale of his or her jersey, that does not mean the player is a professional" (Chambers, 2004, p. C16).

This issue has long been a point of concern for intercollegiate athletic administrators. Walter Byers admitted, in his 1995 biography of his time as NCAA Executive Director (the position equivalent to the Association's president today), that the term "student-athlete," which we have used throughout this text, was concocted by the Association's leadership in the 1950s. It was done to counter the notion that athletic scholarships constituted pay and, therefore, were subject to taxation and worker's compensation payment for injuries. The term was created to give the public impression that scholarship recipients were students first and foremost, not paid employees of their school.

Student-athletes' images in advertising

In 2007, the NCAA began to consider amending the 1992 legislation noted above to allow companies to use student-athletes in advertising campaigns. Currently, companies are permitted to include pictures and images of student-athletes in ads as long as the student-athlete makes no specific endorsement. Also, companies are allowed to show only their name and logo in any such ad. Proposed new guidelines would permit the inclusion of products or services in an ad that would include student-athletes, with the existing proviso that the student-athletes refrain from specific endorsements. The new rules would also provide guidance in how to deal with ads in evolving new mediums.

The NCAA itself has already garnered criticism of its use of student-athletes in new media. In 2005, then-corporate partner Pontiac used video highlights of football games next to images of its cars as part of a Web-based promotional campaign seeking to induce viewers to vote for their favorite play of the season. In 2008, broadcast partner CBS announced it was creating a fantasy Division I football league using student-athletes' names instead of generic players like "#8 Oklahoma QB." Current bylaws prohibit companies from trading on the likenesses or images of specific athletes. The NCAA has not tried to stop CBS from creating the game, but it has warned its corporate partner that the new fantasy league could jeopardize student-athlete eligibility. CBS believes it can run the league legally because of an earlier federal appeals court ruling that permitted a company that ran a professional baseball fantasy league to use players' names and likenesses without compensation because they are in the public domain. The CBS site will not charge entry fees or offer prize money, but could generate significant revenue from sponsorships and advertising. CBS said it has plans for a men's Division I college basketball league as well (Smith, 2007; Moser, 2008).

As with the licensed product incidents, critics argue that any student-athletes used in ads would be further exploited, as they would receive no compensation for the appearance and have no control over how their images were used. Amy Perko, executive director of the Knight Foundation, called the proposed ad rules change "misguided," but Michael Rogers, faculty athletics representative from Baylor University and chair of the NCAA's agents and amateurism subcommittee, who helped craft the new guidelines, responded that "there was some fear originally that it would allow a student-athlete to hold up a can of soda and say, 'Buy this, drink this.' That's not what we are doing" (Moser, 2008, p. A32). Of the fantasy league, Perko commented: "The NCAA exists to protect the integrity of the rules and to protect student-athletes from being exploited. . . . I think it's clear that the CBS program is in violation of [the NCAA's] amateurism rules" (Moser, 2008, p. A32).

Knight Commissioner member Nick Buoniconti, a former defensive standout for the NFL's Miami Dolphins and a member of the board of trustees at the University of Miami (Florida), chided the NCAA for what he called a "weak response" to CBS. He added, "I've always thought the NCAA doesn't act as an advocate for student-athletes but represents universities . . . . [The NCAA needs to] go back and review what [its] purpose is" (Carey, 2008, p. 10C). NCAA official Wally Renfro noted that while many might take issue with CBS and the NCAA's response, "The association does not own the publicity rights of student-athletes, and that's what this case is about" (Carey, 2008, p. 10C).

Christine Plonsky of Texas, who contributed to the legislative draft for the ad bylaw change, believes that the proposal still protects student-athletes from exploitation:

> There are many, many ways that we can present messages where the company's message is definitely attached to the activity, but you're not asking a student-athlete to endorse or in any way back the actual product. . . . [Audiences are] sophisticated enough to know what they're being dealt in a commercial or sponsorship message. (Smith, 2007, p. A36)

The student-athletes who comprise the NCAA's Division I Student-Athlete Advisory Committee supported the proposed amendment, as did Chris Lefton, a University of Tennessee men's basketball player, who said, "It's good for the school, it's good for the players, and good for the team," but also suggested that if players' names and pictures are used, "why not pay them?" (Moser, 2008, p. A15). The move was tabled in late 2007 when a group of presidents expressed concern over the nature of the proposal (Smith, 2007).

In July 2009, former UCLA and NBA player Ed O'Bannon further contested this issue, filing a class action lawsuit against the NCAA and IMG College, claiming that former student-athletes should be compensated for the use of their images and likenesses in TV ads, video games, and apparel. O'Bannon was encouraged to file the claim by former adidas, Nike, and Reebok shoe-deal impresario Sonny Vaccaro and his wife and business partner Pam. The male Vaccaro now considers himself an advocate for student-athletes' rights, and claimed the suit was filed because "[The NCAA and IMG College] don't own [the student-athletes], and they're going to have to explain it . . . to explain how they can rule over [student-athletes] and nobody questions them" (Garcia, 2009b, p. 7C). O'Bannon, MVP in UCLA's 1995 title-winning national championship game, now works in marketing and sales for a Las Vegas, Nevada, car dealership, and alleges that his likeness is used in the "classic teams" portion of EA Sports' *NCAA Basketball 09* video game. He said he agreed to be the face of the suit because of the issue of fairness rather than money. "If your likeness is being sold, you should be compensated," said O'Bannon. "This is about going after what's right" (Thamel, 2009, p. B16). An NCAA spokesperson said of the suit, "The NCAA categorically denies any infringement on former or current student-athlete likeness rights" (Garcia, 2009a, p. 1C) and "to claim the NCAA profits off student-athlete likenesses is also pure fiction" (Thomas, 2010, p. B16).

At issue in the suit is the "08-3a form," a waiver that student-athletes are required to sign that permits the NCAA and its licensees to use student-athlete names and likenesses without compensating them. Lead attorney Michael Hausfeld predicted that the case would eventually be joined by thousands of former Division I football and men's basketball student-athletes (Garcia, 2009a). How this suit proceeds could have a significant impact on all intercollegiate licensing and marketing deals. In February 2010, a federal district court denied the NCAA's motion to dismiss the case, and a handful of former student-athletes (including two members of the 1966 NCAA champion Texas Western men's basketball team), had joined the case (Thomas, 2010).

Pay for play

While critics might still argue that there can be no integrity where exploitation exists, supporters of the current student-athlete grant-in-aid system state that any pay-for-play system would have to give equal payments to female sports, as Title IX dictates, so few athletic departments actually earn enough to support any sort of compensation package.

NCAA 2008 settlement. In February 2008, the NCAA agreed to settle an federal anti-trust suit that will provide more compensation for student-athletes. Under the settlement of the suit, filed by four former football and men's basketball student-athletes, the NCAA will reallocate up to $228 million over the next five years to help the more than 150,000 Division I student-athletes in all sports pay for basic expenses not covered by athletic grants-in-aid. The settlement allows more money to go to student-athletes for out-of-pocket expenses such as personal travel. The lawsuit accused the NCAA of creating a hardship for student-athletes by capping the amount of athletic and institutional aid they could receive.

Under the agreement, the NCAA said it would consider legislation that would allow schools to extend athletic aid beyond the current five-year limit, and award multi-year grants, as suggested in the 2006 report from the NCAA Presidential Task Force on the Future of Division I Intercollegiate Athletics. One expert, Michael McCann, an assistant professor at Mississippi College School of Law, said the deal may "help soften some of the critique" that NCAA players are forbidden to share in the revenues generated by the enterprise, as "there's a growing sense that athletes aren't being treated as well as they should, given how much money college sports brings in" (Wolverton, 2008a, p. A20). The price tag for the settlement could be extremely costly for athletic departments after the five-year period—as much as $1 million a year.

Given the financial situations of some programs, University of Oklahoma AD Joe Castiglione predicts: "I can see this as a precursor for reduction of varsity sports and limiting participation opportunities on certain campuses" (Wolverton, 2008a, p. A20). Such additional payments, says Darin Spease, senior associate AD at University of North Carolina at Charlotte, could create conflicts between certain schools: "The small group of 'profitable' schools" he says, "could add yet another attractive component to their offer that would further widen the gulf that exists from a recruiting perspective" (Wolverton, 2008b, p. A15). Also at issue here is the potential that compensation of student-athletes could lead to the establishment of an employee-employer relationship between schools and student-athletes, which would impact the taxable nature of departmental revenues and possibly lead to schools being forced to pay unemployment insurance and worker's compensation benefits for injuries.

Change in tax status. The factor that most deters any viable pay-for-play system for student-athletes is that such payments would then change the tax status of all athletic income, making it susceptible to state and federal taxation. Or, as former NCAA head Walter Byers wrote, "The federal tax code has indeed replaced amateurism as the rationale for the current rule book" (Rushin, 1997, p. 6). Because of this, any proposals that suggest such payments are stillborn.

An additional perspective on the issue of tax exempt status was provided in May 2009 by the Congressional Budget Office (CBO), a non-partisan research arm of the U. S. Congress. At that time, the CBO released a report entitled, *Tax Preferences for Collegiate Sports.* According to CBO director Douglas Elmendorf, the report was prepared at the request of Senator Charles Grassley (R- IA), ranking member of the Senate Finance Committee, because

> . . . concerns have arisen that some activities undertaken by colleges and universities are only loosely connected to educating students and might be viewed as unrelated to the schools' tax-favored purpose. . . . Sports in many universities have become highly commercialized. The large sums generated through advertising and media rights by schools with highly competitive sports programs raise the questions of whether those sports programs have become side businesses for schools and, if they have, whether the same tax preferences should apply to them as to schools in general. (Congressional Budget Office, 2009, Preface; Wolverton, 2009)

The report attempted to address this issue by comparing Division I athletic departments' share of revenue derived from commercial sources with that of the rest of the schools' activities to assess the extent of athletic department commercialization. It also discussed some of the issues that might arise if Congress were to decide to alter the treatment of these programs in the tax code. The report broadly defined a "commercial activity" as activities that "provide a good or service in exchange for a fee in a market that also includes taxed businesses." In this case, the examples included ticket sales, shared revenues from championship games, sales of media rights, and advertising. The CBO based its study on data collected in 2006 by the *Indianapolis Star* newspaper under the Freedom of Information Act, and data on total revenues for those schools from the U. S. Department of Education (Congressional Budget Office, 2009, Summary). The study reached the following conclusions:

- Division I athletic departments obtain a considerably larger share of their revenues from commercial activities than do other parts of the schools that house them.

- Bowl Subdivision programs generate 60 to 80 percent of their revenues from activities that can be described as commercial.

- Championship Subdivision and programs without football generate only 20 to 30 percent of revenues from these activities.

- Removing the major tax preferences currently available to these athletic departments would be unlikely to alter significantly the nature of these programs or to garner significant tax revenues, because as long as athletic departments remained a part of a larger nonprofit environment, schools would have considerable opportunity to shift revenue, cost, or both between their taxed and untaxed sectors.

The report does suggest several policy options available to Congress if it is perceived that these athletic programs are too commercial, but, as noted above, the moves would have little significant impact. For example, Congress could limit the deduction of charitable giving to athletic funds, a significant revenue sources for departments. If these tax breaks were eliminated, however donors could shift their giving to a university fund and simply restrict their gift to athletics. Nathan Tublitz of the Coalition on Intercollegiate Athletics commented that the report "ignored the basic principle that nonprofit organizations are granted their special nonprofit status by the IRS to further their missions, which in the case of universities and colleges is exclusively educational" (Wolverton, 2009, p. A23). But Glenn Wong, a professor of sport management at the University of Massachusetts, commented that the report could lead to positive changes reflecting the educational mission of schools: "I would love to see the tax code reshaped in a way that would encourage institutions, if they want to retain their contributions and deductions, to maintain their sports programs also" (p. A23).

Agents

Because of what many critics call as exploitation—the inability of intercollegiate athletes to share in the revenues generated by certain intercollegiate athletics programs—these critics argue that student-athletes are susceptible to contact with boosters or professional agents before the period permitted by NCAA legislation. The plight is familiar, as described by author Michael Lewis (2007): "God help the [student-athlete] who is caught breaking (NCAA rules). Each year some player who grew up with nothing is tempted by a booster's offer of a car, or some cash, and is never heard from again" (p. 1-11).

The earliest example of agent-athlete involvement was in 1925, when Charles C. Pyle (a.k.a., "Cash and Carry"), a theater owner and stage producer, met University of Illinois running back Harold "Red" Grange, the "Galloping Ghost"—college football's first superstar. Pyle became Grange's manager and negotiated his professional contract with the Chicago Bears of the fledgling National Football League, which stipulated that Grange receive 50 percent of the Bears' home game ticket revenues—of which Pyle got half. Pyle organized many of Grange's endorsement deals and postseason barnstorming tours, and his drawing power was so strong that he is credited with saving the inchoate NFL, although Pyle and Grange also organized a short-lived competitor league in the late 1920s (Carroll, 1999).

This business relationship was viewed as controversial because the arrangement between the two began several months before Grange's senior season, which led to rumors that he would be deemed ineligible. As soon as his last game of his senior season was over, Grange told reporters that he was dropping out of school to play professionally. Illinois head coach Bob Zuppke tried to talk Grange out of it, saying: "Keep away from professionalism. . . . Football isn't a game to play for money." Grange replied that Zuppke made a living out of teaching and coaching football, "so what's the difference if I make a living playing football?" (Carroll, 1999, pp. 98–99). Many coaches and others associated with the college game at the time were staunch opponents of professional football, in part because it was seen as a possible competitor for media attention and fan interest, and in part because many held sacred the notion of intercollegiate football as a bastion of the amateur ideal.

Although Grange's decision goes back nearly a century, the elements that fueled the debate surrounding his decision still resonate, and there are still questions from some on how an agent's acting on behalf of a coach is acceptable but not for a student-athlete with remaining years of intercollegiate eligibility. And another factor that complicates the agent concern is the lack of restrictions as to who can become an agent. This lack of formalized approval, along with intense competition among agents to sign clients, means that prospective professional players are particularly vulnerable to putting their intercollegiate careers in jeopardy.

Perhaps the most notorious agent/student-athlete interactions occurred in the mid-1980s, when Norby Walters and Lloyd Bloom were working to establish themselves by representing aspiring professional athletes. Walters had once owned a bar in Brooklyn that was shut down because of violence and prostitution. Then he moved into the music entertainment industry, where he served as agent for acts such as Miles Davis, Luther Vandross, and Janet Jackson. He later joined forces with Bloom, a former high school football player who had never been recruited to play collegiately and had once worked as a bouncer at Studio 54, the famed 1970s New York City disco mecca. The duo moved into athlete representation, forming World Sports & Entertainment, and became famous by spending huge sums of cash—estimated at $800,000—and squiring clients on trips and to concerts. With the money, they signed at least 30 clients, including five first-round picks in the 1987 NFL draft. The players who took the money, including Purdue defensive back Ron Woodson, Ohio State wide receiver Cris Carter, and University of Alabama basketball forward Derrick McKey, did so before their intercollegiate eligibility expired, a violation of NCAA bylaws.

Walters and Bloom were also alleged to have used violence to enter the market by sending hitmen to rough up rival agents who signed away former clients and to threaten clients who considered leaving the firm. One FBI tape caught Bloom threatening to break the hands of Southern Methodist wide receiver Ron Morris if he signed with another agent. It was also alleged that some of the Big 10 and Southeastern Conference student-athletes who signed with the firm attempted to shave points in football and basketball games. Iowa running back Ronnie Harmon, who later admitted to owing the pair more than $54,000, aroused suspicion when he fumbled four times in the first half and dropped a pass in the end zone in a 45–28 Rose Bowl loss to UCLA in 1986. The allegations were never proven.

The contracts the pair forced players to sign were also extremely one-sided, giving full power-of-attorney over financial affairs to the agents and giving them 6 percent, up front, of any contract signed by the player (including bonuses), and 10 percent of the player's endorsement income. The end for the duo came in 1989, when they were convicted by a federal jury of five counts of racketeering and fraud. Walters was sentenced to five years in prison and five years' probation; Bloom received three years of each. Both forfeited hundreds of thousands of dollars in criminal penalties (Neff, 1987; Fiffer, 1989a, 1989b).

There is no shortage of similar incidents of agents and student-athlete involvement since the macabre misdealings of Walters and Bloom, but one high-profile case involving Heisman Trophy winning and former University of Southern California (USC) running back Reggie Bush indicates that elements of need and exploitation that fuel such relationships still exist. In 2006, Bush left USC after his junior year and was selected second overall in that year's NFL Draft by the New Orleans Saints, signing a contract that would guarantee him more than $26 million. According to various reports, while a student-athlete at USC, Bush and his family allegedly received cash and gifts totaling close to $300,000 from a prospective sports marketing agency, New Era Sports & Entertainment, formed in San Diego (Bush's hometown) by Lloyd Lake, Michael Michaels, and LaMar Griffin (Bush's stepfather).

Mike Ornstein is also alleged to have given cash and gifts to Bush and his family while Bush was still enrolled at USC. Bush's ties to Ornstein began when he served as an intern in Ornstein's office in the summer of 2005 (Yaeger, 2008). After declaring for the draft, Bush hired Ornstein as his marketing agent, and Joel Segal to represent him in his future contract negotiations. The move was not a surprise, because during a meeting the previous December between Lake and LaMar Griffin, Griffin told Lake: "I said it's going to be his decision. And no matter what his word said, you're talking to a 22-year-old kid that's looking at the opportunity of a lifetime. He's the best player in college football. And I got to tell you, he's got to look at all avenues" (p. 139). Soon thereafter, Lake and Michaels sought to file suit against Bush, claiming that Bush and his parents had defrauded them out of $3.2 million in what was termed "lost business capital and monies" given to Bush and his family. When news of the suit became public before the draft, the Houston Texans, the team with the first pick in the 2006 NFL Draft, asked Bush to clarify the situation surrounding the suit. After hearing his side, the Texans opted to select University of North Carolina defensive lineman Mario Williams instead of Bush.

The suit brought by Lake and Michaels was settled out of court for approximately $300,000, but the pair sued again in 2007 to recoup the nearly $300,000 in cash and gifts they claimed to have given Bush and his family during his sophomore and junior seasons. Bush is fighting this latter suit, which as of 2010 remained unsettled, with his lawyers claiming that Lake, a convicted felon who has served prison time, has no credibility. The NCAA's enforcement personnel began to review the case soon thereafter, with the case assigned to Rich Johanningmeier, associate director of enforcement, and Angie Cretors, assistant director of agents, gambling, and amateurism. After Lake filed his second suit against Bush, he agreed to meet with Johanningmeier and Cretors in November 2007 at the office of his attorneys in Pasadena, California, to discuss Bush's involvement with New Era Sports & Entertainment (as of March 2010, Michael's deposition in the civil lawsuit against Bush had been postponed because of a delay in the arrival of legal paperwork [Klein, 2010]). USC officials had not been invited to participate in the meeting, even though, according to Todd Dickey, the school's senior vice-president and general counsel, "we have repeatedly requested to be included in all interviews and all aspects of the investigation" (Yaeger, 2008, p. 215).

In February 2010, USC AD Mike Garrett and school president Steven Sample appeared before NCAA's Division I Committee on Infractions in regard to allegations that Bush and former USC basketball player O.J. Mayo received extra benefits while they were at USC (Klein, 2010). If investigators conclude that either accepted improper benefits from a prospective sports agent, he could be deemed retroactively ineligible, forcing USC to forfeit games. USC could also receive sanctions if it were shown that administrators and coaches knew or should have known about the alleged benefits. Those involved with these machinations believe that officials at USC, including head football coach Pete Carroll and assistant coach Todd McNair, knew about the payments to Bush. (Following the disappointing 2009 season, Carroll left USC to return to the NFL as head coach of the Seattle Seahawks.) Some believe that USC penalized its men's basketball program for amateurism and booster involvement infractions to avoid heavy NCAA levies on its high-profile grid program.

Cases involving agent misdeeds don't necessarily involve lowlifes or wannabees. One example involves Tim Norling, an agent working for the established and successful firm LMM Sports Management, which has represented numerous NFL first-round draft picks, including 2007's Number 1, former LSU QB JaMarcus Russell (Mullen, 2008). In August 2008, Norling allegedly took University of Oregon offensive tackle Fenuki Tupou to dinner, paid for it, and slipped him five $20 bills in their parting handshake. After the incident, Tupou informed Oregon athletic department officials about it, and was then suspended by the school for the Ducks' first game of the season. Department officials notified the NCAA and the NFL Players Association (the union that represents players in bargaining matters with the NFL and also certifies player agents) about the incident. Norling and LMM deny that this happened. Ethan Lock, principal owner of LMM, responded: "We have a 25-year history of not doing anything like this. We don't engage in this type of conduct and we don't condone it. This is appalling to us." LMM officials also claimed that Oregon athletic department personnel never contacted them to verify Tuopu's claim (p. 19).

Many states have passed laws that criminalize behaviors by agents that jeopardize the amateur status of intercollegiate student-athletes. In addition, in 2004, then-President George W. Bush signed into federal law a bill championed by Congressman Bart Gordon of Tennessee and Tom Osborne of Nebraska, the legendary University of Nebraska head football coach who has since returned there to serve as AD. The law is designed to protect student-athletes from predatory agents who make false or misleading statements in encouraging student-athletes to turn pro. The law permits schools and state attorneys general to take legal action if an agent violates provisions of the law (Yaeger, 2008). It is true that many agents have acted in unscrupulous ways to attract and retain prospective clients, resulting in damaged reputations to student-athletes and schools alike. But if the facts pertaining to Reggie Bush and New Era Sports & Entertainment prove true, there is ample evidence of unscrupulous behavior by all parties involved.

Fan conduct

Examples of bad fan behavior, especially at Division I men's basketball games, are plentiful. In January 2008, UCLA and future first-round NBA pick Kevin Love traveled to Eugene, Oregon, to take on Pac-10 rival University of Oregon (UO). Love grew up in Oregon, and his father, Stan, is the sixth-leading scorer in UO history.

Before the game, Love received more than 30 threatening messages on his cellphone from members of the "Pit Crew," UO's rabid 1,500-member fan club, which had acquired Love's number and circulated it among its members. One message stated: "If you guys win, we'll come to your house and kill your family"; another said: "We'll find your hotel room and blow your fucking head off with a shotgun" (Wahl, 2008, p. 40). Love immediately cancelled his service. But the abuse continued at the game, and included barbs and projectiles aimed at Love's family, causing Love's grandmother to break into tears. One sign read, "Kevin Loves Jon Amaechi," suggesting a link between Love and the openly gay former NBA player. Said Love's father:

> There were six-year-old kids with signs saying "Kevin Love Sucks." It was the grossest display of humanity I've ever been involved with. To think I'm sitting at the school where I played ball, and just because my kid didn't pick Oregon he gets abused like that? . . . The NCAA and league commissioners and athletic directors need to put a stop to it. I'm all for creative, loud, and funny fans. But don't target one guy, don't threaten him on the phone, don't tell him you're going to break his legs or get him after the game. (p. 44)

Players themselves are critical of such behavior, especially in the setting of institutions of higher education. Former University of North Carolina standout Tyler Hansbrough said, "A lot of [people on] campuses talk about equal rights" but "it seems like, when students get together at a big event, their behavior goes against what colleges are saying" (p. 42).

What is the responsibility of schools to deal with rude and abusive behavior from student fans? Georgia Tech AD Dan Radakovich argued that it's difficult to restrain students and that schools are unwilling to forfeit the advantage of playing at home. But some coaches believe that contemporary fan conduct has crossed a line. Michigan State University head men's basketball coach Tom Izzo complained that "the abuse that fans are bringing day-to-day, whether it's on talk radio or in the stands, is going to ruin the game eventually" (Wahl, 2008, p. 42). Georgia Tech head men's hoop coach Paul Hewitt differs, saying, "It was much worse 20 years ago." He remembers when, growing up as a fan of Georgetown University, he saw opposing fans bait star center Patrick Ewing by throwing bananas on the floor and holding up signs that read, "Patrick Ewing can't read this" (Torre, 2008, p. 43). Another notorious outburst occurred in 1988, when Arizona State University fans chanted "PLO, PLO" (for the Palestine Liberation Organization) at rival University of Arizona guard Steve Kerr. His father, Malcolm Kerr, president of the American University of Beruit, had just been assassinated by terrorists in Lebanon. An Arizona State fan later justified the abuse in a letter to Kerr, claiming, "There's no way you can understand . . . some of the things we've had to put up with when we've gone to Arizona over the years" (Glier, 2008, p. C17).

Some of the increasing improper conduct has been prompted by technology, such as the personal information posted by student-athletes themselves on their personal web pages. The Oregon fans noted above once printed a thousand copies of an embarrassing photo of a Stanford player that had been posted on Facebook.

Not surprisingly, many negative actions are fueled by excessive alcohol consumption. One study found that students at the University of Texas drink more on football game days than on Halloween, New Year's Eve, or the last day of fall semester classes (Borzi, 2009). One school that is notorious for its student fan imbibing is the University of Colorado (CU), long identified as the nation's top party school. According to one study, 72 percent of the students binge drink (Smith,

2006). The campus is surrounded by 60 bars and liquor stores, and an informal poll there showed that most students attending football games were drunk at nearly every game they attended. One administrator at the school noted that football was a significant part of the school's binge-drinking culture, commenting: "The students start early in the morning and don't stop. . . . A couple of years ago, we found a student in the bushes who was turning blue. He blew a .40 [blood alcohol level]. He survived, but it happens all the time" (Smith, 2006, p. 84). One fraternity pledge didn't survive, dying from a related drinking binge in 2004 (Wahl, 2008).

As a result of this connection to alcohol, fans at Folsom Field, Colorado's home football venue, are considered to be among the worst behaved in the country. In 2001, after the Buffaloes won the Big 12 championship, 500 students set at least seven fires in an off-campus neighborhood, which was home to many students. City police had to use pepper spray and a military-style armored truck to clear the streets. In 2005, during a 30–3 loss to rival Nebraska, students littered the field with debris until game officials ordered two sections of students cleared in the fourth quarter. The next season, campus police stepped up enforcement, ejecting nearly 70 students from each of CU's first two home games. To deal with these game-day issues, CU employs 70 armed police officers and 300 ushers and security guards and has 25 video cameras placed throughout the stadium. One CU senior says, "You only get hassled if you're ridiculously drunk. I mean, we're all drunk. It's the drunk ones who act stupid that you have to watch for. . . . [However], when you get caught up in the moment, anything can happen" (Smith, 2006, pp. 83–84).

In response to the issue, other schools have begun to take steps to deal with heavy alcohol consumption and associated negative behavior. The University of Minnesota opened a new on-campus football stadium at which alcohol is not sold—costing the school an estimated $1 million in revenue. Alcohol is permitted, however, in campus parking lots for tailgating. Student season-ticket holders who have been ejected from a game for intoxication offenses can attend future games only by submitting to a blood alcohol breath analyzer. Students under age 21 must be alcohol-free; students 21 or older cannot exceed a blood alcohol content (BAC) level of 0.08. Students who fail BAC tests can have their tickets revoked. According to the director of the school's student conduct office, the message to ejected students is that to come to a game in the future, you have to prove sobriety. Students have been supportive of the measures, as evidenced by the comments of one student who was entered into the Check BAC program: "The cops aren't going up to people who look fine and say, 'Are you drinking?' They're going up to people who are out of control. I think anyone who is in the program pretty much deserves it" (Borzi, 2009, p. B17).

Minnesota has had a history of underage drinking problems, including campus disturbances after the school's men's ice hockey team won the 2003 NCAA Division I championship, which caused $150,000 in damages. In the first six games at the new facility, 78 people (including 56 students) were ejected for alcohol-related disturbances. Toben Nelson, public health professor at the school commended the policy, but doubted that it would significantly reduce binge drinking on campus (Borzi, 2009).

Many schools and the NCAA that have established financial relationships with beer companies have been found to be hypocritical and complicitous. The Center for Science in the Public Interest is working to get schools to join its Campaign for Alcohol-Free Sports TV. In recent years, the beer industry has spent about $60 million annually on advertising during televised intercollegiate athletic events, which equaled about 10 percent of annual TV spending (Brogan, 2004). NCAA men's basketball tournament games led all other major telecasted sporting events in the number of alcohol-related advertisements. Beer industry officials deny that their ads are targeted toward underage drinkers and claim that there is no evidence that advertising encourages such behavior. They also note that nearly 90 percent of intercollegiate athletics viewers are of legal drinking age, as are 57 percent of college students. An Anheuser-Busch spokesperson said of the ads: "I think it's ethical and good business. We want to be where our customers are." An NCAA spokesperson echoed this, stating: "We don't feel [the ads] are inconsistent with our mission" (Brogan, 2004, p. 4C). The NCAA does restrict alcohol ads to 14 percent (60 seconds per hour) of total advertising content during broadcasts of its tournaments, but conference and individual school policies vary.

Nearly three-quarters of college and universities ban alcohol ads on their campuses, and some schools, such as the University of Arizona, reject financial relationships with alcohol makers. But the University of Missouri, two hours west of the St. Louis headquarters of Anheuser-Busch, welcomes its relationship with the company and its impact on the athletic department budget. Said associate AD Mario Mocca: "Anheuser-Busch is our No. 1 corporate client when it comes to cash. We are proud of our affiliation. We have to deal with real-world revenue issues" (Brogan, 2004, p. 4C). A student at the University of Maryland supports a ban on alcohol ads during intercollegiate athletic events but doubts it would impact student drinking habits: "If it's a moral stand, schools should not accept money from the beer industry. But students are going to drink whether they see the ads or not" (Brogan, 2004, p. 4C).

School nicknames and mascots

A final ethical issue faced by intercollegiate athletics organizations involves the depiction of and context in which their logos, marks, nicknames, and mascots are viewed. This issue has been raised specifically by those who are offended by the way schools portray Native American mascots. Institutions that have been affected include Dartmouth (originally founded in the early 1700s to teach Christianity to Native Americans); Stanford (whose football team was dubbed the "Indians" because former football coach Glenn "Pop" Warner had come from the Carlisle Indian Industrial School in Pennsylvania, where he had coached Native American football and Olympic standout Jim Thorpe); and the University of Tennessee at Chattanooga (which dropped Native American nicknames and mascots four decades ago). Other organizations, however, have responded to accusations from organizations such as the National Coalition Against Racism in Sports and Media, and the National Congress of American Indians by claiming that their depictions are meant to honor Native Americans and their heritage.

In 2005, the NCAA Executive Committee (consisting predominantly of Division I school presidents) announced a policy, set to go into effect the following year, that would prohibit athletic programs that included what it deemed to be hostile and abusive imagery from hosting NCAA postseason contest and banned the use of similarly viewed Indian nicknames by teams, coaches, players, cheerleaders, band members, and others. Initially, 19 schools were ruled ineligible for postseason play based on their nicknames and logos. Exhibit 12.4 lists these schools and their nicknames.

Several schools and politicians criticized the proposal, including then-Florida governor Jeb Bush, who complained: "The folks that made these decisions need to

| EXHIBIT 12.4 | Schools initially deemed ineligible for postseason under the 2006 NCAA nickname and logo policy. |

Alcorn State University Braves

Arkansas State University Indians

Bradley University Braves

Carthage College Redmen

Catawba College Indians

Central Michigan University Chippewas

Chowan University Braves

College of William and Mary Tribe

Florida State University Seminoles

Indiana University (PA) Indians

McMurry University Indians

Midwestern State University Indians

Mississippi College Choctaws

Newberry College Indians

Southeastern Oklahoma State University Savages

University of Illinois Fighting Illini

University of Louisiana-Monroe Indians

University of North Dakota Fighting Sioux

University of Utah Utes

Source: Wolverton, 2006a. Copyright 2006, *The Chronicle of Higher Education.* Reprinted with permission.

get out more often" (Powell, 2005, p. 3). Others questioned the NCAA's legal right to impose the prohibition and the manner in which the policy was formulated. The Board of Directors normally hands down legislative changes, but in the case of this measure, the Executive Committee—considered to be a governance body that does not typically enact legislation—passed the policy without any input from the membership. As a result, the NCAA said it would consider appeals of the ban on a school-by-school basis. By April 2006, most of the schools were removed from the list after changing their nicknames (for Southwestern Oklahoma State, this meant changing from the "Savages" to the "Savage Storm"), or by getting support for the nickname from the eponymous tribe.

One such case occurred when the Seminole Tribe of Florida and the Seminole Nation of Oklahoma endorsed the nickname and imagery used at Florida State University (FSU). Indeed, the Florida tribe helped FSU create the costume for Chief Osceola, the school's mascot, who appears at home football games riding a horse to plant a flaming spear at midfield, even though none of these actions have any connection to actual Seminole history. In response, Bernard Franklin, NCAA senior vice president for governance and membership, stated that the organization "recognizes the many different points of view on this matter, particularly within the Native American community. The decision of a namesake sovereign tribe, regarding when and how its name and imagery can be used, must be respected even when others may not agree" (Wolverton, 2006, p. A 44).

By 2007, five schools (Arkansas State University, Alcorn State University, McMurry University, University of Illinois, University of North Dakota) remained on the non-compliance list. Bradley University was on a five-year watch list after retaining the nickname "Braves" but dropping its Native American mascot and logos. Illinois retired its mascot, Chief Illiniwek, but certain groups at the school continue to use the mascot and related imagery at on-campus events, as the NCAA policy covers only athletic events. Newberry (South Carolina) College, a private school of 925 undergraduates and a member of the Division II South Atlantic Conference, initially chose to fight the edict to change but later relented, and as of 2010, had yet to come up with a replacement moniker. AD Andy Carter noted that the school was seeking the imprimatur of a local tribe to keep "some semblance of Indian regalia," but in the meantime the school's team uniforms bear only the school name (Wolverton, 2006a; Saulny, 2007; Redden, 2008).

Another school that initially contested the NCAA dicta, but also later relented, was the College of William and Mary (W&M), a Division I member of the Colonial Athletic Association, with an enrollment of 5,500 undergraduates, located in Williamsburg, Virginia. W&M, a state-supported school, is the second-oldest institution of higher education in America, chartered by England's King William III and Queen Mary II in 1693. In October 2006, then-school president Gene Nichol sent to members of the school's faculty and staff a report on the NCAA's investigation of the school's nickname, the "Tribe," and its athletic logos to determine whether they violated the Association's new standards. The nickname had been "Indians" until the mid-1980s, when the school amended it to "Tribe" because the former nickname was "deemed potentially offensive and inappropriate."

In defending the "Tribe" nickname and logo, Nichol said a school task force had concluded that the nickname "powerfully and pointedly describes the remarkable sense of attachment and commitment that William and Mary students, staff, and faculty feel toward one another and their institution," that the term "appropriately highlights the defining, historical connection between the College and the education of Native Americans" (citing that the principal element of the College's founding mission was the education of indigenous peoples), and that "regional Virginia tribal leaders, with whom we have consulted, indicate that they clearly do not consider William and Mary's use of the term 'Tribe' to be 'hostile and abusive.'" The defense quoted Chief William Miles of the local native Pamunkey Tribe: "I speak for my tribe in saying there is no perception whatsoever that William and Mary uses the term 'Tribe' in a negative way" (Walker, 2003, pp. 1–2).

Although the NCAA approved the nickname, agreeing with the school that it reflected the school's sense of community and shared common purpose, it ruled that the logo—the letters "W" and "M" linked, with two feathers attached—was potentially hostile and abusive. After a denied appeal, Nichol explained his unwillingness to pursue the case via a lawsuit:

> First, failing to adhere to the NCAA logo ruling would raise the substantial possibility that William and Mary athletes would be foreclosed from competing at the level their attainment and preparations merit. . . . I will not make our athletes pay for our broader disagreements with a governing association. . . . Second, . . . I am loath to divert further energies and resources to an expensive and perhaps multi-faceted lawsuit over an athletic logo. . . . I know, of course, that more than one member of our understandably disgruntled community would likely be willing to help finance litigation against the NCAA. Those dollars are better spent in scholarship programs. Third, . . . I am unwilling to allow [the school] to become the symbol and lodestar for a prolonged struggle over Native American imagery that will likely be miscast and misunderstood—to the detriment of the institution. (Nichol, personal communication, October 11, 2006)

In 2010, W&M introduced a new mascot, a griffin (a mythical beast with lion's body and an eagle's head), picked after a selection process that lasted 16 months and garnered 800 proposed submissions from stakeholders. A list of five finalists (which also include a king and queen, a phoenix, a pug, and a wren), was released in December 2009. Despite the new mascot, the school retained the use of the nickname "tribe" to refer to its teams (Crump, 2010). See the case study below for more on mascot issues.

The University of North Dakota (UND) did not drop the logo fight. After hearing from a Sioux leader who said his tribe opposed the use of the nickname, the NCAA denied UND's appeal in April 2006. Soon thereafter, North Dakota Attorney General Wayne Stenehjem filed the suit on behalf of the school to continue using its "Fighting Sioux" nickname and imagery (Wieberg, 2007). The roots of the dispute can be traced back to 2001, when UND alumnus Ralph Engelstad donated $100 million to the school, half of which was to build an eponymous hockey arena on campus. The arena, which was originally predicted to cost $50 million, is actually owned and operated by one of Engelstad's companies and is leased to the school for $1 a year and located on 30 acres of land that the company leases from the school for the same amount.

Engelstad, a Las Vegas casino owner and real estate and construction magnate, also had been accused of being an admirer of Nazism. Media outlets reported that he had hosted parties on Adolf Hitler's birthday and that he kept a large collection of Third Reich memorabilia. Engelstad graduated from UND in 1954, having been a backup on the school's hockey team. He had already donated $5 million to UND in 1988 to upgrade the school's former hockey arena after years of cultivation by school officials. Soon thereafter, Engelstad fought successfully a move by the school to replace its logo, nearly identical to that of the Chicago Blackhawks of the National Hockey League, with a more abstract version, when he threatened to withhold any future donations. The threat also earned him a guarantee from the school that it would not drop the "Fighting Sioux" nickname (another example of schools being put in compromising positions when seeking to curry favor with prospective donors). A former member of the UND alumni association board admitted:

> We do a little dance to his tune because he's got a lot of money. . . . No one talks about it openly, but everyone hopes the university can get more from Engelstad, perhaps the biggest donation in history. They're talking about a half-billion dollars. The bottom line is that the school won't do anything to jeopardize that. (Dohrmann, 2001, pp. 46, 49)

In 1999, the university released a new logo designed to appease Engelstad. The logo received considerable public criticism (nine native tribes from North Dakota and South Dakota had previously asked the school to stop using the nickname and logo), so then-school president Charles Kupchella formed a committee to study the issue. After Kupchella indicated that he agreed with the tribes, Engelstad threatened to stop construction of the new arena on which he said he had already donated $35 million if Kupchella didn't endorse the new logo and existing nickname. The state's board of higher education later voted to retain both the logo and the nickname.

Opponents say that Engelstad placed too many of the Fighting Sioux logos throughout the arena, which critics also dubbed "Fort Engelstad," and overspent on construction out of spite, to use up the entire $100 million he initially pledged to the school. The final product seemed to support this notion, as each of the stadium's seats is leather; granite tiles from India cover all the floors; Italian chandeliers illuminate the lobby; the scoreboard alone cost $2 million; and the grounds include a 400-foot hedge that spells out "Fighting Sioux" to be read by planes flying overhead (Dohrmann, 2001).

Following the denial of appeal in 2006, a temporary injunction from North Dakota District Judge Lawrence Jahnke allowed UND to play a first-round football playoff game at home in November 2007. A month before this date, however, the school and the NCAA settled the suit. Under the terms of the settlement, the university had three years to obtain approval of the mascot from the two Sioux tribes with a significant presence in the state (the Spirit Lake Tribe and the Standing Rock Tribe). If the tribes were to approve the mascot by November 2010, the university would receive a waiver from the NCAA. If the tribes failed to approve the mascot, the university would have to adopt a new logo and mascot that do not violate the policy. If the university keeps the mascot without tribe approval, it will be subject to NCAA restrictions. Peter Johnson, a UND spokesman, said the school felt vindicated: "We don't believe anything that happens at this institution or that we do can be described as hostile or abusive" (Sander, 2007, p. 1). Experts also said that a court might have found fault with the way the NCAA enacted the entire mascot policy (Wolverton, 2006a; Wieberg, 2007; Davey, 2009).

In September 2009, the Spirit Lake Tribe approved the nickname in a referendum (67 percent in favor), with the tribe's governing council later approving a resolution giving UND "perpetual" use of both the logo and the nickname, but the Standing Rock Tribe was opposed. At that point, the state Board of Education, which sets policy for North Dakota's public universities, decided to retire the mascot if the Standing Rock Tribe did not approve it by the end of October of that year. At that point, some members of the Spirit Lake Tribe secured a temporary restraining order against this plan and filed suit to retain the nickname, stating that the name honors their heritage. Said tribal member Frank Black Cloud, "When you hear them announce the name at the start of the hockey game, it gives you goosebumps. They are putting us up on a pinnacle" (Davey, 2009, p. A16; Wetzel, 2009). The Spirit Lake Tribe members say that many Native Americans who oppose the nickname are from other non-Sioux tribes who are jealous of the attention the nickname brings. Opponents claim that those who support the nickname are secretly behind the new suit that would block the banning of the nickname, a charge the plaintiffs deny. Attorney Patrick Morley, who represents the Spirit Lake tribe members in the lawsuit, stated flatly: "[Arena officials] are not paying me and they are not my client. I am not accepting a cent from anybody but [the tribe members] (Wetzel, 2009, p. 1).

The suit was unsuccessful. North Dakota Northeast District Court Judge Michael Sturdevant ruled that the Board does have the constitutional right to decide and to act on the nickname issue. Sturdevant, a graduate of UND's law school, criticized the state Board of Education and its failure to "seize upon the opportunity to preserve an honored tradition," but he threw out the suit nonetheless. In response, a board spokesperson said the suit "would have established a terrible precedent" in limiting the board's authority (Judge Throws Out, 2009, p. A16).

The issue came to a conclusion in April 2010, when the state Board of Higher Education decided to retire the Fighting Sioux logo and nickname and directed Chancellor Bill Goetz to advise UND President Robert Kelley to begin the transition. Although the state Supreme Court had recently affirmed the district court ruling striking down an injunction sought by several members of the Spirit Lake tribe, board president Richie Smith directed Goetz to send a letter to Kelley recommending the transition begin (Haga, 2010). UND president Kelley responded to the ruling with this statement:

In my 40 years in higher education, I have never met a more passionate alumni base or a more dedicated faculty, staff and student body than we have at UND. Our alums are a tremendous asset to this university . . . and I understand their strong feelings toward the Fighting Sioux identity. There are great memories and accomplishments attached to it. As a result, many will find it difficult to say goodbye to the nickname and logo. But by working together, our gain will be greater than our loss. I want to reassure our students and alumni—and all friends of the University—that we will make sure we appropriately retire the Fighting Sioux nickname and logo. (Statement, 2010, p. 1)

questions for you to consider

1. Based on the facts in the case, why has the mascot issue been so problematic for UND's administrators and athletic department managers?

2. If you were asked to advise on how UND should approach the process of determining nickname and logo, what measures should the school take to address all concerns and stakeholder groups, as promised by President Kelley?

At the University of Denver (DU), a private school with 5,300 undergraduates located in the capital of Colorado and a member of the Division I Atlantic Sun Conference for most sports, the school's nickname—the Pioneers—doesn't seem to fall into the category of hostile or abusive to anybody. Still in 1999, school officials decided to change its mascot from "Denver Boone," a cartoon character festooned with a beard and coonskin cap like the noted American frontier figure Daniel Boone, to a red-tailed hawk named "Ruckus." Boone, drawn by Walt Disney in 1968, was shelved for his "lack of gender inclusiveness and the changing image of the university," according to the student newspaper, the *Clarion* (Mascot Watch, 2008, p. A6; Richardson, 2008, p. 1).

The rationale for the change, according to school chancellor Robert Coombe, was that some thought Denver Boone was a symbol of Western expansionism, and that "the old Boone figure is one that does not reflect the broad diversity of the DU community" (Mascot Watch, 2008, p. A6). The university addressed the mascot question in 2008 through a History and Traditions Task Force, which decided to retire Boone permanently after critics argued that he represented an era of Western imperialism and was offensive to women and minority groups. Monica Kumar, president of the undergraduate student body, who served on the committee, stated that "the name 'Boone' is linked to Daniel Boone, and to people of Native American ancestry, it's sensitive because he was part of a movement that pushed Native Americans to the side. We are a university that has been very sensitive to diversity and one of our objectives is to be inclusive . . . and this was an opportunity for us to come together and show our inclusiveness" (Richardson, 2008, p. 1).

But some students and alumni have lobbied to bring back Boone ever since 1998. In a university survey taken in 2008, in response to a resurgent "Bring back Boone" movement, 87 percent of student and alumni respondents held a favorable opinion of the cartoon figure and wanted to see his return. Students and fans have called for Boone's return, and some come to hockey games dressed in Boone-like garb amidst chants of "We want Boone!" And there is a campus concert series called "Boonestock." Still, Coombe states that Ruckus will remain and urged Boone fans to discuss "what it means to be a Pioneer, for today and the future" (Mascot Watch, 2008, p. A6). Mike Rosen, a DU alumnus and local radio talk-show host and commentator, called the decision "annoying but not surprising. It's an example of the hyper-sensitive, politically correct epidemic in higher education as well as secondary education. Are they going to do away with the name 'pioneer'? I would think that would be at least as offensive as the mascot" (Richardson, 2008, p. 1).

Sacred Heart University, a private Catholic school with 4,000 undergraduates located in Fairfield, Connecticut, and a member of the Division I Metro Atlantic Athletic Conference, also uses the nickname "Pioneers." This school went in the other direction from DU in 2007 and unveiled a new 6'7" mascot named "Big Red," who looks like a bigger version of Denver Boone. DU's Kumar called Big Red "incredibly offensive, like if you took an Asian mascot and called it 'Big Yellow'" (Richardson, 2008, p. 2). But Sacred Heart officials were unapologetic about the decision to add a Daniel Boone–style mascot. Said a school spokesperson: "When Sacred Heart University was founded in 1963, it charted a new direction within American Catholicism, as the very first university to be led and staffed by the laity. Our mascot, Big Red, embodies this pioneering spirit that we proudly embrace. Big Red's name and red hair were inspired by our school color, red" (p. 2).

These changes have meant the emergence of a business opportunity for Dave Raymond, the man behind (or rather, inside) the Phillie Phanatic, one of professional sport's first and best-known mascots. Raymond's father "Tubby" was the former longtime successful head coach at the University of Delaware, and his brother Chris was former head football coach at Division III Colby College in Waterville, Maine. Dave parlayed his former $25-a-game intern gig as mascot for Major League Baseball's Philadelphia Phillies into a business, Raymond Entertainment Group. The company has five full-time employees, plus artists and a costume maker, and makes costumes and develops and trains mascots for sports organizations at a cost of $40,000 or more.

Raymond developed a new mascot for East Stroudsburg (Pennsylvania) University (ESU), a public school with 7,200 students and a member of the Division II Pennsylvania State Athletic Conference. ESU sought bids from 10 mascot companies in 2007 to develop a new mascot costume after the school had dropped its Native American imagery but kept its "Warriors" nickname. The school's vice-president for student affairs said, "We're not getting rid of the concept of Warriors, but we're also not going back to the Native American concept. We're going to do what's best for the entire community" (Branch, 2008, p. Y-9). ESU picked Raymond's bid, and he initially pitched the concept of a bear, a wolf, or a frontiersman. Focus groups at the school preferred the bear, which the company depicted as wearing red-colored Roman legionnaire garb.

After the final version was approved—with a cape—the design became reality. The entire process took 18 months, and the final version was presented to the school's nine-person mascot committee, composed of faculty, alumni, students, and athletic department personnel in September 2008. Raymond donned the costume and burst into the committee meeting in character. "It's one thing to stuff it in a box and send it to them," he said. "It's a different thing to have the character walk in the room" (p. Y–9). The committee approved, and the mascot, dubbed "Burgy" through an online selection that attracted 4,000 voters, made its public debut at the school's homecoming football game on October 4. According to Brenda Friday, ESU's associate director of university relations who oversaw the effort, the time and money spent "were so worth it. And we've only just begun to see the benefit of this," as future community appearances were scheduled, and a second costume and second and third performers were being trained to meet demand (p. Y-9).

CONCLUSION

Within the context of contemporary intercollegiate athletics, reform efforts have been a part of the landscape for nearly as long as colleges have competed against each other. From the so-called Carnegie Report to the *Second Century Imperatives*, organizations associated with higher education have sought to understand the management challenges and to offer possible solutions to align the operations of athletic programs with the mission and goals of higher education. Managers and stakeholders have had to contend with a variety of issues that have challenged the ethical framework of the enterprise, including hazing and other criminal behaviors of student-athletes, student-athlete gender identity and how it impacts competitive equity, whether student-athletes should be able to share in revenues generated through intercollegiate athletics programs, the influence of agents in endangering student-athlete eligibility, rude and dangerous fan conduct at competitions, and the NCAA's decision to ban nicknames judged to demean Native Americans. Some of these issues are not new, but the continued growth and popularity of intercollegiate athletics, coupled with its situation in the realm of higher education, means that intercollegiate athletic managers must be ready to address concerns relating to these topics as they arise.

PRACTITIONER perspective:

CHRISTINE PLONSKY, Director of Women's Athletics, The University of Texas

Finances and budgets play a large role in the efforts of intercollegiate athletic managers. These same financial factors are among the key elements addressed in nearly all the reform efforts outlined in this chapter. As evidenced by the quotes by Christine Plonsky, Director of Women's Athletics at The University of Texas (UT), cited earlier in the chapter, managers in her position have to deal with ethical issues as they impact nearly every aspect of their jobs. Plonsky has served in her current position since 2001, and directs UT's 11-sport women's athletics program. She is the liaison with multimedia rights holder IMG College, which does business with the Longhorns Sports Network (LSN). The LSN staff represents corporate sponsorship sales for UT Athletics and the Frank Erwin Center, including the elements appearing in signage, game-day publications, consumer and retail promotions, and video.

Plonsky also supervises UT's trademark and licensing staff, which works directly with The Collegiate Licensing Company, part of IMG College. In addition, she serves on the NCAA Committee on Academic Performance and the President's Task Force on Commercialization. Her past NCAA service includes five years with the Division I Management Council (chair, January 2003–April 2004). Plonsky also is a former member of the National Association of Collegiate Directors of Athletics (NACDA) Executive Committee and the Board of Directors of the National Association of Collegiate Marketing Administrators. Plonsky worked as women's SID at Iowa State from 1979–81 and first joined the UT Athletics staff in January 1982 as women's sports information director. She was named Big East Conference office director of public relations in July 1986 and spent seven years with the league in public relations and assistant/associate commissioner capacities. In the interview for this book, Plonsky was asked to respond to questions concerning issues outlined in this chapter.

Q: *In the chapter we discussed proposed NCAA legislation to amend existing rules relating to how companies advertise their products and services in association with pictures and images of student-athletes. What are your feelings about this rule change, which has been tabled by Division I presidents?*

A: There is no place on a college campus where private funding is not essential with regard to helping an academic or student service unit meet the mission of the university. The McCombs Business School (at The University of Texas) has several labs (such as mock stock exchanges) sponsored by corporations. In intercollegiate athletics, self-sourced funds are the rule rather than the exception, so any sponsorship decision that helps underwrite opportunities for men's and women's athletics operations is literally no different from underwriting these academic areas. The difference is in the exposure and the exposing vehicles. If you don't attend the McCombs School of Business, you might not see the sponsorships there. But in intercollegiate sports we have public venues, and because of media coverage, the sponsorship is more visible.

Several comments, including those of student-athletes, believe that the revenues generated from intercollegiate sports such as football and men's basketball are achieved outside the mission of higher education and, thus, should be taxable as well as shared directly with student-athletes. How do you respond to these comments?

I find it offensive that individuals want to separate fundraising activities by gender and apply any concept of tax. Our men and women student-athletes are engaging in an institutionally approved activity with a mission that aligns with the goals of the university. Every single athletics staff member has an obligation to work toward identifying sources of funds [for athletics], as most states do not permit academic dollars or tax dollars to support intercollegiate athletics.

Most state universities are not fully funded by legislative dollars. At Texas, funds from the state account for less than 13 percent of the academic budget, so private giving and gifts are paying for the academic infrastructure, with other dollars generated by tuition, fees, and other sources. As long as men and women student-athletes are kept far from employer-employee protocols and remain on merit-based grants, there should be only the current Internal Revenue Service code applied to particular donations that support student-athlete opportunities and services.

The University of Texas, like many other Division I athletic departments, has financial relationships with shoe and apparel companies, such as Nike, that require their coaches and student-athletes to wear their products. How does Texas balance these sponsorship and endorsement agreements with the NCAA's Principle of Amateurism?

Faculty and staff members often serve as spokespersons for businesses, serve on boards, and participate in research projects funded by companies. As long as activities that tie an employee coach to a service are approved by the institution in terms of how the coach serves that company, these activities seem similar.

The student-athletes are not put in a position to do anything other than participate in their activity. They do not shill the product, nor do they endorse it. I imagine students on campuses sit in buildings built by private funds, in computer labs where the equipment is procured through gifts and donations. Again, if we apply filters that exist across campus for non-athletic activities, many similarities would be found.

The escalating Division I coaches' salaries have become another source of criticism regarding the excesses of intercollegiate athletics expenditures. How does Texas balance the need to stay competitive, control costs, and pay these increasing salaries?

Salaries for all institutional positions are now market-driven, and faculty members are as highly recruited as coaches to and away from our institution. One must be mindful that athletic directors are accountable to their institutions to maintain balanced budgets, and if the market drives coaches' salaries to extraordinary levels, sources to pay those salaries must be found.

What is the appropriate role for organizations like the Knight Commission and the Coalition on Intercollegiate Athletics in prompting the ethical operation of intercollegiate athletic departments?

These groups provide discussion, discourse, and sentiment. However, these groups often lack adequate representation of individuals "in the trenches" of intercollegiate athletics, such as active coaches, and high-profile men and women student-athletes. There also appears to be a lack of academic services employees who can speak directly to student-athlete experiences and what is derived from today's intercollegiate athletic environment.

The Second Century Imperatives report indicates that cost-containment is a key issue facing intercollegiate athletic managers. Is this finding accurate, or are there more important reform issues facing you and your colleagues?

Cost-containment is a term that is often misapplied. If facilities are bereft of short- and long-term maintenance, cost-containment may not be applicable. Cost-containment should not preclude institutions from providing the best health care, academic services, and life skills training for student-athletes.

questions TO CONSIDER

1. Compare the findings of the major reform reports outlined in the chapter. How are they similar, and how do they differ?
2. Which of these reports presents the most applicable suggestions for reform?
3. We learned of several ethical issues facing departmental managers. Of those discussed, which do you think most significantly impacts student-athletes on your campus?
4. Of the issue you identified in the previous question, how would you suggest that athletic department managers and school administrators improve the participation experience for your school's student-athletes?
5. Based on her comments in the text and in her interview, explain why Christine Plonsky is so committed to the current financial arrangements that fund The University of Texas athletic programs, and why she argues these arrangements are ethical.

references

Borzi, P. (2009, November 19). After the tailgate, the breathalyzer. *New York Times*, p. B17.

Brady, E., & Libit, D. (2006, March 9). Alarms sound over Facebook time. *USA Today*, pp. 1C–2C.

Branch, J. (2008, December 14). Dressed to hug. *New York Times*, pp. Y1, Y9.

Brenner, S. (2003, September 22–28). Texas-sized effort aims to please Nike. *Street & Smith's SportsBusiness Journal*, p. 21.

Brogan, P. (2004, March 16). Do beer ads, college sports mix? *USA Today*, p. 4C.

Burke, M. (2008, September 1). The most powerful coach in sports. *Forbes*. Accessed December 3, 2008, from: http://www.forbes.com

Byers, W., with Hammer, C. (1995). *Unsportsmanlike conduct: Exploiting college athletes*. Ann Arbor: University of Michigan Press.

Carey, J. (2008, October 25). NCAA unlikely to wage war on fantasy site. *USA Today*, p. 10C.

Carroll, J.M. (1999). *Red Grange and the rise of modern football*. Urbana: University of Illinois Press.

Chambers, M. (2004, March 31). Colleges' jersey sales raise ethics concerns. *New York Times*, pp. C15, C16.

Charter of the Coalition on Intercollegiate Athletics (2003). Accessed July 8, 2008, from: http://www.uoneuro.uoregon.edu/~tublitz/COIA/Charter.html

Coalition on Intercollegiate Athletics. (2007). *Framing the future: Reforming intercollegiate athletics*. Accessed July 8, 2008, from: http://www.uoneuro.uoregon.edu/~tublitz/COIA/PTF%20report%20%20Dec%2005.htm

Colleges Slight Academic Programs to Fuel Athletics. (2008, September 22–28). *Street and Smith's SportsBusiness Journal*, p. 38.

Congressional Budget Office. (2009, May). *Tax preferences for college sports* (Publication No. 3005). Washington, DC: Author.

Crump, M. (2010, April 06). Griffin selected as mascot. *The Flat Hat*. Accessed April 18, 2010, from: http://flathatnews.com/content/73317.

Davey, M. (2009, December 9). In twist, tribe fights for college nickname. *New York Times*, pp. A16, A25.

DiBiaggio, J.A. (1991, January/February). Cosmetic change versus real reform. *Academe*, 77 (1), pp. 21–22.

DiBiaggio, J.A. (1992, Spring). Our last, best chance for athletic reform. *College Board Review*, 163, pp. 27–38.

Dohrmann, G. (2001, October 8). Face-off. *Sports Illustrated*, pp. 44–49.

Dohrmann, G. (2007, August 13). Trouble in paradise. *Sports Illustrated*, pp. 60–64.

Duffy, B. (2000, February 13). A matter of rite and wrong. *Boston Globe*, pp. D1, D17.

Fiffer, S. (1989a, April 14). Two sports agents convicted of fraud and racketeering. *New York Times*. Accessed July, 8, 2008, from: http://query.nytimes.com/gst/fullpage.html

Fiffer, S. (1989b, June 20). Two sports agents get prison terms. *New York Times*. Accessed July, 8, 2008, from: http://query.nytimes.com/gst/fullpage.html

Garcia, M. (2009a, July 22). NCAA sued over player likenesses. *USA Today*, p 1C.

Garcia, M. (2009b, July 22). O'Bannon wants his cut. *USA Today*, p 7C.

Gardiner, A. (2001, February 4). Vermont hockey wounds heal after hazing scandal. *USA Today*. Accessed July 1, 2008, from: http://www.usatoday.com/sports/hockey/shc/2001-02-04-vthazing.htm

Glier, R. (2008, February 22). Putting civility back into the game, if not into the stands. *New York Times*, p. C17.

Greenhouse, S.(2009, November 18). Labor fight ends in win for students. *New York Times*, pp. B1, B4.

Grossfeld, S. (2006, March 3). Addressing issue. *Boston Globe*, pp. C1, C10.

Haga, C. (2010, April 08). Higher ed board votes to retire UND Fighting Sioux nickname, logo. *The Forum of Fargo*. Accessed April 18, 2010, from: http://www.inforum.com/event/article/id/274767/publisher_ID/1/.

Judge Throws Out Lawsuit over University's Nickname. (2009, December 19). *New York Times*, p. A16.

Klein, G. (2010, March 4). USC football: Deposition postponed in civil lawsuit against Reggie Bush. *Los Angeles Times*. Accessed March 21, 2010, from: http://latimesblogs.latimes.com/sports_blog/2010/03/usc-football-ncaa-hearing-reggie-bush-michael-michaels-lloyd-lake-pete-carroll.html

Knight Foundation Commission on Intercollegiate Athletics. (1991). *Keeping faith with the student-athlete: A new model for intercollegiate athletics*. Charlotte, NC: Knight Foundation.

Knight Foundation Commission on Intercollegiate Athletics. (1992). *A solid start*. Charlotte, NC: Knight Foundation.

Knight Foundation Commission on Intercollegiate Athletics. (1993). *A new beginning for a new century*. Charlotte, NC: Knight Foundation.

Lewis, M. (2007, November 11). Serfs of the turf. *New York Times*, pp. 1–11.

Macris, G. (2007, October 3). Salve Regina forfeits 5 games because of hazing incident. Accessed July 8, 2008, from: http://www.projo.com/sports/content/SALVEHAZE_10-03-07_607BPRG.330367c.html

Mascot Watch. (2008, November 14). *Chronicle of Higher Education*, p. A6.

McDonagh, E., & Pappano, L. (2008). *Playing with the boys: Why separate is not equal in sports*. New York: Oxford University Press.

Moser, K. (2008, August 15). New fantasy football league tests NCAA's rules on amateur status. *Chronicle of Higher Education*, p. A15.

Mullen, L. (2008, September 15–21). Agency wants its say after fast resolution of Oregon suspension. *Street & Smith's SportsBusiness Journal*, p. 19.

Naughton, J. (1997, July 25). Athletes on top-ranked teams lack grades and test scores of other students. *Chronicle of Higher Education*, pp. A43–A44.

NCAA Presidential Task Force on the Future of Division I Intercollegiate Athletics. (2006). *The Second Century imperatives: Presidential leadership—institutional accountability*. Indianapolis: NCAA.

Neff, C. (1987, August 3). Agents of turmoil. *Sports Illustrated*. Accessed July 8, 2008, from: http://cnnsi.printthis.click ability.com/pt/cpt?action=cpt&title=Norby+Walters+ stormed.html

Oppenhuizen, K. (2008, July 28). Monitoring sites with a hawkeye. *USA Today*, p. 9C.

Powell, R.A. (2005, August 24). Florida State can keep its Seminoles. Accessed June 30, 2008, from: http://www. nytimes.com/2005/08/24/sports/24mascot.html

Redden, J. (2008, August 1). Mascot watch. *Chronicle of Higher Education*, p. A4.

Richardson, V. (2008, December 27). Denver axes mascot "Boone" in diversity drive. *Washington Times*. Accessed July 24, 2009, from: http://www.washingtontimes.com/news/2008/ dec/27/denver-axes-mascot-boone-in-diversity-drive

Rushin, S. (1997, March 3). Inside the moat. *Sports Illustrated*. Accessed August 7, 2008, from: http://find.galegroup.com/itx

Sack, A.L., & Staurowsky, E.J. (1998). *College athletes for hire: The evolution and legacy of the NCAA's amateur myth*. Westport, CT: Praeger.

Sander, L. (2007, October 26). U. of North Dakota and NCAA settle lawsuit over "Fighting Sioux" mascot. *Chronicle of Higher Education*. Accessed June 30, 2008, from: http:// chronicle.com/news/article/3317/u-of-north-dakota-and- ncaa-settle-lawsuit-over-fighting-sioux-mascot

Sander, L. (2009, October 30). The Knight Commission at 20: Still keeping watch over college sports. *Chronicle of Higher Education*, p. A17.

Sandomir, R. (2006, May 18). College athletes acting badly: It's all there on the web. *New York Times*, p. C18.

Saulny, S. (2007, October 28). University reverses policy to allow mascot's return. *New York Times*, p. 15.

Savage, H.J. (1929). *American college athletics*. New York: Carnegie Foundation for the Advancement of Teaching.

Schmidt, R. (2007). *Shaping college football: The transformation of an American sport, 1919–1930*. Syracuse, NY: Syracuse University Press.

Smith, L. (2007, October 5). NCAA proposal would let colleges cash in on player images. *Chronicle of Higher Education*, pp. A1, A36.

Smith, L.C. (2006, December 18). The party is out of control. *ESPN Magazine*, pp. 80–84.

Sperber, M. (1993). *Shake down the thunder: The creation of Notre Dame football*. New York: Henry Holt.

St. John, W. (2004). *Rammer jammer yellow hammer: A journey into the heart of fan mania*. New York: Crown Publishers.

Statement of UND President Robert O. Kelley (2010, April 09). The University of North Dakota. Accessed April 11, 2010, from: http://nickname.und.edu/logo/?p=25.

Telander, R. (1989). *The hundred yard lie*. New York: Simon and Schuster.

Thamel, P. (2009, July 22). Suit raises concern over N.C.A.A. licensing practices. *New York Times*, p. B16.

Thamel, P. (2009, December 27). A last man off the bench rides a blog and an attitude to stardom. *New York Times*, p. 8-9.

Thelin, J.R. (1996). *Games colleges play: Scandal and reform in intercollegiate athletics*. Baltimore: Johns Hopkins Press.

Thomas, K. (2009, October 30). Call to curb athletic spending strikes some as unrealistic. *New York Times*, p. B15.

Thomas, K. (2010, March 11). Ex-players join suit vs. NCAA. *New Yark Times*, p. B16.

Torre, P.S. (2008, March 3). Pattern of abuse. *Sports Illustrated*, p. 43.

Wahl, G. (2008, March 3). Over the top. *Sports Illustrated*, pp. 40–44.

Walker, B. (2003, November 5). "Tribe" refers to community, Nichol states in a report to the NCAA. *W & M News*. Accessed June 26, 2008, from: http://www.wm.edu/news/ ?id=5338

Wertheim, L.J. (2007, March 5). The program: Portrait of a powerhouse. *Sports Illustrated*, pp. 55–69.

Wetzel, D. (2009, November 9). Arena official denies role in UND nickname lawsuit. *Indian Country News*. Accessed December 15, 2009, from: http://indiancountrynews.net

Whiteside, K. (2004, September 1). College athletes want cut of action. *USA Today*, p. 5C.

Wieberg, S. (2007, January 9). Brand stands by nickname ban, but judge wants group, N. Dakota to settle case. *USA Today*, p. C8.

Wolverton, B. (2006a, May 12). Mascot dispute escalates. *Chronicle of Higher Education*, pp. A43–A44.

Wolverton, B. (2006b, June 2). Hazing photos spur debate on complicity of coaches. *Chronicle of Higher Education*, pp. A1, A37–A38.

Wolverton, B. (2008a, January 18). NCAA nears settlement in antitrust case that could raise aid to athletes. *Chronicle of Higher Education*, p. A20.

Wolverton, B. (2008b, February 8). NCAA will pay big to settle antitrust lawsuit. *Chronicle of Higher Education*, pp. A1, A15.

Wolverton, B. (2009, May 29). Commercialization in college sports may have 'crossed the line,' report says. *Chronicle of Higher Education*, p. A23.

Yaeger, D., with Henry, J. (2008). *Tarnished Heisman: Did Reggie Bush turn his final college season into a six-figure job?* New York: Pocket Books.

Appendices

Contest and playing and practice season information for selected Division I sports.				APPENDIX	A.1

SPORT	FIRST PRACTICE DATE	FIRST CONTEST DATE	MAXIMUM NUMBER OF CONTESTS/DATES OF COMPETITION	END OF REGULAR PLAYING SEASON	LENGTH OF PLAYING SEASON
Football	Date that permits 40 "practice units" before first scheduled contest	Sept. 3, 2009; Sept. 2, 2010	12 (BS) 11 (CS)	Second Saturday or Sunday in December	See previous
Men's Ice Hockey	Oct. 3, 2009; Oct. 2, 2010	Oct. 3, 2009; Oct. 2, 2010	34	Last day of final exams for academic year	132 days (can consist of two segments of consecutive days)
Women's Ice Hockey	Sept. 19, 2009; Sept. 18, 2010	Sept. 19, 2009; Sept. 18, 2010	34	Last day of final exams for academic year	132 days (can consist of two segments of consecutive days)
Men's Soccer	Date that permits 21 "practice units" before the first scheduled contest	Sept. 1, 2009; Sept. 1, 2010	20	Last day of final exams for academic year	132 days (can consist of two segments of consecutive days)
Women's Soccer	Date that permits 21 "practice units" before the first scheduled contest	Aug. 28, 2009; Aug. 27, 2010	20	Last day of final exams for academic year	132 days (can consist of two segments of consecutive days)
Baseball	February 1 of each year (regular season) September 1 of each year (fall practice)	Feb. 26, 2010; Feb. 25, 2011 (regular season) Sept. 1 (fall practice)	56	Conclusion of Championship (regular season); Nov. 30 (fall)	132 days (can consist of two segments)
Softball	September 1 or first day of classes, whichever occurs first	Feb. 11, 2010; Feb. 11, 2011	56	Conclusion of Championship	132 days (can consist of two segments)

Source: 2008-09 NCAA Division I Manual, 2008, pp. 218–219, 223, 249, 261, 263.

APPENDIX **A.2**	Contest and playing and practice season guidelines for selected Division II sports.

SPORT	FIRST PRACTICE DATE	FIRST CONTEST DATE	MAXIMUM NUMBER OF CONTESTS/DATES OF COMPETITION	END OF REGULAR PLAYING SEASON
Football	Regular season: 21 days prior to the first contest	Regular: Thursday preceding August 30	11	Regular season: Conclusion of DII Championship;
	Spring: February 15	Spring: None allowed		Spring: No later than 7 calendar days prior to the date of final exams
M/W Basketball	Pre-season conditioning: Beginning of academic year	November 15	27	DII Championship game
	On-court: October 15			
M/W Soccer	Regular season: 17 days prior to the first permissible contest	Regular: Thursday preceding August 30	Regular: 20	Conclusion of DII Championship
	Spring: February 15	Spring: February 15	Spring: 5 dates of competition	
Baseball/ Softball	Regular season: January 10 or the first day of classes, whichever occurs first	Regular: February 1	56	Regular: Conclusion of DII Championship
	Fall: September 7 or the first day of classes, whichever occurs first	Fall: September 7 or the first day of classes, whichever occurs first		Fall: November 15

Source: 2008-09 NCAA Division II Manual, 2008, pp. 174–175.

| Contest and playing and practice season guidelines for selected Division III sports. | | | | | APPENDIX A.3 |

SPORT	FIRST PRACTICE DATE	FIRST DATE OF COMPETITION	MAXIMUM NUMBER OF CONTESTS / DATES OF COMPETITION	END OF REGULAR PLAYING SEASON	MAXIMUM LENGTH OF PLAYING SEASON
Football	Date that permits 25 practice opportunities prior to first intercollegiate contest	The Friday or Saturday 11 weeks before the first round of the DIII championship or the Thursday prior to Labor Day when the first permissible contest falls on Labor Day weekend	10	Conclusion of DIII Championship	18 weeks between start of preseason and end of regular season
M/W Basketball	October 15	November 15	25	Conclusion of DIII Championship	19 weeks between start of preseason and end of regular season
M/W Ice Hockey	September 7 or first day of classes for fall term	September 7 or first day of classes for fall term	25	Conclusion of DIII Championship	19 weeks (traditional and non-traditional segments combined)
M/W Soccer	TS: Date that permits 16 practice opportunities prior to first intercollegiate game NTS: February 1	TS: September 1 or the preceding Friday if September 1 falls on a Saturday, Sunday, or Monday NTS: February 1	TS: 20 NTS: 1 date of competition	TS: Conclusion of DIII Championship NTS: First day of final exams for the regular academic year	18 weeks (traditional and non-traditional segments combined)
Baseball/ Softball	September 7 or first day of classes for fall term	September 7 or first day of classes for fall term	TS: 40 NTS: 1 date of competition	TS: Conclusion of DIII Championship NTS: October 30	19 weeks (traditional and non-traditional segments combined)

Source: 2008-09 NCAA Division III Manual, 2008, pp. 128–131, 139, 141, 150, 157, 167, 169.

APPENDIX   A.4   NCAA Division II legislative process.

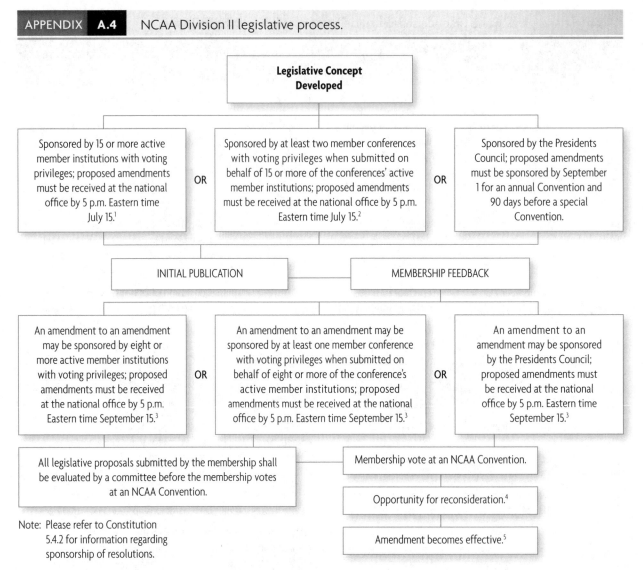

Note: Please refer to Constitution 5.4.2 for information regarding sponsorship of resolutions.

1. Proposals must be submitted in writing by each institution's president or chancellor or the president's or chancellor's designated representative. Proposals must be submitted electronically through the Legislative Services Database for the Internet (LSDBi).

2. Proposals must be submitted in writing by the chief elected or executive officer of the conferences on behalf of their active member institutions and must be signed by the chairs of the conferences' official presidential administrative groups (or at least two presidents or chancellors of a conference's member institutions if a conference does not have a presidential administrative group). Proposals must be submitted electronically through the Legislative Services Database for the Internet (LSDBi).

3. If the amendment-to-amendment does not increase the modification specific in the original proposal, the amendment to a proposed amendment for an annual Convention must be submitted in writing and received at the national office not later than 5 p.m. Eastern time November 1. In addition, the Presidents Council may propose amendments-to-amendments at the time of the Convention without meeting the submission deadlines provided the proposed amendments are approved by at least two-thirds of the Council and copies are distributed before or during the Division II business session.

4. Before the adjournment of any Convention, an affirmative or negative vote on an amendment may be subjected to one motion for reconsideration of that action by any member that voted on the prevailing side in the original consideration.

5. All amendments shall become effective not earlier than the first day of August after adoption by the Convention delegates. However, if a voting delegate wishes to propose an immediate effective date, or to propose any other effective date before the first day of August, a two-thirds majority of all delegates present and eligible to vote on the amendment is required to approve the date. Those amendments designated as being effective immediately shall become effective on adjournment of the Convention.

Source: NCAA, 2010.

NCAA Division III legislative process.   APPENDIX   A.5

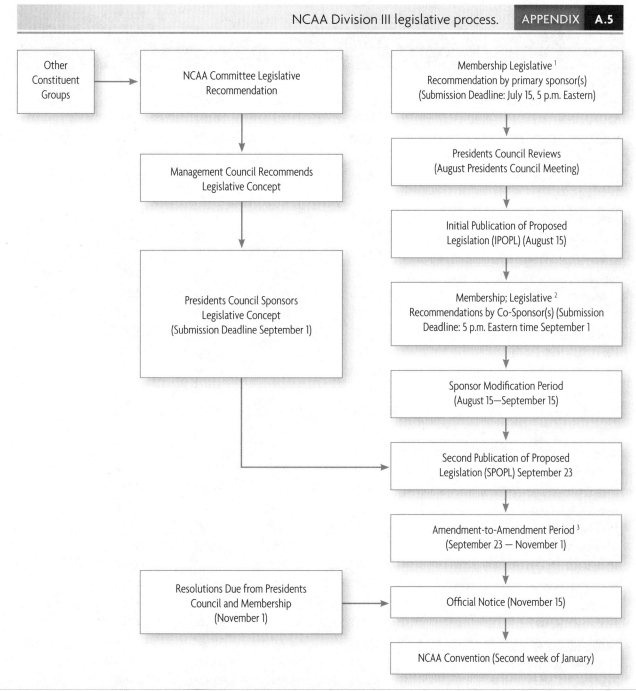

1 Per NCAA Constitution 5.3.4.1-(b) and -(c), legislative recommendations from the membership may be sponsored by 20 or more active member institutions with voting privileges or two or more voting member conferences. Per Constitution 5.3.5.3.1.1, at least one of the sponsors of a conference sponsored amendment or at least 10 of the 20 individual institution sponsors must meet the July 15 deadline.

2 Per Constitution 5.3.5.3.1.1, the second co-sponsor of a conference sponsored amendment or the additional 10 individual institutions must meet the deadline of 5 p.m. Eastern time September 1 or the amendment will be automatically withdrawn.

3 Per Constitution 5.3.4.2, an amendment to an amendment may be sponsored by the Presidents Council, 20 or more active member institutions with voting privileges or two or more voting member conferences.

Source: NCAA, 2010.

APPENDIX	A.6	Median salaries of athletic department personnel.

POSITION	ALL SCHOOLS	DOCTORAL GRANTING	MASTER'S GRANTING	BACHELOR'S GRANTING	TWO-YEAR
Head trainer	$50,000	$65,000	$47,853	$46,000	$43,389
Asst. trainer/ physical therapist	36,000	39,138	34,967	35,785	41,389
Ticket manager	42,000	48,391	36,021	41,492	-
Head coach, football	80,000	194,155	78,298	67,596	57,528
Offensive coordinator, football	57,000	129,000	45,485	43,185	-
Defensive coordinator, football	56,170	116,805	50,000	41,450	-
Asst. coach, football	40,197	80,535	38,493	34,866	-
Head coach, baseball	52,200	79,570	51,758	45,240	50,122
Asst. coach, baseball	33,567	43,650	31,128	25,320	35,457
Head coach, men's basketball	70,224	189,644	69,898	55,167	51,089
Asst. coach, men's basketball	42,557	68,220	39,369	30,950	32,451
Head coach, women's basketball	63,000	126,697	62,007	50,962	46,844
Asst. coach, women's basketball	38,596	51,500	36,329	30,589	31,275
Head coach, cross country	41,212	51,500	36,242	37,000	-
Head coach, track and field	52,083	70,075	48,790	44,248	-
Head coach, cc and t/f	52,108	60,200	49,786	49,450	-
Head coach, skiing	49,750	49,255	49,750	49,864	-
Head coach, swimming/diving	52,550	59,964	46,370	48,725	-
Head coach, men's golf	46,305	55,184	40,359	36,947	-
Head coach, men's gymnastics	80,000	81,218	-	-	-
Head coach, men's ice hockey	81,480	136,010	68,095	75,387	-
Head coach, men's lacrosse	50,617	75,258	49,200	47,007	-
Head coach, men's rowing	52,297	60,040	51,058	51,801	-
Head coach, men's soccer	47,603	63,829	44,177	44,610	-
Head coach, men's tennis	43,445	52,693	39,483	40,096	-
Head coach, men's volleyball	51,599	64,852	47,825	42,097	-
Head coach, wrestling	50,991	64,528	46,803	44,785	-
Head coach, field hockey	47,698	62,525	42,005	45,000	-
Head coach, women's golf	45,181	60,088	37,170	34,525	-
Head coach, women's gymnastics	63,516	69,000	53,957	-	-
Head coach, women's ice hockey	56,526	89,065	49,171	53,400	-
Head coach, women's lacrosse	46,275	56,820	42,138	43,900	-
Head coach, women's rowing	55,139	60,000	43,469	49,200	-
Head coach, women's soccer	46,468	59,093	43,692	43,385	-
Head coach, softball	45,328	60,087	42,785	41,350	44,355
Head coach, women's tennis	45,933	54,562	38,526	39,105	-
Head coach, women's volleyball	47,917	67,946	45,420	43,518	40,000

Source: "Median salaries," 2008. Copyright 2008, *The Chronicle of Higher Education*. Reprinted with permission.

Index